# Pro SAP Scripts, Smartforms, and Data Migration

## ABAP Programming Simplified

**Sushil Markandeya**

Apress®

*Pro SAP Scripts, Smartforms, and Data Migration*

Sushil Markandeya
Saket, New Delhi, India

ISBN-13 (pbk): 978-1-4842-3182-1               ISBN-13 (electronic): 978-1-4842-3183-8
https://doi.org/10.1007/978-1-4842-3183-8

Library of Congress Control Number: 2017961575

Cover image by Freepik (`www.freepik.com`)

Managing Director: Welmoed Spahr
Editorial Director: Todd Green
Acquisitions Editor: Nikhil Karkal
Development Editor: Matthew Moodie
Technical Reviewer: Srivastava Gauraw
Coordinating Editor: Prachi Mehta
Copy Editor: Lori Jacobs

Distributed to the book trade worldwide by Springer Science+Business Media New York, 233 Spring Street, 6th Floor, New York, NY 10013. Phone 1-800-SPRINGER, fax (201) 348-4505, e-mail `orders-ny@springer-sbm.com`, or visit `www.springeronline.com`. Apress Media, LLC is a California LLC and the sole member (owner) is Springer Science + Business Media Finance Inc (SSBM Finance Inc). SSBM Finance Inc is a **Delaware** corporation.

For information on translations, please e-mail `rights@apress.com`, or visit `http://www.apress.com/rights-permissions`.

Apress titles may be purchased in bulk for academic, corporate, or promotional use. eBook versions and licenses are also available for most titles. For more information, reference our Print and eBook Bulk Sales web page at `http://www.apress.com/bulk-sales`.

Any source code or other supplementary material referenced by the author in this book is available to readers on GitHub via the book's product page, located at `www.apress.com/978-1-4842-3182-1`. For more detailed information, please visit `http://www.apress.com/source-code`.

Printed on acid-free paper

*To those of my trainees who persuaded me that my classroom training material can be transformed into books.*

# Contents

# About the Author

**Sushil Markandeya** is a B.E. from Osmania University (1973) and M.E. (Electrical Engineering) from B.I.T.S.—Pilani. (1975) In 1977, he shifted to Information Technology. He has always been involved in creating business application software on various platforms.

Since July 2006, he has been doing corporate training in SAP ABAP for people just out of college. Some of the major Indian corporate clients he has trained for are Accenture, Wipro group Sony India, Mphasis (part of H.P), ITC Info tech., Hyundai Motor, Godrej Info tech., CGI, Orient Cements, and Sopra India.

He, along with Kaushik Roy, authored the book: *SAP ABAP—Hands-On Test Projects with Business Scenarios* (Apress, 2014).

Presently, he is located in Delhi, India.

# About the Technical Reviewer

**Srivastava Gauraw** is a SAP Technofunctional Consultant. He holds several certificates in SAP. He has been working as an independent consultant providing his services in development, training, and documentation, and troubeshooting queries during SAP implementation. He has expertise in ABAP, HANA, Workflow, and other technical and functional aspects of SAP.

# Acknowledgments

The manuscript submitted by the author to the publisher goes through a series of processes, mostly of an editorial nature, to produce the book. My acknowledgements to the following editorial and allied personnel of Apress (in chronological order of my first interaction with them)

| | |
|---|---|
| Mr. Nikhil Karkal | Acquisitions Editor |
| Mr. Celestin Suresh John | Senior Editor |
| Ms. Prachi Mehta | Coordinating Editor |
| Mr. Matthew Moodie | Lead Development Editor |

Acknowledgements to the personnel of Springer and Apress who worked behind the scenes to produce this book.

Acknowledgements to the technical reviewer Mr. Srivastava Gauraw.

# Introduction

The present book *Pro SAP Scripts, Smartforms, and Data Migration*, is a sequel to our earlier book *SAP ABAP—Hands-On Test Projects with Business Scenarios*. It is perceived by enterprises or corporates that an entry-level ABAP consultant must be well grounded in the topics contained in the two books. Personnel trained in classrooms on the topics contained in the two books were included as a shadow resource in the SAP project teams. Subsequently, after three to six months, the shadow resource graduated to a tangible resource in the project teams.

The books come from the training material created for the corporate trainings by the authors. They can now serve as training material for classroom training, individual learning, and reference material for experienced consultants.

## Target Audience

The book is basically addressing people who want to learn *SAP Scripts*, *Smartforms*, and Data *Migration* afresh and people who have been working in these areas for a few years (0-4 years). People with experience in these areas will find this book useful as a reference in the context of doing things.

## Target Audience Prerequisites

Ideally, people who want to read this book should have read the book *SAP ABAP—Hands-On Test Projects with Business Scenarios* **and** grasped the concepts presented in that book. Alternatively, to be able to comprehend the contents of the present book, the reader should have been exposed to the following areas of ABAP:

- ABAP dictionary—domains, data elements, tables, text tables, structures, database views, search helps, etc.
- ABAP language elements—declarations, arithmetic, string manipulation, conditions, looping, etc.
- Reporting—classical and ALV
- Internal tables—filling, retrieval, initialization, etc.
- Modularization—includes, subroutines, and function modules
- Open SQL
- Selection screens
- Dynpro programming
- ABAP debugger, messages, field symbols, etc.
- Familiarity with the basic functional module database tables of sales and purchase

Though project experience is not essential, the target audience must have worked extensively in the ABAP workbench environment in the areas mentioned previously.

# Book's Approach

This book's major thrust is on the "doing" part: to be able to create objects and programs required as per a defined context or scenario.

The book, for most part, uses a scenario-orientated presentation. Concepts and features are communicated through illustrative examples and scenarios. Wherever possible, business scenarios are used to communicate concepts and features.

The book is a completely practical approach, demonstrating and conveying the topics and features through demonstration and hands-on examples.

The demonstration and hands-on exercise objects, including the programs, rely on some of the SAP functional module database tables being populated. This is assured if the reader is logged on to an IDES (Internet demonstration and evaluation system) server or system. An IDES server is now a de facto system for all SAP training-related activities. Specifically, SAP functional module database tables used for demonstration and hands-on exercises in the book are the basic database tables of sales and purchase. Most people with nil or little exposure to business and the commercial world relate to the business areas of sales and purchase.

All the hands-on exercises in the book are performed using SAP sales and purchase functional module database tables.

*The author strongly insists that you perform the demonstration and hands-on exercises as you read a chapter and come to the exercises, not defer to performing them after completing a chapter or the book. It should not be just reading but reading and simultaneously performing the demonstration and hands-on exercises.*

# Resources

The book is complemented and supplemented with an E-resource containing various objects including a source program created during the performance of the demonstration and hands-on exercises in the book. We recommend that you read the document *A Guide to Use E-resource*, located in the folder E_RESOURCE before you commence reading the book.

Most source programs in the E-resource are also listed in the book. Some source programs of E-resource are partially listed in the book and some are not listed in the book. This is indicated in the respective chapters.

In addition to the book and the E-resource, you will use the following additional resources:

- You must have connectivity to the SAP system, specifically, a SAP IDES server. Your log-in user id must be able to create, edit, and delete objects in the ABAP workbench environment. Your log-in user id must be able to access and update data of SAP functional module database tables.

- Apart from book reading, some extra reading is required.

  - You will need to read extra theory and description not exposited in the book.

  - You need to refer to some detailed information like all formatting options available in the SAP Script environment, a complete list of SAP Script control commands, etc.

The material for most of the above-mentioned readings is available in freely downloadable PDF documents from the following link http://www.easymarketplace.de/online-pdfs.php. You will not violate any copyright law by downloading the documents from this link. These are PDF documents of SAP version 4.6C. Though the documents are older version, they will largely serve your purposes.

Download the following PDF documents from the link http://www.easymarketplace.de/online-pdfs.php. For downloading a specific document, click the link (consolut mirror) against the document title.

- BC Style and Form Maintenance **BCSRVSCRFORM.pdf**

- SAP Smart Forms (BC-SRV-SCR) **BCSRVSCRSF.pdf**

- BC Basis Programming Interfaces **BCDWBLIB.pdf**

  (Consider topics of data transfer only)

You will need to refer (not read) to these documents for information during chapter readings. If you do want to read these documents, preferably, do not read them while you are reading a chapter. Read these documents between chapters. At what stage you are to refer to which of these documents is indicated in the book's chapters.

- After completing a chapter, you can also visit the SAP portal of online documentation. You can look up the chapter's topic in the online documentation.

# Conventions Used in the Book

The following conventions were used in the book:

- All ABAP workbench object names appear in upper case or capitals

- All references to ABAP workbench objects you are expected to be exposed to (as a prerequisite) appear in lower case. For example, program, data element, message class, and so on.

- Generally, terms which are supposedly new to the first-time reader of topics in the book will appear in *italics*. All components of topics covered will appear in *italics*. The topic itself will not appear in *italics*. For example, the topic SAP Script—no *italics*. SAP Script components: *Form, Style*—in *italics*. SAP Script fonts—no *italics*, because you are expected to know what fonts are.

- All nomenclatures or screen field labels in the running text will appear in *italics*.

# Conclusion

A caution on similar sounding terms: function module and functional module. A function module is part of the ABAP modularization feature. A functional module is, loosely, a SAP functional area like sales or purchase.

So on to stimulating reading. Not just readings though, the exercises should be performed simultaneously with the readings.

# CHAPTER 1

■ ■ ■

# SAP Script–Forms, Styles, and Standard Texts

SAP script is essentially a tool for the presentation of business data. Business data is presented in a SAP environment using mostly reporting tools: WRITE statement, ALV (ABAP List Viewer) function modules, and ALV classes—the ALV functionalities. SAP script provides a special case of business data presentation. In business applications, data has to be presented in modes other than the tabulated mode produced by the WRITE statement and ALV functionalities.

A specific type of business document layout might require separate font types and font sizes to be used in different parts of the business document. Its layout might require separate font styling (bold, italic, underlining, etc.) in different parts of the business document. The layout might also require the incorporation of graphics (e.g., a company logo). It might require the output of formatted long text, (e.g., the *terms & conditions* in a purchase order). Figure 1-1 shows the rough layout of a business document-type purchase order highlighting the previously mentioned special output requirements.

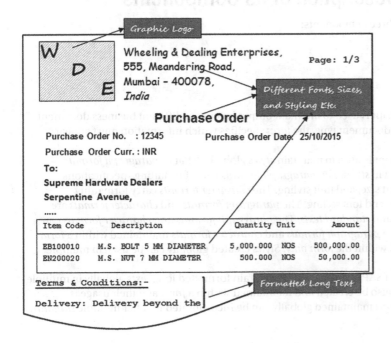

***Figure 1-1.*** *Rough layout of a purchase order highlighting special output requirements*

© Sushil Markandeya 2017
S. Markandeya, *Pro SAP Scripts, Smartforms, and Data Migration*,
https://doi.org/10.1007/978-1-4842-3183-8_1

ABAP environment reporting tools (i.e., the WRITE statement and ALV functionalities) do not provide the facilities that could produce an output like the one shown in Figure 1-1. Hence, we have SAP script, the tool to create and maintain business document layouts and produce business documents.

SAP script is used to format and generate business document types like purchase requisitions, requests for quotations, purchase orders, sales orders, delivery notes, invoices, credit memos, debit memos, invoice cancellations, and so on.

SAP script can also be used to generate a list or report like a customer-wise sales summary, and so on, which you normally generate using the WRITE statement or the ALV functionalities. In this chapter and the next, we will generate lists or reports using SAP script as part of the hands-on exercises in the current and next chapter. But the deployment of SAP script instead of the WRITE statement or ALV functionalities to generate a report would require extra effort and time. Thus, in real-life scenarios, this extra effort and time to produce a report must be justifiable.

Most business documents are sent to business partners—customers and vendors. In our discussions, a specific business document means one particular business document, bearing a business document number (e.g., one invoice or one purchase order). A specific business document might have multiple pages, depending on the size of the stationery (A4, letter, etc.) used to output the business document and the number of items in the document. Every business document must contain the page number on every document page along with the total number of pages in that specific business document.

If you output multiple business documents (multiple business document numbers) at a time (e.g., more than one purchase order), then each purchase order's page numbering must start from 1.

In our discussions, the word "styling" has been used to mean imparting font styles: bold, italic, and underline.

SAP in its documentation and screens uses the term SAPscript. I am using the term SAP script. Let both these terms be considered as synonymous.

With this introduction, I will proceed to describe the components of SAP script.

# SAP Script—A Brief Description of Its Components

SAP script consists of the following three components:

- *Forms*

- *Styles*

- *Standard texts*

The *forms* component of SAP script is used to maintain output layouts of different business document types. That is, for a specific business document type, the *form* specifies which information must appear where in what format.

The *styles* component of SAP script is used to maintain *styles* globally. That is, *paragraph formats* and *character formats* are maintained in *styles*. The *paragraph formats* carry formatting specifications like margins, indenting, font type, font size, and font styling. The *character formats* carry formatting specifications like font type, font size, and font styling. The *paragraph formats* and *character formats* are applied to information on the *forms* and *standard texts*. The *paragraph formats* and *character formats* can also be maintained within a *form*. The *paragraph formats* and *character formats* maintained within a *form* are local to the *form* and can be used within the *form* only. *Styles* created globally can be used in multiple *forms* and *standard texts*.

The *standard texts* component of SAP script is used to maintain formatted long texts globally in multiple languages. Formatted long texts can also be created and maintained within a *form* and their usage is restricted to the *form*. The *standard text* maintained globally can be incorporated in other multiple *standard texts* as well as multiple *forms*.

# An Overview of SAP Script Form Elements

A SAP script *form* is essentially a layout framework of a business document type. It contains the specifications of a business document type layout: what information appears where and in what format. An enterprise requires a specific business document type, say, the purchase order, to be output in a particular layout; the layout of a business document type will generally map to a SAP script *form*.

SAP script has a relationship with the language key. The following sections introduce the SAP script relationship with the language key. You will be able to relate to the SAP script relationship with the language key better if you are familiar with the basic features of the elements of a SAP script form.

Mostly, we will refer to the SAP script form as just form.

A form consists of several elements (subobjects or components).

## Form Header

Like all workbench objects, a *form* also stores information: *created by*, *date created*, *package*, and so on. The workbench objects store such information as object attributes. The *forms* store this information as part of the *header* information. The *form header* contains additional information: *form* classification, translations allowed languages, page setup, and so on.

## Pages or Page Formats

A *page* element of a *form* is not a physical page of a business document. A *page* element of a *form* maps to a page format of a business document type. A specific business document type can be output in more than one format. For example, let us assume that an enterprise requires the company logo for a specific business document type, say, a purchase order, to appear only on the first page when a purchase order outputs in multiple pages; that is, the pages other than the first page of a purchase order will not contain the company logo. So, in this example, the purchase order has the following two page formats:

- the first page of the purchase order containing the company logo and

- page(s) other than the first page of the purchase order without the company logo.

Corresponding to these two page formats, the purchase order *form* will have two *pages*. Though the SAP documentation refers to this *form* element as a *page*, we will refer to this *form* element as a *page format* so as not to confuse it with the physical pages of a business document.

SAP script as well as smartforms refer to the page sizes A4, letter size, etc., as *page formats*. But I will refer to the different formats in which a business document outputs as *page formats*.

Figure 1-2 graphically conveys the idea of the multiple *page formats*. In Figure 1-2, a specific purchase order, number 12345, runs into three physical pages marked as 1/3, 2/3, and 3/3.

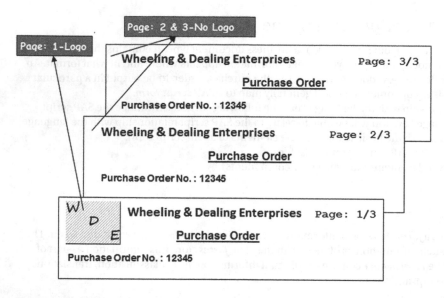

**Figure 1-2.** *Business document type purchase order with two page formats*

You may output more than one purchase order at a time. Each purchase order will output in one or more physical pages. The purchase orders being output will have a company logo appearing only on the first page of every purchase order.

Although Figure 1-2 shows only one purchase order, you can visualize the case of multiple purchase orders. Suppose two purchase orders, numbers 12345 and 12346, are being output. Purchase order 12345 consists of three physical pages, but suppose purchase order 12346 contains four physical pages. The company logo will appear on the first page of purchase order 12345 and the first page of purchase order 12346. There will be two *page formats* for the purchase order: one *page format* containing the company logo and the second *page format* without the company logo. Suppose we designate the *page format* containing the company logo as format-I and the *page format* without the company logo as format-II. Then page number 1 of purchase order numbers 12345 and 12346 will output with *page format* format-I. The pages other than page number 1 of the purchase order numbers 12345 and 12346 will output with *page format* format-II. In the example described, the *form* consisted of two *page formats*.

It is mandatory for a *form* to have a minimum of one *page format*, but a *form* may have more than two *page formats*.

## Windows and Page Windows

The *windows* and the *page windows* are two separate *form* elements. They are being described together because they go together. A *page window* cannot exist without being assigned to a *window*. A *page window* is a physical area on a *page format*. A *page window* is defined by the following:

- Left margin,

- Upper margin,

- Width, and

- Height

These dimensions are essential for the definition of a *page window*. The width and height have to be specified; the left and upper margins need not be explicitly specified – default values are assumed.

It is necessary to assign a *page window* to the *form* element *window*. In the *form* environment, four types of *windows* can be defined.

- Constant *window* (CONST)
- Variable *window* (VAR)
- Graph or Grid screen *window* (GRAPH)
- Main *window* (MAIN)

A constant *window* differs from a variable *window* in the following way: *page windows* of identical (constant) dimensions in different *page formats* can be assigned to a constant *window*. *Page windows* of identical or differing dimensions in different *page formats* can be assigned to a variable *window*. Recall that the dimensions of a *page window* are left margin, upper margin, width, and height.

A graph *window* can contain only graphics. Graphics can also be located in a constant or a variable or the main *window*.

There can be any number of constant *window*s, variable *window*s, and graph *window*s in a *form*. Only one *page window* of a *page format* can be assigned to each of a constant, variable, or graph *window*.

There can only be one main *window* in a *form*. In a *page format*, the main *window* can contain a maximum of 99 multiple *page windows*.

## Paragraph Formats

In the *form* element *paragraph formats*, you specify font type, font size, styling, margins, page protection, tab spacing, etc. The *paragraph formats* are applied to the contents of a *form*. A *form* must have a minimum of one *paragraph format*.

## Character Formats

In the *form* element *character formats*, you specify font type, font size, styling, bar code, etc. The *character formats* are applied to the contents of a *form*.

The *paragraph formats* are applicable to an entire paragraph in a *form* or a document; the *character formats* are applicable to parts within a paragraph of a *form* or a document.

## Text Elements

The *form* elements *page format, windows, page windows, paragraph formats,* and *character formats* constitute the output layout framework and formatting specifications. The actual contents of a business document to be output are contained in the *form* element *text elements*. The *form* element *text elements* are not to be confused with the *text elements* attached to ABAP programs. They are completely different entities.

## Documentation

A *form* also consists of technical documentation referred as *documentation*. The *documentation* will be used by the ABAP developers for *form* maintenance, and as such it does not affect the business document output layout and output contents.

## Form Elements–A Diagrammatic Representation

Figure 1-3 is a rough diagrammatic representation of the *form* and its elements.

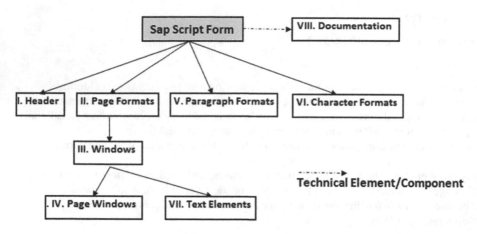

***Figure 1-3.*** *SAP script form elements*

In Figure 1-3, the *form* element *windows* is shown under *form* element *page formats*. *Windows* can be created independent of *page formats*. But the contents of *windows* (*text elements*) cannot be output without the *windows* being assigned to *page windows* which are part of *page formats*. Hence, the *windows* are shown under *page formats* in Figure 1-3.

This section provided a brief description of the different *form* elements. I discuss the *form* elements in the section "A Detail on SAP Script *Form* Elements—a Tour of the *form* MEDRUCK."

## Style Elements and Standard Text

A style consists of a header, paragraph formats, and character formats. The paragraph formats and character formats in styles are similar to the paragraph formats and character formats in forms.

The *standard text* is the word processing tool in the SAP script environment. The *standard text* consists of a *header* and text. The textual matter in the *standard text* can be formatted by applying the *paragraph formats* and *character formats* of *styles*.

# SAP Script Form and ABAP Print Programs

The SAP script *form* is used to design the layout of business document types, including formatted long text. However, there is no facility to retrieve data from database tables in the SAP script *forms* environment. Thus, the data originating from database tables which is to appear in the business document is retrieved and processed in an ABAP program. Hence, an ABAP program, called the print program, is associated with a SAP script *form*.

Data is sent by the print program and received by the SAP script *form* in terms of individual fields or columns (elementary data objects). The individual fields can, of course, be components of a structure or structure fields as well. I describe this transfer of data from the print program to the SAP script *forms* in detail in the section "A Detail on SAP Script *Form* Elements."

# Generating Business Documents Using SAP Script— Architecture

This section describes the basic architecture of the generation of business documents using the SAP script *form, depicted in* Figure 1-4.

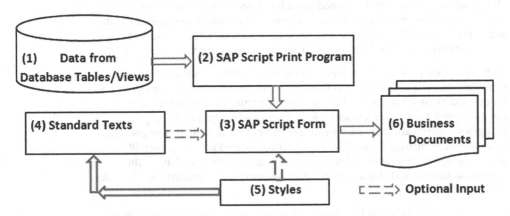

***Figure 1-4.*** *Generating business documents using SAP script—Architecture*

Figure 1-4 marks the process steps as (1), (2), (3), (4), (5), and (6).

1. Process step (1) involves retrieving all the data required to produce the business documents. For example, if your business document type is purchase orders, then some of the main database tables from which data will have to be retrieved are

   - LFA1        Vendor Name and Address

   - T005T       Country Texts

   - EKKO        Purchasing Document Header Information

   - EKPO        Purchasing Document Item Information

   - EKET        Scheduling Agreement Schedule Lines

   - MAKT        Material Description Texts

   Here we are not getting into the issue of how to retrieve the required data. Suffice it to say that at this stage we just have to understand that the required data will have to be retrieved by the print program into appropriately defined internal tables (typical client server processing). The process will involve retrieval of specific and selective business documents through a SELECT-OPTIONS input statement or an equivalent in the print program.

2. Once we retrieve the data, it may be ordered or sorted by the print program (process step (2)). The print program will set up appropriate looping procedures to send field-wise data to the SAP script *form*.

3.    Process step (3) involves the receipt of data to be output by the SAP script *form* from the print program. The SAP script *form* specifies the business document type layout—that is, which information is to output on which area of a page? The SAP script *form* will apply formatting specifications like font type, font size and styling, etc. (through *character formats* and *paragraph formats*), to the output information.

4.    The *standard texts* to be incorporated into a business document can be specified while designing or creating the SAP script *form*. The *standard texts* are then static to the *form*. Optionally, the *standard texts* to be incorporated into a business document can be specified at runtime (dynamic), shown in process step (4).

5.    A *form* can have *paragraph formats* and *character formats* created within the *form*. The *paragraph formats* and *character formats* created within the *form* are applied to the information or content for formatting. The *form* may also use *paragraph formats* and *character formats* created in *styles* and apply the *paragraph formats* and *character formats* of *styles* to the information or content to be output. Similarly, *standard texts* being incorporated into the *form* will use *paragraph formats* and *character formats* created in *styles* and apply the *paragraph formats* and *character formats* of *styles* to these *standard texts*. Process step (5) reflects this.

6.    In process step (6) in Figure 1-4, the generation of the business document occurs.

I describe the transfer of data from the print program to the SAP script form in the section "An Overview of SAP Script Form Elements."

# SAP Script Relationship with Client Code

SAP supplies ready-to-use *forms* for every standard business document type. These ready-to-use *forms* are located in client 000. You can copy the ready-to-use SAP delivered *forms* in client 000 to the logged-in client in the customer's namespace (name starting with Y/Z, etc.). You can then carry out modifications and customize the copied *forms* as per requirements (customized *forms*) of the enterprise.

When a SAP script print program refers to a *form*, the runtime system at first tries to locate the referred *form* in the logged-in client. If the referred *form* is not available in the logged-in client, the runtime system will look for the *form* in client 000 as a default. So if the SAP-delivered ready-to-use *forms* suit your requirements without any modifications whatsoever, you can use them without copying them from client 000 into other clients. In this way, the *forms* in client 000 are accessible in other clients for reference in the print programs and displaying in transaction code SE71. *Forms* existing in clients other than 000 are accessible for reference in print programs and displaying in transaction code SE71 only in that client.

You can copy SAP script *forms* from any client (source) into the logged-in client (destination). In the copying process, the destination client is always the logged-in client.

The client considerations described in context of *forms* also apply to *styles*.

The *standard texts* are incorporated into *forms* and also into other *standard texts*. The *standard texts*, while being incorporated into *forms* or into other *standard texts*, must exist in that client (i.e., the logged-in client or the client in which processing is occurring). With *standard texts*, unlike with *forms* and *styles*, there is no default access to client 000.

You can copy *standard texts* from any client (source) into the logged-in client (destination). In the copying process, the destination client is always the logged-in client.

In the ABAP workbench environment, all the objects that we create, like programs, ABAP dictionary objects, screens, interfaces, classes, transaction codes, messages, etc., are cross client or client independent. All these objects are to be assigned a package. The SAP script is one instance where you have to assign a package and the object is client dependent as well.

# SAP Script Relationship with Language Key

When you create a SAP script *form*, the logged-in language key is stored in the header information of the *form*. This is called the original language of the *form*. If the *form* exists in multiple languages, it will have different language versions. For modifications for a form with multiple language versions, you will have to use the following procedure:

- To carry out modifications to one or more *form* elements—*page formats, windows, page windows, paragraph formats, character formats*—you need to open the original language version of the *form*.

- To carry out modifications to the *form* elements *text element* and/or *documentation,* you need to open the respective language version of the *form*.

For example, suppose you created a *form* when you were logged in with language key = EN (or English) and then you created two other language versions of the *form*: German and French. Now the *form* exists in three language versions: English, German, and French, but the original language of the *form* is English.

With this scenario in mind, if you want to carry out modifications to

- One or more of the following *form* elements—*page formats, windows, page windows, paragraph formats, character formats*—you need to open the original language version of the *form* (i.e., the English version of the *form*). If you open either the German or French version of the *form*, the *form* elements—*page formats, windows, page windows, paragraph formats, character formats*—are disabled for editing.

- The *form* element *text element* or *documentation*, you need to open the respective language version of the *form*.

As mentioned in the section "SAP Script Relationship with Client Code," all the SAP-delivered ready-to-use *forms* are located in client 000. The original language of all the SAP delivered ready-to-use *forms* is German. If you are editing a copy of a SAP delivered *form* and want to carry out modifications to one or more of the *form* elements: *page formats, windows, page windows, paragraph formats, character formats*, you need to open the German language version of the *form*.

In the context of the foregoing discussion regarding the relationship of *forms* with language key, the *form* elements *page formats, windows, page windows, paragraph formats*, and *character formats* are language independent and the *form* elements *text elements* and *documentation* are language dependent.

The language key considerations described in context of *forms* also apply to *styles*. To carry out modifications to *styles*, you must open the original language version of the *style*.

To carry out modifications to *standard text*, you need to open the respective language version of the *standard text*.

# Navigation and Transaction Codes

In this section I describe navigations within the SAP script and the various transactions codes available to operate SAP script.

- SAP script *forms* are maintained in transaction code SE71–*form* painter.

- On the opening screen of transaction code SE71, select Environment ➤ Style to navigate to the screen for maintaining *styles*. Alternatively, you can use transaction code SE72 to navigate directly to the opening screen for maintaining *styles*.

- To navigate to the screen for maintenance of *standard texts*, select Environment ➤ Standard Text from the opening screen of transaction SE71. Alternatively, you can use the transaction code SO10 to navigate directly to the screen for maintenance of *standard texts*.

- To view available fonts, font particulars, and maintenance of fonts, navigate from the SE71 opening screen with the menu option Environment ➤ Administration ➤ Font. You can navigate to the font maintenance screen directly with transaction code SE73.

- For format conversion, navigate from the SE71 opening screen with the menu option Environment ➤ Administration ➤ Format Conversion. Using transaction code SE74, you can navigate to the format conversion screen directly.

- For settings, navigate from the SE71 opening screen with the menu option Environment ➤ Administration ➤ Settings. Using transaction code SE75, you can navigate to settings screen directly.

- To import graphics into the SAP database, navigate from the SE71 opening screen with the menu option Environment ➤ Administration ➤ Graphics. Using transaction code SE78, you can navigate to import graphics screen directly.

- Use transaction code SE76 for the translation of SAP script *forms*.

- Use transaction code SE77 for *style* conversion (i.e., *style* translation).

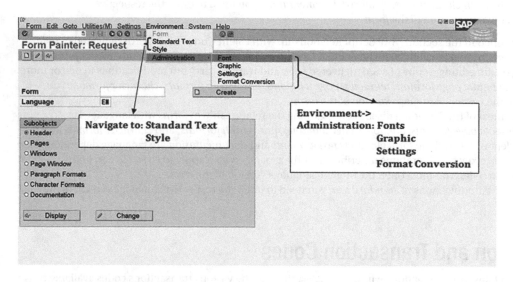

***Figure 1-5.*** *Transaction Code SE71—Form Painter: opening screen.*

Figure 1-5 shows the opening screen of transaction code SE71—Form Painter.
Table 1-1 summarizes the navigations and different transaction codes for operating SAP script.

**Table 1-1.** *SAP Script Navigations*

| Trans. Code | Description | Navigation Through Menu Selection from SE71 Screen |
|---|---|---|
| SE71 | *Forms* maintenance | |
| SE72 | *Style* maintenance | Environment ➤ Style |
| SE73 | Font maintenance | Environment ➤ Administration ➤ Font |
| SO10 | *Standard text* maintenance | Environment ➤ Standard Text |
| SE74 | Format conversion | Environment ➤ Administration ➤ Format Conversion |
| SE75 | SAP script settings | Environment ➤ Administration ➤ Settings |
| SE78 | Import graphics | Environment ➤ Administration ➤ Graphics |
| SE76 | SAP script *form* translation | |
| SE77 | SAP script *style* conversion | |

## Transaction Code SE74—Format Conversion

Transaction code SE74 has the following options:

- Import of RTF document template files (SAP environment) into *forms* and *styles*.

- Export from *forms* and *styles* into RTF document template Files (SAP environment).

- Import Word document templates (Prototypes) into RTF document template files.

- Format conversions in SAP script texts. With this option you can copy all or specific *character formats* and *paragraph formats* from source *form* or *style* to a destination *form* or *style*.

## Transaction Code SE75–SAP script Settings

The following options are available in transaction code SE75:

- Maintain text objects (TEXT, etc.) and text IDs (ST, etc.). Ready-to-use text objects and text IDs are available. You can create your own text objects and text IDs as well.

- Maintain graphical objects and graphical IDs. Ready-to-use graphical object (GRAPHICS) and graphical ID (BMAP) are available. You can create your own graphical objects and graphical IDs as well.

- Maintain standard symbols. Ready-to-use standard symbols are available like for month names, (symbol name = %%SAPSCRIPT_MMMM_01 and symbol value = January), month short names, week names, week short names. Standard symbols are language dependent. You can create your own standard symbols. When you specify a standard symbol in a SAP script *text element*, it will be replaced by its value at runtime.

# Fonts in SAP Script Environment

The SAP script environment supports its own font families. These font families contain some of the commonly used fonts: *Courier, Gothic, Times Roman,* and so on. But some other commonly used fonts in Microsoft office, *Arial, Comic Sans MS,* etc., are not available in the SAP script environment. If you want to use these Microsoft office fonts in the SAP script environment, you need to import them. Only the true type fonts (ttf font files) can be imported into the SAP script environment.

## Font Families

The SAP-delivered as well as -imported fonts, font sizes, and font styling available in the SAP script environment can be viewed through transaction code SE73. To view the available (delivered and imported) fonts, navigate to the opening screen of transaction code SE73 as shown in Figure 1-6.

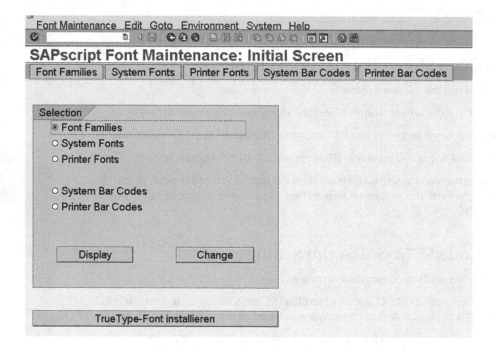

*Figure 1-6. Transaction code SE73 opening screen–SAP script font maintenance*

If you select the first Radio button and click the display or change button, all the font families available in the SAP script environment are listed (see Figure 1-7).

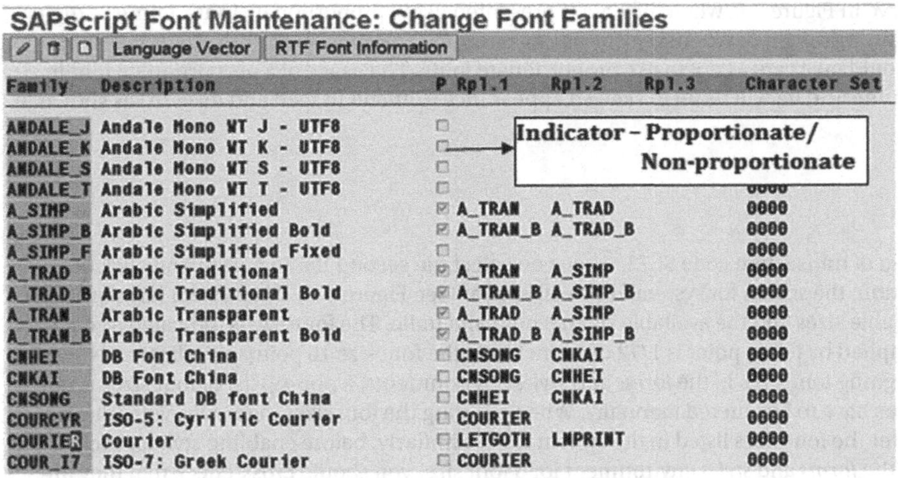

**SAPscript Font Maintenance: Change Font Families**

| Family | Description | P | Rpl.1 | Rpl.2 | Rpl.3 | Character Set |
|--------|-------------|---|-------|-------|-------|---------------|
| ANDALE_J | Andale Mono WT J - UTF8 | ☐ | | | | |
| ANDALE_K | Andale Mono WT K - UTF8 | ☐ | | | | |
| ANDALE_S | Andale Mono WT S - UTF8 | ☐ | | | | |
| ANDALE_T | Andale Mono WT T - UTF8 | ☐ | | | | 0000 |
| A_SIMP | Arabic Simplified | ☑ | A_TRAN | A_TRAD | | 0000 |
| A_SIMP_B | Arabic Simplified Bold | ☑ | A_TRAN_B | A_TRAD_B | | 0000 |
| A_SIMP_F | Arabic Simplified Fixed | ☐ | | | | 0000 |
| A_TRAD | Arabic Traditional | ☑ | A_TRAN | A_SIMP | | 0000 |
| A_TRAD_B | Arabic Traditional Bold | ☑ | A_TRAN_B | A_SIMP_B | | 0000 |
| A_TRAN | Arabic Transparent | ☑ | A_TRAD | A_SIMP | | 0000 |
| A_TRAN_B | Arabic Transparent Bold | ☑ | A_TRAD_B | A_SIMP_B | | 0000 |
| CNHEI | DB Font China | ☐ | CNSONG | CNKAI | | 0000 |
| CNKAI | DB Font China | ☐ | CNSONG | CNHEI | | 0000 |
| CNSONG | Standard DB font China | ☐ | CNHEI | CNKAI | | 0000 |
| COURCYR | ISO-5: Cyrillic Courier | ☐ | COURIER | | | 0000 |
| COURIER | Courier | ☐ | LETGOTH | LNPRINT | | 0000 |
| COUR_I7 | ISO-7: Greek Courier | ☐ | COURIER | | | 0000 |

Language Vector | RTF Font Information

Indicator – Proportionate/Non-proportionate

*Figure 1-7. SAP script Font Maintenance-fonts/font families available*

A preview of the fonts is not available. I have marked the font attribute check box for a font's being a proportionate or non-proportionate in Figure 1-7.

## Proportionate and Non-proportionate Fonts

With the non-proportionate fonts (also called the mono-spaced fonts), all the characters occupy the same horizontal space or width. A typical example of non-proportionate font is the *courier* font family.

With the proportionate fonts, each character occupies different horizontal space or width. For example, the slender characters like 1 (numeral one) or I (ninth alphabet) occupy less horizontal space when compared to the elongated characters like 8 or A, B, and so on. The *Times Roman* font family is a typical example of a proportionate font.

Figure 1-8 shows the output of three ten-digit numbers using the proportionate and non-proportionate fonts. The first number consists of all 1s (slender character), the second number consists of all 8s (elongated character). The third number is the sum of the first two numbers—all 9s (elongated character). The three numbers are presented in a proportionate font on the left side and in a non-proportionate font on the right side.

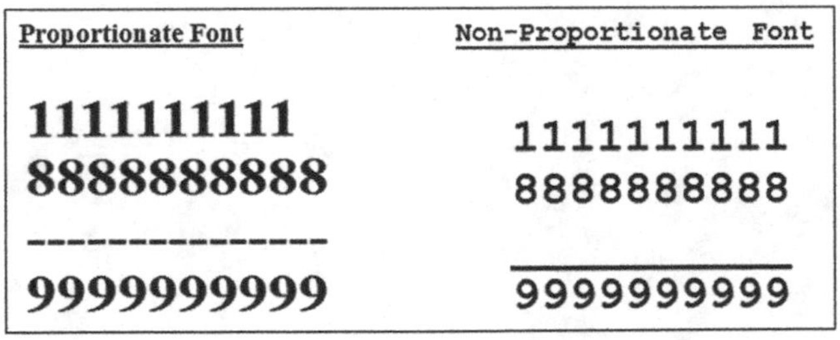

| Proportionate Font | Non-Proportionate Font |
|--------------------|------------------------|
| **1111111111** | 1111111111 |
| **8888888888** | 8888888888 |
| **9999999999** | 9999999999 |

*Figure 1-8. Presentation of numeric data in proportionate and non-proportionate fonts*

As you can observe in Figure 1-8, when the data is presented using proportionate fonts, numeric digits 1 and 8 are substantially misaligned. Whenever presenting currency amounts, inventory quantities or any numeric data, you should take care as not to use proportionate fonts. The usage of a proportionate font in the presentation of numeric data will result in skewed appearance (difficult to read and discern) as shown in Figure 1-8.

## System Fonts

On the opening screen of transaction code SE73, when you select the second Radio button and click the display or change button, the screen for system fonts will appear (see Figure 1-9). The system fonts are a list of fonts with the available sizes and the available styling: bold and italic. The font size is indicated as deci points or points multiplied by ten (a point is 1/72 of an inch). So the font size 16 points is indicated as 160, and so on. When assigning font sizes in the *forms* and *styles* environments, a pop-up list of font sizes is not available; the font sizes have to be entered manually. When entering the font sizes manually, you must be sure that you only enter the font sizes listed in the system fonts. Similarly, before enabling styling, such as bold and/or italic, in the *forms* and *styles* environment for a font size, you should cross-check that they are available through the reference to the system fonts. The system font list shown in Figure 1-9 is a partial list of the font *courier*.

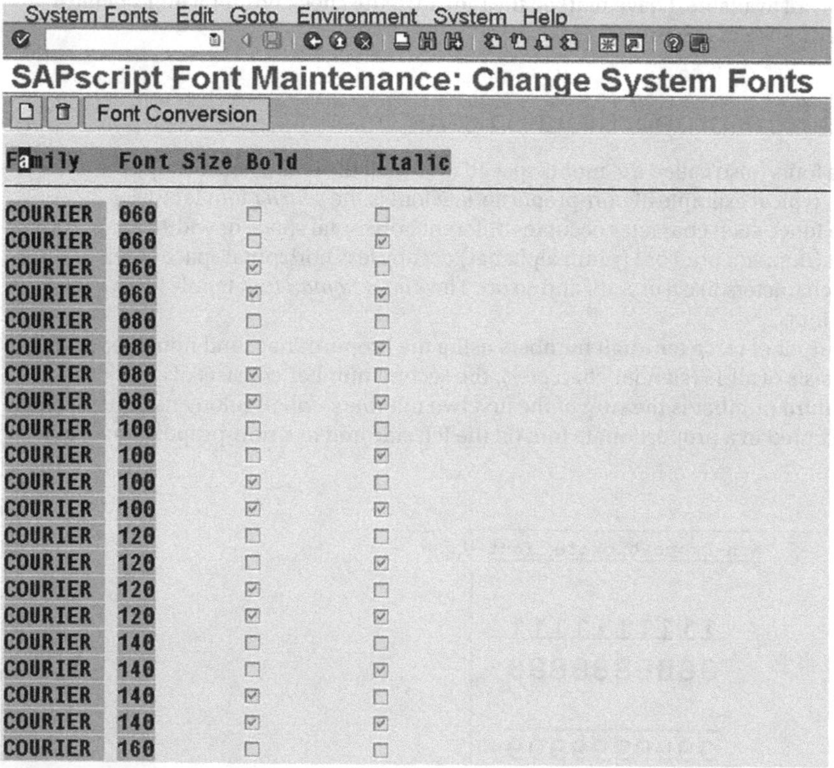

| Family | Font Size | Bold | Italic |
| --- | --- | --- | --- |
| COURIER | 060 | ☐ | ☐ |
| COURIER | 060 | ☐ | ☑ |
| COURIER | 060 | ☑ | ☐ |
| COURIER | 060 | ☑ | ☑ |
| COURIER | 080 | ☐ | ☐ |
| COURIER | 080 | ☐ | ☑ |
| COURIER | 080 | ☑ | ☐ |
| COURIER | 080 | ☑ | ☑ |
| COURIER | 100 | ☐ | ☐ |
| COURIER | 100 | ☐ | ☑ |
| COURIER | 100 | ☑ | ☐ |
| COURIER | 100 | ☑ | ☑ |
| COURIER | 120 | ☐ | ☐ |
| COURIER | 120 | ☐ | ☑ |
| COURIER | 120 | ☑ | ☐ |
| COURIER | 120 | ☑ | ☑ |
| COURIER | 140 | ☐ | ☐ |
| COURIER | 140 | ☐ | ☑ |
| COURIER | 140 | ☑ | ☐ |
| COURIER | 140 | ☑ | ☑ |
| COURIER | 160 | ☐ | ☐ |

*Figure 1-9. Font maintenance–system fonts*

## Printer Fonts, System Bar Codes, and Printer Bar Codes

Under Printer Fonts (the third Radio button on the SE73 opening screen), you can view the font versions already assigned to print devices. You can also assign font versions to print devices.

Under System Bar Codes (the fourth Radio button on the SE73 opening screen), you can view the bar codes available. You can create your own bar codes as well.

Under Printer Bar Codes (the fifth Radio button on the SE73 opening screen), you can view the bar codes already assigned to print devices. You can also assign bar codes to print devices.

Chapter 4 will demonstrate and cover the bar code output.

## True Type Font Installation

You can install or import additional fonts in the SAP script environment. The additional fonts to be installed have to be true type and must have been installed as true type font files in the operating system. The fonts to be installed must have the operating system font files and font matrix files available.

The installation of fonts from the operating system files into the SAP script environment cuts across operating systems and output device drivers. It involves the installation of font matrix files into the SAP script environment.

Installing fonts from the operating system into the SAP script environment is an elaborate process and involves the execution of operating system commands. You can refer to the SAP online document "SAP Printing Guide (BC-CCM-PRN)" for a detailed description of how to do it.

Here, I am demonstrating a procedure is to install a non-proportionate ttf file (Arial monospaced for SAP) from the Microsoft windows operating system into the SAP script environment.

For the non-proportionate font we are installing, we do not intend to use font matrix file.

The font installation procedure generally involves the font versions regular, bold, and italic and bold + italic to be installed in separate steps. The non-proportionate font Arial monospaced for SAP does not have an italic version. So you need to perform two steps, one for installation of the regular version of the font and the second step for installation of the bold version of the font. The procedure involves the assignment of installed font versions to device types (printer devices).

## Installing the Font

To install ttf files from the Microsoft (MS) windows operating system, navigate to the transaction code SE73 opening screen. At the bottom, click the button *True Type Font installation*. A screen will appear as shown in Figure 1-10.

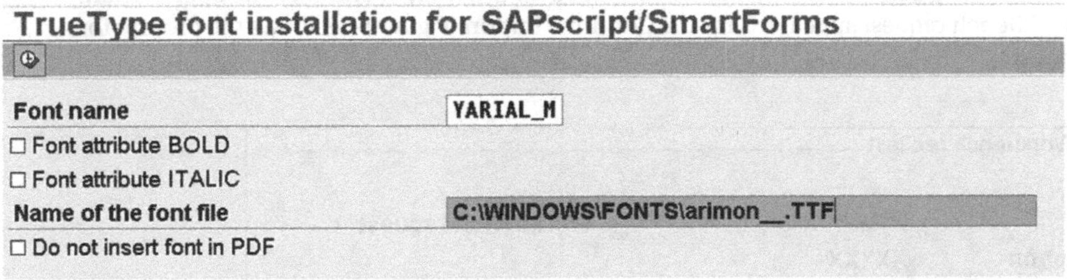

**TrueType font installation for SAPscript/SmartForms**

| | |
|---|---|
| Font name | YARIAL_M |
| ☐ Font attribute BOLD | |
| ☐ Font attribute ITALIC | |
| Name of the font file | C:\WINDOWS\FONTS\arimon__.TTF |
| ☐ Do not insert font in PDF | |

*Figure 1-10.* *True type font installation—Regular I*

Install the regular version of the non-proportionate ttf Arial monospaced of SAP from the MS windows operating system. We entered the name of the font to be installed as YARIAL_M (maximum namespace of eight characters). A font name need not start with Y or Z, but it is a good practice to have installed font names starting with Y/Z. This is the name by which the font will be referred to in the SAP script environment. We entered the ttf operating system file name along with the drive, folder location, and file's secondary name (ttf). The entry of the file name along with the folder location and the file's secondary name is necessary. The name of the font file for regular version is arimon__.TTF. The value C:\WINDOWS\FONTS\arimon__. TTF has been entered in the field *Name of the font file* as shown in Figure 1-10. Since the regular version of the font is being installed, we must ensure that the check box fields *Font attribute BOLD* and *Font attribute ITALIC* are disabled. Next, we should click the execute button or function key F8. An open file dialog box appeared as shown in Figure 1-11.

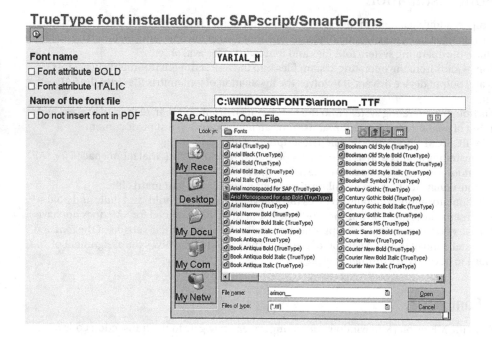

**Figure 1-11.** *True Type Font Installation—Regular II*

In the open file dialog box, select the Arial mono spaced for SAP font ttf and click the open button. A prompt for workbench request appears. Click the Continue button. Figure 1-12 shows the prompt for workbench request.

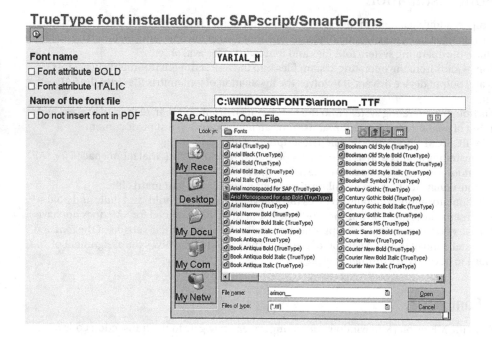

**Figure 1-12.** *True type font installation—Regular III: prompt for workbench request*

A dialog box to enter *RTF font info* should appear. Enter the *RTF font info* as shown in Figure 1-13 and click the Continue button.

RTF font info for PC txt editr
RTF text
\fmodern\fcharset &&& Arial monospaced for SAP

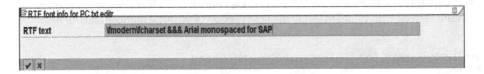

***Figure 1-13.*** *True type font installation—Regular IV: Prompt for RTF font info*

The RTF info has been entered based on the following guidelines available at the site:

`http://msdn.microsoft.com/en-us/library/aa140301(v=office.10).aspx`

If the ttf file gets installed successfully, it is reported through a screen like the one shown in Figure 1-14.

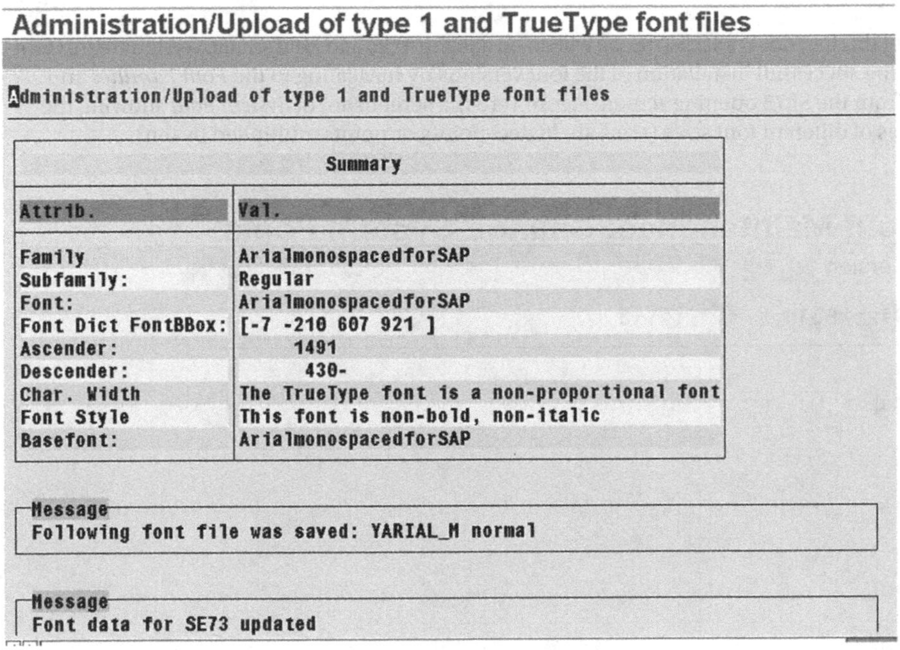

Administration/Upload of type 1 and TrueType font files
Administration/Upload of type 1 and TrueType font files
Summary
Attrib.
Val.
Family
ArialmonospacedforSAP
Subfamily:
Regular
Font:
ArialmonospacedforSAP
Font Dict FontBBox:
[-7 -210 607 921 ]
Ascender:
1491
Descender:
430-
Char. Width
The TrueType font is a non-proportional font
Font Style
This font is non-bold, non-italic
Basefont:
ArialmonospacedforSAP
Message
Following font file was saved: YARIAL_M normal
Message
Font data for SE73 updated

***Figure 1-14.*** *True type font installation—Regular: Successful installation)*

We installed the regular version of the font Arial monospaced for SAP. We repeated the same steps to install the bold version of the same font. The *Font name* should be the same as for the regular the version (i.e., YARIAL_M). The name of the font file for the bold version is arimonbd.TTF, which must be entered in the field *Name of font file* along with the folder name, etc. The check box *Font attribute BOLD* must be enabled. Figure 1-15 shows the initial screen with values to install the bold version of the Arial monospaced for SAP.

## TrueType font installation for SAPscript/SmartForms

| | |
|---|---|
| **Font name** | YARIAL_M |
| ☑ Font attribute BOLD | |
| ☐ Font attribute ITALIC | |
| **Name of the font file** | C:\WINDOWS\FONTS\arimonbd.TTF |
| ☐ Do not insert font in PDF | |

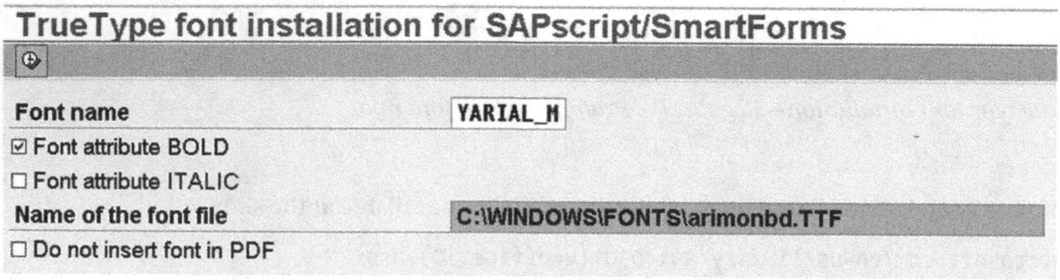

*Figure 1-15.* *True type font installation—Bold version*

An italic version of this font does not exist. So we will not install the italic and bold + italic versions of this font.

We can confirm the successful installation of the font versions by navigating to the *Font Families* and *System Font* screens from the SE73 opening screen. Figure 1-16 is a screenshot of *System Font* showing the YARIAL_M font entries of different font sizes (sizes are in deci points or points multiplied by ten).

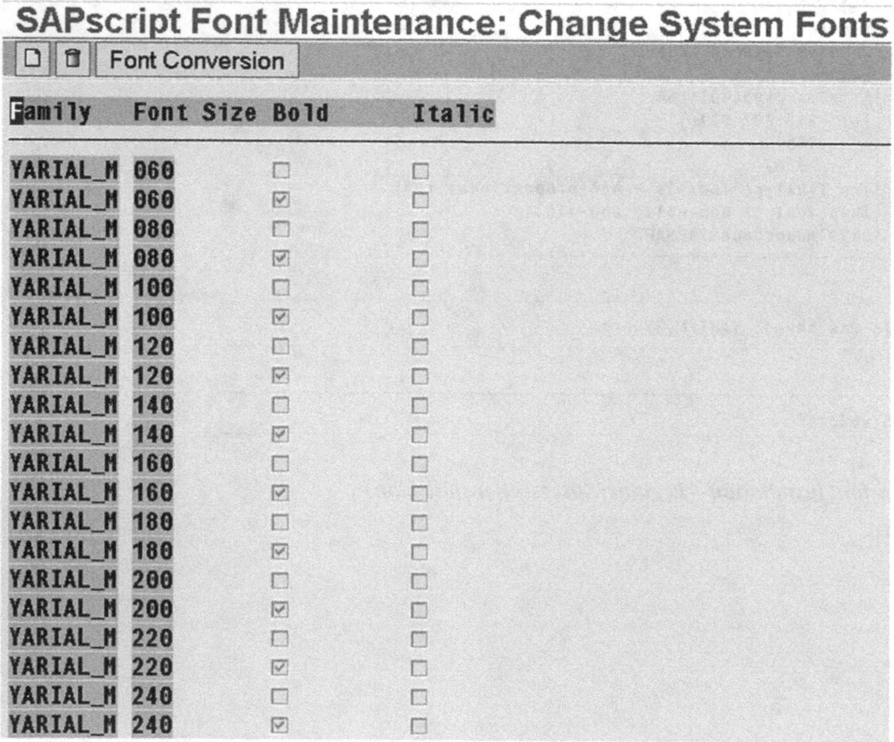

## SAPscript Font Maintenance: Change System Fonts

☐ 🗑 Font Conversion

| Family | Font Size | Bold | Italic |
|---|---|---|---|
| YARIAL_M | 060 | ☐ | ☐ |
| YARIAL_M | 060 | ☑ | ☐ |
| YARIAL_M | 080 | ☐ | ☐ |
| YARIAL_M | 080 | ☑ | ☐ |
| YARIAL_M | 100 | ☐ | ☐ |
| YARIAL_M | 100 | ☑ | ☐ |
| YARIAL_M | 120 | ☐ | ☐ |
| YARIAL_M | 120 | ☑ | ☐ |
| YARIAL_M | 140 | ☐ | ☐ |
| YARIAL_M | 140 | ☑ | ☐ |
| YARIAL_M | 160 | ☐ | ☐ |
| YARIAL_M | 160 | ☑ | ☐ |
| YARIAL_M | 180 | ☐ | ☐ |
| YARIAL_M | 180 | ☑ | ☐ |
| YARIAL_M | 200 | ☐ | ☐ |
| YARIAL_M | 200 | ☑ | ☐ |
| YARIAL_M | 220 | ☐ | ☐ |
| YARIAL_M | 220 | ☑ | ☐ |
| YARIAL_M | 240 | ☐ | ☐ |
| YARIAL_M | 240 | ☑ | ☐ |

*Figure 1-16.* *System font screen showing installed true type font YARIAL_M*

We will have to assign the installed font versions and font sizes to a device type—that is, a physical output device of a particular make and model.

## Assigning the Font to a Device Type

The device types are assigned to output devices (logical output devices). To know the device types supported by the application server(s), you can use the transaction code SPAD. On the opening screen of the transaction code SPAD, select an output device from the pop-up list. In the IDES server we used, the single output device is LP01. After entering the output device, click the first display button. Figure 1-17 shows the screen.

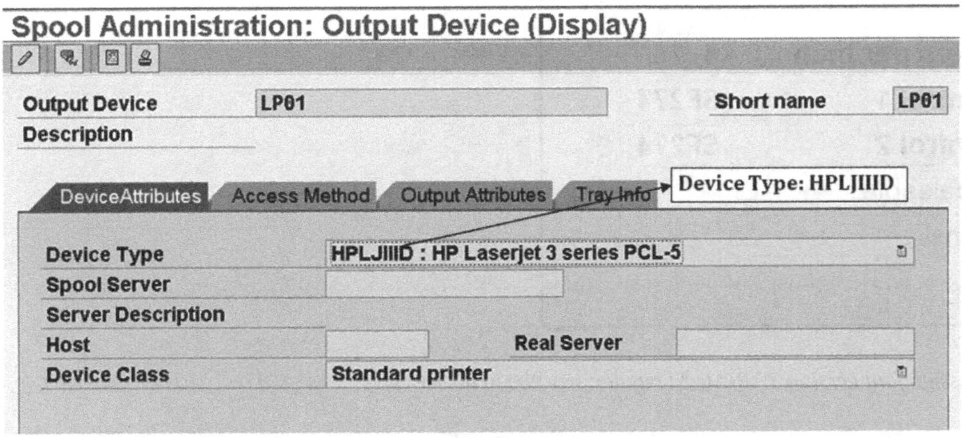

**Spool Administration: Output Device (Display)**

| Output Device | LP01 | | Short name | LP01 |
| Description | | | | |

DeviceAttributes | Access Method | Output Attributes | Tray Info → **Device Type: HPLJIIID**

| Device Type | HPLJIIID : HP Laserjet 3 series PCL-5 | |
| Spool Server | | |
| Server Description | | |
| Host | | Real Server | |
| Device Class | Standard printer | |

*Figure 1-17. Transaction code SPAD—output device and device type*

We will have to assign the installed font versions and sizes to the device type. (In our case, the device type is HPLJIIID.)

To assign installed font versions and sizes to the device type, you should navigate to transaction code SE73. On the opening screen of transaction code SE73, select the Radio button *Printer Fonts* and click the change button.

The device type HPLJIIID can be located in the device type list. Double-click the device type HPLJIIID. The font versions and sizes assigned to the device type HPLJIIID should appear as in Figure 1-18.

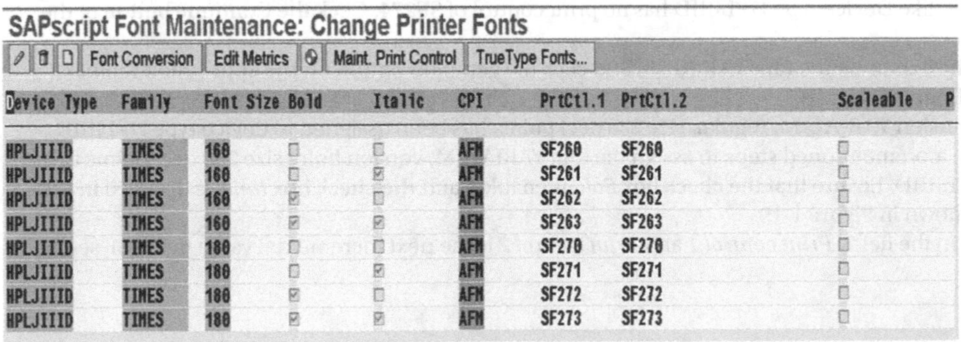

**SAPscript Font Maintenance: Change Printer Fonts**

Font Conversion | Edit Metrics | Maint. Print Control | TrueType Fonts...

| Device Type | Family | Font Size | Bold | Italic | CPI | PrtCtl.1 | PrtCtl.2 | Scaleable | P |
|---|---|---|---|---|---|---|---|---|---|
| HPLJIIID | TIMES | 160 | ☐ | ☐ | AFM | SF260 | SF260 | ☐ | |
| HPLJIIID | TIMES | 160 | ☐ | ☑ | AFM | SF261 | SF261 | ☐ | |
| HPLJIIID | TIMES | 160 | ☑ | ☐ | AFM | SF262 | SF262 | ☐ | |
| HPLJIIID | TIMES | 160 | ☑ | ☑ | AFM | SF263 | SF263 | ☐ | |
| HPLJIIID | TIMES | 180 | ☐ | ☐ | AFM | SF270 | SF270 | ☐ | |
| HPLJIIID | TIMES | 180 | ☐ | ☑ | AFM | SF271 | SF271 | ☐ | |
| HPLJIIID | TIMES | 180 | ☑ | ☐ | AFM | SF272 | SF272 | ☐ | |
| HPLJIIID | TIMES | 180 | ☑ | ☑ | AFM | SF273 | SF273 | ☐ | |

*Figure 1-18. Screen—assign font version and size to device type*

To assign font versions and sizes to a device type, click the Create button on the application toolbar (the third button from the left). When you clicking the Create button, a dialog box pops up as in Figure 1-19.

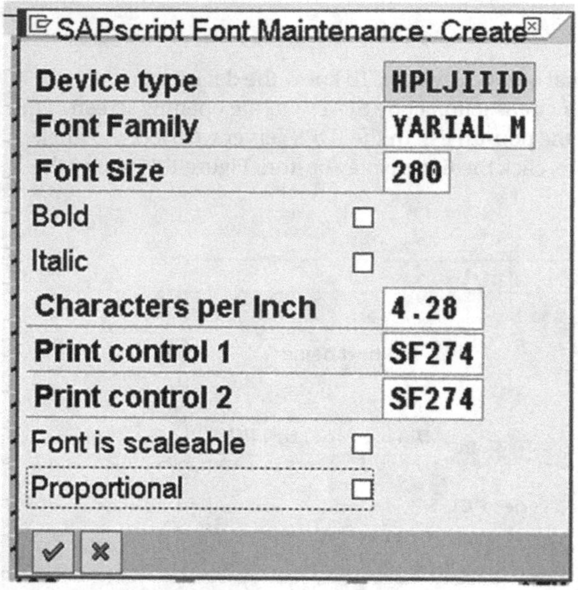

**Figure 1-19.** *Assign font version YARIAL_M regular, size 280 to device type*

As you can observe from Figure 1-19, we are assigning font version YARIAL_M Regular (installed earlier), size 280 deci points (28 points) to device type HPLJIIID. The font size has to be specified in deci points only. We are now assigning the regular version of font YARIAL_M to the device type, so we ensured that the check boxes *Bold* and *Italic* are disabled.

The value in the field *Characters per Inch* (4.28) has been calculated on the basis of the value ten characters per inch for a font size of 120 deci points (12 points).

The value in the fields *Print control 1* and *Print control 2* (SF274) is the next incremental value in the SF series (*Print control 1* and *Print control 2* are for portrait and landscape mode, respectively).

As the installed font YARIAL_M is non-proportionate, you must ensure that the check box *Proportionate* is disabled. We have not installed the font matrix files, so the check box *Font is scalable* is disabled.

After filling in the field values in the dialog box of Figure 1-19, click the Continue button. A message alert will appear, like Device type HPLJIIID has no print control of SF274. Click the Continue button of the message alert.

Position the cursor on the font YARIAL_M and click the generate button on the application toolbar. (Third button from the right)

The font version YARIAL_M, regular, size 280 deci points has been assigned to device type HPLJIIID.

Repeat the aforementioned steps to assign the font YARIAL_M, version bold, size 280 deci points to device type HPLJIIID. Ensure that the check box *Bold* is enabled and the check box *Italic* is disabled in the dialog box as shown in Figure 1-19.

The value in the fields *Print control 1* and *Print control 2* is the next incremental value in the SF series (i.e., SF275).

We have to create the print controls SF274 and SF275. To create the print controls, you have to be on the screen *SAP script Font Maintenance: Change Printer Fonts* for the device type HPLJIIID. This is the same screen we used to assign font versions and sizes to the device type (the screen in Figure 1-19). Position the cursor on the print control SF274. Click the application toolbar button *Maintain Print Control* (second button from the right). The dialog box for maintaining print controls, shown in Figure 1-20, should pop up.

| SAPscript Font Maintenance: Maintain Print Control | ⊠ |
|---|---|
| Device type | **HPLJIIID** |
| Print control | **SF274** |
| | |
| Variant | 1 |
| Hexadecimal switch | X |
| Standard setting | |
| Control Char. Seq. | 1B28304E1B287330703132683130763073306233454 |

**Figure 1-20.** *Create print control SF274*

Copy and paste the value in the field *Control Char.Seq.* from the COURIER font (i.e., from SF001). Accept default values for other fields on the screen. Click the Continue button, which creates the print control SF274.

In a similar manner, we can create the print control SF275.

We have installed the regular and the bold versions of the non-proportionate Arial monospaced for SAP font from the operating system into SAP script as YARIAL_M. This font does not have an italic version. We assigned this font, only for size 280 deci points, to the device type HPLJIIID. So, in the SAP script environment, we can only use the size 280 deci points of this font. If we want to use other sizes of this font, we will have to perform the assignment process of the font size to the device type, a cumbersome process. If the font matrix file of the font is installed, this may not be necessary. If the font matrix file of the font is installed in the SAP script environment, we can enable the check box *Font is scalable* (Figure 1-19) when assigning the font to a device type. In this manner, you can avoid assigning different font sizes to a device type.

I will use the installed font YARIAL_M in the demonstrative exercises.

# A Note on Naming Convention of Objects in the Book

The maximum namespace for a font name is eight characters. Whenever possible, we will be using a uniform naming convention for objects created for demonstration and as part of hands-on exercises in the book. In the present context of naming the imported font, we do not have enough characters to be able to identify the imported font name as per our naming convention.

As per our naming convention, all objects created for demonstration and as part of hands-on exercises will start with YCH##, ## indicating the chapter number we are in, like YCH01 . . . for objects created in Chapter 1, and so on. In most cases, we are also indicating a specific workbench object serial number like YCH01_01_<prog> for the first program in the chapter 1, YCH01_01_<view> for the first view in Chapter 1, and so on. Sometimes the namespace does not have enough characters to provide for a serial number. Sometimes we are only creating one or two objects categories and not specifying a serial number.

I suggest that you create your objects with names starting with the letter Z; the remaining characters in your object names can be the same as my object names. With this naming convention for your object names, co-relating your objects with my objects becomes easy. You can upload my objects from the E-resource into your server. My uploaded objects can serve as reference. Please read the document *A Guide to Use E-resource* available in the E_RESOURCE folder for this book (www.apress.com/9781484212345).

# Form Graphics–Import Graphics

You can incorporate graphics like a company logo into a *form*. The graphics to be incorporated into a *form* must be in the document server of the SAP database. You can import either a BMP (file saved with *Microsoft windows paint*) or a TIF graphic file of the operating system into the document server of the SAP database.

I will demonstrate the import of a BMP graphic file (created in *Microsoft windows paint*) into the document server. This imported graphic will be incorporated into *forms* as a company logo subsequently in our exercises. Before the BMP file is imported, you must ensure that the size of the graphic in the originating file is such that it can be incorporated as a company logo—approximately between one and two inches square. When you create a graphic in *Microsoft windows paint*, your actual graphic image may be lying in the top left corner, but by default, the white background of the graphic occupies a full page. Ensure that you remove the white background. We are using a simple graphic file which will serve the purpose of a demonstration. For the graphic import being demonstrated here, the originating BMP file looks like the one in Figure 1-21:

***Figure 1-21.*** *Import graphics—originating BMP file opened in MS windows paint*

Having identified the BMP file, let us go about importing it into the document server of the SAP database.

To import a graphic into the document server of the SAP database, we navigate to the opening screen of transaction code SE78. We click the *Stored on Document Server* node and then click the *Graphics General Graphics* subnode. Select the *BMAP Bitmap Images* folder. The screen should looked like the one in Figure 1-22.

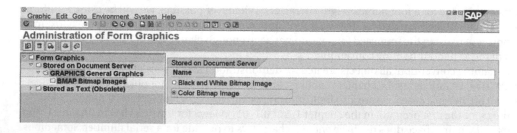

***Figure 1-22.*** *Import graphics—transaction code SE78 opening screen*

Click the import button on the application toolbar, the first button from the left. The dialog box for graphic file selection, etc. appears as shown in Figure 1-23.

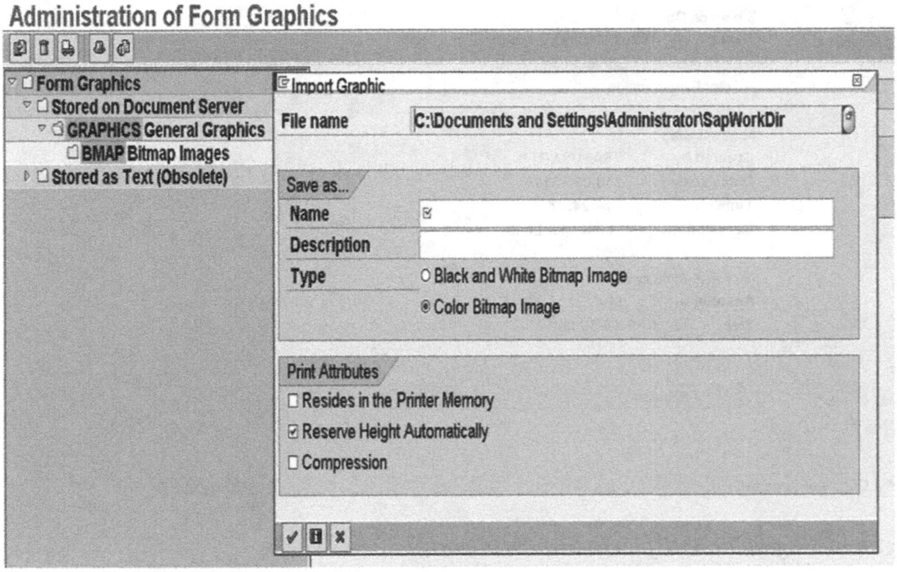

**Figure 1-23.** *Import graphics—dialog box to select graphic file, etc*

In the dialog box, enable the *Color Bitmap image* check box; enter a *Name* and a *Description* for the graphic. The name of the graphic need not start with Y/Z, but it is a good practice to do so. The graphic name was entered as YCH01_COMPANY_LOGO, following our naming convention. The default values were accepted for the *Print Attributes*. To make a selection of the BMP graphic file, press function key F4 in the field *File name*. The file selection dialog box appears. Select the BMP graphic file with the folder as: C:\temp\GRAPHIC_LOGO.bmp. After all the fields are entered, the screen appears as in Figure 1-24.

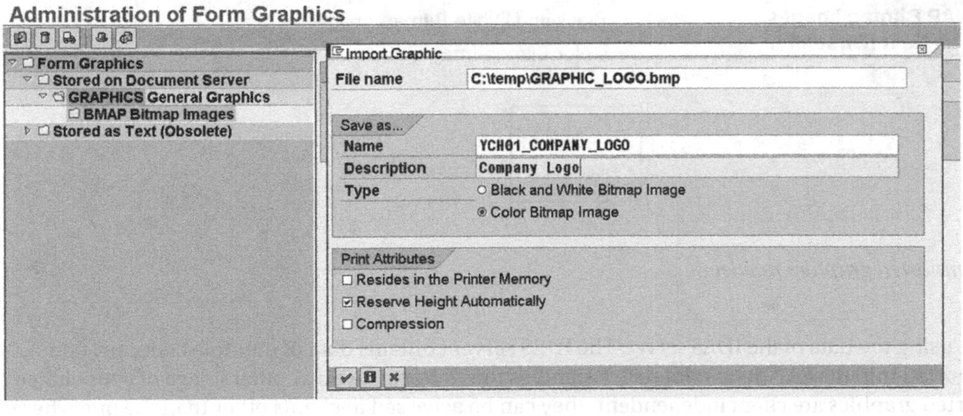

**Figure 1-24.** *Import graphics—dialog box with all the values entered*

Click the Continue button of the dialog box. If the graphic BMP file is successfully imported, a status message appears on the status bar as shown in Figure 1-25.

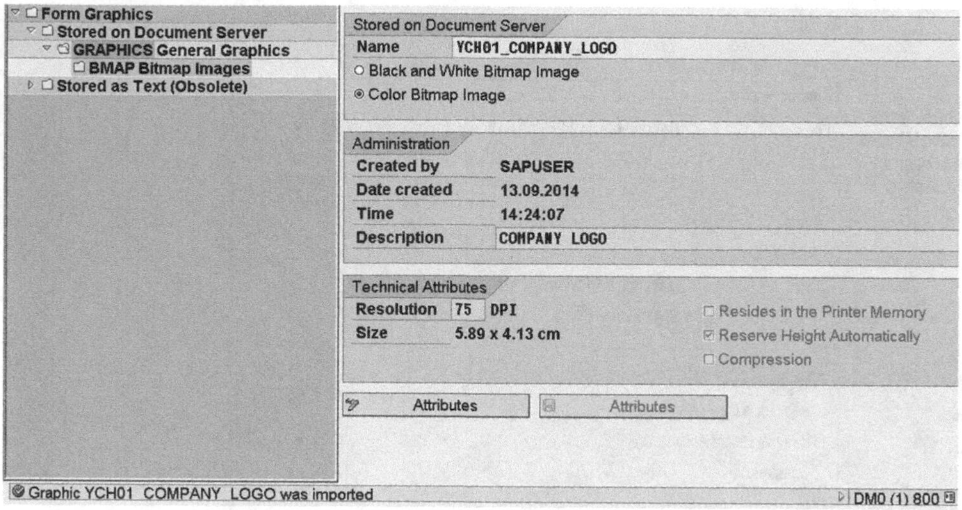

*Figure 1-25. Import graphics—graphic BMP file successfully imported*

This was the procedure to import a graphic BMP file into the document server of the SAP database. A preview of the imported graphic is available by clicking the preview button on the application toolbar (the first button from the right). Figure 1-26 shows a preview of our imported graphic.

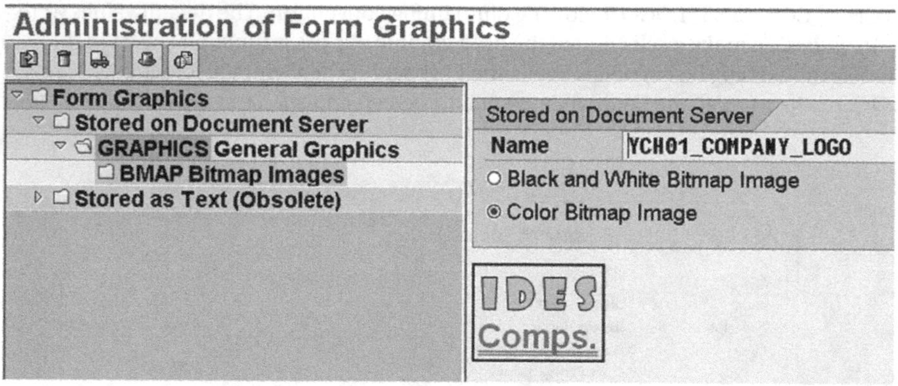

*Figure 1-26. Imported graphics preview*

We will be using the data of the IDES server. The IDES server contains data of multiple company codes. The image imported into the SAP document server signifies this. You can use any other image of your choice.

The imported graphics are client independent; they can be accessed in clients other than the one where they were imported. No package needs to be assigned to the imported graphics.

The imported graphics can be deleted—the button on the application toolbar is available to perform the operation.

We will use this imported graphic in our exercises. The BMP file is also available in the E-resource if you want to use it.

# Forms: Searching and Classification

Before proceeding to elaborate descriptions of *form* elements, I would like to touch upon the following two aspects of the *form*:

- *Form* classifications and sub classifications

- Searching for specific *forms*

The SAP-delivered ready-to-use *forms* residing in client 000 are assigned to classifications and subclassifications based on functional modules and submodules with which the *form* is associated. For example, the SAP ready-to-use *form* for purchase order is assigned to classification *Materials Management* and subclassification *Purchasing*. The name (technical name) of this *form* is MEDRUCK. Another example is the SAP ready-to-use *form* for delivery note, which is assigned to classification *Sales Distribution*, subclassification *Shipping*, and sub-subclassification *Delivery notes, picking lists*. The name (technical) of this *form* is RVDELNOTE.

The classifications (highest-level nodes), subclassifications (second and lesser levels of nodes), down to the *form* (last level of node) constitute a tree-like hierarchical structure. This tree-like hierarchical structure of *forms* and classifications is referred as the *SAP script Form Tree*.

Most SAP-delivered ready-to-use *forms* are assigned to classification and subclassification. *Forms* not assigned to any classification, subclassification nodes are assigned to the *unclassified* node.

To view the *SAP script Form Tree*, navigate to the opening screen of transaction code SE71. In the field *Form*, press function key F4. The screen shown in Figure 1-27 will appear.

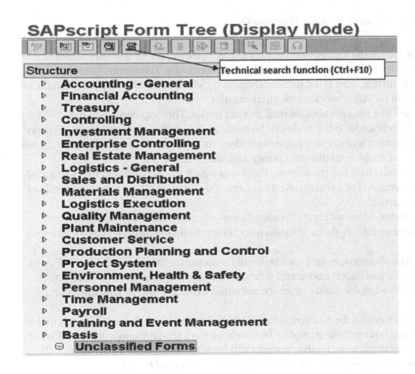

*Figure 1-27. SAP script Form Tree*

If we want to locate the *form* for purchase orders, click the node *Materials Management* and then click the subnode *Purchasing* as shown in Figure 1-28:

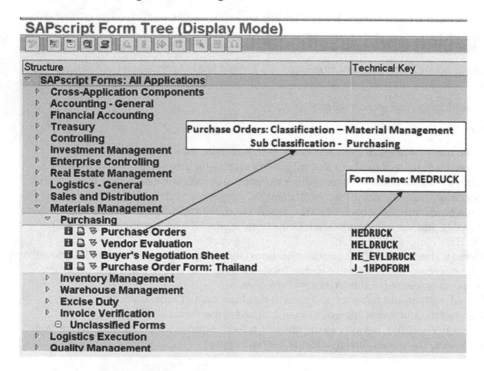

**Figure 1-28.** *SAP script Form Tree—locating the form Purchase Order*

The *SAP script Form Tree* facilitates the location and access to *forms*, especially by SAP functional consultants. The *SAP script Form Tree* is somewhat like an application hierarchy. The name of the purchasing document *form* is MEDRUCK. This is the technical name by which ABAP developers will refer to it, just like any other object name in the ABAP workbench environment.

The *unclassified* node appears as a kind of subnode under other nodes. This appearance of the *unclassified* node as a kind of subnode under other nodes is the same as the *unclassified* node appearing on the *SAP Script Form Tree* opening screen without any node expanded. Its appearance as a subnode facilitates the user's ability to view *unclassified* forms from different nodes and subnodes.

Recalling the relationship of *forms* with the client code, the *forms* which will be visible in the *SAP script Form Tree* will be all the language versions of *forms* residing in client 000 as well as all the language versions of *forms* residing in the logged-in client.

As part of our hands-on exercises, when we create custom *forms*—that is, modify copies of SAP-delivered ready-to-use *forms*—we can classify them. If we do not classify them, the *forms* will be assigned to the unclassified node.

We can create our custom classifications. In fact, we can totally manipulate the *SAP script Form Tree* to our requirements: insert, move, edit, and delete nodes and subnodes. The manipulation of the *SAP script Form Tree* will be demonstrated following the hands-on exercises when we create and modify forms and classify them in Chapter 2.

An alternative to locating *forms* through the *SAP script Form Tree* is locating *forms* through a search dialog box. We can invoke the search dialog box by clicking the fifth button from the left on the application toolbar of the *SAP script Form Tree* screen. This application toolbar button (fifth from the left) is marked in Figure 1-27 (technical search function). Figure 1-29 shows the search dialog box referred as *Find Forms*.

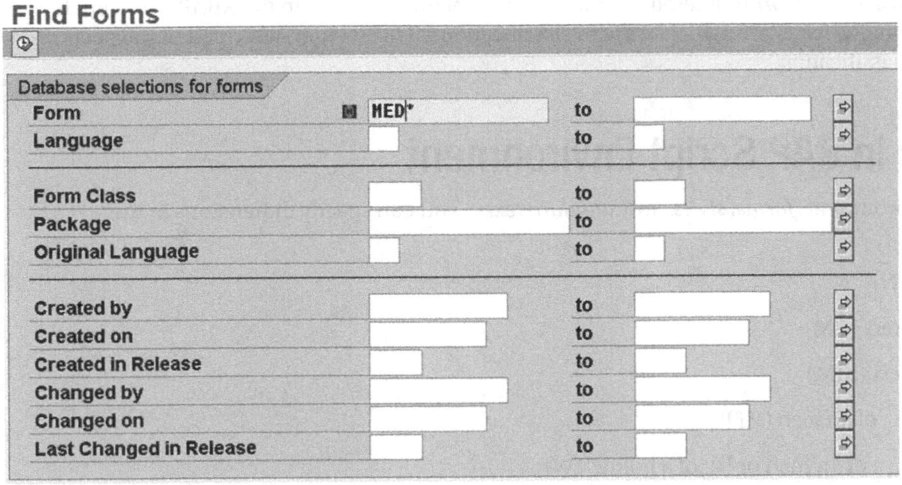
Find Forms
Database selections for forms
Form
MED*
to
Language
to
Form Class
to
Package
to
Original Language
to
Created by
to
Created on
to
Created in Release
to
Changed by
to
Changed on
to
Last Changed in Release
to

***Figure 1-29.*** *Find Forms—dialog box*

For the value(s) entered in the dialog box of Figure 1-29, all the language versions of *forms* whose names start with MED in client 000 and the logged-in client must appear in the list. Figure 1-30 shows part of the *Find Forms* list.

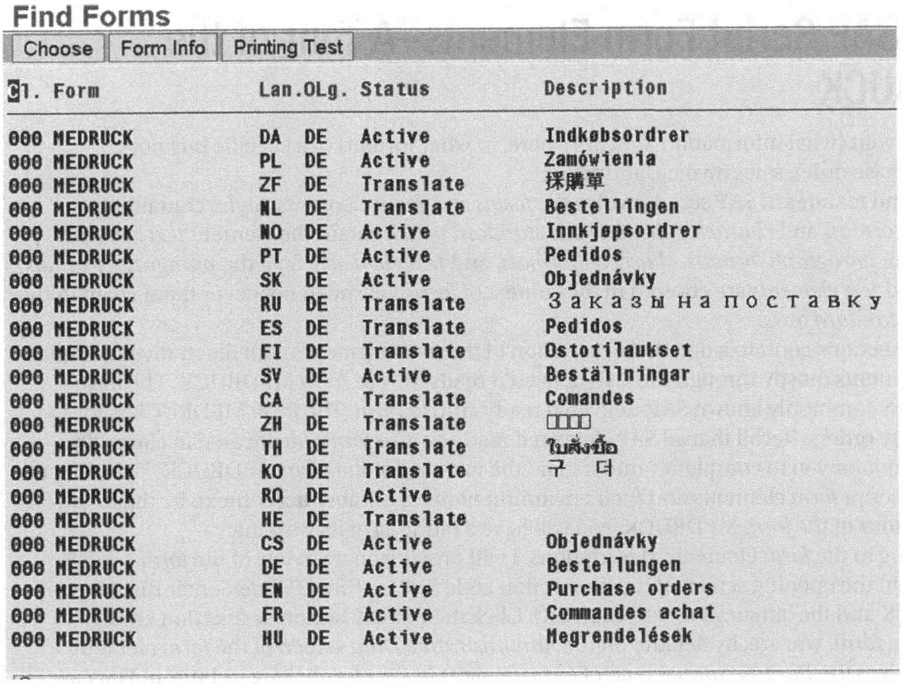
Find Forms
Choose
Form Info
Printing Test
Cl. Form Lan.OLg. Status Description
000 MEDRUCK DA DE Active Indkøbsordrer
000 MEDRUCK PL DE Active Zamówienia
000 MEDRUCK ZF DE Translate 採購單
000 MEDRUCK NL DE Translate Bestellingen
000 MEDRUCK NO DE Active Innkjøpsordrer
000 MEDRUCK PT DE Active Pedidos
000 MEDRUCK SK DE Active Objednávky
000 MEDRUCK RU DE Translate Заказы на поставку
000 MEDRUCK ES DE Translate Pedidos
000 MEDRUCK FI DE Translate Ostotilaukset
000 MEDRUCK SV DE Active Beställningar
000 MEDRUCK CA DE Translate Comandes
000 MEDRUCK ZH DE Translate □□□□
000 MEDRUCK TH DE Translate ใบสั่งซื้อ
000 MEDRUCK KO DE Translate 구 더
000 MEDRUCK RO DE Active
000 MEDRUCK HE DE Translate
000 MEDRUCK CS DE Active Objednávky
000 MEDRUCK DE DE Active Bestellungen
000 MEDRUCK EN DE Active Purchase orders
000 MEDRUCK FR DE Active Commandes achat
000 MEDRUCK HU DE Active Megrendelések

***Figure 1-30.*** *Result of Find Forms.*

The location and access to *forms* differed from the location of other objects in the ABAP workbench environment. Additionally, *forms* are associated with classifications. This section described two aspects of *forms*: location and classification.

# Dimensions in SAP Script Environment

In the SAP script environment (*forms, styles,* and *standard texts*), you can specify dimensions in the following units:

- Inches (IN)

- Centimeters (CM)

- Millimeters (MM)

- Points–$1/_{72}$ of an inch (PT)

- Twips–$1/_{1440}$ of an Inch or $1/_{20}$ of a point (TW)

- Number of lines for vertical measure; example: 10 lines top margin (LN)

- Number of columns or characters for horizontal measure; example: 10 characters/columns left margin (CH)

You need to specify dimensions for *page windows*; margins, indents, and so on, of *paragraph formats* and tab spaces. When specifying dimensions, you can use any of the units from the foregoing list.

# A Detail on SAP Script Form Elements–A Tour of the Form MEDRUCK

A *form* maps to the layout (what information appears where, in what format) of a specific business document type: purchase order, sales invoice, and so on.

Most concepts and features of SAP script involve the *forms* and *form* elements. *Styles* contain the elements *paragraph formats* and *character formats*. The *standard texts* contain the element *text elements*. The *forms* also contain *paragraph formats, character formats,* and *text elements*. So if the *paragraph formats, character formats,* and *text elements* are covered in the context of *forms*, we need not cover them again in the context of *styles* and *standard texts*.

The succeeding sections contain a detailed description of the *form* elements with illustrative examples. I explain the *form* elements mostly through the SAP-delivered ready-to-use *form* MEDRUCK. The *form* MEDRUCK is the most commonly known SAP-delivered ready-to-use *form*. The *form* MEDRUCK is for the generation of purchase orders. Recall that all SAP-delivered ready-to-use *forms* are located in client 000.

The objective is not for you to completely understand the working of the *form* MEDRUCK. The objective is to present the SAP script *form* elements and their environment in a non-abstract context. By the time you are through with the tour of the *form* MEDRUCK, you will have a fair idea of its working.

Before proceeding to the *form* elements' descriptions, I will provide an overview of the *form's* application toolbar. On the opening screen of the transaction code SE71—*Form Painter*: enter the name of the *form* as MEDRUCK and the language as DE (German). Click the display button or function key F7.

When you enter a *form*, you are, by default, on the *Administrative Data* screen of the *form* element *header*. You can switch to the *Basic Settings* screen of *form* element *header* by clicking its button. You can switch or navigate to the different elements of the *form* by clicking the button of the corresponding *form* element. Figure 1-31 shows the application toolbar of a *form* screen.

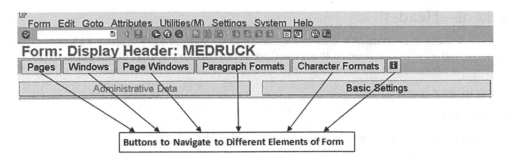

**Figure 1-31.** *Application toolbar of a form*

The first button to the right of the application toolbar represents the *form documentation*, to navigate to *form* element *documentation*. This button contains only an icon without any text.

To navigate to the *form* element *windows*, click the button *Windows*. The screen will appear as in Figure 1-32.

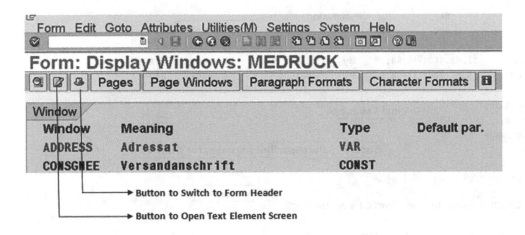

**Figure 1-32.** *Screen for Form element: Window*

When you navigate to the screen of a particular *form* element, the corresponding button of the *form* element disappears on the application toolbar. In Figure 1-32, on the screen of *form* element *windows*, two buttons on the application toolbar are marked (second and third buttons from the left; these two buttons contain icons without any text).

By clicking the second button from the left on the application toolbar, you navigate to the *form* element: *text elements*. This button appears on the application toolbar only when you are either on the *windows* screen or on the *page windows* screen. The *form* element *text elements* is located in the form element *windows* (Figure 1-3).

By clicking the third button from the left on the application toolbar (picture of a hat), you navigate back to the *form* element *header*.

The navigation from one *form* element to another is available through the menu option *Goto* as well.

The following sections provide detailed descriptions of *form* elements.

# Form Element—Header

The first of the *form* elements is the *header*. A *header* contains attribute information like *created by, last changed by, package,* and so on (maintained by the system), as well as substantial extra information. The *header* is further categorized into the following:

- Administrative Data

- Basic Settings

Figure 1-33 shows a screenshot of the *Administrative Data* of the *form* MEDRUCK.

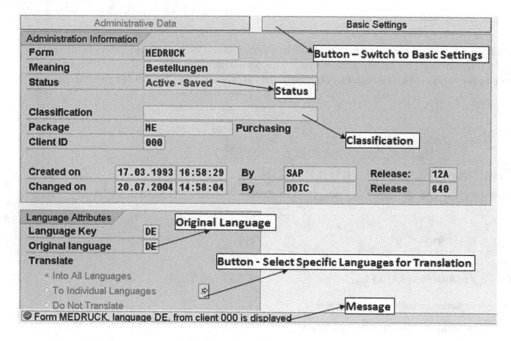

***Figure 1-33.*** *Form element—header: Administrative Data*

The *form* in Figure 1-33 has been opened in display mode in the original language version (i.e., DE). The message on the status bar is alerting the user of the client 000 to the location of the *form*.

The field *Classification* is blank. The *form* MEDRUCK is assigned a two-level classification, Materials Management ➤ Purchasing. If a *form* is assigned a single-level classification, the classification appears in this field, *Forms* assigned to multilevel classifications as well as unclassified *forms* will contain blanks in the field *Classifications*. When we create or define custom nodes, subnodes and assign our custom *forms* to subnodes, the field *Classification* of our custom *forms* contains the immediate subnode text to which the custom *form* is assigned. (Refer to the concluding part of the section "Classifying forms" in Chapter 2.)

The Radio buttons at the left bottom of the screen specify the *form* translations. When you create a new *form*, the button marked as *Languages for Selection* enables you to select languages into which the new *form* can be translated or the languages in which the *form* can be maintained. When you press this button, a dialog box appears listing all the SAP supported languages with check boxes to enable or disable language selections for translation.

Other fields on the screen of Figure 1-33 are self-explanatory.

When you click the button *Basic Settings*, a screen as shown in Figure 1-34 will appear.

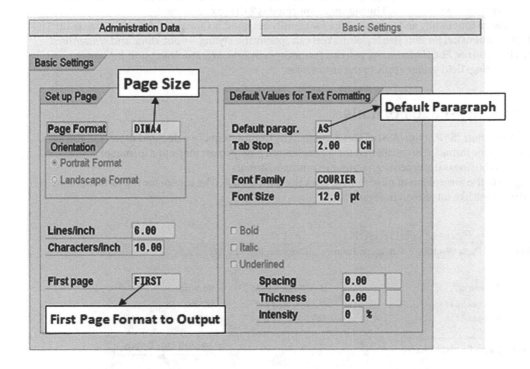

***Figure 1-34.*** *Form element—header: Basic Settings.*

*Basic Settings* consists of several elements.

## Set Up Page Area

You can specify the page alignment through Radio buttons: *Portrait Format* or *Landscape Format*. You can specify the page size or dimensions through a pop-up list. In Figure 1-34, the page size DINA4 has been assigned. DINA4 has the following dimensions: 210MM X 297MM in *Portrait Format*. DINA4 is the German name of A4 size stationery. Most common stationery sizes like A3, letter, and so on, are available in the pop-up list.

Next you can specify the vertical density in terms of lines/inch and horizontal density in terms of characters/inch. When you specify dimensions in lines and characters within a *form*, the SAP script *form* maintenance system uses the values assigned here to convert the lines and characters into physical dimensions (inches, centimeters, etc.).

You have to specify the *page format* which should output first when you generate the business document. This is entered in the field *First page*. For the MEDRUCK *form*, the value assigned is FIRST. Assigning a value to the field *First page* is mandatory.

## Default Values for Text Formatting Area

In this area, you specify the default paragraph which is mandatory. The default paragraph value assigned is AS. You further specify the tab spaces. The tab space specified is 2 CH (2 characters).

Next you assign font family and font size. The font family assigned is Courier and the font size is 12PT (or points). The dimension for font size is points. You can specify the styling—*Bold, Italic* and *Underlined*—through the check boxes. For *Underlining,* you can further specify *Spacing, Thickness,* and *Intensity.*

The *Basic Settings* field values apply to the entire *form.*

## Form Element—Page Formats

Recall from the section "SAP Script-A Brief Description of Its Components," we decided to refer to the *form* element *page* as *page format.* Also recall that the *form* element *page format* maps to a format of a business document type. A business document can output in multiple formats.

To navigate to the *form* element *page format,* click the button *Page.* The screen for the *form* element *page format* will look like the screen in Figure 1-35.

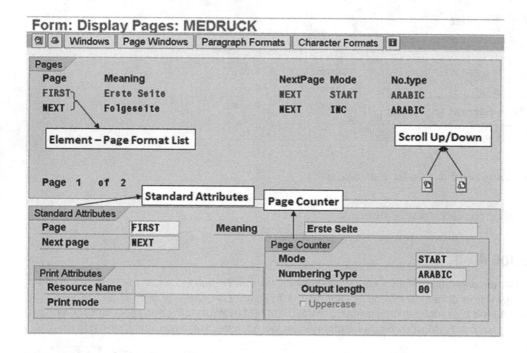

***Figure 1-35.*** *Form element—Pages format: FIRST*

In Figure 1-35, the top section under the heading *Pages* is a listing of *page format* elements. The *form* MEDRUCK has two *page formats:* FIRST and NEXT. You can select one element of the list by double-clicking the element. When you initially enter the screen, the first element in the list is selected by default; the selected element appears in blue with default screen color settings. When you navigate to any of the other *form* elements—*windows, page windows, paragraph formats* and *character formats*—a similar element list will appear.

The namespace of *form* elements *page formats*, *windows*, and *page windows* is a maximum of eight characters.

In Figure 1-35, the *page format* FIRST has been selected. You provide meaning or short text for every element. In the lower part of the screen, under the section on the left, *Standard Attributes*, the particulars of the selected *form* element *page format* appear. The first two fields in the section are *Page*, containing the value FIRST, and *Meaning*, or the short text. This is the name of the *page format* element—namespace of eight characters, case insensitive. All *form* element names are case insensitive. In the next field *Next page* is entered in the value NEXT. This is an indication to the SAP script runtime system to output which *page format* after the FIRST. Entry in this field is mandatory.

In the area *print Attributes*, in the field *Resource Name*, you can optionally enter a paper tray name as the source of stationery.

In the field *Print mode*, you can specify through a pop-up list whether you require printing on one side or both sides of the stationery. Table 1-2 provides pop-up list values with descriptions.

*Table 1-2.* *Page Format—Standard Attributes—Print Mode*

| Print mode | Description |
| --- | --- |
|  | Default: no change of print mode |
| S | SIMPLEX MODE |
| D | DUPLEX MODE (Printing on Both Sides) |
| T | TUMBLE DUPLEX MODE (Printing on Both Sides) |

Under the section on the bottom right of the screen *Page Counter*, you can indicate the how the page number will be operated upon and output for the *page format*. The field *Mode* in this section can be assigned a value from a pop-up list. A list of available values from the pop-up list along with descriptions and comments appears in Table 1-3.

*Table 1-3.* *Page Format—Page Counter—Mode*

| Mode | Description | Comments |
| --- | --- | --- |
| INC | Increasing counter by 1 | Running number. Page Format NEXT has been assigned this value. |
| HOLD | Not changing counter | Do not disturb counter value. |
| START | Setting counter to 1 | Initialize at the start of a new business document. Page Format FIRST has been assigned this value. (Figure 1-28) |

The next field under the section *Page Counter* is *Numbering Type*. You can assign a value to the field from a pop-up list. The field denotes how the page number will output on the business document (decimal numeral, Roman numeral, letters, etc.). The pop-up list values with the descriptions appear in Table 1-4.

**Table 1-4.** *Page Format—Page Counter—Numbering Type*

| Numbering Type | Description | Comments |
| --- | --- | --- |
| ARABIC | Numbering with Arabic or decimal numerals | Numerals 1, 2, 3 . . . |
| CHARACTER | Fixed character | |
| LETTERS | Numbering with letters | |
| ROMAN | Numbering with Roman numerals | Roman numerals I, II... |

In the field *Output Length* in the section *Page Counter*, you can optionally enter the number of columns to output the page number.

The field *Uppercase* (check box) in the section *Page Counter* enables you to make Roman numerals and letters of page numbers appear in upper case only.

I have described all the fields of the screen of *page format* FIRST.

Figure 1-36 shows a screenshot of *page format* NEXT.

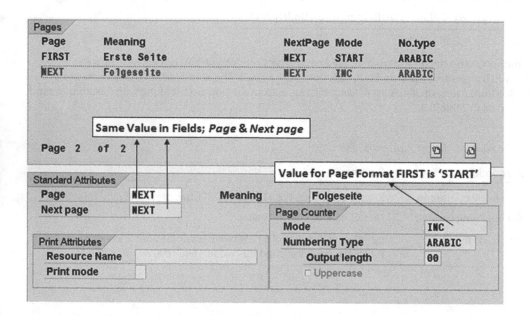

**Figure 1-36.** *Form element—Page format: NEXT*

In Figure 1-36, note the value of field *Next page* as NEXT. This value indicates which *page format* to use after the first physical page using *page format* NEXT is full.

The value of field *Mode* is INC; that is, increment the page counter by 1 every time a physical page is full.

# Form Elements–Windows and Page Windows

Our discussion in this section will involve both *windows* and *page windows*. The two *form* elements go together. A *page window* cannot exist without being assigned to a *window*. A *page window* does not have an identification or name of its own. Practically, a *window* not assigned to a *page window* (unused *window*) makes no sense. Hypothetically, you can create a *window* and not assign it a *page window*, but then this is a waste.

The *form* element *window* is independent of the *form* element *page format*. A *window* is not located inside a *page format*. A *page window* is located inside a *page format*, and a *page window* has to be mandatorily assigned to a *window*.

For *window* types constant, variable, and graph, only one *page window* of a *page format* can be assigned to a *window*. There can be any number of constant, variable, and graph *windows* in a *form*.

For *window* type main, multiple (maximum of 99) *page windows* of a *page format* can be assigned to the main *window*. There can only be one main *window* in a *form*. The name of the main *window* can be 'MAIN' only.

To navigate to the *windows* screen in the *form* MEDRUCK, click the button *Windows* on the application toolbar.

Figure 1-37 shows a screenshot of the *windows* of the *form* MEDRUCK:

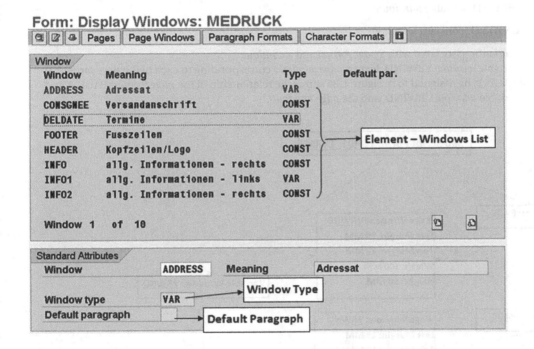

***Figure 1-37.*** *Form element—Window: ADDRESS*

As you can observe in Figure 1-37, there are ten *windows* in the *form* MEDRUCK. Eight of the ten *windows* are visible in the element list in Figure 1-37. Scrolling down will make the rest of the two *windows* appear.

The list appears in alphabetic ascending order.

A default paragraph can be optionally assigned to a *window* (bottom of Figure 1-37). This assignment overrides the default paragraph assignment in the *basic settings* of the *form header*.

A meaning or short text is provided for every element.

Other fields in Figure 1-37 are self-explanatory.

I am diverting a bit for a while from the *form* MEDRUCK to explain the relationship between *page formats, windows,* and *page windows* as well as the concept of *windows* and *page windows* in the context of presentation or output of data—especially repetitive data. The term "repetitive data" is explained in the section "Window Type Main—Operation and Considerations." I will revert to the *form* MEDRUCK after I have discussed the relationship between *page formats, windows,* and *page windows,* as well as the concept of *windows* and *page windows* in the context of presentation of data.

## Relationship Between Page Formats, Windows, and Page Windows

I will explain the relationship between the *form* elements *page formats, windows,* and *page windows* with a specific example. Consider a *form* YCH01_DFRM. Let it consist of the following two *page formats*:

- PAGE_1
- PAGE_2

Let it consist of the following two *windows*:

- VRWIND (variable *window*)
- CNWIND (constant *window*)

A *page window* is associated with a *page format* and a *window.*

For the variable *window* VRWIND, let two *page windows* corresponding to each of the *page formats,* PAGE_1 and PAGE_2, be assigned to it. Figure 1-38 shows the relationship of the *page formats* PAGE_1 and PAGE_2 the variable *window* VRWIND, and the *page windows.*

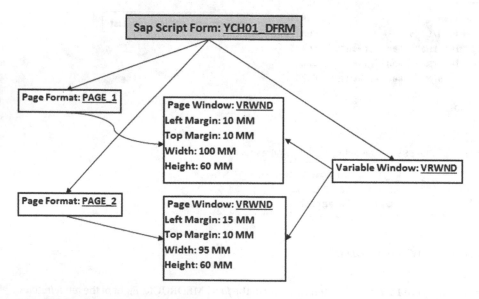

***Figure 1-38.*** *Relationship between page formats, variable windows, and page windows*

The dimensions of the two *page windows* (i.e., left margin, top margin, width, and height) assigned to the variable *window* VRWIND have been deliberately made different.

For the constant *window* CNWIND, let two *page windows* corresponding to each of the *page formats* PAGE_1 and PAGE_2 be assigned to it. Figure 1-39 shows the relationship of the *page formats* PAGE_1, PAGE_2, constant *window* CNWIND, and the *page windows*.

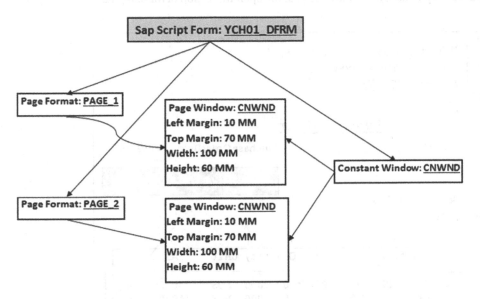

***Figure 1-39.*** *Relationship between page formats, constant windows, and page windows*

The dimensions of the two *page windows* (i.e., left margin, top margin, width, and height) assigned to the constant *window* CNWIND are identical.

The relationship between *page formats*, a graph *window,* and *page windows* is identical to the relationship between *page formats*, a variable *window,* and *page windows* depicted in Figure 1-38.

It is apparent that you can avoid using constant *windows*.

I will elaborate on the relationship between *page formats*, the main *window*, and *page windows* with specific examples during coverage of the *form* element *text elements*.

## Window Type Main—Operation and Considerations

A main *window* differs considerably from the other *window* types in operation and behavior. When a new *form* is created, the main *window* gets created by default automatically. The main *window* is to be used for data (data for most part means fields) which is repeating within a page and repeating from page to page. I will refer to this data which is repeating within a page and repeating from page to page as repetitive data.

To clarify the idea of presentation of repetitive data, let us revert to the business document type purchase order introduced in the opening section of this chapter. The emphasis now is on the output of items/materials of the purchase order. The data of items—material code, description, quantity, and amount—in the purchase order or most business documents constitutes the repetitive data. In terms of SAP table fields, the repetitive data in the purchase order is MATNR, MAKTX, MENGE, MEINS, and NETWR. Figure 1-40 reproduces the purchase order introduced in the opening section of this chapter.

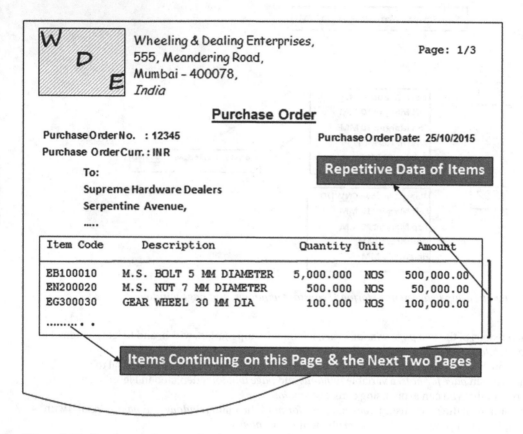

***Figure 1-40.*** *Purchase order—emphasis on output of items*

The purchase order shown in Figure 1-40 runs for three pages: 1/3, 2/3, and 3/3.

A purchase order or a business document might contain one or *n* number of items. You assign an area of a physical page for the item data to be output. This area can accommodate certain number of items in a single physical page. If the number of items in a purchase order exceeds the number of items which can be accommodated in a single physical page, the document must extend and continue to output in the next page and the next page and so on until all the items in a purchase order are output.

The output of repetitive data is implemented in the *forms* by locating the repetitive data in a *page window* assigned to the *main window*.

When only one *page window* of a *page format* is assigned to the main *window*, the *page window* behaves like a stretchable frame. As you continually fill such a *page window* with data, when the current page is full, a page break is generated automatically, the output of the data continues in the *page window* on the next page. This process continues until the filling of data into *page window* ceases.

If more than one *page window* of a *page format* is assigned to the main *window*, then the process of filling data in the *page window* is as follows: Let us consider the case of two *page windows* of a *page format* assigned to the main *window* and the same process will apply to the case of more than two *page windows* of a *page format* assigned to the main *window*.

When two *page windows* of a *page format* are assigned to the main *window*, data filling will take place in the first *page window* of a *page format* assigned to the main *window*. When the first *page window* of a *page format* assigned to the main *window* is full, data filling by default will continue in the second *page window* of a *page format* assigned to the main *window* on the same page. When the second *page window* of a *page format* assigned to the main *window* is full, an automatic page break occurs, and data filling will continue in the first *page window* of a *page format* assigned to the main *window* in the next page. This process continues until data filling ceases. The operation of main *window* with a single *page window* and multiple *page windows* will be demonstrated in demonstration exercises III and IV.

## Window Types Other Than Main Window–Operation and Considerations

For the three *window* types—constant, variable, and graph—the contents of the *page windows* assigned to these *window* types appear on every physical page which outputs for the *page format* in which the *page windows* exist.

For the *window* type graph, if the size of the graphic/picture is larger than the *page window* size, the graphic/picture will overshoot the boundaries of the *page window* and occupy the neighboring *page windows*.

When a *page window* is assigned to any of the two *window* types—constant and variable—and you try to include more data more than the physical size of this *page window* can accommodate, the extra data gets truncated. The size of a *page window* is essentially its height and width.

# Form Elements–Windows and Page Windows: Tour of Form MEDRUCK Continued

I will resume the descriptions of *form* elements through the tour of MEDRUCK in this section. The *form* element next in line for description is the *page windows*.

To view the *page windows* of the *form* MEDRUCK, click the button *Page Windows* on the application toolbar. The screen will look as shown in Figure 1-41.

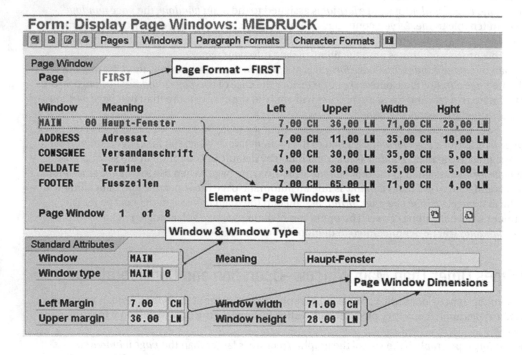

**Figure 1-41.** *Form element—Page window: MAIN 00 for page format FIRST*

The very first field on the screen is the *page format* (*page* in SAP terminology). Recall that *page windows* are located in *page formats*. The value in this field is FIRST. The *page windows* listed in the element list belong to the *page format* FIRST. There are eight *page windows* in the *page format* FIRST.

The first of the *page windows* appearing in the element list is the *page window* assigned to MAIN *window* marked as 00. The names of the *page windows* are the same as the names of their corresponding *window*s. As the MAIN *window* can be assigned to multiple *page windows,* the *page windows* assigned to MAIN *window* are numbered 00-98 by default.

Under the element list, in the *Standard Attributes* area, the dimensions left margin, upper margin, window width, and window height appear.

The *page windows* horizontal dimensions have been expressed in characters (CH) and vertical dimensions have been expressed in lines (LN).

Following the *page window(s)* assigned to MAIN *window*, the list of remaining *page windows* appears in alphabetic ascending order.

You can double-click these *page windows* and view their *Standard Attributes*.

If you select in the field *Page* (nee *page format*) the value equal to NEXT from the pop-up list, *page windows* of *page format* NEXT will appear in the element list. This is shown in Figure 1-42.

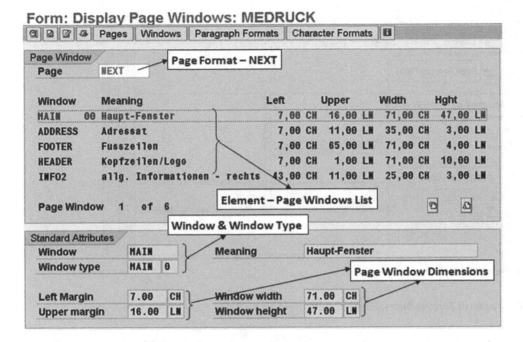

*Figure 1-42. Form element—Page window: MAIN 00 for Page Format—NEXT*

There are six *page windows* in the *page format* NEXT.

In Figures 1-41 and 1-42, we have viewed the layout of a *page format* with its *page windows* in non-graphical mode. The layout of a *page format* with its *page windows* can be viewed with the *Graphical Form Painter*. To view a *page format* with its *page windows* in graphical mode, make the following menu selection: Settings ➤ Form Painter. On making this menu selection, the dialog box of *User Specific Settings* as shown in Figure 1-43 appears:

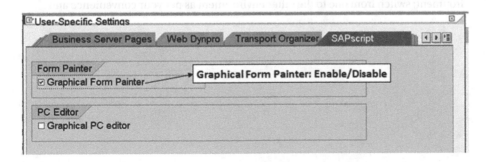

*Figure 1-43. Form Painter setting—Graphical/Non-Graphical*

Enable the check box of *Graphical Form Painter*, and click the Continue button.
The *Graphical Form Painter* will display the *page windows* of *page format* FIRST as shown in Figure 1-44.

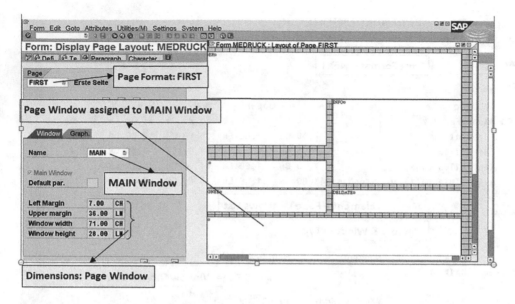

***Figure 1-44.*** *Graphical Form Painter—Page Format: FIRST*

All of the white rectangular areas on the right of the screen are *page windows* of the *page format* FIRST.

You can select the *page format* NEXT from the drop-down list at the top left corner of the screen marked as *page format*. You can then view the *page windows* of the *page format* NEXT in the *Graphical Form Painter*.

There is no way to close the *Graphical Form Painter* dialog box on *form* screen; you can minimize it though.

The only way to close the *Graphical Form Painter* dialog box is make the menu selection Settings ➤ Form Painter and disable the *Graphical Form Painter* check box in the *User Specific Settings*.

The *Graphical Form Painter* is a tool to maintain (create, change, position/reposition, and delete) *windows* and *page windows* together in a graphical environment. I will describe the operations in the *Graphical Form Painter* when we perform exercises. You can use *Graphical Form Painter* or operate in the non-graphical environment; switch from one to the other environment as per your convenience and requirements.

# Form Element–Paragraph Formats

The *form* element *paragraph formats* are formatting specifications applied to the contents of a *form*. The contents of a *form* are located in the *form* element *text elements*. To navigate to the *paragraph formats* in the MEDRUCK *form*, click the *paragraph formats* button of the application toolbar. The screen will look like the one in Figure 1-45.

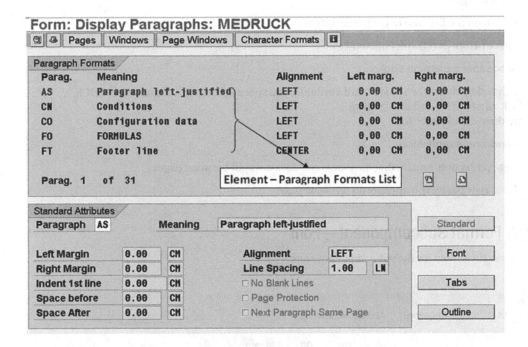

**Figure 1-45.** *Form element—Paragraph Formats AS: subcomponent standard*

There are 31 *paragraph formats* in the *form* MEDRUCK. The first of the *paragraph formats*, AS, is displayed. A *paragraph format* namespace is a maximum of two characters, the name starts with an alphabet; the second character can be alphanumeric.

As for any other component, you enter meaning or short text.

A *paragraph format* consists of four subcomponents. Each of these subcomponents is accessible through four push buttons marked *Standard*, *Font*, *Tabs*, and *Outline*. The four push buttons appear at the bottom right of the screen as shown in Figure 1-45. By default, the subcomponent *Standard* is selected.

A description of each of the four subcomponents follows.

## Paragraph Format Subcomponent—Standard

Figure 1-45 shows the standard attributes of the subcomponent *Standard*. In this subcomponent, on the left side of the screen, you specify

- Left margin

- Right margin

- Indent on the first line of the paragraph

- Space before paragraph commences

- Space after paragraph ends

On the right side of the screen of standard attributes, you specify paragraph alignment (BLOCK, CENTER, LEFT, and RIGHT) and line spacing.

There are three check boxes for:

- Blank line: suppression

- Page protection: ensure that the paragraph does not spill between pages

- Next: new paragraph appears on the same page

## Paragraph Format Subcomponent—Font

Figure 1-46 shows the screen for the subcomponent *Font*:

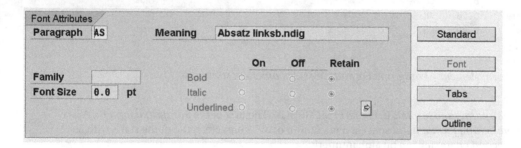

*Figure 1-46. Form element—Paragraph format AS: subcomponent Font*

You can select a font from a pop-up list in the field *Family* (left side of the screen, under the field *Paragraph*). The font size is to be entered manually. The dimension for font size is points. A preview of fonts is unavailable, so, before using or assigning a font family and size, check whether the font family and size is available in the *System Fonts* as well as *Printer Fonts*. No values are assigned to the font fields; it implies that font family and size assigned in prior setting (i.e., the *Basic Settings* of the *form Header*) are applicable (see Figure 1-34).

In Figure 1-46, on the right side of the screen, you can specify font styling: bold, italic, and underlined. There are three Radio buttons for each styling: bold, italic, and underlined. You can click the Radio button *On* to enable the specific styling, click the Radio button *Off* to disable the specific styling, and click the Radio button *Retain* to retain the prior style settings (i.e., the *Basic Settings* of the *form Header* are applicable) (see Figure 1-34). You can assign underlying attributes like thickness, intensity, and so on, by using the button appearing alongside the underlined Radio button.

## Paragraph Format Subcomponent—Tabs

Figure 1-47 shows the screen for the subcomponent *Tabs*.

Tabs
Paragraph AS
Meaning
Absatz linksb.ndig
Tab – Width
Tab – Unit
Tab – Alignment
Number
Tab position
Alignment
1
2
3
0.00
0.00
0.00
Standard
Font
Tabs
Outline

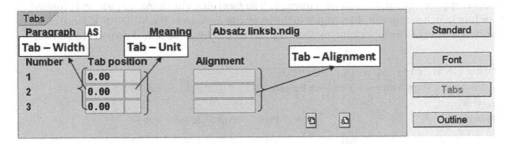

***Figure 1-47.*** *Form element—Paragraph format AS: subcomponent Tabs*

This subcomponent of the *paragraph format* allows you to establish tab stops; these tab stops override the tab stops created in the *Basic Settings* of the *form Header*.

The tab width or space is the space from the left *page window* margin. The units can be any of the horizontal space units: CH, CM, IN, MM, PT, or TW.

If the tab stops in a *paragraph format* are fewer than in the *Basic Settings* of the *form Header*, the tab stops in the *Basic Settings* of the *form Header* are used for the rest of the line.

You can specify alignment of text with the tab stop through a pop-up list in the field marked as *Tab—Alignment* in Figure 1-47. In addition to the alignments—left, right and center—you can also specify alignment with sign and alignment with comma character.

I next describe the last of the *paragraph format* subcomponents: *Outline*.

## Paragraph Format Subcomponent—Outline

Using the subcomponent *Outline* of the *paragraph format*, you can create paragraph names or numbers, chain paragraph names or numbers, and output chained paragraph names or numbers. You can specify margins to use, when you output chained paragraph names or numbers. The screen for subcomponent *Outline* will look like the one in Figure 1-48.

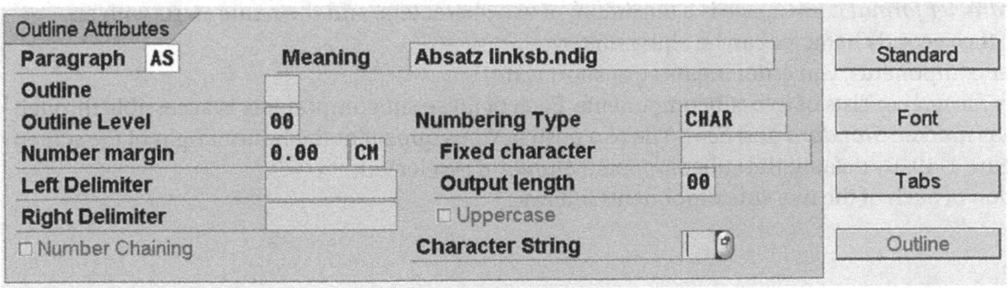

Outline Attributes
Paragraph AS
Meaning
Absatz linksb.ndig
Outline
Outline Level 00
Numbering Type CHAR
Number margin 0.00 CM
Fixed character
Left Delimiter
Output length 00
Right Delimiter
Uppercase
Number Chaining
Character String
Standard
Font
Tabs
Outline

***Figure 1-48.*** *Form element—Paragraph format AS: Subcomponent Outline*

From here we move on to a description of the *form* element *character formats*.

# Form Element–Character Formats

The *form* element *character formats* are formatting specifications applied to the contents of a *form*. As discussed previously, the contents of a *form* are located in the *form* element *text elements*. The *form* element *paragraph formats* is applied to format an entire paragraph. The *form* element *character formats* is applied to format parts or blocks in a paragraph. To navigate to the *character formats* in the MEDRUCK *form*, click the *character formats* button of the application toolbar. The screen will look like that shown in Figure 1-49.

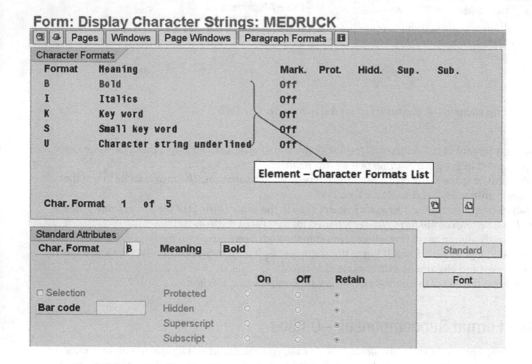

***Figure 1-49.*** *Form element—Char.Format B: subccomponent Standard*

There are five *character formats* in the *form* MEDRUCK. The first of the *paragraph formats* B is displayed. A *character format* namespace is a maximum of two characters, and the name starts with an alphabet letter; the second character can be alphanumeric.

As for other components, you enter meaning or short text.

A *character format* consists of two subcomponents. Each of these subcomponents is accessible through two push buttons marked *Standard* and *Font*. The two push buttons appear at the bottom right of the screen as shown in Figure 1-49. By default, the subcomponent *Standard* is selected.

A description of each of the two subcomponents follows.

## Character Format Subcomponent—Standard

Figure 1-49 shows the standard attributes of the subcomponent *Standard*. In this subcomponent, on the left side of the screen, you can enable the check box *Selection* to indicate bar code output. You can then select a bar code from the pop-up list.

On the right side of the screen of standard attributes, there are four Radio buttons with legends. Table 1-5 lists the legends and descriptions.

***Table 1-5.*** *Character Format—Standard Attributes*

| Legend | Description |
| --- | --- |
| Protected | The text assigned to this character format will output in one line, not spill over between lines |
| Hidden | The text will not output |
| Superscript | The text is output half a line higher |
| Superscript | The text is output half a line Lower |

We proceed next to the subcomponent *Font*.

## Character Format Subcomponent—Font

Figure 1-50 shows the screen for the subcomponent *Font*.

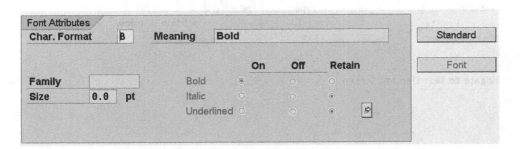

***Figure 1-50.*** *Form element—Char.Format B: subcomponent Font*

The subcomponent *Font* of element *character format* is identical to the subcomponent *Font* of the element *Paragraph format* (Figure 1-46). Before using or assigning a font family and size, check whether the font family and size are available in the *System Fonts* as well as *Printer Fonts*. No values have been assigned to the font fields; it implies that font family and size assigned in the prior setting are effective. The font assignments of *character format* override the font assignments of *Paragraph format*.

From here we move on to a description of the *form* element *text elements*.

# Form Element—Text Elements

The six *form* elements described so far (*header, page formats, windows, page windows, paragraph formats,* and *character formats*) involve only the layout and formatting specifications of a *form* (how and where to output). The contents of a *form* are contained in the *form* element *text elements* (what to output).

We introduced and elaborated the six *form* elements mostly in the context of the SAP-delivered ready-to-use *form* MEDRUCK. We will also introduce the *form* element *text element* in the context of the *form* MEDRUCK. Then we will get out of the context of the *form* MEDRUCK and create simple *forms* of our own. While creating our own *forms*, we will use the concepts of the six *form* elements described earlier and demonstrate the various features of the *form* element *text elements*. These *forms* of our own will be demonstrative in nature; that is, they will demonstrate mostly the features of the *form* elements. These *forms* of our own will not involve full-fledged business scenarios. The *forms* of our own (custom *forms*) involving full-fledged business scenarios will be created and tested in Chapter 2.

First, let us view *text elements* in the main *window* of the form MEDRUCK. Recall, the *text elements* are located in a *window*. Also recall that repetitive data (i.e., the item data of purchase orders) is located in the main *window*.

Open the German version (language key DE) of the *form* MEDRUCK in display mode from the opening screen of the transaction code SE71.

To navigate to the *text element* screen of the main *window* of the *form* MEDRUCK, click the button *Windows* on the application toolbar. Scroll down (not if all ten *windows* are visible) and select the main *window* in the element list. Figure 1-51 shows the screen of the main *window*.

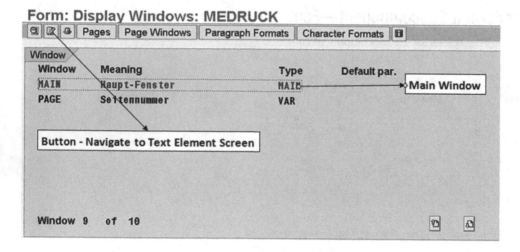

*Figure 1-51. Select Window Main, Button to navigate to text elements*

Click the button *text element* on the application toolbar (second button from the left, marked in Figure 1-51).

The *text element* screen like the one shown in Figure 1-52 will appear.

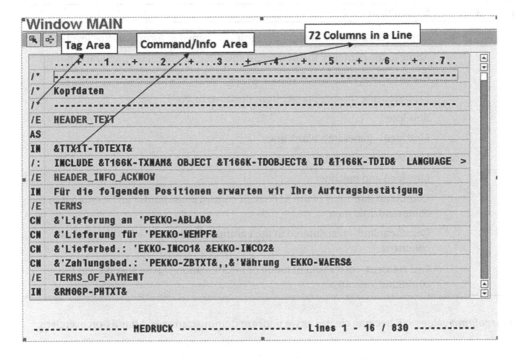

*Figure 1-52.* *Form MEDRUCK—Main Window, text element screen*

You use the text editor to make entries in the *text element* screen. As shown in Figure 1-52, the *text element* screen is divided into two areas or sections: the *Tag Area* and the *Command/Info Area*.

The text editor has a menu bar (not shown in Figure 1-52) to carry out various operations.

The *text elements* can be named or identified. There can be any number of named *text elements* in a *window*. There can be, at the very beginning, one unnamed *text element* in a *window*.

The description of each of the *text element* areas—*Tag Area* and *Command/Info Area*—follows.

## Text Element—Format Column or Tag Area

In Figure 1-52, one area is marked as the *Tag Area*. In the SAP documentation the *Tag Area* is referred to as *format column*. A *format column* can contain a two-character tag indicating the type of entry in the area marked *Command/Info Area*. For example, if the *format column* contains /: (forward slash and a colon), you can enter any of the repertoire of ABAP-like statements in the *Command/Info Area*. The repertoire of ABAP-like statements supported in the *text elements* of a *form* is called SAP script control commands. The SAP script control commands with explanations can be found in the PDF document "BC Style and Form Maintenance," part of the supplementary resource to be used with this book (www.apress.com/9781484212345).

Table 1-6 lists the *format column* values with explanations.

***Table 1-6.*** *Format Column Values with Explanations*

| Format Column Value | Explanation |
| --- | --- |
| * | Apply to the contents, default paragraph assigned at form/window level |
| <para name> | Apply to the contents, the paragraph specified (2-character paragraph name) |
| | Continuous text |
| = | Extended line (line extending from previous line(s)) |
| ( | Raw line |
| / | Line feed—generate a blank line |
| /= | Line feed and extended line |
| /( | Line feed and raw line |
| /: | Command line—any of the SAP script control commands can be entered in the command/info area |
| /* | Comment line—text entered in the command/info area will be treated as comment |
| /E | Text element—text element name or identification will be specified in the command/info area |

The *format column* values will become clearer as we perform demonstrative and hands-on exercises.

# Text Element—Command/Info Area

The *Command/Info Area* of the *text element* in Figure 1-52 shows 72 visible columns in a line. But a line can extend beyond 72 columns to a maximum of 132 columns by making the menu selection Edit ➤Page Left/ Right. The visibility of 72 columns in a single line is the limit of the text editor.

When the *format column* value is an * (asterisk) or a two-character paragraph name, data or information will be specified in the *command/info area*. The data in the *command/info area* can be string/text literals and variables. Data specification in the *command/info area* (literals and variables) can run into multiple lines. The continuation to the next line is indicated with the tag assigned a value '=' (equal to). The literals are entered as they are without enclosing single quotes. The variable data or information in the *command/info area* is specified by enclosing the variable name in ampersands (&). For instance, &KNA1-KUNNR& specifies that you want to output the variable KUNNR which is a component of the structure KNA1 declared in the SAP script print program. This is the way data is received from the SAP script print program into the SAP script *form* environment. Several types of variables can be specified in the *command/info area* of *text elements*.

## Program Symbols

The values of elementary data objects declared with the DATA and TABLES in the SAP script print program (ABAP program) are transferred to identically named variables in the *text element* enclosed in ampersands (&). These variables in the *text element* enclosed in ampersands deriving their values from identically named elementary data objects in the print program are called program symbols. The values in the program symbols are as they are output. For example, let the value of amount of a purchasing document item be stored or be available in the data object EKPO-NETWR. This data object is declared in the SAP script print program. The value is stored in packed decimal notation (two decimal digits per byte, etc.). If you specify a program symbol or variable in the *text element* of a *form* as &EKPO-NETWR&, the value available in this program symbol is stored in character notation (two bytes per character in Unicode 16). The amount will be stored as it outputs, that is, with the thousand separators, a decimal character, and a sign. Figure 1-53 shows, on the left, the data as stored in the data object EKPO-NETWR (SAP script print program), and on the right, data as stored in the program symbol &EKPO-NETWR&.

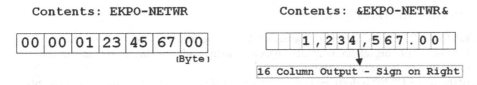

**Figure 1-53.** *Data transfer from print program data object to program symbol*

## Text Symbols

The text symbol can be declared within a *text element* of the SAP script *form* with a SAP script control command DEFINE. The text symbol names need to be enclosed within ampersands. The text symbols store information equivalent to the ABAP elementary type C. They can assume values not greater than 80 characters. If more than 80 characters have to be stored, they have to be split and stored in multiple text symbols up to a maximum of 255 characters which can output in a single line. The text symbols in the SAP script *form text element* environment are distinct from the text symbols defined in the text elements of an ABAP program. Following is an example of text symbol definition and assignment:

```
/: DEFINE &ENTERPRISE_NAME& = 'Apress Publishers'
```

SAP script control commands unlike ABAP statements are not terminated by a period (.) as in the control command above. The namespace of a text symbol is a maximum of 34 characters including the enclosing ampersands.

# System Fields Available Within the SAP Script Form Environment

It can be any of the variables available in the SAP script *form* environment including the system fields available in ABAP programs with the prefix SY- like SY-DATUM, SY-REPID, and so on.

The System fields in the SAP script *form* environment are further categorized.

## System Symbols

Some system symbols are &DATE&, &TIME&, &MONTH&, &PAGE&, &NAME_OF_MONTH&, &NEXTPAGE&, &ULINE&, and &VLINE&.

## Standard Symbols

The standard symbols can be viewed with the transaction code SE75 SAP script settings ➤ standard symbols. The standard symbols are language dependent. You can create your own standard symbols and assign values to them. At runtime the standard symbols are replaced by their values.

## General SAP script Fields

Some general SAP script fields are &SAPSCRIPT-SUBRC&, &SAPSCRIPT-FORMPAGES& (total number of pages in a business document), and &SAPSCRIPT-JOBPAGES&.

## SYST Fields or System Fields in the ABAP Programming Environment

The system fields of the ABAP programming environment with the prefix SY- are available in the SAP script environment. They must be specified with the prefix SYST- instead of the prefix SY-. The STST fields are set by the SAP script runtime environment instead of the ABAP runtime environment.

## &USR03&—Structure for User Info

The structure USR03 in the SAP script environment contains information from the user address data for a user-like user id: address, telephone, telefax, language key, etc. The user address data is available in the DDIC transparent table of the same name (i.e., USR03).

If a data object of the name USR03 is declared in the SAP script print program, then the contents of this data object is copied to the SAP script symbol &USR03&, else, SAP script runtime system loads the values for the logged-in user into this symbol from the user address data table USR03.

With the SAP script system fields, there are instances of redundancy, like the application server date being available in SYST field &SYST-DATUM& as well as in system symbol &DATE&, the application server time being available in SYST field &SYST-UZEIT& as well as in system symbol &TIME&, and so on.

In the *text element* screens of the *form* MEDRUCK described by us until now, the text editor being used in the screenshots is a non-graphical editor. You can switch to a graphical text editor by using the menu options Goto ➤ Configure Editor or Goto ➤ Change Editor in the text editor screen.

We will be using the non-graphical text editor only throughout this book.

The non-graphical editor of *text elements* is a line editor. Copying and pasting operations with this editor are thus extremely cumbersome and awkward (ctrl+Y, etc.). Whenever you want to perform copying and pasting operations in the *text elements* environment, you can switch to the graphical text editor.

I will cover the features of *text elements* (control commands and formatting features) in detail as we perform demonstrative examples in the current chapter and business scenario examples in Chapter 2.

I will defer a description of the last of the *form* element *documentation* to a later stage, when we create forms for business scenarios.

Now that I have completed descriptions of the elements of a *form* in the context of the SAP-delivered *form* MEDRUCK, we will create *forms* and print programs to demonstrate the basics of *forms*, *styles*, and *standard texts*.

# Demonstration I

We will create our first *form* to demonstrate the following:

- Creation of a *form* with a single *page format*

- Inclusion of a graphic image in a graphic *window* of the *form*

- Inclusion of literal text in a variable *window* of the *form*

- Creation and application of *paragraph formats* and *character formats* to the literal text in the variable *window*

- Test print or print preview the *form* from the SAP script environment

In this demonstration, we are not using the main *window*.

So, let us proceed to the creation of a *form* that will demonstrate the foregoing features.

## Form Header

We navigated to the *SAP script Form Maintenance: Initial Screen*—transaction code SE71. We entered the *form* name as YCH01_01_FST_FRM (maximum namespace of 16 characters) in the field *Form*. We clicked the Create button (you can alternatively press the function key F5). An information alert "Form YCH01_01_FST_FRM language EN is not available in client ###" appeared. We clicked the Continue button. The *Administration Data* screen of the element *header* appeared. We entered a meaningful text in the field *Meaning*. We clicked the *Basic Settings* button. On this screen, we selected the DINA4 stationery in portrait mode—210MM width and 297MM height. For the rest, we accepted the defaults proposed by the *form* maintenance system.

## Page Format

Next, we will create one *page format*. We clicked the application toolbar button *Pages*. We are on the *Pages* screen. The element list is empty. Once you are on any element screen (*Pages, Windows*, etc.) if you want to create a new element, make the following menu selection: Edit ➤ Create Element (Shift+F6). When this menu selection was made, a dialog box appeared for input of element name (*page format* name) and meaning or short text. Figure 1-54 shows the dialog box with the entered values.

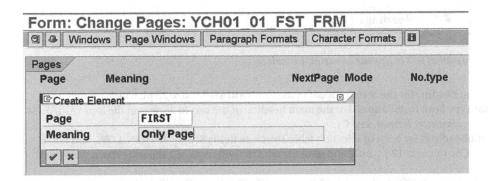

*Figure 1-54.* *Create Form YCH01_01_FST_FRM—Page format FIRST*

We clicked the Continue button and accepted the default values for the fields of the standard attributes. We did not enter any value in the field *Next page*. The *page format* FIRST is created.

## Specifications of the Text in the Variable Window

The text we are planning to locate in the variable *window* is a short write-up on the description of the structure of selection tables. The selection tables, if you recall, are data objects created with the SELECTION-SCREEN statement SELECT-OPTIONS or the data declarative statement RANGES. The *paragraph formats* and the *character formats* that we create will depend on how we want to present the text in the variable *window*. We could have selected any random text; we have selected the text related to a description of the structure of selection tables because readers can relate to it. The appearance of the text should be as shown in Figure 1-55.

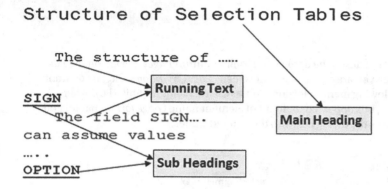

***Figure 1-55.*** *Rough layout of text to appear in variable window*

We want the main heading for the text to appear in the font YARIAL_M, size 28 pt, which we uploaded in the section "True Type Font Installation." For the main heading of the text to appear in the font YARIAL_M will require a separate *character format,* say, C1.

We want the subheadings for each of selection table structure fields SIGN, OPTION, LOW, and HIGH to appear in the font Courier, size 12 pt, bold and underlined. This will require a separate *character format,* say, C2.

We will have one *paragraph format,* say P1, with all the default values. We will designate this as the default paragraph. For our running text, we require a *paragraph format,* say, P2 with five characters indenting on the first line of the paragraph and one line gap at the end of the paragraph. When we use or output with the uploaded font YARIAL_M; the characters in one line are almost touching the characters in the next line. To resolve this and create a small gap between two lines, we will use a *paragraph format,* say, P3, with a value equal to 2 in the field *Line Spacing*. Assigning a value 2 to the field *Line Spacing* to produce a gap between lines has been determined by trial and error. The value in all the other fields will be the default values.

To sum up, we have two *character formats* and three *paragraph formats* in the *form.*

## Paragraph Formats

Let us create *paragraph formats*. We clicked the application toolbar button *paragraph formats*. On the screen of the *paragraph formats*, we made the menu selection Edit ➤ Create Element. The dialog box for input of element name (*paragraph format* name) and meaning or short text appeared. Figure 1-56 shows the dialog box with the entered values.

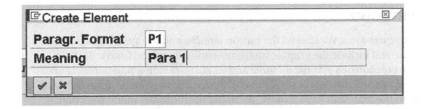

*Figure 1-56.* *Create Form YCH01_01_FST_FRM—Paragr.Format P1*

We clicked the Continue button. We accepted the default values for the fields of the standard attributes, fonts, tabs, and so on.

In a similar manner, we set about creating a second *paragraph format* P2. For the *paragraph format* P2, in the *Standard Attributes* area, we assigned the field *Indent 1st line* (indent first line in the paragraph) a value 5 CH (5 characters) and the field *Space After* a value of 1 LN (1 line). Figure 1-57 shows these entered values for *paragraph format* P2.

| Paragraph Formats | | | | | |
|---|---|---|---|---|---|
| **Parag.** | **Meaning** | **Alignment** | **Left marg.** | **Rght marg.** | |
| P1 | Para 1 | LEFT | 0,00 CH | 0,00 CH | |
| P2 | Para 2 | LEFT | 0,00 CH | 0,00 CH | |

Parag.  2  of  2

| Standard Attributes | | | | |
|---|---|---|---|---|
| Paragraph | P2 | Meaning | Para 2 | Standard |
| Left Margin | | CH | Alignment | LEFT | Font |
| Right Margin | | CH | Line Spacing | 1.00 LN | |
| Indent 1st line | 5 | CH | ☐ No Blank Lines | | Tabs |
| Space before | | CH | ☐ Page Protection | | |
| Space After | 1 | LN | ☐ Next Paragraph Same Page | | Outline |

*Figure 1-57.* *Create Form YCH01_01_FST_FRM—Paragraph Formats P1 and P2*

We created a third *paragraph format* P3, with default values for all fields except the field *Line Spacing*. In the field *Line Spacing*, we entered the value 2.00 LN (2 lines).

## Complete Mandatory Entries in the Form Header

Now that we have created a *page format* and three *paragraph formats*, we have to complete the mandatory entries in the *basic settings* of the *form* element *header*. So we clicked the button for *Header* (picture of hat) and clicked the button *Basic Settings*. In the field *First page*, we entered the value FIRST (*page format*); next, in the field *Default paragr.*, we entered the value P1. These are mandatory fields.

## Windows and page windows

Next, let us create *windows* and *page windows*. We clicked the button *windows* on the application toolbar. We have to create a graphic *window* and include the graphic image we earlier imported from a BMP file into the SAP document server. The creation of a graphic *window* and its corresponding *page window* and the inclusion of the graphic image from SAP document server into the *page window* can be done only with *graphical form painter*. To switch to the *graphical form painter*, we made the following menu selection: Settings ➤ Form Painter. When the *User Specific Settings* dialog box appeared, we enabled the check box for *graphical form painter* and clicked the Continue button. With *graphical form painter*, the window of the *graphical form painter* appeared. We clicked the mouse right button to invoke the context menu as shown in Figure 1-58:

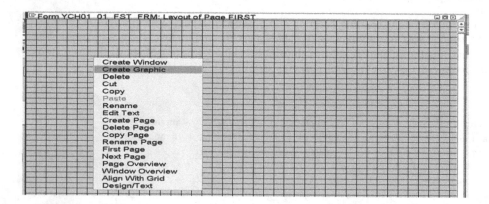

***Figure 1-58.*** *Create Form YCH01_01_FST_FRM—graphical form painter*

We selected the option *Create Graphic* from the context menu options. With the *graphical form painter*, you can create, simultaneously, a graphic *window* and its corresponding *page window* and have a graphic image from the SAP document server incorporated into the *page window* of the graphic *window*. When we selected the option *Create Graphic* in the context menu, the dialog box *Include Graphics* appeared.

We pressed the function key F4 in the field *Name* of this dialog box. Another dialog box, *Find Graphic*, appeared. We entered the pattern YCH* in the field *Name* and enabled the check box *Color Bit Map Image* as shown in Figure 1-59.

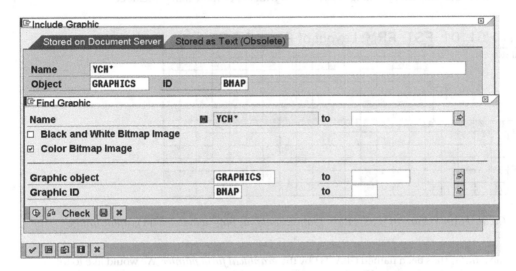

***Figure 1-59.*** *Create Form YCH01_01_FST_FRM—Include Graphic dialog box*

We clicked the execute button on the *Find Graphic* dialog box. A selection list with graphic image name(s) starting with YCH appeared as shown in Figure 1-60.

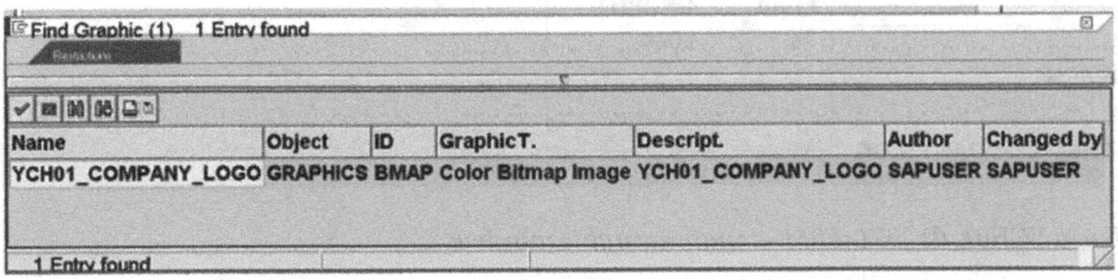

| Name | Object | ID | GraphicT. | Descript. | Author | Changed by |
|---|---|---|---|---|---|---|
| YCH01_COMPANY_LOGO | GRAPHICS | BMAP | Color Bitmap Image | YCH01_COMPANY_LOGO | SAPUSER | SAPUSER |

***Figure 1-60.*** *Create Form YCH01_01_FST_FRM—include Graphic Selection list*

When the graphic image is selected from the list, the *graphical form painter* created a graphic *window* with the name GRAPH1, and a *page window* to which the graphic *window* GRAPH1 was assigned, and included or incorporated the graphic image inside the *page window*. Figure 1-61 shows the graphic *window* by the name GRAPH1 and its corresponding *page window* with the graphic image included.

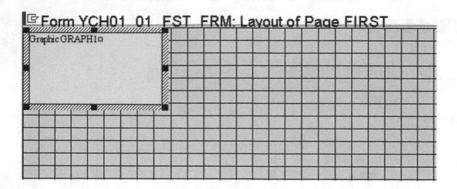

*Figure 1-61.* *Create Form YCH01_01_FST_FRM—graphic window, page window with graphic image*

The graphic *window* has been named GRAPH1 by the *graphical form painter*. We would like to follow our own naming patterns/conventions. We are renaming the graphic *window* GRAPH1 to LOGO. We can rename windows with the renaming option in the context menu. When the renaming selection was made from the context menu, a dialog as shown in Figure 1-62 appeared.

| Window | Graph. | | Rename Window or ⊠ | |
| --- | --- | --- | --- | --- |
| | | | From | GRAPH1 |
| | | | To | LOGO |
| Name | GRAPH1 ▫ | | | |
| | | | ✓ ✗ | |
| Meaning | YCH01_COMPANY_LOG | | | |

*Figure 1-62.* *Create Form YCH01_01_FST_FRM—rename graphic window*

The graphic *window* was renamed as LOGO. We switched back to the non-graphical mode, changed the meaning or short text (*window*) and adjusted or rounded the *Left margin* and *Upper margin* from 2MM to 5MM (*page window*). This is shown in Figure 1-63.

| Standard Attributes | | | | |
| --- | --- | --- | --- | --- |
| Window | LOGO | Meaning | LOGO | |
| Window type | GRAPH | | | |
| Left Margin | 5.00 MM | Window width | 40.64 MM | |
| Upper margin | 5.00 MM | Window height | 29.81 MM | |

*Figure 1-63.* *Create Form YCH01_01_FST_FRM—Graphic window, Page window*

The issue of using *graphical form painter* or operating in non-graphical mode for maintaining *forms* is a matter of personal convenience and choice. In specific contexts, as for the creation of graphic *window, graphical form painter* is a must. If you want to be accurate to a fraction of a millimeter for the dimensions of *page windows*, it is advisable to do so in non-graphical mode.

For variable, constant, and graphic *windows*, with the *graphical form painter*, you can create a *window* and its corresponding *page window* at one go. For variable and constant *windows*, in the non-graphical mode, you can create a *window* and its corresponding *page window* in two separate steps. You can create *windows* and the corresponding *page windows* with the *graphical form painter*, but the dimensions of the *page windows* might not be accurate to a fraction of a millimeter. You can then adjust or assign exact dimensions accurate to a fraction of a millimeter in the non-graphical mode.

Of course, you can switch from one mode to the other at any time. It is a good practice to visually view the final *page windows* layout of a *form* in *graphical form painter*. We will, for most part in the book, use the non-graphic mode to create *windows* and *page windows* and switch to the *graphical form painter* to create graphic *windows* and to visually review the *page window* layouts.

If you want to view the *text element* of the *window* LOGO from the *window* screen, click the button of *text element* (the second button from the left) and a screen like the one shown in Figure 1-64 will appear.

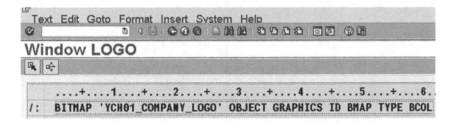

***Figure 1-64.*** *Create Form YCH01_01_FST_FRM—Window LOGO: text element*

You can observe that the *text element* screen of *window* LOGO is in display mode. It contains one line only. The content of *format column* is '/:' meaning that the line is a SAP script control command. The control command is to include or incorporate a graphic image from the SAP document server into the *page window* of the graphic *window*. The control command was generated by the SAP script *form* maintenance system.

We could have located the graphic image inside a constant or variable or even a main *window*. The disadvantage of it is that we would have had to adjust the *page window* dimensions (the width and the height) manually as per the graphic image size. In the case of graphic *window*, the *page window* dimensions (the width and the height) were automatically generated as per the size of the graphic image being included or incorporated. Moreover, in the case of a constant or a variable *window*, the control command to include the graphic image would not have been generated. To include a graphic image in a *page window* assigned to a constant or variable *window*, you make the following menu selection on the *text element* screen: Insert ➤ Graphics. The menu selection will pop up the dialog box *Include Graphic* and you can search for graphic image(s) and make a selection. After you make the selection, the control command to include the graphic image is generated. You can create a graphical *window* with its corresponding *page window* and the graphic image included in it as we have and subsequently change the *window* to the variable or constant type. You can perform this part—the change of *window* type from graphic to a variable or a constant *window* type—as an additional exercise.

The context menu in the *graphical form painter* has other options: Cut, Copy, Paste, Delete, etc.

We next created a variable *window* and its corresponding *page window*. We intend to locate text in the *text element* of the variable *window*.

To create a variable *window*, we clicked the application toolbar button *windows*. On the screen of the *windows*, make the menu selection Edit ➤ Create Element. The dialog box for input of element name (*window* name) and meaning or short text appeared. We entered the *window* name as VARIABLE and a meaningful short text. We clicked the Continue button. The *window* VARIABLE was created.

We have to create a *page window* which will be assigned to the variable *window* VARIABLE. To create a *page window*, we clicked the application toolbar button *page windows*. On the screen of the *page window*, we made the menu selection Edit ➤ Create Element. A dialog box for assignment of the *page window* to a *window* as shown in Figure 1-65 appeared.

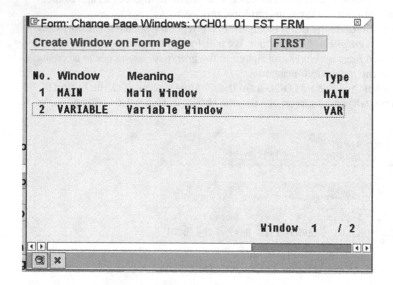

**Figure 1-65.** *Create Form YCH01_01_FST_FRM—Assign Window VARIABLE to page window*

Notice in Figure 1-65 that only the *windows* available for assignments appear in the list. (The *window* LOGO, already assigned, does not appear in the list.) We double-clicked the *window* VARIABLE to assign it to the *page window*. After the assignment of the *window*, we entered the following values for the *page window* dimensions:

*Left margin* 46MM, *Upper margin* 5MM, *Window width* 160MM, *Window height* 190MM

We have created all the *windows* and *page windows* planned in this demonstration. Let us visually view layout of the *page windows* in the *graphical form painter*. Figure 1-66 shows the layout of the *page windows* in the *graphical form painter*.

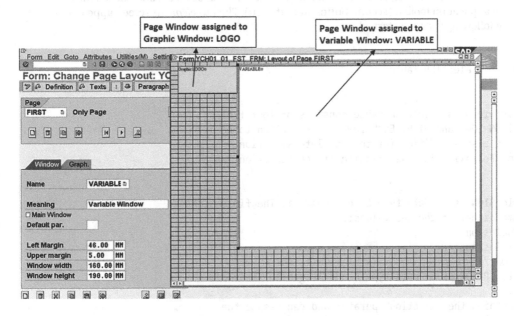

***Figure 1-66.*** *Create Form YCH01_01_FST_FRM—Page Window layout*

## Character Formats

We need to create two *character formats*, C1 and C2, each to be applied to the main heading and subheading of the text, respectively. The procedure to be followed to create *character formats* is the same one we followed to create other *form* elements. We clicked the application toolbar button *character formats*. We made the menu selection Edit ➤ Create Element. A dialog box for element *name* and *meaning* appeared.

For the *character format* C1, we assigned the font YARIAL_M, size 28PT. For the *character format* C2, we retained the default font Courier, size 12PT, and enabled bold and underline Radio buttons.

Figure 1-67 shows the screen with the two-*character format* C1 and C2.

| Character Formats | | | | | | |
|---|---|---|---|---|---|---|
| **Format** | **Meaning** | **Family** | **Size** | **Bold** | **Italic** | **Undl** |
| C1 | YARIAL_M Monospaced 28 | YARIAL_M | 28,0 | | | |
| C2 | Courier 12 Bold & Underlined | COURIER | 12,0 | On | | On |

Char. Format   2   of   2

| Font Attributes | | | | | | |
|---|---|---|---|---|---|---|
| **Char. Format** | **C2** | **Meaning** | Courier 12 Bold & Underlined | | | Standard |
| | | | **On** | **Off** | **Retain** | Font |
| Family | COURIER | Bold | ◉ | ○ | ○ | |
| Size | 12.0 pt | Italic | ○ | ○ | ◉ | |
| | | Underlined | ◉ | ○ | ○ | |

***Figure 1-67.*** *Create Form YCH01_01_FST_FRM—Character Formats*

# Text in Text Element

We will proceed to fill up the *text element* of the variable *window* VARIABLE with text. We clicked the button *Windows* on the application toolbar, ensured the *window* VARIABLE was selected, and clicked the button *text elements* on application toolbar (second button from the left). The *text elements* screen appeared. We entered the following text in the text editor:

```
P1
P3 Structure of Selection Tables
P1
P1
P2 The structure of a selection table consists of four fields:
= SIGN, OPTION LOW, and HIGH. Each row of a selection table
= constitutes a sub-condition for the complete selection
= criterion. Following is a description of the selection table
= fields:
P1 SIGN
P2 The field SIGN is of data type C and length 1. The field SIGN
= can assume either of the two values:.
P2 I for inclusion
P2 E for exclusion
P1 <C2>OPTION</>
P2 The field OPTION is of data type C and length 2. The field

= OPTION contains the selection operator and can assume the
= following values:
P2 If the field HIGH contains INITIAL value, the field OPTION can
= assume any of these values: EQ, NE, GT, GE, LT, LE, CP, and NP
= (Single values or single pattern values)
P2 If the field HIGH is not INITIAL, the field OPTION can assume any of
= these values: BT and NB. (Range values)
P1 LOW
P2 The data type and length of the field LOW is derived from the data
= object or the type to which the selection table variable is referring.
P1 HIGH
P2 The data type and length of the field HIGH is also derived from the data
= object or the type to which the selection table variable is referring.
```

The first two columns/characters in every line represent the value in the *format column—paragraph format* name (P1/P2/P3) or the equal character (=) to indicate free-flowing text. The text on the right side in every line represents *command/info* area; the gap between the *format column* and *command/info area* is for readability. After the application of *paragraph formats* and the *character formats* and depending upon the width of the *window*, the free-flowing text will word wrap or soft carriage returns will be inserted during output of the free-flowing text as in any word processor.

You can enter the text manually here, in the *text element* environment, or you can upload text from an operating system ITF file into a user clipboard and insert the uploaded text from the user clipboard into the *text element*. Following are the steps with menu options: (1) Goto ➤ User Clipboard ➤ User Clipboard 1, 2, 3, 4 or 5; (2) Clipboard ➤ Upload; (3) Ctrl+S (save); (4) Function key F3 (return from clipboard to *text element*; and (5) Insert ➤ Clipboard ➤ User Clipboard ➤ Clipboard 1, 2, 3, 4 or 5. You can copy text in the *text element* and paste into a clipboard and then download the text from the clipboard to an operating system file (the reverse process of upload).

Once, the foregoing text is entered, the *character formats* have to be applied to the main heading (Structure of Selection Tables) and the subheadings (SIGN, OPTION, LOW, and HIGH). Let us start the application of *character formats* with the main heading. We position the cursor on the first column of the *command/info* area and make the menu selection Format ➤ Character as shown in Figure 1-68.

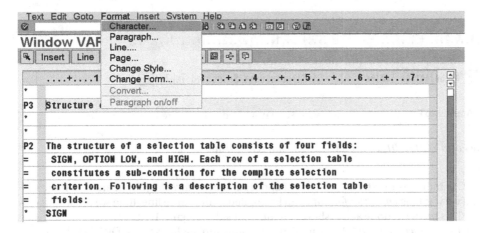

***Figure 1-68.*** *Create Form YCH01_01_FST_FRM—menu: apply Character format*

When we make the menu selection, the selection list of *character formats* appears as shown in Figure 1-69.

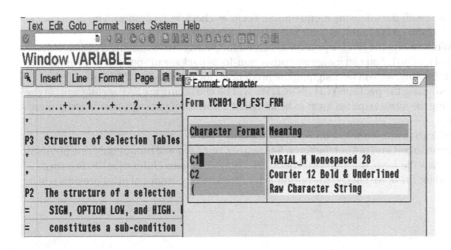

***Figure 1-69.*** *Create Form YCH01_01_FST_FRM—Format: Character pop-up list*

We select the *character format* C1. When you select and assign a *character format*, the SAP script *form* maintenance system applies the selected *character format* only to the first word from where the cursor was positioned when the menu selection was made for *character format* selection. In our present case the *character format* C1 was applied to the first word of the main heading, that is, 'Structure.' This is shown on the left side of Figure 1-70.

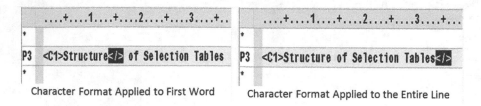

Character Format Applied to First Word          Character Format Applied to the Entire Line

*Figure 1-70.* *Create Form YCH01_01_FST_FRM—apply character format*

In Figure 1-70, <C1> indicates the starting column of application of a *character format* and </> indicates the ending column. If we want the *character format* C1 to be applied to the entire line, then we must shift </> to the end of the line. This has been done and is shown on the right side of Figure 1-70.

In a like manner, the *character format* C2 was applied to the four subheadings SIGN, OPTION, LOW, and HIGH. We exited the *text element* screen to navigate back to the language-independent area of the *form* (*Heading, page formats, windows,* etc.).

## Test or Print Preview Form

We performed the *form check* with the following menu option: Form ➤ check ➤ Definition. The *form* check generated the following alert: No errors found in form YCH01_01_FST_FRM.

We saved the *form*. While saving the *form*, a prompt appeared for package assignment. We assigned the predefined package YCH_BC401. You can assign any other non-local package of your choice. For all the workbench objects we are creating, we will be assigning the predefined local package $TMP. Only for the SAP script *forms*, we are assigning the package YCH_BC401. We will be classifying the SAP script *forms* at the end of Chapter 2. Classifying the *forms* requires them to be assigned a non-local package, hence assignment of the package YCH_BC401.

We activated the *form* with the menu selection Form ➤ Activate

We are now in a position to test and output the *form*. Remember, our *form* will output only one physical page. To test and print preview the *form*, the following menu selection was made: Utilities(M) ➤ Printing Test. A dialog box appeared for *Print*; we clicked the button *Print Preview*. The output of print preview will be like the one in Figure 1-71.

**Print Preview of LP01 Page 00001 of 00001**

```
Structure of Selection
Tables

      The structure of a selection table consists of four
fields: SIGN, OPTION LOW, and HIGH. Each row of a selection
table constitutes a sub-condition for the complete selection
criterion. Following is a description of the selection table
fields:

SIGN
      The field SIGN is of data type C and length 1. The field
SIGN can assume either of the two values:.

      I for inclusion

      E for exclusion

OPTION
      The field OPTION is of data type C and length 2. The
field OPTION contains the selection operator and can assume
the following values:

      If the field HIGH contains INITIAL value, the field
OPTION can assume any of these values: EQ, NE, GT, GE, LT, LE,
CP, and NP (Single values or single pattern values)

      If the field HIGH is not INITIAL, the field OPTION can
```

*Figure 1-71. Form YCH01_01_FST_FRM—output*

If you scroll down, you can view the rest of the text for the subheadings LOW and HIGH.

## Recapitulation

We have implemented all the specifications listed at the commencement of this demonstration.
To recapitulate, we performed the following:

- Created a *form*.

- Created a single *page format*.

- Created a graphic *window* with the corresponding *page window*; included an
  imported bit map image from the SAP document server into the graphic *window*.

- Created *paragraph formats* and *character formats* to be applied to format the text in
  the variable *window* as per formatting specifications described.

- Created a variable *window* with the corresponding *page window* and included text in
  the variable *window text element area*.

- Saved and activated the *form*. Print previewed the *form* from the SAP script *form*
  environment.

This was a demonstration. We did not need a SAP script print program. We did not have variable data to be output. We could carry out the testing and demonstration from within the SAP script *form* environment.

# Demonstration II

In this demonstrative exercise, we will produce the same output as in demonstration I but with a major difference in approach. In demonstration I, the text was created directly in the variable *window's text element* area. In the present exercise, we will create the text separately as *standard text*. The *standard text* created with transaction code SO10 can be incorporated in multiple *forms*. The *standard text* can be included in other *standard texts* as well.

The standard text environment does not support local paragraph formats and character formats. The standard text can use a style. The paragraph formats and character formats located in a style can be used to format text maintained in standard texts.

In this demonstrative exercise, we are creating, for the first time, two SAP script components: style and standard text.

Our demonstration exercise involves the following steps:

1. We will create a *style* YCH01_01 (transaction code SE72). We will locate *paragraph formats* P1, P2, and P3 and *character formats* C1 and C2 within this style. The *paragraph formats* P1, P2, and P3 and *character formats* C1 and C2 in the *style* are identical to the *paragraph formats* P1, P2, and P3 and *character formats* C1 and C2 we created in the *form* YCH01_FST_FRM.

2. We will create *standard text* YCH01_01_SEL_TABLES and enter or upload into it our text relating to selection tables. We will associate our *standard text* with the *style* YCH01_01. We will use the *paragraph formats* P1, P2, and P3 and *character formats* C1 and C2 in *style* YCH01_01 to format the *standard text*.

3. We will create a *form* YCH01_02_SEC_FRM with a single *page format*. We will create a graphic *window* LOGO and its corresponding *page window* and include within it the imported bmp image from the document server.

4. We will create a variable *window* VARIABLE and its corresponding *page window* and include within it the formatted *standard text* with a control command.

5. We will test print or print preview the *form* YCH01_02_SEC_FRM from the SAP script environment.

Let us proceed to performing the five steps.

## Create Style YCH01_01

We navigated to the transaction code SE72 opening screen. We entered YCH01_01 (maximum namespace of eight characters) in the field *Style*. We clicked the Create button (you can alternatively press the function key F5). We clicked the button *paragraph formats* on the application toolbar. We created three *paragraph formats* P1, P2, and P3. The method to create *paragraph formats* in *styles* is the same as in *forms*—menu option Edit ➤ Create Element, and so on. The *paragraph formats* P1, P2, and P3 created in this *style* are identical to the *paragraph formats* we created in the *form* YCH01_01_FST_FRM in the demonstration I exercise.

Figure 1-72 is a screenshot of the created *paragraph formats*.

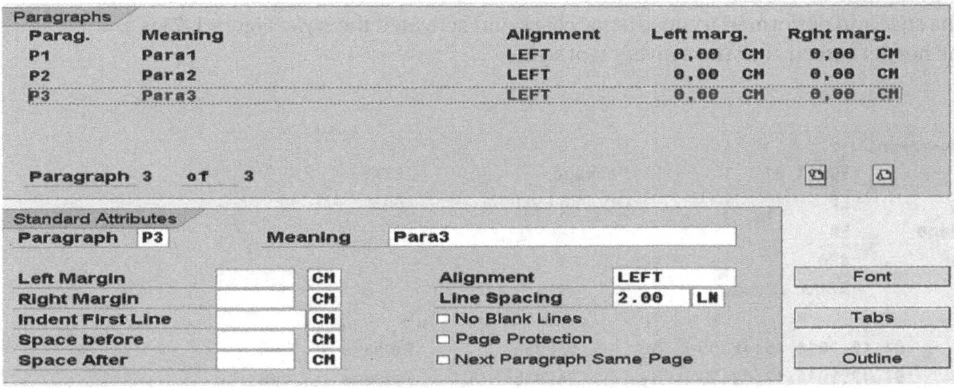

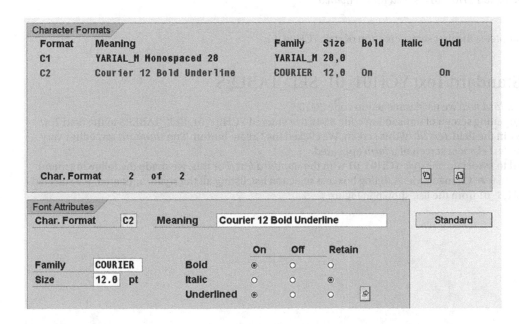

**Figure 1-72.** *Style YCH01_01—Paragraph formats*

In a similar manner, we created the *character formats* C1 and C2 identical to the *character formats* C1 and C2 created in the demonstration I exercise.

Figure 1-73 is a screenshot of the created *character formats* C1 and C2.

**Figure 1-73.** *Style YCH01_01—Character Formats*

Next, we need to assign the *paragraph format* P1 as the default paragraph. So we clicked the button header (picture of hat, second button from the right) on the application toolbar. We entered the value P1 in the field *Default paragraph* on the screen in Figure 1-74.

We saved the *style* and performed a consistency check and activated the *style*. Figure 1-74 is a screenshot of the header screen after the activation of *style*.

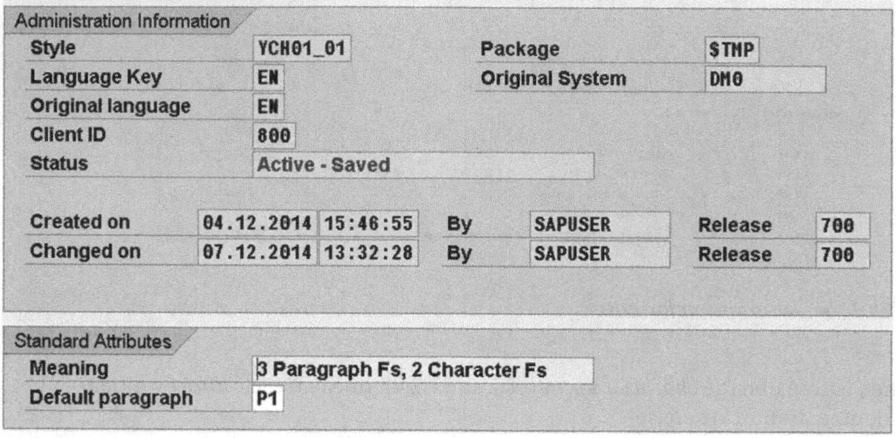

| Administration Information | | | |
|---|---|---|---|
| Style | YCH01_01 | Package | $TMP |
| Language Key | EN | Original System | DM0 |
| Original language | EN | | |
| Client ID | 800 | | |
| Status | Active - Saved | | |

| Created on | 04.12.2014 | 15:46:55 | By | SAPUSER | Release | 700 |
|---|---|---|---|---|---|---|
| Changed on | 07.12.2014 | 13:32:28 | By | SAPUSER | Release | 700 |

| Standard Attributes | |
|---|---|
| Meaning | 3 Paragraph Fs, 2 Character Fs |
| Default paragraph | P1 |

**Figure 1-74.** *Style YCH01_01—saved and activated*

This completes the first step—creation of *style* YCH0q_01.

# Create Standard Text YCH01_01_SEL_TABLES

To create *standard text*, we used transaction code SO10.

On the opening screen of transaction code SO10, we entered YCH01_01_SEL_TABLES in the field *Text Name* and ST in the field *Text Id.* of this screen. We clicked the Create button. The *standard text* editor very similar to the *text element* screen of a *form* appeared.

We need to associate our *style* YCH01_01 with the *standard text*. For this, we made the following menu selection: Format ➤ Change Style. A dialog box or a selection list, listing all the *styles*, appeared. We selected our style YCH01_01 from the list, shown in Figure 1-75.

```
Format: Change Style                                            [X]

Form SYSTEM

 Style     Meaning

 S_DEVSCR  Devbook Paragraph Formatting
 S_DOCUP1  Printing Online Documentation
 S_DOCURM  Online display (SO70)
 S_DOCUS1  Online Display (SO70)
 S_GLOSS1
 S_JPTEST  SAPscript test style set
 S_OFFICE  SAPoffice paragraph formatting
 S_STERMC  Comment Editor for Terminology
 S_TEST    Barcodes, fonts, fontsizes
 S_TEST01  SAPscript test style 01
 S_TEST02  SAPscript test style 02
 S_TEST_D  SAPscript test info draft
 S_UDMP1   Stil für UDM-Druck generiert
 S_UDMP3   Stil für UDM-Druck generiert
 VVSRG_DV  Style for Reg. Rep. PRF List
 WF_NOTES  Style of notes in workflow
 YCH01_01  3 Paragraph Fs, 2 Character Fs

 ✓ Choose   ✤ Attributes   ▯ ▥ ▨ ✕
```

*Figure 1-75. Standard text YCH01_01_SEL_TABLES—Change Style*

Once, we choose a *style* (YCH01_01) through this process, all the *paragraph formats* and the *character formats* of the *style* can be applied to the *standard text* for formatting.

We have to have the text relating to selection tables in the *standard text*. You can enter the text manually as in the demonstration I exercise or you can upload it from a downloaded operating system file. The text is available in the subfolder STANDARD_TEXTS of the Chapter 1 folder of the E-resource (www.apress.com/9781484212345). The ability to directly download and upload text is available only in the *standard text* environment and only through clipboards in the *text element* environment of a *form*. I am demonstrating the uploading of the text file into the *standard text*. To upload the text file into *standard text*, we made the following menu selection, Text ➤ Upload, as shown in Figure 1-76.

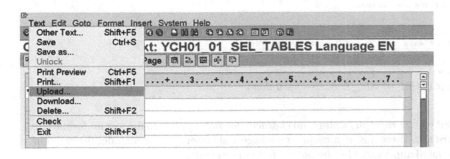

*Figure 1-76. Standard text YCH01_01_SEL_TABLES—menu selection to upload text file*

A dialog box to make a file format selection appeared. We selected the file format ITF as shown in Figure 1-77.

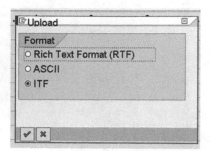

*Figure 1-77.* *Standard text YCH01_01_SEL_TABLES—file format selection to upload*

When you press the Continue button, a file selection dialog box as shown in Figure 1-78 appears.

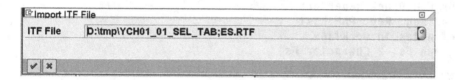

*Figure 1-78.* *Standard text YCH01_01_SEL_TABLES—file to upload*

The screen after the file was uploaded looks like the one in Figure 1-79.

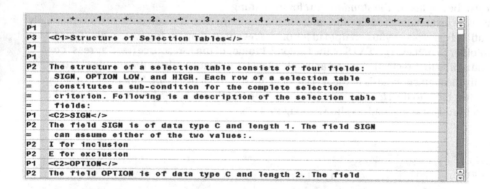

*Figure 1-79.* *Standard text YCH01_01_SEL_TABLES—file upload*

The text was uploaded with *paragraph formats* and *character formats* applied to the text for formatting.

We saved the *standard text*. There was no prompt for package assignment. This concludes the creation of text that will be incorporated into a variable *window* of a *form* to be created.

## Create Form YCH01_02_SEC_FRM, Page Format FIRST, Graphic Window LOGO, etc.

We entered YCH01_02_SEC_FRM in the field *Form* on the screen of *SAP script Form Maintenance* (transaction code SE71). We clicked the Create button. We clicked the Continue button on the information alert: *Form* YCH01_02_SEC_FRM language EN is not available in client ###. We entered a meaningful text in the field *Meaning*. We clicked the *Basic Settings* button. On this screen, we selected the DINA4 stationery in portrait mode—210MM width and 297MM height. For the rest, we accepted the defaults proposed by the *form* maintenance system.

We clicked the button *Pages* (*page formats*) on the application toolbar. We created a *page format* FIRST. We clicked the button *paragraph format* on the application toolbar. We created a *paragraph format* P1.

We assigned values to the mandatory fields of the *header*. Next, we clicked the button for *header* (picture of hat) and clicked the button *basic settings*. In the field *First page*, we entered the value FIRST, (*page format*) next; in the field *Default paragr.*, we entered the value P1.

Switching to *graphic form painter*, we created a graphic *window* and its corresponding *page window*, like the one we created in the demonstration I exercise, locating the same bit map image YCH01_COMPANY_LOGO from the document server. We renamed the graphic *window* as LOGO. For the *page window* of the graphic *window* LOGO, we adjusted the *Left margin* and *Upper margin* fields to 5mm.

## Create a Variable Window VARIABLE, Page Window and Include Standard Text

In this step, we first created a variable *window* VARIABLE. On the application toolbar, we clicked the button *windows* and made the following menu selection: Edit ➤ Create Element. In the element dialog box, we entered the *window* name as VARIABLE and text. We clicked the Continue button. The *window* VARIABLE was created.

We next clicked the button *page windows* on the application toolbar and made the following menu selection: Edit ➤ Create Element. We assigned the *window* VARIABLE to the *page window*. We entered the dimensions of this *page window* as *Left margin* 46MM , *Upper margin* 5MM , *Window width* 160MM, and *Window height* 190MM. Switching to the *graphic form painter*, we visually viewed the layout of the *page windows* and confirmed that the layout is as per the specifications.

After the creation of the *windows* and *page windows*, the *window* screen will look like the one Figure 1-80 and the *page windows* screen like the one in Figure 1-81.

**Form: Change Windows: YCH01_02_SEC_FRM**

| Pages | Page Windows | Paragraph Formats | Character Formats |

| Window | Meaning | Type | Default par. |
| --- | --- | --- | --- |
| LOGO | YCH01_COMPANY_LOGO | GRAPH | |
| MAIN | Main Window | MAIN | |
| VARIABLE | Variable Window | VAR | |

*Figure 1-80.* *Form YCH01_02_SEC_FRM—Windows*

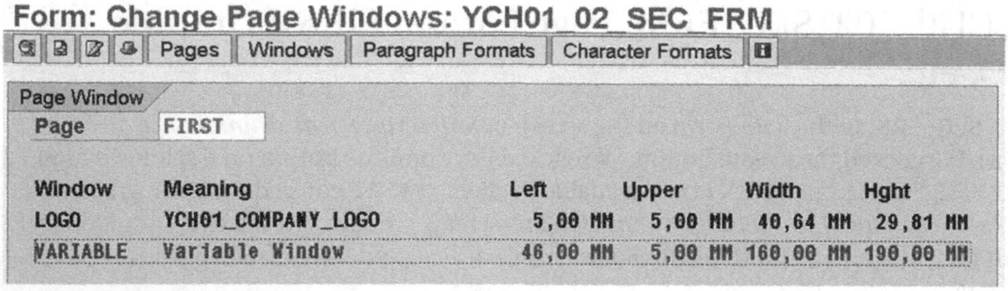

Form: Change Page Windows: YCH01_02_SEC_FRM
Pages
Windows
Paragraph Formats
Character Formats
Page Window
Page FIRST
Window Meaning Left Upper Width Hght
LOGO YCH01_COMPANY_LOGO 5,00 MM 5,00 MM 40,64 MM 29,81 MM
VARIABLE Variable Window 46,00 MM 5,00 MM 160,00 MM 190,00 MM

***Figure 1-81.*** *Form YCH01_02_SEC_FRM—Page Windows*

We now have to incorporate the standard text (created earlier in step 2) into the variable *window* VARIABLE.

On the *windows* or *page windows screen,* we clicked the *text element* button on the application toolbar. In the text editor, we made the following menu selection, Insert ➤ text ➤ Standard, as shown in Figure 1-82.

Text Edit Goto Format Insert System Help
Window VARIABL
Insert
Line
Format
Symbols
Text
Clipboard
Characters
Graphics...
Standard... Ctrl+Shift+F5
Documentation...
Hypertext...

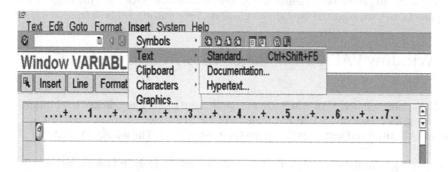

***Figure 1-82.*** *Form YCH01_02_SEC_FRM—menu selection to include standard text*

An *Insert Text* dialog box appeared as shown in Figure 1-83.

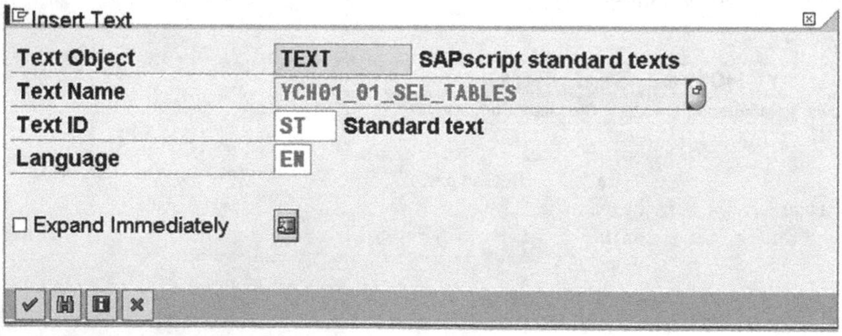

Insert Text
Text Object TEXT SAPscript standard texts
Text Name YCH01_01_SEL_TABLES
Text ID ST Standard text
Language EN
Expand Immediately

***Figure 1-83.*** *Form YCH01_02_SEC_FRM—insert Standard text*

After entering the values as shown in Figure 1-83, we clicked the Continue button which generated the control command to include the standard text as shown in Figure 1-84.

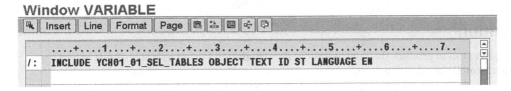

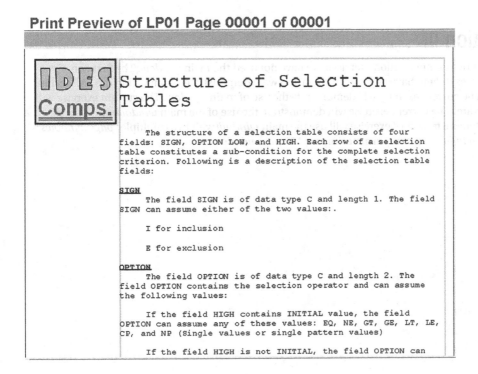

*Figure 1-84.* Form YCH01_02_SEC_FRM—control command to include standard text

We navigated back to the previous screen. We saved the *form*. We assigned the package YCH_BC401. You can assign any other non-local package of your choice.

We performed check with the following menu selection: Form ➤ Check ➤ Definition. The *form* check generated the following alert: No errors found in form YCH01_02_SEC_FRM.

We activated the form with the following menu selection: Form ➤ Activate.

This completes step 4.

## Test Print Form YCH01_02_SEC_FRM

Our *form* will output only one physical page. To test and print preview the *form*, we made the following menu selection: Utilities(M) ➤ Printing Test. A dialog box appeared for *Print*; we clicked the button *Print Preview*. The output of print preview will be like the one in Figure 1-85.

*Figure 1-85.* Form YCH01_02_SEC_FRM—output

The output is identical to the output produced by the *form* in demonstration I. In demonstration I, we did not use any style and standard text, whereas we used a style and standard text to produce the output in the current demonstration.

## Recapitulation

Demonstration II set out to produce the same output as demonstration I using *style* and *standard text*. To recall, we performed the following steps:

1. Created a *style*, consisting of three *paragraph formats* and two *character formats*.

2. Created *standard text* and uploaded text from an operating system file.

3. Created a *form*.

   a. Created a single *page format*.

   b. Created a graphic *window* with the corresponding *page window*; included an imported bit map image from the SAP document server into the graphic *window*.

   c. Created a variable *window* with the corresponding *page window*; included *standard text* in the variable *window*.

   d. Saved and activated the *form*.

4. Print previewed the *form* from the SAP script *form* environment.

Again, we did not have variable data to be output. So, we could carry out the testing from within SAP script *form* environment.

# Demonstration III

Until now, in the first two demonstration exercises, we have not used the main *window*. The first two demonstration exercises did not have any variable data and were demonstrated from within the SAP script *form* environment. The current exercise will demonstrate the use of main *window*. The current exercise will also use a print program. The current exercise will demonstrate the use of the main *window* with a single *page window*. The Demonstration IV exercise will use the main *window* with two (multiple) *page windows*. Recall that the main *window* can contain a maximum of 99 *page windows*.

Suppose; we are required to produce a list of materials from the table MAKT using a SAP script form. The output layout will be as specified in Table 1-7.

***Table 1-7.*** *List of Materials—Output Layout*

| Field Description | Field Name | Column Span | Width in Columns |
|---|---|---|---|
| Serial Number | DATA: SRL_NO TYPE SY-TABIX | 01-05 | 05 |
| | | 06-06 | 01 |
| Material Code | MAKT-MATNR | 07-24 | 18 |
| | | 25-25 | 01 |
| Material Description | MAKT-MAKTX | 26-65 | 40 |

The output should be as shown in Figure 1-86.

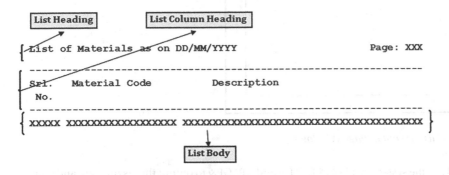

***Figure 1-86.*** *List of materials—output*

Since the output involves a large volume of variable data, we need to have a print program that will retrieve data and send it to SAP the script *form*. This demonstration exercise will involve a *form* and a corresponding print program.

We need to repetitively output the three fields SRL_NO, MAKT-MATNR, AND MAKT-MAKTX in a page and from page to page. The three fields constitute the body of the report. Recall that the data that repeats within a page and repeats from page to page is to be located in the main *window*.

For the *form* to generate the list of materials, we will have a single *page format*; we will locate the list body in the main *window* and the list heading along with the list column heading in a variable *window*.

The variable *window* will have a corresponding *page window* in which we will locate list headings. The main *window* will contain one *page window* in which we will locate the data of list body. The *page window* of the main *window* will continually receive one row of data (through a LOOP...ENDLOOP process in the print program) and output it until the *page window* is full. At the point the *page window* is full, a page break is triggered and output continues in the *page window* assigned to the main *window* of a new page. This process continues until all the data is output.

The *page windows* layout will look like the one in Figure 1-87.

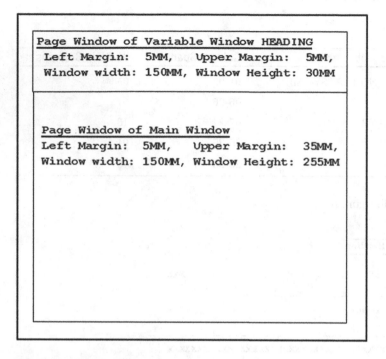

*Figure 1-87.* *List of materials—layout of Page Windows*

The list heading will use the system symbols &DATE& and &PAGE& to output the 'as on' date and page number, respectively.

The print program will use five function modules related to the operation of *forms* from an ABAP program. Table 1-8 lists these function modules with explanations.

***Table 1-8.*** *Main Function Modules Used to Operate Forms*

| Function Module | Explanation |
| --- | --- |
| OPEN_FORM - Exporting: <form name> and <language> | Physical location of the existence of a form and setup. Analogous to open file. |
| START_FORM - Exporting: <form name> and <language> | Throughout our exercises, we are calling the function module START_FORM before the beginning of output of a business document. The calling of this function module ensures output starts on a new page and page counter &PAGE& initialized to 1. |
| | When the output of a business document is concluded, we are calling the function module END_FORM. |
| | In the present scenario, we are producing a list of materials. We will consider the entire material list as a single business document. Hence we will call the function module START_FORM once before the commencement of output of the material list, after calling the function module OPEN_FORM. |
| | And we will call the function module END_FORM once after the conclusion of output of the material list, before calling the function module CLOSE_FORM. |
| WRITE_FORM – Exporting <text element name> and <window name> | Send data from the elementary data objects of the print program to identically named program symbols in the specified named *text element* of specified *window*. |
| END_FORM | Refer to the note on START_FORM. |
| CLOSE_FORM | A form opened has to be closed for output of form to appear. Analogous to close file. |

A description of these function modules can be found in the manual BC Style and Form Maintenance. You can also refer to the function modules' documentation.

So, let us proceed to create a *form* and subsequently, the print program—an ABAP program.

Our demonstration exercise involves the following steps:

1.   Create a *form* YCH01_03_MLIST1 with a single *page format*. In the *Basic Settings*, assign font Courier size 10PT (points).

2.   Create a variable *window* HEADING and its corresponding *page window*. Fill in the *text element* LIST_HEADING of this variable *window* as per the list and column headings of Figure 1-86.

3.   Create a *page window* for the main *window*. Fill in the *text element* LIST_DATA of the main *window* as per the list body of Figure 1-86. Check and activate the *form*.

4. Create an ABAP program YCH01_01_MLIST_ONE_MWINDOW (print program) to retrieve and load data from the database table MAKT into an internal table. Call the function modules OPEN_FORM and START_FORM. Set up a LOOP… ENDLOOP process to fetch data one row at a time from the internal table into the structure and send the data to main *window* of the *form* using the function module WRITE_FORM. After the ENDLOOP, call the function modules END_FORM and CLOSE_FORM. Perform program check and program activation.

5. Test the *form* YCH01_03_MLIST1 by executing the program YCH01_01_MLIST_ONE_MWINDOW.

Let us proceed to perform the five steps.

## Create Form YCH01_03_MLIST1, Page Format FIRST, etc.

We entered YCH01_03_MLIST1 in the field *Form* on the screen of *SAP script Form Maintenance* (transaction code SE71). We clicked the Create button. We clicked the Continue button on the following information alert: *Form* YCH01_03_MLIST1 language EN is not available in client ###. We entered meaningful text in the field *Meaning*. We clicked the *Basic Settings* button. On this screen, we selected the DINA4 stationery in portrait mode—210MM width and 297MM height—and we changed the font size to 10PT. For the rest, we accepted the defaults proposed by the *form* maintenance system.

We clicked the button *Pages* (*page formats*) on the application toolbar. We created a *page format* FIRST with the following menu selection: Edit ➤ Create Element, etc. In the field *Next page*, we entered the value FIRST. This is an indication to the SAP script runtime system as to what *page format* to output following the output of the first page. When we test a *form* from within the SAP script *form* environment, this field should be left blank.

We clicked the button *paragraph format* on the application toolbar. We created a *paragraph format* P1 with default values.

We must assign values to the mandatory fields of the *header*. So we clicked the button for *header* (picture of hat) and clicked the button *Basic Settings*. In the field *First page*, we entered the value FIRST (*page format*); next, in the field *Default paragr.*, we entered the value P1.

This completes step 1.

## Create Variable Window, Its Corresponding Page Window, Create Text Element, etc.

To create a variable *window*, we clicked the button *windows* on the application toolbar and made the following menu selection: Edit ➤ Create Element. In the element dialog box, we entered the *window* name as HEADING and text. We clicked the Continue button. The window HEADING was created.

Next, we clicked the button *page windows* on the application toolbar, made the following menu selection: Edit ➤ Create Element. We assigned the *window* HEADING to the *page window*. We entered the dimensions of this *page window* as *Left margin* 5MM, *Upper margin* 5MM, *Window width* 150MM, and *Window height* 30MM.

After the creation of the *page window*, the *page windows* dimension area screen will look like the one in Figure 1-88:

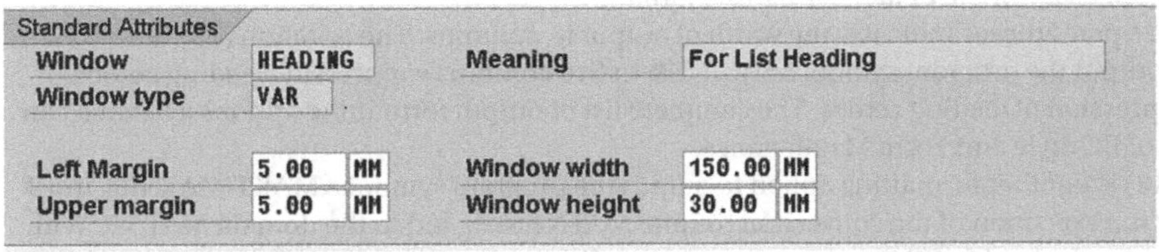

*Figure 1-88. Form YCH01_03_MLIST1—page window of Window HEADING*

We clicked the *text element* button. In the text editor, we entered the name of the *text element* as LIST_HEADING; we entered text for the list heading and the list column heading as per the output layout of Figure 1-86. The text editor screen with the entered values will look like the one in Figure 1-89:

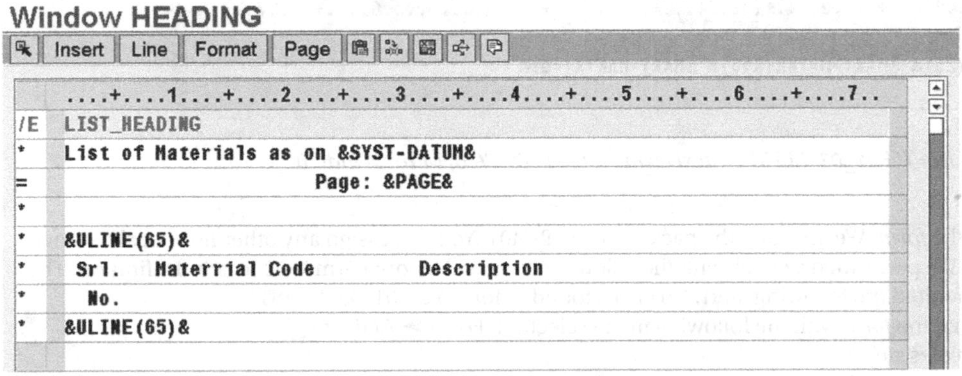

*Figure 1-89. Form YCH01_03_MLIST1—text element LIST_HEADING of Window HEADING*

&ULINE& is the system symbol to generate a horizontal line. The number in the parenthesis (65) indicates the number of columns in the horizontal line. (Refer to Table 1-7.)

We navigated back to previous screen. Save the *form*. This concludes step 2.

# Create Page Window for the Main Window, Create Text Element, etc.

To create a *page window* to be assigned to the main *window*, we clicked the button *page windows* on the application toolbar and made the following menu selection: Edit ➤ Create Element. We assigned the *window* main to the *page window*. We entered the dimensions of this *page window* as *Left margin* 5MM, *Upper margin* 35MM, *Window width* 150MM, *Window height* 255MM. Switching to the *graphic form painter*, we visually viewed the layout of the *page windows* and confirmed that the layout is as per the requirements.

Next, we created the *text element* LIST_DATA in the main window. We clicked the *text element* button. In the text editor we entered the following:

```
/E LIST_DATA
* &SRl_NO(Z5)& &MAKT-MATNR(K18)& &MAKT-MAKTX(40)&
```

The first line identifies (format area value /E) the *text element*—LIST_DATA.

The second line has program symbols for the three program variables: SRL_NO, MAKT-MATNR, and MAKT-MAKTX. This constitutes the list body. One line corresponds to one material. The asterisk (*) in the *format area* indicates the usage of the default *paragraph format*.

The number in the parentheses indicates the width of output in columns. The notation (Z5) is a formatting option to output the program symbol &SRL_NO& in five columns suppressing leading zeroes. The letter Z is for suppression of leading zeroes. The complete list of output formatting options available can be found in the manual BC Style and Form Maintenance.

The notation (K18) is another formatting option to output the program symbol &MAKT-MATNR& in 18 columns suppressing the execution of the conversion routine MATN1 assigned to the domain MATNR. With the formatting option (K), the field MATNR, will output with leading zeroes. By default the material code field MATNR outputs with leading zeroes suppressed.

The notation (40) is to output the program symbol &MAKT-MAKTX& in 40 columns.

The text editor screen with the entered values will look like the one in Figure 1-90.

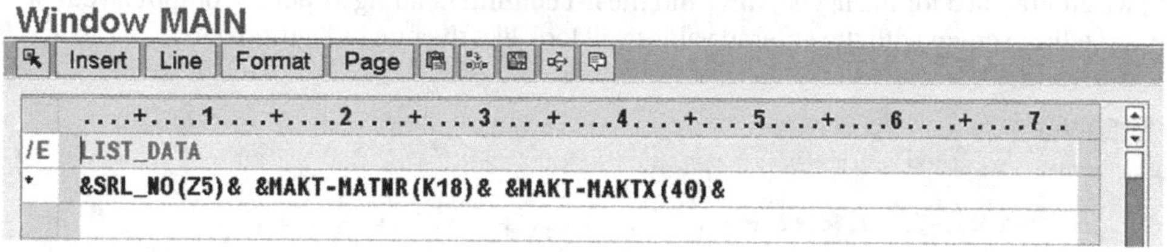

**Window MAIN**

*Figure 1-90. Form YCH01_03_MLIST1—text element LIST_DATA of Main Window*

We saved the *form*. We assigned the package YCH_BC401. You can assign any other non-local package of your choice. We performed a check with the following menu selection: Form ➤ Check ➤ Definition. The *form* check generated the following alert: No errors found in form YCH01_03_MLIST1.

We activated the *form* with the following menu selection: Form ➤ Activate.

This completes step 3.

# Create an ABAP Program YCH01_01_MLIST_ONE_MWINDOW (Print Program), etc.

We created a program YCH01_01_MLIST_ONE_MWINDOW (transaction code SE38).

The source program follows. The source with the comment lines should convey the new features and logic of the program.

```
REPORT YCH01_01_MLIST_ONE_MWINDOW.

* Material List in SAP Script Form (YCH01_03_MLIST1) **

*Declare data: structure MAKT, internal table MAKT_TAB, SRL_NO*
** *****
** Load internal table MAKT_TAB, sort MAKT_TAB by MATNR *****
** *****
** CALL FUNCTION MODULE OPEN_FORM, CALL FUNCTION MODULE START_FORM *****
** *****
** CALL FUNCTION MODULE WRITE_FORM - list heading in v window *
** *****
```

```
** LOOP AT MAKT_TAB INTO MAKT *****
** Assign SY-TABIX to SRL_NO *****
** CALL FUNCTION MODULE WRITE_FORM - list body in main window *
** ENDLOOP *****
** *****
** CALL FUNCTION MODULES END_FORM, CLOSE_FORM *****

TABLES MAKT.
DATA: MAKT_TAB TYPE STANDARD TABLE OF MAKT,
 SRL_NO TYPE SY-TABIX.
START-OF-SELECTION.
SELECT * FROM MAKT INTO TABLE MAKT_TAB UP TO 1000 ROWS WHERE SPRAS = SY-LANGU.
SORT MAKT_TAB BY MATNR.
CALL FUNCTION 'OPEN_FORM'
 EXPORTING
 FORM = 'YCH01_03_MLIST1'
 LANGUAGE = SY-LANGU
 .
IF SY-SUBRC <> 0.
 MESSAGE ID SY-MSGID TYPE SY-MSGTY NUMBER SY-MSGNO
 WITH SY-MSGV1 SY-MSGV2 SY-MSGV3 SY-MSGV4.
ENDIF.
CALL FUNCTION 'START_FORM'
 EXPORTING
 FORM = 'YCH01_03_MLIST1'
 LANGUAGE = SY-LANGU
 .

IF SY-SUBRC <> 0.
 MESSAGE ID SY-MSGID TYPE SY-MSGTY NUMBER SY-MSGNO
 WITH SY-MSGV1 SY-MSGV2 SY-MSGV3 SY-MSGV4.
ENDIF.

CALL FUNCTION 'WRITE_FORM'
 EXPORTING
 ELEMENT = 'LIST_HEADING'
 WINDOW = 'HEADING'
 .
 IF SY-SUBRC <> 0.
 MESSAGE ID SY-MSGID TYPE SY-MSGTY NUMBER SY-MSGNO
 WITH SY-MSGV1 SY-MSGV2 SY-MSGV3 SY-MSGV4.
 ENDIF.
LOOP AT MAKT_TAB INTO MAKT.
 SRL_NO = SY-TABIX.
 CALL FUNCTION 'WRITE_FORM'
 EXPORTING
 ELEMENT = 'LIST_DATA'
 WINDOW = 'MAIN'
 .
 IF SY-SUBRC <> 0.
 MESSAGE ID SY-MSGID TYPE SY-MSGTY NUMBER SY-MSGNO
```

```
WITH SY-MSGV1 SY-MSGV2 SY-MSGV3 SY-MSGV4.
 ENDIF.
ENDLOOP.
CALL FUNCTION 'END_FORM'
 .
IF SY-SUBRC <> 0.
 MESSAGE ID SY-MSGID TYPE SY-MSGTY NUMBER SY-MSGNO
 WITH SY-MSGV1 SY-MSGV2 SY-MSGV3 SY-MSGV4.
ENDIF.
CALL FUNCTION 'CLOSE_FORM'
 .
IF SY-SUBRC <> 0.
 MESSAGE ID SY-MSGID TYPE SY-MSGTY NUMBER SY-MSGNO
 WITH SY-MSGV1 SY-MSGV2 SY-MSGV3 SY-MSGV4.
ENDIF.
```

In the program, as we are in a training paradigm and testing state, we have restricted the retrieval of data from the database table MAKT to 1,000 rows. We are also retrieving material descriptions in the logged-in language (WHERE SPRAS = SY-LANGU) though our list and column headings will always appear in English.

This completes step 4.

## Test form YCH01_03_MLIST1, Execute Program YCH01_01_MLIST_ONE_MWINDOW

We executed the program YCH01_01_MLIST_ONE_MWINDOW; the print dialog box popped up. We clicked the button *Print Preview*. The output will look like that in Figure 1-91:

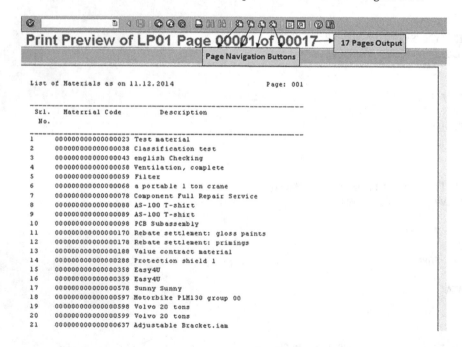

*Figure 1-91. Form YCH01_03_MLIST1—Print Preview*

The 1,000 materials are output in 17 pages as shown in Figure 1-91. You can navigate to different pages with page navigation buttons: first page, previous page, next page, and last page marked in Figure 1-91. This is the end of demonstration III.

## Recapitulation

Demonstration III produced a material description list using a SAP script *form*. We used the main *window* for the first time. The main *window* used a single *page window*. We used a print program. Practically every *form* will use a print program. All our forthcoming exercises will have a print program. The first two demonstration exercises were very basic: they used no variable data and could be demonstrated and tested without a print program. We also introduced five function modules to operate *forms* from the print program. We used program symbols and three system symbols. We also used a few output formatting options.

# Form Check Text

There are two types of checks you need to perform on a *form*. One type of check that we have performed until now is the check for the *form* definition. You perform this check with the following menu selection: Form ➤ Check ➤ Definition. When you perform this check, the SAP script *form* maintenance system validates the *form* definition; that is, it checks for default *paragraph format* assignment and first *page format* assignment, for *page windows* over shooting the page boundaries, etc. We will refer to this check as the definition check.

The second type of check is performed on *text elements*. Let us perform the second type of check on the *form* YCH01_03_MLIST1 in transaction code SE78. We opened the *form* in edit mode. You perform this second type of check with the following menu selection, Form ➤ Check ➤ Texts, as shown in Figure 1-92.

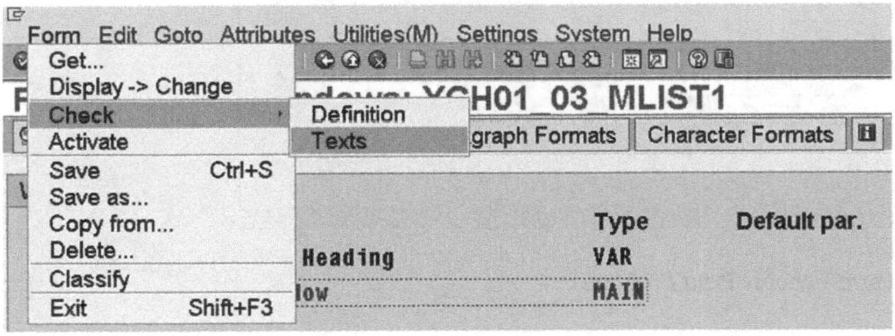

*Figure 1-92.* Form Check—Texts

When you perform this check, the SAP script *form* maintenance system validates the program symbols; that is, it checks whether the program symbols in *text elements* are declared or defined as elementary data objects in the print program. Apart from the program symbols, when you commit an error in specifying any of the system symbols or text symbols or standard symbols, this is reported as an unknown symbol. For example, if you entered &SYST-UNAME& by mistake as &SYSS-UNAME&, the same will be reported as an unknown symbol.

It checks for the existence of *paragraph formats* and *character formats* used in the *text elements*. It checks for the existence of the included *standard texts*. It also checks the syntax of control commands. We will refer to this check as the text check. You can also perform this check from within the *text element* environment with the following menu selection: Text ➤ Check.

Let us perform a text check on the *form* YCH01_03_MLIST1. On the *form* screen, we made the menu selection as shown in Figure 1-92. A dialog box appeared for selection of checks as shown in Figure 1-93.

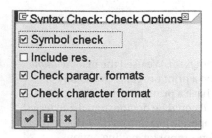

**Figure 1-93.** *Text check for form—Check Options*

As no *standard text* is being included in this *form*, we disabled the second check box in the dialog box. We clicked the Continue button. This popped up the dialog box to choose Print Programs, shown in Figure 1-94.

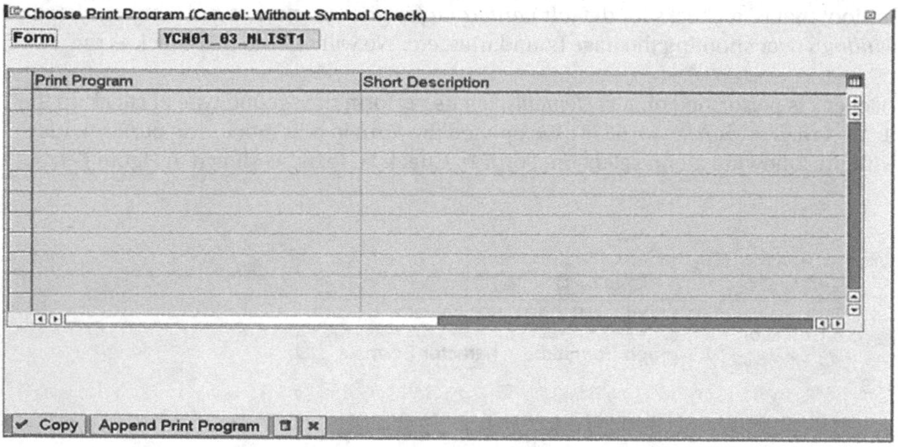

**Figure 1-94.** *Text check for Form—choose Print Program*

We clicked the button *Append Print Program*. A dialog box appeared for entering the print program name or making a selection from a full/filtered selection list. After entering the print program name, we clicked the copy button. We returned to the dialog box to choose Print Program with the print program entry. Next, we clicked the row selector of the print program entry. The screen looked like the one in Figure 1-95:

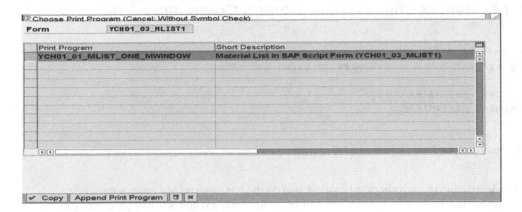

*Figure 1-95. Text check for form—Print Program selected*

We clicked the copy button of the dialog box to choose Print Program. The SAP script *form* maintenance system performed the text check and issued an alert. Our *text elements* do not contain any errors. The following alert was issued: The text is syntactically correct.

To demonstrate an erroneous situation in the *text elements*, we deliberately misspelled two program symbols &MAKT-MATNR& as &MAT-MATNR& and &MAKT-MAKTX as &MAKT-MAKTS& in the main *window*. We then performed the text check. The text check produced error report as shown in Figure 1-96.

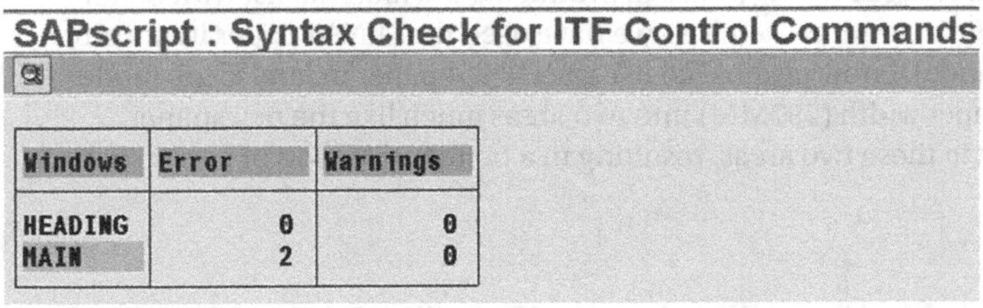

**SAPscript : Syntax Check for ITF Control Commands**

| Windows | Error | Warnings |
|---------|-------|----------|
| HEADING | 0 | 0 |
| MAIN | 2 | 0 |

*Figure 1-96. Text check for form—Window-wise summary of errors*

The error reporting is a *window*-wise summary. Two errors were reported in the main *window*. When we clicked a summary line of a *window*, a detailed list of errors for the selected *window* appeared as shown in Figure 1-97:

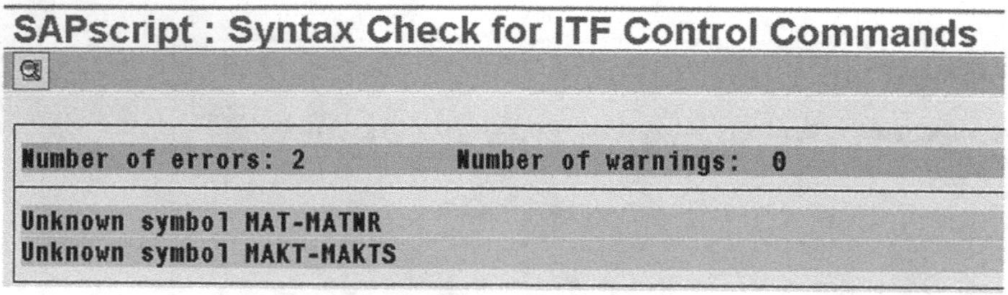

**SAPscript : Syntax Check for ITF Control Commands**

Number of errors: 2          Number of warnings:  0

Unknown symbol MAT-MATNR
Unknown symbol MAKT-MAKTS

*Figure 1-97.* *Text check for form—window detail of errors*

This was a description of a text check to be performed on the *text elements* of a *form*. A form gets activated even with errors in the *text elements*. You should perform the text check before proceeding to activate a *form*.

# Demonstration IV

In this exercise, as in demonstration III, we will use the main *window*. But, instead of using the main *window* with a single *page window* as in demonstration III, we will use the main *window* with two (multiple) *page windows*. We will produce the same output of material list with two *page windows* assigned to the main *window*.

If you observe the material list output of demonstration III in Figure 1-91, you will notice lot of empty space adjoining the material description. We are making a case of producing the material list with better space utilization. Until now, in all our demonstration exercises, we have used the DINA4 paper in portrait mode: 210MM by 297MM (the default mode). I now propose to use the DINA4 paper in landscape mode: 297MM by 210MM. We will divide the paper width (297MM) into two areas much like the newspaper columns. We will output the material list in these two areas, resulting in a better utilization of paper space.

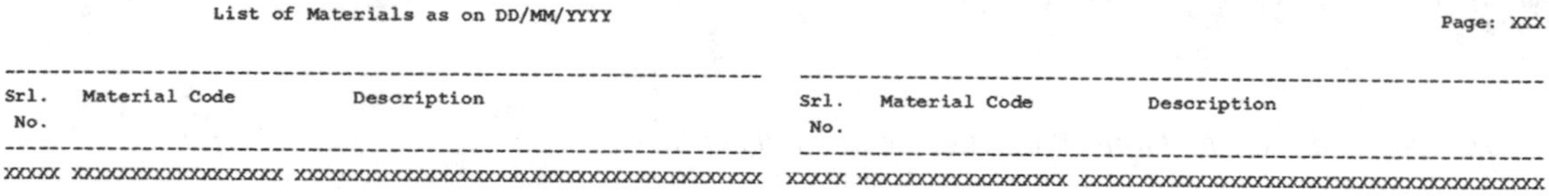

```
        List of Materials as on DD/MM/YYYY                                                                          Page: XXX

------------------------------------------------------------        ------------------------------------------------------------
Srl.    Material Code        Description                            Srl.    Material Code        Description
No.                                                                 No.
------------------------------------------------------------        ------------------------------------------------------------
XXXXX  XXXXXXXXXXXXXXXX  XXXXXXXXXXXXXXXXXXXXXXXXXXXXXXXXXXXX        XXXXX  XXXXXXXXXXXXXXXX  XXXXXXXXXXXXXXXXXXXXXXXXXXXXXXXXXXXXXX
```

*Figure 1-98.* *List of Materials—output in two page windows in main window*

The two areas will map to two *page windows* assigned to the main *window*. Figure 1-98 shows a rough sketch of the output.

The output will commence in the first *page window* or the left-side area of the page. When this first *page window* or the left-side area is full, output will commence in the second *page window* or the right-side area of the page. When this second *page window* or the right-side area is full, a page break will be triggered and output will commence in the first *page window* or the left-side area of the new page. This process will continue until all the data is output.

For the *form* to generate the list of materials in the manner shown in Figure 1-96, we will have a single *page format*. We will locate the list heading and column heading in two variable *windows* with their corresponding *page windows*. We will locate the list heading in the first of the two variable *windows*. We will locate the list column heading in both of the two variable *windows*

We will locate the list body in the main *window*. The main window will have two *page windows*. The *page windows* layout will look like the one in Figure 1-99.

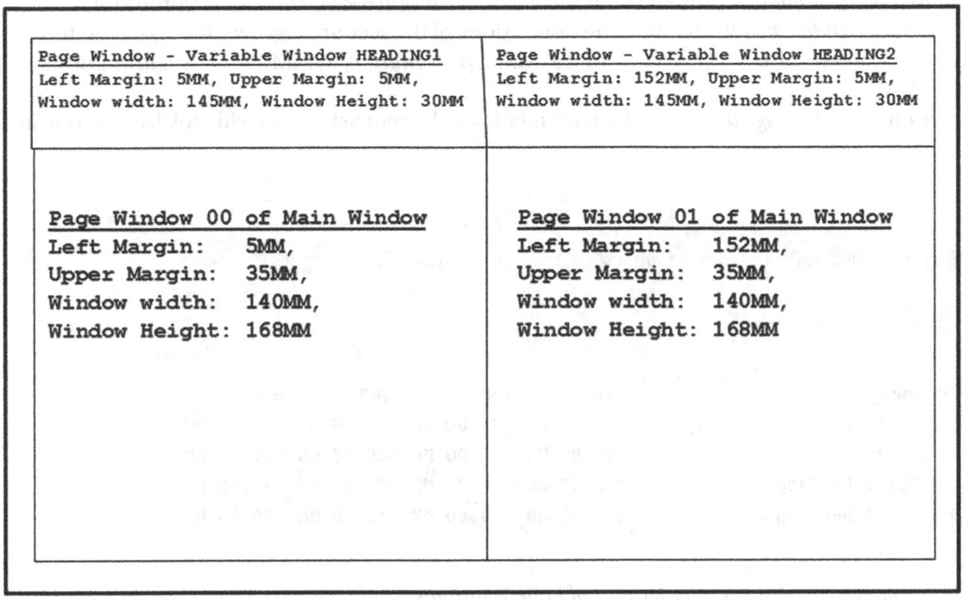

```
┌─────────────────────────────────────────────┬─────────────────────────────────────────────┐
│ Page Window - Variable Window HEADING1        │ Page Window - Variable Window HEADING2        │
│ Left Margin: 5MM, Upper Margin: 5MM,          │ Left Margin: 152MM, Upper Margin: 5MM,        │
│ Window width: 145MM, Window Height: 30MM      │ Window width: 145MM, Window Height: 30MM      │
├─────────────────────────────────────────────┼─────────────────────────────────────────────┤
│                                               │                                               │
│ Page Window 00 of Main Window                 │ Page Window 01 of Main Window                 │
│ Left Margin:     5MM,                          │ Left Margin:     152MM,                        │
│ Upper Margin:    35MM,                         │ Upper Margin:    35MM,                         │
│ Window width:    140MM,                        │ Window width:    140MM,                        │
│ Window Height:   168MM                         │ Window Height:   168MM                         │
│                                               │                                               │
└─────────────────────────────────────────────┴─────────────────────────────────────────────┘
```

**Figure 1-99.** *List of materials—layout of Page Windows*

# Create Form YCH01_04_MLIST2

We entered YCH01_04_MLIST2 in the field *Form* on the screen of *SAP script Form Maintenance* (transaction code SE71). We clicked the Create button. We clicked the Continue button on the following information alert: Form YCH01_04_MLIST2 language EN is not available in client ###. We entered a meaningful text in the field *Meaning*. We clicked the *Basic Settings* button. On this screen, we changed the font size to 10PT.

We clicked the button *Pages* (*page formats*) on the application toolbar. We created a *page format* FIRST. We made the following menu selection: Edit ➤ Create Element, etc. In the field *Next page*, we entered the value FIRST.

We clicked the button *paragraph format* on the application toolbar. We created a *paragraph format* P1 with default values.

We must complete the assignment of values to the mandatory fields of the *header*. So we clicked the button for *header* (picture of hat) and clicked the button *Basic Settings*. In the field *First page*, we entered the value FIRST (*page format*); next, in the field *Default paragr.*, we entered the value P1.

To create variable *windows*, we clicked the button *windows* on the application toolbar and made the following menu selection: Edit ➤ Create Element. In the element dialog box, we entered the *window* name as HEADING1 and text. We clicked the Continue button. The window HEADING1 was created. In a like manner, we created the second variable *window* HEADING2.

We then clicked the button *page windows* on the application toolbar and made the following menu selection: Edit ➤ Create Element. We assigned the *window* HEADING1 to the *page window*. We entered the dimensions of this *page window* as *Left margin* 5MM, *Upper margin* 5MM, *Window width* 145MM, *Window height* 30MM. We created another *page window*; we assigned this *page window* to the variable *window* HEADING2. The dimensions of this *page window* will be *Left margin* 152MM, *Upper margin* 5MM, *Window width* 145MM, *Window height* 30MM.

We created two *page windows* to be assigned to the main *window*. The dimensions of the first *page window* assigned to the main *window* (numbered as 00) was *Left margin* 5MM, *Upper margin* 35MM, *Window width* 140MM, *Window height* 168MM. The dimensions of the second *page window* assigned to the main *window* (numbered as 01) was *Left margin,* 152MM *Upper margin,* 35MM *Window width* 140MM, *Window height* 168MM.

After the creation of all the *page windows*, the *page windows* element list screen will look like the one in Figure 1-100.

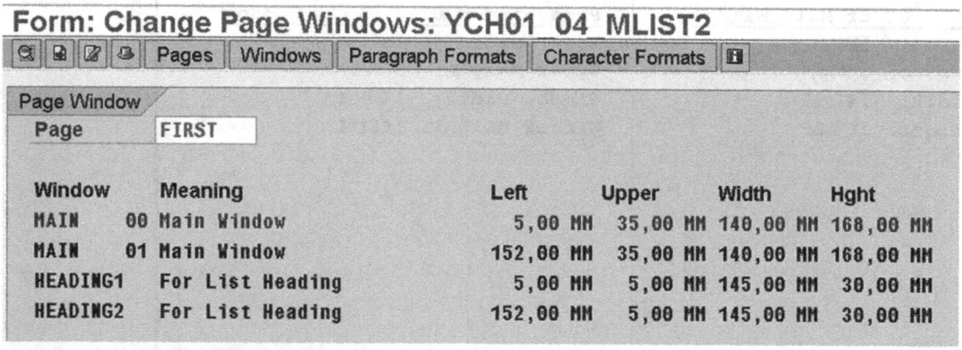
Form: Change Page Windows: YCH01_04_MLIST2
Pages
Windows
Paragraph Formats
Character Formats
Page Window
Page FIRST
Window Meaning Left Upper Width Hght
MAIN 00 Main Window 5,00 MM 35,00 MM 140,00 MM 168,00 MM
MAIN 01 Main Window 152,00 MM 35,00 MM 140,00 MM 168,00 MM
HEADING1 For List Heading 5,00 MM 5,00 MM 145,00 MM 30,00 MM
HEADING2 For List Heading 152,00 MM 5,00 MM 145,00 MM 30,00 MM

***Figure 1-100.*** *Form YCH01_04_MLIST2element list of Page Windows*

Switching to the *graphic form painter,* we visually viewed the layout of the *page windows* and confirmed that the layout is as per the requirements.

We now have to create the *text elements* for the three *windows*: HEADING1, HEADING2, and main. We started with the variable *window* HEADING1. We ensured that the variable *window* HEADING1 is selected on the *windows* screen. We clicked the *text element* button on the application toolbar. The screen after entry in text editor looked like the one in Figure 1-101.

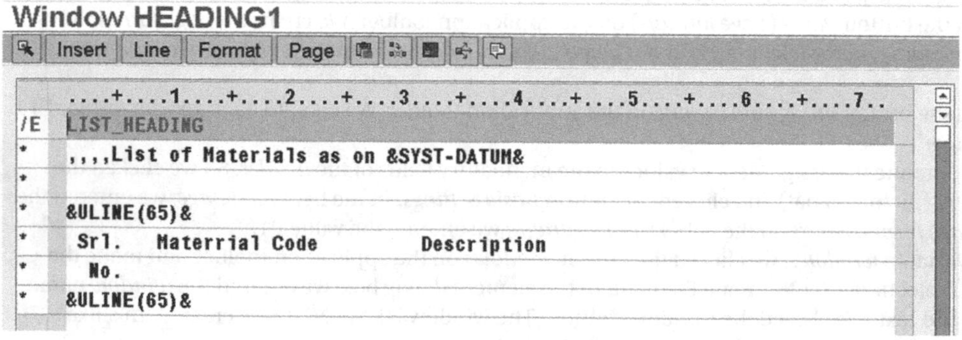
Window HEADING1
Insert
Line
Format
Page
....+....1....+....2....+....3....+....4....+....5....+....6....+....7..
/E LIST_HEADING
* ,,,,List of Materials as on &SYST-DATUM&
*
* &ULINE(65)&
* Srl. Materrial Code Description
* No.
* &ULINE(65)&

***Figure 1-101.*** *Form YCH01_04_MLIST2—text element of Window HEADING1*

The four commas (,,,,) in the second line of the text editor screen are to insert tab spaces. You use two commas to insert a single tab space. Tab space is specified in the *basic settings*. (Refer to Figure 1-34.) Tab stops are specified in the *Tabs* area of *paragraph formats*. (Refer to Figure 1-47.) We did not specify any tab stops in the *paragraph formats* of any of our *forms*. On our system, by default, when a *form* is created, tab space of 1CM is assigned in the *basic settings*. So, in our present context, using two commas (,,) is inserting 1CM of space and using four commas (,,,,) is inserting 2CM of space.

For the variable *window* HEADING2, the screen after entry in text editor looked like the one in Figure 1-102.

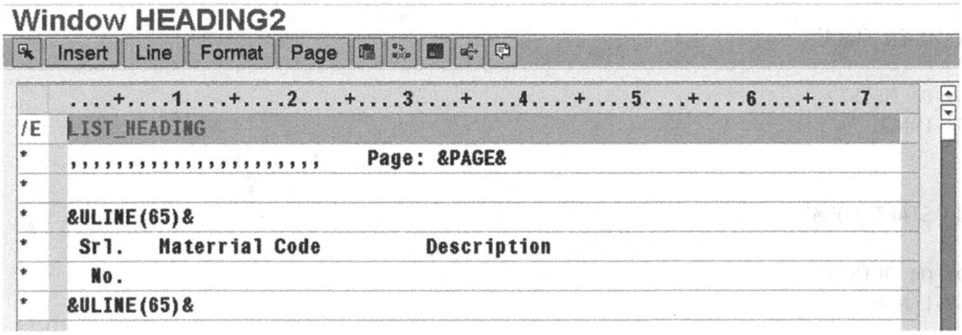

## Window HEADING2

| Insert | Line | Format | Page | | | | |
|---|---|---|---|---|---|---|---|

```
....+....1....+....2....+....3....+....4....+....5....+....6....+....7..
/E  LIST_HEADING
*      ,,,,,,,,,,,,,,,,,,,,,        Page: &PAGE&
*
*   &ULINE(65)&
*   Srl.    Materrial Code        Description
*   No.
*   &ULINE(65)&
```

*Figure 1-102.* *Form YCH01_04_MLIST2—text element of Window HEADING2*

The *text element* name LIST_HEADING is identical in both the variable *windows* HEADING1 and HEADING2.

For the main *window* the screen after entry in text editor looked like the one in Figure 1-103.

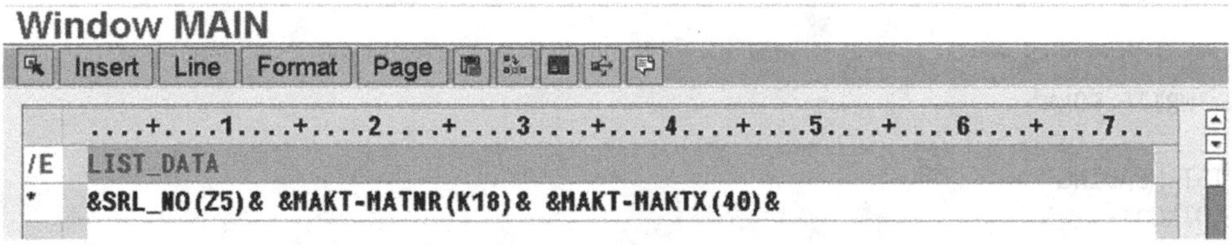

## Window MAIN

| Insert | Line | Format | Page | | | | |
|---|---|---|---|---|---|---|---|

```
....+....1....+....2....+....3....+....4....+....5....+....6....+....7..
/E  LIST_DATA
*   &SRL_NO(Z5)& &MAKT-MATNR(K18)& &MAKT-MAKTX(40)&
```

*Figure 1-103.* *Form YCH01_04_MLIST2—text element of Main Window*

We saved the *form*. We assigned the package YCH_BC401. You can assign any other non-local package of your choice. We performed the definition check with the following menu selection: Form ➤ Check ➤ Definition. The *form* check generated the following alert: No errors found in form YCH01_04_MLIST2.

## Create and Test ABAP Program YCH01_02_MLIST_TWO_MWINDOWS (Print Program)

We created a program YCH01_02_MLIST_TWO_MWINDOWS (transaction code SE38). This program is very similar to the program YCH01_01_MLIST_ONE_MWINDOW. When calling the function modules OPEN_FORM and START_FORM, the formal parameter FORM has to be provided with a value YCH01_04_MLIST2. This is the name of the *form* of our current exercise. The source lines for calling these two function modules will be as follows:

```
CALL FUNCTION 'OPEN_FORM'
 EXPORTING
 FORM = 'YCH01_04_MLIST2'
 LANGUAGE = SY-LANGU
 .

CALL FUNCTION 'START_FORM'
 EXPORTING
 FORM = 'YCH01_04_MLIST2'
 LANGUAGE = SY-LANGU
 .
```

Our headings—list heading and list column headings—appears in two variable windows. Hence the function module WRITE_FORM (before LOOP AT... statement) to output headings is to be invoked twice. The source lines will be as follows:

```
CALL FUNCTION 'WRITE_FORM'
 EXPORTING
 ELEMENT = 'LIST_HEADING'
 WINDOW = 'HEADING1'
 .

CALL FUNCTION 'WRITE_FORM'
 EXPORTING
 ELEMENT = 'LIST_HEADING'
 WINDOW = 'HEADING2'
 .
```

Except for these differences, the rest of the program YCH01_02_MLIST_TWO_MWINDOWS is identical to the earlier program YCH01_01_MLIST_ONE_MWINDOW. So the full source is not listed here but available in the E-resource (www.apress.com/9781484212345). We performed syntax check and activated the program YCH01_02_MLIST_TWO_MWINDOWS.

We reverted to the *form* screen and performed the text check with the following menu option: Form ➤ Check ➤ Text. The *form* check generated the following alert: The text is syntactically correct. We activated the *form* with the following menu selection: Form ➤ Activate.

# Test Form YCH01_04_MLIST2, Execute Program YCH01_02_MLIST_TWO_MWINDOWS

When we executed the program YCH01_02_MLIST_TWO_MWINDOWS, the output looked as shown in Figure 1-104.

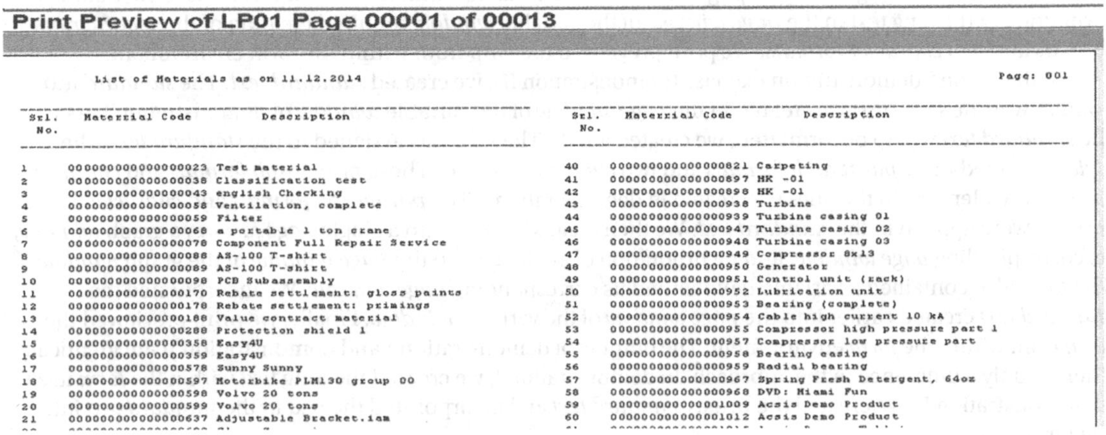

Print Preview of LP01 Page 00001 of 00013

List of Materials as on 11.12.2014 Page: 001

| Srl. No. | Materrial Code | Description | Srl. No. | Materrial Code | Description |
|---|---|---|---|---|---|
| 1 | 000000000000000023 | Test material | 40 | 000000000000000821 | Carpeting |
| 2 | 000000000000000038 | Classification test | 41 | 000000000000000897 | HK -01 |
| 3 | 000000000000000043 | english Checking | 42 | 000000000000000898 | HK -01 |
| 4 | 000000000000000058 | Ventilation, complete | 43 | 000000000000000938 | Turbine |
| 5 | 000000000000000059 | Filter | 44 | 000000000000000939 | Turbine casing 01 |
| 6 | 000000000000000068 | a portable 1 ton crane | 45 | 000000000000000947 | Turbine casing 02 |
| 7 | 000000000000000078 | Component Full Repair Service | 46 | 000000000000000948 | Turbine casing 03 |
| 8 | 000000000000000088 | AS-100 T-shirt | 47 | 000000000000000949 | Compressor 8x13 |
| 9 | 000000000000000089 | AS-100 T-shirt | 48 | 000000000000000950 | Generator |
| 10 | 000000000000000098 | PCB Subassembly | 49 | 000000000000000951 | Control unit (rack) |
| 11 | 000000000000000170 | Rebate settlement: gloss paints | 50 | 000000000000000952 | Lubrication unit |
| 12 | 000000000000000178 | Rebate settlement: primings | 51 | 000000000000000953 | Bearing (complete) |
| 13 | 000000000000000188 | Value contract material | 52 | 000000000000000954 | Cable high current 10 kA |
| 14 | 000000000000000288 | Protection shield 1 | 53 | 000000000000000955 | Compressor high pressure part 1 |
| 15 | 000000000000000358 | Easy4U | 54 | 000000000000000957 | Compressor low pressure part |
| 16 | 000000000000000359 | Easy4U | 55 | 000000000000000958 | Bearing casing |
| 17 | 000000000000000578 | Sunny Sunny | 56 | 000000000000000959 | Radial bearing |
| 18 | 000000000000000597 | Motorbike PLM130 group 00 | 57 | 000000000000000967 | Spring Fresh Detergent, 64oz |
| 19 | 000000000000000598 | Volvo 20 tons | 58 | 000000000000000968 | DVD: Miami Fun |
| 20 | 000000000000000599 | Volvo 20 tons | 59 | 000000000000001009 | Acsis Demo Product |
| 21 | 000000000000000637 | Adjustable Bracket.iam | 60 | 000000000000001012 | Acsis Demo Product |

***Figure 1-104.*** *Program YCH01_02_MLIST_TWO_MWINDOWS—output*

As can be observed, with two *page windows* assigned to the main *window*, the 1,000 rows output in 13 pages compared to 17 pages with one *page window* assigned to the main *window* in demonstration III.

This concludes demonstration IV.

# Recapitulation

Demonstration IV produced a material list. From the output of demonstration III, we contrived a scenario of underutilization of paper space in the output. We set out to improve the paper space utilization in demonstration IV. Demonstration IV has produced the same output as that of demonstration III in a different format, resulting in better paper space utilization. In practical terms, it is unlikely that a material list will be produced using SAP script *forms*. The objective of demonstrations III and IV was to convey in familiar terms the output mechanism with single *page window* assigned to the main *window* and multiple *page windows* assigned to the main *window*.

# Conclusion

This chapter has introduced you to the SAP script as a tool for maintaining business document layouts.

You have learned about the components of SAP script: *forms, styles,* and *standard texts*.

You were given a brief description of the elements of a *form* as well as *window* types.

I described the relationship of SAP script and client code. I also described the relationship of SAP script and language key.

You learned how fonts exist in the SAP script environment. I described and demonstrated the import of operating system font files into the SAP script environment. I also described and demonstrated the import of a BMP graphic image file into the SAP document server.

A detailed description of elements of *form* was presented through a tour of the SAP-delivered ready-to-use *form* MEDRUCK.

We performed four demonstration exercises to highlight some basic core features of *forms*.

The first demonstration exercise (demonstration I) involved the creation of a *form* with a single *page format*, a graph *window*, its corresponding *page window*, and incorporation of an image into the *page window* of the graph *window*. The *form* also contained a variable *window* and its corresponding *page window*. We created long text in the *page window* of the variable *window*. The long text was formatted. The formatting of the long text in the *page window* of the variable *window* required creation of three *paragraph formats* and two *character formats*. We print previewed the *form* from within the *form* environment.

In the second demonstration exercise (demonstration II), we created *standard text*. The *standard text* content was the same text we created in the *page window* of the variable *window* of demonstration I. As the *standard text* was to be formatted, we created a *style*. The *style* was assigned to the *standard text*. The *style* contained three *paragraph formats* and two *character formats*. These *paragraph formats* and *character formats* are identical to the ones we created in demonstration I. The *paragraph formats* and *character formats* were applied to the *standard text*. We then created a *form* with a single *page format*, a graph *window*, its corresponding *page window*, and incorporation of an image into the *page window* of the graph *window*. The *form* also contained a variable *window* and its corresponding *page window*. We incorporated the *standard text* created earlier into the *page window* of the variable *window*. Finally, we print previewed the *form* from within the *form* environment. The outputs of demonstration I and demonstration II are identical. There is only a difference in the approach. In demonstration I, we created the long text within the *form* itself; in demonstration II, we created the text as *standard text* and incorporated the text in the *standard text* into the *form*.

Demonstration III highlighted the location of repetitive data in the main *window*. We undertook to produce a list of materials using a SAP script *form*. The material list fields had to be repetitively output. So they had to be located in the *page window* assigned to the main *window*. We used a single *page window* assigned to the main *window* to output material list fields. We used a variable *window* with its corresponding *page window* to output the material list heading. We created a named *text element* for the main *window* as well as the variable *window*. This exercise required data to be retrieved and processed, so we had to code a print program. We used five function modules—OPEN_FORM, START_FORM, WRITE_FORM, END_FORM, and CLOSE_FORM—for the interaction of the *form* with the print program.

Demonstration IV highlighted the assignment of two (multiple) *page windows* to the main *window*. I contrived a case where demonstration III did not use paper space optimally. I set about to use the paper space more optimally than in demonstration III. I planned to output two columns of material list data on a page much like the newspaper columns. The output of two columns of material list data on a page required two *page widows* to be assigned to the main *window*. The exercise demonstrated in a simple and effective manner the operation of two or more *page windows* assigned to the main *window*. The data of demonstrations III and IV is identical; the difference was in the presentation of the data.

In Chapter 2, we will create *forms*, their corresponding print programs, and required workbench objects for specified business scenarios.

# CHAPTER 2

∎∎∎

# SAP Script–Hands-on Exercises

Chapter 1 introduced you to SAP script as a tool to maintain business document layouts. It described the SAP script environment, its components, and the different tools available to maintain the layout of business documents. I focused for the most part on the *form* component of SAP script. Creating and maintaining business document layouts involves working mostly with *forms*. Chapter 1 also described print programs (ABAP programs) associated with *forms* and the transfer of data from the print programs to SAP script *forms* and *standard texts*. You were exposed to the function modules used in the print program to interact with *forms*. Demonstration exercises were performed to highlight and convey different concepts of SAP script. In this chapter, we will apply SAP script features introduced in Chapter 1 to implement business scenarios. I use the term "hands-on exercises" for the implementation of business scenarios.

We will perform the following five hands-on exercises involving the creation and modifications of *forms* in this chapter:

- Output vendors' address labels of a specific company code.

- Output custom purchase order.

- Output custom purchase order involving invocation of external subroutine from SAP script *text element* and invocation of function modules in the external subroutine.

- Make a copy of the SAP delivered *form* MEDRUCK and customize it.

- Produce customer-wise sales summary of a specific company code using SAP script *form*.

Apart from performing the hands-on exercises of creation and modification of *forms*, we will create our own nodes and sub nodes and assign our *forms* to the subnodes of the SAP script *form* tree.

Detailed implementation of the hands-on exercises follows.

## Hands-on Exercise I–Output Vendors' Address Labels of a Specific Company Code

Sometimes, an enterprise communicates with its business partners (customers or vendors) through postal mail. The enterprise would like to have the address of the business partners printed on address labels or stickers. The address labels will be stuck on envelopes containing communicating material to be sent to business partners.

We will produce the address labels for vendors. The address labels will output for a specific company code. We will create a SAP script *form* layout to produce the address labels. We will create a print program and related workbench objects to produce the address labels for vendors.

© Sushil Markandeya 2017
S. Markandeya, *Pro SAP Scripts, Smartforms, and Data Migration*,
https://doi.org/10.1007/978-1-4842-3183-8_2

# Output Specification and Layout

We will output vendors' address labels on DINA4 stationery in landscape mode—297MM width and 210MM height. We will output 15 address labels on a single sheet of DINA4 stationery in landscape mode. We will locate three address labels in one row and five address labels in one column with appropriate margins and gaps. Each of the address labels will be 93MM in width 38MM in height. All of our address label data repeats within a page and repeats from page to page. Hence, for the *form* to output address labels, we will only use the main *window*. Each of the 15 address labels will map to a *page window* of the main *window*. Each *page window* will contain the address of one vendor. The *page windows* will be numbered from 00 to 14. Figure 2-1 shows a rough layout of the address labels or *page windows*.

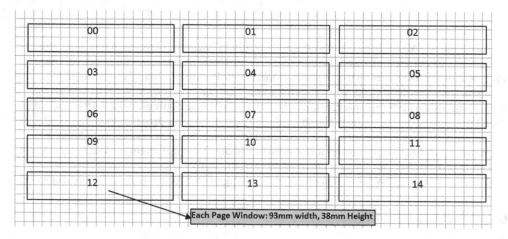

***Figure 2-1.*** *Layout of vendors' address labels*

Table 2-1 lists the dimensions of the 15 *page windows*.

***Table 2-1.*** *Dimensions of 15 Page Windows*

| Page Window Number | Dimensions | | | |
| --- | --- | --- | --- | --- |
| 00 | Left margin 5MM | Upper margin 5MM | Window width 93MM | Window height 38MM |
| 01 | Left margin 102MM | Upper margin 5MM | Window width 93MM | Window height 38MM |
| 02 | Left margin 199MM | Upper margin 5MM | Window width 93MM | Window height 38MM |
| 03 | Left margin 5MM | Upper margin 4MM | Window width 93MM | Window height 38MM |
| 04 | Left margin 102MM | Upper margin 46MM | Window width 93MM | Window height 38MM |
| 05 | Left margin 199MM | Upper margin 46MM | Window width 93MM | Window height 38MM |

*(continued)*

**Table 2-1.** (*continued*)

| Page Window Number | Dimensions | | | |
|---|---|---|---|---|
| 06 | Left margin 5MM | Upper margin 87MM | Window width 93MM | Window height 38MM |
| 07 | Left margin 102MM | Upper margin 87MM | Window width 93MM | Window height 38MM |
| 08 | Left margin 199MM | Upper margin 87MM | Window width 93MM | Window height 38MM |
| 09 | Left margin 5MM | Upper margin 128MM | Window width 93MM | Window height 38MM |
| 10 | Left margin 102MM | Upper margin 128MM | Window width 93MM | Window height 38MM |
| 11 | Left margin 199MM | Upper margin 128MM | Window width 93MM | Window height 38MM |
| 12 | Left mrgin 5MM | Upper margin 169MM | Window width 93MM | Window height 38MM |
| 13 | Left margin 102MM | Upper margin 169MM | Window width 93 MM | Window height 38MM |
| 14 | Left margin 199MM | Upper margin 169MM | Window width 93MM | Window height 38MM |

## Output Considerations

When outputting the address labels, we will call the function module START_FORM at the beginning of a page and the function module END_FORM at the end of a page. That is, our document consists of only one page. We will call the function module START_FORM before commencing to fill the first *page window* in a page. We will call the function module END_FORM after filling the last (15th) *page window* in a page. The calling of the function module END_FORM after filling the last (15th) *page window* in a page and the subsequent calling of the function module START_FORM will ensure a page break for the next vendor address to be output and that next vendor address will output in the first *page window* of the next page.

In Chapter 1, I described the operation of multiple *page windows* located in the main *window*. To recapitulate, initially, the first *page window* will be filled with data. When the first *page window* is full, the second *page window* will be filled with data, and so on, until all the *page windows* in the page are fully filled up. When all the *page windows* of a page are filled up fully, a page break is triggered and this process of data filling will continue in the first *page window* of the next page. This process continues until the data is exhausted.

The operation of multiple *page windows* (15 in our present case) in the main *window* suits our present purpose with one exception. Suppose, when we output a vendor address in the first *page window*, the first *page window* does not get filled up fully because the specific vendor address is short and crisp. Then, since the first *page window* is not full, the address of second vendor will start outputting in the residual space of the first *page window*. This phenomenon could occur for subsequent *page windows* as well. This is not desirable. We want every vendor address to output in a fresh *page window* instead of commencing output in the residual remaining space of current *page window*.

The calling of function modules START_FORM and END_FORM at the beginning and end of a page, respectively, ensures that the first vendor address in a page outputs in the first *page window* of a page. We have to ensure that the second vendor address in a page outputs in the second *page window* (not in the residual space of the first *page window*), the third vendor address outputs in the third *page window,* and so on until the 15th vendor address outputs in the 15th *page window*.

In the SAP script *text element* environment, we can ensure that output commences in a new *page window* instead of in the residual space of current *page window* with the following control command:

```
NEW-WINDOW
```

Though the control command does not contain the phrase *page window*, the semantics of this control command is to commence output in a new *page window* instead of in the residual space of the current *page window*.

In our present context, we want to issue the control command NEW-WINDOW only for *page windows* 2 to 15. For this purpose, we will maintain a counter whose value signifies the *page window* being output in the SAP script ABAP print program. We will check the contents of this counter in the SAP script *text element* environment and issue the control command NEW-WINDOW accordingly. The ABAP program lines and SAP script *text element* control commands will look as follows:

ABAP program lines:

```
DATA: COUNTER(2)TYPE N,
      LFA1_STRU TYPE ....
      LFA1_TAB......TYPE .....
.....
LOOP AT LFA1_TAB INTO LFA1_STRU.
.......
 IF COUNTER = 0.
  CALL FUNCTION 'START_FORM'...
 ENDIF.
 COUNTER = COUNTER + 1.
 CALL FUNCTION 'WRITE_FORM'...
.......
 IF COUNTER = 15.
  CALL FUNCTION 'END_FORM'...
  COUNTER = 0.
 ENDIF.
ENDLOOP.
.....
```

Control commands:

```
/: IF &COUNTER& <> '01'
/: NEW-WINDOW
/: ENDIF
```

The variable COUNTER has been declared as type N to make the IF control command comparison simpler. Recall from Chapter 1 that all the program symbol values in the SAP script *text element* environment are character oriented.

## Inputs

We need to output vendor addresses. All of the vendor address data is available in the vendor primary table LFA1 and through the field ADRNR in the table ADRC. As we are outputting vendor addresses of a specific company code, we need to link the two tables LFA1 and LFB1. We have created a database view (YCH02_LFA1_LFB1) of these two tables. The *Table/Join Conditions* tab of the database view will be as follows:

```
LFB1          LFA1    MANDT    =    LFB1    MANDT
LFA1          LFA1    LIFNR    =    LFB1    LIFNR
```

The *View Flds* tab of the database view has the fields shown in Table 2-2.

*Table 2-2.* *Fields in the Database View YCH02_LFA1_LFB1*

| Srl. No. | Field/Table | Srl. No. | Field/Table |
|----------|-------------|----------|-------------|
| 01 | MANDT / LFA1 | 10 | ORT02 / LFA1 |
| 02 | LIFNR / LFA1 | 11 | PFACH / LFA1 |
| 03 | BUKRS / LFB1 | 12 | PSTL2 / LFA1 |
| 04 | LAND1 / LFA1 | 13 | PSTLZ / LFA1 |
| 05 | NAME1 / LFA1 | 14 | REGIO / LFA1 |
| 06 | NAME2 / LFA1 | 15 | STRAS / LFA1 |
| 07 | NAME3 / LFA1 | 16 | ADRNR / LFA1 |
| 08 | NAME4 / LFA1 | 17 | ANRED / LFA1 |
| 09 | ORT01 / LFA1 | | |

The view YCH02_LFA1_LFB1 is our sole input.

## *Text element* contents in the main *window*

We need to format the individual vendor addresses according to the postal convention of country of the individual vendor. The SAP script *form's text element* environment provides the wherewithal for formatting individual vendor addresses according to the postal convention of each individual vendor country.

The respective primary tables (LFA1 and KNA1) maintain business partners' (vendors and customers) addresses. These addresses are also maintained in the *business address services* table ADRC as per the postal convention of individual business partner's country (the recipient country). The table ADRC is accessed through the field ADRNR. The field ADRNR is available in the table structures LFA1 and LFB1.

In the SAP script *text element* environment, a set of control commands is available to output the addresses as per postal convention of a country. The set of control commands is as follows:

```
/: ADDRESS <options & parameters>
/: .....
/: ENDADDRESS
```

The set of control commands outputs the addresses as per postal convention of recipient country as well as provides additional customizing features. Read up on this set of control commands in the PDF document "Style and Form Maintenance."

The set of control commands to output the addresses as per postal convention of recipient country internally uses the function module ADDRESS_INTO_PRINTFORM.

The *text element* in the main *window* of the *form* YCH02_01_ADR_STK will have the following contents:

```
/E ADDRESS
/: IF &COUNTER& <> '01'
/: NEW-WINDOW
/: ENDIF
/: IF &LFA1_STRU-ADRNR(K)& = ' '
/: ADDRESS PARAGRAPH DP
/:   TITLE    &LFA1_STRU-ANRED&
```

```
/:  NAME      &LFA1_STRU-NAME1&, &LFA1_STRU-NAME2&, &LFA1_STRU-NAME3&
/:  STREET    &LFA1_STRU-STRAS&
/:  POBOX     &LFA1_STRU-PFACH&  CODE &LFA1_STRU-PSTL2&
/:  CITY      &LFA1_STRU-ORT01&, &LFA1_STRU-ORT02&
/:  POSTCODE &LFA1_STRU-PSTLZ&
/:  COUNTRY   &LFA1_STRU-LAND1&
/:  REGION    &LFA1_STRU-REGIO&
/:  FROMCOUNTRY &T001-LAND1&
/:  ENDADDRESS
/:  ELSE
/:  ADDRESS PARAGRAPH DP
/:   ADDRESSNUMBER &LFA1_STRU-ADRNR(K)&
/:  FROMCOUNTRY &T001-LAND1&
/:  ENDADDRESS
/:  ENDIF
```

The set of control commands checks the value of the field ADRNR. If this field has a value, the address is output from the table ADRC; otherwise, the individual address fields from the table LFA1 specified under the ADDRESS.....ENDADDRESS set of control commands are output.

## Source program

The print program for the SAP script *form* YCH02_01_ADR_STK is as follows:

```
REPORT  YCH02_01_PPRG_YCH02_01_ADR_STK.

**********************************************************
* Address Labels for Vendors of a Specific Company Code **
* Use SAP script Form: YCH02_01_ADR_STK              **
**********************************************************

TYPES: BEGIN OF LFA1_STRU_TP,
        LIFNR    TYPE LIFNR,
        ADRNR    TYPE ADRNR,
        ANRED    TYPE ANRED,
        NAME1    TYPE NAME1_GP,
        NAME2    TYPE NAME2_GP,
        NAME3    TYPE NAME3_GP,
        NAME4    TYPE NAME4_GP,
        STRAS    TYPE STRAS_GP,
        PFACH    TYPE PFACH,
        PSTL2    TYPE PSTL2,
        ORT01    TYPE ORT01_GP,
        ORT02    TYPE ORT02_GP,
        PSTLZ    TYPE PSTLZ,
        LAND1    TYPE LAND1_GP,
        REGIO    TYPE REGIO,
      END OF LFA1_STRU_TP.

TABLES: T001.
DATA: LFA1_TAB     TYPE STANDARD TABLE OF LFA1_STRU_TP,
      LFA1_STRU    TYPE LFA1_STRU_TP,
      COUNTER(2)   TYPE N.
```

```
**********************************************************
PARAMETERS: COMP_CD   TYPE KNB1-BUKRS DEFAULT 3000
            VALUE CHECK.
**********************************************************
START-OF-SELECTION.
SELECT SINGLE * FROM T001 WHERE BUKRS = COMP_CD.

SELECT LIFNR ADRNR ANRED NAME1 NAME2 NAME3 NAME4 STRAS
       PFACH PSTL2 ORT01 ORT02 PSTLZ LAND1 REGIO
       FROM YCH02_LFA1_LFB1
       INTO TABLE LFA1_TAB
       WHERE BUKRS = COMP_CD.
SORT LFA1_TAB BY LIFNR.
**********************************************************
CALL FUNCTION 'OPEN_FORM'
 EXPORTING
   FORM                             = 'YCH02_01_ADR_STK'
   LANGUAGE                         = 'E'
       .
IF SY-SUBRC <> 0.
 MESSAGE ID SY-MSGID TYPE SY-MSGTY NUMBER SY-MSGNO
        WITH SY-MSGV1 SY-MSGV2 SY-MSGV3 SY-MSGV4.
ENDIF.

**********************************************************
LOOP AT LFA1_TAB INTO LFA1_STRU.

 COUNTER = COUNTER + 1.

 IF COUNTER = '01'.
  CALL FUNCTION 'START_FORM'
   EXPORTING
     FORM                           = 'YCH02_01_ADR_STK'
     LANGUAGE                       = 'E'
         .
  IF SY-SUBRC <> 0.
   MESSAGE ID SY-MSGID TYPE SY-MSGTY NUMBER SY-MSGNO
          WITH SY-MSGV1 SY-MSGV2 SY-MSGV3 SY-MSGV4.
  ENDIF.

 ENDIF.

 CALL FUNCTION 'WRITE_FORM'
  EXPORTING
    ELEMENT                         = 'ADDRESS'
    WINDOW                          = 'MAIN'
        .
 IF SY-SUBRC <> 0.
  MESSAGE ID SY-MSGID TYPE SY-MSGTY NUMBER SY-MSGNO
         WITH SY-MSGV1 SY-MSGV2 SY-MSGV3 SY-MSGV4.
 ENDIF.
```

```
IF COUNTER = '15'.
 COUNTER = 0.
 CALL FUNCTION 'END_FORM'
         .
 IF SY-SUBRC <> 0.
  MESSAGE ID SY-MSGID TYPE SY-MSGTY NUMBER SY-MSGNO
          WITH SY-MSGV1 SY-MSGV2 SY-MSGV3 SY-MSGV4.
 ENDIF.

 ENDIF.

ENDLOOP.
*****************************************
CALL FUNCTION 'CLOSE_FORM'
       .
IF SY-SUBRC <> 0.
 MESSAGE ID SY-MSGID TYPE SY-MSGTY NUMBER SY-MSGNO
         WITH SY-MSGV1 SY-MSGV2 SY-MSGV3 SY-MSGV4.
ENDIF.
```

# Creation of Form YCH02_01_ADR_STK and Print Program YCH02_01_PPRG_YCH02_01_ADR_STK

In transaction code SE71, we created a *form* YCH02_01_ADR_STK. We made the page orientation as landscape. The *form* consisted of a single *page format* ONLY_PG. The *form* consisted of single *paragraph format* DP. The font family assigned to the *paragraph format* DP is Courier and the font size is 10 points. In the *basic settings* of the *form* attributes, we assigned the default paragraph as DP and assigned the first page as ONLY_PG. We also adjusted the *Lines/inch* to 7.2 and *Characters/inch* to 12.

We assigned the next page for *page format* ONLY_PG as ONLY_PG.

The *form* consists of only the main *window*. We created 15 *page windows* as per Table 2-1. In the main *window text element*, we entered the control commands shown under 'Text element contents in the main window.'

We saved the *form* and assigned the package YCH_BC401. You can assign this package or any other non-local package of your choice.

We created an ABAP program YCH02_01_PPRG_YCH02_01_ADR_STK with the lines as shown under the headings 'Source program.' We performed a syntax check and activated this program.

In the transaction code SE71, we performed a *form* definition check as well as the *form* texts check on the *form* YCH02_01_ADR_STK and activated it.

The *form* YCH02_01_ADR_STK and the source program YCH02_01_PPRG_YCH02_01_ADR_STK are available in the E-resource for this book (www.apress.com/9781484212345).

## Output

We executed the program YCH02_01_PPRG_YCH02_01_ADR_STK. We executed the program with the company code value equal to 3000. The output will look as shown in Figures 2-2 and 2-3.

**Print Preview of LP01 Page 00001 of 00036**

```
Electronic Components Distributor      José Fernandez                  KBB Schwarze Pumpe
Tower Lane 1082                        Via Rioja 1                     D-99999 FRANKENTHAL/PFALZ
FOSTER CITY CA  94404

                                       11111 MEXIKO CITY
                                       MEXICO




Company                                Company                         Sedona Suppliers
Express Vendor Inc                     AluCast                         PO Box 34446
2550 North Racine Ave                  HILLSBOROUGH NJ  22086          RIMROCK AZ  12224
CHICAGO IL  60614




Intercompany Resources to Belgium      Intercompany Resources Canada   Firma
CANADA                                 CANADA                          C.E.B. BERLIN
                                                                       Kolping Str. 15
                                                                       D-12001 BERLIN
```

***Figure 2-2.*** *Output of program YCH02_01_PPRG_YCH02_01_ADR_STK—page 1/36)*

**Print Preview of LP01 Page 00035 of 00036**

```
N. A. Sealing Company                  Interstate Transport Comp.      Total Chemical Company
PHILADELPHIA PA                        PHILADELPHIA PA                 PHILADELPHIA PA




Supplier - One                         Manufacturer Valencia Foundry   Company
1000 Industrial Hwy                    Valencia Foundry                Contra Pak
NEW ORLEANS LA  70112                  2300 McBean Parkway             Contra Pack
                                       VALENCIA CA  91355              500 Washington Ave
                                                                       MEMPHIS TN  30101




American Sports Distributor            Sports Distributors             Paper Suplies
PO Box 1000                            Postfach 7900                   Postfach 9500
PHILADELPHIA PA  10003                 D-61962 HOCKENHEIM              D-12001 BERLIN
```

***Figure 2-3.*** *Output of program YCH02_01_PPRG_YCH02_01_ADR_STK—page 35/36*

The output will depend on the number of vendors for the specified company code. In the present case, the output consists of 36 pages.

# Hands-on Exercise Recapitulation

In this hands-on exercise, we used the feature of multiple *page windows* in the main *window* to output the address labels of vendors. The feature of multiple *page windows* in the main *window* was introduced in demonstration IV in Chapter 1.

We wanted to ensure that each vendor address commences output in a new *page window* instead of commencing output in the residual space, if any, of the current *page window*. To implement this requirement, we introduced the control command NEW-WINDOW.

To ensure that the vendor address outputs as per the postal convention of the recipient country, we introduced the set of control commands ADDRESS.....ENDADDRESS.

We used the five function modules: OPEN_FORM, START_FORM, WRITE_FORM, END_FORM and CLOSE_FORM. These function modules are invariably used in the print program's interaction with SAP script *forms*.

You are already familiar with the rest of the print program and *form* features used in the hands-on exercise.

# Hands-on Exercise II—Output Custom Purchase Order

In this hands-on exercise, we will create a *form*, its corresponding print program, and other required workbench objects to output standard purchase orders. SAP delivers *forms* for all commonly used enterprise business documents. The SAP delivered *forms* have their corresponding print programs. In Chapter 1, via a tour of the SAP delivered *form* for purchasing document MEDRUCK, I introduced the various features and concepts of *forms*. In real-life SAP implementation projects, copies are made of SAPdelivered *forms* in the Y/Z namespace. The copied *forms* are then modified and customized as per requirements. A copy of a SAP delivered *form* modified and customized as per requirements will use the print program associated with the original SAP delivered *form*, so a new print program is not required to be created. The advantages of this approach of copying and customizing SAP delivered *forms* is that you do not have to create a *form* from scratch and do not have to code its corresponding complex print program.

The present hands-on exercise gives me an occasion and the scope to expose you to the process of creating from scratch a complex *form* for a business document that outputs standard purchase orders, as well as to introduce you to more features of *text elements* of *forms*. In one of the succeeding hands-on exercises, we will copy the SAP delivered *form* MEDRUCK into Y namespace and customize it as per laid-out specifications.

## Hands-on Exercise–Scope and Limits

The present hands-on exercise will output the standard purchase orders, somewhat similar in looks to the one produced by the SAP delivered *form* MEDRUCK. But the *form* MEDRUCK produces not just purchase orders but all other purchasing documents like purchase requisitions, request for quotations, and so on. The objective of this exercise is to allow you to create from scratch a complex *form*, its associated print program, and the deployment of the *form* to output standard purchase orders.

In the present hands-on exercise, it is assumed that the purchase orders submitted for output are new purchase orders and not the purchase orders for which full or partial deliveries have been made.

The present hands-on exercise assumes that there is only one consignee/delivery address for all the items of a purchase order and only one delivery date for all the items of a purchase order.

The present hands-on exercise also assumes that there is only one term of delivery for all the items of a purchase order.

## Output and Layout Specification

We will output standard purchase orders on DINA4 stationery in portrait mode—210MM width and 297MM height. We will output a graphic logo in a graphic *window* and item data in the main *window*. The rest of the data will be output in variable *windows*.

There will be two *page formats* for the purchase order: FIRST and NEXT. The first page of a purchase order will output with the *page format* FIRST; if a purchase order runs into multiple pages, all the pages other than the first page of a purchase order will output with the *page format* NEXT.

The area of purchase order above the item area of *page format* FIRST will be as shown in Figure 2-4.

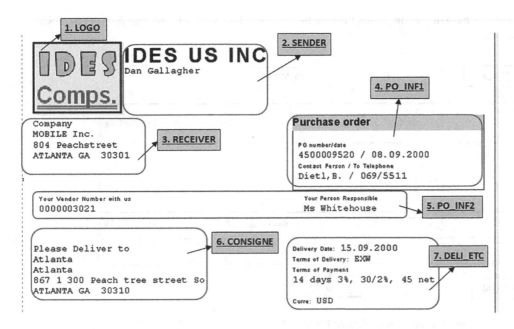

*Figure 2-4. Custom purchase order page format FIRST—I*

The areas bounded by rectangles with rounded corners represent *windows* with their corresponding *page windows*. The *windows* with their corresponding *page windows* are numbered for convenience. There is one graphic *window* and six variable *windows* with their corresponding *page windows*. The contents of *windows* and their corresponding *page windows* will be as follows:

1.  The company logo is located in the LOGO *window*.

2.  The *window* SENDER (sender of purchase order) contains the sender's name and address, that is, the company code name and address.

3.  The *window* RECEIVER (receiver of purchase order) contains the receiver's name and address, that is, the vendor's name and address.

4.  The *window* PO_INF1 contains the following information:

    •  Document type, in our context 'Purchase order,' since we restricted our scope to output normal new purchase orders.

    •  Purchase order number and date.

    •  Contact person and telephone number.

5.  The *window* PO_INF2 contains vendor code and vendor person responsible.

6.  The *window* CONSIGNE contains the delivery plant/branch office address.

7.  The *window* DELI_ETC contains the following information:

    •  Delivery date

    •  Terms of delivery

    •  Terms of payment

    •  Currency

103

The area of purchase order containing the item header, item data, total, etc., of *page format* FIRST will be as in Figure 2-5.

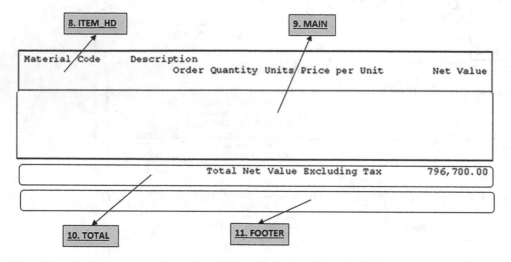

**Figure 2-5.** *Custom purchase order page format FIRST—II*

8. The *window* ITEM_HD contains the column heading text for item data: 'Material code,' 'Description,' etc.

9. The *window* MAIN contains the item data (data which is repeating in a page and repeating page to page). The item data is being output in two lines. The first line outputs material code and description. The second line outputs order quantity, units, price per unit, and net value.

10. The *window* TOTAL contains a purchase order's total net value. For a specific purchase order, the total net value must output on the last page of a purchase order

11. We have not located any information in the *window* FOOTER. You might choose to locate some information in this *window*.

For the second *page format* NEXT, its *windows* and *page windows* layout will be as shown in Figure 2-6:

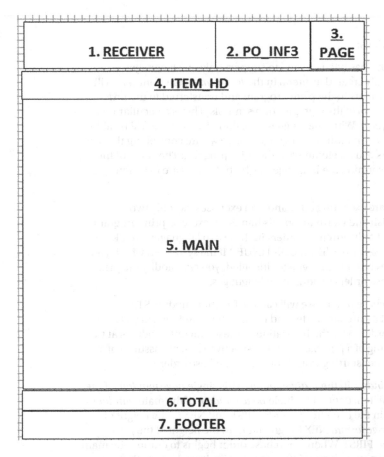

*Figure 2-6. Custom purchase order page format NEXT —windows and page windows layout*

The *window* PO_INF3 contains the purchase order number and date.

The *window* PAGE contains a running page number along with the total number of pages in a purchase order. The page number will start from 1 for each purchase order. The total number of pages will be the number of pages in a purchase order.

As in the SAP delivered *form* MEDRUCK, the page number is being output from the second page of a purchase order; the page number information does not appear in the first page of a purchase order.

The other *windows* and *page windows* in the *page format* NEXT are common to the *page format* FIRST. The height of *page window* of the main *window* in the *page format* NEXT is greater than its corresponding *page window* in the *page format* FIRST.

This concludes the output specification and layout.

# Output Considerations

Following are some output considerations:

- The hands-on exercise *form* has been created to support only one language: English. All the text normally created as literal in the *text element* environment will be retrieved from data elements in the print program and transferred to the *text element* environment of the *form* through program symbols. This is a peculiar way of handling the texts in a *form*. With one language version of a *form*, we will be able to output the purchase order in multiple languages, since we are controlling the text language through the texts of data elements in the print program. The value of the field EKKO-SPRAS will determine the language in which the texts are to be fetched from data elements.

- The system on which we are executing our hands-on exercises has only two languages installed: English and German. So this hands-on exercise print program has been created to accept only purchase orders in these two languages. (IF EKKO-SPRAS <> 'D' AND EKKO-SPRAS <> 'E' .....CONTINUE.) If the system on which you are executing the exercises has more languages installed, you can modify the print program to accept purchase orders in additional languages.

- When outputting the purchase orders, we will call the function module START_FORM at the beginning of a purchase order and the function module END_FORM at the end of a purchase order. With the invocation of these function modules at the commencement and ending of a purchase order, respectively, we are assured of a page break and page number starting from 1 for every purchase order.

- We have only one *page window* in the *main window*. This single *page window* of the main *window* receives the item data. This single *page window* of the main *window* has different dimensions in the two *page formats* FIRST and NEXT. The height of the *page window* in the *page format* NEXT is greater than the height of the *page window* in the *page format* FIRST. When a purchase order begins to output, the main *window page window* of the *page format* FIRST will receive item data continually. If the item data for all the items is received and the main *window page window* in the *page format* FIRST is not completely filled up, it is a case of a purchase order not extending to the second page. At the end of outputting all items, the total needs to be output. After the total is output, the output of the purchase is completed and the commencement of output of the next purchase order if any will start. This was the case of a purchase order that runs into one page only.

- Let us consider the case of a purchase order that runs into more than one page. When a purchase order begins to output, the main *window page window* of the *page format* FIRST will receive the item data continually until the main *window page window* in the *page format* FIRST is full. When the main *window page window* in *page format* FIRST is full, a page break will be triggered, and data will continue to output in the main *window page window* of the *page format* NEXT; this process will go on until all the item data of a purchase order is received and output.

- Three addresses are being output: (1) sender or company code name and address; (2) receiver or vendor name and address; (3) consignee or delivery address. We want the sender or company code name to output in font type Helve and font size 28 points. This requires applying *character format* to the company code name field. To be able to apply *character format* to the company code name field, we are not using the ADDRESS.....ENDADDRESS set of control commands to output the sender or company code name and address. Using the field ADRNR of table T001, we are retrieving the address of company code from the table SADR. The retrieved address from the table SADR is formatted as per the company code country's postal convention by calling the function module ADDRESS_INTO_PRINTFORM. This function module takes input addresses and returns the formatted address as per the country's postal convention. This function module is also internally used by the ADDRESS.....ENDADDRESS set of control commands. The other two addresses, that is, the receiver or vendor address and consignee or delivery address, are output using the ADDRESS.....ENDADDRESS set of control commands.

- The item header and item data are being output enclosed in boxes as shown in Figure 2-5. You can produce boxes or frames using the control command BOX..... The document type 'Purchase Order' is output using control command BOX.....with shading option (grayish background). You can specify the x-axis, y-axis, width, and height of the box when issuing the control command BOX. You can also specify the thickness of box or frame boundary line (dimension used is Twip, $\frac{1}{1440}$ of an inch) and shading effect. The control command BOX by default starts from the *page window* assigned to the *window* in which it is issued. But by specifying negative x-axis and y-axis values, you can have the box start from a position prior to the current position. Similarly, by specifying positive x-axis and y-axis values, you can have the box start from a position ahead of the current position. The box size is not constrained by *page window* boundaries and can cut across the *page window* boundaries. Two control commands, POSITION and SIZE, go along with the control command BOX. For a detailed description of these control commands, refer to the PDF document "BC Style and Form Maintenance."

- The item data is output in two lines: the first line outputting material code and description and the second line outputting order quantity, units, price per unit, and net value. We do not want the two lines constituting the detail of an item to split between two pages but output on the same page. To ensure that the two lines constituting the detail of an item output on the same page, we are using the control commands PROTECT.....ENDPROTECT. Whatever lines you locate between the control commands PROTECT.....ENDPROTECT will output on the same page, equivalent to RESERVE <lines> ABAP statement used in the context of ABAP statement WRITE.

- We are using the SAP script system symbol &PAGE& to output page numbers of a purchase order. We are using the general SAP script field &SAPSCRIPT-FORMPAGES& to output the total number of pages of a purchase order. We are using SAP script system symbol &nextpage& (&nextpage& value is zero for the last page of a document) to ascertain the last page of a purchase order and output the total net value only on the last page of a purchase order.

- We are using some of the SAP script *text element* formatting options like output length specification, zero suppression, left-side space compression, right justification, suppression of conversion routine, etc. Refer to the detailed description of formatting options in the PDF document "BC Style and Form Maintenance."

- We plan to output some of the information of purchase order in a font type and size other than the default font type Courier 12, etc. So we created a few *character formats* to output information in font type and size other than the default.

This concludes the output considerations.

# Data Inputs and Data Input Considerations

The two main sources of data to output the purchase orders with custom *form* are the tables EKKO, purchasing document header, and EKPO, purchasing document item.

We will retrieve data from EKKO with the SELECT..... ENDSELECT loop. You can choose to load EKKO data into an internal table and loop from the internal table. A SELECT-OPTIONS statement is provided to be able to choose the purchase orders to be output.

The data relating to the company code of a purchase order being processed will be retrieved from the tableT001—SELECT SINGLE * FROM T001 WHERE BUKRS = EKKO-BUKRS. The address of the company code is retrieved from the table SADR- SELECT SINGLE * FROM SADR WHERE ADRNR = T001-ADRNR. The function module ADDRESS_INTO_PRINTFORM will return ten lines of address of the company code formatted as per the postal convention of the country of the company code which is output in the *window* SENDER.

The data relating to the vendor of a purchase order being processed will be retrieved from the vendor primary table LFA1 - SELECT SINGLE * FROM LFA1 WHERE LIFNR = EKKO-LIFNR.

The set of control commands ADDRESS.....ENDADDRESS will retrieve the vendor address through the field LFA1-ADRNR and will output the vendor address as per the recipient country's postal convention which is being output in the *window* RECEIVER.

The document type (purchase order) along with the field nomenclatures or labels for purchase order number and date are retrieved from table T166U as follows:

```
SELECT SINGLE * FROM T166U WHERE BSTYP = EKKO-BSTYP AND
 BSART = EKKO-BSART AND SPRAS = EKKO-SPRAS AND DRUVO = '1'.
```

The 'contact person' and 'to telephone' are retrieved from the table T024 like SELECT SINGLE * FROM T024 WHERE EKGRP = EKKO-EKGRP.

The terms of payment are retrieved from the table T052 like SELECT SINGLE * FROM T052 WHERE ZTERM = EKKO-ZTERM. The function module FI_PRINT_ZTERM is used to retrieve the terms-of-payment text.

We require the material description in our output. For this reason, we are using a database view of the tables EKPO and MAKT joined by the fields MANDT and MATNR. The name of this view is YCH02_EKPO_MAKT. This view will contain material descriptions in all the languages. In the print program, at any time, we will retrieve from this view only the items pertaining to a specific purchase order being currently output. When the data is retrieved from this view for a specific purchase order, we will retrieve material descriptions of items of a purchase order being output in the language of the purchase order as follows:

```
SELECT * FROM YCH02_EKPO_MAKT INTO TABLE ITEM_TAB
  WHERE EBELN = EKKO-EBELN
    AND BUKRS = EKKO-BUKRS
    AND SPRAS = EKKO-SPRAS.    "Load itab from View
```

The consignee (deliver to plant/branch office address) is retrieved through the view field YCH02_EKPO_MAKT-ADRNR from the first item record of the purchase order, alternatively through YCH02_EKPO_MAKT-ADRN2 and again alternatively from table T001W through YCH02_EKPO_MAKT-WERKS. The consignee data will be retrieved for the first item of a purchase order, assuming that it is the same for all other items in the purchase order.

The delivery date is retrieved from the table EKET as follows:

```
SELECT SINGLE * FROM EKET WHERE EBELN = YCH02_EKPO_MAKT-EBELN
 AND EBELP = YCH02_EKPO_MAKT-EBELP.
```

Again this will be retrieved for the first item of a purchase order, assuming that it is the same for all other items in the purchase order.

Table 2-3 provides a list of the tables/views with fields used. A field of a table/view is deemed to be used when it is appearing in the output or occurs in subsequent WHERE condition(s):

*Table 2-3. List of Tables and Views with the Fields*

| Srl. No. | Table/View | Table/View Fields used | | |
|---|---|---|---|---|
| 01 | EKKO - Purchasing document header | EBELN | BUKRS | EKGRP |
| | | BEDAT | LIFNR | ZTERM |
| | | BSTYP | ADRNR | INCO1 |
| | | BSART | VERKF | |
| | | SPRAS | WAERS | |
| 02 | YCH02_EKPO_MAKT - Database view of tables: purchasing document item EKPO and material descriptions MAKT | EBELN | MATNR | MAKTX |
| | | EBELP | MENGE | |
| | | WERKS | MEINS | |
| | | ADRNR | NETPR | |
| | | ADRN2 | NETWR | |
| 03 | LFA1 - Vendor primary | ANRED | PFACH | LAND1 |
| | | NAME1 | PSTL2 | REGIO |
| | | NAME2 | ORT01 | |
| | | NAME3 | ORT02 | |
| | | NAME4 | PSTLZ | |
| 04 | T001 - Company code | ADRNR | | |
| 05 | SADR - Address Management: Company Data | ANRED | PFACH | LAND1 |
| | | NAME1 | PSTL2 | REGIO |
| | | NAME2 | ORT01 | |
| | | NAME3 | ORT02 | |
| | | NAME4 | PSTLZ | |
| 06 | T024 - Purchasing Groups | EKNAM, EKTEL | | |
| 07 | T166U - Headings in Purchasing Document Printout | DRTYP, DRNUM | | |
| 08 | T001W - Plants/Branches | ANRED | PFACH | LAND1 |
| | | NAME1 | PSTL2 | REGIO |
| | | NAME2 | ORT01 | |
| | | NAME3 | ORT02 | |
| | | NAME4 | PSTLZ | |
| 09 | EKET - Scheduling Agreement Schedule Lines | EINDT | | |
| 10 | T052 - Terms of Payment | ZTERM | | |

The nomenclatures or labels for the fields are retrieved from data elements' long texts using the function module WCGW_DATA_ELEMENT_TEXT_GET. Most table fields' existing data element texts do not suit us; that is, the texts of these existing data elements do not correspond with the texts of the proposed output. So, for this hands-on exercise, we have created our own data elements and created texts for these data elements in the two languages: English and German. There are a total of 16 data elements; their English and German texts are available in the E-resource for this book (www.apress.com/9781484212345). The German texts available in the E-resource were created using the Google translator.

The nomenclatures or labels for fields as a rule are specified through literals in the *text element* environment of the SAP script *form*. This is the practice in all the SAP delivered *forms* as well as the *forms* we have created until now. By making the nomenclatures or labels for fields as program symbols or variables in *text element* environment of the SAP script *form*, we are making the *form* itself language independent.

This concludes the data input and data input considerations.

# Creation of SAP Script Form, Print Program, and Related Workbench Objects

To output purchase orders using custom *form*, we will be creating the following workbench objects:

- A database view using the tables EKPO and MAKT.

- A SAP script *form*.

- A print program for the SAP script *form*.

- A database view using the tables EKKO and LFA1. This database view will be used in an elementary search help.

- An elementary search help. This elementary search help uses the database view consisting of tables EKKO and LFA1. This elementary search help is being attached to the SELECT-OPTIONS field in the print program

A description for how to create these workbench objects follows.

## Database View YCH02_EKPO_MAKT

We created a database view YCH02_EKPO_MAKT with the table EKPO as the primary table and table MAKT as a secondary table. The tables are to be joined through the fields MANDT and MATNR. The database view consists of fields listed in Table 2-4.

*Table 2-4.* *Fields in the Database View YCH02_EKPO_MAKT*

| Srl. No. | Field/Table | Srl. No. | Field/Table |
|----------|-------------|----------|-------------|
| 01 | MANDT / EKPO | 08 | ADRN2 / EKPO |
| 02 | EBELN / EKPO | 09 | MATNR / EKPO |
| 03 | EBELP / EKPO | 10 | MENGE / EKPO |
| 04 | SPRAS / MAKT | 11 | MEINS / EKPO |
| 05 | BURKS / EKPO | 12 | NETPR / EKPO |
| 06 | WERKS / EKPO | 13 | NETWR / EKPO |
| 07 | ADRNR / EKPO | 14 | MAKTX / MAKT |

We performed the consistency check and activated the database view.

## SAP Script Form YCH02_02_PORDER1

We created a *form* YCH02_02_PORDER1. Within the *form*, we created a *paragraph format* DP with default values. Further, we created a *page format* FIRST. In the *basic settings* of the *form* attributes, we assigned the default paragraph as DP and assigned the first page as FIRST.

We created *page format* NEXT. We assigned the next page for *page format* FIRST as NEXT. And we assigned the next page for *page format* NEXT as NEXT.

For *page format* FIRST, we created *windows* and their corresponding *page windows* as per the entries in Table 2-5.

***Table 2-5.*** *Page Format FIRST—Windows and Page Windows*

| Window & Page Window | Page Window Dimensions | Contents |
|---|---|---|
| 1.LOGO | Left margin : 5.00MM<br>Upper margin : 5.00MM<br>Window width : 46.64MM<br>Window height : 29.81MM | Company Logo<br>'YCH01_COMPANY_LOGO' OBJECT<br>GRAPHICS ID<br>BMAP TYPE BCOL |
| 2.SENDER | Left margin : 46.00MM<br>Upper margin : 5.00MM<br>Window width : 145.00MM<br>Window height : 30.00MM | Company code name & address<br>&ADRS-LINE1&..... &ADRS-LINE9& |
| 3.RECEIVER | Left margin : 5.00MM<br>Upper margin : 35.00MM<br>Window width : 115.00MM<br>Window height : 30.00MM | &EKKO-ADRNR(K)& etc. |
| 4.PO_INF1 | Left margin : 120.00MM<br>Upper margin : 35.00MM<br>Window width : 85.00MM<br>Window height : 30.00MM | &T166U-DRTYP& &T166U-DRNUM&<br>&EKKO-EBELN& &EKKO-BEDAT&<br>&YCH02_EKNAM& &YCH02_EKTEL&<br>&T024-EKNAM& &T024-EKTEL& |
| 5.PO_INF2 | Left margin : 5.00MM<br>Upper margin : 65.00MM<br>Window width : 200.00MM<br>Window height : 20.00MM | &YCH02_LIFNR(30) & &YCH02_VERKF&<br>&EKKO-LIFNR(K)& &EKKO-VERKF& |
| 6.CONSIGNE | Left margin : 5.00MM<br>Upper margin : 85.00MM<br>Window width : 115.00MM<br>Window height : 30.00MM | &YCH02_CONSG&<br>&YCH02_EKPO_MAKT-ADRNR(K)& or<br>&YCH02_EKPO_MAKT-ADRN2(K)& or<br>&SADR-ANRED&..... etc. |
| 7.DELI_ETC | Left margin : 120.00MM<br>Upper margin : 85.00MM<br>Window width : 85.00MM<br>Window height : 30.00MM | &YCH02_EINDT& &EKET-EINDT&<br>&YCH02_INCO1& &EKKO-INCO1&<br>&YCH02_ZBTXT&<br>&ZBTXT_STRU&<br>&WAERS& &EKKO-WAERS& |

*(continued)*

**Table 2-5.** (*continued*)

| Window & Page Window | Page Window Dimensions | Contents |
|---|---|---|
| 8.ITEM_HD | Left Mmargin : 5.00MM<br>Upper margin : 115.00MM<br>Window width : 200.00MM<br>Window height : 20.00MM | &YCH02_MATNR& &YCH02_MAKTX&<br>&YCH02_MENGE(R14)& &YCH02_MEINS(5)&<br>&YCH02_NETPR(R14)& &NETWR(R15)& |
| 9.MAIN | Left margin : 5.00MM<br>Upper margin : 135.00MM<br>Window width : 200.00MM<br>Window height : 137.00MM | &YCH02_EKPO_MAKT-MATNR(18K)&<br>&YCH02_EKPO_MAKT-MAKTX(40)&<br>&YCH02_EKPO_MAKT-MENGE(14)&<br>&YCH02_EKPO_MAKT-MEINS(5)&<br>&YCH02_EKPO_MAKT-NETPR(14)&<br>&YCH02_EKPO_MAKT-NETWR(15)& |
| 10.TOTAL | Left margin : 5.00MM<br>Upper margin : 272.00MM<br>Window width : 200.00MM<br>Window height : 10.00MM | &YCH02_TOTAL_NET_E& &TOTAL& |
| 11.FOOTER | Left margin : 5.00MM<br>Upper margin : 282.00MM<br>Window width : 200.00MM<br>Window height : 10.00MM | Footer text if any |

For *page format* NEXT, we created *windows* and their corresponding *page windows* as per the entries in Table 2-6.

**Table 2-6.** *Page Format NEXT—Windows and Page Windows*

| Window & Page Window | Page Window Dimensions | Contents |
|---|---|---|
| 1.RECEIVER | Left margin : 5.00MM<br>Upper margin : 5.00MM<br>Window width : 115.00MM<br>Window height : 30.00MM | &EKKO-ADRNR(K)& etc. |
| 2.PO_INF3 | Left margin : 120.00 MM<br>Upper margin : 5.00 MM<br>Window width : 65.00 MM<br>Window height : 30.00 MM | &YCH02_LIFNR(30)& &YCH02_VERKF&<br>&EKKO-LIFNR(K)& &EKKO-VERKF& |
| 3. PAGE | Left margin : 185MM<br>Upper margin : 5.00MM<br>Window width : 20MM<br>Window height : 30MM | &YCH02_PAGE&<br>&PAGE(R2)&/&SAPSCRIPT-FORMPAGES(C2)& |
| 4.ITEM_HD | Left margin : 5.00MM<br>Upper margin : 35.00MM<br>Window width : 200.00MM<br>Window height : 20.00MM | &YCH02_MATNR& &YCH02_MAKTX&<br>&YCH02_MENGE(R14)& &YCH02_MEINS(5)&<br>&YCH02_NETPR(R14)& &NETWR(R15)& |

(*continued*)

**Table 2-6.** (*continued*)

| Window & Page Window | Page Window Dimensions | Contents |
|---|---|---|
| 5.MAIN | Left margin : 5.00MM<br>Upper margin : 55.00MM<br>Window width : 200.00MM<br>Window height : 217.00MM | &YCH02_EKPO_MAKT-MATNR(18K)&<br>&YCH02_EKPO_MAKT-MAKTX(40)&<br>&YCH02_EKPO_MAKT-MENGE(14)&<br>&YCH02_EKPO_MAKT-MEINS(5)&<br>&YCH02_EKPO_MAKT-NETPR(14)&<br>&YCH02_EKPO_MAKT-NETWR(15)& |
| 6.TOTAL | Left margin : 5.00MM<br>Upper margin : 272.00MM<br>Window width : 200.00MM<br>Window height : 10.00MM | &YCH02_TOTAL_NET_E& &TOTAL& |
| 7.FOOTER | Left margin : 5.00MM<br>Upper margin : 282.00MM<br>Window width : 200.00 MM<br>Window height : 10.0MM | Footer text if any |

We created the following *character formats*.

**Table 2-7.** *Character Format List*

| Character Format Name | Description | Font Type /Family | Font Size | Bold |
|---|---|---|---|---|
| CD | Helve 14 - For Document Type | HELVE | 14,0 | On |
| CS | For Sender Name in 16 pts | HELVE | 16,0 | On |
| CT | For Sender Name in 28 pts | HELVE | 28,0 | On |
| HS | Helve 8 – For Field Nomenclature | HELVE | 8,0 | |

We are using the *character format* CD to output the text of the document type.

Depending on the number of characters in the field company code name, we are employing two *character formats*: CS and CT.

We are using the *character format* HS to output field nomenclature/labels.

The graph *window* LOGO will contain the following in its *text element*:

```
/:  BITMAP 'YCH01_COMPANY_LOGO' OBJECT GRAPHICS ID  BMAP TYPE BCOL
```

We created the following in the *text element* area of the *window* SENDER:

```
/E      SENDER
/:      IF &LENGTH& > '15'
*       <CS>&ADRS-LINE0&</>
/:      ELSE
*
*       <CT>&ADRS-LINE0&</>
```

```
/:      ENDIF
*       &ADRS-LINE1&
*       &ADRS-LINE2&
*       &ADRS-LINE3&
*       &ADRS-LINE4&
*       &ADRS-LINE5&
*       &ADRS-LINE6&
*       &ADRS-LINE7&
*       &ADRS-LINE8&
*       &ADRS-LINE9&
```

We created the following in the *text element* area of the *window* RECEIVER:

```
/:      IF &EKKO-ADRNR(K)& = ' '
/:      ADDRESS PARAGRAPH DP
/:        TITLE     &LFA1-ANRED&
/:        NAME      &LFA1-NAME1&, &LFA1-NAME2&, &LFA1-NAME3&, &LFA1-NAME4&
/:        STREET    &LFA1-STRAS&
/:        POBOX     &LFA1-PFACH&  CODE &LFA1-PSTL2&
/:        CITY      &LFA1-ORT01&, &LFA1-ORT02&
/:        POSTCODE &LFA1-PSTLZ&
/:        COUNTRY   &LFA1-LAND1&
/:        REGION    &LFA1-REGIO&
/:        FROMCOUNTRY &T001-LAND1&
/:      ENDADDRESS
/:      ELSE
/:      ADDRESS PARAGRAPH DP
/:        ADDRESSNUMBER &EKKO-ADRNR(K)&
/:      FROMCOUNTRY &T001-LAND1&
/:      ENDADDRESS
/:      ENDIF
```

We created the following in the *text element* area of the *window* PO_INF1:

```
/:      BOX FRAME 15 TW
/:      BOX HEIGHT '1.5' LN INTENSITY 14
*       <CD>&T166U-DRTYP&</>
*
*       <HS>&T166U-DRNUM&</>
*       &EKKO-EBELN&&' / 'EKKO-BEDAT&
*       <HS>&YCH02_EKNAM&&' / 'YCH02_EKTEL&</>
*       &T024-EKNAM&&' / 'T024-EKTEL&
```

Create the following in the *text element* area of the *window* PO_INF2:

```
*       <HS>&YCH02_LIFNR(30)&</>,,,,,,,,,,,,,,,,,,<HS>&YCH02_VERKF&</>
*       &EKKO-LIFNR(K)&      ,,,,,,,,,,,,,,,,,,,&EKKO-VERKF&
```

The ,, (commas) generate tab or horizontal spaces. The tab setting in the *form*'s attributes is 1 centimeter. Two commas generate 1 tab space or 1 centimeter.

We created the following in the *text element* area of the *window* CONSIGNE:

```
*        &YCHO2_CONSG&
/:       IF &YCHO2_EKPO_MAKT-ADRNR(K)& = ' ' AND &YCHO2_EKPO_MAKT-ADRN2(K)& = ' '
/:       ADDRESS DELIVERY PARAGRAPH DP
/:          TITLE     &SADR-ANRED&
/:          NAME      &SADR-NAME1&, &SADR-NAME2&, &SADR-NAME3&, &SADR-NAME4&
/:          STREET    &SADR-STRAS&
/:          CITY      &SADR-ORTO1&, &SADR-ORTO2&
/:          POSTCODE  &SADR-PSTLZ&
/:          COUNTRY   &SADR-LAND1&
/:          REGION    &SADR-REGIO&
/:          FROMCOUNTRY &LFA1-LAND1&
/:       ENDADDRESS
/:       ELSE
/:       IF &YCHO2_EKPO_MAKT-ADRNR(K)& <> ' '
/:       ADDRESS DELIVERY PARAGRAPH DP
/:          ADDRESSNUMBER &YCHO2_EKPO_MAKT-ADRNR(K)&
/:                   FROMCOUNTRY &LFA1-LAND1&
/:       ENDADDRESS
/:       ELSE
/:       ADDRESS DELIVERY PARAGRAPH DP
/:          ADDRESSNUMBER &YCHO2_EKPO_MAKT-ADRN2(K)&
/:          FROMCOUNTRY &LFA1-LAND1&
/:       ENDADDRESS
/:       ENDIF
/:       ENDIF
```

We created the following in the *text element* area of the *window* DELI_ETC:

```
*        <HS>&YCHO2_EINDT&:</> &EKET-EINDT&
*        <HS>&YCHO2_INCO1&:</> &EKKO-INCO1&
*        <HS>&YCHO2_ZBTXT&</>
*        &ZBTXT_STRU&
*
*        <HS>&WAERS&:</> &EKKO-WAERS&
```

We created the following in the *text element* area of the *window* ITEM_HD:

```
/E       ITEM_HEAD
/:       BOX HEIGHT 15 MM FRAME 15 TW
/:       IF &PAGE(C)& = '1'
/:       BOX HEIGHT 156 MM FRAME 20 TW
/:       ELSE
/:       BOX HEIGHT 236 MM FRAME 20 TW
/:       ENDIF
*        &YCHO2_MATNR&      &YCHO2_MAKTX&
*                                    &YCHO2_MENGE(R14)& &YCHO2_MEINS(5)&
=        &YCHO2_NETPR(R14)&  &NETWR(R15)&
```

We created the following in the *text element* area of the *window* MAIN:

```
/E       ITEM_DATA
/:       PROTECT
*        &YCHO2_EKPO_MAKT-MATNR(18K)& &YCHO2_EKPO_MAKT-MAKTX(40)&
*                                 &YCHO2_EKPO_MAKT-MENGE(14)&
=          &YCHO2_EKPO_MAKT-MEINS(5)& &YCHO2_EKPO_MAKT-NETPR(14)&
=          &YCHO2_EKPO_MAKT-NETWR(15)&
/:       ENDPROTECT
```

We created the following in the *text element* area of the *window* TOTAL:

```
/E       TOTAL
/:       IF &NEXTPAGE(C)& = 'O'
*        ,,,,,,,,,,,,,,       &YCHO2_TOTAL_NET_E&,,&TOTAL(15)&
/:       ENDIF
```

We created the following in the *text element* area of the *window* PAGE:

```
*        &YCHO2_PAGE&
*        &PAGE(R2)&/&SAPSCRIPT-FORMPAGES(C2)&
```

We created the following in the *text element* area of the *window* PO_INF3:

```
*
*
*        <HS>&T166U-DRNUM&</>
*        &EKKO-EBELN& &' / 'EKKO-BEDAT&
```

After creating the *form* elements as described in the preceding pages, we saved the *form*. We assigned the package YCH_BC401. You can assign the same or any other non-local package of your choice.

We have un-named, or default, *text elements* in the following *windows*: LOGO, RECEIVER, PO_INF1, PO_INF2, CONSIGNE, DELI_ETC, PO_INF3, and PAGE.

We have named *text elements* in the following *windows*: SENDER, ITEM_HEAD, MAIN, and TOTAL. We do not have multiple named *text elements* in a *window*; we have only one named *text element* in each of these *windows*.

In the present context, except for the main *window*, we need not have named *text elements* in the *windows*. For the main *window*, we need to continually send repetitive data from the print program through the function module WRITE_FORM. The function module WRITE_FORM requires the *text element* name as a mandatory parameter. Hence we need to have a named *text element* in the main *window*.

# Print Program YH02_02_PPRG_YCH02_02_PORDER1 for SAP Script Form

We created an ABAP program YCH02_02_PPRG_YCH02_02_PORDER1. This will be the print program for the *form* YCH02_02_PORDER1. The source lines of the print program are as follows:

```
REPORT   YCHO2_02_PPRG_YCHO2_02_PORDER1.


**********************************************
* Print Program of Form: YCHO2_02_PORDER1 **
* Purchase Order Output with Custom Form  **
**********************************************


*********** Data Declarations**************
**********************************************
TABLES: EKKO,     "Purchasing Doc Header
        LFA1,     "Vendor Primary
        T001,     "Company Code
        SADR,     "Address Management - Company Code &
                  "Organizational Units
        ADRS,     "Address Management - Structure
        T024,     "Purchasing Groups
        T166U,    "Labels in Purchasing Document Print out
        YCHO2_EKPO_MAKT, "View with Purchasing Doc Items &
                         "Material Texts
        T001W,    "Plant & Branches
        EKET,     "Material Delivery Dates
        T052.     "Payment Terms

DATA: ITEM_TAB   TYPE STANDARD TABLE OF YCHO2_EKPO_MAKT.

DATA: LENGTH(2)      TYPE N, "Length of Company Code Name
      PCNT           TYPE I, "Number of POs output
      TOTAL          TYPE BWERT, "Total for a Purchase Order

*Data Declarations - to Store Long Texts from Data Elements*
************************************************************
      YCHO2_EKNAM    TYPE STRING, "contact person
      YCHO2_EKTEL    TYPE STRING, "to telephone
      YCHO2_LIFNR    TYPE STRING, "your vendor no with us
      YCHO2_VERKF    TYPE STRING, "your person responsible
      YCHO2_CONSG    TYPE STRING, "please deliver to
      YCHO2_EINDT    TYPE STRING, "delivery date
```

117

```
       YCH02_INC01      TYPE STRING, "terms of delivery
       YCH02_ZBTXT      TYPE STRING, "terms of payment
       WAERS            TYPE WAERS,  "currency code
       YCH02_MATNR      TYPE STRING, "material code
       YCH02_MAKTX      TYPE STRING, "description
       YCH02_MENGE      TYPE STRING, "order quantity
       YCH02_MEINS      TYPE STRING, "units
       YCH02_NETPR      TYPE STRING, "price per unit
       NETWR            TYPE STRING, "net value
       YCH02_PAGE       TYPE STRING, "page
       YCH02_TOTAL_NET_E  TYPE STRING. "total net excl tax

***** Data Declarations - Payment Terms *****
**********************************************
DATA: BEGIN OF ZBTXT_STRU,
      STR(50),
      END OF ZBTXT_STRU,
      ZBTXT_TAB LIKE STANDARD TABLE OF ZBTXT_STRU.
***********************************************
SELECT-OPTIONS PO_NOS FOR EKKO-EBELN MATCHCODE OBJECT
     YCH02_01_EKKO_LFA1_SH.

********************Fill Selection Table ***********
*****************************************************
INITIALIZATION.
PO_NOS-SIGN   = 'I'.
PO_NOS-OPTION = 'EQ'.
PO_NOS-LOW    = '4500004823'.
APPEND PO_NOS TO PO_NOS.

PO_NOS-LOW    = '4500009520'.
APPEND PO_NOS TO PO_NOS.

********************Main Program ***********
*******************************************
START-OF-SELECTION.

CALL FUNCTION 'OPEN_FORM' "OPEN_FORM (once)
 EXPORTING
   FORM                          = 'YCH02_02_PORDER1'
   LANGUAGE                      = 'E'
        .
IF SY-SUBRC <> 0.
 MESSAGE ID SY-MSGID TYPE SY-MSGTY NUMBER SY-MSGNO
        WITH SY-MSGV1 SY-MSGV2 SY-MSGV3 SY-MSGV4.
ENDIF.
```

```
*****Main Loop *****
********************

SELECT * FROM EKKO WHERE EBELN IN PO_NOS.

 IF ( EKKO-SPRAS <> 'D' AND EKKO-SPRAS <> 'E' )
    OR EKKO-BSTYP <> 'F'      OR ( EKKO-BSART <>'NB'
    AND EKKO-BSART <> 'PO' ).
  CONTINUE.
 ENDIF.


 SELECT SINGLE * FROM LFA1 WHERE LIFNR = EKKO-LIFNR.
                                     "Get Vendor
 IF EKKO-ADRNR = ' '.

  EKKO-ADRNR = LFA1-ADRNR.
 ENDIF.


 SELECT SINGLE * FROM T001
               WHERE BUKRS = EKKO-BUKRS. "Get Company Code

 SELECT SINGLE * FROM T166U WHERE BSTYP = EKKO-BSTYP
                              AND BSART = EKKO-BSART
                              AND SPRAS = EKKO-SPRAS
                              AND DRUVO = '1'.
                              "Get Title for Document

 SELECT SINGLE * FROM T024
               WHERE EKGRP = EKKO-EKGRP.
                          "Get Purchasing Group
 SELECT SINGLE * FROM T052 WHERE ZTERM = EKKO-ZTERM.
                                     "Get Payment Terms

*****Retrieve Payment Terms Text *****
 CALL FUNCTION 'FI_PRINT_ZTERM'
   EXPORTING
    I_ZTERM         = EKKO-ZTERM
    I_LANGU         = EKKO-SPRAS
    I_XT052U        = 'X'
    I_T052          = T052
   TABLES
    T_ZTEXT         = ZBTXT_TAB
 .

 READ TABLE ZBTXT_TAB INTO ZBTXT_STRU INDEX 1.

*****Retrieve Long Texts from Data Elements*****
 PERFORM GET_TEXT_DE USING 'YCH02_EKNAM' EKKO-SPRAS YCH02_EKNAM.
 PERFORM GET_TEXT_DE USING 'YCH02_EKTEL' EKKO-SPRAS YCH02_EKTEL.
 PERFORM GET_TEXT_DE USING 'YCH02_LIFNR' EKKO-SPRAS YCH02_LIFNR.
 PERFORM GET_TEXT_DE USING 'YCH02_VERKF' EKKO-SPRAS YCH02_VERKF.
 PERFORM GET_TEXT_DE USING 'YCH02_CONSG' EKKO-SPRAS YCH02_CONSG.
```

119

```
PERFORM GET_TEXT_DE USING 'YCH02_EINDT' EKKO-SPRAS YCH02_EINDT.
PERFORM GET_TEXT_DE USING 'YCH02_INC01' EKKO-SPRAS YCH02_INC01.
PERFORM GET_TEXT_DE USING 'YCH02_ZBTXT' EKKO-SPRAS YCH02_ZBTXT.
PERFORM GET_TEXT_DE USING 'WAERS'       EKKO-SPRAS WAERS.

PERFORM GET_TEXT_DE USING 'YCH02_MATNR' EKKO-SPRAS YCH02_MATNR.
PERFORM GET_TEXT_DE USING 'YCH02_MAKTX' EKKO-SPRAS YCH02_MAKTX.
PERFORM GET_TEXT_DE USING 'YCH02_MENGE' EKKO-SPRAS YCH02_MENGE.
PERFORM GET_TEXT_DE USING 'YCH02_MEINS' EKKO-SPRAS YCH02_MEINS.
PERFORM GET_TEXT_DE USING 'YCH02_NETPR' EKKO-SPRAS YCH02_NETPR.
PERFORM GET_TEXT_DE USING 'NETWR'       EKKO-SPRAS NETWR.
PERFORM GET_TEXT_DE USING 'YCH02_PAGE'  EKKO-SPRAS YCH02_PAGE.
PERFORM GET_TEXT_DE USING 'YCH02_TOTAL_NET_ETAX' EKKO-SPRAS
  YCH02_TOTAL_NET_E.

**********
  CALL FUNCTION 'START_FORM' "START_FORM (every purchase order)
    EXPORTING
      FORM                    = 'YCH02_02_PORDER1'
      LANGUAGE                = 'E'
          .
IF SY-SUBRC <> 0.
  MESSAGE ID SY-MSGID TYPE SY-MSGTY NUMBER SY-MSGNO
        WITH SY-MSGV1 SY-MSGV2 SY-MSGV3 SY-MSGV4.
ENDIF.

*****Company Code Name & Address *****
SELECT SINGLE * FROM SADR WHERE ADRNR = T001-ADRNR.
                          "Get Address of Company Cd
SADR-ANRED = ' '. "No Title for Company Code Name
CLEAR ADRS.
MOVE-CORRESPONDING SADR TO ADRS.

CALL FUNCTION 'ADDRESS_INTO_PRINTFORM'
  EXPORTING
    ADRSWA_IN                       = ADRS
  IMPORTING
    ADRSWA_OUT                      = ADRS
        .

LENGTH = STRLEN( ADRS-LINE0 ).

PERFORM WRITE_FRM USING 'SENDER' 'SENDER'.

*****Loop for Items *****
SELECT * FROM YCH02_EKPO_MAKT
        INTO TABLE ITEM_TAB "Load itab from View
        WHERE EBELN = EKKO-EBELN
              AND BUKRS = EKKO-BUKRS
              AND SPRAS = EKKO-SPRAS.
```

```
PERFORM WRITE_FRM USING 'ITEM_HD' 'ITEM_HEAD'.

TOTAL = 0. "Initialize for Purchase order

LOOP AT ITEM_TAB INTO YCHO2_EKPO_MAKT.

  IF SY-TABIX = 1.

    SELECT SINGLE * FROM T001W
                 WHERE WERKS = YCHO2_EKPO_MAKT-WERKS.
    MOVE-CORRESPONDING T001W TO SADR. "Get Delivery Address

    SELECT SINGLE * FROM EKET "Get Delivery Date
                 WHERE EBELN = YCHO2_EKPO_MAKT-EBELN
                   AND EBELP = YCHO2_EKPO_MAKT-EBELP.

  ENDIF.

  PERFORM WRITE_FRM USING 'MAIN' 'ITEM_DATA'.
  TOTAL = TOTAL + YCHO2_EKPO_MAKT-NETWR.
ENDLOOP.

*****Item Loop Over ******
 PERFORM WRITE_FRM USING 'TOTAL' 'TOTAL'.

 CALL FUNCTION 'END_FORM' "ENd_FORM (every purchase order)
      .
 IF SY-SUBRC <> 0.
  MESSAGE ID SY-MSGID TYPE SY-MSGTY NUMBER SY-MSGNO
        WITH SY-MSGV1 SY-MSGV2 SY-MSGV3 SY-MSGV4.
 ENDIF.
 PCNT = PCNT + 1.
ENDSELECT.
*****Main Loop Over *****

CALL FUNCTION 'CLOSE_FORM' "CLOSE_FORM (once)
     .
IF SY-SUBRC <> 0.
 MESSAGE ID SY-MSGID TYPE SY-MSGTY NUMBER SY-MSGNO
       WITH SY-MSGV1 SY-MSGV2 SY-MSGV3 SY-MSGV4.
ENDIF.

IF PCNT = 0.
 MESSAGE S000(YCHO2_MCLASS) DISPLAY LIKE 'W'."No Data - Output
ENDIF.
```

```
**********************************
*****Subroutine for WRITE_FORM *****
**********************************
FORM WRITE_FRM USING VALUE(WINDOW) VALUE(ELEMENT).

 CALL FUNCTION 'WRITE_FORM'
  EXPORTING
   ELEMENT                       = ELEMENT
   WINDOW                        = WINDOW
           .
 IF SY-SUBRC <> 0.
  MESSAGE ID SY-MSGID TYPE SY-MSGTY NUMBER SY-MSGNO
          WITH SY-MSGV1 SY-MSGV2 SY-MSGV3 SY-MSGV4.
 ENDIF.

ENDFORM.


*****************************************************
*Subroutine to Retrieve Long Texts from Data Elements *
*****************************************************
FORM GET_TEXT_DE USING VALUE(DE_NAME) VALUE(LANG) RET_TEXT.
DATA: LTEXT TYPE SCRTEXT_L.

 CALL FUNCTION 'WCGW_DATA_ELEMENT_TEXT_GET'
   EXPORTING
    I_DATA_ELEMENT              = DE_NAME
    I_LANGUAGE                  = LANG
   IMPORTING
    E_SCRTEXT_L                 = LTEXT

          .

RET_TEXT = LTEXT.
ENDFORM.
*****End Program *****
```

The data objects into which we are retrieving long texts from data elements have been given the same names as the names of the data elements, that is, YCH02_EKNAM, YCH02_EKTEL...., etc. The TYPE of these data objects is STRING. New data elements have been created only for the fields where the texts of the fields' data elements have not corresponded with the proposed output texts. When the texts of fields' data elements have corresponded with the proposed output texts, we have retrieved texts from these data elements and not created new data elements—WAERS, NETWR.

Within the program, we are processing purchasing documents fulfilling the following conditions:

- Language key of purchasing documents equal to D or E.

- Purchasing document category (field BSTYP) is purchase order. – BSTYP value equal to F.

- Purchasing document types (field BSART) is standard purchase order. – BSART value equal to NB or PO.

Purchasing documents not fulfilling these conditions are bypassed.

```
IF ( EKKO-SPRAS <> 'D' AND EKKO-SPRAS <> 'E' ) OR EKKO-BSTYP <> 'F'
   OR ( EKKO-BSART <> 'NB' AND EKKO-BSART <> 'PO' ).
  CONTINUE.
 ENDIF.
```

You can incorporate these conditions in WHERE clause itself if you want.

If we make selections of purchasing documents through the search help attached to the SELECT-OPTIONS field PO_NOS, we are assured of its processing or outputting. But if we enter any random numbers of purchasing document numbers, they might or might not be processed as some/all of them might not fulfill one or more of the conditions (i), (ii), and (iii).

The function modules OPEN_FORM, CLOSE_FORM, START_FORM, END_FORM, and WRITE_FORM, discussed earlier, do not need any explanation here. The program is also using the following function modules:

| | |
|---|---|
| FI_PRINT_ZTERM | to retrieve text of terms of payment |
| ADDRESS_INTO_PRINTFORM | to convert address to postal convention format of a country |
| WCGW_DATA_ELEMENT_TEXT_GET | to retrieve texts of data elements |

In transaction code SE91, we created a message class YCH02_MCLASS, and a message number 000 as 'No Data Processed for Output' to report the instance of no data processed and output.

With the comments provided in the program, it is expected that you comprehend the logic and flow of the print program.

## Database View YCH02_EKKO_LFA1

We created a database view YCH02_EKKO_LFA1 with the table EKKO as the primary table and table LFA1 as a secondary table. The tables are to be joined through the fields MANDT and LIFNR. The database view consists of fields listed in Table 2-8.

*Table 2-8.* *Fields in the Database View YCH02_EKKO_LFA1*

| Srl. No. | Field/Table | Srl. No. | Field/Table |
|---|---|---|---|
| 01 | MANDT / EKKO | 06 | BSTYP / EKKO |
| 02 | EBELN / EKKO | 07 | BSART / EKKO |
| 03 | LIFNR / LFA1 | 08 | BEDAT / EKKO |
| 04 | SPRAS / EKKO | 09 | WAERS / EKKO |
| 05 | BURKS / EKKO | 10 | NAME1 / LFA1 |

The selection condition of the database view YCH02_EKKO_LFA1 will be as follows:

```
EKKO    SPRAS    EQ    'D'     OR
EKKO    SPRAS    EQ    'E'     AND
EKKO    BSTYP    EQ    'F'     AND
EKKO    BSART    EQ    'NB'    OR
EKKO    BSART    EQ    'PO'
```

These conditions—(i) purchasing documents of language key equal to D or E, (ii) purchasing document category equal to F, (iii) purchasing document type equal to PO or NB—will ensure that rows fulfilling the conditions will appear in the search help selection list.

We performed a consistency check and activated the database view.

## Elementary Search Help YCH02_01_EKKO_LFA1_SH

We created an elementary search help YCH02_01_EKKO_LFA1_SH using the database view YCH02_EKKO_LFA. The search help parameters will look like those in Table 2-9:

*Table 2-9.* *Elementary Search Help YCH02_01_EKKO_LFA1_SH*

| Search help parameter | IMP | EXP | Lpos | Spos |
|---|---|---|---|---|
| EBELN | | X | 1 | 1 |
| BUKRS | | | | 2 |
| SPRAS | | | | 3 |
| BEDAT | | | 2 | |
| WAERS | | | 3 | |
| LIFNR | | | 4 | 4 |
| NAME1 | | | 5 | 5 |

We performed a consistency check and activated the elementary search help.

## Check and Activate Form

In transaction code SE71, we performed a *form* definition check as well as the *form* texts check on the *form* YCH02_02_PORDER1 and activated it.

The *form* YCH02_02_PORDER1 and the source program YCH02_02_PPRG_ YCH02_02_PORDER1 are available for upload from the E-resource file for this book (www.apress.com/9781484212345).

## Output

As mentioned previously, we are using the data of the IDES server for the hands-on exercises (as preferably you should). We have identified two purchase orders which serve our purpose for testing the output: purchase order numbers 4500004823 and 4500009520. The purchase order number 4500004823 language key is D and the purchase order number 4500009520 language key is E. This enables us to test the output in the two languages. The purchase order number 4500009520 has 53 items and is running into four pages, enabling us to test a multiple-page purchase order. We are filling the selection table PO_NOS with these two specific purchase order numbers. (Refer to the INITIALIZATION event code in the print program).

We executed the program YCH02_02_PPRG_ YCH02_02_PORDER1. The output of the two purchase orders is running into five pages: purchase order number 4500004823 (German) outputs in one page and purchase order number 4500009520 (English) outputs in four pages. The output will look like as shown in Figures 2-7, 2-8, 2-9, 2-10, 2-11, and 2-12:

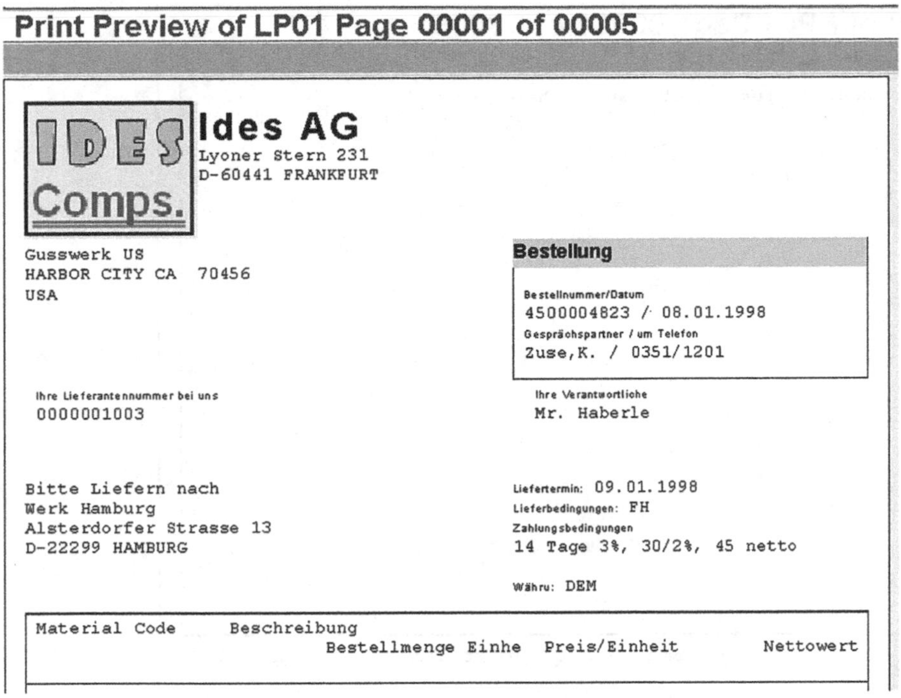

**Print Preview of LP01 Page 00001 of 00005**

**Ides AG**
Lyoner Stern 231
D-60441 FRANKFURT

Comps.

Gusswerk US
HARBOR CITY CA  70456
USA

**Bestellung**

Bestellnummer/Datum
4500004823 / 08.01.1998
Gesprächspartner / um Telefon
Zuse,K. / 0351/1201

Ihre Lieferantennummer bei uns
0000001003

Ihre Verantwortliche
Mr. Haberle

Bitte Liefern nach
Werk Hamburg
Alsterdorfer Strasse 13
D-22299 HAMBURG

Liefertermin: 09.01.1998
Lieferbedingungen: FH
Zahlungsbedingungen
14 Tage 3%, 30/2%, 45 netto

Währu: DEM

| Material Code | Beschreibung | | | | |
|---|---|---|---|---|---|
| | | Bestellmenge | Einhe | Preis/Einheit | Nettowert |

*Figure 2-7. Output of custom purchase order form: PO No. 4500004823—I*

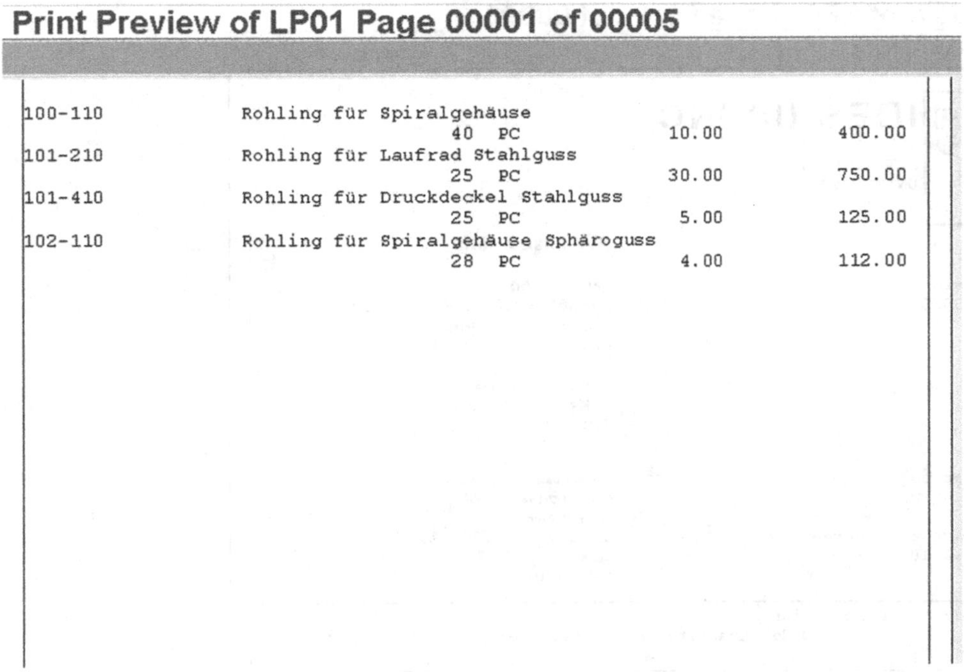

**Print Preview of LP01 Page 00001 of 00005**

| 100-110 | Rohling für Spiralgehäuse | | | | |
|---|---|---|---|---|---|
| | | 40 | PC | 10.00 | 400.00 |
| 101-210 | Rohling für Laufrad Stahlguss | | | | |
| | | 25 | PC | 30.00 | 750.00 |
| 101-410 | Rohling für Druckdeckel Stahlguss | | | | |
| | | 25 | PC | 5.00 | 125.00 |
| 102-110 | Rohling für Spiralgehäuse Sphäroguss | | | | |
| | | 28 | PC | 4.00 | 112.00 |

*Figure 2-8. Output of custom purchase order form: PO No. 4500004823—II*

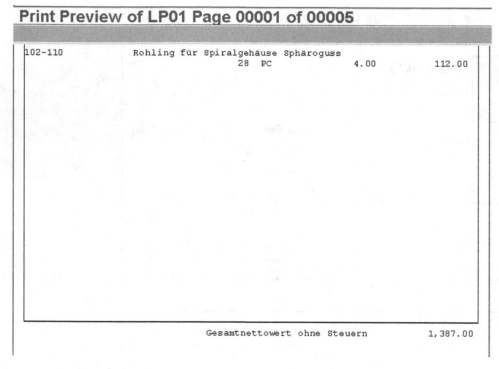

**Figure 2-9.** *Output of custom purchase order form: PO No. 4500004823—III*

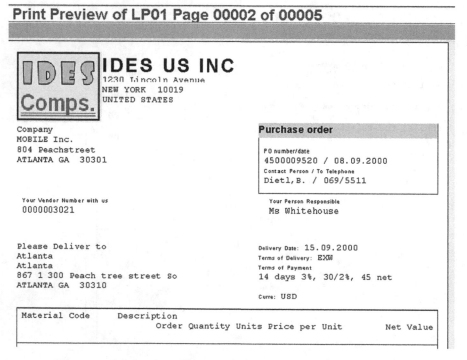

**Figure 2-10.** *Output of custom purchase order form: PO No. 4500009520—I*

## Print Preview of LP01 Page 00002 of 00005

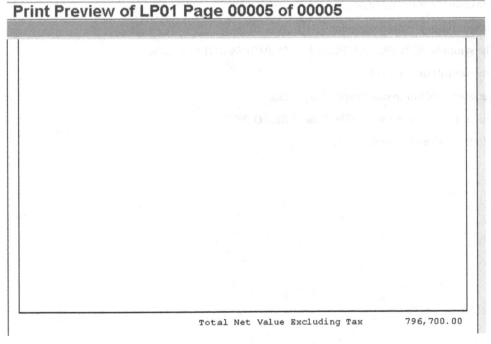

| ISA-0002 | AKAN DE LUXE | | | | |
|---|---|---|---|---|---|
| | | 100 | PC | 265.00 | 26,500.00 |
| ISA-0003 | VANITY | | | | |
| | | 100 | PC | 160.00 | 16,000.00 |
| ISA-0009 | PRIDE | | | | |
| | | 100 | PC | 240.00 | 24,000.00 |
| ISA-0010 | SONIC | | | | |
| | | 100 | PC | 240.00 | 24,000.00 |
| ISA-0011 | TWIN LETTI | | | | |
| | | 100 | PC | 250.00 | 25,000.00 |
| ISA-0012 | V.W. | | | | |
| | | 100 | PC | 260.00 | 26,000.00 |
| ISA-0018 | SLING | | | | |
| | | 100 | PC | 150.00 | 15,000.00 |
| ISA-0019 | TEMPO | | | | |
| | | 100 | EA | 480.00 | 48,000.00 |
| ISA-0020 | BUDONG | | | | |
| | | 100 | PC | 480.00 | 48,000.00 |
| ISA-0021 | EDGE | | | | |
| | | 100 | PC | 480.00 | 48,000.00 |
| ISA-0022 | FUJI | | | | |
| | | 100 | PC | 380.00 | 38,000.00 |
| ISA-0023 | LETTI | | | | |
| | | 100 | PC | 370.00 | 37,000.00 |
| ISA-0024 | MACHINE | | | | |
| | | 100 | PC | 405.00 | 40,500.00 |
| ISA-0025 | NOBILE 2 | | | | |
| | | 100 | PC | 410.00 | 41,000.00 |
| ISA-0027 | COSMO | | | | |
| | | 100 | PC | 543.00 | 54,300.00 |
| ISA-1000 | KAPPA | | | | |
| | | 100 | PC | 100.00 | 10,000.00 |

*Figure 2-11.* *Output of custom purchase order form: PO No. 4500009520—II*

## Print Preview of LP01 Page 00005 of 00005

| | Total Net Value Excluding Tax | 796,700.00 |
|---|---|---|

*Figure 2-12.* *Output of custom purchase order form: PO No. 4500009520—III*

# Hands-on Exercise Recapitulation

In this hands-on exercise, we created a *form* to output purchase orders. We also created the related print program and associated workbench objects. The aim was to go through the process of creating and deploying a *form* of a business document from scratch.

The material descriptions in the output of purchase orders were retrieved from the database table MAKT. This is not necessary. The material description of each of the items is available in the field TXZ01 of the database table EKPO. In fact, the preferred way is to use the field TXZ01.

The output might not be 100% usable in a real-life situation, but it is not far from it.

We retrieved the data to output purchase orders from the print program and the 11 tables. Apart from the function modules used to interact with the *form*, the print program also invoked the following function modules:

```
ADDRESS_INTO_PRINTFORM        To format address as per a country's postal
convention
WCGW_DATA_ELEMENT_TEXT_GET    To retrieve data element texts
FI_PRINT_ZTERM                To obtain text of terms of payment
```

The deployment of the *form* to produce purchase orders involved the creation of two database views, an elementary search help, a message class, and a message.

A specialty of this exercise is the maintenance and retrieval of texts used in *text elements* from data elements. The maintenance of texts of *text elements* in data elements has made the *form* language independent. Though we have chosen data elements, the texts can be maintained in any place that supports the maintenance of multiple language short texts like text symbols of ABAP programs. Another alternative is to locate the texts in SAP script standard symbols—transaction code SE75. But we are using the texts in data elements in a parallel hands-on exercise in Chapter 4 with smartforms. The smartforms cannot access the SAP script standard symbols.

In the *text element* environment of the *form*, the following new features were used:

- The control command BOX

- Various output formatting options

- The symbols: &PAGE&, &SAPSCRIPT-FORMPAGES& &NEXTPAGE&

- The control command IF

- Generation of tab spaces by specifying commas

- The control commands PROTECT and ENDPROTECT

This concludes the hands-on exercise II.

# Hands-on Exercise III—Output Custom Purchase Order—Use Control Command PERFORM

In real-life SAP implementation projects, for the most part, copies made of SAPdelivered *forms* into the Y/Z namespace are modified and customized. When a copy of a SAP delivered *form* is made into the Y/Z namespace and the copied *form* is then modified and customized as per requirements, there is no access to the print program. In this scenario of copying and customizing a delivered *form*, you can make modifications only to the *form*. If you wanted to include some functionality involving ABAP code, you could do this through the limited repertoire of ABAP-like control commands in the *text element* environment of the *form*. If you wanted to retrieve some data with SELECT statements or wanted to call a function module, the set of control commands does not support these statements. The control commands do support execution of external subroutines through the control command PERFORM..... So if you want to incorporate ABAP functionality into a copy of a SAP delivered *form*, you could implement the ABAP functionality in an external subroutine and invoke this external subroutine from within the *text element* environment of a *form* with the control command PERFORM.....

When you execute the control command PERFORM.., the parameter passing between the *text element* environment of the *form* and the external subroutine is rudimentary and crude. Moreover, variables or text symbols declared in the *text element* environment with the control command DEFINE support only character-oriented types with a maximum length of 80 characters. Hence the returned values from the external subroutine to the *text element* environment can only be character-oriented data with a maximum length of 80 characters. Within the ambit of these constraints, you can incorporate extra ABAP functionality to the copied versions of SAP delivered *forms*.

## Output, Layout Specification, and Output Considerations

In this hands-on exercise, we will produce a custom purchase order just as we did in the hands-on Exercise II, with additions involving the invocation of an external subroutine. The custom purchase order being output in this exercise is identical to the one produced with hands-on exercise II except that, additionally, we will output the purchase order total amount expressed in text or words. To produce the purchase order total amount in words, we will have to use the function module SPELL_AMOUNT.

The function module SPELL_AMOUNT takes three main input parameters: (1) the amount to be converted to text, (2) currency key (ISO currency key), and (3) language key for the language in which the text is to be returned. The function module returns the text in a data object declared with reference to the ABAP dictionary structure SPELL: DATA RET_TEXT TYPE SPELL. The text corresponding to the value before the decimal is returned in the field WORD of the data object declared with reference to ABAP dictionary structure SPELL. The text corresponding to the value after the decimal is returned in the field DECWORD of the data object declared with reference to ABAP dictionary structure SPELL. Refer to the documentation of the function module SPELL_MODULE for further details.

We can call the function module SPELL_AMOUNT from within the print program. But we are not going to do so. We are going to invoke an external subroutine from the *text element* environment of the *form* and call the function module SPELL_AMOUNT in the external subroutine. I am resorting to this approach to introduce you to the nitty-gritty of invoking external subroutines from the *text element* environment of the *form*. Also, this is a way to demonstrate the incorporation of ABAP functionality in a copy of a delivered *form*. In the next hands-on exercise, we are going to repeat this procedure of invoking an external subroutine from the *text element* environment in a copy of the SAP delivered *form* MEDRUCK.

We will output the purchase order total amount in words under the purchase order total amount. We will output the purchase order total amount in words in an additional *page window* assigned to a new *window* (*window* name is IN_WORDS). Just like the purchase order total amount appearing on the last page of a purchase order, the purchase order total amount in words must appear on the last page of a purchase order. So the additional *page window* must be located in both the *page formats*: FIRST and NEXT. To be able to accommodate the additional *page window* (height 20MM) to output the purchase order total amount in words, we are reducing the height of *page window* in the main *window* (item data) by 20MM in both the *page formats* FIRST and NEXT. Except for this additional *page window* all other *page windows* of *page formats* FIRST and NEXT are the same as in hands-on exercise II. The *page format* FIRST consists of 12 *windows* and *page windows*. The *page format* NEXT consists of 8 *windows* and *page windows*. The modified and revised layouts of *page formats* FIRST and NEXT are as shown in Figures 2-13 and 2-14.

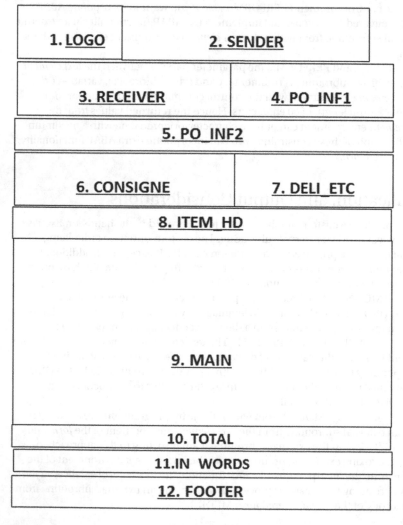

*Figure 2-13.* *Custom purchase order page format FIRST—windows and page windows layout*

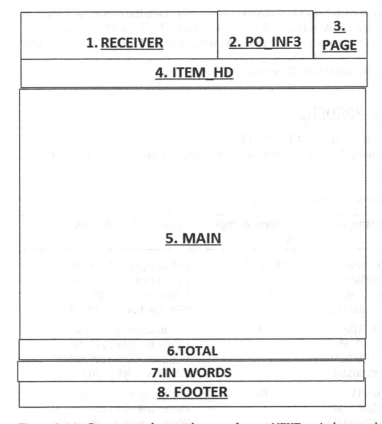

*Figure 2-14. Custom purchase order page format NEXT—windows and page windows layout*

With the *page format* layouts decided, we will proceed to the creation of all the required workbench objects.

## Creation of SAP Script Form, Print Program, and Related Workbench Objects

For this exercise, we can use the workbench objects database views, elementary search help, and message created for hands-on exercise II.

## Print Program YCHO2_03_PPRG_YCHO2_03_PORDER2 for SAP Script Form

We created an ABAP program YCHO2_03_PPRG_YCHO2_03_PORDER2. All the lines of the print program of hands-on exercise II were copied into the current program and the following modifications were made:

```
DATA..
....
YCHO2_INWORDS      TYPE STRING. "total amount in words
......
WAERS_LT               TYPE WAERS,
.......
START-OF-SELECTION.
......
PERFORM GET_TEXT_DE USING 'YCHO2_INWORDS' EKKO-SPRAS YCHO2_INWORDS.
```

The extra lines incorporated into the copied version of hands-on exercise II are the non-italic lines.

In the *text element* area of the *window* IN_WORDS, we defined a text symbol named &WAERS&. In order to avoid a conflict of names, we have renamed the ABAP program variable WAERS to WAERS_LT from the previous hands-on exercise.

We saved, performed a syntax check, and activated the program.

## SAP Script Form YCH02_03_PORDER3

We copied the *form* YCH02_02_PORDER1 to YCH02_03_PORDER2.

For *page format* FIRST, the *windows* and their corresponding *page windows* will be as per the entries in Table 2-10:

***Table 2-10.*** *Page Format FIRST—Windows and Page Windows*

| Window & Page Window | Page Window Dimensions | Window & Page Window | Page Window Dimensions |
|---|---|---|---|
| 1.LOGO | Left margin : 5.00MM<br>Upper margin : 5.00MM<br>Window width : 46.64MM<br>Window height : 29.81MM | 7.DELI_ETC | Left margin : 120.00MM<br>Upper margin : 85.00MM<br>Window width : 85.00MM<br>Window height : 30.00MM |
| 2.SENDER | Left margin : 46.00MM<br>Upper margin : 5.00MM<br>Window width : 145.00MM<br>Window height : 30.00MM | 8.ITEM_HD | Left margin : 5.00MM<br>Upper margin : 115.00MM<br>Window width : 200.00MM<br>Window height : 20.00MM |
| 3.RECEIVER | Left margin : 5.00MM<br>Upper margin : 35.00 MM<br>Window width : 115.00 MM<br>Window height : 30.00 MM | 9.MAIN | Left margin : 5.00MM<br>Upper margin : 135.00 MM<br>Window width : 200.00MM<br>Window height : 117.00MM |
| 4.PO_INF1 | Left margin : 120.00MM<br>Upper margin : 35.00MM<br>Window width : 85.00MM<br>Window height : 30.00MM | 10.TOTAL | Left margin : 5.00MM<br>Upper margin : 252.00MM<br>Window width : 200.00MM<br>Window height : 10.00MM |
| 5.PO_INF2 | Left margin : 5.00MM<br>Upper margin : 65.00MM<br>Window width : 200.00MM<br>Window height : 20.00MM | 11.IN_WORDS | Left margin : 5.00MM<br>Upper margin : 262.00MM<br>Window width : 200.00MM<br>Window height : 20.00MM |
| 6.CONSIGNE | Left margin : 5.00MM<br>Upper margin : 85.00MM<br>Window width : 115.00MM<br>Window height : 30.00MM | 12.FOOTER | Left margin : 5.00MM<br>Upper margin : 282.00MM<br>Window width : 200.00MM<br>Window height : 10.00MM |

For *page format* NEXT, the *windows* and their corresponding *page windows* will be as per the entries in table 2-11:

***Table 2-11.*** *Page Format NEXT—Windows and Page Windows*

| Window & Page Window | Page Window Dimensions | Window & Page Window | Page Window Dimensions |
|---|---|---|---|
| 1.RECEIVER | Left margin : 5.00MM<br>Upper margin : 5.00MM<br>Window width : 115.00MM<br>Window height : 30.00MM | 5.MAIN | Left margin : 5.00MM<br>Upper margin : 55.00MM<br>Window width : 200.00MM<br>Window height : 197.00MM |
| 2.PO_INF3 | Left margin : 120.00MM<br>Upper margin : 5.00 MM<br>Window width : 65.00MM<br>Window height : 30.00MM | 6.TOTAL | Left margin : 5.00MM<br>Upper margin : 252.00MM<br>Window width : 200.00MM<br>Window height : 10.00MM |
| 3. PAGE | Left margin : 185.00MM<br>Upper margin : 5.00MM<br>Window width : 20.00MM<br>Window height : 30.00MM | 7. IN_WORDS | Left margin : 5.00MM<br>Upper margin : 262.00MM<br>Window width : 20.00MM<br>Window height : 30.00MM |
| 4.ITEM_HD | Left margin : 5.00MM<br>Upper margin : 35.00 MM<br>Window width : 200.00MM<br>Window height : 20.00MM | 8.FOOTER | Left margin : 5.00MM<br>Upper margin : 282.00MM<br>Window width : 200.00MM<br>Window height : 10.00MM |

In the *text element area* of the *window* IN_WORDS, we entered the following:

```
/: IF &NEXTPAGE(C)& = '0'
/: DEFINE &AMOUNT& = &TOTAL&
/: DEFINE &SPRAS&  = &EKKO-SPRAS&
/: DEFINE &WAERS&  = &EKKO-WAERS&
/: DEFINE &IN_WORD1& = ' '
/: DEFINE &IN_WORD2& = ' '
/: PERFORM CALL_SPELL_AMOUNT IN PROGRAM YCH02_04_SROUTINE_POOL
/:   USING &AMOUNT&
/:   USING &SPRAS&
/:   USING &WAERS&
/:   CHANGING &IN_WORD1&
/:   CHANGING &IN_WORD2&
/: ENDPERFORM
*  &YCH02_INWORDS& &IN_WORD1&
*               &IN_WORD2&
/: ENDIF
```

In this *window* IN_WORDS, we have deliberately not named the *text element*. If a name is assigned to this *text element*, an explicit execution of the function module WRITE_FORM will be required in the print program to output the contents in the *text element*. Recall that the function module WRITE_FORM requires the *window* name and the *text element* name as parameters.

We want the amount in text or words to appear only on the last page of a purchase order, hence the control command IF for condition testing.

The control command DEFINE is to define text symbols or variables in the *text element* environment. The text symbols are character oriented and contain data as it is output. For instance, when we assign the program symbol &TOTAL& (total amount excluding tax) to the text symbol &AMOUNT&, the text symbol &AMOUNT& will contain, apart from the numerals, a decimal or period and thousand separators (commas). We have assigned the program symbols to text symbols as follows:

```
&AMOUNT& = &TOTAL&,
&WAERS&, = &EKKO-WAERS&
&SPRAS& = &EKKO-SPRAS&
```

We are passing these assigned text symbols as parameters to the external subroutine when we could have passed the program symbols directly as parameters to the external subroutine. We are doing so, since we designed the external subroutine to be generic. We will be using this external subroutine again in our next hands-on exercise as well. When external subroutines are called from the SAP script *text element* environment, parameters are passed as parameter name and parameter value. There is no concept of formal parameters and actual parameters. In the subsequent text, I describe the parameter passing for external subroutines called from the SAP script *text element* environment.

The control command PERFORM must specify the subroutine name along with the program (name) in which the subroutine is located. You can locate external subroutines either in an executable program or a subroutine pool. We have located subroutine CALL_SPELL_AMOUNT in the subroutine pool YCH01_04_ SROUTINE_POOL. The parameters passed with the keyword USING are considered input parameters and the parameters passed with the keyword CHANGING are considered output parameters. The control command PERFORM must be concluded by the control command ENDPERFORM.

When an external subroutine is invoked from the SAP script *text element* environment, the parameters are received in the external subroutines in two internal tables. The first internal table contains input parameters or the parameters passed by using the keyword USING. The second internal table contains output parameters or the parameters passed by using the keyword CHANGING. Each row in the internal tables corresponds to one parameter. The structure of these two internal tables corresponds to the ABAP dictionary structure ITCSY. The structure ITCSY contains two fields: the first field NAME (type CHAR, length 130) contains the name of the parameter; the second field VALUE (type CHAR, length 255) contains the value of the parameter. The name of the parameters are stored without the ampersands or &s. In the formal parameter specification area of the external subroutine, you must specify the tables with the key phrase TABLES <internal table name> STRUCTURE ITCSY..... The parameter values have to be extracted from the internal tables with the READ.....WITH KEY statements. Before exiting the external subroutine, you have to insert the return parameter values in the corresponding rows of the internal table of output parameters.

We saved the *form*. We assigned the package YCH_BC401. You can assign any other non-local package of your choice. We performed a *form* definition check as well as the *form* texts check on the *form* YCH02_03_ PORDER2 and activated it.

The *form* YCH02_03_PORDER2 and the print program YCH02_03_PPRG_ YCH02_03_PORDER2 are available for upload in the E-resource file for this book (www.apress.com/9781484212345).

## Subroutine Pool YCH02_04_SROUTINE_POOL and Subroutine CALL_SPELL_AMOUNT

In transaction code SE38, we created a subroutine pool YCH02_04_SROUTINE_POOL. Within this subroutine pool, we located the subroutine CALL_SPELL_AMOUNT. The lines of the subroutine are as follows:

```
REPORT  YCH02_04_SROUTINE_POOL.


*****************************************************
* Sub Routine Pool used with SAP Script Forms:     **
* YCH02_03_PORDER2 & YCH02_04_MEDRUCK              **
*                                                  **
*****************************************************


FORM CALL_SPELL_AMOUNT TABLES INPUT_TAB  STRUCTURE ITCSY
                              OUTPUT_TAB STRUCTURE ITCSY.


*****************************************************
* Input Parameters:  AMOUNT, SPRAS, WAERS          **
* Output Parameters: IN_WORD1, IN_WORD2            **
*****************************************************


* Data Declaration
*******************
DATA: STR(140)           TYPE C,
      STR1(70)           TYPE C,
      STR2(70)           TYPE C,
      STR_TAB            LIKE STANDARD TABLE OF STR1,
      SPELL             TYPE SPELL,
      AMT(8)             TYPE P DECIMALS 2,
      SPRAS             TYPE SY-LANGU,
      LEN               TYPE I,
      WAERS             TYPE WAERS,
      SAP_WAERS         TYPE TCURC-WAERS,
      ISO_WAERS         TYPE TCURC-ISOCD.

* Extract Parameters from INPUT_TAB
********************************
READ TABLE INPUT_TAB WITH KEY 'AMOUNT'.

DO.
 REPLACE:',' WITH ' ' INTO INPUT_TAB-VALUE.
 IF SY-SUBRC <> 0.
  REPLACE: '.' WITH ' ' INTO INPUT_TAB-VALUE.
  IF SY-SUBRC <> 0.
   EXIT.
  ENDIF.
 ENDIF.
ENDDO.
```

```
CONDENSE INPUT_TAB-VALUE NO-GAPS.
MOVE INPUT_TAB-VALUE TO AMT.
AMT = AMT / 100.

READ TABLE INPUT_TAB WITH KEY 'SPRAS'.
SPRAS = INPUT_TAB-VALUE.

READ TABLE INPUT_TAB WITH KEY 'WAERS'.
WAERS = INPUT_TAB-VALUE.
MOVE WAERS TO SAP_WAERS.

* Convert SAP currency code to ISO currency code
*************************************************
CALL FUNCTION 'CURRENCY_CODE_SAP_TO_ISO'
  EXPORTING
    SAP_CODE           = SAP_WAERS
  IMPORTING
    ISO_CODE           = ISO_WAERS
  EXCEPTIONS
    NOT_FOUND          = 1
    OTHERS             = 2
                  .
IF SY-SUBRC <> 0.
 MESSAGE ID SY-MSGID TYPE SY-MSGTY NUMBER SY-MSGNO
         WITH SY-MSGV1 SY-MSGV2 SY-MSGV3 SY-MSGV4.
 EXIT.
ELSE.
  MOVE ISO_WAERS TO WAERS.
ENDIF.

* Call Function Module SPELL_AMOUNT
***********************************
CALL FUNCTION 'SPELL_AMOUNT'
  EXPORTING
    AMOUNT            = AMT
    CURRENCY          = WAERS
    FILLER            = ' '
    LANGUAGE          = SPRAS
  IMPORTING
    IN_WORDS          = SPELL
  EXCEPTIONS
    NOT_FOUND         = 1
    TOO_LARGE         = 2
    OTHERS            = 3.

IF SY-SUBRC = 0.

 CONCATENATE SPELL-WORD WAERS SPELL-DECIMAL
  INTO STR SEPARATED BY SPACE.
ELSE.
 MESSAGE ID SY-MSGID TYPE SY-MSGTY NUMBER SY-MSGNO
```

```
          WITH SY-MSGV1 SY-MSGV2 SY-MSGV3 SY-MSGV4.
 EXIT.
ENDIF.

* Split STR into Two Lines
**************************
CALL FUNCTION 'YCH02_01_SPLIT_STRING'
  EXPORTING
    STRING_TO_SPLIT                 = STR
  TABLES
    STABLE                          = STR_TAB
 EXCEPTIONS
   IMPORT_PARAMETER_TYPE_INVALID    = 1
   RETURN_TABLE_ELEMENT_NOT_TYPEC   = 2
   OTHERS                           = 3
                     .
IF SY-SUBRC <> 0.
 MESSAGE ID SY-MSGID TYPE SY-MSGTY NUMBER SY-MSGNO
        WITH SY-MSGV1 SY-MSGV2 SY-MSGV3 SY-MSGV4.
 EXIT.
ENDIF.

* Update Values in OUTPUT_TAB Table
***********************************
READ TABLE STR_TAB INTO STR1 INDEX 1.

READ TABLE OUTPUT_TAB WITH KEY 'IN_WORD1'.
IF SY-SUBRC = 0.
 OUTPUT_TAB-VALUE = STR1.
 MODIFY OUTPUT_TAB INDEX SY-TABIX.
ENDIF.

READ TABLE STR_TAB INTO STR2 INDEX 2.

READ TABLE OUTPUT_TAB WITH KEY 'IN_WORD2'.
IF SY-SUBRC = 0.
 OUTPUT_TAB-VALUE = STR2.
 MODIFY OUTPUT_TAB INDEX SY-TABIX.
ENDIF.

*BREAK-POINT.
ENDFORM. "CALL_SPELL_AMOUNT
```

At the entry of the subroutine, input parameters are being extracted: READ TABLE INPUT_TAB WITH KEY 'AMOUNT', and so on.

The value of the parameter AMOUNT will contain thousand separators (commas) and a decimal. To convert the AMOUNT value containing thousand separators and a decimal into ABAP pre-defined type P (packed decimal), the thousand separators and the decimal are removed. The process of removing the decimal is equivalent to multiplying the number by 100. To restore the value of AMOUNT, it is divided by 100 after removal of thousand separators and the decimal.

Similarly, the other input parameters are extracted with the statements READ TABLE INPUT_TAB WITH KEY.....

The function module CURRENCY_CODE_SAP_TO_ISO is called to convert the SAP currency key to the ISO currency key. The function module SPELL_AMOUNT will convert the amount into text in the language provided as the input parameter.

The function module YCH02_01_SPLIT_STRING is used to split the single string STR into two strings: IN_WORD1 and IN_WORD2. The function module YCH02_01_SPLIT_STRING splits a string into multiple strings without breaking a word. Since the string returned by the function module SPELL_AMOUNT can exceed 80 characters, we are splitting it into two strings of 70 characters each. We expect the text will not exceed two lines. (140 characters). The function module YCH02_01_SPLIT_STRING is available in the E-resource file for this book (www.apress.com/9781484212345). You can create a function group or pool. You can create the function module YCH02_01_SPLIT_STRING, locate it in your created function group, and upload into the function module the lines from the E-resource file for this book (www.apress.com/9781484212345). Activate the function group and the function module. You have to create the messages associated with the function module YCH02_01_SPLIT_STRING as well.

```
Message no. 006        Input Parameter has to be TYPE 'C',
Message no. 007        Output Table Element has to be TYPE 'C')
```

Before exiting the subroutine, the output parameters values are stored in the appropriate rows of the internal table OUTPUT_TAB with the READ TABLE OUTPUT_TAB WITH KEY...... and MODIFY statements.

The comments in the subroutine program should help you to comprehend the logic and flow of the subroutine

We saved, performed a syntax check, and activated the program YCH02_04_SROUTINE_POOL. The program YCH02_04_SROUTINE_POOL is available in the E-resource file for this book (www.apress.com/9781484212345).

# Output

We will choose the same two purchase orders we used for testing the output in our previous hands-on exercise: purchase order numbers 4500004823 and 4500009520. The purchase order number 4500004823 language key is D and the purchase order number 4500009520 language key is E.

We executed the program YCH02_03_PPRG_ YCH02_03_PORDER2. The output will be the same as in the previous hands-on exercise except for the additional information of amount being expressed in text. So we are showing only that part of the output containing the amount in text. The output of the two purchase orders, the first in German and the second in English, will look as shown in Figures 2-15 and 2-16.

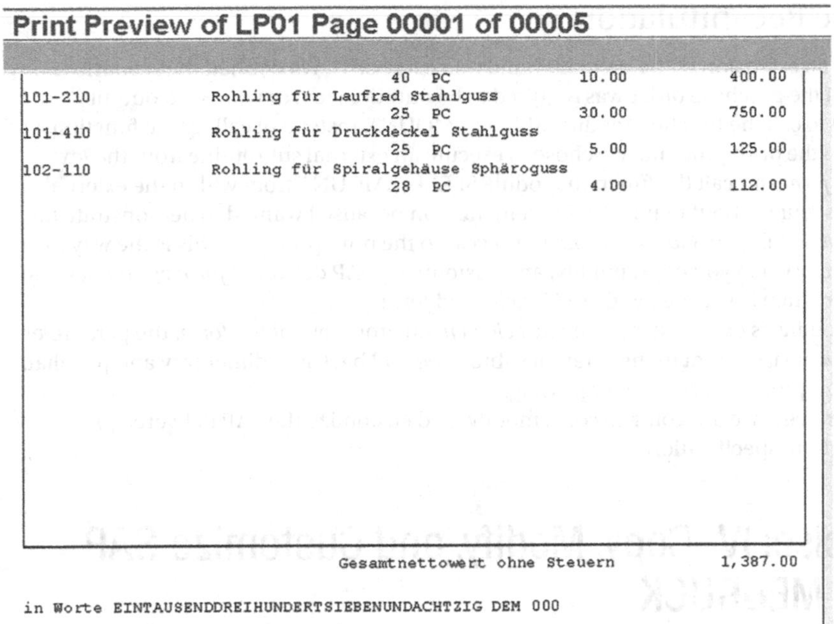

## Print Preview of LP01 Page 00001 of 00005

```
                              40   PC          10.00        400.00
101-210         Rohling für Laufrad Stahlguss
                              25   PC          30.00        750.00
101-410         Rohling für Druckdeckel Stahlguss
                              25   PC           5.00        125.00
102-110         Rohling für Spiralgehäuse Sphäroguss
                              28   PC           4.00        112.00
```

```
                      Gesamtnettowert ohne Steuern        1,387.00
```

in Worte EINTAUSENDDREIHUNDERTSIEBENUNDACHTZIG DEM 000

*Figure 2-15.* *Output of custom purchase order form: PO No. 4500004823*

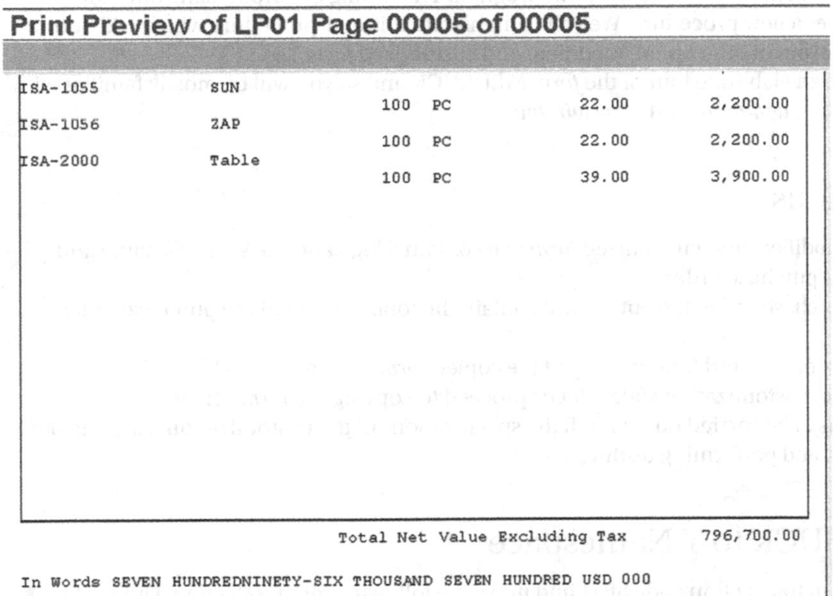

## Print Preview of LP01 Page 00005 of 00005

```
ISA-1055        SUN
                              100  PC          22.00      2,200.00
ISA-1056        ZAP
                              100  PC          22.00      2,200.00
ISA-2000        Table
                              100  PC          39.00      3,900.00
```

```
                      Total Net Value Excluding Tax     796,700.00
```

In Words SEVEN HUNDREDNINETY-SIX THOUSAND SEVEN HUNDRED USD 000

*Figure 2-16.* *Output of custom purchase order form: PO No. 4500009520*

## Hands-on Exercise Recapitulation

This hands-on exercise was an extension of the previous hands-on exercise II. We defined the scenario in which the total amount of the purchase order was required to be output in text or words. To output the amount in text, we need to call the function module SPELL_AMOUNT. Instead of calling the function module SPELL_AMOUNT in the print program, we chose to execute an external subroutine from the *text element* environment of the *form* and call the function module SPELL_AMOUNT from within the external subroutine. I resorted to this round-about manner of implementation because I wanted to demonstrate the manner of adding ABAP functionality to a *form* without the access to the print program. This is the way to incorporate ABAP functionality when you copy, modify, and customize a SAP delivered *form* as you have no access to modify the print program associated with a SAP delivered *form*.

When an external subroutine is executed from the *text element* environment of the *form*, the parameter passing from the *text element* environment to the external subroutine and back is rudimentary and peculiar. Exercise III demonstrated this process of parameter passing.

In the next hands-on exercise, we are going to copy, modify, and customize the SAP delivered *form* MEDRUCK according to laid-out specifications.

# Hands-on Exercise: IV–Copy, Modify, and Customize SAP Delivered Form MEDRUCK

In this hands-on exercise, we will copy the SAP delivered *form* MEDRUCK into Y namespace. We will modify and customize the copied *form*. The modifications will involve the deletion of a *page window* and the creation of new *windows* and their corresponding *page windows*. The modification will also involve incorporation of ABAP functionality by invoking external subroutines from the *text element* environment of this *form*. Remember, we do not have access to the print program. The testing of output using our modified and customized *form* involves a new procedure. We will demonstrate this new procedure which will output purchase orders as per the layout of our copied, modified, and customized *form*.

In Chapter 1, you made an elaborate tour of the *form* MEDRUCK and so you will be mostly familiar with its elements (e.g., *page formats*, *windows*, and *page windows*).

## Output Specifications

The output of our copied, modified, and customized *form* will contain a logo and the sender's name and address on the first page of a purchase order.

On the last page of a purchase order, the output will contain the total amount of the purchase order expressed in text.

The rest of the layout, contents, and functionality of the copied *form* will be retained.

With this specification of customization stated, let us proceed to copying the *form* MEDRUCK, identifying the modifications to be carried out to fulfill the specifications of the customization, carrying out the identified modifications, and performing testing.

## Copy Form MEDRUCK to Y Namespace

To copy a *form*, we navigate to transaction code SE71 and make the following menu selection: Utilities(M) ➤ Copy from client.

A screen appeared prompting for *form* to be copied, source client, target *form* name, etc. Recall, all the SAP delivered *forms* reside in client 000 and the destination client of copied *form* is the logged-in client. Figure 2-17 shows the screen with the entered values.

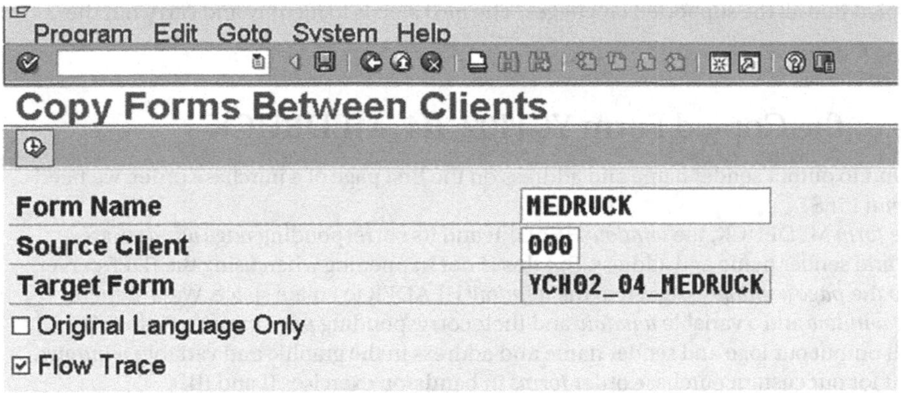

Program  Edit  Goto  System  Help

## Copy Forms Between Clients

| Form Name | MEDRUCK |
|---|---|
| Source Client | 000 |
| Target Form | YCH02_04_MEDRUCK |

☐ Original Language Only
☑ Flow Trace

*Figure 2-17.* *Copy form MEDRUCK from Client 000 to YCH02_04_MEDRUCK into logged-in client*

We clicked the execute button. A prompt appeared for assigning a package. We assigned the package YCH_BC401. You can assign any other non-local package of your choice. A successful copy generated an alert as shown in Figure 2-18.

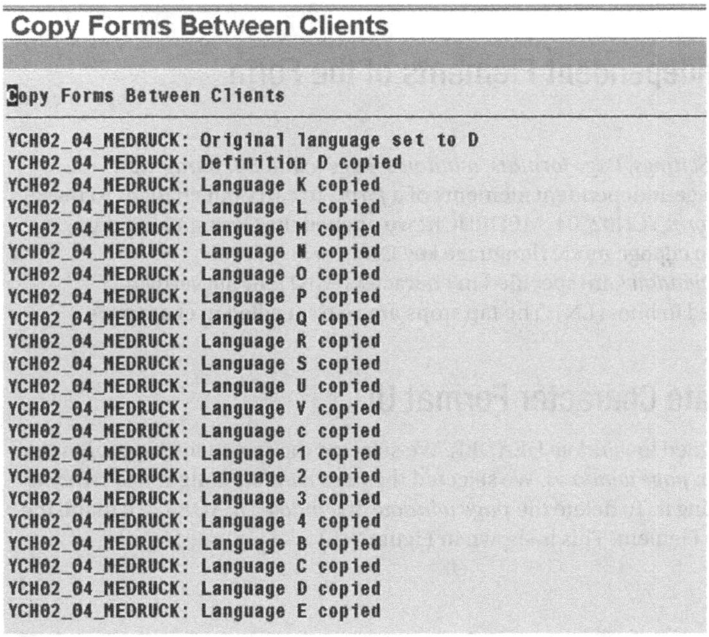

## Copy Forms Between Clients

Copy Forms Between Clients

```
YCH02_04_MEDRUCK: Original language set to D
YCH02_04_MEDRUCK: Definition D copied
YCH02_04_MEDRUCK: Language K copied
YCH02_04_MEDRUCK: Language L copied
YCH02_04_MEDRUCK: Language M copied
YCH02_04_MEDRUCK: Language N copied
YCH02_04_MEDRUCK: Language O copied
YCH02_04_MEDRUCK: Language P copied
YCH02_04_MEDRUCK: Language Q copied
YCH02_04_MEDRUCK: Language R copied
YCH02_04_MEDRUCK: Language S copied
YCH02_04_MEDRUCK: Language U copied
YCH02_04_MEDRUCK: Language V copied
YCH02_04_MEDRUCK: Language c copied
YCH02_04_MEDRUCK: Language 1 copied
YCH02_04_MEDRUCK: Language 2 copied
YCH02_04_MEDRUCK: Language 3 copied
YCH02_04_MEDRUCK: Language 4 copied
YCH02_04_MEDRUCK: Language B copied
YCH02_04_MEDRUCK: Language C copied
YCH02_04_MEDRUCK: Language D copied
YCH02_04_MEDRUCK: Language E copied
```

*Figure 2-18.* *Successful copy of form MEDRUCK from client 000 to YCH02_04_MEDRUCK*

The *form* was copied into all the supported languages. The next step is to identify and carry out the modifications.

## Modifications to the Copied Form YCH02_04_MEDRUCK

To position our logo and to output sender name and address on the first page of a purchase order, we need space in the *page format* FIRST.

In the copy of the *form* MEDRUCK, the *window* HEADER and its corresponding *page window* are meant to output logo and sender name and address. But this is not happening when using the IDES server data. So we will delete the *page window* assigned to the *window* HEADER to create space. We will then incorporate a graphic *window* and a variable *window* and their corresponding *page windows* into this vacated space. We will output our logo and sender name and address in the graphic and variable *windows*, the same way we did it for our custom purchase order *forms* in hands-on exercises II and III.

To output the total amount of a purchase order expressed as text on the last page of the purchase order, we will reduce the height of the *page windows* assigned to the main *window* in both the *page formats* FIRST and NEXT. We will create a new *window* IN_WORDS. The reduction in height of the *page windows* assigned to the main *window* in both the *page formats* FIRST and NEXT will accommodate *page windows* to be assigned to the newly created *window* IN_WORDS. The total amount of a purchase order expressed as text will appear in the *page windows* assigned to the *window* IN_WORDS. This is identical to the manner of outputting the total amount of a purchase order expressed as text in hands-on exercise III.

First, we will carry out modifications to the language-independent elements of the *form*.

## Modifications to Language-Independent Elements of the Form YCH02_04_MEDRUCK

We navigated to transaction code SE71. *Settings*, *Page formats*, *windows*, *page windows*, *paragraph formats* and *character formats* are language-independent elements of a *form*. To carry out changes to these language-independent elements of the *form* YCH02_04_MEDRUCK, we opened the German language (original language) version of this *form* in change mode (language key DE).

The horizontal dimensions of *page windows* are specified in characters (CH) and the vertical dimensions of *page windows* are specified in lines (LN). The tap stops are also specified in characters.

## Delete Window HEADER, Create Character Format UL

We want to delete the *page window* assigned to *window* HEADER. We selected the screen for *page windows* by clicking the application toolbar button *page windows*. We selected the *page window* assigned to *window* HEADER by locating it and double-clicking it. To delete the *page window* of *window* HEADER, we made the following menu selection: Edit ➤ Delete Element. This is shown in Figure 2-19.

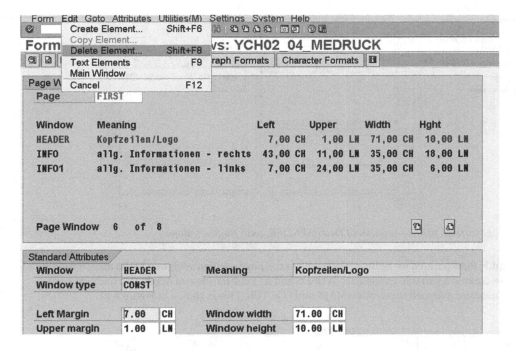

**Figure 2-19.** *Page format: FIRST—delete page window assigned to window HEADER*

This will delete the *page window* assigned to the variable *window* HEADER.
We created a *character format* UL with font family Helve and font size 24 points as follows:

```
UL        For Sender Name in 24 pts        HELVE     24,0
```

The *character format* UL will be applied to the output of company code name.
Next, we proceeded to *page format* modifications.

## Modifications in Page Format FIRST of the Form YCH02_04_MEDRUCK

Next, we have to create the *windows* LOGO, SENDER, and their corresponding *page windows* in the *page format* FIRST. We switched to the graphic *form* painter. In the graphic *form* painter, we created the *windows* LOGO, SENDER, and their corresponding *page windows* in the *page format* FIRST. This is shown in Figure 2-20.

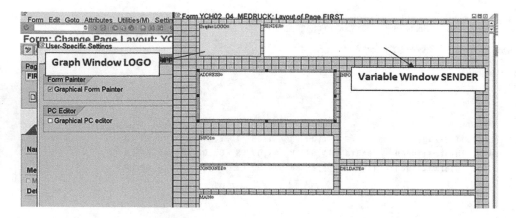

**Figure 2-20.** *Page format: FIRST—windows LOGO, SENDER, with page windows*

In the graphic *form* painter, we reduced the height of the *page window* assigned to the main *window* by two lines. We created a variable *window* IN_WORDS and its *page window* of height two lines in space between *page windows* assigned to *windows* MAIN and FOOTER. This is shown in Figure 2-21.

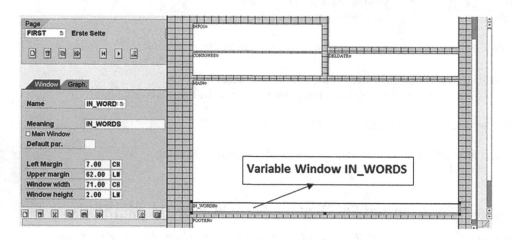

**Figure 2-21.** *Page format: FIRST—window IN_WORDS with page window*

The element list of *page windows* after the creation of the *windows* LOGO, SENDER, IN_WORDS with the corresponding *page windows* marked is shown in Figure 2-22.

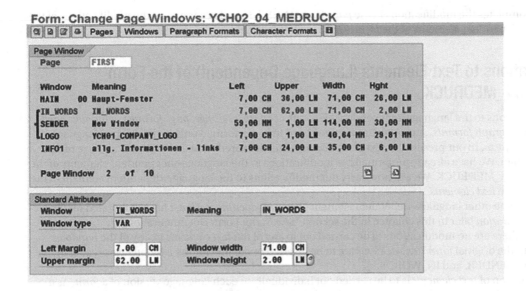

**Figure 2-22.** *Page format: FIRST—page window element list*

The dimensions of these *page windows* is as follows:

```
Page
Window    Left Margin    Upper margin    Win width    Win height
=============================================================
LOGO        7 CH           1 LN          46.64 mm     29.01 mm
SENDER      59mm           1 LN          114mm        30 mm
IN_WORDS    7 CH          62 LN          71 CH        2 LN
```

This completes the modifications in the *page format* FIRST.

# Modifications in Page Format NEXT of the Form YCH02_04_MEDRUCK

The logo and sender name and address appear only on the first page of a purchase order. For this reason, we need not assign *page windows* to the *windows* LOGO and SENDER for the *page format* NEXT.

The total amount of the purchase order in text must appear on the last page of a purchase order. If a purchase order outputs in one page only, the first page of the purchase order will also be its last page. There should be a provision to output the text of total amount of the purchase order in *page format* FIRST. We have already created the *window* IN_WORDS and assigned this *window* to a *page window* in the *page format* FIRST. This part of the modification is over.

If a purchase order outputs in more than one page, the first page of the purchase order will not be its last page. There should be a provision to output the text of total amount of the purchase order in *page format* NEXT. So, we assigned a *page window* to the *window* IN_WORDS in the *page format* NEXT. The dimensions of this *page window* are as follows:

IN_WORDS    Left Margin:7 CH    Upper margin: 61 LN    Win width: 61 CH    Win height: 2 CH

This completes the modifications in the *page format* NEXT. This also completes the modifications of the language-independent elements of the *form* YCH01_04_MEDRUCK.

## Modifications to Text Elements (Language Dependent) of the Form YCH02_04_MEDRUCK

The modifications to the language-independent elements of a *form* (*settings, page formats, windows, page windows, paragraph formats,* and *character formats*) need to be performed only in the original language version of the *form*. In our present context of modifying a SAP delivered *form*, the original language of the *form* is German. We have already performed the modifications to the language-independent elements of the *form* YCH02_04_MEDRUCK. We will now carry out modifications to the language-dependent element of the *form*, that is, the *text elements*.

There is one other language-dependent element of a *form: documentation*. I have elaborated on the *form documentation* later in this chapter, in the section "SAP Script Form Documentation."

In fact, there are no modifications to be carried out to any of the *text elements* in any of the *windows* belonging to the original *form*. *Text elements* are to be inserted or created for the *windows* we created in the *form*: LOGO, SENDER, and IN_WORDS.

The creation of *text elements* is to be carried out individually in each language version of a *form*. As a test case, we will create *text elements* in the two language versions of the *form*: German and English

We will, first, create *text elements* in the German-language version of the *form*. Thus we must ensure that we are in change mode of the German-language version of the *form* YCH02_04_MEDRUCK. Only after we have created the *text elements* in the German-language version of the *form* can we commence to create the *text elements* in the English-language version of the *form*. When you carry out modification to the *text elements* of a *form* in a language other than the original language of the *form*, the *form* maintenance system expects the original language version of the *form* to be in active mode. In our present context, when we are creating/modifying the *text elements* in the English-language version of the *form*, the German-language version of the *form* must be in active mode.

Since the *text elements* have one-to-one association with the *windows*, I will describe the creation of *text elements window*-wise.

## Create Text Elements in the German-Language Version of the Form YCH02_04_MEDRUCK

Entries in the *text element* area will be created *window*-wise as shown in the next sections.

### Text Element in Window LOGO

We created the graph *window* LOGO and its *page window* with the graphical *form* painter in the German-language version of the *form*. The *form* creation system automatically generated the control command to insert a graphic image in the *text element* area of the *window* LOGO. You can confirm this by navigating to the *text element* area of the *window* LOGO. The control command to insert a graphic image is in display mode; it cannot be modified. An image can be inserted in any of the *window* types: graph, constant, variable, and main. We chose to locate the graphic image or logo in a graph *window* because, in this way, the *form* creation system generated the dimensions of the *page window* automatically as identical to the size of the image. But locating the image in a graph *window* does not allow us to modify the *text elements* in the *window*. If you navigate to the *text element* area of the *window* LOGO in the English-language version or any language other than the German-language version, you will find the *text element* area empty and not editable. The *text element* area, being language dependent, has to be entered and filled individually for each language version. The *text element* area is in non-editable because that is how it is for a graph *window*.

We want the logo to appear on the first page of a purchase order for the German version as well as the English version. We are assured of the logo being output for the German language; the *text element* area has the control command to incorporate an image. But in the English version of the *form*, the *text element* area is empty and non-editable. To be able to insert the control command for incorporation of image in the *text element* area of the *window* LOGO in the English-language version of the *form*, we are changing the *window* type from graph to variable for the *window* LOGO. This is shown in Figure 2-23.

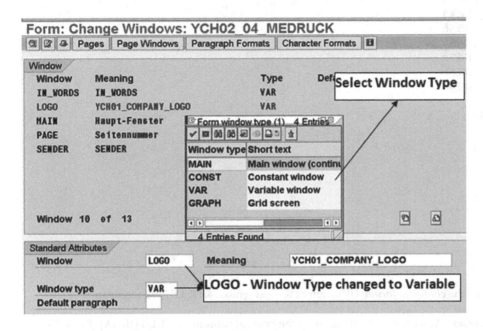

**Figure 2-23.** *Window LOGO—Change window type from graph to variable*

We can change the *window* type in this manner after the creation of a *window*.

In the German-language version of the *form*, we do not need to change anything in the *text element* area of the *window* LOGO. We only needed to change the *window* LOGO type from graph to variable, which we have done.

## Text Element in Window SENDER

The following was entered in the *text element* area of the *window* SENDER:

```
/: IF &PAGE(C)& = 1
/: DEFINE &TE_LINE0& = ' '
/: DEFINE &TE_LINE1& = ' '
/: DEFINE &TE_LINE2& = ' '
/: DEFINE &TE_LINE3& = ' '
/: DEFINE &TE_LINE4& = ' '
/: DEFINE &TE_LINE5& = ' '
/: DEFINE &TE_LINE6& = ' '
/: DEFINE &TE_LINE7& = ' '
/: DEFINE &TE_LINE8& = ' '
```

```
/: DEFINE &TE_LINE9& = ' '
/: PERFORM GET_FORMAT_SENDER_ADDRESS IN PROGRAM YCH02_04_SROUTINE_POOL
/: USING &T001-ADRNR(K)&
/: CHANGING &TE_LINE0&
/: CHANGING &TE_LINE1&
/: CHANGING &TE_LINE2&
/: CHANGING &TE_LINE3&
/: CHANGING &TE_LINE4&
/: CHANGING &TE_LINE5&
/: CHANGING &TE_LINE6&
/: CHANGING &TE_LINE7&
/: CHANGING &TE_LINE8&
/: CHANGING &TE_LINE9&
/: ENDPERFORM
*  <UL>&TE_LINE0&</>
*  &TE_LINE1&
*  &TE_LINE2&
*  &TE_LINE3&
*  &TE_LINE4&
*  &TE_LINE5&
*  &TE_LINE6&
*  &TE_LINE7&
*  &TE_LINE8&
*  &TE_LINE9&
/: ENDIF
```

We have applied the *character format* UL to output the text symbol &TE_LINE0& (company code name).

From within the *text element* area, we are invoking the external subroutine GET_FORMAT_SENDER_ADDRESS located in the subroutine pool program YCH02_04_SROUTINE_POOL. We already located the subroutine CALL_SPELL_AMOUNT in the subroutine pool YCH02_04_SROUTINE_POOL while performing hands-on exercise III. The subroutine pool now has two subroutines. The source lines of external subroutine GET_FORMAT_SENDER_ADDRESS in subroutine pool YCH02_04_SROUTINE_POOL are as follows:

```
************************************************************
FORM GET_FORMAT_SENDER_ADDRESS TABLES
                            INPUT_TAB  STRUCTURE ITCSY
                            OUTPUT_TAB STRUCTURE ITCSY.
************************************************************
* Input Parameters:  ADRNR                                 *
* Output Parameters: TE_LINE0, TE_LINE1, TE_LINE2, TE_LINE3,*
*                    TE_LINE4, TE_LINE5, TE_LINE6, TE_LINE7,*
*                    TE_LINE8, TE_LINE9                     *
************************************************************
* Data Declaration
*****************
TABLES: SADR, ADRS.   "Address Management - Table & Structure

DATA: ADRNR           TYPE ADRNR,
      LENGTH(2)       TYPE N,
      LEN(1)          TYPE N,
      KEY(128)        TYPE C.
```

```
FIELD-SYMBOLS: <FS1>, <FS2>.

* Extract Parameters from INPUT_TAB
**********************************
READ TABLE INPUT_TAB WITH KEY 'T001-ADRNR'.
IF SY-SUBRC <> 0.
 EXIT.
ENDIF.


ADRNR = INPUT_TAB-VALUE.

* Get Company Code Name & Address to Int. Postal Forma t
******************************************************
SELECT SINGLE * FROM SADR "Get Address of Company Cd
                   WHERE ADRNR = ADRNR.
SADR-ANRED = ' '. "No Title for Company Code Name
CLEAR ADRS.
MOVE-CORRESPONDING SADR TO ADRS.

CALL FUNCTION 'ADDRESS_INTO_PRINTFORM'
 EXPORTING
   ADRSWA_IN                       = ADRS
 IMPORTING
   ADRSWA_OUT                      = ADRS

         .

IF SY-SUBRC <> 0.
 EXIT.
ENDIF.

LENGTH = STRLEN( ADRS-LINE0 ).

* Update Values in OUTPUT_TAB Table
**********************************
DO 10 TIMES.
 LEN = SY-INDEX - 1.
 CONCATENATE 'TE_LINE' LEN INTO KEY.
 READ TABLE OUTPUT_TAB WITH KEY KEY.

 IF SY-SUBRC = 0.
  CONCATENATE 'ADRS-LINE' LEN INTO KEY.
  ASSIGN (KEY) TO <FS1>.
  OUTPUT_TAB-VALUE = <FS1>.
  MODIFY OUTPUT_TAB INDEX SY-TABIX.
 ENDIF.

ENDDO.
*BREAK-POINT.
ENDFORM. "GET_FORMAT_SENDER_ADDRESS
```

Within the subroutine GET_FORMAT_SENDER_ADDRESS, we are retrieving the name and address of the company code through the field T001-ADRNR from the table SADR. We are formatting the company code name and address as per the postal convention of the country of the company code by calling the function module ADDRESS_INTO_PRINTFORM. We are resorting to this procedure instead of using the ADDRESS.....ENDADDRESS set of control commands to be able to apply *character format* to a specific field of the name and address of the company code. In our custom purchase order hands-on exercises II and III, the code we have located in the subroutine was located within the print programs. In our present exercise, we do not have access to the print program, hence the external subroutine. We are applying the *character format* UL to output the company code name.

We have used feature of field symbols in the subroutine. You must be sufficiently exposed to the field symbols to follow their usage in the subroutine. You have already been exposed to the extraction of parameters and the insertion of return parameter values in an external subroutine called from within the *text element* environment of a *form*.

For the English-language version of this *form*, in the *text element* area of the *window* SENDER, the same entries have to appear. We can manually enter these same entries when we edit or change the English-language version of this *form*. But the preferred way would be to copy these *text element* entries into any of the five user clipboards and paste from the user clipboard. To select and copy *text element* entries into a user clipboard, it is better to switch to the graphical editor. To switch to graphical editor in the *text element* environment, we made the following menu selection: Goto ➤ Change Editor or Goto ➤ Configure Editor. This is shown in Figure 2-24.

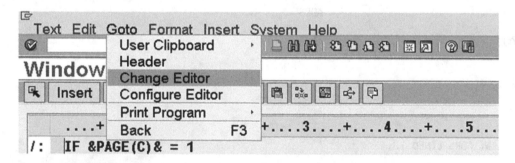

***Figure 2-24.*** *Text element environment—menu option to switch to graphic editor*

Once we are in the graphic editor, we selected the entire text in the *window* SENDER as it is shown in Figure 2-25. To insert the selected text into the user clipboard 1, we made the following menu selection: Edit ➤ Copy to User Clipboard ➤ User Clipboard 1. This is shown in Figure 2-25:

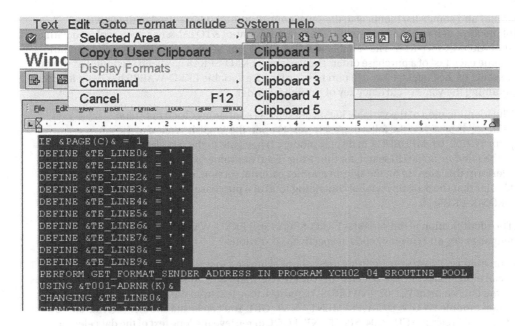

*Figure 2-25. Text element environment—menu option to copy text to user clipboard 1*

The user clipboard 1 now contains the text of the *window* SENDER. The user clipboards in the *text element* environment of *form*s are just like the non-volatile buffers in the ABAP editor. You can copy, view, and change the contents of a user clipboard from within the *text element* environment with the following menu option: Goto ➤ User Clipboard ➤ Clipboard 1/2/3/4/5. We switched back to the non-graphical editor by again making the menu selection shown in Figure 2-25. We proceed to the *window* IN_WORDS next.

## Text Element in Window IN_WORDS

The following was entered in the *text element* area of the *window* IN_WORDS:

```
/: IF &NEXTPAGE(C)& = 'O'
/: DEFINE &AMOUNT& = &KOMK-FKWRT&
/: DEFINE &SPRAS&  = &EKKO-SPRAS&
/: DEFINE &WAERS&  = &EKKO-WAERS&
/: DEFINE &IN_WORD1& = ' '
/: DEFINE &IN_WORD2& = ' '
/: PERFORM CALL_SPELL_AMOUNT IN PROGRAM YCHO2_04_SROUTINE_POOL
/:  USING &AMOUNT&
/:  USING &SPRAS&
/:  USING &WAERS&
/:  CHANGING &IN_WORD1&
/:  CHANGING &IN_WORD2&
/: ENDPERFORM
*      &IN_WORD1&
*      &IN_WORD2&
/: ENDIF
```

This is similar and somewhat identical to the set of control commands we used in the *window* IN_WORDS of the *form* of hands-on exercise III. The program symbol &TOTAL& has been replaced with the program symbol &KOMK-FKWRT&. The variable KOMK-FKWRT has been identified as the one containing the 'Total net value excl. tax' of a purchase order. The variables EKKO-SPRAS has been identified as the one containing the value of the language key of a purchase order. The variable EKKO-WAERS has been identified as the one containing the value of currency key of a purchase order.

- The identification of the variable KOMK-FKWRT as containing 'Total net value excl. tax' is based on the following exercise: (1) open the English version of the *form* YCH02_04_MEDRUCK in display mode; (2) navigate to the text *element area* of the *window* main; (3) search for the string 'Total net value excl. tax' – ctrl+F etc. (Perform this exercise on the side, in another external session, etc.) You will be able to infer that the program symbol containing total of a purchase order excluding tax is &KOMK-FKWRT&

- The identification of the variables EKKO-SPRAS and EKKO-WAERS as containing the language key and currency code, respectively, is obvious.

In hands-on exercise III, we were prefixing the amount expressed in text with 'In Words.' You can do so if you want. You can either enter the text as literal: 'in Worten' (German) and 'In Words' (English). Or, you can use the long text of the data element YCH02_INWORDS. To retrieve long text from the data element, you will have to use the function module WCGW_DATA_ELEMENT_TEXT_GET. You can locate another external subroutine in the subroutine pool program YCH02_04_SROUTINE_POOL to retrieve the long text of the data element.

For the English version of this *form*, in the *text element* area of the *window* IN_WORDS, the same entries have to appear. We again need to select and copy the text in the *window* IN_WORDS into one of the user clipboards. To select text, we switched to the graphical editor by making the menu selection: Goto ➤ Change Editor or Goto ➤ Configure Editor. We selected the entire text in the *window* IN_WORDS. To insert the selected text into the user clipboard 2, we made the following menu selection: Edit ➤ Copy to User Clipboard ➤ User Clipboard 2. This inserted the entire text in the *window* IN_WORDS into the user clipboard 2.

We saved the *form*. We performed a *form* definition check as well as the *form* texts check on the *form* YCH02_04_MEDRUCK. To perform the *form* text check, we used the print program SAPLMEDRUCK. The print program SAPLMEDRUCK is a function pool. The *form* texts check will generate an error and quite a few warnings. We ignored them. We activated the *form*. The German-language version (original language) has to be active to enable changes in other language versions of the *form*.

This completes the task of the creation of *text elements* in the German-language version of the *form*.

# Create Text Elements in the English-Language Version of the Form YCH02_04_MEDRUCK

We need to create the *text elements* in the English-language version of the *form* YCH02_04_MEDRUCK for the *windows* LOGO, SENDER, and IN_WORDS.

We used transaction code SE71 to open the English-language version of the *form* YCH02_04_MEDRUCK in change mode. Before opening the English-language version of this *form,* it is to be ensured that the original language version (German) of this *form* is in active mode.

As *text elements* are mapped one to one with the *windows*, we will proceed to create *text elements* *window*-wise.

## Text Element in Window LOGO

We inserted the following in the *text element* area of the *window* LOGO:

```
/: BITMAP 'YCH01_COMPANY_LOGO' OBJECT GRAPHICS ID  BMAP TYPE BCOL
```

Since the *text element* consists of a single line, it was not considered worthwhile to copy it into a user clipboard. This is all we need to create in the *text element* area of the *window* LOGO.

## Text Element in Window SENDER

We had copied the text in the *window* SENDER while in the German-language version of the *form* into the user clipboard 1. We now have to paste or insert the text from the user clipboard 1 into the *text element* area of the *window* SENDER. To paste text from the user clipboard 1, we made the following menu selection in the *text element* environment of *window* SENDER: Insert ➤ User Clipboard ➤ Clipboard 1. This is shown in Figure 2-26.

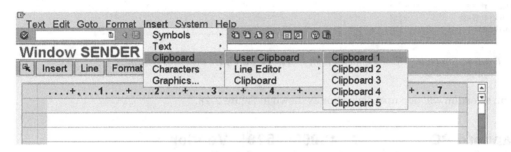

***Figure 2-26.*** *Insert/paste text from user clipboard 1 into text element area of window SENDER*

This pasted contents of the user clipboard 1 into the *text element* area of the *window* SENDER. That is all.

## Text Element in Window IN_WORDS

To paste text from the user clipboard 2, we made the following menu selection in the *text element* environment of *window* IN_WORDS: Insert ➤ User Clipboard ➤ Clipboard 2. This pasted contents of the user clipboard 2 into the *text element* area of the *window* IN_WORDS.

We created *text elements* in the *windows* LOGO, SENDER, and IN_WORDS for the English-language version of the *form*. We performed *form* check and activated the English-language version of the *form*.

We now have the German and English versions of the *form* YCH02_04_MEDRUCK active and ready for testing. If we decide that our test case for the *form* will support the two languages, German and English, our modification and customization of the *form* YCH02_04_MEDRUCK ends.

# Output

We want to test the output of the *form* YCH02_04_MEDRUCK. The print program of the *form* YCH02_04_MEDRUCK is SAPLMEDRUCK, a function pool. We cannot execute this program. Thus I am introducing a simple procedure to test the output of the *form* YCH02_04_MEDRUCK. We will test the output of the *form* YCH02_04_MEDRUCK with purchase order numbers 4500004823 and 4500009520. These are the same two purchase orders we used for testing the output in our hands-on exercises II and III. The purchase order number 4500004823 language key is D and the purchase order number 4500009520 language key is E.

We used the transaction code ME22N—change purchase order—to test the output of the *form* YCH02_04_MEDRUCK. Within this transaction code, we can assign to a specific purchase order, a SAP script *form* to be used for output. The procedure involves assigning each purchase order a *form* to be used to output it, a somewhat cumbersome process if you are outputting purchase orders on a mass scale. In our present scenario, we are not intending to output large number of purchase orders, so it will serve our purposes.

We navigated to the screen of transaction code ME22N. To select a purchase order, we made the following menu selection: Purchase Order ->Other Purchase Order. This is shown in Figure 2-27:

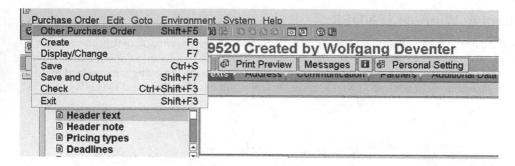

**Figure 2-27.** *Transaction code: ME22N—menu item to select a purchase order for editing*

This menu selection will pop up a dialog box as shown in Figure 2-28.

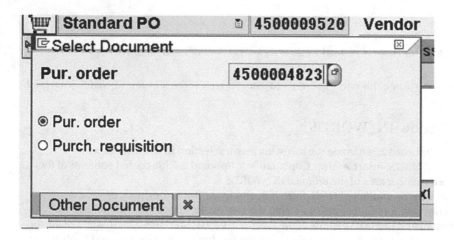

**Figure 2-28.** *Transaction code: ME22N—Select Document*

There is a selection list facility available. We manually entered purchase order number 4500004823 (German purchase order). We clicked the continue Other Document button. This fetched purchase order number 4500004823 for editing as shown in Figure 2-29.

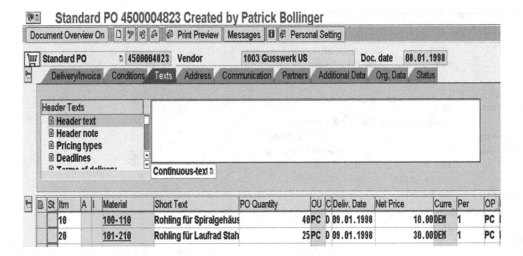

**Figure 2-29.** *Purchase order number: 4500004823—change/edit*

We clicked the application toolbar button Messages. A screen like the one shown in Figure 2-30 appeared.

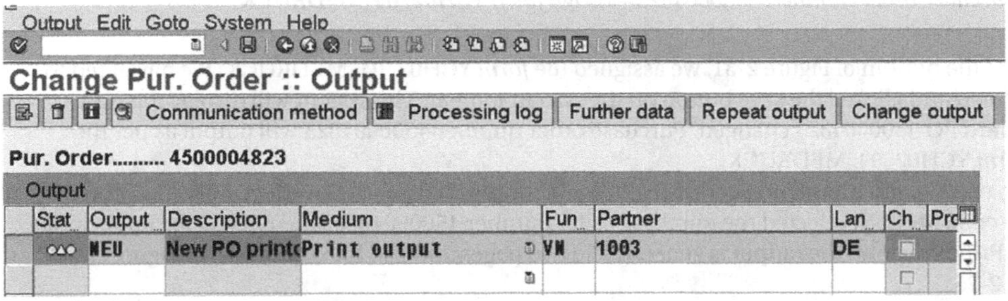

**Figure 2-30.** *Purchase order number: 4500004823—output/messages*

We selected the row as shown in Figure 2-30. If a row does not exist, create a row with the values from the Figure 2-30. We clicked the application toolbar button Communication Method. The screen as shown in Figure 2-31 appeared.

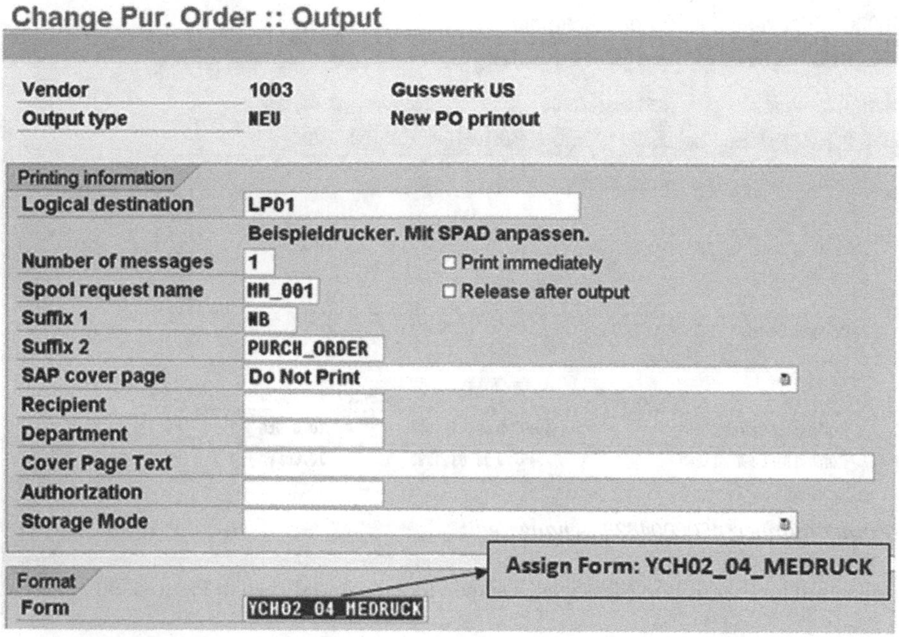

## Change Pur. Order :: Output

| | | |
|---|---|---|
| Vendor | 1003 | Gusswerk US |
| Output type | NEU | New PO printout |

**Printing information**

| | |
|---|---|
| Logical destination | LP01 |
| | Beispieldrucker. Mit SPAD anpassen. |
| Number of messages | 1 □ Print immediately |
| Spool request name | HH_001 □ Release after output |
| Suffix 1 | NB |
| Suffix 2 | PURCH_ORDER |
| SAP cover page | Do Not Print |
| Recipient | |
| Department | |
| Cover Page Text | |
| Authorization | |
| Storage Mode | |

**Assign Form: YCH02_04_MEDRUCK**

**Format**

**Form**   YCH02_04_MEDRUCK

*Figure 2-31. Purchase order number: 4500004823—assign form YCH02_04_MEDRUCK*

As shown at the bottom of Figure 2-31, we assigned the *form* YCH02_04_MEDRUCK. We navigated to the previous screen and clicked the save button on the system toolbar. The system will display the status message 'Standard PO 4500004823 changed'. Purchase order number 4500004823 will output as per the layout of the *form* YCH02_04_MEDRUCK.

We have to execute the transaction code ME22n again for the change to take effect. So, we executed the transaction code ME22N, selected the purchase order number 4500004823, and clicked the application toolbar button Print Preview. The output is generated in two pages and will look as shown in Figures 2-32, 2-33, 2-34, and 2-35:

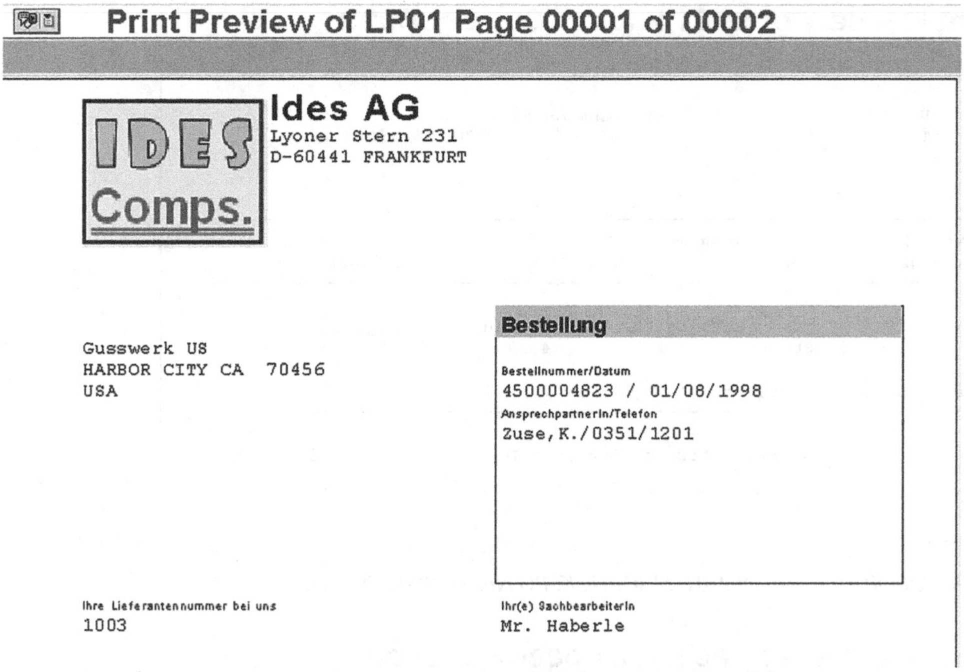

### Ides AG
Lyoner Stern 231
D-60441 FRANKFURT

Gusswerk US
HARBOR CITY CA  70456
USA

**Bestellung**

Bestellnummer/Datum
4500004823 / 01/08/1998
Ansprechpartnerln/Telefon
Zuse,K./0351/1201

Ihre Lieferantennummer bei uns
1003

Ihr(e) Sachbearbeiterln
Mr. Haberle

*Figure 2-32.  Output with form YCH02_04_MEDRUCK: PO No. 4500004823—I*

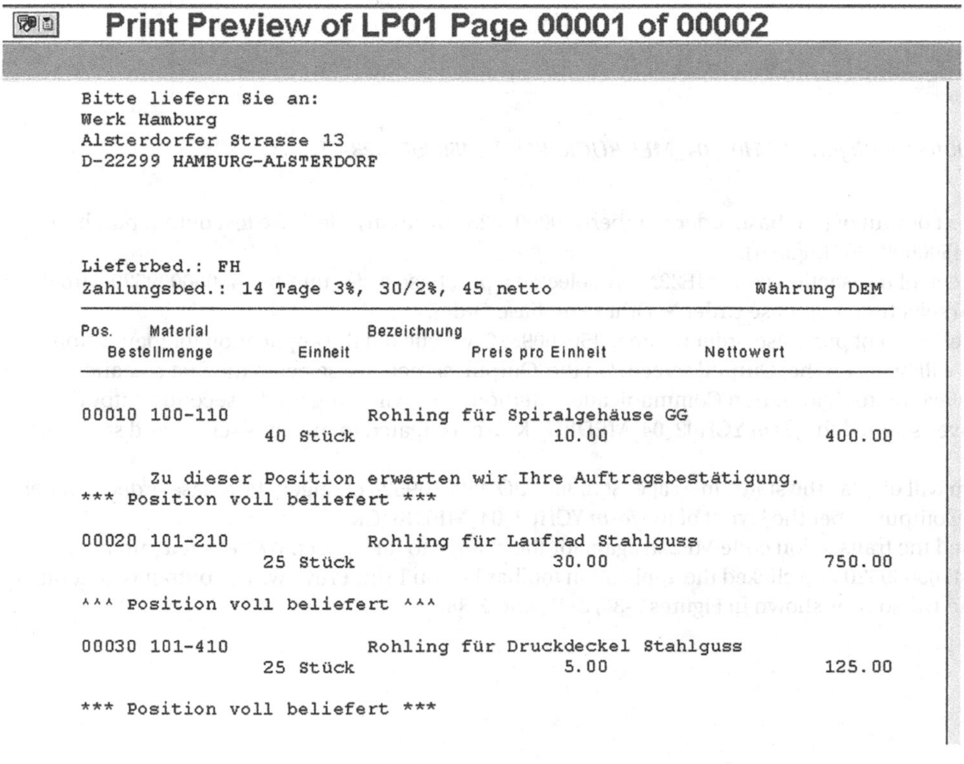

```
Bitte liefern Sie an:
Werk Hamburg
Alsterdorfer Strasse 13
D-22299 HAMBURG-ALSTERDORF




Lieferbed.: FH
Zahlungsbed.: 14 Tage 3%, 30/2%, 45 netto              Währung DEM

Pos.  Material          Bezeichnung
   Bestellmenge       Einheit      Preis pro Einheit      Nettowert
_____

00010 100-110          Rohling für Spiralgehäuse GG
                 40 Stück            10.00                   400.00

      Zu dieser Position erwarten wir Ihre Auftragsbestätigung.
*** Position voll beliefert ***

00020 101-210          Rohling für Laufrad Stahlguss
                 25 Stück            30.00                   750.00

^^^ Position voll beliefert ^^^

00030 101-410          Rohling für Druckdeckel Stahlguss
                 25 Stück             5.00                   125.00

*** Position voll beliefert ***
```

*Figure 2-33.  Output with form YCH02_04_MEDRUCK: PO No. 4500004823—II*

**Print Preview of LP01 Page 00002 of 00002**

```
Gusswerk US                          Bestellnummer/Datum              Seite
HARBOR CITY CA  70456                4500004823 / 01/08/1998  2
USA


Pos.   Material                Bezeichnung
       Bestellmenge            Einheit       Preis pro Einheit        Nettowert


00040 102-110                 Rohling für Spiralgehäuse Sphäroguss
                    28 Stück                    4.00                    112.00

*** Position voll beliefert ***


                       Gesamtnettowert ohne Mwst DEM              1,387.00
```

*Figure 2-34.* *Output with form YCH02_04_MEDRUCK: PO No. 4500004823—III*

**Print Preview of LP01 Page 00002 of 00002**

```
        EINTAUSENDDREIHUNDERTSIEBENUNDACHTZIG DEM 000
```

*Figure 2-35.* *Output with form YCH02_04_MEDRUCK: PO No. 4500004823—IV*

This was test output of purchase order number 4500004823 (German). Next, we test output purchase order number 4500009520 (English).

On the screen of transaction code ME22N, we selected a purchase order number 45000009520 with the following menu selection: Purchase Order ➤ Other Purchase Order.

After the selection of purchase order number 4500009520, we clicked the application toolbar button Messages. This will bring up the 'Output' screen. On the 'Output' screen, we selected the first row and clicked the application toolbar button Communication Method. This will bring up the second 'Output' screen, where we assigned the *form* YCH02_04_MEDRUCK. We navigated to previous screen and saved the purchase order.

The system will display the status message 'Standard PO 4500009520 changed'. Purchase order number: 4500000520 will output as per the layout of the *form* YCH02_04_MEDRUCK.

We executed the transaction code ME22n again for the change to take effect. We selected purchase order number 4500009520 and clicked the application toolbar button Print Preview. The output is generated in ten pages and will look as shown in Figures 2-36, 2-37, and 2-38.

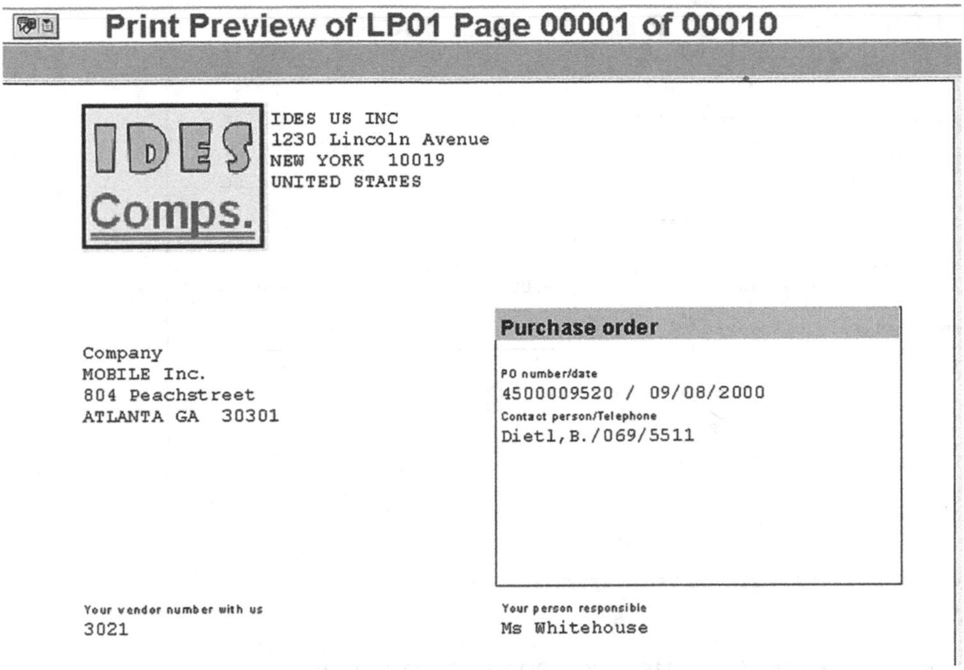

IDES US INC
1230 Lincoln Avenue
NEW YORK   10019
UNITED STATES

Company
MOBILE Inc.
804 Peachstreet
ATLANTA GA   30301

**Purchase order**

PO number/date
4500009520  /  09/08/2000
Contact person/Telephone
Dietl,B./069/5511

Your vendor number with us
3021

Your person responsible
Ms Whitehouse

*Figure 2-36.  Output with form YCH02_04_MEDRUCK: PO No. 4500009520—1/10*

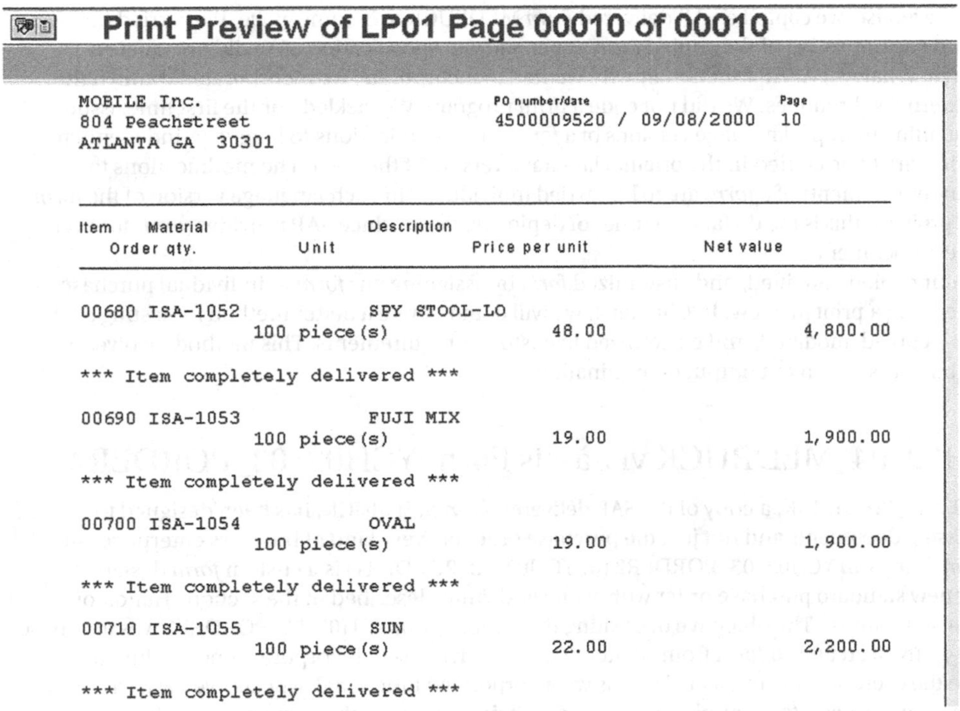

MOBILE Inc.
804 Peachstreet
ATLANTA GA   30301

PO number/date
4500009520 / 09/08/2000

Page
10

| Item | Material | Description | | | |
|------|----------|-------------|------|------|------|
| | Order qty. | Unit | Price per unit | | Net value |
| 00680 | ISA-1052 | SPY STOOL-LO | | | |
| | 100 piece(s) | | 48.00 | | 4,800.00 |
| *** Item completely delivered *** | | | | | |
| 00690 | ISA-1053 | FUJI MIX | | | |
| | 100 piece(s) | | 19.00 | | 1,900.00 |
| *** Item completely delivered *** | | | | | |
| 00700 | ISA-1054 | OVAL | | | |
| | 100 piece(s) | | 19.00 | | 1,900.00 |
| *** Item completely delivered *** | | | | | |
| 00710 | ISA-1055 | SUN | | | |
| | 100 piece(s) | | 22.00 | | 2,200.00 |
| *** Item completely delivered *** | | | | | |

*Figure 2-37.  Output with form YCH02_04_MEDRUCK: PO No. 4500009520—10/10*

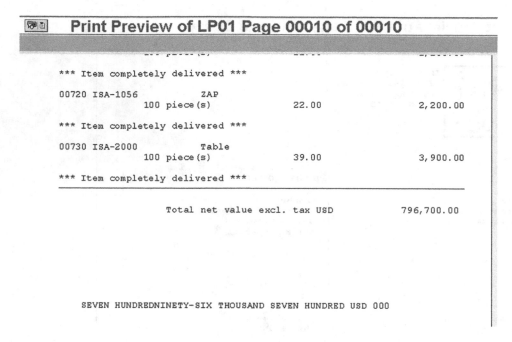

*Figure 2-38.* *Output with form YCH02_04_MEDRUCK: PO No. 4500009520—10/10*

## Hands-on Exercise Recapitulation

In this hands-on exercise, we copied a SAP delivered *form* MEDRUCK to Y namespace. We carried out modification and customization of the copied *form* as per laid-out specifications. We did not create a *form* from scratch. Whatever ABAP functionality we wanted to incorporate, we incorporated through the invocation of external subroutines. We did not code a print program. We tackled, for the first time, issues related to maintaining multiple language versions of a *form*. The modifications to language-independent elements of a *form* are to be carried in the original language version of the *form*. The modifications to language-dependent elements of a *form* are to be carried individually in each language version of the *form*. In real-life SAP projects, this is the de facto manner of deploying *forms*, since SAP provides *forms* for every standard business document.

We tested our copied, modified, and customized *form* by assigning our *form* to individual purchase orders and generating a print preview. In Chapter 4, we will demonstrate a better method for testing SAP delivered *forms*—copied, modified, and customized to customer requirements. This method involves a concept called business document output determination.

## Form YCH02_04_MEDRUCK vis-à-vis Form YCH02_03_PORDER2

The *form* YCH02_04_MEDRUCK, a copy of the SAP delivered *form* MEDRUCK, has been designed to produce purchasing documents and not just the purchase order of every kind of business enterprise—it is a generic *form*. The *form* YCH02_03_PORDER2 (or YCH02_02_PORDER1) is a custom *form* designed to produce just new standard purchase order with scope and limits described in the section "Hands-on Exercise—Scope and Limits." The objective of creating the custom *form* YCH02_03_PORDER2 was to expose you to the nitty-gritty of creating a *form* from scratch. The objective was to incorporate enough functional aspects to make the exercise fairly realistic. Even as we incorporated functional aspects, we have tried not to make the functional aspects too complex as to shift the main focus from the *form* complexities to the functional complexities.

In our custom *form* YCH02_03_PORDER2, the field EKPO-EBELP, the item number, is not appearing in the output. The field EKPO-EBELP is an important reference field and must appear in the purchasing document output. In our custom *form*, we are picking up the material description texts from the table MAKT. The material description texts in the purchasing document language are contained in the table EKPO itself. The field name is TXZ01. The form YCH_02_04_MEDRUCK is using this field to output material description texts.

The *form* YCH_02_04_MEDRUCK is checking and outputting the delivery status of each item. Our custom *form* is assuming the standard purchase being output to be new purchase orders without any deliveries.

The *form* YCH_02_04_MEDRUCK is using more than 70 database tables. You can check this out in the global data area of the print program SAPLMEDRUCK. We are using just 11 database tables in the print program of our custom *form* YCH02_03_PORDER2. I am trying to get across the fact that there is a substantial difference between a generic *form* and a custom *form*.

# Hands-on Exercise V—Output Customer-wise Sales Summary of a Company Code—Use SAP Script Form

To round off the hands-on exercises in this chapter, we will create a SAP script *form* and its corresponding print program which will produce a report much like a report produced by the features of classical reporting or ALV functionalities. We will create a *form* as a layout of a customer-wise sales summary and its corresponding print program. A report produced by a SAP script *form* should use the extra formatting features like different fonts and different font styling in different parts of the output, enclose outputs in box-like frames, impart shading effect, and so on. The usage of the extra formatting features of SAP script *forms* will warrant the deployment of SAP script *forms* over that of classical reporting or ALV functionalities.

## Output Specification and Layout

Let us assume that a customer-wise sales summary is required with the following specifications:

- The column headings and the body of the report should be enclosed in box-like frames.

- The column headings and the body of the report should appear in shaded backgrounds

- The column headings of the report should appear in bold font

Figure 2-39 shows a rough layout of the report.

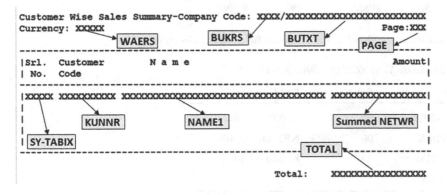

*Figure 2-39.* *Customer-wise sales summary—rough layout*

The number of Xs indicates the number of column positions for the field. The column headings and the body of the report will appear in a gray shaded background (not shown in this rough layout). The field names are marked. Most of the marked fields originate from tables. In the next section, "Data Inputs," the originating tables of the fields will be identified. Some of the marked fields do not originate from tables: PAGE is a SAP script system symbol, SY-TABIX is a system field, and TOTAL is a variable declared in the ABAP print program.

The output will be generated with data from the IDES server. The IDES server contains data for a number of company codes; each company code operates in a specific currency. So it becomes necessary to process and generate the customer-wise sales summary of a specified company code at a time separately. The print program can provide for input of company code for which the customer-wise sales summary is to be generated through a PARAMETERS statement.

We will proceed to the identification of inputs and the processing of input involved in producing an output as shown in Figure 2-39.

# Data Inputs

To produce the output of Figure 2-39, we will be required to access the following tables and their fields:

**Table 2-12.** *Tables and Their Fields Required to Output Customer-wise Sales Summary*

| Srl. No. | Table | Field | Field Description |
|---|---|---|---|
| 01 | T001 – Company code data | BUTXT | Company Code Name |
| 02 | | WAERS | Currency Key of Company Code |
| 03 | KNA1 Customer primary | KUNNR | Customer Code/Number |
| 04 | | NAME1 | Customer Name |
| 05 | VBRK-Billing document, header | BUKRS | Company Code |
| 06 | | NETWR | Total Net Amount |
| 07 | | KURRF | Exchange rate |

We are creating a database view YCH02_VBRK_KNA1 consisting of the tables VBRK and KNA1. The join conditions will be as follows:

| KNA1 | | VBRK | MANDT | = | KNA1 | MANDT |
|---|---|---|---|---|---|---|
| VBRK | | VBRK | KUNAG | = | KNA1 | KUNNR |

The *View Flds* tab of the database view has the following fields, shown in Table 2-13:

**Table 2-13.** *Fields in the Database View YCH02_VBRK_KNA1*

| Srl. No. | Field/Table | Srl. No. | Field/Table |
|---|---|---|---|
| 01 | MANDT / VBRK | 05 | BUKRS / VBRK |
| 02 | VBELN / VBRK | 06 | NETWR / VBRK |
| 03 | KUNNR / KNA1 | 07 | KURRF / VBRK |
| 04 | NAME1 / KNA1 | | |

The currency of each billing document can be different. We have to convert the amount NETWR of individual billing documents into the currency of the company code by multiplying the amount field NETWR with the exchange rate field KURRF With the converted amounts; we have to summarize the data customer-wise. We are using the COLLECT statement to generate customer-wise summarized sales data.

## SAP Script Form YCH02_05_SALESSUM

In transaction code SE71, we created the *form* YCH02_05_SALESSUM.

We will output customer-wise sales summary on DINA4 stationery in portrait mode—210 MM width and 297MM height.

We created a *page format* ONLY_PG with the default values. We assigned the next page for *page format* ONLY_PG as ONLY_PG. We created a *paragraph format* OP with default values. In the *basic settings* of the *form* attributes, we assigned the default paragraph as OP and assigned the first page as ONLY_PG.

We created a *character format* BL. We accepted all default values, including the font family as Courier and font size as 12 points. We enabled the bold Radio button. The *character format* BL will be applied to the column headings of the report to make them appear in bold lettering.

For the only *page format* ONLY_PG, we created the *windows* and their corresponding *page windows* as per the entries in Table 2-14. The horizontal dimensions of the *page windows* have been specified in characters (CH) and the vertical dimensions of the *page windows* have been specified in lines (LN).

*Table 2-14.* *Page Format ONLY_PG—Windows and Page Windows*

| Window & Page Window | Page Window Dimensions |
|---|---|
| 1.HEADING | Left margin : 5 CH<br>Upper margin : 1 LN<br>Window width : 73 CH<br>Window height : 7 LN |
| 2.MAIN | Left margin : 5 CH<br>Upper margin : 7 LN<br>Window width : 73 CH<br>Window height : 57 LN |
| 3.GTOTAL | Left margin : 5 CH<br>Upper margin : 64 LN<br>Window width : 73 CH<br>Window height : 2 LN |

The entries in the text elements *window*-wise will be as shown in the next sections.

## Text Element in Window HEADING

The following was entered in the *text element* area of the *window* HEADING:

```
* Customer Wise Sales Summary-Company Code: &T001-BUKRS&/&T001-BUTXT&
* Currency: &T001-WAERS&,,,,,,,,,,,,,,,,,,,,,,,,,,        Page:&PAGE(C3)&
/: POSITION YORIGIN 4 LN
/: BOX HEIGHT 61 LN FRAME 14 TW INTENSITY 8
/: BOX HEIGHT 3 LN FRAME 21 TW INTENSITY 16
*
* <BL> Srl.  Customer      N a m e</>
= <BL>                               Amount</>
* <BL> No.  Code</>
```

## Text Element in Window MAIN

The following was entered in the *text element* area of the *window* MAIN:

```
/E ITEM_DATA
*  &SRL_NO(Z5)& &CUST_SUMM_STRU-KUNNR(K10)& &CUST_SUMM_STRU-NAME1(35)&
=  &CUST_SUMM_STRU-NETWR(R17)&
```

The data to the main *window* has to be sent repeatedly with an explicit call of function module WRITE_FORM, hence naming of the *text element* with the /E ITEM_DATA in the main *window*.

## Text Element in Window TOTAL

The following was entered in the *text element* area of the *window* TOTAL:

```
/: IF &NEXTPAGE(C)& = '0'
*
*  ,,,,,,,,,,,,,,,,,,,,,,        Total: &TOTAL(17)&
/: ENDIF
```

After creation of the *form* elements as described, we saved the *form*. We assigned the package YCH_BC401. You can assign the same or any other non-local package of your choice.

We have un-named or default *text elements* in the following *windows*: HEADING and TOTAL. We have a named *text elements* in the main *window*.

# Print Program YCH02_05_PPRG_YCH02_05_SALESUM for SAP Script Form YCH02_05_SALESUM

We created an ABAP program YCH02_05_PPRG_YCH02_05_SALESUM. This will be the print program for the *form* YCH02_05_SALESUM. The source lines of the print program are as follows:

```
REPORT   YCH02_05_PPRG_YCH02_05_SALESUM.

**************************************************
* Print Program for Form: YCH02_05_SALESUM      **
* Customer Wise Sales Summary of a Company Code **
**************************************************

TYPES: BEGIN OF CUST_SUMM_TP,
        KUNNR       TYPE KUNNR,
        NAME1       TYPE NAME1_GP,
        KURRF       TYPE KURRF,
        NETWR       TYPE NETWR,
       END OF CUST_SUMM_TP.

TABLES: T001.

DATA: CUST_SUMM_TAB  TYPE STANDARD TABLE OF CUST_SUMM_TP,
      CUST_SUMM_STRU TYPE CUST_SUMM_TP,
      SRL_NO         TYPE SY-TABIX,
      TOTAL          TYPE NETWR.

************************************************************
PARAMETERS COMP_CD TYPE VBRK-BUKRS DEFAULT 3000 VALUE CHECK.

START-OF-SELECTION.

SELECT SINGLE * FROM T001 WHERE BUKRS = COMP_CD.

SELECT KUNNR NAME1 KURRF NETWR FROM YCH02_VBRK_KNA1 INTO
       CUST_SUMM_STRU WHERE BUKRS = COMP_CD.

 CUST_SUMM_STRU-NETWR = CUST_SUMM_STRU-NETWR * CUST_SUMM_STRU-KURRF.
 CUST_SUMM_STRU-KURRF = 0.

 COLLECT CUST_SUMM_STRU INTO CUST_SUMM_TAB.
ENDSELECT.

IF LINES( CUST_SUMM_TAB ) = 0.
 MESSAGE S001(YCH02_MCLASS) DISPLAY LIKE 'E'. "No Data
 EXIT.
ENDIF.
```

```
SORT CUST_SUMM_TAB BY KUNNR.

CALL FUNCTION 'OPEN_FORM'
 EXPORTING
    FORM                          = 'YCH02_05_SALESUM'
    LANGUAGE                      = 'E'
         .
IF SY-SUBRC <> 0.
 MESSAGE ID SY-MSGID TYPE SY-MSGTY NUMBER SY-MSGNO
         WITH SY-MSGV1 SY-MSGV2 SY-MSGV3 SY-MSGV4.
ENDIF.

CALL FUNCTION 'START_FORM'
 EXPORTING
    FORM                 = 'YCH02_05_SALESUM'
    LANGUAGE             = 'E'
         .
IF SY-SUBRC <> 0.
 MESSAGE ID SY-MSGID TYPE SY-MSGTY NUMBER SY-MSGNO
         WITH SY-MSGV1 SY-MSGV2 SY-MSGV3 SY-MSGV4.
ENDIF.

LOOP AT CUST_SUMM_TAB INTO CUST_SUMM_STRU.
 SRL_NO = SY-TABIX.
 TOTAL = TOTAL + CUST_SUMM_STRU-NETWR.

 CALL FUNCTION 'WRITE_FORM'
  EXPORTING
     ELEMENT                      = 'ITEM_DATA'
     WINDOW                       = 'MAIN'
          .
 IF SY-SUBRC <> 0.
  MESSAGE ID SY-MSGID TYPE SY-MSGTY NUMBER SY-MSGNO
          WITH SY-MSGV1 SY-MSGV2 SY-MSGV3 SY-MSGV4.
 ENDIF.

ENDLOOP.
************************************

CALL FUNCTION 'END_FORM'
         .
IF SY-SUBRC <> 0.
 MESSAGE ID SY-MSGID TYPE SY-MSGTY NUMBER SY-MSGNO
         WITH SY-MSGV1 SY-MSGV2 SY-MSGV3 SY-MSGV4.
ENDIF.
```

```
CALL FUNCTION 'CLOSE_FORM'
        .
IF SY-SUBRC <> 0.
 MESSAGE ID SY-MSGID TYPE SY-MSGTY NUMBER SY-MSGNO
         WITH SY-MSGV1 SY-MSGV2 SY-MSGV3 SY-MSGV4.
ENDIF.
*****End Program *****
```

We saved, performed a syntax, check and activated the program.

## Check and Activate Form

In transaction code SE71, we performed a *form* definition check as well as the *form* texts check on the *form* YCH02_05_SALESUM and activated it.

The *form* YCH02_05_SALESUM and the source program YCH02_05_PPRG_YCH02_05_SALESUM are available for upload in the E-resource file for this book (www.apress.com/9781484212345).

## Output

We executed the program YCH02_05_PPRG_YCH02_05_SALESUM. We executed it with the company code 3000. The company code 3000 has substantial billing document data. The output will look as shown in Figures 2-40, 2-41, and 2-42.

### Print Preview of LP01 Page 00001 of 00002

```
Customer Wise Sales Summary-Company Code: 3000/IDES US INC
Currency: USD                                          Page:1
```

| Srl. No. | Customer Code | N a m e | Amount |
|---|---|---|---|
| 1 | 0000000255 | Emma Bull | 2,207.00 |
| 2 | 0000000257 | John Evans | 2,299.00 |
| 3 | 0000000258 | Roger Zahn | 1,912.00 |
| 4 | 0000000260 | Chelsa Quinn Yates | 2,124.00 |
| 5 | 0000000262 | Robert Jensen | 3,720.00 |
| 6 | 0000000266 | Charles Scott | 2,995.00 |
| 7 | 0000000272 | Joe Masson | 748.00 |
| 8 | 0000000281 | Tracy Collins | 1,567.50 |
| 9 | 0000000470 | Alex Lynch | 11,860.80 |
| 10 | 0000000471 | Steve Martin | 8,415.50 |
| 11 | 0000000473 | Albert Brooks | 10,911.80 |
| 12 | 0000000474 | Edward Burns | 12,427.70 |
| 13 | 0000000481 | Peter King | 10,542.10 |
| 14 | 0000000482 | Douglas Barker | 1,614.26 |
| 15 | 0000000504 | Janett Adams | 2,957.16 |
| 16 | 0000000505 | David Lynch | 366.00 |
| 17 | 0000001508 | Deutsche Computer AG | 3,012.50 |
| 18 | 0000003000 | Thomas Bush Inc. | 7,602.00 |
| 19 | 0000003001 | Industrial Supplies Inc. | 4,320.00 |
| 20 | 0000003028 | Live Insurance Inc. | 12,038.25 |
| 21 | 0000003034 | Insurance Company | 299.00 |
| 22 | 0000003060 | Candid International Technology | 28,089.25 |
| 23 | 0000003221 | Andyna and Dynana Laboratories, Inc | 6,153.60 |
| 24 | 0000003250 | Department of Defense | 50,000.00 |
| 25 | 0000003251 | Palo Alto Airways Inc. | 202,496.00 |
| 26 | 0000003261 | Hotel Alfonso Del Vida | 3,571.00 |

*Figure 2-40. Customer-wise sales summary: company code 30000—1/2*

**Print Preview of LP01 Page 00002 of 00002**

```
Customer Wise Sales Summary-Company Code: 3000/IDES US INC
Currency: USD                                              Page:2

Srl.   Customer    N a m e                             Amount
No.    Code

58     0000300719  Hall Manufacturing             12,313,262.00
59     0000301090  Townsend Company                    2,350.00
60     0000401075  LORI WINTER                           862.00
61     0000401076  MARIE WITENBURG                       862.00
62     0000401078  MARIE ZDROK                           862.00
63     0000401079  LORI ZINNY                            862.00
64     0000401081  JANET ZUSSIN                          862.00
65     0000401082  JANE CASTILLO                         862.00
66     0000401083  JANE SANCHEZ                          862.00
67     0000401258  ALAN FAITH                            862.00
68     0000401259  JIM FARAIZL                           862.00
69     0000401260  ALAN FARRAR                           862.00
70     0000401262  JAMES FERENCY                         862.00
71     0000401263  BILL FERNANCE                       3,165.10
72     0000401264  BILL FERRARA                          862.00
73     0000401266  ALAN FINER                            862.00
74     0000401267  JAMES GRUPER                          862.00
75     0000401268  JOHN GRÖNROS                          862.00
76     0000401269  ALAN GUETTEL                          862.00
77     0000401270  BEN GUIER                             862.00
78     0000401272  ALAN GWARA                            862.00
79     A300015     IDES AG                             2,000.00
80     CMS0000001  Crocodile Enterprise                4,495.00
81     IDESCUST    IDES Customer                      21,000.00
```

*Figure 2-41.* *Customer-wise sales summary: company code 30000—2/2*

```
                         Total:     54,469,355.10
```

*Figure 2-42.* *Customer-wise sales summary: company code 30000—2/2 total*

## Hands-on Exercise Recapitulation

In this hands-on exercise, we created a *form* and a print program and required workbench objects to produce not a business document but a report—customer-wise sales summary of a specific company code. The source of data of the report was the tables VBRK (billing document header), KNA1 (customer primary), and T001 (company code). The *form* consisted of a variable *window* with the corresponding *page window* to output the report heading. The body of the report was located in the *page window* assigned to the main *window*. A second variable *window* with its *page window* was used to output the total. The report column heading was produced in bold lettering. The report column heading and body was enclosed in a box-like frame with background shading.

While processing data for the report, we did not filter out or skip billing document data not relating to actual sales like pro forma invoices, etc. (VBTYP = 'U', etc.). In the training and teaching paradigm we are in, this can be overlooked. If you are very particular, you can incorporate the condition to skip the data not relating to actual sales in the WHERE condition of SELECT statement as follows:

```
SELECT KUNNR NAME1 KURRF NETWR FROM YCH02_VBRK_KNA1 INTO
    CUST_SUMM_STRU WHERE BUKRS = COMP_CD
    AND VBTYP NE 'U' AND.....
```

# Classifying Forms

In Chapter 1, in the section "Forms: Searching and classification," I mentioned that the SAP delivered ready-to-use *forms* residing in client 000 are assigned to classifications and subclassifications based on functional modules and submodules with which the *form* is associated. These classifications and subclassifications are presented as nodes and subnodes in a tree-like hierarchical structure. At the leaf level (lowest level, no further subnodes) the SAP script *forms* are assigned. These classifications and subclassifications are to be used by SAP functional consultants to locate a particular *form*. The tree-like hierarchical structure is called the *form* tree.

All the nine *forms* we created until now have been located under the unclassified *forms* node by default. We will now re-locate these nine forms from the unclassified node to nodes and subnodes which we will now create.

We can totally manipulate the *form* tree to our requirements: insert, edit, move, and delete nodes and subnodes. In the present instance, we will create a node at the highest level named 'My Node.' Under this node, we will create two subnodes: 'Demonstration Exercises' and 'Hands-on Exercises.' Under the subnode 'Demonstration Exercises,' we will re-locate the four *forms* we created in Chapter 1. Under the subnode 'Hands-on Exercises,' we will re-locate the five *forms* we created in Chapter 2. Figure 2-43 shows our part of the proposed *form* tree.

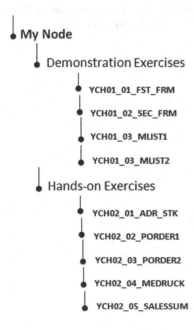

*Figure 2-43.* *Proposed part of own form tree*

We have termed the subnodes under the two sub nodes "Demonstration Exercises" and "Hands-on Exercises" as sub-subnodes. Let us go about creating our nodes, subnodes, and sub-subnodes. A prerequisite to locating *forms* under nodes other than the unclassified node is that they should have been assigned non-local packages. When we created the *forms* in Chapter 1 and this chapter, we assigned the package YCH_BC401 to all the *forms* to enable us to re-locate our *forms* under nodes other than an unclassified node.

To manipulate the *form* tree, we can navigate from the opening screen of transaction code SE71—menu selection: Utilities(M) ➤ Classify Multiple Forms. Alternatively, we can navigate from the change screen of a specific *form*—menu selection: Forms ➤ Classify. We made the following menu selection, Utilities(M) ➤ Classify Multiple Forms, from the opening screen of SE71 screen. The system popped up the following alert:

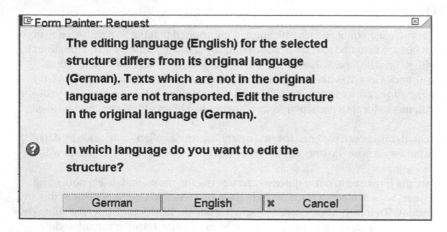

**Figure 2-44.** *Alert—classify multiple forms*

We selected the English language. The *form* tree screen appeared. On the *form* tree screen, we made the following menu selection: Edit ➤ Insert Node ➤. Add to same level as shown in Figure 2-45.

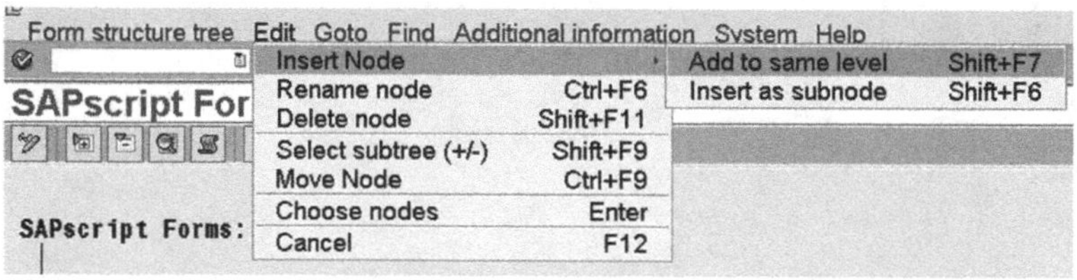

**Figure 2-45.** *Form tree—menu selection to create node*

When this menu selection was made, the dialog box shown in Figure 2-46 appeared.

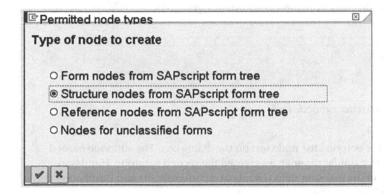

*Figure 2-46. Form tree—create node: select node type*

We selected the Radio button with nomenclature Structure nodes from SAP script *form* tree and clicked the Continue button. A dialog box to input the node text or node name appeared as shown in Figure 2-47.

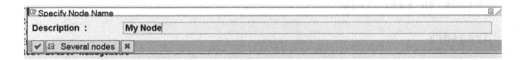

*Figure 2-47. Form tree—create node: enter node text*

After entering the node text, we clicked the Continue button on the dialog box. The node named My Node was created. Next, we selected this node and made the menu selection Edit ➤ Insert Node ➤ Insert as a subnode. Figure 2-48 shows the menu selection.

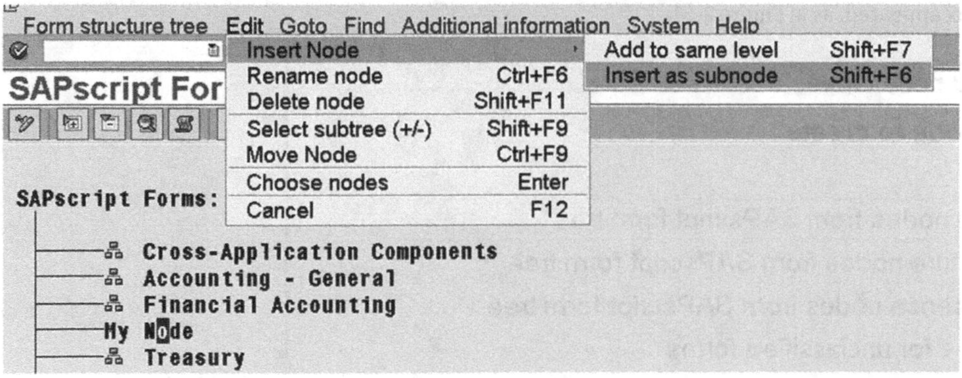

*Figure 2-48. Form tree—menu selection to create subnode*

With this menu selection, the dialog box as shown in Figure 2-46 appeared. We again selected the Radio button with nomenclature Structure nodes from SAP script *form* tree and clicked the Continue button. A dialog box to input the node text or node name appeared as shown in Figure 2-49:

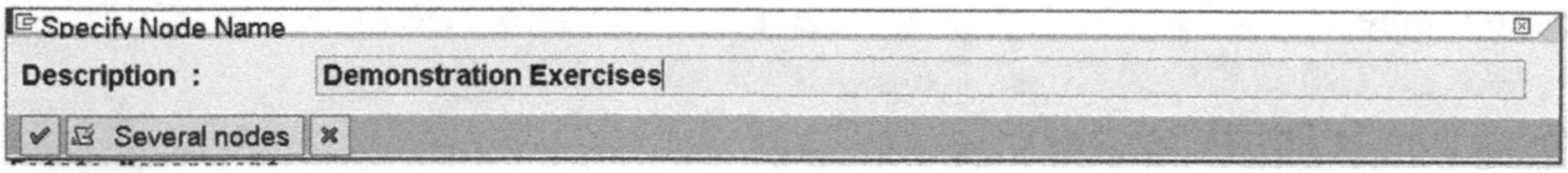

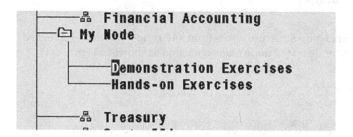

***Figure 2-49.*** *Form tree—create sub node: enter subnode text*

We clicked the Continue button after entering the node text on the dialog box. The subnode named Demonstration Exercises was created. In a similar manner, we created the second subnode, Hands-on Exercises. The screen after the creation of the two subnodes (Demonstration Exercises and Hands-on Exercises) will look as shown in Figure 2-50.

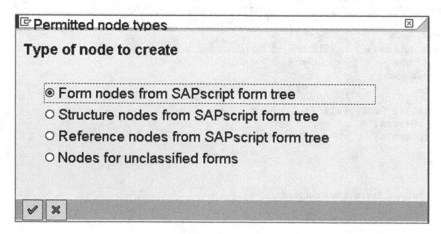

***Figure 2-50.*** *Form tree—a node, two subnodes created*

Next, we have to create the sub-subnodes corresponding to each of the four *forms* under the subnode Demonstration Exercises. And we have to create sub-subnodes corresponding to each of five *forms* under the subnode Hands-on Exercises. First, we will create sub-subnodes under the subnode Demonstration Exercises. So we positioned the cursor on the subnode Demonstration Exercises and made the menu selection Edit ➤ Insert Node ➤ Insert as subnode. When we made this menu selection, a Permitted node types dialog box appeared, as in Figure 2-51.

***Permitted node types***

**Type of node to create**

⊙ Form nodes from SAPscript form tree
○ Structure nodes from SAPscript form tree
○ Reference nodes from SAPscript form tree
○ Nodes for unclassified forms

***Figure 2-51.*** *Form tree—create a node type: form nodes from SAP script form tree*

We selected the first Radio button, as we want this node to be assigned a *form* (lowest level of *form* tree) We clicked the Continue button. A dialog box for input of *form* name appeared. We entered the name of the *form* as YCH02_01_FST_FRM. Figure 2-52 illustrates.

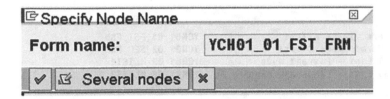

*Figure 2-52. Form tree—create a node type: form nodes from SAP script form tree and assign form name*

We clicked the Continue button. The sub-subnode was created. In a similar manner, we created three more sub-subnodes under the subnode Demonstration Exercises corresponding to the *forms* YCH01_02_SEC_FRM, YCH01_03_MLIST1 and YCH01_04_MLIST2. The screen after the creation of these four sub-subnodes will look as shown in Figure 2-53.

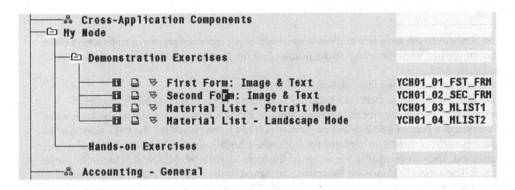

*Figure 2-53. Form tree—four sub-subnodes created*

We shifted the node My Node up. We used the third button from the right on the application toolbar to select the node. We used the first button from the right to move the node after selection. Against the sub-subnode, the short text/description of the *form* appears. The name of the *form* appears to the right of the short text. The name of the *form* is termed the "technical name." The fourth button from the left on the application toolbar acts as a toggle to make the technical name appear or disappear.

In a similar manner, we created five sub-subnodes under the subnode Hands-on Exercises. The five sub-subnodes correspond to the *forms* YCH02_01_ADR_STK, YCH02_02_PORDER1, YCH02_03_PORDER2, YCH02_04_MEDRUCK, and YCH02_05_SALESSUM.

The screen after the creation of the nine sub-subnodes will look as shown in Figure 2-54.

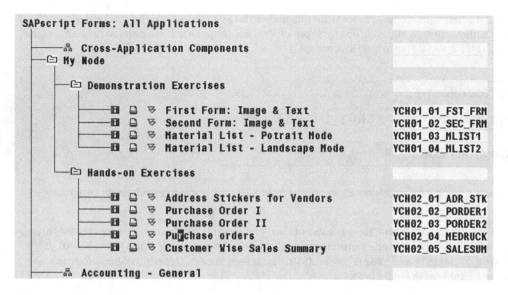

**Figure 2-54.** *Form tree—nine sub-subnodes created*

We saved the changes to the *form* tree and navigated back to the opening screen of transaction code SE71. We have accomplished what we set out to do: manipulate the *form* tree to incorporate nodes and subnodes as per Figure 2-43.

This was a demonstration of the manipulation of the *form* tree.

When you open a SAP delivered *form* (like MEDRUCK) using transaction code SE71, the field *classification* on the *form's Administrative data* screen contains blanks. When you open a custom-created or -customized version of a copy of a SAP delivered *form* which has been classified, the field *classification* on the *form's Administrative data* screen contains the immediate higher-level subnode to which the *form* has been assigned. You can verify this. We assigned the form YCH02_04_MEDRUCK to the subnode Hands-on Exercises. The subnode Hands-on Exercises is assigned to the node My Node. When you view the *Administrative settings* screen of the *form* YCH02_04_MEDRUCK, the field *classification* contains the value of the immediate higher-level subnode, that is, Hands-on Exercises. Figure 2-55 illustrates.

## Form: Change Header: YCH02_04_MEDRUCK

| Pages | Windows | Page Windows | Paragraph Formats | Character Formats | ■ |

| Administrative Data | | Basic Settings |

**Administration Information**

| Form | `YCH02_04_MEDRUCK` |
| Meaning | `Purchase orders` |
| Status | `Active - Saved` |

> Immediate Higher Level Sub Node: 'Hands-on Exercises'

| Classification | `Hands-on Exercises` |
| Package | `YCH_BC401` |
| Client ID | `800` |

**Figure 2-55.** *Form YCH_02_04_MEDRUCK—Value in the field: Classification*

This concludes the brief on *form* tree.

# SAP Script Form Documentation

The SAP script *documentation* is a language-dependent element or component of SAP script *forms*. The other language-dependent element of SAP script *forms* was *text element*. Being language dependent, the *documentation* has to be entered and maintained individually for each language version of the *form*. In the *documentation* area, the developer can provide detailed technical documentation for a *form*.

The SAP script *form* maintenance system by default generates or creates skeletal template *documentation* as the *form* is created and modified. This template *documentation* consists of subheadings for the *form*, each of the *page formats*, *windows*, and named *text elements*. The name of the *form* and its elements, *page formats*, *windows*, and named *text elements* appear in the first line of the subheading and are not editable The short texts entered during the creation of the *form and its* elements, *page formats*, and *windows* appear in the second line of the subheadings of the template *documentation* and are editable. There are no subheadings for the *form* elements *paragraph formats* and *character formats* in the template *documentation*. The developer can add text under the generated template subheadings and can insert and add further subheadings and text.

To reach the *documentation* area of a *form* from the opening screen of the SE71 transaction, select the last Radio button and click the change or display button. To reach the *documentation* area of a *form* from within the *form* screen, make the following menu selection: Goto ➤ Forms Documentation. The *documentation* area is identical to the *text element* area of a *form*.

We created *documentation* for the *form* YCH02_02_PORDER1. It is not comprehensive but will serve as a demonstration. Figure 2-56 shows the initial part of the *documentation*. The subheadings for the *form*, *page formats* FIRST and NEXT, and *window* CONSIGNE are marked in the Figure 2-56.

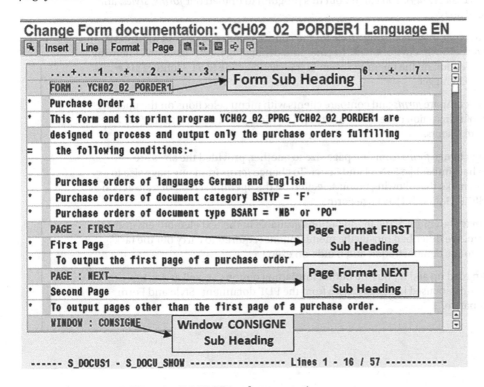

*Figure 2-56.* *Form YCH02_02_PORDER1—documentation*

When you delete a *form* element like a *page format* or a *window* or a *text element*, the *form* element *documentation* text along with the subheading gets deleted in the original language version of the *form*. But the deletion of a *form* element like a *page format* or a *window* or a *text element* does not delete the *form* element *documentation* text along with the subheading in the language versions of *form* other than the original language version. In the language versions other than the original language version of the *form*, only after deletion of the *documentation* text under the subheading is deleted does the subheading get deleted.

You can delete all of the entered *documentation* text in a specific language version of a *form* with the following menu selection: Utilities(M) ➤ Documentation ➤ Delete.

You can print or print preview the *documentation* of a specific language version of a *form* with the following menu selection: Utilities(M) ➤ Documentation ➤ Print.

You can try out the following menu selection: Utilities(M) ➤ Documentation ➤ Clean Up.

You can look up the *documentation* of the copy of SAP delivered *form* YCH02_04_MEDRUCK. A major portion of the *documentation* text is contained under the main *window* subheading.

# SAP Script Tidbits

Following are some miscellaneous tidbits of SAP script *forms*:

- You can download *forms*, *styles*, and *standard texts* to the application server or presentation server files. These downloaded files can be ported to or uploaded into other systems. The downloading of *forms*, *styles*, and *standard texts* to files and subsequent uploading of these files to other systems is enabled with the ABAP program RSTXSCRP. We have used this program to download our *forms*, *styles*, and *standard texts* to make them part of our E-resource file for this book (www.apress. com/9781484212345). You can try out this program to upload our *forms*, *styles*, and *standard texts*.

- You can enter into debugging mode for the control commands issued in the SAP script *text element* environment. To enter into debugging mode, make the following menu selection on the opening screen of transaction code SE71: Utilities(M) ➤ Activate Debugger.

- You can compare *forms* and compare clients with menu selections on the opening screen of transaction code SE71: Utilities(M) ➤ Compare Forms, Utilities(M) ➤ Compare Clients.

- You can change *forms* from one page size to another, provided the sizes are somewhat similar like DINA4 and Letter. To change *forms* from one page size to another, make the following menu selection on the opening screen of transaction code SE71: Utilities(M) ➤ Page Format.

- You can try out more of the menu options available in the text element environment of a form. We described mostly the menu options required to carry out the tasks related to the demonstration and hands-on exercises.

- You can read up and try out the output formatting options as well as control commands not used in our exercises from the PDF document "Style and Form Maintenance."

# Conclusion

For the most part, this chapter consisted of implementations of specific business scenarios using the SAP script concepts and features introduced and described in Chapter 1. I called the implementation of the business scenarios hands-on exercises. We performed five hands-on exercises in this chapter.

In the first hands-on exercise, we created a *form*, a print program, and other required workbench objects to produce vendors' address labels for a specific company code.

In the second hands-on exercise, we created a *form*, a print program, and other required workbench objects to output standard purchase orders. The speciality or peculiarity of the *form* was that it can generate multiple language outputs with a single language version of the *form*. This was implemented through all text in the *text element* area of the *form* originating from the data element text.

In the third hands-on exercise, we extended the *form* of the second hands-on exercise to demonstrate how to incorporate ABAP program functionality by calling an external subroutine from within the *form's text element* environment.

The fourth hands-on exercise modified and customized a copy of the SAP delivered *form* MEDRUCK to output purchasing documents. The modifications and customizations were carried out as per laid-out specifications. The output was tested by assigning individual *forms* to purchasing documents in transaction code ME22N.

The fifth hands-on exercise involved a *form* to output a customer-wise sales summary of a specific company code. The hands-on exercise demonstrated that a list normally produced with reporting features like ABAP WRITE statement and ALV functionalities can also be produced using a *form* and a print program.

We concluded the chapter with the following:

- A description of manipulating the SAP script *form* tree.

- A description of the *form* element *documentation*. The *form* element *documentation* is language dependent like the *form* element *text element*.

- SAP script *form* miscellaneous tidbits

# CHAPTER 3

■ ■ ■

# Smartforms—Forms, Styles, and Text Modules

Smartforms, like SAP script, is also a tool for the presentation of business data. Smartforms is a kind of enhancement of SAP script and has more facilities and features than SAP script. But since Smartforms, like SAP script, is used to achieve the same ends——create and maintain business document layouts—I will describe the features of Smartforms vis-à-vis the SAP script. I will assume that you are familiar and conversant with the SAP script features: that you have perused the first two chapters of this book and performed all the demonstration and hands-on exercises in those chapters.

Smartforms, like the SAP script, has the same three components.

- Forms

- Styles

- Text modules (equivalent of standard texts in SAP scripts)

As in case of SAP scripts, we are going to focus primarily on the *form* component of Smartforms.

We will be performing the same demonstration and hands-on exercises we performed in Chapters 1 and 2 in the coverage of SAP scripts. As I will be describing the Smartforms *forms* features on a basis parallel to the SAP script *forms* features, I will start off by (1) highlighting the major similarities and differences of SAP script *forms* and Smartforms *forms,* (2) describing the extra features and facilities in Smartforms compared to those of SAP script, and (3) listing the objects created in in SAP script environment which are also available for use in Smartforms environment.

SAP in its documentation uses the term Smart Forms. I am using the term Smartforms. Let both these terms be considered as synonymous.

## SAP script and Smartforms—Similarities and Differences

The SAP script *form* element *header* is similar to the Smartforms *form* element *form attributes*. The Smartforms *form* element *form attributes* does not have the ability to specify page orientation: portrait/landscape.

The SAP script *form* element *page* (which we referred as *page format*) is identical to the Smartforms *form* element *page*. In this chapter and in Chapter 4, I will refer to the Smartforms *form* element *page* as *page format*. The Smartforms *form* element *page format* has the ability to specify page orientation: portrait/landscape.

The SAP script *form* element *text element* is identical to the Smartforms *form* element *text*. In fact, you can operate the same text editor in Smartforms *forms* as the text editor you operated in SAP script *forms*. The control commands of SAP script *form* environment are not available in the Smartforms *form* environment. In some places the Smartforms *form* element *text* is referred to as *text element*. I will refer to the Smartforms *form* element *text* as *text*.

© Sushil Markandeya 2017
S. Markandeya, *Pro SAP Scripts, Smartforms, and Data Migration,*
https://doi.org/10.1007/978-1-4842-3183-8_3

Equivalent to the SAP script *form* element *documentation* is the Smartforms *form* element *form information*. The Smartforms *form* element *form information* is generated totally by the Smartforms *form* maintenance system, there is no facility for the developer to modify or change the *form information* generated by the Smartforms *form* maintenance system.

A Smartforms *form* cannot have *paragraph formats* and *character formats* defined within it. The *paragraph formats* and *character formats* can only be defined within Smartforms *styles*. Smartforms *styles* can be assigned at different levels of a *form* like at the level of a *form, text,* and so on. The *paragraph formats* and *character formats* of assigned Smartforms *styles* can be applied to *texts* of a Smartforms *form*.

The SAP script *form* elements *windows* and *page windows* are combined into one element in the Smartforms *forms* and are called *windows*. The element *window* in a Smartforms *form* is equivalent to the element *page window* in a SAP script *form*. So the element *window* of a *form* in Smartforms is a physical area of a *page format* defined by a left margin, an upper margin, a *window* width, and a *window* height.

The formatting facilities in SAP script *form* element *text elements* are available in the Smartforms *form* *text* environment (zero suppression: (Z), space compression: (C), right-justification (R), etc.). You can find a complete list of formatting options in the table *Formatting Options for Fields* of the manual BC-SRV-SCR.

The main *window* in a SAP script *form* can have multiple *page windows*. We used this feature very effectively to output repetitive data down and across as well as across and down as demonstrated in demonstration IV in Chapter 1 and hands-on exercise I in Chapter 2. The ability in the main *window* to output repetitive data across is not available in the Smartforms *forms*. You can output repetitive data only down and not across in the main *window* of Smartforms *forms*. This is because the Smartforms *forms* do not contain an element equivalent of *windows* of SAP script *forms*.

A Smartforms *form* has lot more elements, which will introduced and described in detail at a later stage.

When a Smartforms *form* is activated, a function module is generated. This generated function module has to be called from an ABAP program which we will call the driver program in the context of Smartforms (called an application program in the manual BC-SRV-SCR). The ABAP program was called print program in the context of SAP script. Since the Smartforms *form's* interaction with the driver program is via calling the generated function module, the Smartforms *form* has a parameter interface similar to a function module parameter interface. So a Smartforms *form* can receive data from the driver program of all data types: elementary, structured, and internal tables. Recall, a SAP script *form* could receive only elementary data from the print program.

There is no facility of classification and subclassification of Smartforms *forms* from within the *forms* environment, so there is no organization of Smartforms *forms* into a *forms* tree to facilitate location of *forms* by functional consultants.

The Smartforms *forms* and *styles,* unlike the SAP script *form* and *styles,* and like all workbench objects, is cross client. The Smartforms *forms* and *styles* have no relationship with the client.

You cannot open different language versions of Smartforms *form* or *style* as you could for SAP script *forms* and *styles*. To open a specific language version of a Smartforms *form* or *style*, you should be logged into the language.

# Extra Features and Facilities in Smartforms over SAP Script

A *form* of Smartforms is represented as a graphical tree. Elements of a *form* are organized in a tree-like hierarchical structure with nodes and subnodes. *Form* elements (i.e., tree nodes and subnodes) can be cut, copied, pasted, dragged, and dropped like in any graphic environment.

You can impart color to texts. When you select font family, font size, and so on, in the Smartforms *style* environment, you can assign color to a font. A maximum of 64 colors is available. A preview of fonts is also available.

A Smartforms *form* has a *global definition* area. In this *global definition* area, you can declare your own types as you do in an ABAP program with the TYPES statement. You can also declare, in the *global definition* area, data objects of all types: elementary, structured, internal tables, etc. These data objects declared in the *global definition* area of a *form* can be used anywhere within the *form*. Since internal tables can be declared in the *global definition* area of a *form* and internal tables can be parameters of a *form*, there are facilities or constructs to process internal tables—LOOP AT.....within a *form*. You can also define field-symbols in the *global definition* area of a *form* and use them anywhere in a *form*. You can locate subroutines (*form* routines) in the *global definition* area of a *form* and invoke them from anywhere in a *form*.

Within a Smartforms *form*, you can create nodes for incorporation of ABAP code. This ABAP code goes beyond the control commands in a SAP script *form* environment. For example, you could not call a function module from within a SAP script *form*. But you can call/invoke function modules from within a Smartforms *form*. You cannot use a SELECT statement within a SAP script *form*. But you can use a SELECT statement within a Smartforms *form*, and so on.

You output variables in the Smartforms *form* environment in the same manner you outputted variables in the SAP script *form* environment: by enclosing the variable in ampersands (&). In the SAP script *form* environment, you could refer to the variables only by enclosing them in ampersands—called program symbol, text symbol and so on. The value of a variable enclosed in ampersands is the value as it is output, not as it is internally stored. In the Smartforms *form* environment, you will refer to variables in nodes of ABAP code without enclosing them in ampersands and the value is the value as it is internally stored (as in a normal ABAP program).

Before a Smartforms *form* commences processing, the Smartforms runtime system jumps to the INITIALIZATION event of the *form*. In this INITIALIZATION event, you can locate substantial ABAP code including code for retrieving data: SELECT.....statements.

The Smartforms *form* has the elements *tables* and *templates* to output repetitive data in a formalized manner.

The Smartforms *form* can be used with ABAP web dynpro to input data.

You can generate XML output with a Smartforms *form*.

# SAP Script Objects Available in Smartforms Environment

The following objects created and maintained in the SAP script environment are available in the Smartforms environment:

The BMP/TIFF operating system graphic files imported into the SAP document server using transaction code SE78 are available for incorporation in the Smartforms environment.

The font families, with their sizes, styling, etc., assigned to the installed printer devices in the SAP script environment are available in the Smartforms environment. That is, SAP delivered font families as well as the font families installed through transaction code SE73 and assigned to installed printer devices are available in the Smartforms environment.

The bar codes, SAP delivered, as well as the bar codes installed through transaction code SE73 and assigned to installed printer devices are available in the Smartforms environment.

Texts (long texts) are maintained as *text modules* in the Smartforms environment. The *text module* is parallel or equivalent to the *standard texts* in SAP scripts. A *text module* can be incorporated into other *text modules* and Smartforms *forms*. You can also incorporate the SAP script component *standard* texts maintained with transaction code SO10 into *text modules* and Smartforms *forms*.

# Smartforms *Form* Elements and Smartforms *Form* Environment

Our discussions and descriptions will focus on the *form* element of Smartforms. The two other Smartforms elements—*styles* and *text modules*—do not need to be explained elaborately. As and when we create *styles* and *text modules*, I will describe them and the descriptions accompanying their creation will suffice. I followed a similar approach when covering SAP scripts in Chapter 1.

Mostly, we will refer to the Smartforms *form* as just *form*.

As we mentioned earlier, the *form* and its elements appear as nodes and subnodes of a hierarchical tree. I will introduce and explain the *form* elements and *form* environment through a copy of the SAP delivered purchasing document *form* YSM_SMB40_MMPO_A (original *form* name /SMB40/MMPO_A). I am resorting to the use of a copy of the original since the original will not permit the operation of context menus. The objective is not for you to completely understand the working of the *form* YSM_SMB40_MMPO_A. The objective is to present the *form* elements and environment in a non-abstract context. By the time you are through with the tour of the *form* YSM_SMB40_MMPO_A, you will have a fair idea of its operation.

When you open this *form* in edit mode, the initial screen presented to the developer will look like the one in Figure 3-1.

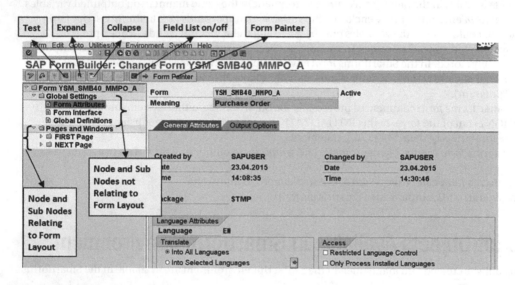

**Figure 3-1.** *Form YSM_SMB40_MMPO_A—Initial Screen*

As you can see, the *form* tree appears on the left. Attributes or information related to the selected *form* tree node appears on the right. Attributes or information related to the selected *form* tree node might be contained in more than one tab screen. A detailed description of the different areas of this screen follows.

As you can see in Figure 3-1, there are two main nodes in the hierarchical Smartforms *form* tree: (1) *Global Settings* and (2) *Pages and Windows*. An elaborate description of these two nodes along with the associated environment follows.

## Application Toolbar

Following is a description of the application toolbar:

- The first button from the left is the universal button to toggle between change and display modes.

- The second button from the left is the universal button for syntax check.

- The third button from the left is the universal button to activate .

- The fourth button from the left is for testing a *form* from within the *form* environment.

- The fifth button from the left is to expand a node/subnode.

- The sixth button from the left is to collapse a node/subnode.

- The second button from the right is to make the field list appear/disappear. The field list contains all the fields declared in the global definitions, fields from *form interface parameters* and the Smartforms system fields. The field list appears in the bottom left corner.

- The first button from the right is to make the *form painter* appear/disappear. The *form painter* appears to the right of the form tree. The *form painter* is similar to the graphic *form painter* in SAP script.

- Apart from these application toolbar buttons, additional functionalities are available through menu options. These menu options will be introduced at appropriate junctures.

## Menu Bar and Menu Options

Figures 3-2 and 3-3 shows the four main menu options and suboptions:

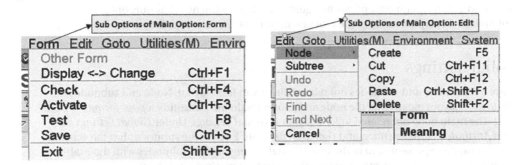

*Figure 3-2. Smartforms form—menu options: Form and Edit*

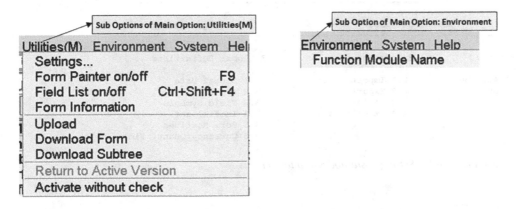

*Figure 3-3. Smartforms form—menu options: Utilities(M) and Environment*

Following is a description of the menu bar options and suboptions:

- The first of the menu bar options in Figure 3-2 is Form. You can (i) open another *form*; (ii) toggle between change and display mode of the *form*; (iii) check the *form* (validation); (iv) activate the *form*; (v) test the *form*; (vi) save the *form*; and (vii) exit the *form* screen.

- The second of the menu bar options in Figure 3-2 is Edit. You can (i) create, cut copy, paste, and delete nodes; (ii) create, cut copy, paste, and delete subtree; (iii) undo operations; (iv) redo operations; (v) search for a string; (vi) issue next search; and (vii) cancel creation or editing of a *form*.

- The third of the menu bar options in Figure 3-3 is Utilities(M). You can (i) perform settings (described in the following pages); (ii) make the *form painter* appear or disappear; (iii) make the *field list* appear or disappear; (iv) navigate to *form information* (*form documentation*); (v) upload from a presentation server file into the *form*; (vi) download the *form* to presentation server file; (vii) download *subtree* to presentation server file; (vii) return to the active version of the *form;* and (viii) activate the *form* without a check.

- The fourth of the menu bar options in Figure 3-3 is Environment. It has only one suboption: display the name of the function module of the activated form.

## Node: Global Settings

Marked in Figure 3-1 are node and subnodes not related directly to *form* layout. Node and subnodes not related directly to *form* layout means that the node and subnodes do not constitute a *page format* or part of a *page format*. The main node not related to *form* layout is *Global Settings*. Under *Global Settings* are subnodes: *Form Attributes, Form Interface,* and *Global Definitions*. Each of the subnodes has tab screens. Figure 3-4 shows a graphic representation of the node *Global Settings* and its subnodes with their tab screens: the subnodes are marked 1, 2, etc., and the tab screens are marked 1.1, 1.2, etc.

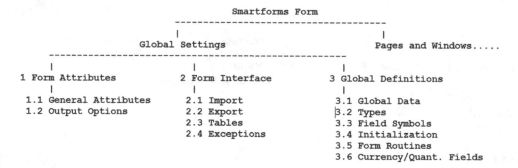

*Figure 3-4. Form node: Global Settings—subnodes and tab screens*

A description of the nodes, subnodes, and their tab screens of the main node *Global Settings* follows.

## Form Attributes

The first of the subnode *Form Attributes* under the node *Global Settings* is similar to *Form Header* of SAP scripts. The subnode *Form Attributes* has two tab screens: *General Attributes* and *Output Options*. Figure 3-1 is in fact a screenshot of the tab screen *General Attributes*. Figure 3-5 shows the tab screen *Output Options*:

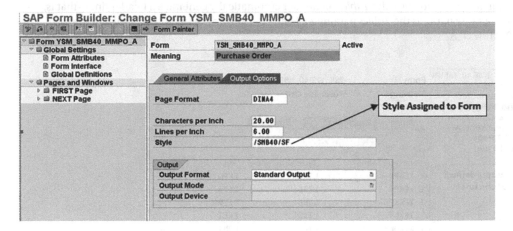

**Figure 3-5.** *Form Attributes——tab screen: Output Options*

You can assign a *style* to a *form* as shown in Figure 3-5. If no *style* is assigned to a *form*, the Smartforms *form* maintenance system assigns the *style* SYSTEM to the *form* by default.

## Form Interface

The second of the subnodes, *Form Interfaces,* under *Global Settings* is similar to a function module parameter interface. It has four tab screens: *Import, Export, Tables,* and *Exceptions*. There are no changing parameters as in function modules. You have to specify your parameters which will be received by the *form* from the ABAP driver program. There are predefined system import parameters, all optional. You can enter your own parameters and exceptions (Defined). Figure 3-6 shows the tab screen *Import*.

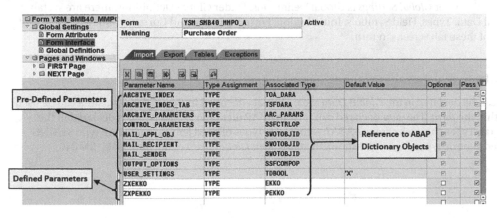

**Figure 3-6.** *Form Interface—tab screen: Import*

185

Mostly, the parameters (i.e., *Import, Export,* and *Tables*) are defined by referring to ABAP dictionary objects. The parameters can also be defined by referring to the predefined generic types or to the fixed length ABAP elementary types—D, F, I, and T—or referring to the ABAP elementary type STRING.

There are no *Export* parameters for the *form* YSM_SMB40_MMPO_A. Thus we are skipping the tab screen *Export.*

In the tab screen *Tables*, you enter the internal table parameters. The internal table parameters are specified in the same way as in function modules. Internal tables can be defined by referring to a structure with the keyword LIKE. Internal tables can be defined by referring to predefined generic types like ANY TABLE, etc. As in function modules, the *Tables* parameter automatically generates a header line—that is, a structure of the same name as the *Tables* parameter. Figure 3-7 shows the tab screen *Tables* of the form YSM_SMB40_MMPO_A.

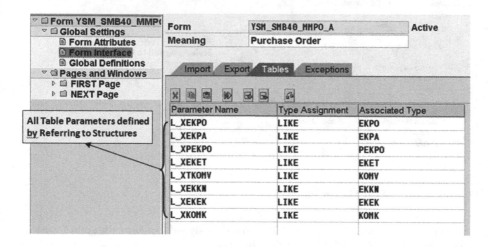

***Figure 3-7.*** *Form Interface—tab screen: Tables*

We are skipping the tab screen *Exceptions* as it is identical to the function module exceptions. There are predefined exceptions; you can enter your own exceptions and raise these exceptions.

# Global Definitions

The third subnode under *Global Settings* is Global Definitions. Under Global Definitions, there are six tab screens: Global Data, Types, Field Symbols, Initialization, Form Routines, and Currency/Quant. Fields. I will describe each of these tab screens in turn.

## Global Data

Data objects can be declared in the *Global Data* area. The data declared in the *Global Data* area can be used anywhere within the *form*. The data declared can refer to ABAP dictionary objects, types declared in the Types screen tab Types (next tab screen), ABAP elementary types of fixed length, and ABAP type STRING and predefined generic types. Figure 3-8 shows the tab screen *Global Data* of the *form* YSM_SMB40_MMPO_A.

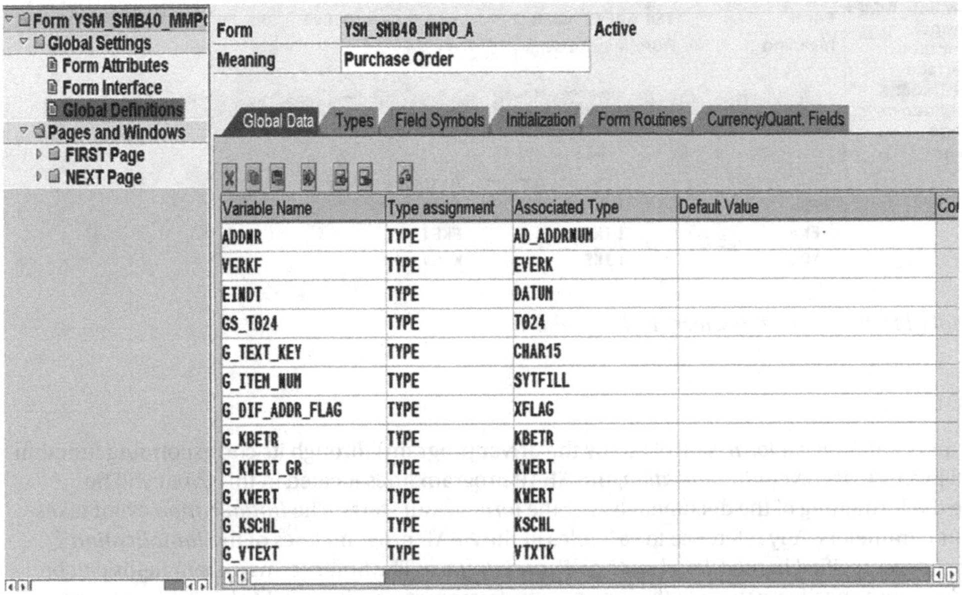

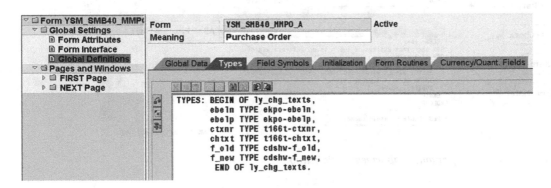

*Figure 3-8.* *Global Definitions—tab screen: Global Data*

## Types

In this tab screen area, you can declare your own types using the keyword TYPES as in an ABAP program. Subsequently, you can declare data in the *form* referring to the types in this area. Figure 3-9 shows the tab screen *Types* of the *form* YSM_SMB40_MMPO_A.

```
TYPES: BEGIN OF ly_chg_texts,
       ebeln TYPE ekpo-ebeln,
       ebelp TYPE ekpo-ebelp,
       ctxnr TYPE t166t-ctxnr,
       chtxt TYPE t166t-chtxt,
       f_old TYPE cdshw-f_old,
       f_new TYPE cdshw-f_new,
       END OF ly_chg_texts.
```

*Figure 3-9.* *Global Definitions—tab screen: Types*

## Field Symbols

You can define field symbols under this tab screen. When a large volume of data is to be processed using the looping process in a *form*, it is advisable to use an assigned field symbol. You can use the variation LOOP AT..... ASSIGNING.....instead of LOOP AT.....INTO..... Instead of fetching rows into a structure, row by row, the LOOP AT..... ASSIGNING.....directly accesses rows in an internal table, thereby improving performance for large volumes of data. You can use field symbols in contexts other than the LOOP AT..... ASSIGNING.....as per requirements. Figure 3-10 shows the tab screen *Field Symbols* of the *form* YSM_SMB40_MMPO_A.

| Field Symbol | Type assignment | Associated Type |
|---|---|---|
| <FS> | LIKE | EKPO |
| <EK> | LIKE | EKET |
| <KO> | LIKE | KOMV |

**Form** YSM_SMB40_MMPO_A **Active**
**Meaning** Purchase Order

Global Data | Types | Field Symbols | Initialization | Form Routines | Currency/Quant. Fields

*Figure 3-10. Global Definitions—tab screen: Field Symbols*

## Initialization

Initialization is an event. When a *form* is invoked (by the driver program) through its corresponding function module, control jumps to the event *Initialization*, the ABAP program lines located in this event will be executed before the formatting of the document as per the *form* layout starts. The *Initialization* event takes input and output parameters. Any reference to variables in the ABAP program lines of the *Initialization* event must have been specified in the *Global Data* or *Form Interface*. The Smartforms system fields can be directly referred without specifying them in the input, output parameters. Figure 3-11 shows the tab screen *Initialization* of the *form* YSM_SMB40_MMPO_A.

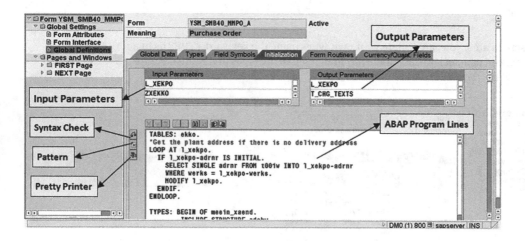

*Figure 3-11. Global Definitions—tab screen: Initialization*

Figure 3-11 has three marked buttons: *Syntax Check, Pattern,* and *Pretty Printer*. The function of these buttons is the same as their function in ABAP editor environment. These buttons exist wherever ABAP program lines are to be maintained in the *form* environment. These buttons exist in the tab screen *Types* (Figure 3-9). The *Syntax Check* button exists on most node screens, subnode screens, and tab screens to perform validity checks.

As you can observe, type has been declared in the ABAP program lines in the *Initialization* event (last visible ABAP program line). This type declaration is local to the *Initialization* event; it can be referred to declare variables only within the *Initialization* event.

## Form Routines

You can locate subroutines within the tab screen *Form Routines*. Each of the subroutines starts with the FORM statement and ends with the ENDFORM statement, just as in ABAP programs. The parameter passing and specification is identical to the parameter passing and specification in ABAP programs. The subroutines located within the tab screen *Form Routines* can be called from anywhere in the *form* with the PERFORM statement.

The buttons *Syntax Check*, *Pattern*, and *Pretty Printer* also appear on this tab screen. The *form* YSM_SMB40_MMPO_A does not contain any subroutines in the tab screen *Form Routines*. Hence, we are skipping a screenshot of this tab screen. In Chapter 4 hands-on exercise II, you are required to locate subroutines in the tab screen *Form Routines*; you will then have the opportunity to see the operation and usage of *Form Routines*.

## Currency Quant. Fields

When you define variables in the *forms Global Data* tab screen of ABAP dictionary types CURR (currency amounts) QUAN (inventory quantities), you need to specify their corresponding ABAP dictionary types CUKY (currency key) and UNIT (unit of measure key). The specification of fields of ABAP dictionary type CUKY for the type CURR variables and the type UNIT for the type QUAN variables is entered in the tab screen *Currency/Quant. Fields*.

There are no entries in this tab screen of the *form* YSM_SMB40_MMPO_A.

This concludes the descriptions of the tab screens of the subnode *Global Definitions* as well as the node *Global Settings*. We designated the node *Global Settings* as the node not directly related to *form* layout. Every *form* will consist of the node *Global Settings* with subnodes *Form Attributes*, *Form Interface*, and *Global Definitions*

# Node: *Pages* and *Windows*

The node *Pages and Windows* contains, as its name suggests, the form's *page formats, windows,* and other *form* layout elements. All the subnodes and the subnodes under the subnodes under the node *Pages and Windows* are being termed "*form* layout elements." The *form* layout elements appear as subnodes to the main node *Pages and Windows*. This node is directly related to the layout of a *form* (i.e., which information will appear where in what format).

Under the main node *Pages and Windows*, you can create *page format* nodes. A *form* must have a minimum of one *page format* and can have any number of *page formats*.

Under a *page format* node you can create nodes of *windows, graphics,* and *addresses*.

Under a *window*, you can create nodes of *texts, tables, templates, flow logics,* and *folders*.

Under an *address*, you can create nodes of *tables, templates, flow logic,* and *folders*.

Figure 3-12 shows a rough graphic representation of the node *Pages and Windows* and its subnodes.

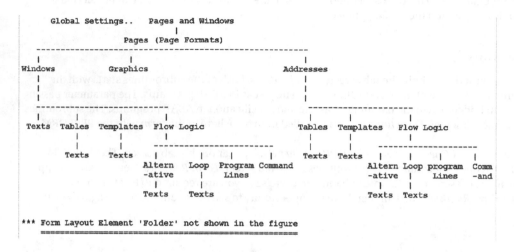

```
     Global Settings..   Pages and Windows
                                |
                    Pages (Page Formats)
       --------------------------------------------------------
       |               |                              |
   Windows         Graphics                       Addresses
       |               |                              |
       |               |                              |
       |               |                              |
   ---------------------------------          ----------------------
    |      |        |        |                  |       |        |
  Texts Tables  Templates Flow Logic         Tables Templates Flow Logic
         |        |        |                          |       |        |
       Texts    Texts  ------------------------     Texts  Texts  --------------------
                        |       |        |      |                  |       |      |    |
                      Altern   Loop  Program Command             Altern Loop program Comm
                      -ative    |    Lines                       -ative  |   Lines  -and
                        |       |                                  |      |
                      Texts   Texts                              Texts  Texts

*** Form Layout Element 'Folder' not shown in the figure
===================================================================
```

***Figure 3-12.*** *Form node: Pages and Windows—subnodes*

Figure 3-12 is a rough representation of the different layout elements under the node *Pages and Windows*. One of the layout elements, *folder,* is not represented in Figure 3-12. The layout elements *tables, templates,* and *loops* contain, apart from the element *text,* additional layout elements not represented in Figure 3-12.

Each of nodes and subnodes in the main node *Pages and Windows* has tab screens. The number of tab screens depends on the layout element type.

Following is a detailed description of *form* layout elements.

## Layout Element: *Page Format*

The Smartforms *form* layout element *page* is identical to the SAP script *form* element *page.* In Chapters 1 and 2, we referred to the *form* element *page* as *page format* (our own terminology) to distinguish it from the physical pages of a business document. We will refer to the Smartforms *form* layout element *page* as *page format.* Each *page format* of a *form* maps to a format of a business document.

When you enter in create mode of a *form* for the first time, the Smartforms *form* maintenance system creates a *page format* by default. It assigns a name to this *page format* starting with the character '%'. In fact, whenever you create a new subnode or a *form* layout element, the Smartforms *form* maintenance system assigns it a default name starting with the character '%'. The Smartforms *form* maintenance system also enters a default short description for a newly created *form* layout element. While creating *forms* of demonstration and hands-on exercises, we are always changing the default names and their corresponding short descriptions.

In the SAP script *form* environment, you were designating one *page format* as the first page of the business document. In the Smartforms *form* environment, the *page format* physically positioned at the top of the tree will be implicitly considered the first page of the business document. So you should be sure to position the *page format* you want to be used as the first page of a business document at the top of the tree.

*Portrait* or *Landscape* is specified in the *page format.* The page orientation in the SAP script *form* environment was specified in the *form* element *header.*

As in SAP script *form page formats,* you specify in the Smartforms *form page format*s, the next page in *page formats.*

190

You can provide for a background picture or graphic (a kind of watermark) for a *page format*.

It is mandatory to have a minimum of one *page format* in a *form*. You can have any number of *page formats* in a *form*.

Other aspects of *page format* are identical to the *page format* in the SAP script *form* environment.

The *form* YSM_SMB40_MMPO_A contains two *page formats*: FIRST and NEXT. Figures 3-13 and 3-14 show the tab screens *General Attributes* and *Output Options* of the *page format* FIRST of this *form*.

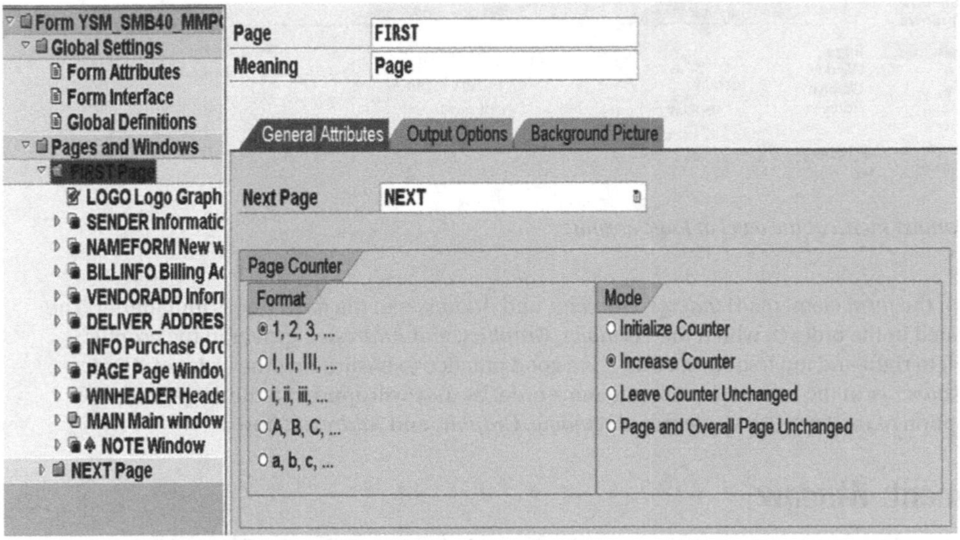

*Figure 3-13.* *Page Format: FIRST—tab screen: General Attributes*

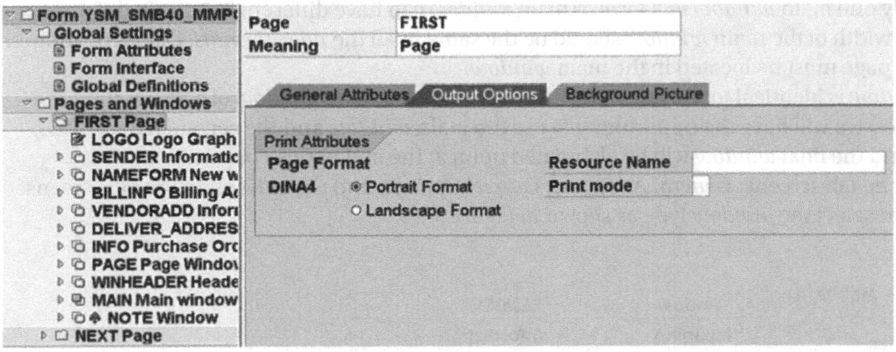

*Figure 3-14.* *Page Format: FIRST—tab screen: Output Options*

You add nodes and subnodes to the *form* tree mostly with the context menu, or equivalent functionalities available in the main menu. You can cut, copy, paste, and delete nodes and subnodes from the context menu.

A *page format* can consist of the following *form* layout elements immediately under it:

- Windows

- Graphics

- Addresses

When you select a *page format* node and invoke the context menu, you can create another *page format* at the same hierarchical level or create one of the layout elements: *Window/Graphic/Address* at the next lower hierarchical level. Figure 3-15 illustrates.

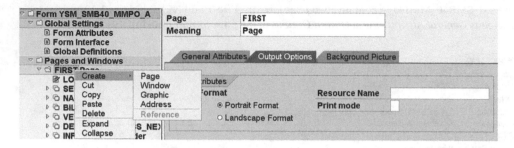

***Figure 3-15.*** *Context menu at the level of Page Format*

The order of the *form* elements *Windows, Graphics,* and *Addresses* in the *form* tree is immaterial. The output is generated in the order in which the *Windows, Graphics,* and *Addresses* appear in the *graphic form painter*: left to right and top to bottom. But, it is a good practice to ensure that the order of *Windows, Graphics,* and *Addresses* in the *form* tree are in the same order as they will appear in the output.

The description of the *form* layout elements *Window, Graphic,* and *Address* follows.

## Layout Element: *Window*

The *window* layout element of a *form* is the same as the *page window* in a SAP script *form*—that is, a physical area in a *page format*. A Smartforms *form window* must necessarily have the following dimensions: *left margin, width, upper margin,* and *height. Windows* can be of four types: main, secondary, copies, and final.

There can be only one main *window* in a *form*. A main *window* can have different heights in different *page formats*, but the width of the main *window* should be the same in all the *page formats*. Data repeating in a page and page to page must be located in the main *window*.

A secondary *window* is identical to the *page window* located in a variable *window* of a SAP script *form*.

In all our exercises, we will have the opportunity to use the main *window* and the secondary *windows*. The copies *window* and the final *window* will be elaborated upon at the end of this chapter.

A window has three tab screens: *General Attributes, Output Options,* and *Conditions*. In the tab screens *General Attributes*, you select the *window* type as shown in Figure 3-16.

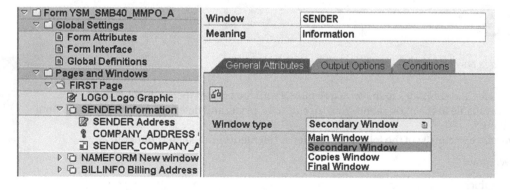

***Figure 3-16.*** *Form layout element window—tab screen: General Attributes*

In the tab screen *Output Options*, you specify the dimensions of the *window*: *Left margin, Width, Upper margin,* and *Height.* You can further specify whether you want a framed outline for the *window* and a shaded background. This is equivalent to the control command BOX in the SAP script *form's text element* environment. Figure 3-17 shows the tab screen *Output Options*.

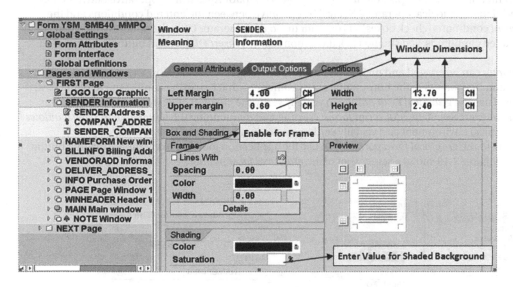

**Figure 3-17.** *Form layout element window—tab screen: Output Options*

In the tab screen *Conditions*, you specify conditions; the output in the window will be generated only if the conditions specified is true. Figure 3-18 shows a screenshot of the screen tab *Conditions*.

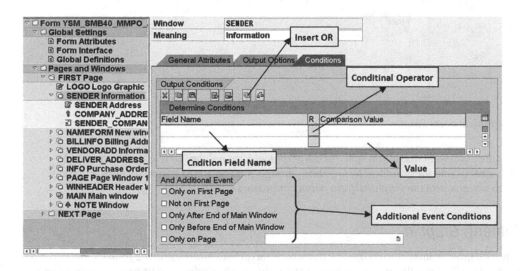

**Figure 3-18.** *Form layout element window—tab screen: Conditions*

193

At the bottom of Figure 3-18 are marked check boxes for *And Additional Event*. The contents of the *window* will output only if the conditions are true. For instance, if you enable the first check box *Only on First Page*, the contents of the *window* will output only on the first page of a business document. The tab screen *Conditions* is available for most *form* layout elements further in the tree hierarchy.

You can enter or create multiple conditions. The logical operator AND will be operative between the multiple conditions. The logical operator AND will be operative between the entered conditions and the *Additional event* conditions (check boxes). If you want the logical operator OR to be operative between any of the entered conditions, you should click the button marked *Insert OR* (second button from right) in Figure 3-18.

The *windows* can be created and maintained in the *graphical form painter* as in SAP scripts. We will create and maintain *windows* in the non-graphical environment—that is, use the context menu of the *form* tree. But we will use the *graphical form painter* to visually verify the creation of *windows*. We followed this procedure in our exercises of the SAP script *forms*: creating and maintaining the *windows* and *page windows* in the non-graphical environment and visually verifying them in the *graphical form painter*.

To navigate to the *graphical form painter*, you use the application toolbar *Form Painter*, the first button from the right. Figurer 3-19 shows a screenshot of the *graphical form painter*.

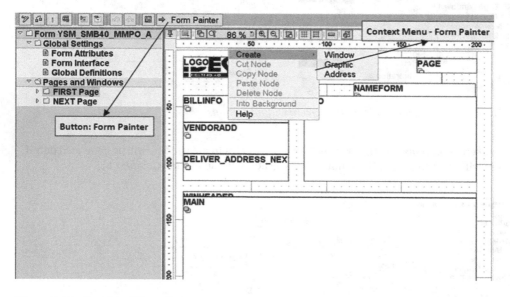

**Figure 3-19.** *Graphical Form Painter*

Most of the time you want maximum space in the *graphical form painter*. So it amounts to a toggle between the tab screens and the *graphical form painter*, though you can adjust boundary lines and have *form* tree, the tab screens, and the *graphical form painter* appearing together.

## Layout Element: *Graphic*

You can incorporate graphic images from the SAP document server into *forms* using the *form* element *graphic*. The *graphic* in the Smartforms *form* is equivalent to the graph *window* and its *page window* in SAP script *forms*. The *form* layout element *graphic* is at the same hierarchical level as the *window* or *address*, directly under *page formats*. The graphic image can be fetched from the selection list (function key F4, etc.) the same way as it is in SAP script. Figure 3-20 shows a screenshot of the tab screen *General Attributes* of *graphic* LOGO.

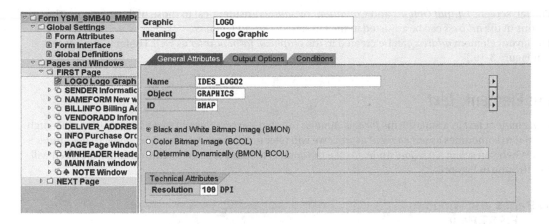

**Figure 3-20.** *Form layout element graphic—tab screen: General Attributes*

The tab screens *Output Options* and *Conditions* of the layout element *graphic* are identical to those of the *windows*. The width and height dimensions of the *graphic* are generated automatically based on the size of the image.

The layout element *graphics* can be created in the *graphical form painter* as well. (Refer to the context menu in Figure 3-19.)

## Layout Element: *Address*

The Smartforms *form* layout element *address* is equivalent to the control commands set ADDRESS.....
ENDADDRESS in the *text element* area of the SAP script *form*. You have to provide the address number; the address will be formatted as per the postal convention of the recipient country. Figure 3-21 shows a screenshot of the tab screen *General Attributes* of *address* SENDER_COMPANY_ADDRESS.

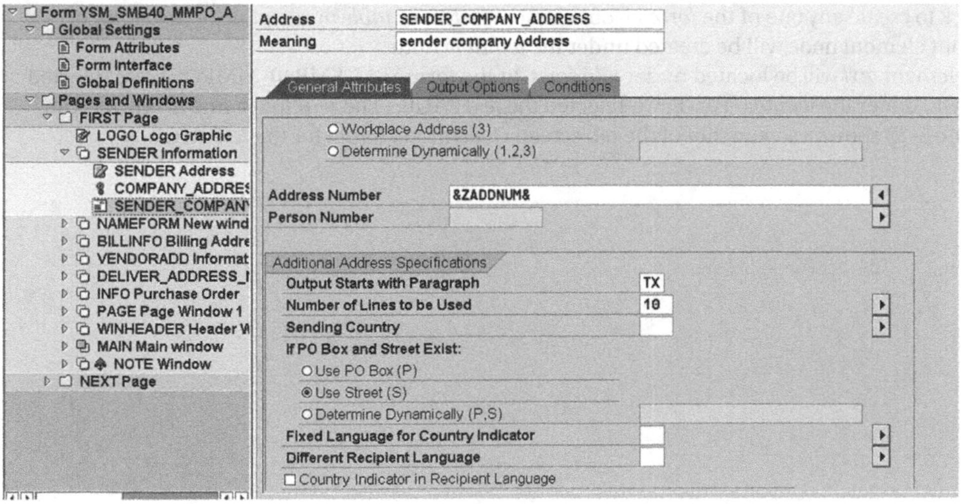

**Figure 3-21.** *Form layout element address—tab screen: General Attributes*

The tab screens *Output Options* and *Conditions* of *address* are identical to those of the *windows*. The dimensions of the *address* can be adjusted in the tab screen *Output Options*.

The layout element *address* can be created in the *graphical form painter* as well. (Refer to the context menu in Figure 3-19.)

## Layout Element: *Text*

The *form* element *text* in a Smartforms *form* is same as the element *text element* in a SAP script *form*. Though it is referred to sometimes as *text element* as well, we will refer to it as *text*. A *text* node can be created under a *window*. When you select a *window* node, invoke the context menu and select *Create* option; the screen will look like the one in Figure 3-22.

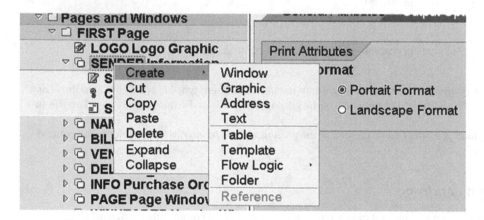

**Figure 3-22.** *Create layout elements within a Window—context menu*

In Figure 3-22, If you click to create any one of the *form* layout elements—*window* or *graphic* or *address*—the layout element node will be created at the same hierarchical level as the selected *window* node. If you click to create any one of the *form* layout elements—*text* or *table* or *template* or *flow logic* or *folder*—the layout element node will be created under the *window* node.

The *form* element *text* will be located under *windows*. In the *form* YSM_SMB40_MMPO_A, we selected the *window* PAGE, under the *window* PAGE, we selected the *text* PAGE. (The *window* name is same as the *text* name) Figure 3-23 shows a screenshot of the tab screen *General Attributes* for the *text* PAGE.

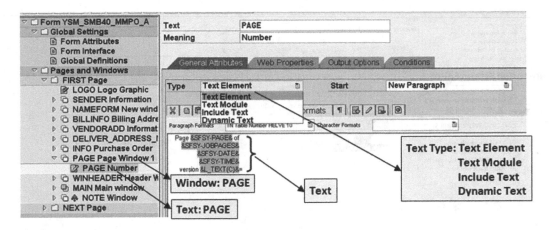

***Figure 3-23.*** *Form layout element text—tab screen: General Attributes I*

As shown in Figure 3-23, you can select a *Text Type* from the drop-down list: *Text Element* or Text Module or *Include Text* or *Dynamic Text*.

When you select the *Text Type* as *Text Element* (default), the text can be entered in the layout element *text* the same way you entered text in the *text element* of SAP script *forms*. You can enter literal text, you can enter variables; the variables have to be enclosed within &s (ampersands) as in the SAP script *form's text element* environment. The variables can be declarations in the *Global Data* area or variables of the *Form Interface* or Smartforms system fields. The text in layout element *text* named PAGE in Figure 3-23 is

```
Page &SFSY-PAGE& of
  &SFSY-JOBPAGES&
      &SFSY-DATE&
      &SFSY-TIME&
 version &L_TEXT(C)&
```

In this text, the variables with the prefix SFSY- are Smartforms system fields. All the output formatting options of SAP script, like zero suppression, space compression, justification, and so on, are available in the Smartforms. In fact, the *Type Text* in Smartforms is identical to the *text element* in SAP script except for the non-availability of SAP script control commands.

When you select the *Text Type* as *Text Module*, you can incorporate a Smartforms *Text module* (equivalent to the *standard text* of SAP script) in the layout element *text*.

When you select the *Text Type* as *Include Text*, you can incorporate the *standard text* of SAP script in the layout element *text*.

When you select *Text Type* as *Dynamic Text*, you can incorporate the *standard text* of SAP script in the layout element *text*. The name of the *standard text* is to be specified at runtime, which is why you call the selection as the *Dynamic Text*.

To the right side of the *Text Type* selection, you can indicate how the text starts from the drop-down list of options: *New Paragraph, New Line,* or *Append directly*. You can enter text in the bottom right white area, but you can enter text using a full screen editor as well. On the left side, next to the *form* tree, there are buttons to navigate to full screen editor and validate the contents of the layout element *text*. Figure 3-24 shows these features.

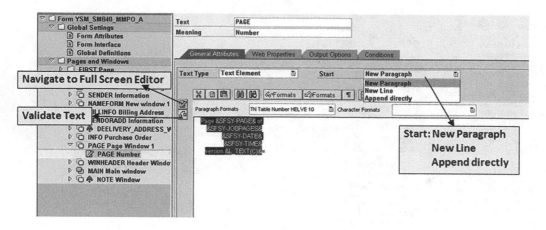

**Figure 3-24.** *Form layout element text—tab screen: General Attributes II*

The buttons to navigate to full screen editor and validate *text* were not visible in Figure 3-23, as the screen was scrolled horizontally to the right. The validation of text would involve, for example, the validation of the variables. The variables should be either valid Smartforms system fields or locatable in the *Global Definitions* area the *Form Interface*. The validation button is available in most elements of a Smartforms *form*.

You can assign a *paragraph format* to text by first selecting the text and then selecting the desired *paragraph format* from a drop-down list. The *paragraph formats* available in the *style* assigned to the layout element or node are available in the drop-down list. *Styles* can be assigned at different hierarchical levels of the *form* tree. The *style* assigned at the lowest node level of the *form* hierarchy is operative in that node. A *style* can be assigned in the tab screen *Output Options*. For example, assume the *style* YCH_03_FORM is assigned in the *Form Attributes* (highest level in the *form* tree hierarchy). The *style* YCH_03_TEXT is assigned in the *text* PAGE. Then the *style* YCH_03_TEXT will be operative on the text of PAGE.

Figure 3-25 shows the *paragraph formats* drop-down list.

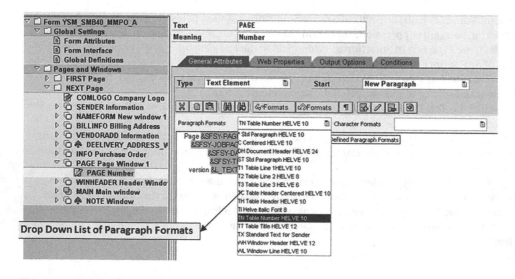

**Figure 3-25.** *Form layout element text—tab screen: General Attributes III*

The *character formats* are applied to texts in an identical manner as *paragraph formats*. Figure 3-26 shows the *character formats* drop-down list.

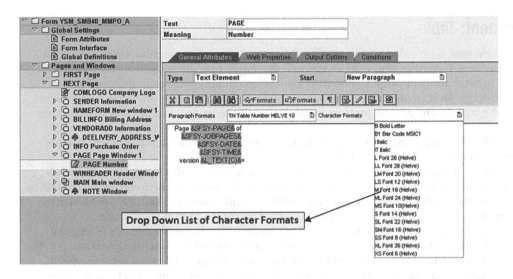

***Figure 3-26.*** *Form layout element text—tab screen: General Attributes IV*

You can enter text in the white area provided or use the full screen editor. We navigated to the full screen editor. The full screen editor will look like the one in Figure 3-27.

***Figure 3-27.*** *Form layout element text—full screen: line editor*

The screen in Figure 3-27 is identical to the line editor of the SAP script *form's text element*. We can switch to a full screen Microsoft Word like text editor with the menu option: Goto ➤ Change Editor. We are not using this full screen Microsoft Word like text editor. While performing exercises in this chapter and the next, we will use the full screen line editor to enter text. To apply *paragraph formats* and *character formats* to text, we will use the *General Attributes* screen (non-full screen) because we can select the text on this screen more easily than in the line editor. Also, the drop-down lists of *paragraph formats* and *character formats* are more easily available on this screen so we will use it to copy/cut and paste text.

The buttons under the tabs over the white text area are self-explanatory.

The next tab screen, *Web Properties,* is used to set properties when the Smartforms *form* is used to input data in the ABAP web dynpro environment. We are skipping this tab screen for now.

The tab screen *Output Options* of the layout element *text* facilitates the provision of a frame and shading to the text just as it does in the layout elements *windows*, *address,* and *graphic.*

The tab screen *Conditions* is identical to the tab screen *Conditions* in the layout elements *windows,* *address,* and *graphic.* The text output can be made conditional by specifying conditions.

## Layout Element: *Table*

The layout element *table* is provided in the Smartforms *form* environment to output repetitive data like the items of a business document. Almost every business document contains repetitive item data. Note that the repetitive data cannot be output without the layout element *table.* We can output repetitive data in the Smartforms *form* environment in the same way we outputted it in the SAP script *text element* environment. The layout element *table* provides features to output repetitive data in the desired manner in a formalized way.

Hypothetically, you can locate the layout element *table* in any type of *window,* but in practical terms, you will locate the element *table* in the main *window.*

The layout element *table* will have a data source: an internal table. A LOOP AT.....INTO/ASSIGNING..... process will operate on the internal table. A structure (INTO) must be specified where one row of data will be fetched from the internal table into the structure. Alternatively, a field symbol (ASSIGNING) defined in the *global settings* node can be specified for serial direct access of a row of the source internal table.

Recall the item data output of hands-on exercise II in Chapter 2. The material number and material description were being output in the first line. The ordered quantity, unit of measure, price, and amount were output in the second line. There were two line formats, or, in Smartforms parlance, two line types. If you plan to have header and footer in the layout element *table,* you may specify line types for header and footer as well.

So the data pertaining to an item may be output in more than one line; that is, one set of literals or variables being output in first line and another set of literals or variables being output in the second line. The layout element *table* will then consist of two line types. The layout element *table* must consist of a minimum of one line type and can consist of any number of line types.

Each field—literal or variable in a line type—to be output is contained in a layout element called a *cell.* If the contents of a *cell* exceed the *cell* width, output is not truncated but continues on the next line. The layout element *cell* is like a cell of an Excel spreadsheet. Grid lines can be provided to *cells* to enhance the output appearance.

The layout element *cell* will contain within it the layout element *text.*

With the layout element *table,* column headings can be output (optional). The column headings are specified in an area designated *Header.* The column headings appearance on first page and/or every page can be controlled with conditional check boxes provided for this purpose.

The item information or the table body is specified in an area designated *Main Area.*

With the layout element *table,* a footer can be output (optional). The footer is specified in an area designated *Footer.* The appearance of the footer at the end of table/last page and/or every page can be controlled with conditional check boxes provided for this purpose. Vertical space has to be explicitly specified for the footer. If the footer content exceeds the vertical space provided, excess footer output gets truncated. Typical footer information could be "grand total" and/or "running total."

Figure 3-28 shows a graphical representation of the layout element *table* with its elements or subcomponents.

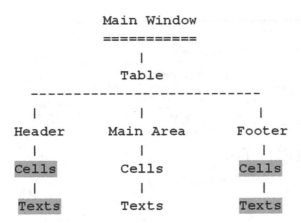

**Figure 3-28.** *Form layout element table—subcomponents*

The indication of optional in Figure 3-28 means that it is not mandatory to locate *cells* in the *header* or *footer*.

## The Layout Element Table in the Form YSM_SMB40_MMPO_A

The *form* YSM_SMB40_MMPO_A, a copy of the original SAP supplied *form* /SMB40/MMPO_A, was created with an older version of Smartforms. This older version of the Smartforms

- Did not have an explicit *main area*. All layout elements under a *table* and not under either a *header* or *footer* are deemed to be implicitly under the *main area*.

- Did not have the layout element *cells*. The layout element *text* was directly under a *table, header,* and *footer*. The text directly under a *table* was considered under the *main area* (i.e., data repeating in a page and page to page).

## Layout element *table–* tab screen *table*

Having described the layout element *table* in general, I will continue with a tour of the *form* YSM_SMB40_MMPO_A in the context of the layout element *table*.

The layout element *table* consists of the five tab screens: *Table, Data, Events, Output Options,* and *Conditions.* Figure 3-29 shows the first tab screen *Table.*

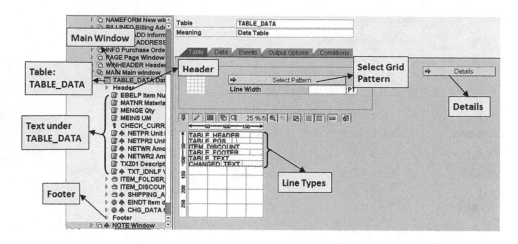

**Figure 3-29.** *Form layout element table—tab screen: Table I*

Figure 3-29 marks the tree node Main *window*. Under the node Main *window*, the layout element *table* named TABLE_DATA is located. Directly under the layout element *table* TABLE_DATA are layout elements (*texts*) EBELP (item number), MATNR (material number/code), MENGE (ordered quantity), MEINS (unit of measure), NETPR (price), and NETWR (amount).

The line types are marked in Figure 3-29. The line types are created on a screen navigated by clicking the button *Details* (marked in Figure 3-29).

Also marked in the figure is the button *Select Grid Pattern*, which is used to select the output grid pattern: grid with only row separators, grid with only column separators, grid with row and column separators, and so on.

The *form* YSM_SMB40_MMPO_A outputs the repetitive item data in the layout element *table* as follows: fields EBELP (item number), MATNR (material number/code), MENGE (ordered quantity), MEINS (unit of measure), NETPR (price), and NETWR (amount) are output in one line. This is a total of six fields. It outputs the field TXZ01 (material description) in the next line under the first line field MATNR (material number/code). It outputs more fields in additional lines like cash discount as per payment terms, etc. I will restrict the discussion to two lines but the concept can be extended to more than two lines.

Since each output line contains different fields, each line constitutes a separate format; these separate line formats are called the line types in the Smartforms environment. The format of the two lines of output described for each item will look as shown in Figure 3-30.

```
------------------------------------------------------------------------
Item   Material Number/Description        Quantity  UOM   Net Price   Net Amount
------------------------------------------------------------------------
  10   ISA-0002                           100.00    PC       266.00    26,660.00
       AKAN DELUXE
```

**Figure 3-30.** *Output item information in two lines*

The line types are created and maintained by clicking the button *Details*. Figure 3-31 shows the screen to create and maintain line types.

Figure 3-31 marks the *Line Type Id* (names): TABLE_HEADER, TABLE_POS, ITEM_DISCOUNT, and so on. Each row with its columns constitutes one line type. Next to the line type names is a Radio button to indicate whether it is a default line type. If you do not specify line type in the *table line*, the default line type is adopted.

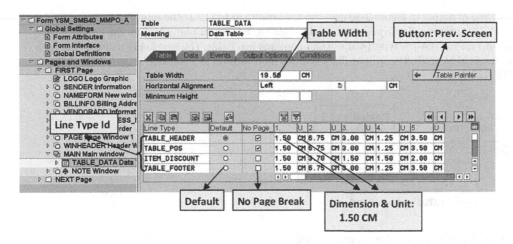

**Figure 3-31.** *Form layout element table—tab screen: Table II*

Next to the *Default* Radio button is a check box to enable page protection (marked as *No Page Break* in Figure 3-31). If the check box is enabled and if the text outputs in more than one line, the multiple lines will output in the same page (i.e., it won't split between pages).

In each line type, you specify the width of each field in the line type. In one column, you specify a number or the width of the field and in the next column you specify the units—CM/MM/CH, etc. For each field, you want to output, you repeat this process. This is marked as *Dimension & Unit* in Figure 3-31. The sum of the widths of the fields must be equal to the *Table Width*.

The first line of output in Figure 3-30 uses the line type TABLE_POS. The line type TABLE_POS has six fields, shown in Figure 3-32.

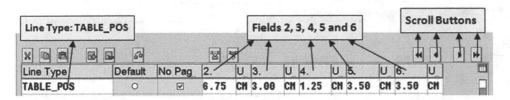

**Figure 3-32.** *Form layout element table—line type TABLE_POS*

In Figure 3-32, the width of first field is not visible. On our system, only the width of five fields is visible. The screen was scrolled to the right. The width of the six fields in line type TABLE_POS is as follows:

```
1.50 CM
6.75 CM
3 00CM
1.25 CM
3.50 CM
3.50 CM
```

The second line of output in Figure 3-30 uses the line type TABLE_TEXT. The line type TABLE_TEXT has only one field, TXZ01 (material description). The field TXZ01 must output aligned under the field MATNR of first line. For this reason the line type TABLE_TEXT contains two fields. The first field's width is the same as the width of the field MATNR. This will be like a dummy field without any contents. Figure 3-33 shows the line type TABLE_TEXT.

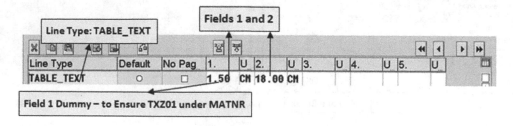

**Figure 3-33.** *Form layout element table—line type TABLE_TEXT*

The width of the two fields in line type TABLE_TEXT is 1.50CM and 18.00CM

## Layout Element Table Tab Screen Data

In the tab screen *Data*, you specify the source of data to the layout element *table*. Figure 3-34 shows a screenshot of the tab screen *Data*.

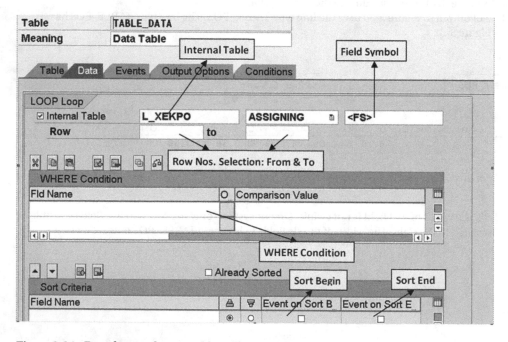

**Figure 3-34.** *Form layout element table—tab screen: Data*

As shown in Figure 3-34, the tab screen Data is equivalent to the LOOP AT.....statement in an ABAP program. There is a provision to fetch data into a structure row by row (INTO) or access row by row directly (ASSIGNING). There is a provision to filter rows fulfilling conditions (WHERE). There is a provision to start processing from a specific row and conclude processing at a specific row. Figure 3-34 marks these provisions.

There is also a provision for specifying sort fields. You can trigger events: *Sort Begin* and *Sort End*. Figure 3-34 marks these. The *Begin Sort* event is triggered when the first row of a specific value of sort field is fetched. The *End Sort* event is triggered when the last row of a specific value of sort field is fetched. These events can be used to produce multiple-level summary outputs like using internal table control level processing in ABAP programs.

## Layout Element Table: Tab Screen Events

The tab screen *Events* in the layout element *table* exists in the older version of Smartforms. In the latest version of Smartforms, the tab screen *Events* is replaced by the tab screen *Calculations*. The tab screen *Calculations* will be explained in hands-on exercise II in Chapter 4.

In the tab screen *Events* in the layout element *table*, you can specify when the *header* and *footer* output must appear. You can also reserve vertical space for the footer. Figure 3-35 shows a screenshot of the tab screen *Events* of the layout element *table*.

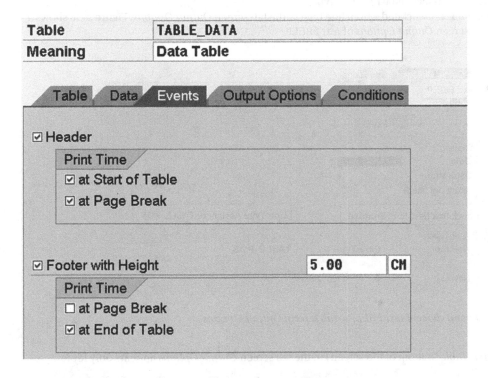

*Figure 3-35. Form layout element table——tab screen: Events*

The tab screens *Output Options* and *Conditions* of layout element *table* are identical to layout elements described earlier.

## Description of Layout Element Table in the Form YSM_SMB40_MMPO_A—Text

In the *form* YSM_SMB40_MMPO_A, the column headings for the item data produced of the layout element *table* TABLE_DATA (under the main *window*) are generated by the text in secondary *window* WINHEADER. You can check this out.

## Layout Element: Text Located in Table

We have already described the layout element *text* located directly under a *window*. The layout element *text* is identical to the element *text element* in SAP script *forms*. When using the current version of Smartforms, the layout element *text* under a *table* is located in the layout element *cell* (see Figure 3-28). I will describe the layout element *text* located inside a *cell* under a *table* in hands-on exercise II in Chapter 4.

But, as mentioned earlier, the *form* YSM_SMB40_MMPO_A was created with an older version of Smartforms. With this older version of Smartforms, the layout element *cell* is nonexistent. The *text* inside the *table* is located in the *header*, the *footer*, and directly under the *table*.

Here I am describing the *text* directly under the *table* TABLE_DATA. The *text* directly under the *table* TABLE_DATA is the repetitive item data: EBELP, MATNR, MENGE, MEINS, NETPR, NETWR, TXZ01, etc. Each of these *texts* is to be associated with a line type.

A layout element *text* is associated with a line type in the tab screen *Output Options*. Figure 3-36 shows a screenshot of the tab screen *Output Options* of *text* EBELP.

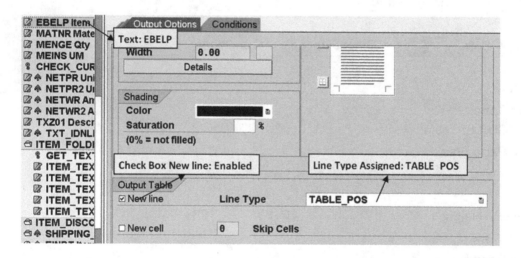

***Figure 3-36.*** *Form layout element text EBELP—tab screen: Output Options*

The area *Output Table* (bottom of the screen) in the tab screen *Output Options* appears only for *text* located inside a *table*.

The *text* EBELP is the first field in the output; hence the check box *New line* is enabled. The *text* EBELP is assigned the line type TABLE_POS.

The *text* MATNR is the second field to be output. The *text* MATNR must output on the same line as the *text* EBELP. Figure 3-37 shows a screenshot of the tab screen *Output Options* of *text* MATNR.

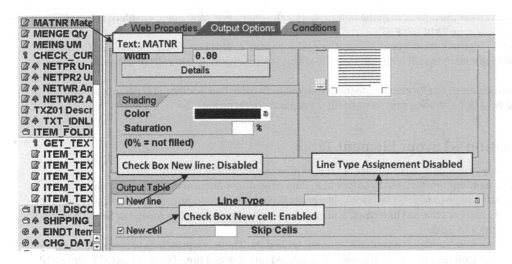

**Figure 3-37.** *Form layout element text MATNR—tab screen: Output Options*

The *text* MATNR is the second field in the output; hence the check box *New line* is disabled. The *text* MATNR is implicitly assigned the line type TABLE_POS. You can explicitly assign a line type only when the check box *New line* is enabled.

The remaining four *texts,* MENGE, MEINS, NETPR, and NETWR, are to output on the same line; hence their *Output Table* area will be identical to that of *text* MATNR.

The *text* TXZ01 must output in next line; it is to be assigned the line type TABLE_TEXT and must output directly under the *text* MATNR. Figure 3-38 shows a screenshot of the tab screen *Output Options* of *text* TXZ01.

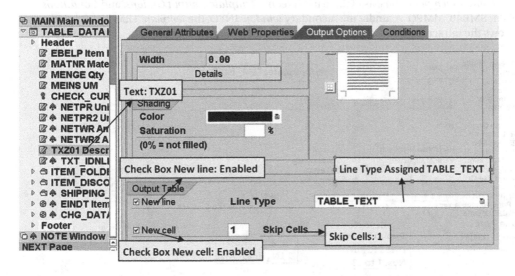

**Figure 3-38.** *Form layout element text TXZ01—tab screen: Output Options*

The *text* TXZ01 is the only field in the output; hence the check box *New line* is enabled. The *text* TXZ01 is assigned the line type TABLE_TEXT.

As shown in Figure 3-38, the field *Skip cells* contains a value 1. This is because the *text* TXZ01 must output aligned with *text* MATNR of the previous line. This is a provision to skip cells to create desired gaps in the output.

The layout element *text* located inside the layout element *table* had additional aspects than the *text* located directly under a *window* and so warranted a separate description.

## Recapitulation—Layout Element Table

I have elaborately covered the layout element *table* as it has a plethora of features.

The layout element *table* is used to output item data of business documents (i.e., data repeating in a page and repeating page to page). The layout element *table* is to be located primarily in the main *window*.

The layout element *table* has line types, and each line type corresponds to a format or formats of field layouts to be output in a line.

The layout element *table* has a source of internal table data. There is a provision to restrict the retrieved data—WHERE conditions, etc. Data is retrieved or accessed one row at a time LOOP AT.....INTO or LOOP AT.....ASSIGNING.

The layout element *table* has a provision to output a header and footer of item data.

The layout element *table* has grid options to select from: grid with only row separators, grid with only column separators, grid with row and column separators, etc.

# Layout Element: *Template*

The layout element *template* is similar to the layout element *table*. In the layout element *table*, the number of rows to be output is determined at runtime. With the layout element *template*, the number of rows to be output is fixed or predetermined.

The layout element *template* consists of three tab screens: *Template, Output Options,* and *Conditions.* In the *form* YSM_SMB40_MMPO_A, under the secondary *window* INFO, the *template* TEM_INFO is located. Figure 3-39 shows the tab screen *Template* of the layout element *template* TEM_INFO.

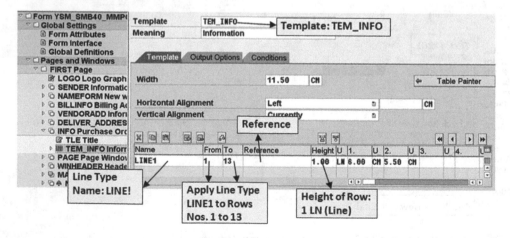

***Figure 3-39.*** *Form layout element template TEM_INFO—tab screen: Template*

As marked in Figure 3-39, a line type is assigned to rows in the output while defining a line type. In the *template* TEM_INFO, the line type LINE1 has been assigned to all 13 lines (1–13) of output, the *template* TEM_INFO, has only one line type LINE1. You have to specify the height of the line type. For the *template* TEM_INFO, the height is specified as 1LN (1 line). The line type LINE1 has two field widths: 6CM and 5.5CM, respectively.

In the *template* TEM_INFO, all the particulars of a purchasing document (document number, document date, document currency, payment terms, etc.), a total of 13 fields, are output. Each field is output in one line. Each field is output with its corresponding label text as follows:

```
Document Number: 12345
Document Date    : 25/06/2015
Vendor                : 4321
Currency              : USD
```

The *texts* with the prefix TLE_ (TLE_EBELN, etc.) indicate the text label of the field; *texts* with the prefix VAL_ (VAL_EBELN, etc.) indicate the value of the field. There are a total of 13 *texts* with the prefix TLE_ and 13 *texts* with the prefix VAL_.

Figure 3-40 shows a screenshot of the tab screen *Output Options* of *text* TLE_EBELN.

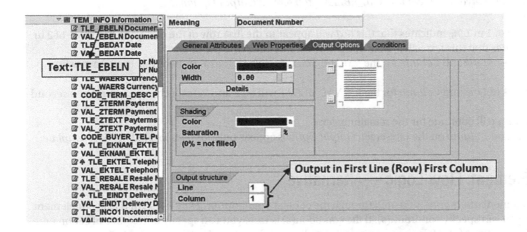

***Figure 3-40.*** *Form layout element text TLE_EBELN—tab screen: Output Options*

In the area *Output structure* at the bottom of the Figure 3-40, *Line* and *Column* are marked. The value of 1 in *Line* indicates that this *text* will appear in the first row of the *template*. The value of 1 in *Column* indicates that this *text* will appear in the first column of the *template*.

Figure 3-41 shows a screenshot of the tab screen *Output Options* of *text* VAL_EBELN.

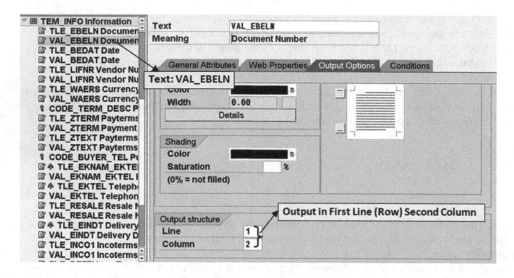

**Figure 3-41.** *Form layout element text VAL_EBELN—tab screen: Output Options*

The value of 1 in *Line* indicates that this *text* will appear in the first row of the *template*. The value of 2 in *Column* indicates that this *text* will appear in the second column of the *template*.

The values of *Line* and *Column* for the *text* TLE_BEDAT will be 2 and 1, respectively (second row first column).

The values of *Line* and *Column* for the *text* VAL_BEDAT will be 2 and 2, respectively (Second row second column).

The pattern will continue for the remaining *texts*.

The *Line* and *Column* on the tab screen *Output Options* appear only for *texts* located inside a *template*.

## Layout Element: Flow Logic —Alternative

The layout element *alternative* is created through the context menu option *Flow Logic*. In the layout element *alternative*, you can specify condition(s). If the condition(s) is true, you can specify one course of action or output; if the condition(s) is false, you can specify an alternative course of action or output. The *form* YSM_SMB40_MMPO_A does not contain the layout element *alternative*.

We will be using the layout element *alternative* in hands-on exercise II in Chapter 4.

## Layout Element: Flow Logic—Loop

The layout element *loop* is created through the context menu option *Flow Logic* With the layout element *loop*, you can establish fetching or accessing of one row of data from an internal table. The retrieval of data can be restricted in the same manner as in the layout element *table*. Figure 3-42 shows tab screen *Data* of layout element *loop* LP_PR_COND.

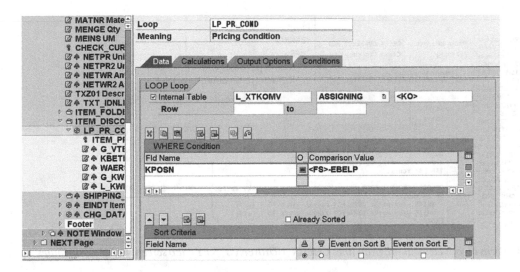

**Figure 3-42.** *Form layout element loop LP_PR_COND—tab screen: Data*

The layout element *loop* will, for the most part, be located in the main *window*. The layout element *loop* LP_PR_COND is located inside the layout element *table* TABLE_DATA.

As in the layout element *table*, there is a provision for specifying sort fields. They operate the same way as in the layout element *table*.

In the tab screen *Calculations*, you can sum, average, and count just like the aggregate functions of open SQL.

## Layout Element: Flow Logic—Program Lines

You can create tree nodes to locate ABAP program lines. The ABAP program lines constitute the layout element *program lines* created through the context menu option *Flow Logic*.

You should take care in locating the node of the layout element *program lines*. Suppose you want to calculate a certain figure and subsequently output it in a layout element *text*. Then, the node of layout element *program lines* to calculate the figure must precede the node for layout element *text* to output the figure.

Figure 3-43 shows the tab screen *General Attributes* of the layout element *program lines* CHECK_CURRENCY_KEY.

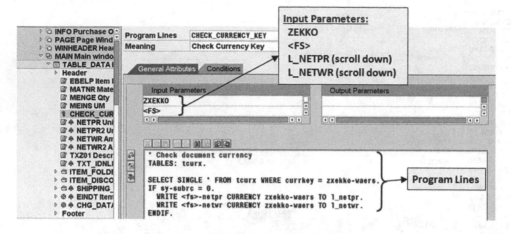

**Figure 3-43.** *Form layout element program lines CHECK_CURRENCY_KEY—tab screen: General Attributes*

The layout element *program lines* are like subroutines. The layout element *program lines* have input and output parameters. All references to variables of *form interface, global definitions,* and *field symbols* within the *program lines* have to be entered in the input/output parameters of the *program lines*. It would have been more appropriate to enter the L_NETPR and L_NETWR as output parameters. The Smartforms system fields with the prefix SFSY- can be referred to directly in the *program lines*.

You can use the ABAP statement for static breakpoints: BREAK-POINT in the *program lines*. You should ensure that the static breakpoints are disabled or deleted after debugging process is over.

The *program line* CHECK_CURRENCY_KEY shown in Figure 3-43 determines the output of the currency fields NETPR and NETWR. The *program line* CHECK_CURRENCY_KEY has four input parameters: ZEKKO, <FS> (these two are visible in Figure 3-43), L_NETPR, and L_NETWR (these two become visible when you scroll down the input parameters).

## Layout Element: Flow Logic—Command

The layout element *command* created through the context menu option *Flow Logic* can be used to branch to a new page from within the main *window* and can be used to reset paragraph numbers and issue print control.

The *form* YSM_SMB40_MMPO_A does not use the layout element *command*. We do not plan to use the layout element *command* in any of our demonstration or hands-on exercises. You can try it out as an exercise.

## Layout Element: *Folder*

The layout element *folder*, strictly speaking, is not a layout element. For this reason, we did not show it in Figure 3-12, a rough representation of the node page and windows and its subnodes. The layout element *folder* is a grouping of layout elements within a *window*. You group layout elements within a *folder*. The layout elements under a *folder* are secondary to this *folder*.

You group layout elements under a *folder* to achieve ends. To illustrate this point, we navigated to the *texts* in the *header* area of the *table* TABLE_DATA of the *form* YSM_SMB40_MMPO_A, shown in Figure 3-44.

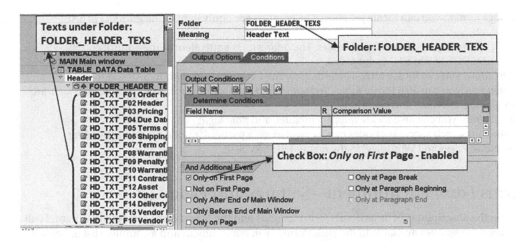

**Figure 3-44.** *Form layout element folder FOLDER_HEADER_TEXS—tab screen: Conditions*

Figure 3-44 shows the tab screen *Conditions* of the *folder* FOLDER_HEADER_TEXS. This *folder* node consists of many *texts*: HD_TXT_FD01..... Sixteen *texts* are visible in the Figure 3-44. On the tab screen *Conditions* in the area *And Additional Events*, the check box *Only on First Page* is enabled. It means that all the *texts*—HD_TXT_FD01..... will output only on the first page of a business document. So instead of specifying the condition on each of the *texts* (more than 16), the *texts* have been located inside a *folder* and the condition specified in the *folder*. The condition specified in the *folder* will apply to all the layout elements in the *folder*.

This was one instance of utility of the *folder*. In Chapter 4, we will use the *folder* to implement page protection. A single item information in a purchasing document or a purchase order outputs in multiple lines (item number, material number ordered quantity, unit of measure, price amount in one line and material description in the next line, etc.). When we output single item information in multiple lines, we desire that the information of one item must not split between pages. We implemented this requirement with the PROTECT.....ENDPROTECT control commands in the SAP script *text element* environment in Chapter 2.

In the Smartforms environment, page protection can be provided in the *paragraph format* of *styles*. But the page protection at the *paragraph format* level does not serve our purpose as each item information line is a new paragraph. This is where we can use the *folder* to implement page protection. All the *texts* inside a *window, table,* etc., requiring page protection can be located in a *folder*. On the tab screen *Output Options* of this *folder*, the check box *Page Protection* is enabled. This will provide page protection for all the *text* in the *folder*. I will demonstrate the use of folder to implement page protection in hands-on exercises II and III in Chapter 4.

# Recapitulation—Node: *Pages and Windows*

We termed the subnodes under the node *pages and windows* as layout elements. Under the node *pages and windows*, what we are calling a *page format* is same as a *page format* in SAP script *forms*.

Under a *page format*, you can locate *windows*. The *windows* are equivalent to *page windows* in SAP script *forms*, physical areas of *page formats*, defined by a left margin, upper margin, width, and height. There are four types of *windows* supported in Smartforms *form*: main, secondary, final, and copies. The main *window* is equivalent to a *page window* of the main *window* in SAP script *forms*. The secondary *window* is equivalent to a *page window* of the variable *window* in SAP script *forms*.

Under a *page format*, you can locate *graphics*. The *graphics* are equivalent to the *graphics* in SAP script *form*.

Under a *page format*, you can locate *addresses*. The *addresses* is equivalent to the control commands ADDRESS......ENDADDRESS in SAP script *forms*

Under a *window*, you can locate *texts*. The *texts* are same as the *text elements* in SAP script *forms*

Under a *window*, you can also locate *tables*, *templates*, and *flow logic*. The components of *flow logic* are *alternative*, *loop*, *program lines*, and *command*.

Under an *address*, you can also locate *tables*, *templates*, and *flow logic*.

You can find out which successor nodes can be created for a particular node under the heading "Successors of Node Pages and Windows" in the manual BC-SRV-SCR.

## Smartforms *Form* Environment—Settings and Field List

Before I wind up the descriptions of Smartforms *form* elements and the Smartforms *form* environment, I will briefly touch upon the settings available in the Smartforms *form* environment and a complete list of fields in the Smartforms *form* environment: fields of *form interface*; fields defined in the *global data*; fields assigned to field symbols and the system fields (prefix SFSY-).

To perform settings in the Smartforms *form* environment, you make the menu selection Unilities(M) ➤ Settings in the *Form Builder* screen. A dialog box for settings as shown in Figure 3-45 will appear.

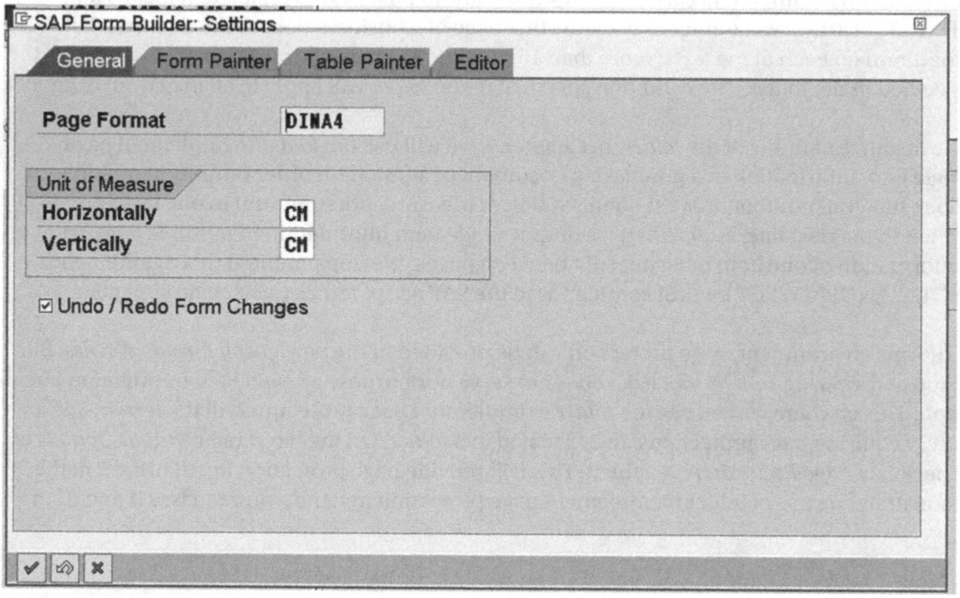

**Figure 3-45.** *Form Builder—Settings*

As shown in Figure 3-45, there are tab screens: *General, Form Painter, Table Painter,* and *Editor.* You can explore these tab screens as an exercise.

You can view the entire collection of fields existing for a *form* and select fields. These fields will be (1) the fields of *form interface*, (2) fields defined in the *global data*, and (3) fields assigned to field symbols and the system fields (prefix SFSY-). To view the fields, you click the second button from the right on the application toolbar. The button acts as a toggle; clicking it will make field appear and disappear. Figure 3-46 shows the field list.

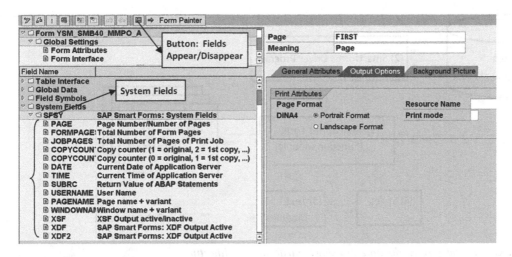

**Figure 3-46.** *Smartforms form list of fields*

Figure 3-46 shows the nodes *Table interface, Global Data, Field Symbols,* and *System Fields.* The nodes above the node *Table interface* are *Import Interface* and *Export Interface.* The nodes *Import Interface* and *Export Interface* are not visible in Figure 3-46 as the screen has been scrolled down. Each of these nodes can be expanded, etc. In Figure 3-46, the node System Field has been expanded to show all the fields with prefix SFSY-.

# Smartforms *Form* and ABAP Driver Program

As with the SAP script *forms*, Smartforms *forms* are used to design the layout of business document types that include formatted long text. The main data originating from the database tables that is to appear in the business document will not be retrieved and processed within the Smartforms environment. Subsidiary data originating from database tables that is to appear in the business document may be retrieved within the Smartforms *form* environment. In the INITIALIZATION event and *Program Lines* of the Smartforms *form*, you can use the SELECT statement. The main data originating from the database tables that is to appear in the business document will mostly be retrieved and processed in an ABAP program. When a Smartforms *form* is activated, a function module is generated. From the ABAP program retrieving the main data, you will call the function module of the Smartforms *form*. Hence an ABAP program is associated with a Smartforms *form*. We are terming the ABAP program associated with a Smartforms *form* "the driver program."

Data is sent by the driver program and received by the SAP script *form* in "*form parameters.*"

# Generating Business Documents Using Smartforms—Architecture

In this section I will describe the basic architecture of the generation of a business document using Smartforms.

Figure 3-47 depicts the architecture for generating business documents using Smartforms.

215

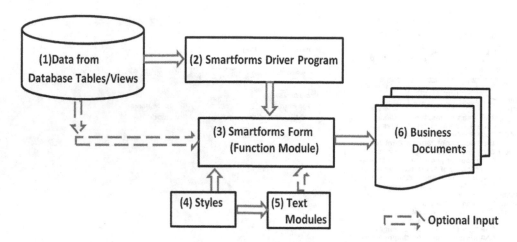

**Figure 3-47.** *Generating business documents using Smartforms—architecture*

In Figure 3-47, the process steps are marked (1), (2), (3), (4), (5), and (6). Following is a description of these process steps:

1. The process step marked (1) in the Figure 1-4 involves retrieving all the data required to produce the business documents. For example, if your business document type is purchase orders, then some of the main database tables from which data will have to be retrieved are

   ```
   LFA1    Vendor Name and address
   T005T   Country Texts
   EKKO    Purchasing Document Header Information
   EKPO    Purchasing Document Item Information
   ```

   The process step marked (1) in Figure 1-4 involves the retrieval of data from database tables and database views by the driver program. The data retrieval could involve retrieval of specific and selective business documents through a SELECT-OPTIONS input statement or equivalent in the driver program.

2. Once the data is retrieved, it may be ordered or sorted by the driver program. The driver program will call the function module of the Smartforms *form*. When calling the function module, data will be passed from the driver program to the *form* through the function module interface parameters.

3. The process step marked (3) in Figure 3-47 involves the receipt of data to be output by the Smartforms *form* from the driver program. Within the *form*, additional data from database tables and database views could be optionally retrieved. In the Smartforms *form*, the business document type layout is specified—t is, which information is to be output on which area of which page.

4. A *form* is assigned a *style* at the level of the form. It can also be assigned *styles* at other lower levels: *text*, etc. The *paragraph formats* and *character formats* of these *styles* are applied to the information or content for formatting. Similarly, *text modules* being incorporated into the *form* will use *paragraph formats* and *character formats* created in *styles* assigned to *text modules* and apply the *paragraph formats* and *character formats* of *styles* to these *texts* in the *text modules*. The process step marked (4) in Figure 3-47 reflects this.

5.   The *text modules* to be incorporated into a business document can be specified while designing or creating the *form*. The *text modules* are then static to the *form*. Optionally, the *text modules* to be incorporated into a business document can be specified at runtime (dynamic). This is shown in process step (5) in Figure 1-4.

6.   The generation of the business document occurs in the process step marked (6) in Figure 3-47.

Throughout the book, we will be using the non-graphical text editor only.

The non-graphical editor of *text elements* is a line editor. Copying and pasting operations with this editor are extremely cumbersome and awkward. (ctrl+y, etc.) Whenever you want to perform copying and pasting operations in the *text elements* environment, you can switch to the graphical text editor.

The features of *text elements* (control commands and formatting features) will be covered in detail as we perform demonstration examples in thid chapter and business scenario examples in Chapter 4.

I will defer a description of the last of the *form* element *documentation* to a later stage, when we create forms for business scenarios.

Now that I have completed the descriptions of the elements of a *form* in the context of the SAP delivered *form* MEDRUCK, we will create *forms* and print programs to demonstrate the basics of *forms*, *styles*, and *standard texts*.

# Demonstration I

We will create our first Smartforms *style* and *form* involving the following:

- Creation of a *style* consisting of *paragraph formats* and *character format*. The *style* is to be assigned to the *form*

- Creation of a *form* with a single *page format*

- Creation of an element graphic and inclusion of a graphic image in the element *graphic* of the *form*

- Creation of a secondary *window* and inclusion of literal long text in the secondary *window* of the *form*

- Application of assigned *style's paragraph formats* and *character formats* to the literal long text in the secondary *window*

- Saving, checking, and activation of the *form*

- Test print or print preview the *form* from within the Smartforms environment

In this demonstration, we are not using the main *window*.

So, let us proceed to the creation of a *style* and a *form* which will involve the activities just listed.

## Recapitulation of Specifications of *Text* in Secondary *Window*

Before we proceed to the creation of a *style*, I will recapitulate the output form of the text to be located in the secondary window of the *form*.

The text we are planning to locate in the secondary *window* is the short write-up on the description of the structure of selection tables. We used this text in demonstrations I and II in Chapter 1. The *paragraph formats* and the *character formats* that we create in the *style* will depend on the presentation of the text in the secondary *window*. To reproduce the appearance of the text of Chapter 1 follow the steps in Figure 3-48.

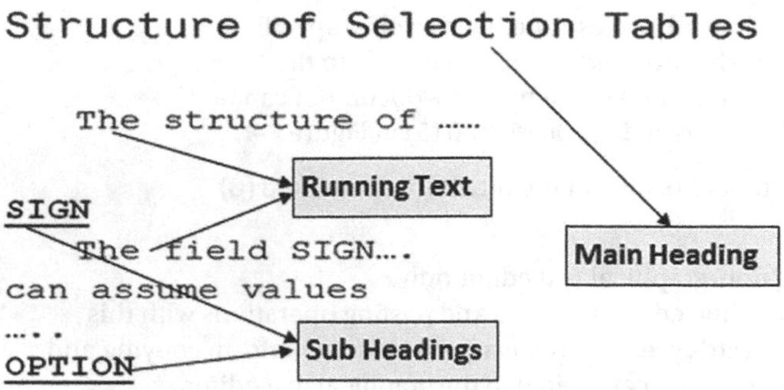

# Structure of Selection Tables

*Figure 3-48.* *Rough layout of text to appear in secondary window*

As the Smartforms supports colors, we will use color for the main heading and subheadings.

We want the main heading for the text to appear in the font family YARIAL_M, font size 28 pt and font color green. For the main heading of the text to appear with these attributes will require a separate *character format,* say, C1.

We want the subheadings for each of selection table structure fields SIGN, OPTION, LOW, and HIGH to appear in the font family Courier, font size 12 pt, font style bold, underlined, and font color blue. This will require a separate *character format,* say, C2.

We will have one *paragraph format,* say, P1, with the default values. We will designate this as the standard or default paragraph. For our running text, we require a *paragraph format,* say, P2, with five characters indenting on the first line of the paragraph and one line gap at the end of the paragraph. When we use or output with the uploaded font YARIAL_M, the characters in one line are almost touching the characters in the next line. To resolve this and create a small gap between two lines, we will use a *paragraph format,* say, P3, with a value equal to 2 in the field *Line Spacing.* Assigning a value 2 to the field *Line Spacing* to produce a gap between lines has been determined by trial and error. The values in all the other fields will be the default values.

To sum up, we will have to create two *character formats*—C1, C2—and three *paragraph formats*—P1, P2, and P3—in the *style.*

## Create *Style*

We navigated to the Smartforms *SAP Smart Form: Initial Screen*——transaction code SMARTFORMS. We ensured that the Radio button *Style* is enabled. We entered the *style* name as YCH03_01 (maximum namespace of 30 characters) in the field *Style.* We could have used a longer name, but we are sticking to the namespace of styles in the SAP script environment. We clicked the Create button (you can alternatively press the function key F5). The screen as shown in Figure 3-49 appeared.

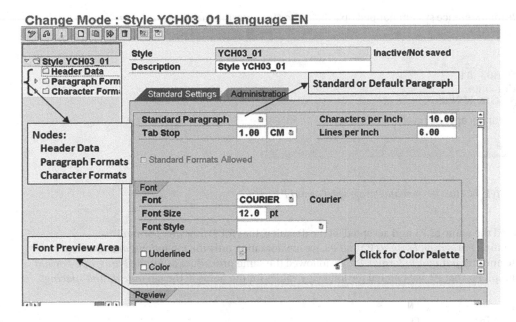

*Figure 3-49.* *Style YCH03_01—Header Data, tab screen: Standard Settings*

The *style*, its elements, or its components are represented as nodes and subnodes of a tree.

In Figure 3-49 the nodes *Header Data, Paragraph Formats,* and *Character Formats* are marked. You can create any number of *paragraph formats* as subnodes under the node *Paragraph Formats.* You can create any number of *character formats* as subnodes under the node *Character Formats.*

Also marked in Figure 3-49 are the area of font preview, a color palette for color selection, and the assignment of a standard paragraph which was termed "the default paragraph" in the SAP script environment.

We changed the default description (meaning/short text). We started off by creating three *paragraph formats.* To create *paragraph formats,* we selected the node *paragraph formats* and invoked the context menu by pressing the mouse right button as shown in Figure 3-50.

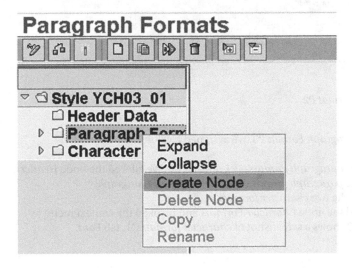

*Figure 3-50.* *Style YCH03_01—context menu to create paragraph formats*

219

The *style* maintenance system popped up a dialog box for entering the *paragraph format* name as shown in Figure 3-51.

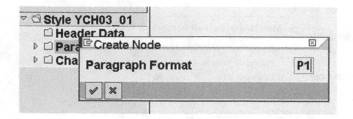

**Figure 3-51.** *Style YCH03_01—create Paragraph Format P1*

We entered the name as P1 and accepted all the default values for *Paragraph Format* P1.

While creating *Paragraph Formats* P2 and P3, we are operating only the tab *indents and spacing*.

To create another *paragraph format,* P2, we followed the same procedure as for the *Paragraph Format* P1. For Paragraph Format P2, we entered the following values for the fields in the tab *indents and spacing*:

```
Space After           1 LN
Indent First Line     5 CH
```

These are marked as shown in Figure 3-52.

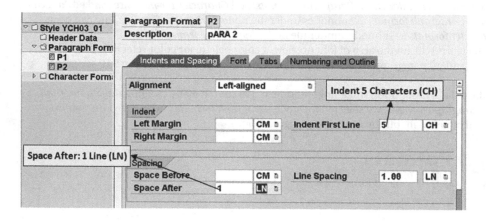

**Figure 3-52.** *Style YCH03_01—Paragraph Format P2*

We created *Paragraph Format* P3. In *Paragraph Format* P3, we assigned a value 2 to the field *Line spacing* in the tab *indents and spacing*.

This completes the creation of the three *paragraph formats*—P1, P2 and P3. We clicked the node *Header Data, Standard Settings* tab. We assigned the *paragraph format* P1 as the *Standard Paragraph*.

Next, we will proceed to the creation of the two *character formats*.

To create *character formats*, we selected the node *Character Formats* and invoked the context menu by pressing the mouse right button. Figure 3-53 shows a screenshot of *character formats* C1, tab *Font*.

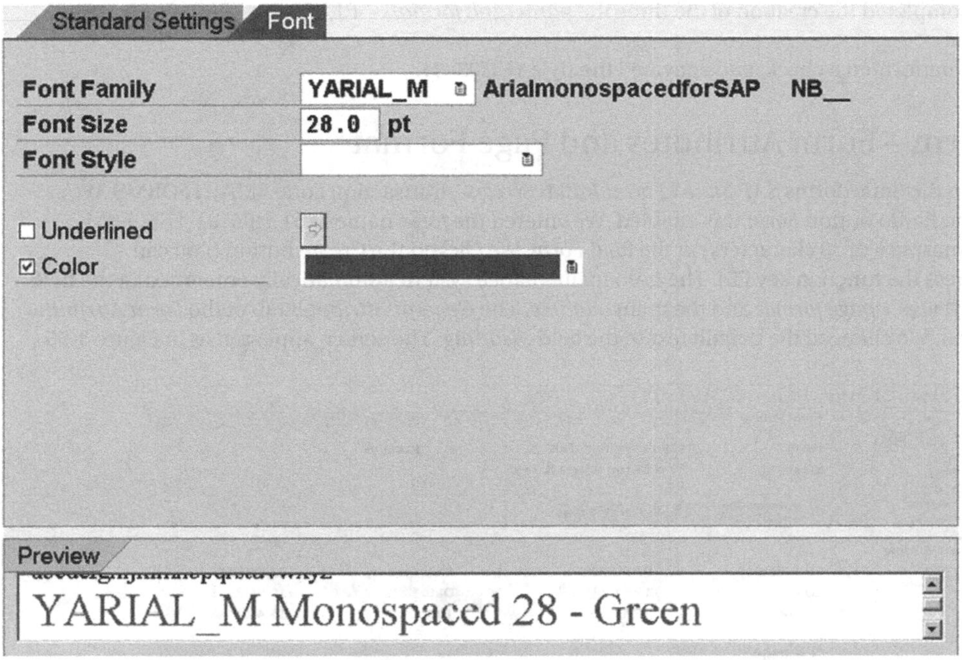

**Figure 3-53.** *Style YCH03_01—Character Format C1*

As shown in Figure 3-53, we assigned the font family YARIAL_M, font size 28 points, and font color green to the *Character Format* C1. *Character Format* C1 will be applied to the main heading of the text in the secondary *window*.

In a like manner, we created *Character Format* C2. *Character Format* C2 has font family Courier (default), font size 12 points (default), and font color blue. *Character Format* C2 has font style bold and underlined. Figure 3-54 shows the entered values for *Character Format* C2.

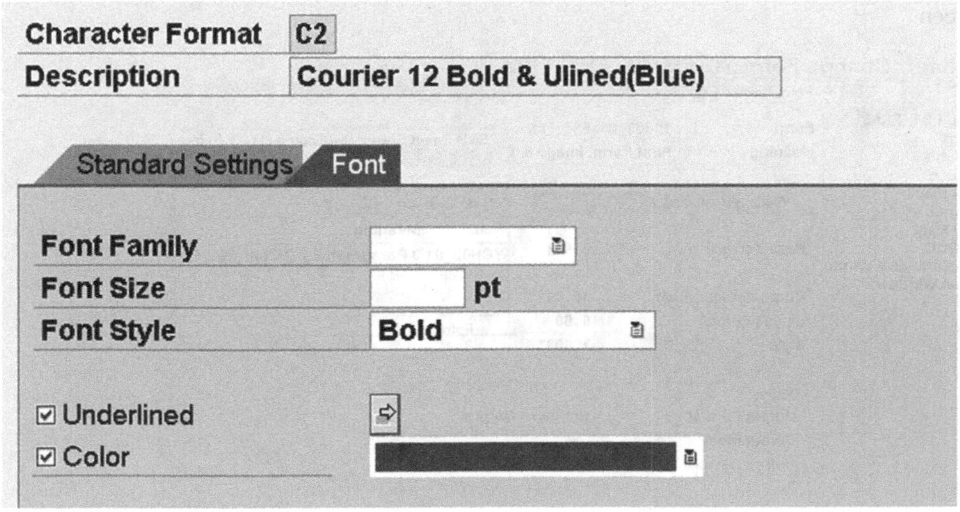

**Figure 3-54.** *Style YCH03_01—Character Format C2*

We have completed the creation of the three the *paragraph formats*—P1, P2, P3—and two *character formats*—C, C2.

We saved, performed a check, and activated the *style* YCH03_01.

## Create Form—Form Attributes and Page Format

We navigated to the Smartforms *SAP Smart Form: Initial Screen*—transaction code SMARTFORMS. We ensured that the Radio button *Form* was enabled. We entered the *form* name as YCH03_01_FST_FRM (maximum namespace of 30 characters) in the field *Form*. We clicked the Create button (you can alternatively press the function key F5). The *form* maintenance system automatically enters text in the field *Meaning* and creates a *page format* and the main *window*. The *General Attributes* tab of the *Form Attributes* screen appeared. We changed the default text in the field *Meaning*. The screen appeared as in Figure 3-55.

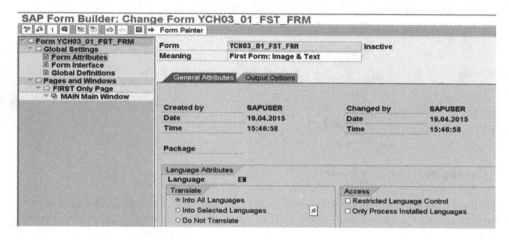

**Figure 3-55.** *Create Form YCH03_01_FST_FRM—form Attributes, General Attributes screen*

We clicked the *Output Options* tab. On the *Output Options* tab screen, we assigned our style YCH03_01. For the other fields on the *Output Options* tab, we accepted the default values. Figure 3-56 shows the *Output Options* tab screen.

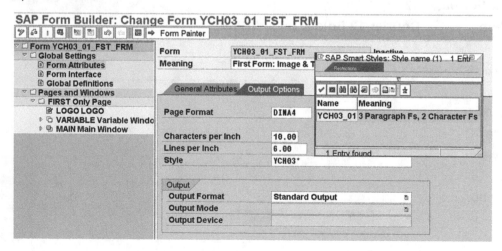

**Figure 3-56.** *Create Form YCH03_01_FST_FRM—form Attributes, Output Options screen*

We clicked the node of *page format*. We changed the name of the automatically created *page format* to FIRST and changed the default text in the field *Meaning*. The *General Attributes* tab of *page format* FIRST appeared as in Figure 3-57.

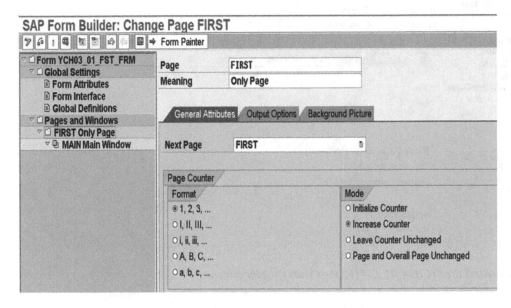

***Figure 3-57.*** *Create Form YCH03_01_FST_FRM—page format FIRST: General Attributes screen*

We are accepting the default values for the *page format* FIRST. You can view the other two tabs of the *page format* FIRST: *Output Options* and *Background Picture*.

## Create *Form—Graphic* and Secondary *Window*

Next, let us create a *graphic* and a secondary *window*. To create a *graphic*, we selected the node of the *page format* FIRST and invoked the context menu by pressing the mouse right button as shown in Figure 3-58.

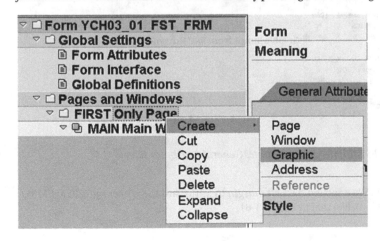

***Figure 3-58.*** *Create Form YCH03_01_FST_FRM—context menu to create graphic*

223

We made the menu selection Create ➤ Graphic. The screen to enter *graphic* particulars appeared like that in Figure 3-59.

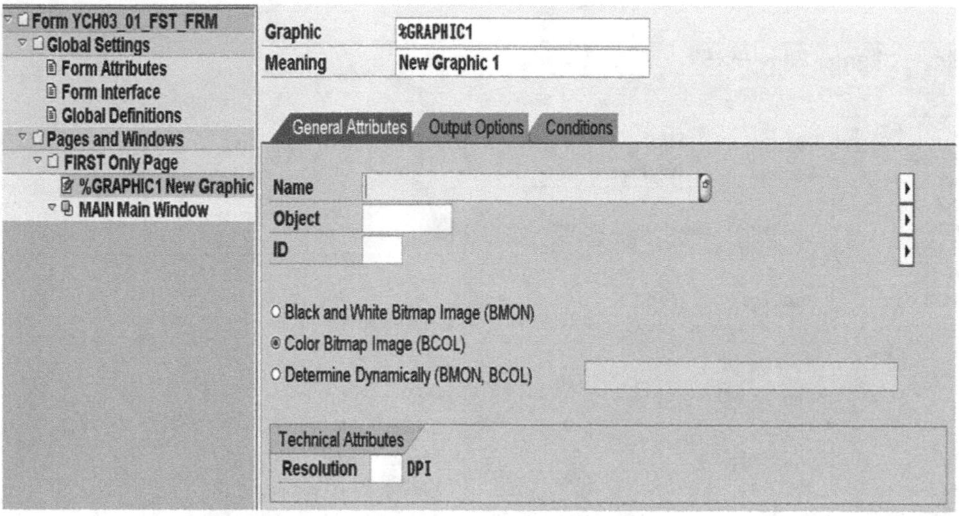

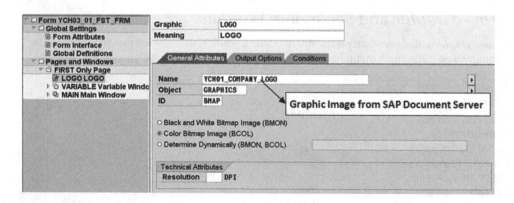

**Figure 3-59.** *Create Form YCH03_01_FST_FRM—Create Graphic screen*

We entered values in the *General Attributes* tab screen. We entered the value YCH01_COMPANY_LOGO the field *Name*. This is the BMP image file we imported into the SAP document server in Chapter 1. You can use the function key F4 to locate it. You can use some other imported image of your choice if you desire so. Next, we changed the *graphic* name to LOGO; we changed the contents of the field *Meaning*.to LOGO. The screen with the entered values should look like that in Figure 3-60.

**Figure 3-60.** *Create Form YCH03_01_FST_FRM—create graphic: General Attributes screen*

We clicked the *Output Options* tab. We adjusted the *Left margin* to 5MM and the *Upper margin* to 5MM. The *Output Options* tab screen should look like that in Figure 3-61.

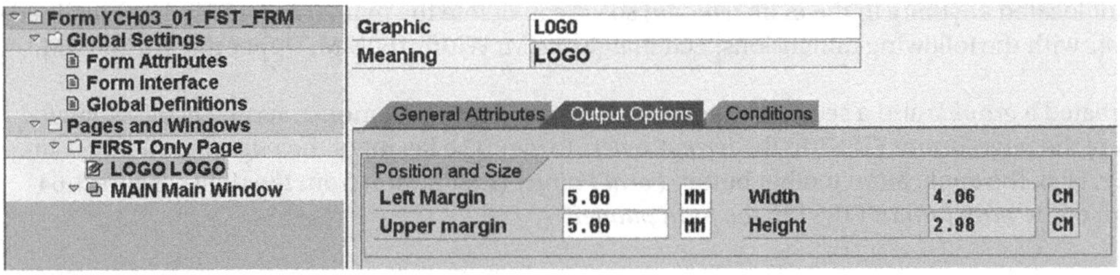

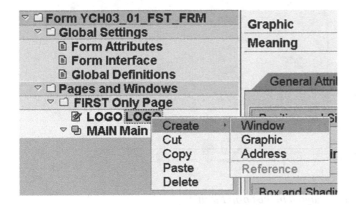

**Figure 3-61.** *Create Form YCH03_01_FST_FRM—create graphic: Output Options screen*

To create a secondary *window*, we clicked the *graphic* node LOGO and invoked the context menu by pressing the mouse right button as shown in Figure 3-62.

**Figure 3-62.** *Create Form YCH03_01_FST_FRM—context menu to Create Window*

We made the menu selection Create ➤ Window. The screen to enter *window* particulars appeared. We want the *window* to be a secondary *window* which is the default. We changed the name of the *window* to VARIABLE (we are retaining the name from the SAP script exercise) and we changed the contents of the field *Meaning*. We clicked on the tab *Output Options*. On the *Output Options* tab screen, we entered *Left margin* as 46MM, *Width* as 160MM, *Upper margin* as 5MM, and *Height* as 190MM. The screen with the entered values should look like that in Figure 3-63.

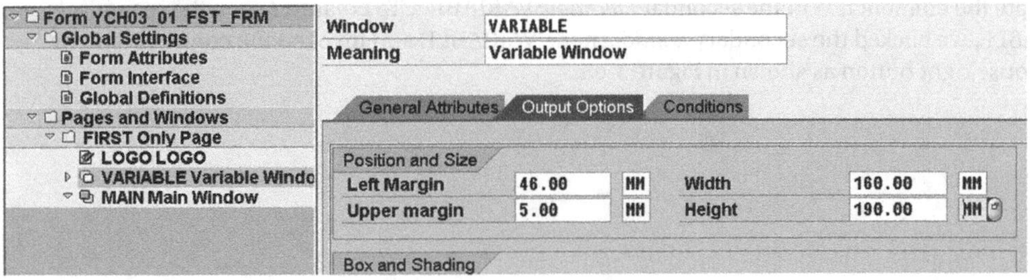

**Figure 3-63.** *Create Form YCH03_01_FST_FRM—create window: Output Options screen*

We have not located anything in the main *window,* so we can delete the main *window.* We have retained the main *window* with the following dimensions: Left margin 5MM, Width 160MM, Upper margin 200MM, Height 5MM.

We have created a *graphic* and a secondary *window* as planned in this demonstration. Let us visually view the layout of the *page format* FIRST in the *form painter.* To view the layout of the *page format* FIRST in the *form painter,* click the application toolbar button *Form Painter* (first button from the right). Figure 3-64 shows the layout of the *page format* FIRST in the *form painter.*

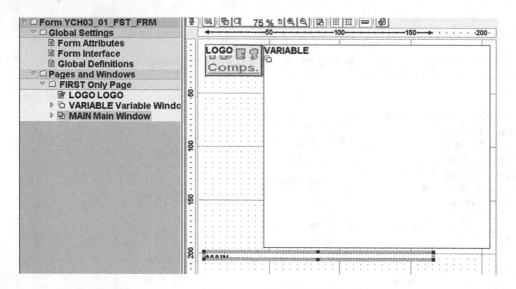

***Figure 3-64.*** *Create Form YCH03_01_FST_FRM—layout in the Form Painter*

The issue of using *graphical form painter* or operating in non-graphical mode for maintaining *forms* is purely a matter of personal convenience and choice. If you need to define elements with exact dimensions, I recommend usage of non-graphical mode of operation.

This completes the creation of a *page format,* a *graphic,* and a secondary *window* of the form YCH03_01_FST_FRM.

## Create *Form—Text*

We need to create the element *text* in the secondary *window* VARIABLE. To create a *text* in the secondary *window* VARIABLE, we clicked the secondary *window* node VARIABLE and invoked the context menu by pressing the mouse right button as shown in Figure 3-65.

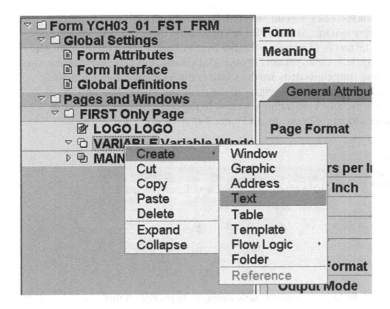

*Figure 3-65.* *Create Form YCH03_01_FST_FRM—Create Text in the secondary window VARIABLE*

We made the menu selection Create ➤ Text as shown in Figure 3-65. When we did so, a screen as shown in Figure 3-66 appeared.

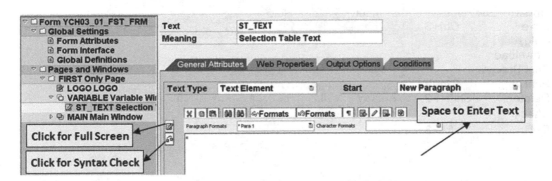

*Figure 3-66.* *Create Form YCH03_01_FST_FRM—screen to Create Text in window VARIABLE*

We changed the name of the text to ST_TEXT and entered suitable description in the field *Meaning* as shown in Figure 3-66.

You can enter text in the area marked *Space to Enter Text* in the Figure 3-66.

Also marked in Figure 3-66 is a button *Click for Full Screen* to navigate to a full screen for text entry. This will be a screen similar in looks to the *text element* screen of SAP script. In the full screen mode, there is an option as in SAP script to operate in graphical or non-graphical text editor. We will be operating all the while in full screen mode for text entry. We will be operating for most part in non-graphical text editor. When we are required to select copying and pasting of text, we will operate in graphical mode of text editor.

For now, we clicked on the button marked *Click for Full Screen* to navigate to the full screen editor. You can enter the text manually by referring to it in Chapter 1. We are uploading the text from an operating system folder file into a user clipboard. The text is, of course, available in the Chapter 1 and Chapter 3 folders of the E-resource file for this book (www.apress.com/9781484212345). The Smartforms *text* environment also provides five user clipboards. In fact, these user clipboards are the same as the SAP script user clipboards.

To upload text into a user clipboard, we first need to navigate to the screen of a user clipboard. To navigate to the user clipboard 5, we made the following menu selection in the *text* environment: Goto ➤ User Clipboard ➤ Clipboard 5. The screen looked like the one in Figure 3-67.

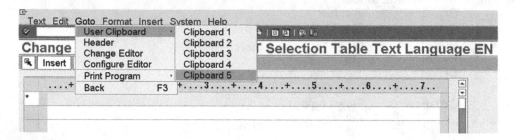

***Figure 3-67.*** *Create Form YCH03_01_FST_FRM—menu selection to navigate to user clipboard*

Once we were on the screen of user clipboard 5, we made the following menu selection to upload text into user clipboard 5: Clipboard ➤ Upload. The screen looked like that in Figure 3-68.

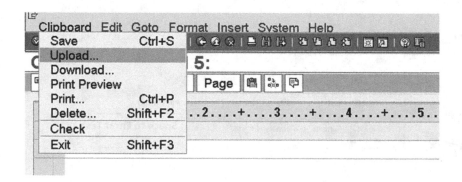

***Figure 3-68.*** *Create Form YCH03_01_FST_FRM—menu selection to upload text into user clipboard*

The menu selection popped up the dialog box to select the file format as shown in Figure 3-69.

Change Clipboard 5:
Insert
Line
Format
Page
....+....1....+....2....+....3....+.
Upload
Format
Rich Text Format (RTF)
ASCII
ITF

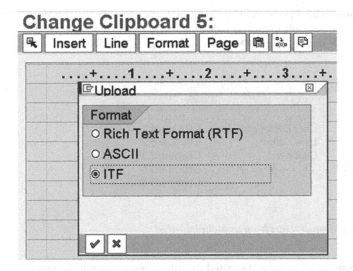

*Figure 3-69. Create Form YCH03_01_FST_FRM—select Upload text format*

We selected the ITF format. The text was downloaded into E-resource file in ITF format. The file selection dialog appeared. We made the selection as D:\TEMP\YCH01_01_SEL_TABLES. You will have to provide your folder location. The text was uploaded from the file into user clipboard 5 and the screen looked like that in Figure 3-70.

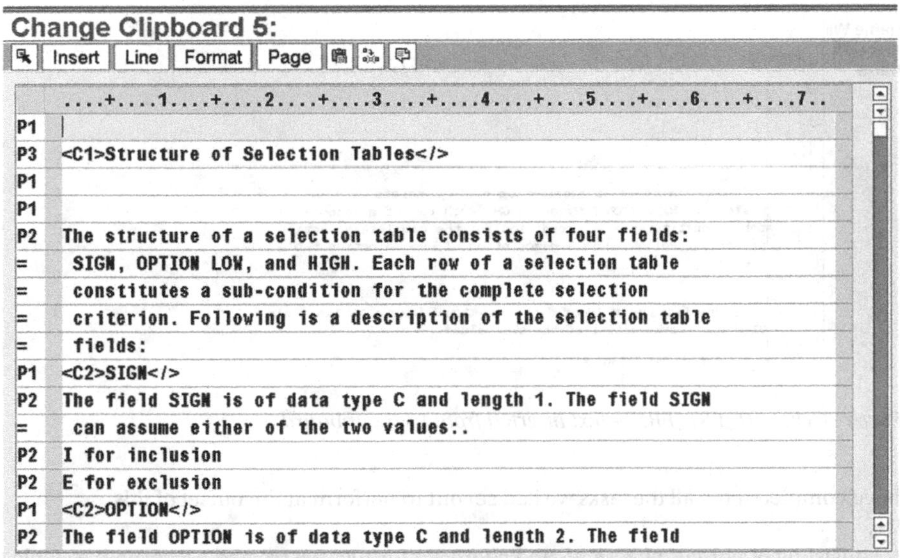

Change Clipboard 5:
Insert
Line
Format
Page
....+....1....+....2....+....3....+....4....+....5....+....6....+....7..
P1
P3 <C1>Structure of Selection Tables</>
P1
P1
P2 The structure of a selection table consists of four fields:
= SIGN, OPTION LOW, and HIGH. Each row of a selection table
= constitutes a sub-condition for the complete selection
= criterion. Following is a description of the selection table
= fields:
P1 <C2>SIGN</>
P2 The field SIGN is of data type C and length 1. The field SIGN
= can assume either of the two values:.
P2 I for inclusion
P2 E for exclusion
P1 <C2>OPTION</>
P2 The field OPTION is of data type C and length 2. The field

*Figure 3-70. Create Form YCH03_01_FST_FRM—text uploaded into clipboard 5*

We navigated from the user clipboard screen back (function key F3) to the *text* screen. We now have to insert the text from user clipboard 5 into the *text* area. We made the following menu selection to insert text from the user clipboard 5: Insert ➤ Clipboard ➤ User Clipboard ➤ Clipboard 5. Figure 3-71 illustrates.

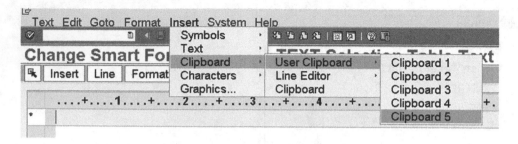

***Figure 3-71.*** *Create Form YCH03_01_FST_FRM—Insert text from user clipboard 5*

The text from user clipboard 5 was inserted into *text* area. We exited the full screen editor. The screen after exiting the full screen editor looked like that in Figure 3-72.

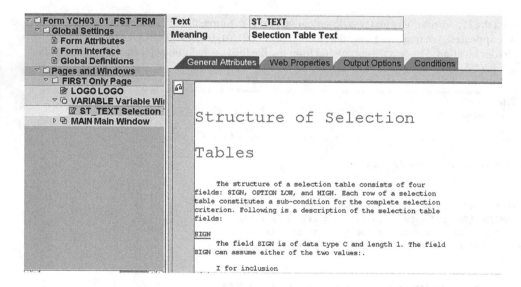

***Figure 3-72.*** *Create Form YCH03_01_FST_FRM—text inserted from user clipboard 5*

At this point we have completed the all the tasks we had set out to perform at the outset of this demonstration exercise.

We created a *style* consisting of *paragraph formats* and *character format*. We created a *form* with a single *page format*. We created an element *graphic* and included a graphic image in the element *graphic* of the *form*. We created a secondary *window* and included text in the secondary *window* of the *form*.

We saved, performed a check, and activated the *form*. We will test print or print preview the *form* from within the Smartforms environment.

## Test or Print Preview *Form*

We are now in a position to test and output the *form*. Recall that our *form* will output only one physical page. Also recall that our activated *form* is a function module. To test and print preview the *form*, we made the following menu selection: Form ➤ Test. The form maintenance system navigated to the Function Builder: Initial Screen—transaction code SE37, shown in Figure 3-73.

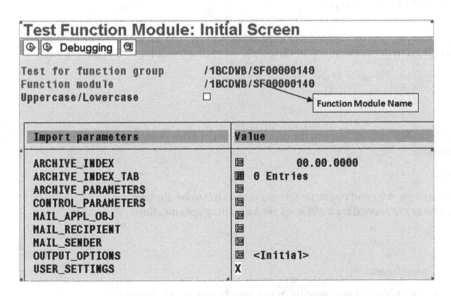

**Figure 3-73.** *Form YCH03_01_FST_FRM—test print/Print Preview I*

We clicked the Execute button on the application toolbar (third button from the left). The *Test Function Module: Initial Screen* appeared as shown in Figure 3-74.

**Test Function Module: Initial Screen**

| ⊕ | ⊕ Debugging | ⊞ |

Test for function group        /1BCDWB/SF00000140
Function module                /1BCDWB/SF00000140
Uppercase/Lowercase            ☐        → Function Module Name

| Import parameters | Value |
| --- | --- |
| ARCHIVE_INDEX | ▣      00.00.0000 |
| ARCHIVE_INDEX_TAB | ▦  0 Entries |
| ARCHIVE_PARAMETERS | ▣ |
| CONTROL_PARAMETERS | ▣ |
| MAIL_APPL_OBJ | ▣ |
| MAIL_RECIPIENT | ▣ |
| MAIL_SENDER | ▣ |
| OUTPUT_OPTIONS | ▣ <Initial> |
| USER_SETTINGS | X |

**Figure 3-74.** *Form YCH03_01_FST_FRM—test print/Print Preview II*

We clicked the Execute button on the application toolbar again (first button from the left). The print dialog box appeared. We clicked the Print Preview button. The output appeared as shown in Figure 3-75.

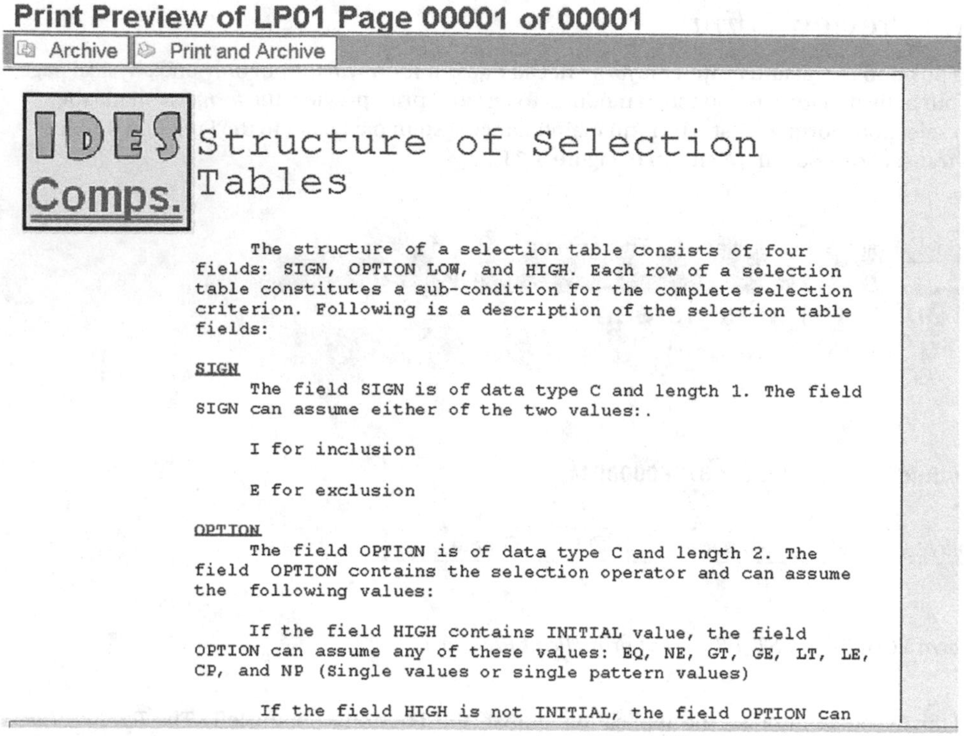

## Print Preview of LP01 Page 00001 of 00001

| 🗎 Archive | ▷ Print and Archive |

**IDES Comps.** Structure of Selection Tables

The structure of a selection table consists of four
fields: SIGN, OPTION LOW, and HIGH. Each row of a selection
table constitutes a sub-condition for the complete selection
criterion. Following is a description of the selection table
fields:

SIGN

The field SIGN is of data type C and length 1. The field
SIGN can assume either of the two values:.

I for inclusion

E for exclusion

OPTION

The field OPTION is of data type C and length 2. The
field  OPTION contains the selection operator and can assume
the  following values:

If the field HIGH contains INITIAL value, the field
OPTION can assume any of these values: EQ, NE, GT, GE, LT, LE,
CP, and NP (Single values or single pattern values)

If the field HIGH is not INITIAL, the field OPTION can

*Figure 3-75. Form YCH03_01_FST_FRM—output*

If you scroll down, you can view the rest of the text for the subheadings LOW and HIGH. The output is identical to the one we produced in demonstration I in Chapter 1, except for the color of the heading and subheadings.

## Recapitulation

We have implemented all the specifications listed at the commencement of this demonstration. We performed the following tasks:

1. Created a *style*.

2. Created *paragraph formats* and *character formats* in the *style* to be applied to format the text in the secondary *window* as per formatting specifications described.

3. Created a *form*

4. Created a single *page format*.

5. Created a *graphic*; included an imported bit map image from the SAP document server into the *graphic*

6. Created a secondary *window* and included text in the secondary *window*.

7. Saved and activated the *form*. Print previewed the *form* from the Smartforms *form* environment.

This was a demonstration. We did not need a driver program. We did not have variable data to be output. We could carry out the testing and demonstration from within Smartforms *form* environment.

# Demonstration II

In this demonstration exercise, we will produce the same output as in demonstration I, but with a major difference in approach. In demonstration I, we created the text directly in the secondary *window*'s *text* area. In the present exercise, we will create the text separately as a *text module*. The *text module* is a component of Smartforms. A *text module* created in the transaction code SMARTFORMS can be incorporated into multiple *forms*. A *text module* can be included in other *text modules* as well.

To format the *text module* we will use the *style* we created in demonstration I.

Our demonstration exercise involves the following steps:

1. We will create *text module* YCH03_01_SEL_TABLES and upload into it our text relating to selection tables. We will associate our *text module* with the *style* YCH03_01. We will use the *paragraph formats* P1, P2, and P3 and *character formats* C1 and C2 in *style* YCH03_01 to format the *text module*.

2. We will create a *form* YCH03_02_SEC_FRM with a single *page format* FIRST. We will create a *graphic* LOGO; include within it the imported bmp image from the SAP document server.

3. We will create a secondary *window* VARIABLE and include within it the formatted *text module* with a control command.

4. We will test print or print preview the *form* YCH03_02_SEC_FRM from the Smartforms environment.

Since this demonstration exercise is for most identical reputation of the demonstration I in this chapter, our descriptions will be somewhat brief and not elaborate. Let us proceed to performing the four steps.

## Create *Text Module* YCH03_01_SEL_TABLES

To create a *text module*, we used the transaction code SMARTFORMS. We ensured that the third Radio button was enabled. We entered YCH03_01_SEL_TABLES in the field *Text Module*. We clicked the Create button. A *text module* editor very similar to the *text* screen of a *form* appeared.

We need to associate the *style* YCH03_01 with the *text module*. To assign the *style* to the *text module*, we clicked the *Management* tab. On the *Management* tab, we assigned the *style* YCH03_01 to the field *Style Name* as shown in Figure 3-76.

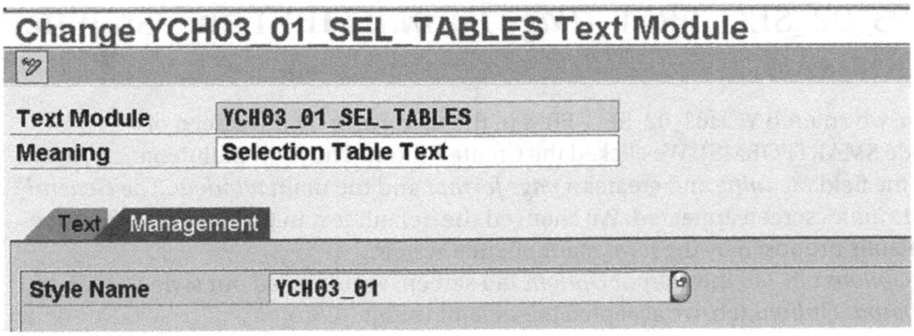

**Change YCH03_01_SEL_TABLES Text Module**

| Text Module | YCH03_01_SEL_TABLES |
| Meaning | Selection Table Text |

Text | Management

| Style Name | YCH03_01 |

*Figure 3-76. Text Module YCH03_01_SEL_TABLE—assign style*

We are inserting the text from user clipboard 5 into the *text module*. The text was uploaded from an operating system file into user clipboard 5 in the previous exercise. Recall that the user clipboards are non-volatile buffers. To insert the text from user clipboard 5 into *text module*, we made the following menu selection, Insert ➤ Clipboard ➤ User Clipboard ➤ Clipboard 5, as shown in Figure 3-77.

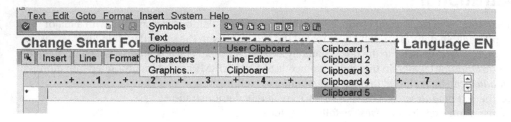

**Figure 3-77.** *Text Module YCH03_01_SEL_TABLES—menu selection to insert text*

The screen after the text is loaded from user clipboard 5 will be as shown in Figure 3-78.

```
     ....+....1....+....2....+....3....+....4....+....5....+....6....+....7..
P1
P3   <C1>Structure of Selection Tables</>
P1
P1
P2   The structure of a selection table consists of four fields:
=      SIGN, OPTION LOW, and HIGH. Each row of a selection table
=      constitutes a sub-condition for the complete selection
=      criterion. Following is a description of the selection table
=      fields:
P1   <C2>SIGN</>
P2   The field SIGN is of data type C and length 1. The field SIGN
=      can assume either of the two values:.
P2   I for inclusion
P2   E for exclusion
P1   <C2>OPTION</>
P2   The field OPTION is of data type C and length 2. The field
```

**Figure 3-78.** *Text Module YCH01_01_SEL_TABLES—text inserted*

The text has been uploaded with *paragraph formats* and *character formats* applied to the text for formatting.

We saved the *text module*. This concludes the creation of text in the *text module* which will be incorporated into a secondary *window* of a *form* to be created.

## Create *Form* YCH03_02_SEC_FRM—*Page Format* FIRST and Graphic *Window* LOGO

To create a Smartforms *form*, we entered YCH03_02_SEC_FRM in the field *Form* on the screen of *Smartforms* (transaction code SMARTFORMS). We clicked the Create button. The *form* maintenance system automatically enters text in the field *Meaning* and creates a *page format* and the main *window*. The *General Attributes* tab of the *Form Attributes* screen appeared. We changed the default text in the field *Meaning*. For the rest, we accepted the defaults proposed by the *form* maintenance system.

We clicked the *Output Options* tab. On the *Output Options* tab screen, we assigned our style YCH03_01. For the other fields on the *Output Options* tab, we accepted the default values.

We clicked the node of *page format*. We changed the name of the automatically created *page format* to FIRST and changed the default text in the field *Meaning*.

We created a *graphic* element LOGO and incorporated the graphic image YCH01_COMPANY_LOGO from the SAP document server into it. This is a repetition of the process described in the demonstration I of this chapter. We clicked the *Output Options* tab. We adjusted the *left margin* to 5MM and the *upper margin* to 5MM. This completes step 2—that is, the commencement of creation of the *form*, a single *page format* in it, and the creation of a *graphic* element with our image incorporated into it.

## Create *Form*—Create a Secondary *Window* VARIABLE and Include *Text Module*

To create a secondary *window*, we clicked the *graphic* node LOGO and invoked the context menu by pressing the mouse right button. We made the following menu selection: Create ➤ Window.

The screen to enter *window* particulars appeared. We want the *window* to be a secondary *window* which is the default. We changed the name of the *window* to VARIABLE (we are retaining the name from the SAP script exercise); we changed the contents of the field *Meaning*. We clicked the tab *Output Options*. On the *Output Options* tab screen, we entered *Left margin* as 46MM, *Width* as 160MM, *Upper margin* as 5MM, and *Height* as 190 MM. All this is again a repetition of what we did in demonstration I in this chapter.

We have not located anything in the main *window,* so we can delete the main *window*. We have retained the main *window* with the following dimensions: Left margin 5MM, Width 160MM, Upper margin 200MM, Height 5MM.

We have created a *graphic* and a secondary *window* as planned in this demonstration. Let us visually view layout of the *page format* FIRST in the *form painter*. To view the layout of the *page format* FIRST in the *form painter*, click the application toolbar button *Form Painter* (first button from the right). Figure 3-79 shows the layout of the *page format* FIRST in the *form painter*.

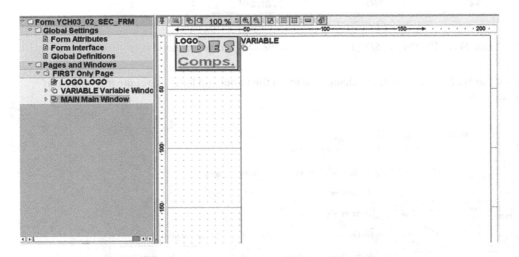

***Figure 3-79.*** *Create Form YCH03_02_SEC_FRM—layout in the Form Painter*

To include the text from the *text module* YCH03_01_SEL_TABLES in the secondary *window*, we have to create the element *text* under the secondary *window* VARIABLE. We selected the node of the secondary *window* VARIABLE and invoked the context menu by clicking the mouse right button. We selected the following context menu: Create ➤ Text.

On the *text* screen, we changed the name of the text to ST_TEXT and entered suitable description in the field *Meaning*. To incorporate a *text module* in the *text* area, we have to select *Text Module* from the dropdown list in the field *Text Type* on the tab *General Attributes*. Figure 3-80 illustrates.

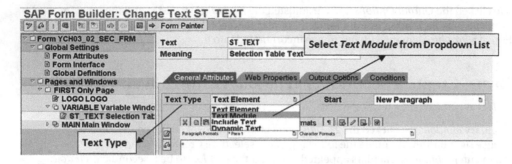

**Figure 3-80.** *Create Form YCH03_02_SEC_FRM—text type selection to incorporate text module*

The form maintenance system prompts with a confirmatory alert as shown in Figure 3-81.

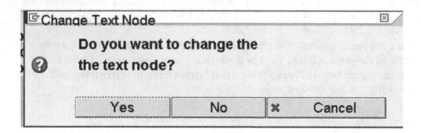

**Figure 3-81.** *Create Form YCH03_02_SEC_FRM—confirmation to change text node*

We clicked the *Yes* button. The screen changed to input the name and language of the *text module* as shown in Figure 3-82.

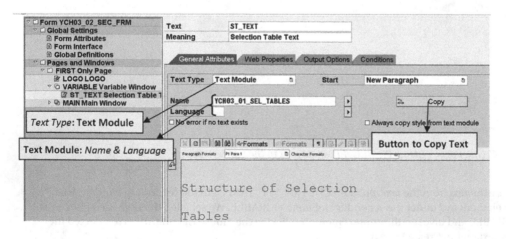

**Figure 3-82.** *Create Form YCH03_02_SEC_FRM—incorporate text module*

We entered the *Name* of *text module* as YCH03_01_SEL_TABLES. The *Language* field was left blank. The Smartforms *form* maintenance system will adopt the logged in language as the language of the *text module*.

The name of the *text module* can be selected from a list—function key F4, etc. The text of the *text module* YCH03_01_SEL_TABLES created in step 1 was incorporated into the element *text* of the secondary *window* VARIABLE. The incorporated text cannot be changed—it is not editable. In Figure 3-82, a button is marked as the Copy button. If you click this Copy button, the incorporated text becomes editable.

We performed a check on the *form* and activated the *form*.

This completes step 3.

## Test Print *Form* YCH03_02_SEC_FRM

Our *form* will output only one physical page. To test and print preview the *form*, we made the following menu selection: Form ➤ Test. The form maintenance system navigated to the Function Builder: Initial Screen—transaction code SE37. We clicked the Execute button on the screen of the function builder. The text function module screen appeared. We clicked the Execute button on this screen. The print dialog box appeared. We clicked the Print Preview button. The output appeared as shown in Figure 3-83.

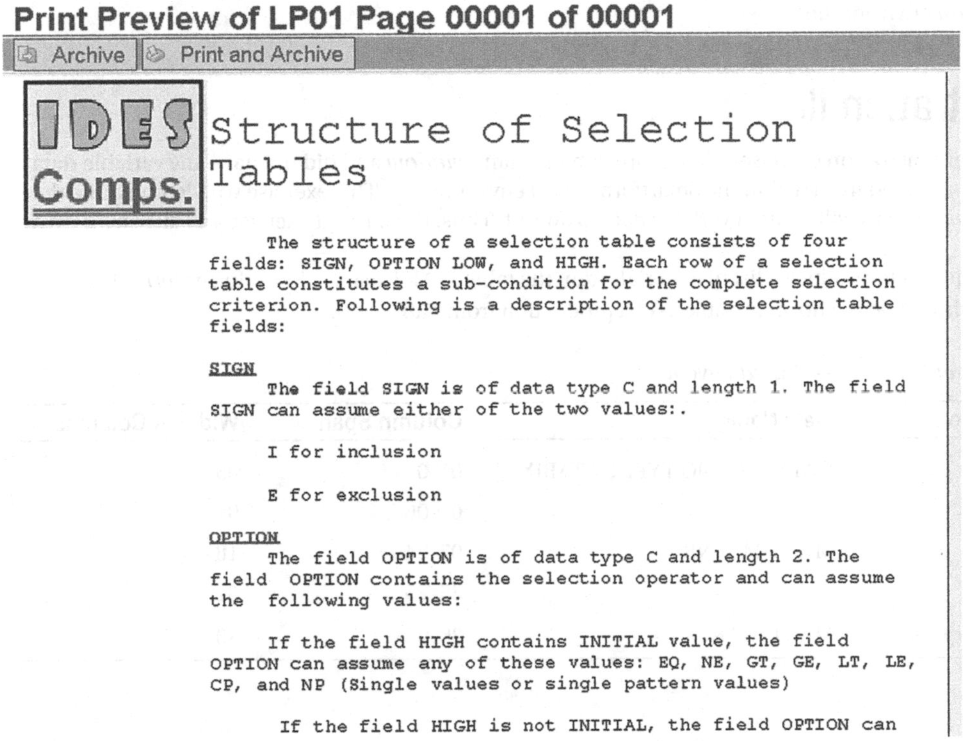

*Figure 3-83. Form YCH03_02_SEC_FRM—output*

The output is identical to the output produced by the *form* of demonstration I in this chapter. In demonstration I, we did not use any *text module*, whereas we used a *text module* to produce the output in the current demonstration.

## Recapitulation

Demonstration II set out to produce the same output as demonstration I in this chapter using *text module*. We performed the following steps:

1. Created *text module*; inserted text from user clipboard 5.

2. Created a *form*.

3. Created a single *page format*.

4. Created a *graphic*; included an imported bit map image from the SAP document server into the *graphic*.

5. Created a secondary *window*; included text from the *text module* in the secondary *window*

6. Saved and activated the *form*.

7. Print previewed the *form* from the Smartforms *form* environment.

Again, we did not have variable data to be output. So, we could carry out the testing from within Smartforms *form* environment.

# Demonstration III

The first two demonstration exercises did not operate the main *window* and did not have any variable data and were demonstrated from within the Smartforms *form* environment. This exercise will demonstrate the use of main *window* and will contain variable data to output. Thus, the current exercise will also use a driver program.

We are required to produce a list of materials from the table MAKT using a Smartforms *form*. The output layout should be as shown in Table 3-1 (reproduction from Table 1-7).

***Table 3-1.*** *List of Materials—Output Layout*

| Field Description | Field Name | Column Span | Width in Columns |
|---|---|---|---|
| Serial Number | DATA: SRL_NO TYPE SY-TABIX | 01-05 | 05 |
| | | 06-06 | 01 |
| Material Code | MAKT-MATNR | 07-24 | 18 |
| | | 25-25 | 01 |
| Material Description | MAKT-MAKTX | 26-65 | 40 |

The output should be like that in Figure 3-84.

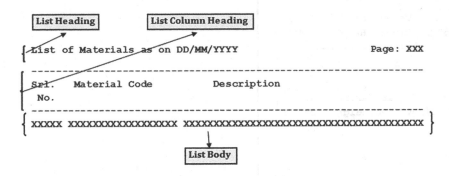

**Figure 3-84.** *List of materials—output*

Since the output involves a large volume of variable data, we need to have a driver program that will retrieve data from a source, load it into an internal table, and send the internal to the Smartforms *form*. This demonstration exercise will involve a *style, a form,* and a corresponding driver program.

We need to repetitively output the three fields SRL_NO, MAKT-MATNR, AND MAKT-MAKTX in a page and from page to page. The three fields constitute the body of the report. Recall that the data that repeats within a page and repeats from page to page is to be located in the main *window.*

For the *form* to generate the list of materials, we will have a single *page format*; we will locate the list body in the main *window* and the list heading along with the list column heading in a secondary *window.*

In the secondary *window,* we will locate list headings. In the main *window* we will locate the data of list body. The main *window* will continually receive one row of data (through a LOOP...ENDLOOP process in the within the *form*) and output it until the main *window* is full. At the point that the main *window* is full, a page break is triggered and output continues in the main *window* of a new page. This process continues until all the data is output.

The layout of *windows* will look like that in Figure 3-85.

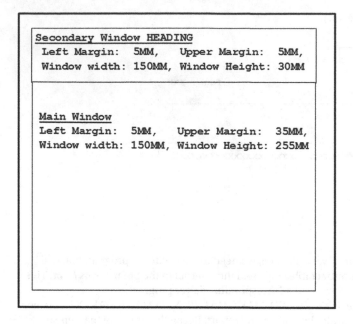

**Figure 3-85.** *List of materials—layout of windows*

The list heading will use the symbols &SYST-DATE& and &SFSY-PAGE& to output the 'as on' date and page number, respectively.

This is a repetition of demonstration III performed in the SAP script environment. The operation of main *window* in the Smartforms *form* environment is being demonstrated in this exercise.

We will load an internal table with data from the database table MAKT. The internal table will be passed as a TABLES parameter while calling the function module of the Smartforms *form*. The rest of the processing (setting up loop, etc.) will be carried out within the Smartforms *form*.

Apart from operating the main *window*, we will be deploying the following features of Smartforms for the first time:

- Using the TYPES statement in the *Global Definitions* area to declare custom types and then referring to the declared custom types to define data.

- Defining data in the *Global Definitions* area.

- Using the LOOP AT..... node to retrieve and process data one row at a time.

- Creating a node to locate ABAP code (program lines) .

So, let us proceed to create a *style*, a *form,* and, subsequently, the driver program.
Our demonstration exercise involves the following steps:

1. We plan to output the material list in font family courier and font size 10 points. This will involve creation and usage of a custom *style* instead of ready-to-use *style* SYSTEM. Hence we will create a *style* YCH03_02.

2. Create a *form* YCH03_03_MLIST1 with a single *page format* FIRST. Declare TYPES and define data in the *Global Definitions*. The *form* will consist of one interface TABLES parameter containing the data to be output.

3. Create a secondary *window* HEADING of dimensions as specified in Figure 3-85. Fill in the *text* area of LIST_HEADING in the secondary *window* as per the list and column headings of Figure 3-84. Create a node of *Program Lines* to assign the system field SFSY-PAGE to global variable PAGE.

4. Adjust the dimensions of the main *window* as specified in Figure 3-85. Create a *loop* element to retrieve and output data from TABLES *form interface* parameter. Fill in the *text* area of LIST_DATA in the main *window* as per the list body of Figure 3-84. Create a node of *Program Lines* to increment the global variable SRL_NO. Check and activate the *form*.

5. Create an ABAP program YCH03_01_MLIST1 (driver program) to retrieve and load data from the database table MAKT into an internal table. Call the function module corresponding to the Smartforms *form*. Perform program check and program activation.

6. Test the *form* YCH03_03_MLIST1 by executing the program YCH03_01_MLIST1.

Let us proceed to perform the six steps.

## Create *Style* YCH03_02

We entered YCH03_02 in the field *Style* on the screen of *SAP Smart Forms: Initial Screen* (transaction code SMARTFORMS) We ensured that the Radio button *Style* was enabled. We clicked the Create button. We entered a meaningful text in the field *Description*. On the *Standard Settings* tab screen, in the font area, we accepted the default font family as Courier. We entered the font size as 10 points.

We created a *paragraph format,* P1, with default values. We assigned *Paragraph Format* P1 as the standard paragraph on the *Standard Settings* tab screen. We saved the *style,* performed a check, and activated the *style*.

We created this *style* to output our material list in font size 10 points instead of the default font size 12 points.

## Create F*orm* YCH03_03_MLIST1, *Page Format* FIRST, etc.

The screenshots appearing in the figures in this exercise were produced after full creation and activation of the *form* and not as the *form* elements were created one by one.

We entered YCH03_03_MLIST1 in the field *Form* on the screen of *SAP Smart Forms: Initial Screen* (transaction code SMARTFORMS). We clicked the Create button. We entered a meaningful text in the field *Meaning*. On the *Output Options* tab of *form attributes* screen, we assigned the *style* YCH03_02. We accepted the default stationery DINA4. Figure 3-86 illustrates

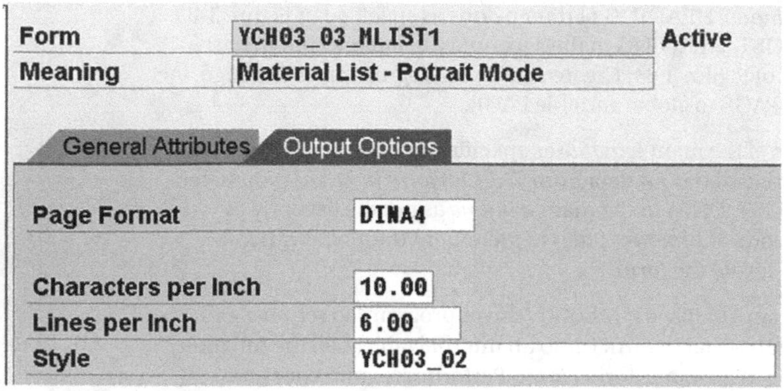

| Form | YCH03_03_MLIST1 | Active |
|---|---|---|
| Meaning | Material List - Potrait Mode | |

**General Attributes** / Output Options

| Page Format | DINA4 |
|---|---|
| Characters per Inch | 10.00 |
| Lines per Inch | 6.00 |
| Style | YCH03_02 |

*Figure 3-86.* *Create Form YCH03_03_MLIST1—assign style*

We clicked *page format* node, changed the name of the *page format* to FIRST, and changed the text in field *meaning*. We selected the default portrait mode210MM width and 297MM height. We assigned the value FIRST to the field *next page*.

We clicked the *Form Interface* node (under *Global Settings*); next we clicked the *Tables* tab. We created a TABLES parameter named MAKT_TAB like the structure of database table MAKT. Figure 3-87 illustrates.

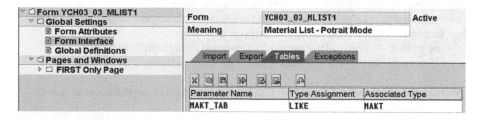

*Figure 3-87.* *Create Form YCH03_03_MLIST1—form interface, tables parameter*

We clicked the *Global Definitions* node (under *Global Settings*); next we clicked the *Types* tab. We created custom types using the TYPES statement as shown in Figure 3-88.

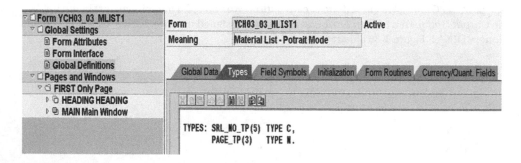

*Figure 3-88.* *Create Form YCH03_03_MLIST1—Global Definitions, declare custom types*

As shown in Figure 3-84, the material list output contains a serial number. We are generating the serial number within Smartforms by incrementing the variable SRL_NO in an ABAP code node. The variable SRL_NO used as a serial number has been declared in the tab *Global Data* of the *Global Definitions* screen. The variable SRL_NO has been declared referring to the type SRL_NO_TP.

We could have used the Smartforms system field SFSY-PAGE to output the page number in the list. We are using a variable PAGE declared in the tab *Global Data* of the *Global Definitions* screen. The variable PAGE has been declared referring to the type PAGE_TP. The use of the global variable PAGE to output page number was for demonstration purposes.

Under the *Global Definitions* screen, we clicked the *Global Data* tab. We declared the global variables required as shown in Figure 3-89.

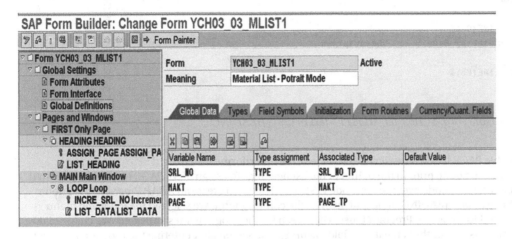

***Figure 3-89.*** *Create Form YCH03_03_MLIST1—Global Definitions, define global data*

The variables SRL_NO and PAGE have already been explained. The structure MAKT will serve the purpose of holding one row of data in LOOP AT node.

## Create Secondary Window, Create Text, etc.

To create a secondary *window*, we clicked the *page format* node FIRST and invoked the context menu by pressing the mouse right button. We selected the menu option Create ➤ Window.

The screen to enter *window* particulars appeared. We want the *window* to be a secondary *window* which is the default. We changed the name of the *window* to HEADING; we changed the contents of the field *Meaning*. We clicked the tab *Output Options*. On the *Output Options* tab screen, we entered *Left margin* as 5MM, *Width* as 150MM, *Upper margin* as 5MM, and *Height* as 30MM. Figure 3-90 shows the secondary *window* HEADING *Output Options* tab screen.

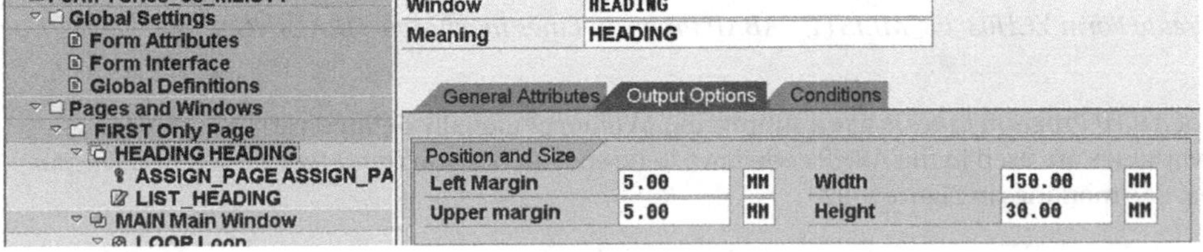

***Figure 3-90.*** *Create Form YCH03_03_MLIST1—secondary window HEADING*

To create a *text* node, we clicked the *window* HEADING node and invoked the context menu by pressing the mouse right button. We selected the menu option Create ➤ Text. When the screen for *text* appeared, we changed the name of the *text* to LIST_HEADING. We also changed the contents of the field *Meaning*. We clicked the full screen Text Editor button and created text as shown in Figure 3-91.

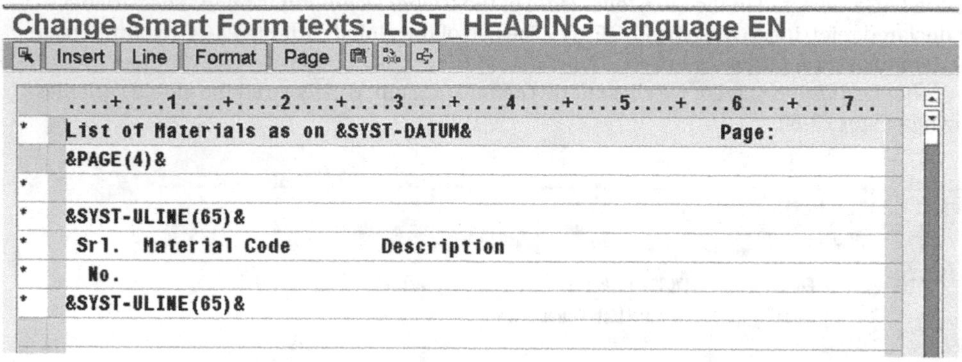

**Change Smart Form texts: LIST_HEADING Language EN**

| 🔍 | Insert | Line | Format | Page | 📋 | ⁝⁝ | ⇦ |

```
....+....1....+....2....+....3....+....4....+....5....+....6....+....7..
*  List of Materials as on &SYST-DATUM&                        Page:
   &PAGE(4)&
*
*  &SYST-ULINE(65)&
*   Srl.   Material Code          Description
*   No.
*  &SYST-ULINE(65)&
```

*Figure 3-91.* *Create Form YCH03_03_MLIST1—text in LIST_HEADING*

The variable PAGE has to be assigned the value of the Smartforms system field SFSY-PAGE. The assignment has to be done prior to the output of the list heading. To assign SFSY-PAGE to PAGE, we created an *ABAP Program Lines* node over the text node LIST_HEADING. To create an *ABAP Program Lines* node, we clicked the *window* HEADING node and invoked the context menu. We selected the following menu option: Create ➤ Flow Logic ➤ Program Lines. The screen for the program lines appeared. We changed the name of the node as well as the value in the field *Meaning*. The screen after entering the program lines will look like the one in Figure 3-92.

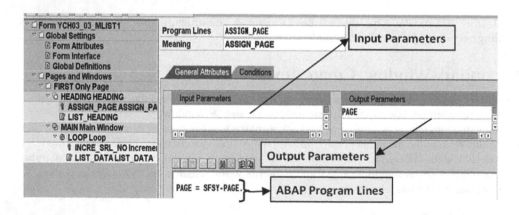

*Figure 3-92.* *Create Form YCH03_03_MLIST1—ABAP Program Lines in window HEADING*

The node of *ABAP Program Lines* is like a subroutine. Whatever globally defined variables and/or *form* interface variables are used in the ABAP code have to be specified in the *Input Parameters* and *Output Parameters* area. See markings in Figure 3-92.

We created the *form* YCH03_03_MLIST1 with a single *page format* FIRST. We assigned the *style* YCH03_02 to this *form*, We created the secondary *window* HEADING. We created the *text* LIST_HEADING in this *window* and incorporated the required text. We created an *ABAP Program Lines* node just above the *text* node TEXT_HEADING. We assigned the variable PAGE to the Smartforms system field SFSY-PAGE in the *ABAP Program Lines* node.

## Adjust Dimensions of Main *Window*, Create *Text* in Main *Window*, etc.

The main *window* is already created by default. We need to adjust its dimensions as per our specifications in Figure 3-85. We entered the dimensions of the main *window* as follows: *Left margin* 5MM, *Upper margin* 35MM, *Width* 150MM, *Height* 255MM on the *Output Options* tab screen of the main *widow*. Switching to the *graphic Form Painter*, we visually viewed the layout of the *windows* and confirmed that the layout is as per the requirements. Figure 3-93 shows the layout of the *windows*.

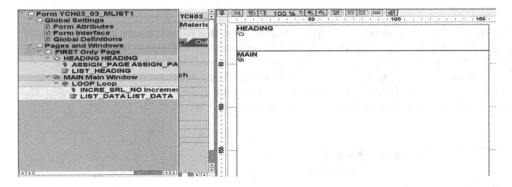

***Figure 3-93.*** *Create Form YCH03_03_MLIST1—windows layout*

We closed the graphic *Form Painter*. We need to create a *loop* element node under the main *window*. The *loop* element under the main *window* retrieves one row at a time from the interface TABLES parameter MAKT_TAB into the structure MAKT. To create a *loop* element node, we clicked the main *window* node, invoked the context menu, and made the following menu selection: Create ➤ Flow Logic ➤ Loop. The screen for the *loop* element appeared. We changed the name of the element to LOOP and entered text in the field *Meaning*. We ensured that the check box for *Internal Table* was enabled entered the internal table name as MAKT_TAB, and ensured that the INTO was selected from the drop-down list and entered MAKT in the field adjoining the INTO. Figure 3-94 illustrates.

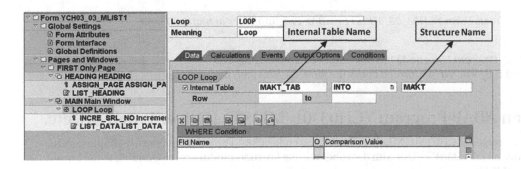

***Figure 3-94.*** *Create Form YCH03_03_MLIST1—Element loop node in main window*

245

We needed to create a *text* node in the main *window* under the *loop* element node. We clicked *loop* element node LOOP and invoked the context menu by pressing the mouse right button. We selected the menu option: Create ➤ Text. When the screen for *text* appeared, we changed the name of the *text* to LIST_DATA. We also changed the contents of the field *Meaning*. We clicked the full screen Text Editor button and created text as shown in Figure 3-95.

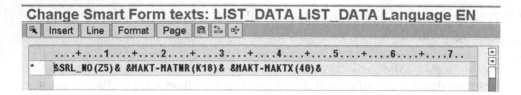

*Figure 3-95.* *Create Form YCH03_03_MLIST1—text in LIST_DATA*

We have to create a node to incorporate the ABAP *Program Lines* that will increment the global variable SRL_NO. This node containing ABAP *Program Lines* must precede the *text* node which outputs the material data. To create an *ABAP Program Lines* node, we clicked the *loop element* LOOP node and invoked the context menu. We chose the following menu option: Create ➤ Flow Logic ➤ Program Lines. The screen for the *Program Lines* appeared. We changed the name of the node as well as the value in the field *Meaning*. The screen after entering the *Program Lines* will look like the one in Figure 3-96:

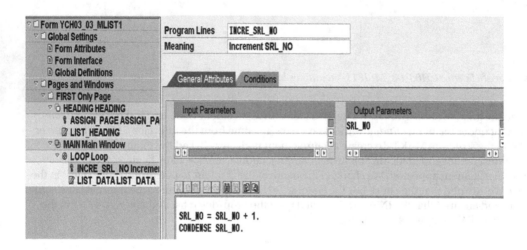

*Figure 3-96.* *Create Form YCH03_03_MLIST1—ABAP Program Lines in main window*

The ABAP *Program Lines* node has one output parameter: SRL_NO.
We saved the *form*. We performed check the *form*. We activated the *form*.

## Create an ABAP Program YCH03_01_MLIST1 (Driver Program), etc.

We created a program YCH03_01_MLIST1 (transaction code SE38). The program is a very simple one. It loads the internal table MAKT_TAB with data and calls the function module corresponding to the form YCH03_03_MLIST1.

The source program is listed in the code that follows.

```
REPORT  YCH03_01_MLIST1.

********************************************************
* Material List in Smartforms Form (YCH03_03_MLIST1) **
* F.M.: /1BCDWB/SF00000143                           **
********************************************************

DATA: MAKT_TAB TYPE STANDARD TABLE OF MAKT.

START-OF-SELECTION.

SELECT * FROM MAKT INTO TABLE MAKT_TAB UP TO 1000 ROWS
    WHERE SPRAS = SY-LANGU.

SORT MAKT_TAB BY MATNR.

CALL FUNCTION '/1BCDWB/SF00000143' "change the FM name as
                                   "per the generated name
  TABLES
    MAKT_TAB                  = MAKT_TAB
  EXCEPTIONS
    FORMATTING_ERROR          = 1
    INTERNAL_ERROR            = 2
    SEND_ERROR                = 3
    USER_CANCELED             = 4
    OTHERS                    = 5
               .
IF SY-SUBRC <> 0.
  MESSAGE ID SY-MSGID TYPE SY-MSGTY NUMBER SY-MSGNO
          WITH SY-MSGV1 SY-MSGV2 SY-MSGV3 SY-MSGV4.
ENDIF.
********************************************************
```

In the program, being in a training paradigm and testing state, we restricted the data from the database table MAKT to 1,000 rows. We are retrieving only material descriptions in the logged-in language (WHERE SPRAS = SY-LANGU), though our list and column headings will always appear in English.

## Test *Form* YCH03_03_MLIST1, Execute Program YCH03_01_MLIST1

We executed the program YCH03_01_MLIST1; the print dialog box popped up. We clicked the button *Print Preview*. The output will look as shown in Figure 3-97.

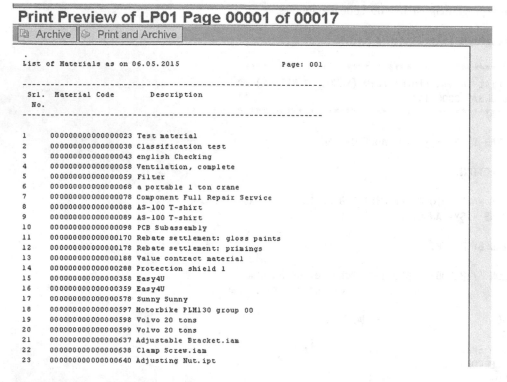

**Figure 3-97.** *Form YCH03_03_MLIST1—Output Print Preview*

The 1,000 materials are output in 17 pages as shown in Figure 3-97. The output is identical to the one produced by demonstration III in Chapter 1. You can scroll down and navigate to other pages of the list.

You can observe that the ABAP program used to output the material list in this exercise is relatively smaller and simpler when compared to its counterpart of SAP script print program.

## Recapitulation

Demonstration III produced a material list using a Smartforms *form*. We output large volume of variable data and so used the main *window* for the first time in Smartforms. The main *window* in Smartforms operates the same way it operates in SAP script. We also used the following for the first time in Smartforms:

- Types tab of the Global Definitions node

- Global Data tab of the Global Definitions node

- The use of Program Lines node

- The use of loop node

# Demonstration IV

In this exercise, as in demonstration III, we will use the main *window*. This exercise is a parallel of demonstration IV in Chapter 1. I will reproduce here the output generated by demonstration IV of Chapter 1.

The variable windows HEADING1 and HEADING2 in demonstration IV in Chapter 1 will exactly map to secondary windows of the same names. The list body will be located in the main *window*.

In Chapter 1, demonstration IV produced a material list in a newspaper columnar manner. The page was divided into two halves: left half of the page and right half of the page. The material list commenced in the left half of the page. When the left half of the page was full, the list continued in the right half of the page. When the right half of the page was full, a page break was triggered and list continued in the left half of a new page. This process of listing in the left half of the page and then the right half of the page continued until all the data was output. We produced the list by setting the page to landscape mode. This approach of listing resulted in effective paper utilization and reduced the size of the list from 17 pages in demonstration III to 13 pages in demonstration IV.

The process of producing the material list in the newspaper columnar manner (described in the preceding paragraph) relied on multiple *page windows* being assigned to the main *window* in the SAP script *form*. When using Smartforms, we do not have the two *form* elements *windows* and *page windows*. We only have *windows* which are equivalent to *page windows* in SAP script. The *page windows* in SAP script and the *windows* in Smartforms are similar elements, physical areas on a *page format* defined by a left margin, an upper margin, a width, and a height. A Smartforms *form* as SAP script *form* can have only one main *window*.

We cannot produce the material list using Smartforms in the facile and easy manner we produced it using the SAP script in Chapter 1. This is one of the instances in which a more recent tool does not carry all the good features of an older previous tool.

In this demonstration exercise we reproduced the output of demonstration IV in Chapter 1, but the reproduction of this output will involve a bit of tweaked programming as you will see.

Figure 3-98—reproduced from Chapter 1—shows a rough sketch of the output to be generated.

```
            List of Materials as on DD/MM/YYYY                                              Page: XXX

    ------------------------------------------------------------    ------------------------------------------------------------
    Srl.    Material Code        Description                        Srl.    Material Code        Description
    No.                                                             No.
    ------------------------------------------------------------    ------------------------------------------------------------
    XXXXX XXXXXXXXXXXXXXX XXXXXXXXXXXXXXXXXXXXXXXXXXXXXXXXXXX        XXXXX XXXXXXXXXXXXXXX XXXXXXXXXXXXXXXXXXXXXXXXXXXXXXXXXXX
```

***Figure 3-98.*** *List of mterials—Output in newspaper column manner in main window*

In demonstration IV in Chapter 1, we were outputting 78 items in a page, the first 39 items appearing in the left half of the page and 40—78 items appearing in the right half of the page. The 40th item appeared alongside the right of the first item, the 41st item appeared alongside on the right of the second item, and so on, until the 78th item appeared alongside the right of 39th item. Figure 3-99 illustrates.

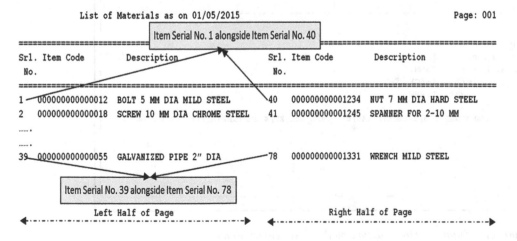

***Figure 3-99.*** *List of materials—depiction of data appearance in output*

Since in Smartforms, there is no concept of multiple *page windows* in the main *window* and multiple main *windows* cannot exist, we will have to organize data in an internal table in the driver program itself as it is to appear as output. We will have an internal table, say, MAKT_TAB, with a structure containing two sets of variables—first set of variables to output in the left half of the page and second set of variables to output in the right half of the page. The structure of the internal table will consist of the following fields:

SRL_NO1
MATNR1
MAKTX1


SRL_NO2
MATNR2
MAKTX2


In the present exercise, the variablesSRL_NO1, MATNR1, and MAKTX1 will output in the left half of the page and the variables SRL_NO2, MATNR2, and MAKTX2 will output in the right half of the page.

The first row in the internal table MAKT_TAB must contain the data for the item serial number 1 in the set of variables or fields SRL_NO1, MATNR1, MAKTX1 and must contain data for the item serial number 40 in the set of variables SRL_NO2, MATNR2, and MAKTX2.

Similarly, the second row in the internal table MAKT_TAB must contain the data for the item serial number 2 in the set of variables SRL_NO1, MATNR, and MAKTX1 and must contain data for the item serial number 41 in the set of variables SRL_NO2, MATNR2, and MAKTX2.

This pattern must continue. These two sets of variables, SRL_NO1, MATNR, MAKTX1 and SRL_NO2, MATNR2, MAKTX2, have to be located in the same line of the main *window*.

To sum up, the Smartforms *form* to output a material list in the manner it was done in demonstration IV of Chapter 1 will have a single *page format*. It will contain two secondary *windows*—HEADING1 and HEADING2. These two secondary *windows* are identical to the variable *windows* HEADING1 and HEADING2 of the SAP script *form* YCH01_04_MLIST1. It will have the main *window* to output the list body. In light of the foregoing descriptions, the layout of the *windows* of the Smartforms *form* YCH03_04_MLIST1 should be like that in Figure 3-100.

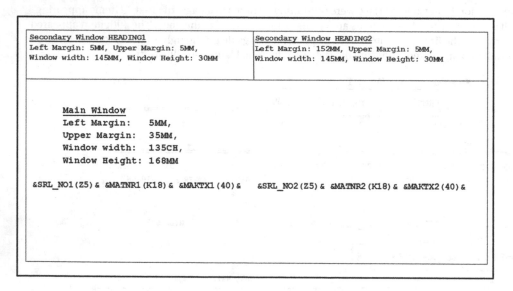

*Figure 3-100.* *List of materials in landscape mode—layout of windows*

Observe that the main *window* width is specified in characters (CH). The six program symbols—SRL_NO1, MATNR1, MAKTX1, SRL_NO2, MATNR2, and MAKTX2—to appear in the *text* area are shown as well in Figure 3-100. They are specified without the prefix of the structure (MAKT-).

Let us proceed to create the *form* YCH03_04_MLIST2, the driver program YCH03_02_MLIST2, and associated workbench objects.

## Create ABAP Dictionary Structure YCH03_2REC_MAKT_STRU

We created an ABAP dictionary structure YCH03_2REC_MAKT_STRU with fields and their respective data elements as specified in the Table 3-2.

*Table 3-2.* *Fields of ABAP Dictionary Structure YCH03_2REC_MAT_STRU*

| Field Name | Data Element Name | Type | Length |
|---|---|---|---|
| SRL_NO1 | SYTABIX | INT4 | 4 |
| MATNR1 | MATNR | CHAR | 18 |
| MAKTX1 | MAKTX | CHAR | 40 |
| SRL_NO2 | SYTABIX | INT4 | 4 |
| MATNR2 | MATNR | CHAR | 18 |
| MAKTX2 | MAKTX | CHAR | 40 |

We performed a check and activated the structure.

## Create *Form* YCH03_04_MLIST2

We created the form YCH03_04_MLIST2 in transaction code SMARTFORMS. We changed the name of the *page format* to FIRST, etc. On the *Output Options* tab of the *Form Attributes* screen, we assigned the *style* YCH03_02. We accepted the default values for all the other fields.

We clicked *Form Interface* node and *Tables* tab and entered one parameter as shown in Figure 3-101.

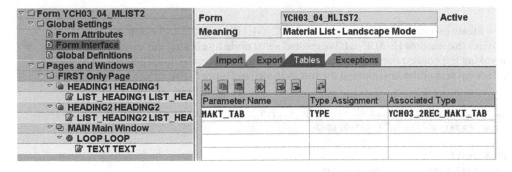

*Figure 3-101.* *Form YCH03_04_MLIST2—Form Interface, Tables Parameter*

We clicked the *Global Definitions* node, *Global Data* tab, and entered one variable as shown in Figure 3-102.

251

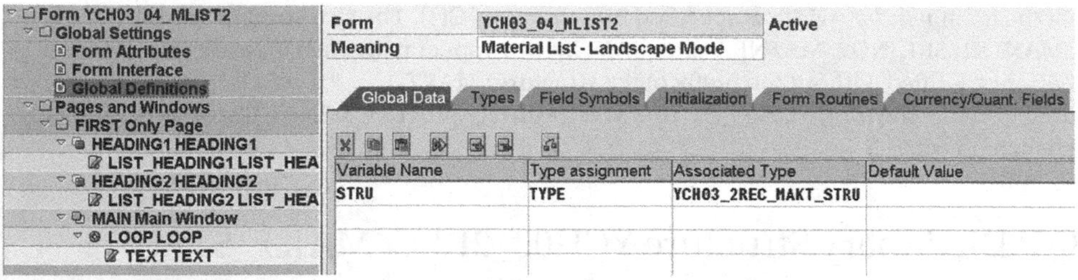

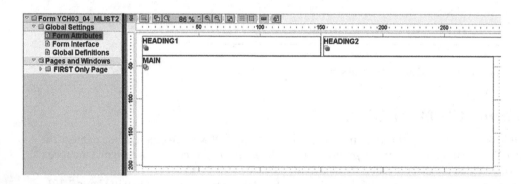

*Figure 3-102. Form YCH03_04_MLIST2—Global Definitions, global data*

We clicked the *page format* FIRST node and invoked the context menu to create the secondary *window* HEADING1 with the following dimensions: *Left margin* 5MM, *Width* 140MM, *Uppermargin* 5MM, and *Height* 30MM.

We created the secondary *window* HEADING2, with the following dimensions: *Left margin* 152MM, *width* 140MM, *Upper margin* 5MM, and *Height* 30MM.

We adjusted the dimensions in the main *window* as *Left margin* 5MM, *Width* 135CH, *Upper margin* 35MM, and *Height* 168MM. The main *window* width is specified in characters (CH).

The layout of the *windows* in *Form Painter* should look like that in Figure 3-103.

*Figure 3-103. Form YCH03_04_MLIST2—layout of windows in Form Painter*

We will now locate text in each of the *windows* HEADING1, HEADING2, and main.

We started with the window HEADING1. We created a *text* node by clicking the *window* node HEADING1, invoking the context menu and making the following menu selection: Create ➤ Text. We switched to full screen text editor and entered the text as shown in Figure 3-104.

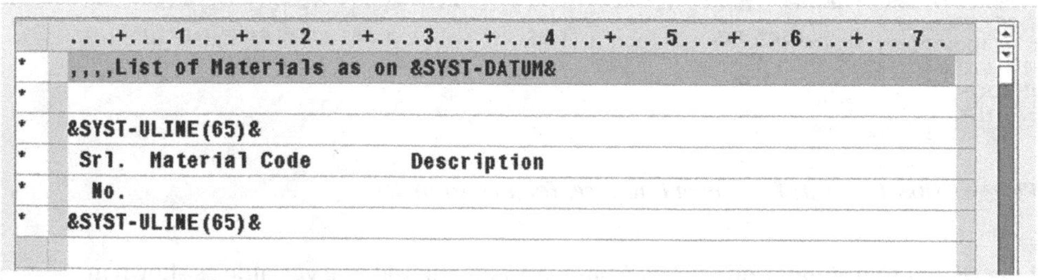

```
....+....1....+....2....+....3....+....4....+....5....+....6....+....7..
,,,,List of Materials as on &SYST-DATUM&

&SYST-ULINE(65)&
 Srl.  Material Code        Description
 No.
&SYST-ULINE(65)&
```

*Figure 3-104. Form YCH03_04_MLIST2—text in window HEADING1*

In a similar manner, we created a *text* node under the *window* node HEADING2, Figure 3-105 shows the text entered in *window* HEADING2.

```
    ....+....1....+....2....+....3....+....4....+....5....+....6....+....7..
*  ,,,,,,,,,,,,,,,,,,,,,,,,           Page: &SFSY-PAGE(3)&
*
*  &SYST-ULINE(65)&
*   Srl.   Material Code      Description
*   No.
*  &SYST-ULINE(65)&
```

**Figure 3-105.** *Form YCH03_04_MLIST2—text in window HEADING2*

We need to create a *loop* element node under the main *window*. The *loop* element under the main *window* will retrieve one row at a time from the interface TABLES parameter MAKT_TAB into the structure STRU. To create a *loop* element node, we clicked the main *window* node, invoked the context menu, and made the following menu selection: Create ➤ Flow Logic ➤ Loop. The screen for the *loop* element appeared. We changed the name of the element to LOOP and entered text in the field *Meaning*. We ensured that the check box for *Internal Table* was enabled, entered the internal table name as MAKT_TAB, ensured that the INTO was selected from the drop-down list, and entered STRU in the field adjoining the INTO. Figure 3-106 illustrates.

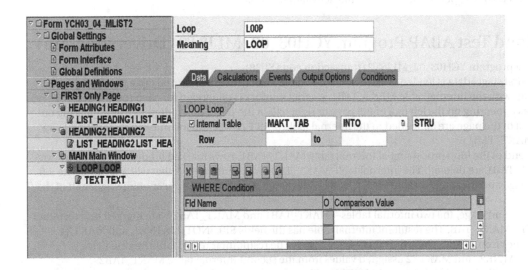

**Figure 3-106.** *Form YCH03_04_MLIST2—LOOP in main window*

Finally, we created a *text* node in the main *window* under the LOOP node; Figure 3-107 shows the text entered.

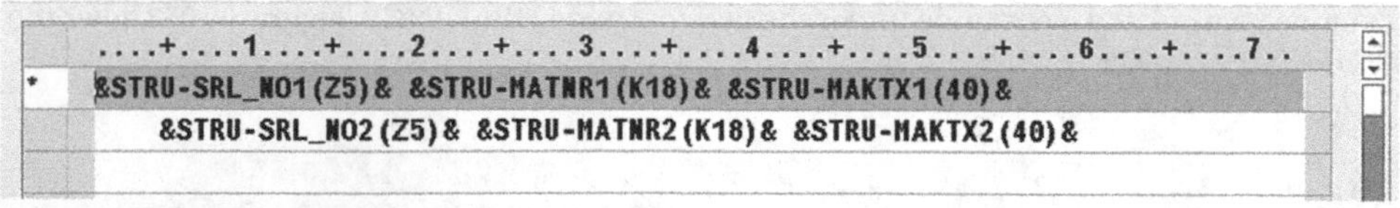

```
....+....1....+....2....+....3....+....4....+....5....+....6....+....7..
* &STRU-SRL_NO1(Z5)& &STRU-MATNR1(K18)& &STRU-MAKTX1(40)&
     &STRU-SRL_NO2(Z5)& &STRU-MATNR2(K18)& &STRU-MAKTX2(40)&
```

*Figure 3-107. Form YCH03_04_MLIST2—text in loop element LOOP*

This completes the *form* creation process.
The *form* consists of the following:

- One parameter of type *Tables* in the *Form Interface*: MAKT_TAB (internal table).

- One entry in the *Global Data*: STRU to hold data of one row fetched from the internal table MAKT_TAB through the *loop* element.

- One *page format* FIRST.

- Two secondary *windows* HEADING1 and HEADING2:

   ✓  *Text* within the secondary *windows* HEADING1 and HEADING2.

- Main *Window:*

   ✓  A *loop* element LOOP within the main *window*

   ✓  *Text* within the *loop* element LOOP.

We saved the *form*, performed a check, and activated the *form*.

# Create and Test ABAP Program YCH03_02_MLIST2 (Driver Program)

We created a program YCH03_02_MLIST2 (transaction code SE38).

In the first stage, data is loaded from the database table MAKT into the internal table MAKT_TAB1. A loop is set up with the internal table MAKT_TAB1. A serial number is generated for each row; each row is identified as appearing on the left half of the page or right half of the page. Rows identified as appearing on the right half of the page are appended to the internal table MAKT_TAB2 and are marked for deletion from the table MAKT_TAB1.

At the end of the loop processing of internal table MAKT_TAB1, rows marked for deletion in the internal table MAKT_TAB1 are deleted. The internal table MAKT_TAB1 will contain rows that will appear on the left half of the page and the internal table MAKT_TAB2 will contain rows that will appear on the right half of the page.

In the second stage, the two internal tables—MAKT_TAB1 and MAKT_TAB2—are merged into resultant internal table MAKT_TAB. The resultant internal table has the fields SRL_NO1, MATNR1, and MAKTX1 assigned values from the first internal table MAKT_TAB1. The resultant internal table has the fields SRL_NO2, MATNR2, and MAKTX2 assigned values from the second internal table MAKT_TAB2.

The fields SRL_NO1, MATNR1, and MAKTX1 will appear on the left half of the page and the SRL_NO2, MATNR2, and MAKTX2 will appear on the right half of the page.

The source list is as follows:

```
REPORT   YCH03_02_MLIST2.

******************************************************
* Material List in Smartforms Form (YCH03_04_MLIST2) **
* F.M.: /1BCDWB/SF00000147                          **
******************************************************

TYPES: BEGIN OF MAKT_STRU_TP.
         INCLUDE STRUCTURE MAKT.
TYPES:   SRL_NO TYPE SY-TABIX,
         END OF MAKT_STRU_TP.

CONSTANTS: THIRTY_NINE TYPE I VALUE 39.
             "no of items in each half of page

DATA: MAKT_TAB1      TYPE STANDARD TABLE OF MAKT_STRU_TP
                       WITH HEADER LINE,
      MAKT_TAB2      TYPE STANDARD TABLE OF MAKT_STRU_TP
                       WITH HEADER LINE,
      MAKT_TAB       TYPE STANDARD TABLE OF
                       YCH03_2REC_MAKT_STRU
                       WITH HEADER LINE.

DATA: QT1            TYPE I,
      RM1            TYPE I,
      RM2            TYPE I,
      OVER1(1)       TYPE C,
      OVER2(1)       TYPE C.

******************************************************
START-OF-SELECTION.

*******************
***** first stage **
*******************
SELECT * FROM MAKT INTO CORRESPONDING FIELDS OF TABLE
  MAKT_TAB1 UP TO 1000 ROWS WHERE SPRAS = SY-LANGU.

SORT MAKT_TAB1 BY MATNR.

LOOP AT MAKT_TAB1 INTO MAKT_TAB1.

 MAKT_TAB1-SRL_NO = SY-TABIX.
 QT1 = SY-TABIX DIV THIRTY_NINE.
 RM1 = SY-TABIX MOD THIRTY_NINE.
 RM2 = QT1 MOD 2.
```

```
IF ( RM1 > 0 AND RM2 = 0 ) OR ( RM1 = 0 AND RM2 > 0 ).
                    "rows on left half of page

  MODIFY MAKT_TAB1.
  CONTINUE.

 ELSEIF ( RM1 > 0 AND RM2 > 0 ) OR ( RM1 = 0 AND RM2 = 0 ).
                    "rows on right half of page

  APPEND MAKT_TAB1 TO MAKT_TAB2.
  MAKT_TAB1-SRL_NO = 9999999.
  MODIFY MAKT_TAB1.
 ENDIF.

ENDLOOP.

DELETE MAKT_TAB1 WHERE SRL_NO = 9999999.

*********************
***** second stage **
*********************
DO.
 CLEAR MAKT_TAB.

 IF OVER1 = ' '.
  READ TABLE MAKT_TAB1 INDEX SY-INDEX.
  IF SY-SUBRC = 0.
   MAKT_TAB-SRL_NO1 = MAKT_TAB1-SRL_NO.
   MAKT_TAB-MATNR1  = MAKT_TAB1-MATNR.
   MAKT_TAB-MAKTX1  = MAKT_TAB1-MAKTX.
  ELSE.
   OVER1 = 'X'.
  ENDIF.
 ENDIF.

 IF OVER2 = ' '.
  READ TABLE MAKT_TAB2 INDEX SY-INDEX.
  IF SY-SUBRC = 0.
   MAKT_TAB-SRL_NO2 = MAKT_TAB2-SRL_NO.
   MAKT_TAB-MATNR2  = MAKT_TAB2-MATNR.
   MAKT_TAB-MAKTX2  = MAKT_TAB2-MAKTX.
  ELSE.
   OVER2 = 'X'.
  ENDIF.
 ENDIF.

 IF OVER1 = 'X' AND OVER2 = 'X'.
  EXIT.
 ENDIF.
```

```
 APPEND MAKT_TAB.
ENDDO.

****************************************************
CALL FUNCTION '/1BCDWB/SF00000147'  "change the name as per the
                                    "name generated by the form
   TABLES
     MAKT_TAB                  = MAKT_TAB
   EXCEPTIONS
     FORMATTING_ERROR          = 1
     INTERNAL_ERROR            = 2
     SEND_ERROR                = 3
     USER_CANCELED             = 4
     OTHERS                    = 5
              .
 IF SY-SUBRC <> 0.
  MESSAGE ID SY-MSGID TYPE SY-MSGTY NUMBER SY-MSGNO
          WITH SY-MSGV1 SY-MSGV2 SY-MSGV3 SY-MSGV4.
  ENDIF.
****************************************************
```

## Test *Form* YCH03_04_MLIST2, Execute Program YCH03_02_MLIST2

When we executed the program YCH03_02_MLIST2, the output looked as shown in Figure 3-108.

**Print Preview of LP01 Page 00001 of 00013**

Archive | Print and Archive

```
        List of Materials as on 06.05.2015                                                          Page: 1

-----------------------------------------------------          -----------------------------------------------------
Srl.  Material Code      Description                            Srl.  Material Code      Description
No.                                                            No.
-----------------------------------------------------          -----------------------------------------------------

   1  000000000000000023 Test material                          40  000000000000000821 Carpeting
   2  000000000000000038 Classification test                    41  000000000000000897 HK -01
   3  000000000000000043 english Checking                       42  000000000000000898 HK -01
   4  000000000000000058 Ventilation, complete                  43  000000000000000938 Turbine
   5  000000000000000059 Filter                                 44  000000000000000939 Turbine casing 01
   6  000000000000000068 a portable 1 ton crane                 45  000000000000000947 Turbine casing 02
   7  000000000000000078 Component Full Repair Service          46  000000000000000948 Turbine casing 03
   8  000000000000000088 AS-100 T-shirt                         47  000000000000000949 Compressor 8x13
   9  000000000000000089 AS-100 T-shirt                         48  000000000000000950 Generator
  10  000000000000000098 PCB Subassembly                        49  000000000000000951 Control unit (rack)
  11  000000000000000170 Rebate settlement: gloss paints        50  000000000000000952 Lubrication unit
  12  000000000000000178 Rebate settlement: primings            51  000000000000000953 Bearing (complete)
  13  000000000000000188 Value contract material                52  000000000000000954 Cable high current 10 kA
  14  000000000000000288 Protection shield 1                    53  000000000000000955 Compressor high pressure part 1
  15  000000000000000358 Easy4U                                 54  000000000000000957 Compressor low pressure part
  16  000000000000000359 Easy4U                                 55  000000000000000958 Bearing easing
  17  000000000000000578 Sunny Sunny                            56  000000000000000959 Radial bearing
  18  000000000000000597 Motorbike PLM130 group 00              57  000000000000000967 Spring Fresh Detergent, 64oz
  19  000000000000000598 Volvo 20 tons                          58  000000000000000968 DVD: Miami Fun
  20  000000000000000599 Volvo 20 tons                          59  000000000000001009 Acsis Demo Product
  21  000000000000000637 Adjustable Bracket.iam                 60  000000000000001012 Acsis Demo Product
  22  000000000000000638 Clamp Screw.iam                        61  000000000000001015 Acsis Demo - Tablets
  23  000000000000000640 Adjusting Nut.ipt                      62  000000000000001016 Acsis Demo - Tablets
```

**Figure 3-108.** *Program YCH03_02_MLIST2—output*

This output is identical to the one produced by demonstration IV in Chapter 1.

## Recapitulation

If you were to compare demonstration IV in this chapter with demonstration IV in Chapter 1, you would realize that it is a better option to use a SAP script *form* than a Smartforms *form* when you need to output repetitive data both down and across the page. The output of repetitive data both down and across the page is facilitated by the support of multiple *page windows* assignation to the main *window* in SAP script *forms*, a facility unavailable in Smartforms *forms*. We managed to reproduce the output of demonstration IV in chapter 1 in this chapter, but it involved considerable tweaked programming, which is totally avoidable if you implement the output using SAP script *forms*.

# Conclusion

This chapter has introduced you to Smartforms as a further tool for maintaining business document layouts.

You have learned about the components of Smartforms: *forms*, *styles*, and *text modules*.

A detailed description of the elements of *form* was presented via a tour of a copy of the SAP delivered ready-to-use *form* /SMB40/MMPO_A.

We performed four demonstration exercises to highlight some basic core features of *forms*.

The first demonstration exercise (demonstration I) involved the creation of a *form* with a single *page format*, a *graphic* element, and incorporation of an image into the *graphic* element. The *form* also contained a secondary *window*. We created long text in the secondary *window*. The long text was formatted. The formatting of the long text in the secondary *window* required application of three *paragraph formats* and two *character formats*. We created the three *paragraph formats* and two *character formats* in a Smartforms *style*. We assigned the *style* to the *form*. We print previewed the *form* from within the *form* environment.

In the second demonstrative exercise (demonstration II) we created a *text module*. The *text module* content was the same text we created in the *secondary window* of demonstration I. The *style* we created in demonstration I was assigned to the *text module*. We then created a *form* with a single *page format* and a *graphic* element and incorporated an image into the *graphic* element. The *form* also contained a secondary *window*. We incorporated the *text module* created earlier into the secondary *window*. Finally, we print previewed the *form* from within the *form* environment. The output of demonstration I and demonstration II is identical. There is only a difference in the approach. In demonstration I, we created the long text within the *form* itself; in demonstration II, we created the text as a *text module* and incorporated the text of the *text module* into the *form*.

The third demonstration exercise (demonstration III) produced the material list using a Smartforms *form*. The material list fields had to be repetitively output, so they had to be located in the main *window*. We used a secondary *window* to output the material list heading. This exercise used the following extra features of Smartforms *forms* for the first time:

- Definition and use of *Types* under *Global Definitions* node

- Declaration and use of *Global Data* under *Global Definitions* node

- Use of *loop* element to retrieve and process row-wise data within the *form*

- Execution of ABAP program lines in a *window*

The fourth demonstration exercise (demonstration IV) attempted to reproduce the output of demonstration IV in Chapter 1. With this exercise, we realized that the SAP script is a better option to output repetitive data across the page.

In Chapter 4, we will create *forms*, their corresponding driver programs, and required workbench objects for specified business scenarios.

## CHAPTER 4

■ ■ ■

# Smartforms–Hands-on Exercises

Chapter 3 introduced you to Smartforms as an enhanced tool, compared to SAP script, to maintain business document layouts. Chapter 3 described the Smartforms environment, its components, and the different tools available to maintain the layout of business documents. As with SAP scripts in Chapter 1, in Chapter 3 we focused for the most part on the *form* component of Smartforms. Creating and maintaining business document layouts involves working mostly with *forms*. Chapter 3 also described driver programs (ABAP programs) associated with *forms* and the transfer of data from the driver programs to Smartforms *forms* through the *form parameters*. Demonstration exercises were performed to highlight and convey different concepts of Smartforms. In the present chapter, we will apply the Smartforms features introduced in Chapter 3 to implement business scenarios. As in Chapter 2, we are terming the implementation of business scenarios as "hands-on exercises."

We will perform the following five hands-on exercises involving creation and modifications of *forms* in this chapter:

- Output vendors' address labels of a specific company code.

- Output purchase orders with a custom *form*.

- Make a copy of SAP delivered *form* /SMB40/MMPO_A for purchase orders and customize it.

- Output material bar code labels.

- Produce customer wise sales summary of a specific company code using Smartforms *form*.

A detailed implementation of the hands-on exercises follows.

## Hands-on Exercise I—Output Vendors' Address Labels of a Specific Company Code

The first of the hands-on exercise involves the production of the address labels for vendors. The address labels will output for a specific company code. We will create a Smartforms *form* layout to produce the address labels. We will create a driver program and related workbench objects to produce the address labels for vendors.

© Sushil Markandeya 2017
S. Markandeya, *Pro SAP Scripts, Smartforms, and Data Migration*,
https://doi.org/10.1007/978-1-4842-3183-8_4

## Output Specification and Layout

We will output vendors' address labels of a specific company code. We will output vendors' address labels on DINA4 stationery in landscape mode—297MM width and 210MM height. We will output 15 address labels on a single sheet of DINA4 stationery in landscape mode. We will locate three address labels in one row and five address labels in one column with appropriate margins and gaps. Each of the address labels will be 93MM wide and 9 lines high. All of our address label data repeats within a page and repeats from page to page. Hence, for the *form* to output address labels, we will only use the main *window*. We will not be able to repeat vendor address data across a page as we were able to do in SAP script with multiple *page windows* assigned to the main *window*. There is no concept of SAP script *window* in Smartforms.

We are reproducing the output of hands-on exercise I, Chapter 2. We are employing Smartforms instead of SAP script now.

We will output the vendor address labels using the font Courier, font size 10 points.

Figure 4-1 shows a rough layout of the address labels as they will output in a page (reproduced from Figure 2-1, Chapter 2).

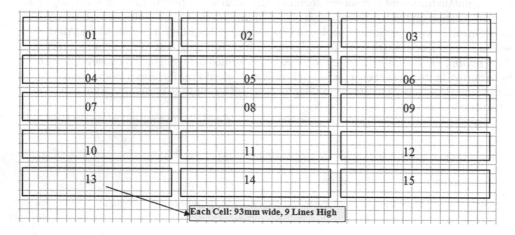

*Figure 4-1.* *Layout of vendors' address labels*

## Output Considerations

We will locate the vendor address data in the Smartforms element *table*. The sole line type of this element *table* will consist of five *cells* (columns) with the widths shown in Table 4-1.

*Table 4-1.* *Line Type of Element Table to Output Three Vendors in a Row*

| | | |
|---|---|---|
| Cell 1 | 93MM | (data) |
| Cell 2 | 04 MM | (gap) |
| Cell 3 | 93 MM | (data) |
| Cell 4 | 04MM | (gap) |
| Cell 5 | 93MM | (data) |

The *cells* with width 93MM will contain vendor address data; the *cells* with width 4MM are meant to create a horizontal gap between vendors' address data. Three vendor addresses will output across in a page and 5 vendor addresses will output down in a page, making a total of 15 vendor addresses to output in a page as shown in Figure 4-1.

The output of *cells* down the page will be the outcome of the operation of the element *table* in the main *window*. The repetition of data across the page will be implemented with some special data declaration and programming in the driver program and the Smartforms *form*.

For repetition of data across a page, I will resort to the procedure similar to the one we used in demonstration exercise IV in Chapter 3.

To be able to pass an internal table to Smartforms with the data of three vendors in one row, in our driver program or application program, we will declare an internal table with the structure or fields shown in Table 4-2.

*Table 4-2.* *Internal Table Structure Containing Three Vendors Data in One Row*

| Field Name | Description |
| --- | --- |
| ANRED1 | Title. This field is unavailable in database table ADRC, so should be picked from database table LFA1 |
| ADRNR1 | Address Number, to retrieve address from database table ADRC |
| SPRAS1 | Language Key of Vendor |
| ANRED2 | |
| ADRNR2 | |
| SPRAS2 | |
| ANRED3 | |
| ADRNR3 | |
| SPRAS3 | |

We have created an ABAP dictionary structure YCH04_LFA1_ADRNR_STRU consisting of the nine fields in Table 4-2.

Through the value of the fields ADRNR1, ADRNR2, and ADRNR3, the vendor addresses will be retrieved from the database table ADRC. The retrieved vendor address numbers along with the titles (ANRED1, ANRED2, and ANRED3) and language keys (SPRAS1, SPRAS2, and SPRAS3) are passed on to the function module ADDRESS_INTO_PRINTFORM. The function module will return the vendor addresses formatted in the postal convention of the recipient country. The vendor addresses will be returned in nine lines. Recall that the maximum number of address lines returned is ten. The number of lines in which the address is to be returned is specified in the field ANZZL of the structure ADRS.

We can insert the *form* element *address* in the *cell* numbers 1, 3, and 5 and provide the address numbers through fields ADRNR1, ADRNR2, and ADRNR3, respectively, to these *cells* of the element *table*. Within the element *address*, the vendor addresses are generated in the postal convention of the recipient country. The function module ADDRESS_INTO_PRINTFORM is used internally. With this approach, the blank lines if any in the address are suppressed in the output and a vendor address might occupy less space than the nine lines we assigned as vertical space to each vendor. Each vendor address must necessarily occupy nine lines of vertical space as per our output specifications. To ensure that each vendor address uniformly occupies nine lines of vertical space, we are retrieving the vendor address from the database table ADRC using the fields ADRNR1/ ADRNR2/ADRNR3, calling the function module ADDRESS_INTO_PRINTFORM explicitly to generate and return the nine lines of vendor addresses in the postal convention of the recipient country. The nine lines of vendor address returned fields are output by inserting the nine address field lines in the element *text* located in the *cells*.

One row in the internal table will contain title, address number, and language key data of three vendors mapping to the three data *cells* (*cell* numbers 1, 3, and 5 in Table 4-1) located in the line type of the element *table*.

To load the internal table with data of three vendors in one row, we will first load an internal table with data of one vendor in one row from the database view YCH02_LFA1_LFB1. We will then transfer the data from the internal table containing data of one vendor per row into the internal table that will contain data of three vendors per row. The database view YCH02_LFA1_LFB1 was created with the database tables LFA1 and LFB1 in Chapter 2. The company code field BUKRS is picked from the database table LFB1.

The ABAP program lines to fetch data from the database view YCH02_LFA1_LFB and load into an internal table with a structure consisting of fields for three vendors will be as follows:

```
TYPES: BEGIN OF INTER_STRU_TP, "one vendor per row
         LIFNR    TYPE LIFNR,
         ANRED    TYPE ANRED,
         ADRNR    TYPE ADRNR,
         SPRAS    TYPE SPRAS,
       END OF INTER_STRU_TP.

TABLES: T001.

DATA: LFA1_TAB    TYPE STANDARD TABLE OF YCH04_LFA1_ADRNR_STRU,
      LFA1_STRU   TYPE YCH04_LFA1_ADRNR_STRU, "ABAP dictionary
                                              "structure:three
                                              "vendors per row
      INTER_TAB   TYPE STANDARD TABLE OF INTER_STRU_TP,
      INTER_STRU  TYPE INTER_STRU_TP,
      COUNTER(1)  TYPE N.

**************************************************************
PARAMETERS: COMP_CD   TYPE KNB1-BUKRS DEFAULT 3000 VALUE CHECK.

**************************************************************
START-OF-SELECTION.

SELECT SINGLE * FROM T001 WHERE BUKRS = COMP_CD.

SELECT LIFNR ANRED ADRNR SPRAS FROM YCH02_LFA1_LFB1
       INTO TABLE INTER_TAB
       WHERE BUKRS = COMP_CD.

IF LINES( INTER_TAB ) = 0.
 MESSAGE S001(YCH02_MCLASS) DISPLAY LIKE 'E'."No Data Retrieved
 EXIT.
ENDIF.

SORT INTER_TAB BY LIFNR.

LOOP AT INTER_TAB INTO INTER_STRU.
 COUNTER = COUNTER + 1.
 CASE COUNTER.
  WHEN 1.
   LFA1_STRU-ANRED1 = INTER_STRU-ANRED.
   LFA1_STRU-ADRNR1 = INTER_STRU-ADRNR.
   LFA1_STRU-SPRAS1 = INTER_STRU-SPRAS.
  WHEN 2.
```

```
  LFA1_STRU-ANRED2 = INTER_STRU-ANRED.
  LFA1_STRU-ADRNR2 = INTER_STRU-ADRNR.
  LFA1_STRU-SPRAS2 = INTER_STRU-SPRAS.
 WHEN 3.
  LFA1_STRU-ANRED3 = INTER_STRU-ANRED.
  LFA1_STRU-ADRNR3 = INTER_STRU-ADRNR.
  LFA1_STRU-SPRAS3 = INTER_STRU-SPRAS.
 ENDCASE.
 IF COUNTER = 3.
  APPEND LFA1_STRU TO LFA1_TAB.
  COUNTER = 0.
  CLEAR LFA1_STRU.
 ENDIF.
ENDLOOP.
.....
```

At the end of LOOP AT......ENDLOOP processing, the internal table LFA1_TAB will contain three vendors' data in one row. The field LIFNR—vendor number—is being fetched from the database view to be able to sort the data vendor number wise.

All that remains to be done in the driver program is to call the function module of the *form* to output vendor address labels.

# Inputs

This is a repeat from a Chapter 2 hands-on exercise: The vendor address data is available in the vendor primary table LFA1 and through the field ADRNR in the table ADRC. As we are outputting vendor addresses of a specific company code, we need to link the two tables LFA1 and LFB1. We are using database view YCH02_LFA1_LFB1 created in Chapter 2. The *Table/Join Conditions* tab of the database view will be as follows:

```
LFB1         LFA1    MANDT   =      LFB1    MANDT
LFA1         LFA1    LIFNR   =      LFB1    LIFNR
```

The *View Flds* tab of the database view has the fields shown in Table 4-3.

*Table 4-3. Fields in the Database View YCH02_LFA1_LFB1*

| Srl. No. | Field/Table | Srl. No. | Field/Table |
|---|---|---|---|
| 01 | MANDT / LFA1 | 10 | ORT02 / LFA1 |
| 02 | LIFNR / LFA1 | 11 | PFACH / LFA1 |
| 03 | BUKRS / LFB1 | 12 | PSTL2 / LFA1 |
| 04 | LAND1 / LFA1 | 13 | PSTLZ / LFA1 |
| 05 | NAME1 / LFA1 | 14 | REGIO / LFA1 |
| 06 | NAME2 / LFA1 | 15 | STRAS / LFA1 |
| 07 | NAME3 / LFA1 | 16 | ADRNR / LFA1 |
| 08 | NAME4 / LFA1 | 17 | ANRED / LFA1 |
| 09 | ORT01 / LFA1 | | |

The view YCH02_LFA1_LFB1 is our sole input.

## Creation of *Style* YCH04_01, *Form* YCH04_01_ADR_STK and Driver Program YCH04_01_DPRG_YCH04_01_ADR_STK

As we plan to output vendor address labels in font Courier, font size 10, we created a *style* YCH04_01 using transaction code SMARTFORMS. In the *style* YCH04_01, for the standard paragraph SP, we assigned the font Courier, font size 10. For the rest, we accepted the default values. Figure 4-2 shows a screenshot of the paragraph SP, *style* YCH04_01.

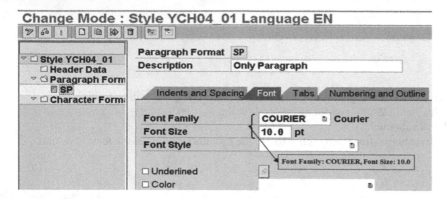

*Figure 4-2.* *Style: YCH04_01—standard paragraph SP*

Next, in transaction code SMARTFORMS, we created the *form* YCH04_01_ADR_STK. We assigned the *style* YCH04_01 in the *Output Options* tab of the *Form Attributes* node. We made the page orientation landscape. The *form* consisted of a single *page format* ONLY_PG.

We assigned the next page for *page format* ONLY_PG as ONLY_PG.

The *form* will contain one import parameter and one table parameter. The *Sending country key* is to be provided to the function module ADDRESS_INTO_PRINTFORM, returning the address in the format of the recipient country's postal convention. The field T001-LAND1 is required from the driver program. I have named the import parameter LAND1. The table parameter is the internal table containing the data of three vendors in a single row. I have named the table parameter LFA1_ADRNR_TAB. Figures 4-3 and 4-4 are screenshots of the tabs *Import* and *Tables* of the node *Form Interface*.

| Parameter Name | Type Assignment | Associated Type |
|---|---|---|
| ARCHIVE_INDEX | TYPE | TOA_DARA |
| ARCHIVE_INDEX_TAB | TYPE | TSFDARA |
| ARCHIVE_PARAMETERS | TYPE | ARC_PARAMS |
| CONTROL_PARAMETERS | TYPE | SSFCTRLOP |
| MAIL_APPL_OBJ | TYPE | SWOTOBJID |
| MAIL_RECIPIENT | TYPE | SWOTOBJID |
| MAIL_SENDER | TYPE | SWOTOBJID |
| OUTPUT_OPTIONS | TYPE | SSFCOMPOP |
| USER_SETTINGS | TYPE | TDBOOL |
| LAND1 | LIKE | T001-LAND1 |

Form Interface
Global Definitions
▽ Pages and Windows
▷ ONLY_PG ONLY PAGE

Import  Export  Tables  Exceptions

*Figure 4-3.* *Form Interface: tab—Import*

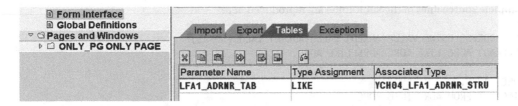

**Figure 4-4.** *Form Interface: tab—Tables*

To operate the function module ADDRESS_INTO_PRINTFORM returning the address in the format of the recipient country's postal convention, we need the structures ADRS and ADRC. Hence the structures have been defined in the *Global Data* tab of the *Global Definitions* node as shown in Figure 4-5.

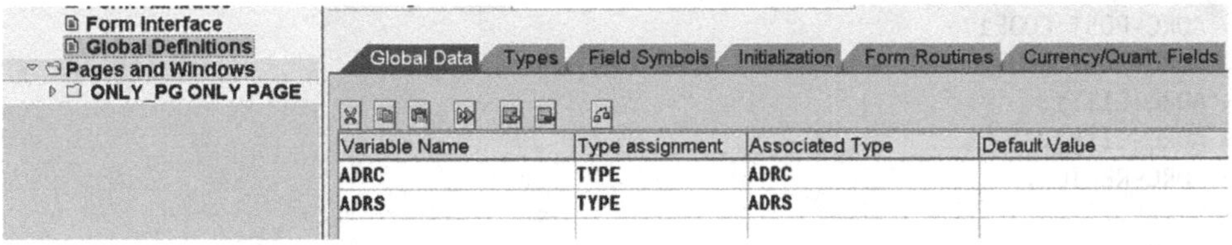

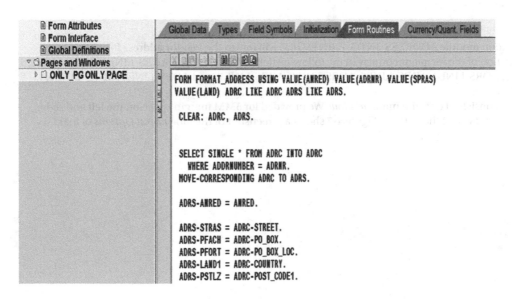

**Figure 4-5.** *Global Definitions: tab—Global Data*

The function module ADDRESS_INTO_PRINTFORM is to be called with three different values: ADRNR1, ADRNR2, and ADRNR3 Address numbers). We located a subroutine in the *Form Routines* tab of the *Global Definitions node*. This subroutine will accept different values of address numbers and call the function module ADDRESS_INTO_PRINTFORM. Figure 4-6 shows the *Form Routines* tab.

```
FORM FORMAT_ADDRESS USING VALUE(ANRED) VALUE(ADRNR) VALUE(SPRAS)
VALUE(LAND) ADRC LIKE ADRC ADRS LIKE ADRS.

    CLEAR: ADRC, ADRS.


    SELECT SINGLE * FROM ADRC INTO ADRC
        WHERE ADDRNUMBER = ADRNR.
    MOVE-CORRESPONDING ADRC TO ADRS.

    ADRS-ANRED = ANRED.

    ADRS-STRAS = ADRC-STREET.
    ADRS-PFACH = ADRC-PO_BOX.
    ADRS-PFORT = ADRC-PO_BOX_LOC.
    ADRS-LAND1 = ADRC-COUNTRY.
    ADRS-PSTLZ = ADRC-POST_CODE1.
```

**Figure 4-6.** *Global Definitions: tab—Form Routines*

The complete source lines of the subroutine are reproduced here.

```
FORM FORMAT_ADDRESS USING VALUE(ANRED) VALUE(ADRNR) VALUE(SPRAS)
     VALUE(LAND) ADRC LIKE ADRC ADRS LIKE ADRS.

 CLEAR: ADRC, ADRS.
 SELECT SINGLE * FROM ADRC INTO ADRC
   WHERE ADDRNUMBER = ADRNR.
 MOVE-CORRESPONDING ADRC TO ADRS.


 ADRS-ANRED = ANRED.
 ADRS-STRAS = ADRC-STREET.
 ADRS-PFACH = ADRC-PO_BOX.
 ADRS-PFORT = ADRC-PO_BOX_LOC.
 ADRS-LAND1 = ADRC-COUNTRY.
 ADRS-PSTLZ = ADRC-POST_CODE1.
 ADRS-PSTL2 = ADRC-POST_CODE2.
 ADRS-ORTO1 = ADRC-CITY1.
 ADRS-ORTO2 = ADRC-CITY2.
 ADRS-REGIO = ADRC-REGION.
 ADRS-SPRAS = SPRAS.
 ADRS-INLND = LAND.
 ADRS-ANZZL = 9.


 CALL FUNCTION 'ADDRESS_INTO_PRINTFORM'
   EXPORTING
     ADRSWA_IN                        = ADRS
   IMPORTING
     ADRSWA_OUT                       = ADRS
             .
ENDFORM.
```

The function module ADDRESS_INTO_PRINTFORM will return the vendor address formatted in the postal convention of the recipient country in the following fields: ADRS-LINE0, ADRS-LINE1, ADRS-LINE2, ADRS-LINE3, ADRS-LINE4, ADRS-LINE5, ADRS-LINE6, ADRS-LINE7, and ADRS-LINE8 (ADRS-LINE0..... ADRS-LINE8).

The *form* consists of only the main *window*. We provided for 5MM margin space on the left and right, 3MM on top, and 2MM at the bottom. Figure 4-7 shows a screenshot of the tab *Output Options* of main *window*.

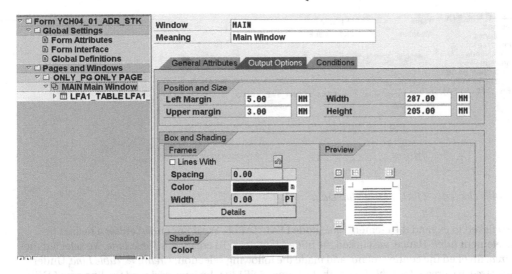

**Figure 4-7.** *Main Window tab—Output Options*

Under Main *Window*, we created an element *table* named LFA1_TAB. To create the element *table*, we selected the node of Main *Window*, invoked the context menu, and made the following selection: *Create* ➤ *Table*. We created a single line type for the element *table* named LINE1. The line type LINE1 consists of five *cells* as per Table 4-1. Figure 4-8 shows the line type LINE1.

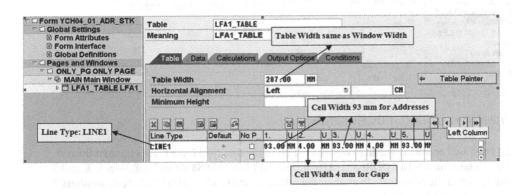

**Figure 4-8.** *Table element—LFA1_TABLE, Line Type: LINE1*

We navigated to the line type screen from the default *Table Painter* screen by clicking the *Details* button. We can navigate back to the *Table Painter* screen by clicking the button *Table Painter*. The element *table* consists of five tabs: *Table, Data, Calculations, Output Options,* and *Conditions.*

After creating the line type, we clicked the *Data* tab. In the *Data* tab, we entered the internal table to be used by the element *table* (i.e., the *tables* parameter in *Form Interface*: LFA1_ADRNR_TAB). Since the *tables* parameter implicitly provides you with a header line, we have specified the same name, LFA1_ADRNR_TAB, as the work area. Figure 4-9 is a screenshot of the tab *Data*.

267

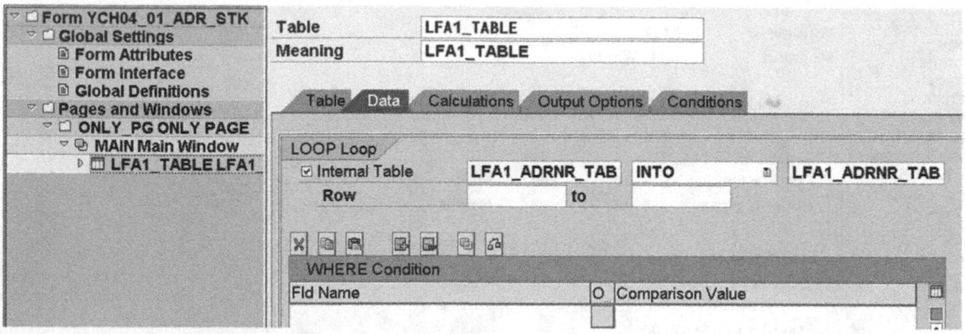

***Figure 4-9.*** *Table element—LFA1_TABLE: tab Data*

Next, we clicked to expand the element *table* node LFA1_TABLE. We do not need either a header or footer for the element *table*. Hence, we clicked the node *Main Area*. To create the *Table Line*, we selected the node *Main Area*, invoked the context menu, and made the following selection: *Create* ➤ *Table Line*. Under the node *Main Area*, we created a *Table Line* with the name LINE1 to which we assigned the line type LINE1. Figure 4-10 illustrates.

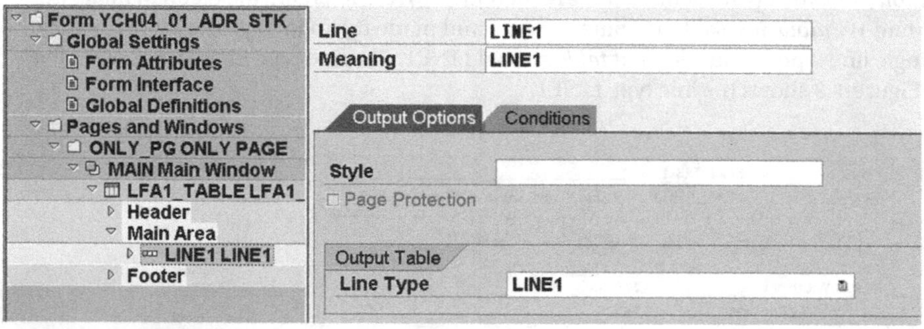

***Figure 4-10.*** *Table element—LFA1_TABLE, line type LINE1*

The node LINE1 will consist of the five *cells* we created in the line type LINE1. We changed the *cell* names from their default names to ADDRESS1, ADDRESS2, and ADDRESS3 for *cell* numbers 1, 3, and 5, respectively. We changed the *cell* names from their default names to GAP1 and GAP2 for *cell* numbers 2 and 4, respectively. Figure 4-11 illustrates.

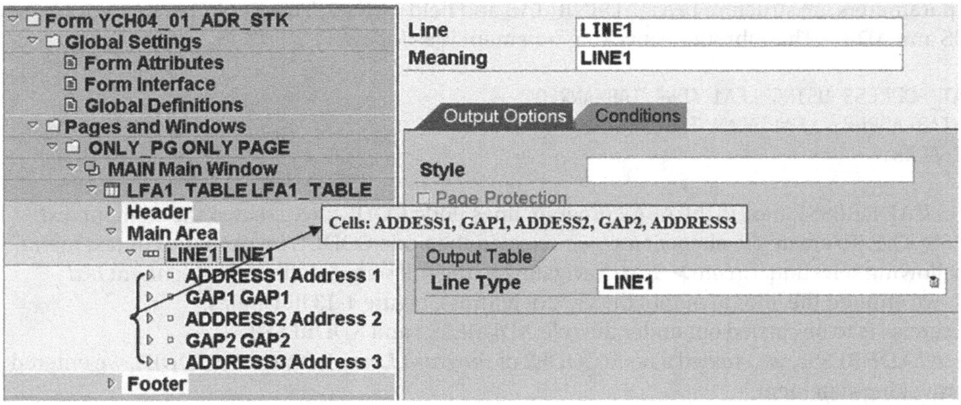

**Figure 4-11.** *Line type—LINE1, cells: ADDRESS1, GAP1, ADDESS2, GAP2, and ADDRESS3*

We need to create the element *text* in the *cells* ADDRESS1, ADDRESS2, and ADDRESS3 and locate the address output variables ADRS-LINE0.....ADRS-LINE8 in the element *text* of each of these nodes.

But before we output the variables, ADRS-LINE0.....ADRS-LINE8 in the element *text* of each of these *cells*, we need to execute the function module ADDRESS_INTO_PRINTFORM. So, under the *cells* ADDRESS1, ADDRESS2, and ADDRESS3, just before the node of element *text*, we need to create nodes for the execution of ABAP *Program Lines*. We will be invoking the subroutine FORMAT_ADDRESS in the *Program Lines*. We earlier located the subroutine FORMAT_ADDRESS in the *Form Routines* tab under the node *Global Definitions*. We are calling the function module ADDRESS_INTO_PRINTFORM in the subroutine FORMAT_ADDRESS for the vendor address to be formatted as per the recipient country's postal convention and return it.

To create the *Program Lines*, we selected the node ADDRESS1, invoked the context menu, and made the following selection: *Create ➤ Flow Logic ➤Program Lines*. Figure 4-12 shows the *Program Lines* node CODE1 that we created under the *cell* ADDRESS1.

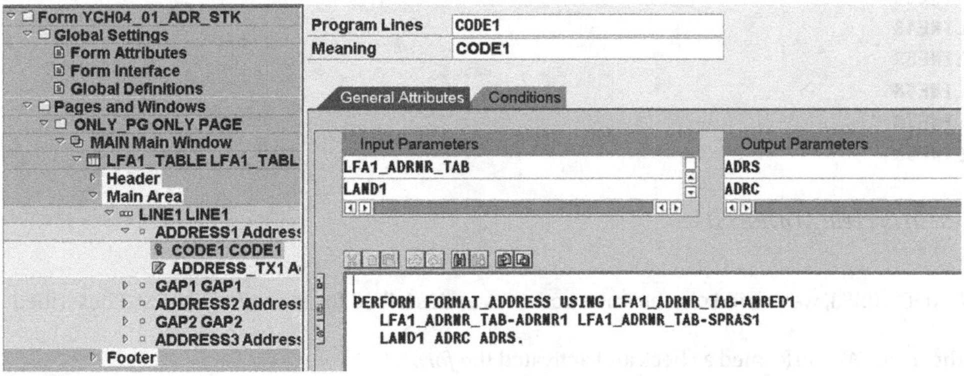

**Figure 4-12.** *Program Lines under the cell ADDRESS1*

The input parameters are structure LFA1_ADRNR_TAB and field LAND1. The output parameters are structures ADRS and ADRC. The subroutine invoking statement is as follows:

```
PERFORM FORMAT_ADDRESS USING LFA1_ADNR_TAB-ANRED1
   LFA1_ADNR_TAB-ADRNR1 LFA1_ADNR_TAB-SPRAS1
   LAND1 ADRC ADRS.
```

Under the *cell* ADDRESS1, next to the ABAP program lines node CODE1, we created the element *text* named ADDRESS_TX1. To create the element *text*, we selected the node CODE1, invoked the context menu, and made the following selection: *Create* ➤ *Text*. Navigating to the full screen editor of the element *text* ADDRESS_TX1, we entered the lines to output the vendor address. Figure 4-13 illustrates.

A similar exercise is to be carried out under the *cells* ADDRESS2 and ADDRESS3.

Under the *cell* ADDRESS2, we created a node CODE2 of *Program Lines*. In the node CODE2, we entered the subroutine invoking statement.

```
PERFORM FORMAT_ADDRESS USING LFA1_ADNR_TAB-ANRED2
   LFA1_ADNR_TAB-ADRNR2 LFA1_ADNR_TAB-SPRAS2
   LAND1 ADRC ADRS.
```

Under the *cell* ADDRESS2, next to the *Program Lines* node CODE2, we created the element *text* named ADDRESS_TX2. Navigating to the full screen editor of the element *text* ADDRESS_TX2, we entered the same lines that we entered as shown in Figure 4-13.

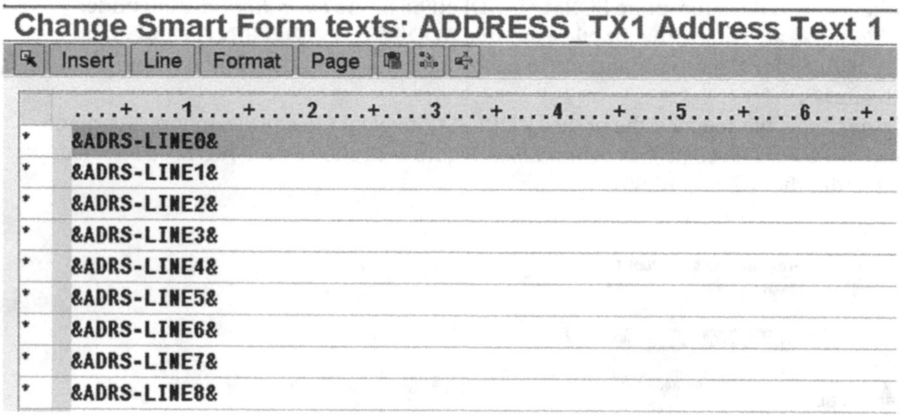

*Figure 4-13.* Text in the cell: ADDRESS1

For the *cell* ADDRESS3, we carried out the same activities as described for the *cell* ADDRESS2 described previously.

We saved the *form*. We performed a check and activated the *form*.

We created an ABAP program YCH04_01_PPRG_YCH04_01_ADR_STK with the lines as shown under 'Source program'. We performed syntax check and activated this program.

Following is the complete source program:

```
REPORT   YCH04_01_DPRG_YCH04_01_ADR_STK.

**********************************************************
* Address Labels for Vendors of a Specific Company Code **
**********************************************************

TYPES: BEGIN OF INTER_STRU_TP,
         LIFNR    TYPE LIFNR,
         ANRED    TYPE ANRED,
         ADRNR    TYPE ADRNR,
         SPRAS    TYPE SPRAS,
       END OF INTER_STRU_TP.

TABLES: T001.

DATA: LFA1_TAB    TYPE STANDARD TABLE OF YCH04_LFA1_ADRNR_STRU,
      LFA1_STRU   TYPE YCH04_LFA1_ADRNR_STRU, "ABAP dictionary
                                              "structure
      INTER_TAB   TYPE STANDARD TABLE OF INTER_STRU_TP,
      INTER_STRU  TYPE INTER_STRU_TP,
      COUNTER(1)  TYPE N.

***************************************************************
PARAMETERS: COMP_CD   TYPE KNB1-BUKRS DEFAULT 3000 VALUE CHECK.

***************************************************************
START-OF-SELECTION.

SELECT SINGLE * FROM T001 WHERE BUKRS = COMP_CD.

SELECT LIFNR ANRED ADRNR SPRAS FROM YCH02_LFA1_LFB1
        INTO TABLE INTER_TAB
        WHERE BUKRS = COMP_CD.

IF LINES( INTER_TAB ) = 0.
 MESSAGE S001(YCH02_MCLASS) DISPLAY LIKE 'E'."No Data Retrieved
 EXIT.
ENDIF.

SORT INTER_TAB BY LIFNR.

LOOP AT INTER_TAB INTO INTER_STRU.
 COUNTER = COUNTER + 1.
 CASE COUNTER.
  WHEN 1.
   LFA1_STRU-ANRED1 = INTER_STRU-ANRED.
   LFA1_STRU-ADRNR1 = INTER_STRU-ADRNR.
   LFA1_STRU-SPRAS1 = INTER_STRU-SPRAS.
```

271

```
  WHEN 2.
    LFA1_STRU-ANRED2 = INTER_STRU-ANRED.
    LFA1_STRU-ADRNR2 = INTER_STRU-ADRNR.
    LFA1_STRU-SPRAS2 = INTER_STRU-SPRAS.
  WHEN 3.
    LFA1_STRU-ANRED3 = INTER_STRU-ANRED.
    LFA1_STRU-ADRNR3 = INTER_STRU-ADRNR.
    LFA1_STRU-SPRAS3 = INTER_STRU-SPRAS.
 ENDCASE.
 IF COUNTER = 3.
  APPEND LFA1_STRU TO LFA1_TAB.
  COUNTER = 0.
  CLEAR LFA1_STRU.
 ENDIF.
ENDLOOP.
************************************************************
IF COUNTER > 0.
 APPEND LFA1_STRU TO LFA1_TAB.
ENDIF.
************************************************************
CALL FUNCTION '/1BCDWB/SF00000149' "change the FM name as
                                   "per the generated name

  EXPORTING
    LAND1                    = T001-LAND1
  TABLES
    LFA1_ADRNR_TAB           = LFA1_TAB
  EXCEPTIONS
    FORMATTING_ERROR         = 1
    INTERNAL_ERROR           = 2
    SEND_ERROR               = 3
    USER_CANCELED            = 4
    OTHERS                   = 5.
IF SY-SUBRC <> 0.
 MESSAGE ID SY-MSGID TYPE SY-MSGTY NUMBER SY-MSGNO
         WITH SY-MSGV1 SY-MSGV2 SY-MSGV3 SY-MSGV4.
ENDIF.
```

The *style* YCH04_01, the *form* YCH04_01_ADR_STK, and the source program YCH04_01_PPRG_ YCH04_01_ADR_STK are available for upload in the E-resource file for this book (www.apress.com/ 9781484212345).

## Output

We executed the program YCH04_01_DPRG_YCH04_01_ADR_STK. We executed the program with the company code value equal to 3000. The output will look like that in Figures 4-14 and 4-15.

**Print Preview of LP01 Page 00001 of 00036**

Archive | Print and Archive

```
Electronic Components Distributor      José Fernandez                  KBB Schwarze Pumpe
Tower Lane 1082                        Via Rioja                       Fasanenstr. 8
FOSTER CITY CA  94404                                                  D-67210 FRANKENTHAL/PFALZ

                                       11111 MEXIKO CITY
                                       MEXICO


Company                                Firma                           Sedona Suppliers
Express Vendor Inc                     AluCast                         PO Box 34446
2550 North Racine Ave                  900 Edison Ave. Suite 300       RIMROCK AZ  12224
CHICAGO IL  60614                      HILLSBOROUGH NJ  08844


Intercompany Resources to Belgium      Intercompany Resources Canada   Firma
CANADA                                 CANADA                          C.E.B. BERLIN
                                                                       Kolping Str. 15
                                                                       D-12001 BERLIN
```

**Figure 4-14.** *Output of program YCH04_01_DPRG_YCH04_01_ADR_STK—page 1/36*

**Print Preview of LP01 Page 00035 of 00036**

Archive | Print and Archive

```
Speedy Transportation Services         Company                         US Chemical - Dallas
Westchester Pike                       US Detergent Co.                 200 Industrial Way
NEWTOWN SQUARE  19073                  1000 Cleaner Way                 DALLAS TX  75252
                                       NEW ORLEANS LA  70112


Universal Chemical Stabilizer Co.      World Colors Incorporated       Global Additives Ltd.
Westchester Pike                       PHILADELPHIA PA                  PHILADELPHIA PA
PHILADELPHIA PA  19101


N. A. Sealing Company                  Interstate Transport Comp.      Total Chemical Company
PHILADELPHIA PA                        PHILADELPHIA PA                 PHILADELPHIA PA
```

**Figure 4-15.** *Output of program YCH04_01_DPRG_YCH04_01_ADR_STK—page 36/36*

The output from our server consists of 36 pages. The output is identical to the one produced by hands-on exercise I in Chapter 2.

## Hands-on Exercise Recapitulation

In this hands-on exercise, using Smartforms, we reproduced the output of hands-on exercise I in Chapter 2.

We deployed the element *table* in Smartforms for the first time. The element *table* has three nodes: *Header*, *Main Area*, and *Footer*. In this hand-on exercise, we had the opportunity to use only the node *Main Area*. In the upcoming exercise, we will have the opportunity to use the other two nodes: *Header* and *Footer*. We defined only one line type in the element *table*. In the upcoming exercise, we will define multiple line types for the element *table*.

In this exercise, instead of using the element *table*, we could have used the element *template*. The element *template* will then have to be located under the element *loop*. The element *template* could have a single row consisting of the same five *cells* we located in the line type of the element *table*. In the element *template*, we can specify the height of a *cell*. With the specification of the height of a *cell* (nine lines in this case), we could locate the element *address* (instead of element *text*) under the *cell*. The Smartforms runtime system will then internally format the address as per the postal convention of recipient country instead of our doing so explicitly by calling the function module ADDRESS_INTO_PRINTFORM.

In demonstration exercise IV in Chapter 3, we realized that we could not produce repetitive information across a page like we can in SAP script. If repetitive information is to be produced across a page, using SAP script is a better option.

# Hands-on exercise II—Output Purchase Orders Using Custom *Form*

In this hands-on exercise, we will create a *form*, its corresponding driver program, and other required workbench objects to output standard purchase orders. To repeat what we stated in Chapter 2, SAP delivers *form*s for all commonly used enterprise business documents. The SAP delivered *form*s have their corresponding driver programs. The various features and concepts of Smartforms *form*s were introduced in Chapter 3 via a tour of the SAP delivered *form* for purchase orders /SMB40/MMPO_A. In real-life SAP implementation projects, copies are made of SAP delivered *form*s into the Y/Z namespace. The copied *form*s are then modified and customized as per requirements. A copy of SAP delivered *form* modified and customized as per requirements will use the driver program associated with the original SAP delivered *form*, so it is not necessary to create a new driver program. The advantages of this approach of copying and customizing SAP delivered *form*s is that you do not have to create a *form* from scratch and do not have to code its corresponding complex driver program.

In the present hands-on exercise, we are creating a *form* to output standard purchase orders, as it gives an occasion and scope to expose you to the process of creating a complex *form* for a business document from scratch as well as to introduce more features of *form*s. In one of the succeeding hands-on exercises, we will copy SAP delivered *form* /SMB40/MMPO_A into Y namespace and customize it as per laid-out specifications.

## Hands-on Exercise—Scope and Limits

The present hands-on exercise will output just the standard purchase orders.

In the present hands-on exercise, it is assumed that the purchase orders submitted for output are new purchase orders and not the purchase orders for which full or partial deliveries have been made.

The present hands-on exercise assumes that there is only one consignee/delivery address for all the items of a purchase order, that there is only one delivery date for all the items of a purchase order, and thatthere is only one term of delivery for all the items of a purchase order.

The objective of this exercise is to give you a feel of creating a complex *form* and its associated driver program from scratch and deploying the *form* to output standard purchase orders.

The same scope and limits existed in the hands-on exercises II and III in Chapter 2. In the present hands-on exercise, we are going to reproduce the output of hands-on exercise III in Chapter 2. That hands-on exercise II produced purchase orders using a custom *form*. Hands-on exercise III in Chapter 2 also produced purchase orders using a custom *form* and introduced you to the process of calling an external subroutine from within the SAP script environment. The process of calling an external subroutine from within the SAP script environment is fairly involved and complex, so we felt that it warranted a separate hands-on exercise. In Chapter 2, we performed two hands-on exercises to produce purchase orders using a custom *form*. Since the issue of calling an external subroutine from Smartforms does not exist, we will perform only one hands-on exercise to produce purchase orders using a custom *form* here.

# Output and Layout Specification

We will output standard purchase orders on DINA4 stationery in portrait mode—210MM width and 297MM height. We will output a graphic logo in the element *graphic*. We will output item data in the main *window*. The rest of all the data will be output in secondary *windows*.

There will be two *page formats* for the purchase order named FIRST and NEXT. The first page of a purchase order will output with the *page format* FIRST; if a purchase order runs into multiple pages, all the pages other than the first page of a purchase order will output with the *page format* NEXT.

The area of purchase order above the item area of *page format* FIRST will be like that in Figure 4-16.

The areas bounded by rectangles with rounded corners represent *windows*. The *windows* are numbered for convenience. There is one element *graphic* and six secondary *windows*. The contents of a *graphic* and *windows* will be as follows:

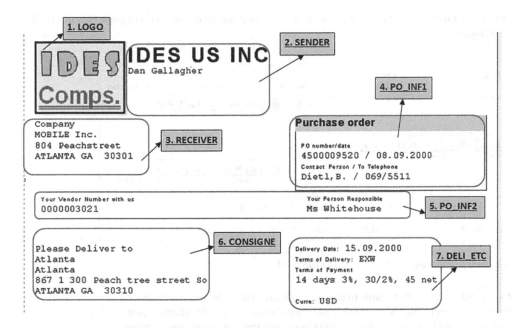

***Figure 4-16.*** *Custom purchase order page format FIRST—I*

1. The company logo is located in the *graphic* LOGO.

2. The *window* SENDER (sender of purchase order) contains the senders' name and address, that is, the company code name and address.

3. The *window* RECEIVER (receiver of purchase order) contains the receivers' name and address, that is, the vendor's name and address.

4. The *window* PO_INF1 contains the following information:

   • Document type, in our context 'Purchase order', since we restricted our scope to output normal new purchase orders.

- Purchase order number and date.

- Contact person and to telephone.

5. The *window* PO_INF2 contains vendor code and vendor person responsible.

6. The *window* CONSIGNE contains the delivery plant/branch office address.

7. The *window* DELI_ETC contains the following information:

    - Delivery date

    - Terms of delivery

    - Terms of payment

    - Currency

The area of the purchase order containing item header, item data, total, and so on of *page format* FIRST will be like that in Figure 4-17.

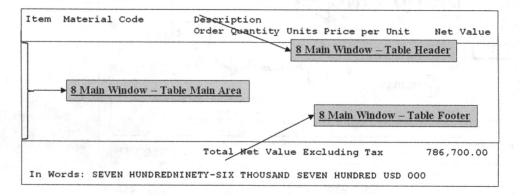

*Figure 4-17.* *Custom purchase order page format FIRST—II*

8. We are using the element *table* to output the item data in the main *window*. In the main *window*, the element *table* will contain the column heading for item data, item data (Data which is repeating in a page and repeating page to page) and footer to output the total and the total expressed in text. The item data is being output in two lines. The first line outputs item number, material code and description. The second line outputs order quantity, units, price per unit and net value. The *header*, *main area* and the *footer* of the element *table* are marked in Figure 4-16.

9. We have not located any information in the *window* FOOTER. You might choose to locate some information in this *window*.

For the second *page format* NEXT, the layout of *windows* will be as shown in Figure 4-18.

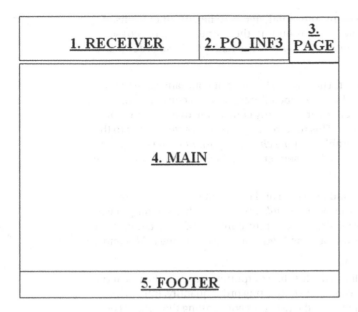

*Figure 4-18.* *Custom purchase order page format NEXT—windows layout*

The *window* PO_INF3 contains the purchase order number and date.

The *window* PAGE contains a running page number along with the total number of pages in a purchase order. The page number will start from 1 for each purchase order. The total number of pages will be the number of pages in a purchase order.

The page number is being output from the second page of a purchase order, the page number information does not appear on the first page of a purchase order.

The other *windows* in the *page format* NEXT are common to the *page format* FIRST. The height of the main *window* in the *page format* NEXT is greater than its corresponding *window* in the *page format* FIRST.

## Output Considerations

- The hands-on exercise *form* has been created to support only one language: English. All the text normally created as literal in the *text* environment will be retrieved from data elements in the INITIALIZATION event of the *form* and transferred to the *text* environment of the *form* through program symbols. This is a peculiar way of handling the texts in a *form*. With one language version of a *form*, we will be able to output the purchase order in multiple languages, since we are controlling the language text through the texts of data elements. The value of the field EKKO-SPRAS will determine the language in which the texts are to be fetched from data elements.

- The system on which we are executing our hands-on exercises has only two languages installed: English and German. So this hands-on exercise driver program has been created to accept only purchase orders in these two languages (IF EKKO-SPRRAS <> 'D' AND EKKO-SPRRAS <> 'E' .....CONTINUE). If the system on which you are executing the exercises has more languages installed, you can modify the driver program to accept purchase orders of additional languages.

- When outputting the purchase orders, we will call the *form* function module from the driver program for each document or purchase order.

- At the end of outputting of all items, the 'Total' needs to be output in terms of number as well as text. After the 'Total' is output, the output of the purchase is completed and the commencement of output of the next purchase order if any will start.

- Three addresses are being output. These are (1) sender or company code name and address, (2) receiver or vendor name and address, and (3) consignee or delivery address. We want the sender or company code name to output in font type Helve and font size 28 points. This requires applying *character format* to the company code name field. To be able to apply *character format* to the company code name field, we have not located the senders' data in the element *address* but in a secondary *window*.

- We will output the item header and item data and item footer (located in the element *table*) with grid lines. The element *table* provides facilities to output with different grid line options. The facility to output the contents of the element *table* with different grid line options will be described when we create the *table* element in the *form*.

- The item data is output in two lines: the first line outputting item number, material code, and description and the second line outputting order quantity, unit, price per unit, and net value. We do not want the two lines constituting the detail of an item to split between two pages but output on the same page, that is, provide page protection for the two lines of item data. Thus, we will locate the element *texts* corresponding to the two lines of item data to the element *folder*. We will enable the check box *Page Protection* in the *Output Options* tab of the element *folder*.

- Since we want the total to be output only at the end, we will enable the check box *Only After End of Main Window* in the *Conditions* tab of the element *texts* of the total.

- We plan to output some of the information of purchase order in font type and size other than the default font type Courier 12, etc. Thus we created a few *character formats* in the *style* YCH04_03. The *style* YCH04_03 is assigned to the *form* to output custom purchase orders. This is to enable output of information in font type and size other than the default.

## Data Inputs and Data Input Considerations

The two main sources of data to output the purchase orders with a custom *form* are the tables EKKO (purchasing document header) and EKPO (purchasing document item).

We will retrieve data from EKKO with the SELECT..... ENDSELECT loop. You can choose to load EKKO data into an internal table and loop from the internal table. A SELECT-OPTIONS statement is provided to be able to choose the purchase orders to be output.

The data relating to the company code of a purchase order being processed will be retrieved from the tableT001.

```
SELECT SINGLE * FROM T001 WHERE BUKRS = EKKO-BUKRS.
```

The address of the company code is retrieved from the table SADR.

```
SELECT SINGLE * FROM SADR WHERE ADRNR = T001-ADRNR.
```

The function module ADDRESS_INTO_PRINTFORM will return ten lines of address of the company code formatted as per the postal convention of the country of the company code which is output in the *window* SENDER.

The data relating to the vendor of a purchase order being processed will be retrieved from the vendor primary table LFA1-SELECT SINGLE * FROM LFA1 WHERE LIFNR = EKKO-LIFNR.

The supply of vendor address number through the field LFA1-ADRNR to the element *address* named RECEIVER will output the vendor address as per the recipient country's postal convention in the *window* RECEIVER.

The document type (purchase Order) along with the field nomenclatures or labels for purchase order number and date are retrieved from table T166U as follows:

```
SELECT SINGLE * FROM T166U WHERE BSTYP = EKKO-BSTYP AND
 BSART = EKKO-BSART AND SPRAS = EKKO-SPRAS AND DRUVO = '1'.
```

The 'contact person' and 'to telephone' are retrieved from table T024 as follows:

```
SELECT SINGLE * FROM T024 WHERE EKGRP = EKKO-EKGRP.
```

The terms of payment are retrieved from the table T052 as follows:

```
SELECT SINGLE * FROM T052 WHERE ZTERM = EKKO-ZTERM.
```

The function module FI_PRINT_ZTERM is used to retrieve the terms of payment text.

The relevant item data (specific fields) is being fetched from the database table EKPO into an internal table declared referring to the ABAP dictionary structure YCH04_ITEM_STRU. Only the items belonging to the specific purchase order being output at a time are fetched into the internal table. The function module of the *form* will receive header data and its corresponding item data of one purchase order as *Form Parameters*.

We are using the field TXZ01 in the database table EKPO to output the material descriptions.

The consignee (deliver to plant/branch office address) is retrieved through the view field EKPO -ADRNR from first item record of the purchase order, alternatively through EKPO -ADRN2 again alternatively from table T001W through EKPO -WERKS. The consignee data will be retrieved for the first item of a purchase order, assuming that it is the same for all other items in the purchase order.

The delivery date is retrieved from the table EKET as follows:

```
SELECT SINGLE * FROM EKET WHERE EBELN = EKPO -EBELN AND EBELP = EKPO -EBELP.
```

Again this will be retrieved for the first item of a purchase order, assuming that it is the same for all other items in the purchase order.

Table 4-4 is a list of the tables with fields used. A field of a table is deemed to be used when it is appearing in the output or occurs in subsequent WHERE condition(s).

*Table 4-4.* *List of Tables with the Fields*

| Srl. No. | Table/View | Table/View Fields used | | |
|---|---|---|---|---|
| 01 | EKKO - Purchasing document header | EBELN | BUKRS | EKGRP |
| | | BEDAT | LIFNR | ZTERM |
| | | BSTYP | ADRNR | INCO1 |
| | | BSART | VERKF | |
| | | SPRAS | WAERS | |
| 02 | YCH02_EKPO_MAKT - Database view of tables: purchasing document item EKPO and material descriptions MAKT | EBELN | MATNR | MAKTX |
| | | EBELP | MENGE | |
| | | WERKS | MEINS | |
| | | ADRNR | NETPR | |
| | | ADRN2 | NETWR | |
| 03 | LFA1 - Vendor primary | ANRED | PFACH | LAND1 |
| | | NAME1 | PSTL2 | REGIO |
| | | NAME2 | ORT01 | |
| | | NAME3 | ORT02 | |
| | | NAME4 | PSTLZ | |
| 04 | T001 - Company code | ADRNR | | |
| 05 | SADR - Address Management: Company Data | ANRED | PFACH | LAND1 |
| | | NAME1 | PSTL2 | REGIO |
| | | NAME2 | ORT01 | |
| | | NAME3 | ORT02 | |
| | | NAME4 | PSTLZ | |
| 06 | T024 - Purchasing Groups | EKNAM, EKTEL | | |
| 07 | T166U - Headings in Purchasing Document Printout | DRTYP, DRNUM | | |
| 08 | T001W - Plants/Branches | ANRED | PFACH | LAND1 |
| | | NAME1 | PSTL2 | REGIO |
| | | NAME2 | ORT01 | |
| | | NAME3 | ORT02 | |
| | | NAME4 | PSTLZ | |
| 09 | EKET - Scheduling Agreement Schedule Lines | EINDT | | |
| 10 | T052 - Terms of Payment | ZTERM | | |

The nomenclatures or labels for the fields are retrieved from data elements' long texts using the function module WCGW_DATA_ELEMENT_TEXT_GET. Most table fields' existing data element texts do not suit us; that is, the texts of these existing data elements do not correspond with the texts of proposed output. So, for this hands-on exercise, we will use the data elements created in Chapter 2. Recall that the data elements in Chapter 2 were created with texts in two languages: English and German. There were a total of 16 data elements; their English and German texts are available for your use in the E-resource file for this book (www.apress.com/9781484212345). We are using one additional data element, YCH04_EBELP, for the field EBELP—item number. We did not output this field in hands-on exercises II and III in Chapter 2.

The nomenclatures or labels for fields as a rule is specified through literals in *text* environment of the Smartforms *form*. This is the practice in all the SAP delivered *forms* as well as the *forms* we have created up to now in Smartforms. By making the nomenclatures or labels for fields as program symbols or variables in *text form*, we are making the *form* itself language independent.

## Creation of Smartforms *Form*, Driver Program, and Related Workbench Objects

To output purchase orders using a custom *form*, we will be creating the following workbench objects:

- An ABAP dictionary structure with the relevant fields of database table EKPO.

- A *style* containing *character formats* to enable output in different fonts and font sizes, etc.

- A Smartforms *form*

- A driver program for the Smartforms *form*

- A database view involving the tables EKKO and LFA1 (created in Chapter 2). This database view will be used in an elementary search help.

- An elementary search help (created in Chapter 2. This elementary search help uses the database view consisting of tables EKKO and LFA1. This elementary search help is being attached to the SELECT-OPTIONS field in the driver program

A description of the creation of these workbench objects follows.

## ABAP Dictionary Structure YCH04_ITEM_STRU

We created an ABAP dictionary structure YCH04_ITEM_STRU containing relevant fields of the database table EKPO. We refer to the structure to declare the internal table. This internal table will be loaded with item data of a specific purchase order being output. The structure consists of the fields listed in Table 4-5.

**Table 4-5.** *Fields in the Structure YCH04_ITEM_STRU*

| Srl. No. | Field Name | Data Element | Srl. No. | Field Name | Data Element |
|----------|-----------|--------------|----------|-----------|--------------|
| 01 | EBELN | EBELN | 07 | NETPR | BPREI |
| 02 | EBELP | EBELP | 08 | NETWR | BWERT |
| 03 | MATNR | MATNR | 09 | ADRNR | ADRNR_MM |
| 04 | WERKS | EWERK | 10 | ADRN2 | ADRN2 |
| 05 | MENGE | BSTMG | 11 | TXZ01 | TXZ01 |
| 06 | MEINS | MEINS | | | |

For the currency amount fields NETPR and NETWR, we filled the columns *Reference table* and *Ref. field* as EKKO and WAERS. For the inventory quantity fields MENGE, we filled the columns *Reference table* and *Ref. field* as YCH04_ITEM_STRU and MEINS. We performed the consistency check and activated the structure.

## Smartforms *Style* YCH04_02

With the transaction code SMARTFORMS, we created a *style* YCH04_02. We created a *paragraph format* SP with the default values. We assigned the *paragraph format* SP as the standard paragraph. We created four *character formats* as listed in Table 4-6.

***Table 4-6.*** *Character Format List in Style YCH04_02*

| Character Format Name | Description | Font Type/Family | Font Size | Bold | Color |
|---|---|---|---|---|---|
| CD | Helve 14 - For Document Type | HELVE | 14,0 | On | |
| CS | For Sender Name in 16 pts | HELVE | 16,0 | On | Green |
| CT | For Sender Name in 28 pts | HELVE | 28,0 | On | Green |
| HS | Helve 8 – For Field Nomenclatures | HELVE | 8,0 | | |

We performed a check and activated the *style* YCH_04_02.

## Smartforms *Form* YCH04_02_PORDER1

We created a *form* YCH04_02_PORDER1 and assigned the *style* YCH04_02 to the *form*.

Smartforms will contain three parameters in the *Form Interface* area. The first parameter will be an *import* parameter—type EKKO—for receiving, from the driver program, the header information of the purchase order being output. The second parameter will be an *import* parameter —type T001—for receiving, from the driver program, the address number information to be used to output the sender address. The third parameter will be a *Tables* parameter—like YCH04_ITEM_STRU—for receiving, from the driver program, the item information of the purchase order being output.

The driver program will retrieve the header, item information of a purchase order, and address number of company code and then call the function module of the *form*. The rest of the information required to be output is retrieved in the *Initialization* event of the *form* itself.

## Node: Form Interface

We entered the *import* (EKKO and T001) and *tables* (IIEM_TAB) parameters in the *Form Interface* area of the *form* as shown in Figures 4-19 and 4-20.

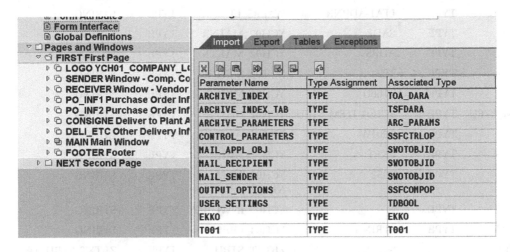

*Figure 4-19.* *Form Interface—Import parameters: EKKO, T001*

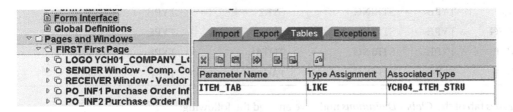

*Figure 4-20.* *Form Interface—Tables parameter: ITEM_TAB*

## Node: Global Definitions

Since so much of data other than the header and item data of a purchase order to be output is being retrieved within the *form*, we need to declare data items in the *Global Data* tab of the *Global Definitions* node. Table 4-7 lists the data items created in the *Global Data* tab of the *Global Definitions* node.

**Table 4-7.** *Data Items in the Global Data Tab*

| Name | TYPE | Reference | Name | TYPE | Reference |
|------|------|-----------|------|------|-----------|
| LFA1 | TYPE | LFA1 | YCH02_ZBTXT | TYPE | STRING |
| VADRNR | TYPE | LFA1-ADRNR | WAERS_LT | TYPE | STRING |
| SADR | TYPE | SADR | YCH02_MATNR | TYPE | STRING |
| ADRS | TYPE | ADRS | YCH02_MAKTX | TYPE | STRING |
| T024 | TYPE | T024 | YCH02_MENGE | TYPE | STRING |
| T166U | TYPE | T166U | YCH02_MEINS | TYPE | STRING |
| YCH04_ITEM_STRU | TYPE | YCH04_ITEM_STRU | YCH02_NETPR | TYPE | STRING |
| T001W | TYPE | T001W | NETWR | TYPE | CHAR15 |
| EKET | TYPE | EKET | YCH02_PAGE | TYPE | STRING |
| T052 | TYPE | T052 | YCH02_TOTAL_ NET_E | TYPE | STRING |
| LENGTH | TYPE | N | YCH02_INWORDS | TYPE | STRING |
| YCH02_EKNAM | TYPE | STRING | YCH04_EBELP | TYPE | STRING |
| YCH02_EKTEL | TYPE | STRING | ZBTXT_STRU | TYPE | ZBTXT_STRU_TP |
| YCH02_LIFNR | TYPE | STRING | ZBTXT_TAB | TYPE | ZBTXT_TAB_TP |
| YCH02_VERKF | TYPE | STRING | STR2 | TYPE | CHAR70 |
| YCH02_CONSG | TYPE | STRING | STR1 | TYPE | CHAR70 |
| YCH02_EINDT | TYPE | STRING | TOTAL | TYPE | NETWR |
| YCH02_INCO1 | TYPE | STRING | PAGE | TYPE | NUM02 |

In the *Types* tab of the *Global Definitions* node, we entered the following:

```
TYPES: BEGIN OF ZBTXT_STRU_TP,
       STR(50),
       END OF ZBTXT_STRU_TP,
       ZBTXT_TAB_TP TYPE STANDARD TABLE OF ZBTXT_STRU_TP.
```

As all of the text and data other than the header and item data of a purchase order to be output is to be retrieved in the *Initialization* event within the *form*, there will be considerable code in the *Initialization* event tab of *Global Definitions* node. The source lines in the *Initialization* event are as follows:

```
DATA: STR(14) TYPE C.
TOTAL = 0. "Initialize for Purchase order

 SELECT SINGLE * FROM LFA1
        WHERE LIFNR = EKKO-LIFNR. "Get Vendor

 IF EKKO-ADRNR = ' '.
 VADRNR = LFA1-ADRNR.
 ELSE.
 VADRNR = EKKO-ADRNR.
```

```
    ENDIF.
*****************************************
   SELECT SINGLE * FROM T166U WHERE BSTYP = EKKO-BSTYP AND
   BSART = EKKO-BSART AND SPRAS = EKKO-SPRAS AND
   DRUVO = '1'.  "Get Title for Document

   SELECT SINGLE * FROM T024
        WHERE EKGRP = EKKO-EKGRP. "Get Purchasing Group
   SELECT SINGLE * FROM T052
        WHERE ZTERM = EKKO-ZTERM. "Get Payment Terms

*****Retrieve Long Texts from Data Elements*****
   PERFORM GET_TEXT_DE USING 'YCH02_EKNAM' EKKO-SPRAS YCH02_EKNAM.
   PERFORM GET_TEXT_DE USING 'YCH02_EKTEL' EKKO-SPRAS YCH02_EKTEL.
   PERFORM GET_TEXT_DE USING 'YCH02_LIFNR' EKKO-SPRAS YCH02_LIFNR.
   PERFORM GET_TEXT_DE USING 'YCH02_VERKF' EKKO-SPRAS YCH02_VERKF.
   PERFORM GET_TEXT_DE USING 'YCH02_CONSG' EKKO-SPRAS YCH02_CONSG.
   PERFORM GET_TEXT_DE USING 'YCH02_EINDT' EKKO-SPRAS YCH02_EINDT.
   PERFORM GET_TEXT_DE USING 'YCH02_INCO1' EKKO-SPRAS YCH02_INCO1.
   PERFORM GET_TEXT_DE USING 'YCH02_ZBTXT' EKKO-SPRAS YCH02_ZBTXT.
   PERFORM GET_TEXT_DE USING 'WAERS'        EKKO-SPRAS WAERS_LT.

   PERFORM GET_TEXT_DE USING 'YCH04_EBELP' EKKO-SPRAS YCH04_EBELP.

   PERFORM GET_TEXT_DE USING 'YCH02_MATNR' EKKO-SPRAS YCH02_MATNR.
   PERFORM GET_TEXT_DE USING 'YCH02_MAKTX' EKKO-SPRAS YCH02_MAKTX.
   PERFORM GET_TEXT_DE USING 'YCH02_MENGE' EKKO-SPRAS YCH02_MENGE.
   PERFORM GET_TEXT_DE USING 'YCH02_MEINS' EKKO-SPRAS YCH02_MEINS.
   PERFORM GET_TEXT_DE USING 'YCH02_NETPR' EKKO-SPRAS YCH02_NETPR.
   PERFORM GET_TEXT_DE USING 'NETWR'        EKKO-SPRAS NETWR.
   WRITE NETWR TO STR RIGHT-JUSTIFIED.
   NETWR = STR. " right justify text

   PERFORM GET_TEXT_DE USING 'YCH02_PAGE'  EKKO-SPRAS YCH02_PAGE.
   PERFORM GET_TEXT_DE USING 'YCH02_TOTAL_NET_ETAX' EKKO-SPRAS YCH02_TOTAL_NET_E.
   PERFORM GET_TEXT_DE USING 'YCH02_INWORDS' EKKO-SPRAS
     YCH02_INWORDS.

*****Retrieve Payment Terms Text *****
   CALL FUNCTION 'FI_PRINT_ZTERM'
     EXPORTING
      I_ZTERM          = EKKO-ZTERM
      I_LANGU          = EKKO-SPRAS
      I_XT052U         = 'X'
      I_T052           = T052
     TABLES
      T_ZTEXT          = ZBTXT_TAB
   .
   READ TABLE ZBTXT_TAB INTO ZBTXT_STRU INDEX 1.
```

```
*****Company Code Name & Address *****
 SELECT SINGLE * FROM SADR WHERE ADRNR = T001-ADRNR.
                            "Get Address of Company Cd
 SADR-ANRED = ' '. "No Title for Company Code Name
 CLEAR ADRS.
 MOVE-CORRESPONDING SADR TO ADRS.

 CALL FUNCTION 'ADDRESS_INTO_PRINTFORM'
  EXPORTING
    ADRSWA_IN                          = ADRS
  IMPORTING
    ADRSWA_OUT                         = ADRS
          .

 LENGTH = STRLEN( ADRS-LINE0 ).
```

The input parameters to the *Initialization* event are EKKO and T001.
Table 4-8 lists the output parameters to the *Initialization* event.

***Table 4-8.*** *Output Parameters—Initialization Event*

| Srl. No. | Parameter | Srl. No. | Parameter |
|----------|-----------|----------|-----------|
| 01 | TOTAL | 16 | YCH02_MAKTX |
| 02 | LFA1 | 17 | YCH02_MENGE |
| 03 | T166U | 18 | YCH02_MEINS |
| 04 | T024 | 19 | YCH02_NETPR |
| 05 | YCH02_EKNAM | 20 | NETWR |
| 06 | T052 | 21 | YCH02_PAGE |
| 07 | YCH02_EKTEL | 22 | YCH02_TOTAL_NET_E |
| 08 | YCH02_LIFNR | 23 | YCH02_INWORDS |
| 09 | YCH02_VERKF | 24 | ZBTXT_TAB |
| 10 | YCH02_CONSG | 25 | ZBTXT_STRU |
| 11 | YCH02_EINDT | 26 | SADR |
| 12 | YCH02_INCO1 | 27 | ADRS |
| 13 | YCH02_ZBTXT | 28 | LENGTH |
| 14 | WAERS_LT | 29 | YCH04_EBELP |
| 15 | YCH02_MATNR | 30 | VADRNR |

There are two subroutines: (1) retrieve text from data elements and (2) convert the total currency amount into text. We have located the two subroutines in the *Form Routines* tab of the *Global Definitions* node. The source lines are as follows:

```
**************************************************************
*****Subroutine to Retrieve Long Texts from Data Elements *****
**************************************************************
FORM GET_TEXT_DE USING VALUE(DE_NAME) VALUE(LANG) RET_TEXT.
DATA: LTEXT TYPE SCRTEXT_L.

  CALL FUNCTION 'WCGW_DATA_ELEMENT_TEXT_GET'
    EXPORTING
      I_DATA_ELEMENT          = DE_NAME
      I_LANGUAGE              = LANG
    IMPORTING
      E_SCRTEXT_L            = LTEXT
          .

RET_TEXT = LTEXT.
ENDFORM.


**********************************
***** Convert TOTAL into Text *****
**********************************
FORM CONV_TOTAL_INTO_TEXT USING VALUE(AMOUNT) VALUE(SPRAS)
                      VALUE(WAERS) STRING1 STRING2.

DATA: STR(140)        TYPE C,
      STR_TAB         TYPE STANDARD TABLE OF CHAR70,
      SPELL           TYPE SPELL,
      LEN             TYPE I,
      SAP_WAERS       TYPE TCURC-WAERS,
      CURR_CD         TYPE TCURC-WAERS,
      ISO_WAERS       TYPE TCURC-ISOCD.

SAP_WAERS = WAERS.
* Convert SAP currency code to ISO currency code
********************************************
CALL FUNCTION 'CURRENCY_CODE_SAP_TO_ISO'
  EXPORTING
    SAP_CODE          = SAP_WAERS
  IMPORTING
    ISO_CODE          = ISO_WAERS
  EXCEPTIONS
    NOT_FOUND         = 1
    OTHERS            = 2
        .
IF SY-SUBRC <> 0.
 MESSAGE ID SY-MSGID TYPE SY-MSGTY NUMBER SY-MSGNO
      WITH SY-MSGV1 SY-MSGV2 SY-MSGV3 SY-MSGV4.
 EXIT.
```

```
ENDIF.
CURR_CD = ISO_WAERS.
* Call Function Module SPELL_AMOUNT
**********************************
CALL FUNCTION 'SPELL_AMOUNT'
  EXPORTING
    AMOUNT           = AMOUNT
    CURRENCY         = CURR_CD
    FILLER           = ' '
    LANGUAGE         = SPRAS
  IMPORTING
    IN_WORDS         = SPELL
  EXCEPTIONS
    NOT_FOUND        = 1
    TOO_LARGE        = 2
    OTHERS           = 3.

IF SY-SUBRC = 0.

 CONCATENATE SPELL-WORD ISO_WAERS SPELL-DECIMAL
   INTO STR SEPARATED BY SPACE.
ELSE.
 MESSAGE ID SY-MSGID TYPE SY-MSGTY NUMBER SY-MSGNO
        WITH SY-MSGV1 SY-MSGV2 SY-MSGV3 SY-MSGV4.
 EXIT.
ENDIF.

* Split STR into Two Lines
**************************
CALL FUNCTION 'YCH02_01_SPLIT_STRING'
  EXPORTING
    STRING_TO_SPLIT                 = STR
  TABLES
    STABLE                          = STR_TAB
  EXCEPTIONS
    IMPORT_PARAMETER_TYPE_INVALID      = 1
    RETURN_TABLE_ELEMENT_NOT_TYPEC     = 2
    OTHERS                             = 3.
IF SY-SUBRC <> 0.
 MESSAGE ID SY-MSGID TYPE SY-MSGTY NUMBER SY-MSGNO
        WITH SY-MSGV1 SY-MSGV2 SY-MSGV3 SY-MSGV4.
 EXIT.
ENDIF.

READ TABLE STR_TAB INTO STRING1 INDEX 1.

READ TABLE STR_TAB INTO STRING2 INDEX 2.
```

For fields of ABAP dictionary types CURR (currency amounts) and QUAN (inventory quantities) defined in the *Global Data tab*, we have to specify the corresponding ABAP dictionary types CUKY (currency key) and UNIT (unit of measure) This is specified in the *Currency/Quant. Fields* tab of *Global Definitions* node.

In the *Global Data* tab, we declared three fields of type CURR: TOTAL, YCH04_ITEM_STRU-NETPR, and YCH04_ITEM_STRU-NETWR one field of type QUAN: YCH04_ITEM_STRU-MENGE.

Figure 4-21 shows the corresponding type CUKY fields and UNIT field specified in the *Currency/Quant. Fields* tab.

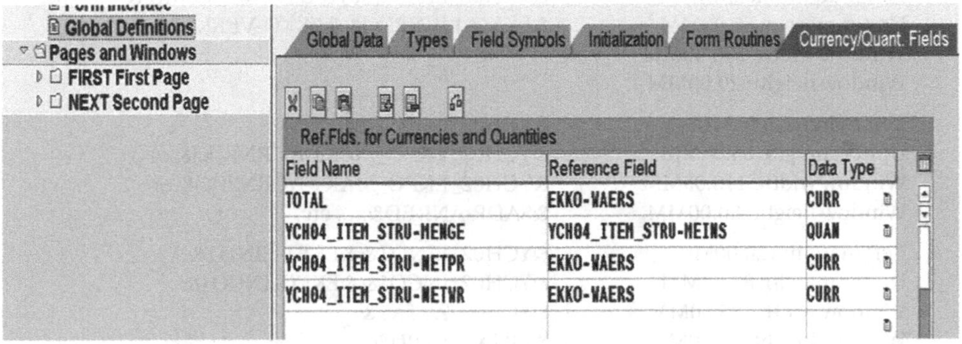

*Figure 4-21.* *Global Definitions—Currency/Quant. fields tab*

These were all the entries created in *Form Interface* and the *Global Definitions* nodes. We next proceed to the creations in *Pages and Windows* nodes.

## Node: Pages and Windows

We renamed the default *page format* created by the Smartforms maintenance system as FIRST.

We created the *page format* NEXT. We assigned the next page for *page format* FIRST as NEXT. And we assigned the next page for *page format* NEXT as NEXT.

For *page format* FIRST, we created *windows* as per the entries in Table 4-9.

*Table 4-9.* *Page Format FIRST—Layout of Windows*

| Window Name | Dimensions | Contents |
|---|---|---|
| 1. LOGO | Left margin: 5.00MM<br>Upper margin: 5.00MM<br>Window width: 46.64MM<br>Window height: 29.81MM | Company Logo<br>'YCH01_COMPANY_LOGO' OBJECT GRAPHICS ID<br>BMAP TYPE BCOL |
| 2. SENDER | Left margin: 46.00MM<br>Upper margin: 5.00MM<br>Window width: 145.00MM<br>Window height: 30.00MM | Company code name & address<br>&ADRS-LINE1&..... &ADRS-LINE9& |
| 3. RECEIVER | Left margin: 5.00MM<br>Upper margin: 35.00MM<br>Window width: 115.00MM<br>Window height: 30.00MM | &EKKO-ADRNR(K)&, etc. |

(*continued*)

***Table 4-9.*** (*continued*)

| Window Name | Dimensions | Contents |
|---|---|---|
| 4. PO_INF1 | Left margin: 120.00MM<br>Upper margin: 35.00MM<br>Window width: 85.00MM<br>Window height: 30.00MM | &T166U-DRTYP& &T166U-DRNUM&<br>&EKKO-EBELN& &EKKO-BEDAT&<br>&YCH02_EKNAM& &YCH02_EKTEL&<br>&T024-EKNAM& &T024-EKTEL& |
| 5. PO_INF2 | Left margin: 5.00MM<br>Upper margin: 65.00MM<br>Window width: 200.00MM<br>Window height: 20.00MM | &YCH02_LIFNR(30) & &YCH02_VERKF&<br>&EKKO-LIFNR(K)& &EKKO-VERKF& |
| 6. CONSIGNE | Left margin: 5.00MM<br>Upper margin: 85.00MM<br>Window width: 115.00MM<br>Window height: 30.00MM | &YCH02_CONSG&<br>&YCH02_EKPO_MAKT-ADRNR(K)& or<br>&YCH02_EKPO_MAKT-ADRN2(K)& or<br>&SADR-ANRED&..... etc. |
| 7. DELI_ETC | Left margin: 120.00MM<br>Upper margin: 85.00MM<br>Window width: 85.00MM<br>Window height: 30.00MM | &YCH02_EINDT& &EKET-EINDT&<br>&YCH02_INCO1& &EKKO-INCO1&<br>&YCH02_ZBTXT&<br>&ZBTXT_STRU&<br>&WAERS& &EKKO-WAERS& |
| 8. MAIN | Left margin: 5.00MM<br>Upper margin: 120.00MM<br>Window width: 200.00MM<br>Window height: 160.00MM | &YCH04_EBELP&<br>&YCH02_MATNR& &YCH02_MAKTX&<br>&YCH02_MENGE(R14)& &YCH02_MEINS(5)&<br>&YCH02_NETPR(R14)& &NETWR(R15)&<br><br>&YCH04_ITEM_STRU-EBELP(4)&<br>&YCH04_ITEM_STRU-MATNR(18K)&<br>&YCH04_ITEM_STRU-TXZ01(40)&<br>&YCH04_ITEM_STRU-MENGE(14)&<br>&YCH04_ITEM_STRU-MEINS(5)&<br>&YCH04_ITEM_STRU -NETPR(14)&<br>&YCH04_ITEM_STRU-NETWR(15)&<br><br>&YCH02_TOTAL_NET_E& &TOTAL&<br>&YCH02_IN_WORDS& &STR1& &STR2& |
| 9. FOOTER | Left margin: 5.00MM<br>Upper margin: 282.00MM<br>Window width: 200.00MM<br>Window height: 10.00MM | Footer text if any |

For *page format* NEXT, we created *windows* as per the entries in Table 4-10.

***Table 4-10.*** *Page Format NEXT—Layout of Windows*

| Window Name | Dimensions | Contents |
|---|---|---|
| 1. RECEIVER | Left margin: 5.00MM<br>Upper margin: 5.00MM<br>Window width: 115.00MM<br>Window height: 30.00MM | &EKKO-ADRNR(K)& etc. |
| 2. PO_INF3 | Left margin: 120.00MM<br>Upper margin: 5.00 MM<br>Window width: 65.00MM<br>Window height: 30.00MM | &YCH02_LIFNR(30)& &YCH02_VERKF&<br>&EKKO-LIFNR(K)& &EKKO-VERKF& |
| 3. PAGE | Left margin: 185MM<br>Upper margin: 5.00MM<br>Window width: 20MM<br>Window height: 30MM | &YCH02_PAGE&<br>&PAGE(R2)&/&SAPSCRIPT-<br>FORMPAGES(C2)& |
| 4. MAIN | Left margin: 5.00MM<br>Upper margin: 35.00MM<br>Window width: 200.00MM<br>Window height: 245.00MM | &YCH04_EBELP&<br>&YCH02_MATNR& &YCH02_MAKTX&<br>&YCH02_MENGE(R14)& &YCH02_<br>MEINS(5)&<br>&YCH02_NETPR(R14)& &NETWR(R15)&<br><br>&YCH04_ITEM_STRU-EBELP(4)&<br>&YCH04_ITEM_STRU-TXZ01(18K)&<br>&YCH04_ITEM_STRU-MAKTX(40)&<br>&YCH04_ITEM_STRU-MENGE(14)&<br>&YCH04_ITEM_STRU-MEINS(5)&<br>&YCH04_ITEM_STRU -NETPR(14)&<br>&YCH04_ITEM_STRU-NETWR(15)&<br><br>&YCH02_TOTAL_NET_E& &TOTAL&<br>&YCH02_IN_WORDS& &STR1& &STR2& |
| 5. FOOTER | Left margin: 5.00MM  Upper margin: 282.00MM<br>Window width: 200.00MM<br>Window height: 10.00MM | Footer text if any |

The *page formats* FIRST and NEXT, when viewed in the *Form Painter*, will look as in Figures 4-22 and 4-23.

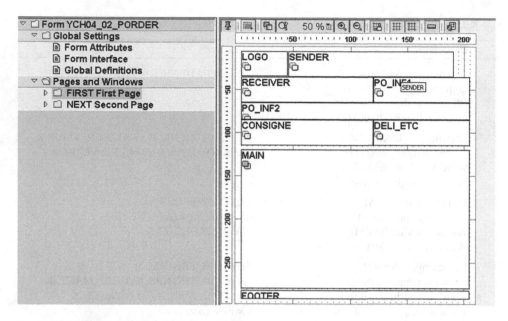

**Figure 4-22.** *Page Format FIRST—view in Form Painter*

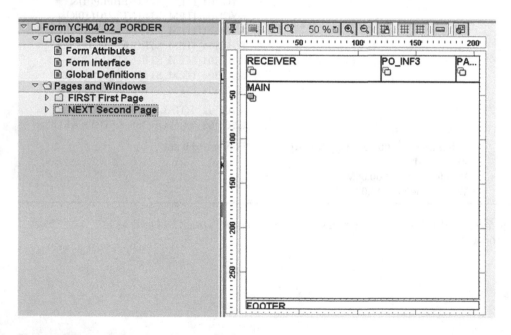

**Figure 4-23.** *Page Format NEXT—view in Form Painter*

We will start creating further elements in the *windows* of the two *page formats.*

## Node: Page Format FIRST

We inserted the element *graphic* named LOGO_GRAPHIC in the secondary *window* named LOGO. We could have located the element *graphic* directly on the *page format* FIRST instead of creating the secondary *window* LOGO and locating the element *graphic* in the *window* as we have done. Figure 4-24 is a screenshot of the *General Attributes* tab of the *graphic* element LOGO_GRAPHIC.

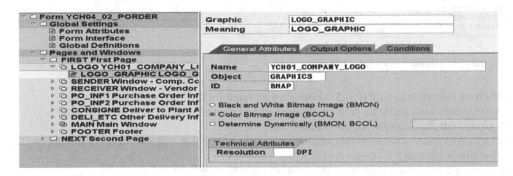

*Figure 4-24.  Graphic Element LOGO_GRAPHIC in window LOGO—tab: General Attributes*

The image from the SAP document server named YCH01_COMPANY_LOGO is assigned to the field *Name*. The image YCH01_COMPANY_LOGO was imported into the SAP document server in Chapter 1.

Since, we want the sender's name in larger font than the other address lines of the sender, we could not insert the element *address* directly into the *window* SENDER. As in Chapter 2, we are retrieving the company code address from the database table SADR, calling the function module ADDRESS_INTO_PRINTFORM to convert and return the address formatted as per the postal convention of the company code country. We are determining the length of the company code name. The code for the retrieval of company code address, its formatting, and determining the length of company code name are located in the *Initialization* event of the *form.*

Depending on the length of company code name, we want to apply different *character formats* to the output of company code name. If the company code name is greater than 15 characters, we are applying the *character format* CS—smaller font size, 16 points; if the length of the company code name is 15 characters or less, we are applying the *character format* CT—larger font size, 28 points.

The process of testing a condition and applying a different *character format* to the output, depending on the testing condition, is implemented with the element *alternative.* The element *alternative* is created with the following context menu option: Create ➤ Flow Logic ➤ Alternative.

In the *window* SENDER, we created the element *alternative* named CONDITION1. Figure 4-25 illustrates.

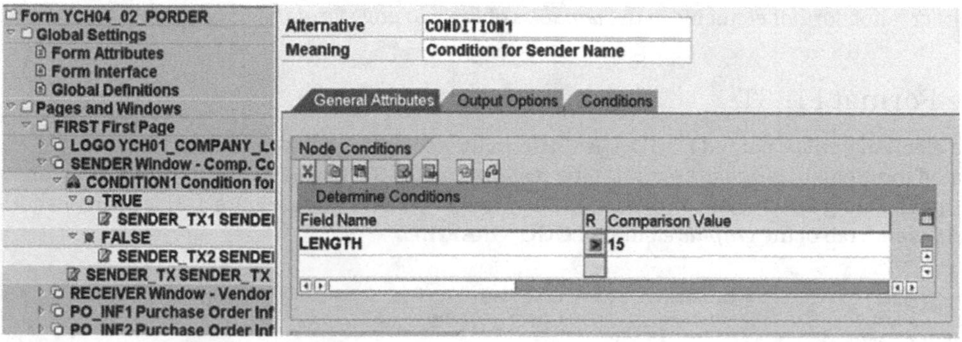

**Figure 4-25.** *Element Alternative—Node Conditions*

The condition we created is LENGTH > 15. Nodes are generated for the true condition and false condition. In the true condition node, we created the element *text* named SENDER_TX1 to output the company code name with *character format* CS—smaller font size.

In the false condition node, we created the element *text* named SENDER_TX2 to output the company code name with *character format* CT—larger font size.

Figures 4-26 and 4-27 show screenshots of SENDER_TX1 and SENDER_TX2.

**Figure 4-26.** *Element Alternative—text: SENDER_TX1*

**Figure 4-27.** *Element Alternative—text: SENDER_TX2*

The rest of the nine address lines of company code are located in the element *text* named SENDER_TX, next to the node FALSE.

We inserted the element *address* named RECEIVER_ADDRESS in the secondary *window* named RECEIVER. We could have located the element *address* directly on the *page format* FIRST instead of creating the secondary *window* RECEIVER and locating the element *address* in the *window* as we have done.

Figure 4-28 is a screenshot of the *General Attributes* tab of the element *address* named RECEIVER_ADDRESS:

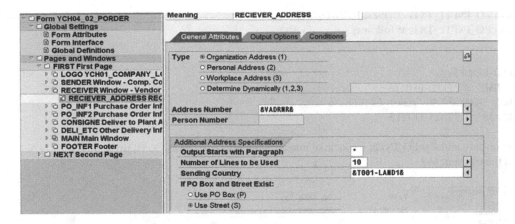

**Figure 4-28.** *Element address RECEIVER_ADDRESS—tab: General Attributes*

The value of the VADRNR specified in the field *Address Number* is derived in the *Initialization* event. In the secondary *window* PO_INF1, we located two *text* elements: PO_INF11_TX and PO_INF12_TX. Figures 4-29 and 4-30 are screenshots of these *text* elements.

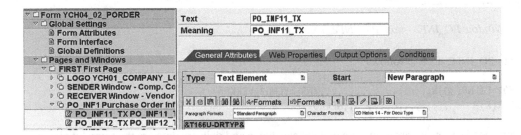

**Figure 4-29.** *Window PO_INF1—text: PO_INF11_TX*

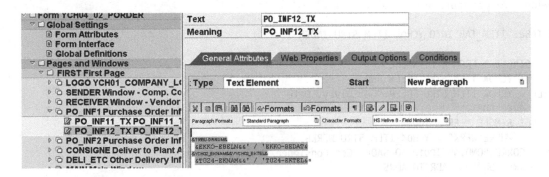

**Figure 4-30.** *Window PO_INF1—text: PO_INF12_TX*

The text in PO_INF11_TX is <CD>&T166U-DRTYP&.</>
The text in PO_INF12_TX is as follows:

```
*
* <HS> &T166U-DRNUM&</>
* &EKKO-EBELN&&' / 'EKKO-BEDAT&
* <HS> &YCH02_EKNAM&&' / 'YCH02_EKTEL&</>
* &T024-EKNAM&&' / 'T024-EKTEL&
```

In the secondary *window* PO_INF2, we located one *text* element: PO_INF2_TX. Figure 4-31 is a screenshot of the element *text*.

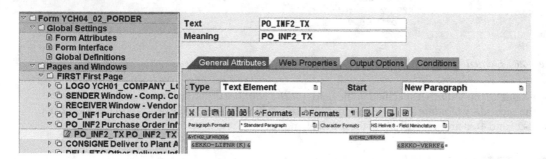

*Figure 4-31.* *Window PO_INF2—text: PO_INF2_TX*

The text in PO_INF2_TX is as follows:

```
* <HS> &YCH02_LIFNR(30)&,,</>,,,,,,,,,,,,,,<HS>&YCH02_VERKF&</>
* &EKKO-LIFNR(K)&    ,,,,,,,,,,,,,,,,,,&EKKO-VERKF&
```

As per our specification, we are assuming that the consignee and delivery date are the same for all the items. We are deriving the consignee address and delivery date from the first item of a purchase order. In the *window* CONSIGNE, we created a node of *program lines* named GET_CONSIGNEE_CODE and located the following ABAP program lines:

```
READ TABLE ITEM_TAB INTO YCH04_ITEM_STRU INDEX 1.

SELECT SINGLE * FROM EKET WHERE
  EBELN = YCH04_ITEM_STRU-EBELN AND
  EBELP = YCH04_ITEM_STRU-EBELP."Get Dlvry. Date
CLEAR: SADR, ADRS.
  SELECT SINGLE * FROM T001W
        WHERE WERKS = YCH04_ITEM_STRU-WERKS.
  MOVE-CORRESPONDING T001W TO SADR."Get Consignee/Delivery Address
 MOVE-CORRESPONDING SADR TO ADRS.

CALL FUNCTION 'ADDRESS_INTO_PRINTFORM'
  EXPORTING
    ADRSWA_IN                       = ADRS
  IMPORTING
    ADRSWA_OUT                      = ADRS.
```

The input parameter to the code is item_tab.

The output parameters to the code are T001W, ADRS, YCH04_ITEM_STRU, and EKET SADR. The consignee address is derived and output as follows:

- If ADRNR is a valid address number, the address is derived and formatted by supplying ADRNR to the element *address* named CONSIGNEE_ADDRESS1.

- If ADRNR is not a valid address number and ADRN2 is a valid address number, the address is derived and formatted by supplying ADRN2 to the element *address* named CONSIGNEE_ADDRESS2.

- If neither ADRNR nor ADRN2 is a valid address number, the address is derived from the plant code YCH04_ITEM_STRU-WERKS; the foregoing ABAP code drives the address, etc.

We have located the element *alternative named* CONSIGNEE_CONDITION1 in the *window* CONSIGNE. We specified in this element *alternative*, the following condition: YCH04_ITEM_STRU-ADRNR NE ' '. Figure 4-32 illustrates.

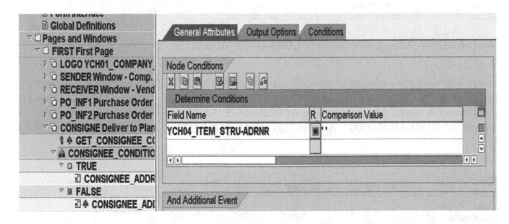

***Figure 4-32.*** *Window CONSIGNE—element alternative: CONSIGNEE_CONDITION1*

Under the node *true*, we inserted the element *address* named CONSIGNEE_ADDRESS1 to which the address number YCH04_ITEM_STRU-ADRNR was supplied. Figure 4-33 illustrates.

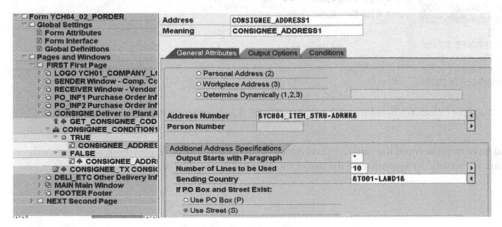

***Figure 4-33.*** *Window CONSIGNE—element address: CONSIGNEE_ADDRESS1*

Under the node *FALSE*, we inserted the element *address* named CONSIGNEE_ADDRESS2 to which the address number YCH04_ITEM_STRU-ADRN2 was supplied. In the *Conditions* tab of the element *address* we inserted the following condition: YCH04_ITEM_STRU-ADRN2 NE ' '. Figure 4-34 illustrates.

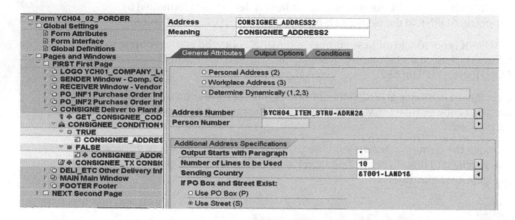

***Figure 4-34.*** *Window CONSIGNE—element address: CONSIGNEE_ADDRESS2*

Next to element *alternative*, we created a *text* node named CONSIGNEE_TX. This *text* node contains the ten lines of address derived from the plant code YCH04_ITEM_STRU-WERKS—ADRS-LINE0.....ADRS-LINE9. In the *Conditions* tab of the element *text* named CONSIGNEE_TX, we inserted the compound condition: YCH04_ITEM_STRU-ADRNR EQ ' ' AND YCH04_ITEM_STRU-ADRN2 EQ ' '. Figure 4-35 illustrates.

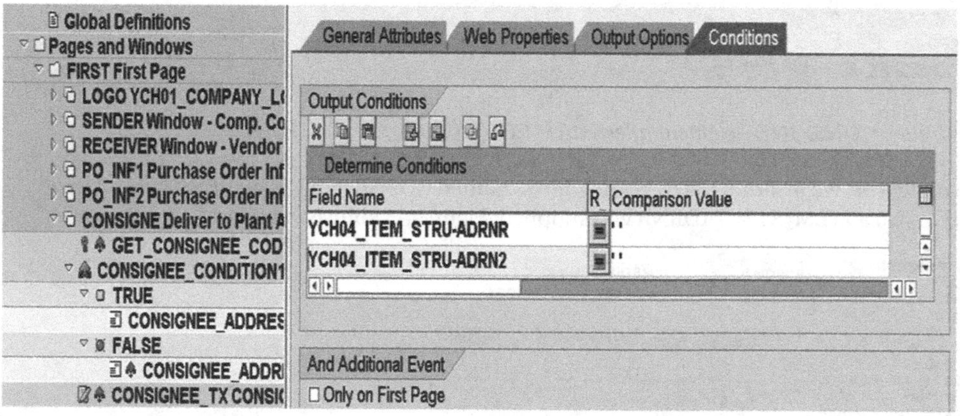

***Figure 4-35.*** *Window CONSIGNE—element text: CONSIGNEE_TX, Conditions tab*

We could have implemented the output of consignee address without the deployment of the element *alternative*. But, we wanted to demonstrate the use of the element *alternative* once more.

In the *window* DELI_ETC, we created the element *text* named DELI_ETC_TX. We entered the following text in the element *text* named DELI_ETC_TX:

```
* <HS>&YCH02_EINDT&</><HS>:</> &EKET-EINDT&
* <HS>&YCH02_INCO1&</><HS>:</> &EKKO-INCO1&
* <HS>&YCH02_ZBTXT&</>
* &ZBTXT_STRU-STR&
*
* <HS>&WAERS_LT&</><HS>:</> &EKKO-WAERS&
```

We plan to output the item information of the purchase order in the element *table*. We plan to output (a) the item column headings in the *header* area of the element *table*, (b) the item data in the *main area* of the element *table*, and (c) the purchase order total amount expressed in numbers and text in the *footer* area of the element *table* (refer to Figure 4-17).

We need to identify the line types to be created in the element *table*. To output the item number, material number, or code and description, we need one line type named, say, LINE1. To output the ordered quantity, unit of measure, price per unit, and net value we need one line type named, say, LINE2.

We can adopt these line types, LINE1 and LINE2, for the column headings of item data as well.

We need one line type to output the total amount with its nomenclature named as FLINE1 and one line type to output the total amount expressed in numbers and text named as FLINE2.

To sum up, we will create four line types in the element *table*.

We created the element *table* named TABLE_ITEMS in the main *window*. We specified the *Table Width* to be the same as Main *Window* width: 200MM.

In the element *table* TABLE_ITEMS, we navigated to the screen of line types by clicking the button *Details*. On the screen of line types, we created the four line types: LINE1, LINE2, FLINE1, and FLINE2. Figure 4-36 shows a screenshot of line types LINE1 and LINE2:

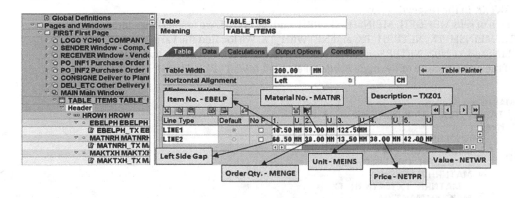

***Figure 4-36.*** *Table TABLE_ITEMS—line types: LINE1, LINE2*

As shown in Figure 4-36, line type LINE1 will accommodate the fields EBELP, MATNR, and TXZ01. It will correspond to the first line of item data. Line type LINE2 will accommodate the fields MENGE, MEINS, NETPR, and NETWR. It will correspond to the second line of item data.

We specified dimensions of all of line type *cells* in millimeters (MM).

We will use the line types LINE1 and LINE2 to output the column headings in the *header* as well as the item data of the element *table*.

Figure 4-37 is a screenshot of line types FLINE1 and FLINE2:

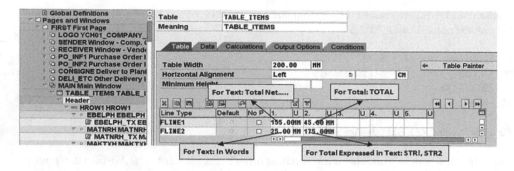

**Figure 4-37.** *Table TABLE_ITEMS—line types: FLINE1, FLINE2*

Having created the requisite line types, we proceeded to create *table lines* under the nodes *header*, *main area*, and *footer* of the element *table* TABLE_ITEMS.

The header text or column headings of item data nust appear on each page of a purchase order. The default settings will ensure this. The *Output Options* tab of the node *header* contains check boxes: *At Start of Table* and *At Page Break*. These two check boxes enable you to control the appearance of column headings of item data.

Starting with the node *header*, we created the *table line* HROW1 to which we assigned the line type LINE1. The *table line* HROW1 will consist of three *cells*. Next, again under the node *header*, next to HROW1, we created the *table line* HROW2 to which we assigned the line type LINE2. The *table line* HROW2 will consist of five *cells* inclusive of the first *cell* to create a gap.

Under the *table line* HROW1, we renamed the *cells* EBELPH, MATNRH, and MAKTXH. Under the *table line* HROW2, we renamed the *cells* GAP, MENGEH, MEINSH, NETPRH, and NETWRH.

Under each of *cells* EBELPH, MATNRH, and MAKTXH, we created the elements *text* named EBELPH_TX, MATNRH_TX, and MAKTXH_TX. We located the variables &YCH04_EBELP&, &YCH02_MATNR&, and &YCH02_MAKTX& in the respective *texts*.

Under each of *cells* MENGEH, MEINSH, NETPRH, and NETWRH, we created the elements *text* named MENGEH_TX, MEINSH_TX, NETPRH_TX, and NETWRH_TX. We located the variables &YCH02_MENGE&, &YCH02_MEINS&, &YCH02_NETPR&, and &YCH02_NETWR& in the respective *texts*. Figure 4-38 is a screenshot of the tree structure of the node *header* of element *table* TABLE_ITEMS.

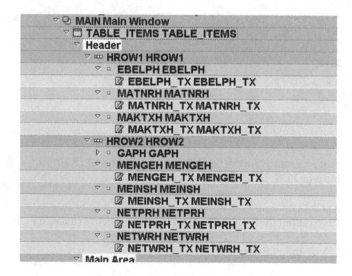

**Figure 4-38.** *Table TABLE_ITEMS—tree structure of node: Header*

This completes the tasks in the *header* of the element *table* TABLE_ITEMS.

Under the node *main area*, we created the *table line* ROW1 to which we assigned the line type LINE1. The *table line* ROW1 will consist of three *cells*. Again, under the node *main area*, we created the *table line* ROW2 to which we assigned the line type LINE2. The *table line* ROW2 will consist of five *cells* inclusive of the first *cell* to create a gap.

Under the *table line* ROW1, we renamed the *cells* EBELP, MATNR, and MAKTX. Under the *table line* ROW2, we renamed the *cells* MENGE, MEINS, NETPR, and NETWR.

Under each of *cells* EBELP, MATNR, and MAKTX, we created the elements *text* named EBELP_TX, MATNR_TX, and MAKTX_TX. We located the variables &YCH04_ITEM_STRU-EBELP(5)&, &YCH04_ITEM_STRU-MATNR(K18)&, and &YCH04_ITEM_STRU-TXZ01(40)& in the respective *texts*.

Under each of *cells* MENGE, MEINS, NETPR, and NETWR, we created the elements *text* named MENGE_TX, MEINS_TX, NETPR_TX, and NETWR_TX. We located the variables &YCH04_ITEM_STRU-MENGE(14)&, &YCH04_ITEM_STRU-MEINS(5)&, &YCH04_ITEM_STRU-NETPR(14)&, and &YCH04_ITEM_STRU-NETWR(15)& in the respective *texts*.

To sum or total the net value of individual items, we created a node of *program lines* named TOTAL_CODE under the *text* node NETWR_TX. The TOTAL_CODE input parameter is YCH04_ITEM_STRU-NETWR and the output parameter is TOTAL. We entered the following ABAP statement:

```
TOTAL = TOTAL + YCH04_ITEM_STRU-NETWR.
```

Figure 4-39 is a screenshot of the tree structure of the node *main area* of element *table* TABLE_ITEMS.

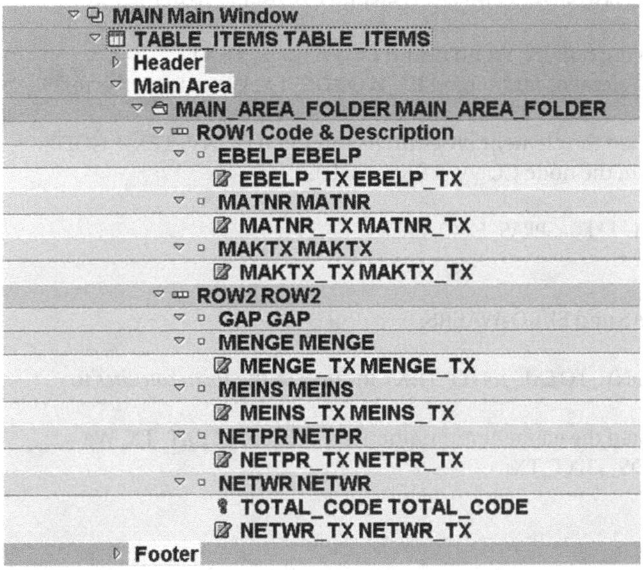

*Figure 4-39. Table TABLE_ITEMS—tree structure of node: Main Area*

This completes the tasks in the *main area* of the element *table* TABLE_ITEMS.

We selected the node *footer* of the element *table* TABLE_ITEMS. We reserved five lines for output of the *table footer*. We enabled the check box *End of Table* to indicate that the *footer* be output only at the end of the item data, that is, the end of the *table*. Figure 4-40 shows the *footer* node.

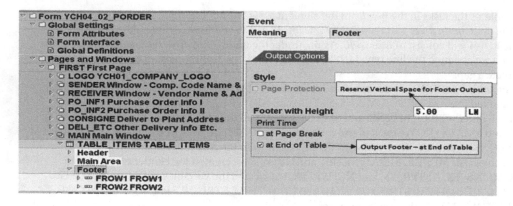

*Figure 4-40.* Table TABLE_ITEMS—Footer settings

Under the node *footer*, we created the *table line* FROW1 to which we assigned the line type FLINE1. The *table line* FROW1 will consist of two *cells*. Next, again under the node *footer*, we created the *table line* FROW2 to which we assigned the line type FLINE2. The *table line* FROW2 will consist of two *cells*.

Under the *table line* FROW1, we renamed the *cells* TOTAL and TOTAL_AMT. Under the *table line* FROW2, we renamed the *cells* IN_WORDS and IN_WORDS_TEXT.

Under each of *cells* TOTAL and TOTAL_AMT, we created the elements *text* named TOTAL_TX and TOTAL_AMT_TX. We entered the text ,,,,,,,,,,&YCH02_TOTAL_NET_E& and &TOTAL(17)& in the *texts* TOTAL_TX and TOTAL_AMT_TX, respectively.

Under the *table line* FROW2, we renamed the *cells* IN_WORDS and IN_WORDS_TEXT.

Under the *cell* IN_WORDS, we created the element *text* named IN_WORDS_TX. We entered the text &YCH02_INWORDS& in the *text* IN_WORDS_TX.

Under the *cell* IN_WORDS_TEXT, we created the element *program lines* named CONV_TEXT_CODE. We entered the following ABAP program lines in the node CONV_TEXT_CODE:

```
PERFORM CONV_TOTAL_INTO_TEXT USING TOTAL EKKO-SPRAS EKKO-WAERS
                         STR1 STR2.
```

Input parameters are TOTAL, EKKO-SPRAS and EKKO-WAERS.

Output parameters are STR1 and STR2.

This is an invocation of the subroutine CONV_TOTAL_INTO_TEXT located in the *form routines* to convert total amount into text.

Under the *cell* IN_WORDS_TEXT, we created the element *text* named IN_WORDS_TEXT_TX. We entered the following text in the *text* IN_WORDS_TEXT_TX:

```
&STR1&
&STR2&
```

Figure 4-41 is a screenshot of the tree structure of the node *Footer* of element *table* TABLE_ITEMS.

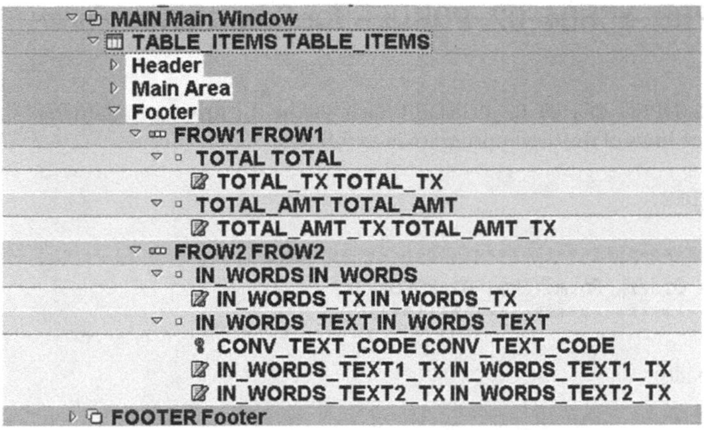

```
▽ ⌂ MAIN Main Window
   ▽ ▦ TABLE_ITEMS TABLE_ITEMS
      ▷ Header
      ▷ Main Area
      ▽ Footer
         ▽ ⚏ FROW1 FROW1
            ▽ ▫ TOTAL TOTAL
               ▨ TOTAL_TX TOTAL_TX
            ▽ ▫ TOTAL_AMT TOTAL_AMT
               ▨ TOTAL_AMT_TX TOTAL_AMT_TX
         ▽ ⚏ FROW2 FROW2
            ▽ ▫ IN_WORDS IN_WORDS
               ▨ IN_WORDS_TX IN_WORDS_TX
            ▽ ▫ IN_WORDS_TEXT IN_WORDS_TEXT
               ⁂ CONV_TEXT_CODE CONV_TEXT_CODE
               ▨ IN_WORDS_TEXT1_TX IN_WORDS_TEXT1_TX
               ▨ IN_WORDS_TEXT2_TX IN_WORDS_TEXT2_TX
   ▷ ⌂ FOOTER Footer
```

*Figure 4-41.* *Table TABLE_ITEMS—tree structure of node: Footer*

This completes the tasks in the *footer* of the element *table* TABLE_ITEMS as well as in the *page format* FIRST.

## Node: Page Format NEXT

In the *page format* NEXT, there are two *windows*—PO_INF3 and PAGE—which differ from the *page format* FIRST. We need to create or insert elements into these two *windows* only. The other *windows* in the *page format* NEXT which are common to the *windows* in *page format* FIRST will already contain elements we created earlier.

In the *window* PO_INF3, we created the element *text* named PO_INF3_TX. We entered the following text in the element *text* named PO_INF3_TX:

```
*
*
*          <HS>&T166U-DRNUM&</>
*            &EKKO-EBELN& &' / 'EKKO-BEDAT&
```

In the *window* PAGE, we created the element *program lines* named ASSIGN_PAGE. We entered the following single line in the element *program lines* named ASSIGN_PAGE:

```
PAGE = SFSY-PAGE.
```

In the *window* PAGE, under the node ASSIGN_PAGE we created the element *text* named PAGE_TX. We entered the following text in the element *text* named PAGE_TX:

```
*          &YCH02_PAGE&
*          &PAGE(Z)&/&SFSY-FORMPAGES(CZ2)&
```

The field PAGE is defined in Global Data area as type NUM02. The field PAGE was assigned the value of SFSY-PAGE for output alignment purpose.

After creating the *form* elements as described in the preceding pages, we saved, performed a consistency check, and activated the *form*.

## Driver Program YH04_02_DPRG_YCH04_02_PORDER for Smartforms *Form:* YCH04_02_PORDER

We created an ABAP program YCH04_02_DPRG_YCH04_02_PORDER. This will be the driver program for the *form* YCH04_02_PORDER. The source lines of the driver program is as follows:

```
REPORT  YCH04_02_DPRG_YCH04_02_PORDER.

****************************************************************
* Driver Program - Custom Purchase Order (Form:YCH04_02_PORDER) *
****************************************************************

TABLES: EKKO,   "Purchasing Doc Header
        T001.   "Company Code

DATA: ITEM_TAB  TYPE STANDARD TABLE OF YCH04_ITEM_STRU, "PO Items
      FORM_NAME TYPE TDSFNAME VALUE 'YCH04_02_PORDER', "Form Name
      FM_NAME   TYPE RS38L_FNAM, "Function Module Name
      CONTROLS  TYPE SSFCTRLOP, "Parameter to Form
      PCNT      TYPE I. "Counter for Number of POS Output

********************************************
SELECT-OPTIONS PO_NOS FOR EKKO-EBELN MATCHCODE OBJECT
    YCH02_01_EKKO_LFA1_SH.

*******************Fill Selection Table ***********
**************************************************
INITIALIZATION.
PO_NOS-SIGN   = 'I'.
PO_NOS-OPTION = 'EQ'.
PO_NOS-LOW    = '4500004823'.
APPEND PO_NOS TO PO_NOS.


PO_NOS-LOW    = '4500009520'.
APPEND PO_NOS TO PO_NOS.


********************************************
START-OF-SELECTION.

CONTROLS-NO_OPEN   = 'X'.
CONTROLS-NO_CLOSE  = 'X'.
CONTROLS-NO_DIALOG = ' '.
CONTROLS-PREVIEW   = 'X'.

 CALL FUNCTION 'SSF_OPEN'
  EXPORTING
    CONTROL_PARAMETERS        = CONTROLS
  EXCEPTIONS
    FORMATTING_ERROR          = 1
    INTERNAL_ERROR            = 2
    SEND_ERROR                = 3
```

```
      USER_CANCELED              = 4
      OTHERS                     = 5.
 IF SY-SUBRC <> 0.
 MESSAGE ID SY-MSGID TYPE SY-MSGTY NUMBER SY-MSGNO
        WITH SY-MSGV1 SY-MSGV2 SY-MSGV3 SY-MSGV4.
 ENDIF.
********************************************

CALL FUNCTION 'SSF_FUNCTION_MODULE_NAME'
  EXPORTING
    FORMNAME                   = FORM_NAME
  IMPORTING
    FM_NAME                    = FM_NAME
  EXCEPTIONS
    NO_FORM                    = 1
    NO_FUNCTION_MODULE         = 2
    OTHERS                     = 3.
IF SY-SUBRC <> 0.
 MESSAGE ID SY-MSGID TYPE SY-MSGTY NUMBER SY-MSGNO
        WITH SY-MSGV1 SY-MSGV2 SY-MSGV3 SY-MSGV4.
ENDIF.

*****Main Loop *****

SELECT * FROM EKKO WHERE EBELN IN PO_NOS.

 IF ( EKKO-SPRAS <> 'D' AND EKKO-SPRAS <> 'E' ) OR
     EKKO-BSTYP <> 'F' OR ( EKKO-BSART <>'NB'
     AND EKKO-BSART <> 'PO' ).
  CONTINUE.
 ENDIF.

 SELECT SINGLE * FROM T001
      WHERE BUKRS = EKKO-BUKRS. "Get Company Code

 SELECT EBELN EBELP MATNR WERKS MENGE MEINS NETPR NETWR ADRNR
        ADRN2 TXZ01 FROM EKPO
        INTO TABLE ITEM_TAB "Load itab from EKPO
        WHERE EBELN = EKKO-EBELN AND BUKRS = EKKO-BUKRS.

 CALL FUNCTION FM_NAME
   EXPORTING
     CONTROL_PARAMETERS         = CONTROLS
     EKKO                       = EKKO
     T001                       = T001
   TABLES
     ITEM_TAB                   = ITEM_TAB
   EXCEPTIONS
     FORMATTING_ERROR           = 1
```

```
      INTERNAL_ERROR                = 2
      SEND_ERROR                    = 3
      USER_CANCELED                 = 4
      OTHERS                        = 5.
  IF SY-SUBRC <> 0.
   MESSAGE ID SY-MSGID TYPE SY-MSGTY NUMBER SY-MSGNO
          WITH SY-MSGV1 SY-MSGV2 SY-MSGV3 SY-MSGV4.
  ENDIF.


  PCNT = PCNT + 1.

ENDSELECT.
****************************************************************

IF PCNT = 0.
  MESSAGE S000(YCH02_MCLASS) DISPLAY LIKE 'W'."No Data Processed
ELSE.

  CALL FUNCTION 'SSF_CLOSE'
    EXCEPTIONS
      FORMATTING_ERROR          = 1
      INTERNAL_ERROR            = 2
      SEND_ERROR                = 3
      OTHERS                    = 4.
  IF SY-SUBRC <> 0.
    MESSAGE ID SY-MSGID TYPE SY-MSGTY NUMBER SY-MSGNO
            WITH SY-MSGV1 SY-MSGV2 SY-MSGV3 SY-MSGV4.
  ENDIF.
ENDIF.
```

We are not calling the function module corresponding to the Smartforms *form* directly. We are calling the function module SSF_FUNCTION_MODULE_NAME and supplying it the name of the *form* in the field FORM_NAME; the function module returns the name of the function module corresponding to the *form* in the field FM_NAME. We are then using the field FM_NAME to call the function module corresponding to the *form*. Henceforth, this will be the practice in all our subsequent hands-on exercises.

The function modules SSF_OPEN and SSF_CLOSE are used to open and close the spool file explicitly. When you call the function module corresponding to a Smartforms *form* without the formal parameter CONTROL_PARAMETERS, the spool file is opened implicitly. Correspondingly, when you exit the function module of a Smartforms *form*, the spool file is closed implicitly. In our current driver program, we are calling the function module corresponding to a Smartforms *form* repeatedly in a loop. We do not want separate spool files to be created for each purchase order output. Hence we are issuing explicit opening and closing of spool files through the function modules SSF_OPEN (once before the looping commences) and SSF_CLOSE (once after the loop processing is over), respectively. When you set the fields NO_OPEN and NO_CLOSE of the structure CONTROLS to 'X' (formal parameter CONTROL_PARAMETERS), the implicit opening and closing of the spool file is suppressed.

Within the program, we are processing purchasing documents fulfilling the following conditions:

- Language key of purchasing documents equal to D or E.

- Purchasing document category (field BSTYP) is purchase order. – BSTYP value equal to F.

- Purchasing document types (field BSART) is standard purchase order. – BSART value equal to NB or PO.

Purchasing documents not fulfilling these conditions are bypassed.

```
IF ( EKKO-SPRAS <> 'D' AND EKKO-SPRAS <> 'E' ) OR EKKO-BSTYP <> 'F'
   OR ( EKKO-BSART <>'NB'    AND EKKO-BSART <> 'PO' ).
  CONTINUE.
 ENDIF.
```

You can incorporate these conditions in WHERE clause itself if you desire to do so.

If we select purchasing documents through the search help attached to the SELECT-OPTIONS field PO_NOS, we are assured of its processing or outputting. But if we enter any random numbers of purchasing documents, they might or might not be processed as some/all of them might not fulfill one or more of the conditions (i), (ii), and (iii).

In Chapter 2, we had created a message class/id YCH02_MCLASS and a message number 000 as 'No Data Processed for Output' to report the instance of no data processed and output. We are using the same message class and message number to report no data situation.

When you read the comments provided in the driver program, I expect that you will be able to comprehend the logic and flow of the driver program.

## Database View YCH02_EKKO_LFA1

We created a database view YCH02_EKKO_LFA1 with the table EKKO as the primary table and table LFA1 as a secondary table in Chapter 2; we are using the same in the present hands-on exercise. We are using the database view YCH02_EKKO_LFA1 in the search help YCH02_01_EKKO_LFA1_SH.

## Elementary Search Help YCH02_01_EKKO_LFA1_SH

We created an elementary search help YCH02_01_EKKO_LFA1_SH using the database view YCH02_EKKO_LFA in Chapter 2; we are using the same in the present hands-on exercise. We attached search help YCH02_01_EKKO_LFA1_SH to the SELECT-OPTIONS variable PO_NOS.

# Output

We are using the same two purchase orders we used in Chapter 2 for testing the output. The identified purchase order numbers are 4500004823 and 4500009520. The purchase order number 4500004823 language key is D and the purchase order number 4500009520 language key is E. This enables us to test the output in the two languages. The purchase order number 4500009520 has 53 items and is running to four pages, enabling us to test a multiple-page purchase order. We are filling the selection table PO_NOS with these two specific purchase order numbers (refer to the INITIALIZATION event code in the driver program).

We executed the program YCH04_02_DPRG_ YCH04_02_PORDER. The output of the two purchase orders is running to five pages, the purchase order number 4500004823 (German) outputs in one page and the purchase order number 4500009520 (English) outputs in four pages. The output will look like that in Figures 4-42, 4-43, 4-44, 4-45, and 4-46.

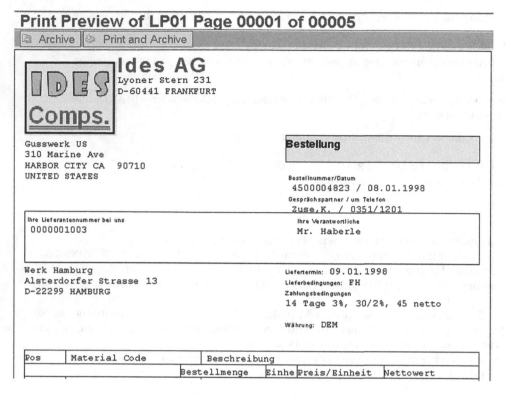

**Figure 4-42.** *Output of custom purchase order form: PO No. 4500004823—I*

| 00010 | 100–110 | Rohling für Spiralgehäuse GG | | | |
| | | | 40 | PC | 10.00 | 400.00 |
| 00020 | 101–210 | Rohling für Laufrad Stahlguss | | | |
| | | | 25 | PC | 30.00 | 750.00 |
| 00030 | 101–410 | Rohling für Druckdeckel Stahlguss | | | |
| | | | 25 | PC | 5.00 | 125.00 |
| 00040 | 102–110 | Rohling für Spiralgehäuse Sphäroguss | | | |
| | | | 28 | PC | 4.00 | 112.00 |
| | Gesamtnettowert ohne Steuern | | | | 1,387.00 |
| in Worte | EINTAUSENDDREIHUNDERTSIEBENUNDACHTZIG DEM 000 | | | | |

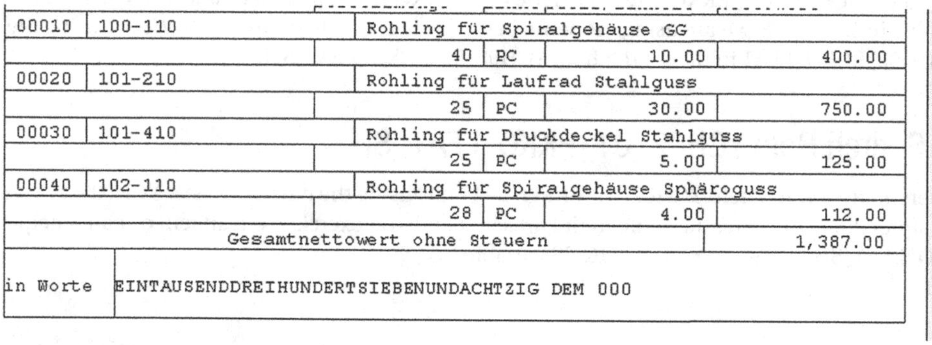

**Figure 4-43.** *Output of custom purchase order form: PO No. 4500004823—II*

## Print Preview of LP01 Page 00002 of 00005

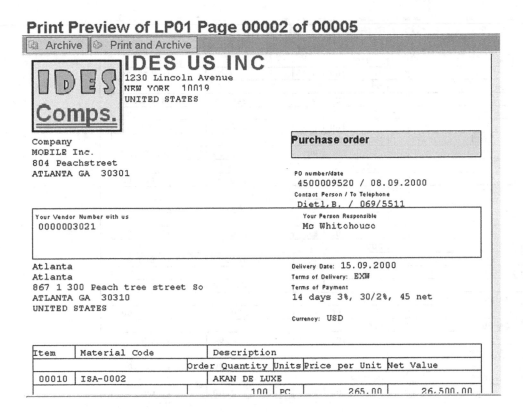

*Figure 4-44. Output of custom purchase order form: PO No. 4500009520—I*

## Print Preview of LP01 Page 00002 of 00005

Archive | Print and Archive

| 00020 | ISA-0003 | VANITY | | | | |
|-------|----------|--------|-----|----|--------|-----------|
| | | | 100 | PC | 160.00 | 16,000.00 |
| 00030 | ISA-0009 | PRIDE | | | | |
| | | | 100 | PC | 240.00 | 24,000.00 |
| 00040 | ISA-0010 | SONIC | | | | |
| | | | 100 | PC | 240.00 | 24,000.00 |
| 00050 | ISA-0011 | TWIN LETTI | | | | |
| | | | 100 | PC | 250.00 | 25,000.00 |
| 00060 | ISA-0012 | V.W. | | | | |
| | | | 100 | PC | 260.00 | 26,000.00 |
| 00070 | ISA-0018 | SLING | | | | |
| | | | 100 | PC | 150.00 | 15,000.00 |
| 00080 | ISA-0019 | TEMPO | | | | |
| | | | 100 | EA | 480.00 | 48,000.00 |
| 00090 | ISA-0020 | BUDONG | | | | |
| | | | 100 | PC | 480.00 | 48,000.00 |
| 00100 | ISA-0021 | EDGE | | | | |
| | | | 100 | PC | 480.00 | 48,000.00 |
| 00110 | ISA-0022 | FUJI | | | | |
| | | | 100 | PC | 380.00 | 38,000.00 |
| 00120 | ISA-0023 | LETTI | | | | |
| | | | 100 | PC | 370.00 | 37,000.00 |
| 00130 | ISA-0024 | MACHINE | | | | |
| | | | 100 | PC | 405.00 | 40,500.00 |
| 00140 | ISA-0025 | NOBILE 2 | | | | |
| | | | 100 | PC | 410.00 | 41,000.00 |

*Figure 4-45. Output of custom purchase order form: PO No. 4500009520—II*

## Print Preview of LP01 Page 00005 of 00005

Archive | Print and Archive

| 00680 | ISA-1052 | SPY STOOL-LO | | | | |
|-------|----------|--------------|-----|----|-------|----------|
| | | | 100 | PC | 48.00 | 4,800.00 |
| 00690 | ISA-1053 | FUJI MIX | | | | |
| | | | 100 | PC | 19.00 | 1,900.00 |
| 00700 | ISA-1054 | OVAL | | | | |
| | | | 100 | PC | 19.00 | 1,900.00 |
| 00710 | ISA-1055 | SUN | | | | |
| | | | 100 | PC | 22.00 | 2,200.00 |
| 00720 | ISA-1056 | ZAP | | | | |
| | | | 100 | PC | 22.00 | 2,200.00 |
| 00730 | ISA-2000 | Table | | | | |
| | | | 100 | PC | 39.00 | 3,900.00 |
| | Total Net Value Excluding Tax | | | | | 796,700.00 |
| In Words | SEVEN HUNDREDNINETY-SIX THOUSAND SEVEN HUNDRED USD 000 | | | | | |

*Figure 4-46. Output of custom purchase order form: PO No. 4500009520—III*

## Hands-on Exercise Recapitulation

In this hands-on exercise, we created from scratch a Smartforms *form* to output purchase orders deployed it.

We produced almost the same output as the one we produced in hands-on exercise III in Chapter 2. The item data along with the column headings and footer was output with grid lines, imparting an appealing visual appearance.

Only the main data to output purchase orders was retrieved in the driver program; the rest of the data was retrieved in the *initialization* event of the *form*. Apart from the function module of the *form*, the driver program also invoked the following function modules:

- SSF_OPEN: To open a spool file

- SSF_FUNCTION_MODULE_NAME: To take a *form* name as input parameter and return corresponding function module name

- SSF_CLOSE: To close a spool file

A specialty of this exercise is the maintenance and retrieval of texts in the *form* from ABAP dictionary data elements. Otherwise the text is entered in the *form* as literal text. The maintenance of texts of the *form* in data elements instead of being entered as literal text has made the *form* language independent.

We used all the three nodes of the element *table*: *header, main area,* and *footer.*

# Hands-on Exercise III–Copy, Modify, and Customize SAP Delivered *Form* /SMB40/MMPO_A, etc.

This hands-on exercise involves copying the SAP delivered purchase order Smartforms *form* /SMB40/ MMPO_A into Y namespace. Next, we are carrying out modifications and customizations to the copied *form* and testing the output of the copied *form*. Testing the output of the copied *form* involves performing output settings. The output settings required to test the output of the copied Smartforms *form* is being introduced in this hands-on exercise. Apart from the output settings, we need to modify SAP driver programs to be able to support output through Smartform *forms*. By default, the SAP driver programs support output through SAP script *forms*. Obviously, the SAP driver programs need to be copied into Y/Z namespace to enable their modification. Hence this hands-on exercise has two stages.

Stage I enables purchase order output with SAP delivered Smartforms *form* /SMB40/MMPO_A. This will involve copying the default SAP driver program SAPFM06P and the include program FM06PE02 into YCH04_ SAPFM06P and YCH04_ FM06PE02, respectively, and modifying these programs so that they support output with Smartforms *form*, and performing global output settings so that the purchase orders output as per the layout of the SAP delivered Smartforms *form* /SMB40/MMPO_A—print preview in transaction code ME22N.

Stage II enables purchase order output with a modified and customized version of a copy of the SAP delivered Smartforms *form*. This will involve copying the SAP delivered Smartforms *form* /SMB40/MMPO_A into Y namespace (YCH04_03_SMB40_MMPO_A), carrying out modifications and customization in the copied *form* YCH04_03_SMB40_MMPO_A as per laid-down specifications, and performing global output settings so that the purchase orders output as per the layout of the modified and customized Smartforms *form* YCH04_03_SMB40_MMPO_A—print preview in transaction code ME22N.

A description of each of the two stages of the hands-on exercise follows.

## A Note on the SAP Delivered Smartforms *Form* /SMB40/MMPO_A

The SAP delivered SAP script form MEDRUCK is designed to generate output of all purchase related documents—requisitions, request for quotations, purchase orders, etc. That is why it is called the form for purchasing documents. With Smartforms, there is a separate form for each of the purchasing documents: requisitions, request for quotations, purchase orders, etc. The SAP delivered Smartforms *form* /SMB40/ MMPO_A generates output for purchase orders.

The SAP delivered Smartforms *form* /SMB40/MMPO_A in our version of IDES server has an error in the *window* SENDER. The *window* SENDER has the element *text* named SENDER. The element *text* SENDER has been assigned *Text Type* as *Text Module*. No *Text Module* name has been assigned which is resulting in the error. To overcome the error, we have copied the *form* /SMB40/MMPO_A into YSM_SMB40_MMPO_A and assigned the element *text* named SENDER the *Text Type* as *Text Element* instead of *Text Module*. We activated the *form:* YSM_SMB40_MMPO_A. The layout of *windows* in the two *page formats* (FIRST and NEXT) of the *form* YSM_SMB40_MMPO_A is identical. The only difference is that they are using different logo graph images.

When invoking the function module of the *form,* the formal *exporting* parameters ZXEKKO and ZXPEKKO may be named differently on your IDES server. Also, the *tables* parameters L_XEKPO, L_XEKPA, L_XPEKPO, L_XEKET, L_XTKOMV, L_XEKKN, L_XEKEK, and L_XKOMK may be named differently on your IDES server. Refer to the *Form* Interface for the names of these parameters.

## Stage I: Enable Purchase Order Output with Smartforms *Form* YSM_SMB40_MMPO_A,

The purchasing document print program SAPFM06P by default does not carry functionality to output purchasing documents using Smartforms *forms*. The functionality of invoking *forms* in fact is incorporated into the include program FM06PE02. So we need to copy the two programs SAPFM06P and FM06PE02 into Y namespace and carry out modifications to the copied programs to incorporate the functionality of calling Smartforms *forms*.

We copied the programs SAPFM06P to YCH04_ SAPFM06P and FM06PE02 to YCH04_ FM06PE02, respectively.

In the program YCH04_ SAPFM06P, we changed only one line: INCLUDE FM06PE02 to INCLUDE YCH04_ FM06PE02. We saved and activated the program YCH04_ SAPFM06P.

In the include program YCH04_ FM06PE02, we incorporated the following lines as data declarations:

```
*************************************
* Extra data defined for smartforms **
*************************************
DATA: FUNC_NAME TYPE RS38L_FNAM,          "Extra for smartforms
      OUTPUT    TYPE SSFCOMPOP,           "Extra for smartforms
      DIALOG    TYPE SSFCTRLOP,           "Extra for smartforms
      XKOMK     TYPE STANDARD TABLE OF KOMK."Extra for smartforms
```

In the include program YCH04_ FM06PE02, we inserted the following lines following the first invocation of the function module ME_READ_PO_FOR_PRINTING:

```
*************modification for smartforms*******
  IF TNAPR-SFORM NE ' '.                      "Extra for smartforms
    CALL FUNCTION 'SSF_FUNCTION_MODULE_NAME'   "Extra for smartforms
         EXPORTING                             "Extra for smartforms
           FORMNAME    = TNAPR-SFORM           "Extra for smartforms
         IMPORTING                             "Extra for smartforms
           FM_NAME     = FUNC_NAME             "Extra for smartforms
         EXCEPTIONS                            "Extra for smartforms
```

```
          NO_FORM              = 1              "Extra for smartforms
          NO_FUNCTION_MODULE = 2               "Extra for smartforms
          OTHERS               = 3.             "Extra for smartforms

  IF SY-SUBRC EQ 0.                            "Extra for smartforms
   DIALOG-NO_DIALOG    = 'X'.                  "Extra for smartforms
   DIALOG-PREVIEW      = 'X'.                  "Extra for smartforms
   DIALOG-LANGU        = L_DOC-XEKKO-SPRAS.    "Extra for smartforms
   OUTPUT-TDDEST       = 'LP01'.               "Extra for smartforms
*  OUTPUT-BCS_LANGU    = L_DOC-XEKKO-SPRAS.    "Extra for smartforms
   OUTPUT-TDNOPREV     = ' '.                  "Extra for smartforms
   OUTPUT-TDNOPRINT    = ' '.                  "Extra for smartforms
   OUTPUT-TDIMMED      = 'X'.                  "Extra for smartforms
   OUTPUT-TDNEWID      = 'X'.                  "Extra for smartforms
   CALL FUNCTION FUNC_NAME                     "Extra for smartforms
        EXPORTING                              "Extra for smartforms
        CONTROL_PARAMETERS = DIALOG            "Extra for smartforms
        OUTPUT_OPTIONS     = OUTPUT            "Extra for smartforms
        USER_SETTINGS      = ' '               "Extra for smartforms
        ZXEKKO             = L_DOC-XEKKO       "Extra for smartforms
        ZXPEKKO            = L_DOC-XPEKKO      "Extra for smartforms
        TABLES                                 "Extra for smartforms
        L_XEKPO            = L_DOC-XEKPO       "Extra for smartforms
        L_XEKPA            = L_DOC-XEKPA       "Extra for smartforms
        L_XPEKPO           = L_DOC-XPEKPO      "Extra for smartforms
        L_XEKET            = L_DOC-XEKET       "Extra for smartforms
        L_XTKOMV           = L_DOC-XTKOMV      "Extra for smartforms
        L_XEKKN            = L_DOC-XEKKN       "Extra for smartforms
        L_XEKEK            = L_DOC-XEKEK       "Extra for smartforms
        L_XKOMK            = XKOMK             "Extra for smartforms
        EXCEPTIONS                             "Extra for smartforms
        FORMATTING_ERROR   = 1                 "Extra for smartforms
        INTERNAL_ERROR     = 2                 "Extra for smartforms
        SEND_ERROR         = 3                 "Extra for smartforms
        USER_CANCELED      = 4                 "Extra for smartforms
        OTHERS             = 5.                "Extra for smartforms
  ELSE.                                        "Extra for smartforms
   CALL FUNCTION 'ME_PRINT_PO'                 "Extra for smartforms
        EXPORTING                              "Extra for smartforms
        IX_NAST            = L_NAST            "Extra for smartforms
        IX_DRUVO           = L_DRUVO           "Extra for smartforms
        DOC                = L_DOC             "Extra for smartforms
        IX_SCREEN          = ENT_SCREEN        "Extra for smartforms
        IX_FROM_MEMORY     = L_FROM_MEMORY     "Extra for smartforms
        IX_TOA_DARA        = TOA_DARA          "Extra for smartforms
        IX_ARC_PARAMS      = ARC_PARAMS        "Extra for smartforms
        IX_FONAM           = TNAPR-FONAM       "Extra for smartforms
        IMPORTING                              "Extra for smartforms
        EX_RETCO           = ENT_RETCO.        "Extra for smartforms
  ENDIF.                                       "Extra for smartforms
ELSE.                                          "Extra for smartforms

*****modification for smartforms over*******
```

We saved and activated the include program YCH04_ FM06PE02. The full source lines of programs YCH04_ SAPFM06P and YCH04_ FM06PE02 are available in the E-resource file for this book (www.apress. com/9781484212345).

To output the purchase orders as per the Smartforms *form*, we have to perform output settings and indicate to the SAP runtime system that a specific Smartforms *form* is to be used to output the purchase orders. By default, the SAP runtime uses SAP delivered standard SAP script *forms* to output business documents (located in client 000).

In Chapter 2, we demonstrated how to output a particular purchasing document using a modified and customized copy of a SAP delivered SAP script *form*. We copied the SAP delivered SAP script *form* for purchasing document MEDRUCK into Y namespace. We modified and customized the copied version of the *form* as per laid-down specifications. We then used the transaction code ME22N—Change Purchasing Document. We selected one specific purchasing document. In the selected purchasing document, we carried out the output settings and part of the output settings was assigning the modified and customized SAP script *form* to the selected purchasing document. The selected purchasing document then output as per the modified and customized *form* layout assigned to it. It worked for one individual selected purchasing document. This process of carrying out output settings in individual purchasing documents served our testing objective in Chapter 2, but in the real-life scenario, this is generally not the manner in which business documents are output or generated using the layout of a modified and customized *form*.

If it was required to output more than one purchasing document using the same modified and customized copy of a SAP delivered SAP script *form*, then it was necessary that the output settings be performed in each of the individual purchasing documents. A better way of ensuring that all purchasing documents output as per the layout of one SAP script or Smartforms *form* is to carry output settings in a global environment. The output settings are carried in the global environment using the transaction code NACE. The transaction code NACE is termed the transaction code for output determination. In the transaction code NACE, the output settings are to be carried out for all the business documents (purchasing documents, billing documents, delivery notes, etc.) to be generated by an enterprise. In the transaction code NACE, you can specify for each business document, the print or driver program to be used, and the SAP script or Smartforms *form* to be used to generate the business document. In the transaction code NACE, you can further specify how a generated business document will reach the business partner (customer/vendor)—hard copy printout, fax or mail, or EDI or Idoc, etc. We are confining our descriptions of transaction code NACE settings to purchasing order hard copy printout.

When you execute the transaction code NACE, the screen in Figure 4-47 appears.

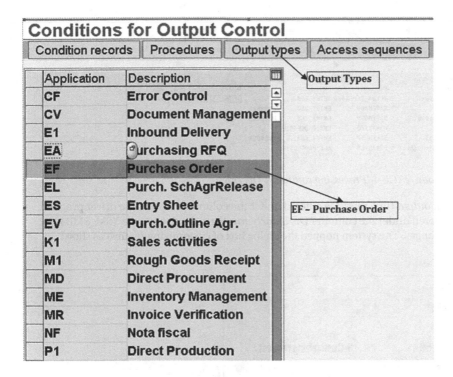

*Figure 4-47.* *Transaction code NACE—Conditions for Output Control*

As marked in Figure 4-47, we have selected the purchase order. We next clicked the application toolbar button: Output Types. The screen shown in Figure 4-48 appeared.

As shown in Figure 4-48, we selected the Output Type NEU and doubled-clicked the node marked *Processing routines*. We toggled for the screen to be in change or edit mode. A screen as shown in Figure 4-49 appeared.

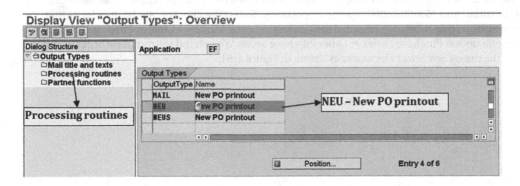

*Figure 4-48.* *Transaction code NACE: Output Types Overview*

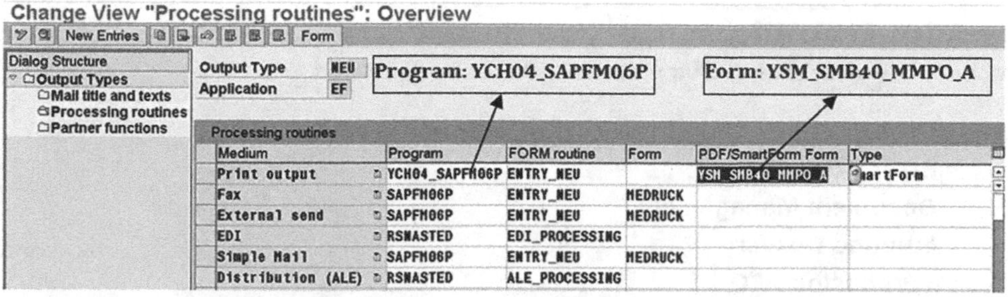

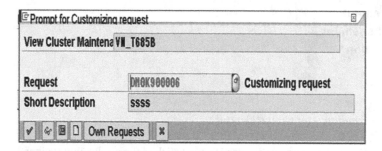

*Figure 4-49.* *Transaction code NACE—"Processing routines": Overview*

Against the entry *Print output* (first row), we entered under the column *program*, the driver program YCH04_SAPFM06P. We entered under the column *PDF/SmartForm Form* the *form* name YSM_SMB40_MMPO_A. We saved the changes. The system popped the dialog box of customizing request as shown in Figure 4-50.

*Figure 4-50.* *Transaction code NACE—Customizing request on saving*

We clicked the Continue button. This concludes the output settings for purchase orders to output using Smartforms *form*.

As in Chapter 2, we will perform the output testing with the two identified purchase order numbers: 4500004823 (German) and 4500009520 (English), respectively. To test the effect of purchase order output settings in transaction code NACE, we executed the transaction code ME22N—Change Purchase Order. We selected the menu option Purchase Order ➤ Other Purchase order. We entered the purchase order number 4500004823 in the dialog box *Select Document* as shown in Figure 4-51.

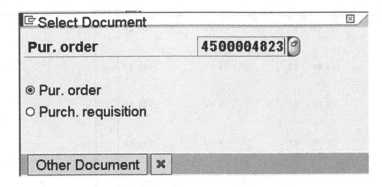

*Figure 4-51.* *Transaction code ME22N—Select Document*

We clicked the Continue button and clicked the *Print Preview* button on the application toolbar. The purchase order number 4500004823 outputted in one page. Figures 4-52 and 4-53 are screenshots of the Print Preview:

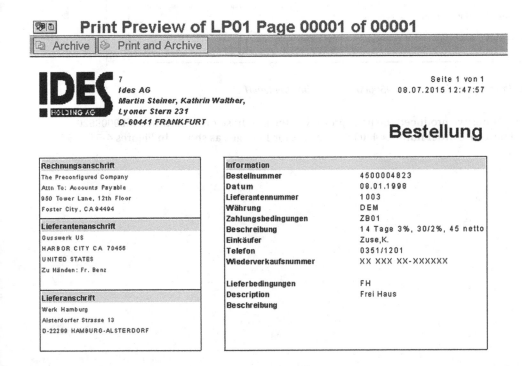

*Figure 4-52.* *Purchase order number 4500004823—Print Preview I*

| Position | Material/Beschreibung | | Menge | Menge | Nettopreis | Nettobetrag |
|---|---|---|---|---|---|---|
| 1 0 | 100-110 | | 40.00 | S T | 10.00 | 400.00 |
| | Rohling für Spiralgehäuse GG | | | | | |
| | Cash Discount | 3.00- % | -12.00 | | | |
| 2 0 | 101-210 | | 25.00 | S T | 30.00 | 750.00 |
| | Rohling für Laufrad Stahlguss | | | | | |
| | Cash Discount | 3.00- % | -22.50 | | | |
| 3 0 | 101-410 | | 25.00 | S T | 5.00 | 125.00 |
| | Rohling für Druckdeckel Stahlguss | | | | | |
| | Cash Discount | 3.00- % | -3.75 | | | |
| 4 0 | 102-110 | | 28.00 | S T | 4.00 | 112.00 |
| | Rohling für Spiralgehäuse Sphäroguss | | | | | |
| | Cash Discount | 3.00- % | -3.36 | | | |
| | | | | | Nettowert | 1,387.00 |
| | | | | | Gesamtbetrag | $ 1,387.00 |

**INSTRUCTIONS TO VENDOR:**

This Purchase Order is subject to the Terms and Conditions incorporated herein by this reference. For a copy of the Terms and Conditions, please refer to the Supplier Guide to Purchasing.

SIGNATURE _____ DATE _____

(Purchasing/Accounting)

*Figure 4-53.* *Purchase order number 4500004823—Print Preview II*

In a like manner, we produced the print preview of the purchase order number 4500009520. The output of purchase order number 4500009520 runs for 12 pages as shown in Figures 4-54, 4-55, 4-56, and 4-57.

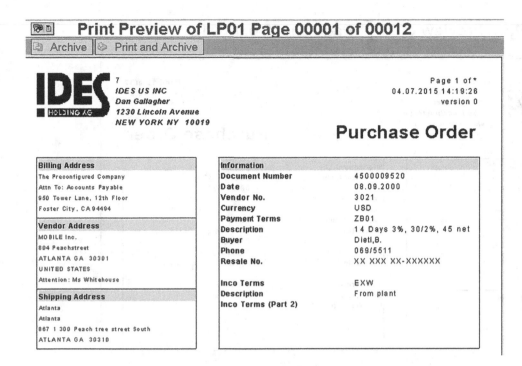

**Figure 4-54.** *Purchase order number 4500009520—Print Preview I*

| Item | Material/Description | | | Quantity | U M | Net Price | Net Amount |
|------|---------------------|------|----------|----------|-----|-----------|------------|
| 1 0 | ISA-0002 | | | 100.00 | PC | 265.00 | 26,500.00 |
| | AKAN DE LUXE | | | | | | |
| | Cash Discount | 3.00- % | -795.00 | | | | |
| 2 0 | ISA-0003 | | | 100.00 | PC | 160.00 | 16,000.00 |
| | VANITY | | | | | | |
| | Cash Discount | 3.00- % | -480.00 | | | | |
| 3 0 | ISA-0009 | | | 100.00 | PC | 240.00 | 24,000.00 |
| | PRIDE | | | | | | |
| | Cash Discount | 3.00- % | -720.00 | | | | |
| 4 0 | ISA-0010 | | | 100.00 | PC | 240.00 | 24,000.00 |
| | SONIC | | | | | | |
| | Cash Discount | 3.00- % | -720.00 | | | | |
| 5 0 | ISA-0011 | | | 100.00 | PC | 250.00 | 25,000.00 |
| | TWIN LETTI | | | | | | |
| | Cash Discount | 3.00- % | -750.00 | | | | |
| 6 0 | ISA-0012 | | | 100.00 | PC | 260.00 | 26,000.00 |
| | V.W. | | | | | | |
| | Cash Discount | 3.00- % | -780.00 | | | | |
| 7 0 | ISA-0018 | | | 100.00 | PC | 150.00 | 15,000.00 |

**Figure 4-55.** *Purchase order number 4500009520—Print Preview II*

319

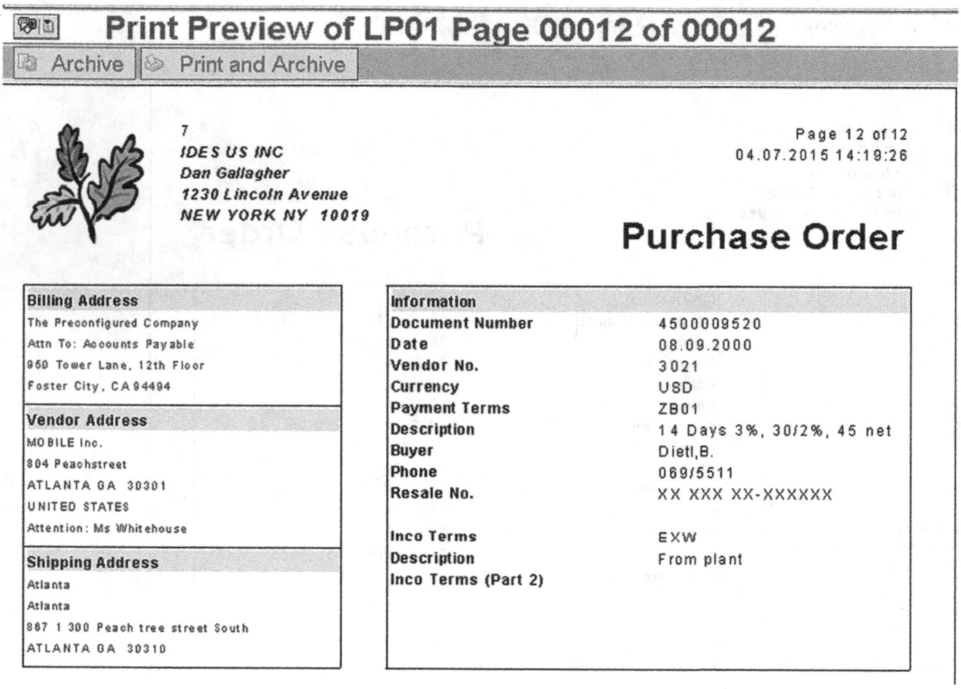

---

### Print Preview of LP01 Page 00012 of 00012

**Archive** | **Print and Archive**

---

7
*IDES US INC*
*Dan Gallagher*
*1230 Lincoln Avenue*
*NEW YORK NY 10019*

Page 12 of 12
04.07.2015 14:19:26

# Purchase Order

| Billing Address | Information | |
|---|---|---|
| The Preconfigured Company | Document Number | 4500009520 |
| Attn To: Accounts Payable | Date | 08.09.2000 |
| 950 Tower Lane, 12th Floor | Vendor No. | 3021 |
| Foster City, CA 94494 | Currency | USD |
| **Vendor Address** | Payment Terms | ZB01 |
| MOBILE Inc. | Description | 14 Days 3%, 30/2%, 45 net |
| 804 Peachstreet | Buyer | Dietl,B. |
| ATLANTA GA 30301 | Phone | 069/5511 |
| UNITED STATES | Resale No. | XX XXX XX-XXXXXX |
| Attention: Ms Whitehouse | | |
| **Shipping Address** | Inco Terms | EXW |
| Atlanta | Description | From plant |
| Atlanta | Inco Terms (Part 2) | |
| 867 1 300 Peach tree street South | | |
| ATLANTA GA 30310 | | |

*Figure 4-56.* *Purchase order number 4500009520—Print Preview III*

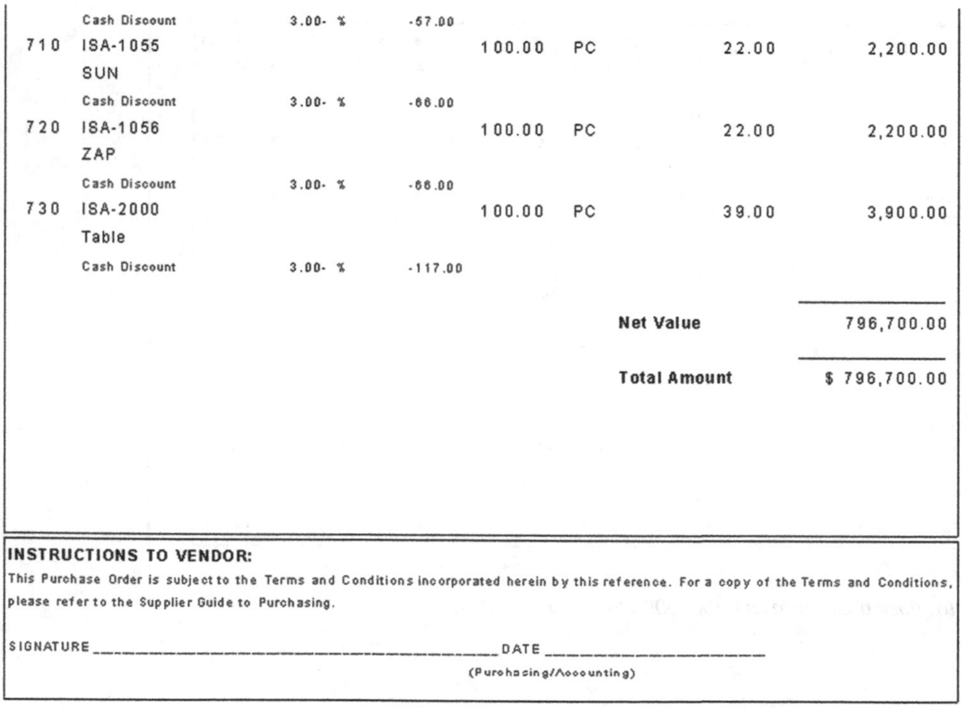

---

| | | | | | | | |
|---|---|---|---|---|---|---|---|
| | Cash Discount | 3.00- % | -57.00 | | | | |
| 710 | ISA-1055 | | | 100.00 | PC | 22.00 | 2,200.00 |
| | SUN | | | | | | |
| | Cash Discount | 3.00- % | -66.00 | | | | |
| 720 | ISA-1056 | | | 100.00 | PC | 22.00 | 2,200.00 |
| | ZAP | | | | | | |
| | Cash Discount | 3.00- % | -66.00 | | | | |
| 730 | ISA-2000 | | | 100.00 | PC | 39.00 | 3,900.00 |
| | Table | | | | | | |
| | Cash Discount | 3.00- % | -117.00 | | | | |

| | |
|---|---|
| **Net Value** | 796,700.00 |
| **Total Amount** | $ 796,700.00 |

**INSTRUCTIONS TO VENDOR:**

This Purchase Order is subject to the Terms and Conditions incorporated herein by this reference. For a copy of the Terms and Conditions, please refer to the Supplier Guide to Purchasing.

SIGNATURE _____ DATE _____
(Purchasing/Accounting)

*Figure 4-57.* *Purchase order number 4500009520—Print Preview IV*

We have completed the first stage of our hands-on exercise, modified copies of driver programs, and performed output settings in the transaction code NACE as to enable output of purchase orders as per the layout of specified SAP delivered Smartforms *form*. We tested the effect of driver program modifications and settings in transaction code NACE by executing transaction code ME22N and producing print preview outputs of identified purchase orders.

We have covered the very basic aspects of transaction code NACE, the aspects that enabled us to output purchase orders using the Smartforms *form*. An elaborate description of transaction code NACE is functional module topic beyond the scope of this book.

## Stage II: Enable Purchase Order Output with a Modified and Customized Copy of Smartforms *Form* /SMB40/MMPO_A

In this second stage of the hands-on exercise, we will modify and customize a copy of the SAP delivered Smartforms *form* /SMB40/MMPO_A and perform output settings in the transaction code NACE as to output purchase orders as per the layout of copied and modified version of the SAP delivered Smartforms *form* /SMB40/MMPO_A.

## Output Specifications

To repeat what I stated in chapter 2, in real-life SAP implementation projects, for the most part, copies made of SAP delivered Smartforms *forms* into the Y/Z namespace are modified and customized. Creation of a *form* from scratch is to be avoided as much as possible.

In this second stage of the present hands-on exercise, we are modifying and customizing the copied version of the SAP delivered purchase order *form* /SMB40/MMPO_A minimally as the focus is on the process of enabling output of purchase orders using a Smartforms *form*.

We are performing the following changes to the copied version of the SAP delivered purchase order *form* /SMB40/MMPO_A:

- We are reducing the bottom margin from 4.7CM to 1.7CM. We are increasing the height of the main *window* from 9.8CM to 12.3CM. We have increased the gap between the *windows* main and NOTE from 0.1CM to 0.6CM.

- The output will contain, on the last page of a purchase order, the total amount of the purchase order expressed in text. The output of the total amount of the purchase order expressed in text on the last page of a purchase order will appear as part of the footer of the element *table* TABLE_DATA.

The complete *page formats*, the layout of *windows* other than main and NOTE, and the entire contents and functionality of the copied *form* /SMB40/MMPO_A, have been retained.

## Copy *Form* YSM_SMB40_MMPO_A to Y Namespace and Modify as per Specifications

On the opening screen of transaction code SMARTFORMS, we selected the menu option Smart Forms ➤ Copy. We copied the SAP delivered purchase order *form* YSM_SMB40_MMPO_A into YCH04_SMB40_MMPO_A.

We opened the copied *form* YCH04_SMB40_MMPO_A in change or edit mode.

We shifted the *window* NOTE down as to render the bottom margin 1.7CM. The dimensions of the *window* NOTE will be as follows: Left margin—0.5CM, Upper margin—25.9CM, *Window* width—19.5CM, and *Window* height—3.0CM.

We increased the height of main *window* from 9.8CM to 12.3CM. The dimensions of the main *window* will be as follows: Left margin—0.5CM, Upper margin—13.0CM, *Window* width—19.5CM, and *Window* height—12.3CM.

We want to output the total amount of the purchase order expressed in text in the footer of the element *table* TABLE _DATA. We will perform the conversion from numbers/digits to text in a subroutine located in the *Form Routines* tab of the *Global Definitions* node. This is identical to the manner we performed this functionality in the previous hands-on exercise *form* YCH04_02_PORDER. We have retained the name of the subroutine as CONV_TOTAL_INTO_TEXT. You can copy the subroutine lines from the *form* YCH04_02_ PORDER into the present *form*. The subroutine CONV_TOTAL_INTO_TEXT returns text in two variables of type C length 70. So we need to define two variables of type C, length 70 in the *Global Data* tab of the node *Global Definitions*. Figure 4-58 illustrates.

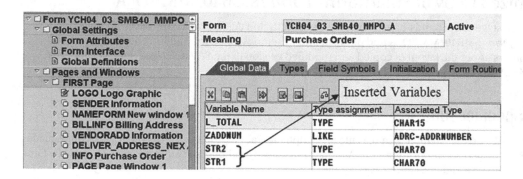

*Figure 4-58.* Form YCH04_03_SMB40_MMPO_A—global data inserted

Next, we clicked the main *window* node. We clicked the node of the element *table* named TABLE _DATA. We clicked the *footer* node of the element *table* named TABLE _DATA. In the *footer* node, next to the last node TOT_VAL2, we created a node CONV_TO_TEXT with the following context menu option: Create ➤ Flow Logic ➤ Program Lines. We inserted the following lines in this node:

```
PERFORM CONV_TOTAL_INTO_TEXT USING G_TOTAL ZXEKKO-SPRAS ZXEKKO-WAERS
 STR1 STR2.
```

Next, we created a node IN_TEXT next to the node CONV_TO_TEXT with the following context menu option: Create ➤ Text. In the text editor of the node IN_TEXT, we inserted the following:

```
ST &STR1&
ST &STR2&
```

Figure 4-59 illustrates.

**Change Smart Form texts: IN_TEXT Output Amount in Text Language EN**

| | Insert | Line | Format | Page | | | |

| | | ....+....1....+....2....+....3....+....4....+....5....+....6....+....7.. | |
|----|------|---|---|
| ST | &STR1& | | |
| ST | &STR2& | | |

*Figure 4-59.* Form YCH04_03_SMB40_MMPO_A—text in IN_TEXT

We have performed the modifications to output the total amount of a purchase order expressed in text as per laid-out specifications. We performed a consistency check and activated the *form* YCH04_03_SMB40_MMPO_A.

On the screen *Processing routines* of transaction code NACE, we assigned the *form* YCH04_03_SMB40_MMPO_A under the column *PDF/SmartForms Form* for the row *Print output* as shown in Figure 4-60.

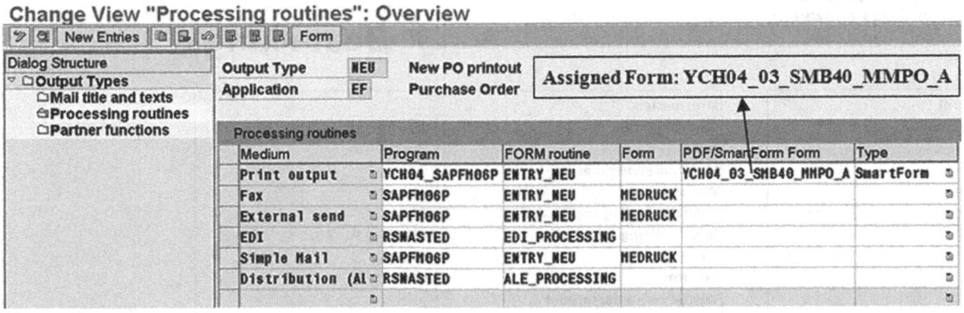

**Change View "Processing routines": Overview**

| Dialog Structure | Output Type | NEU | New PO printout | Assigned Form: YCH04_03_SMB40_MMPO_A | | |
| --- | --- | --- | --- | --- | --- | --- |
| ▽ ◻Output Types | Application | EF | Purchase Order | | | |
| ◻Mail title and texts | | | | | | |
| ⊜Processing routines | | | | | | |
| ◻Partner functions | **Processing routines** | | | | | |

| Medium | Program | FORM routine | Form | PDF/SmartForm Form | Type | |
| --- | --- | --- | --- | --- | --- | --- |
| Print output | ▫ YCH04_SAPFM06P | ENTRY_NEU | | YCH04_03_SMB40_MMPO_A | SmartForm | ▫ |
| Fax | ▫ SAPFM06P | ENTRY_NEU | MEDRUCK | | | ▫ |
| External send | ▫ SAPFM06P | ENTRY_NEU | MEDRUCK | | | ▫ |
| EDI | ▫ RSNASTED | EDI_PROCESSING | | | | ▫ |
| Simple Mail | ▫ SAPFM06P | ENTRY_NEU | MEDRUCK | | | ▫ |
| Distribution (AL | ▫ RSNASTED | ALE_PROCESSING | | | | ▫ |
| | ▫ | | | | | ▫ |

*Figure 4-60.* *Transaction code NACE—assignment of form YCH04_03_SMB40_MMPO_A*

The driver program will remain as YCH04_SAPFM06P. We saved the assignment in transaction code NACE.

## Output

We chose the same two purchase orders which we used earlier, purchase order numbers 4500004823 and 4500009520, for testing. The purchase order number 4500004823 language key is D and the purchase order number 4500009520 language key is E.

We executed the transaction code ME22N—Change Purchase Order. We selected the menu option Purchase Order ➤ Other Purchase order. We entered the purchase order number 4500004823 in the dialog box *Select Document*. We clicked the Continue button and the *Print Preview* button on the application toolbar. The purchase order number 4500004823 outputted in one page. Figures 4-61 and 4-62 are screenshots of the Print Preview.

Print Preview of LP01 Page 00001 of 00001

Archive | Print and Archive

IDES HOLDING AG

7
Ides AG
Martin Steiner, Kathrin Walther,
Lyoner Stern 231
D-60441 FRANKFURT

Seite 1 von 1
08.07.2015 12:47:57

**Bestellung**

**Rechnungsanschrift**
The Preconfigured Company
Attn To: Accounts Payable
950 Tower Lane, 12th Floor
Foster City, CA 94494

**Lieferantenanschrift**
Gusswerk US
HARBOR CITY CA 70456
UNITED STATES
Zu Händen: Fr. Benz

**Lieferanschrift**
Werk Hamburg
Alsterdorfer Strasse 13
D-22299 HAMBURG-ALSTERDORF

| Information | |
|---|---|
| Bestellnummer | 4500004823 |
| Datum | 08.01.1998 |
| Lieferantennummer | 1003 |
| Währung | DEM |
| Zahlungsbedingungen | ZB01 |
| Beschreibung | 14 Tage 3%, 30/2%, 45 netto |
| Einkäufer | Zuse,K. |
| Telefon | 0351/1201 |
| Wiederverkaufsnummer | XX XXX XX-XXXXXX |
| Lieferbedingungen | FH |
| Description | Frei Haus |
| Beschreibung | |

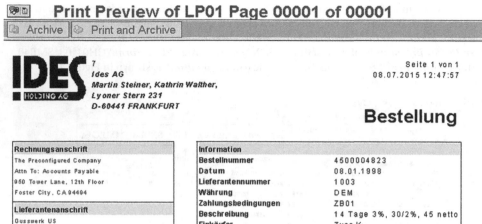

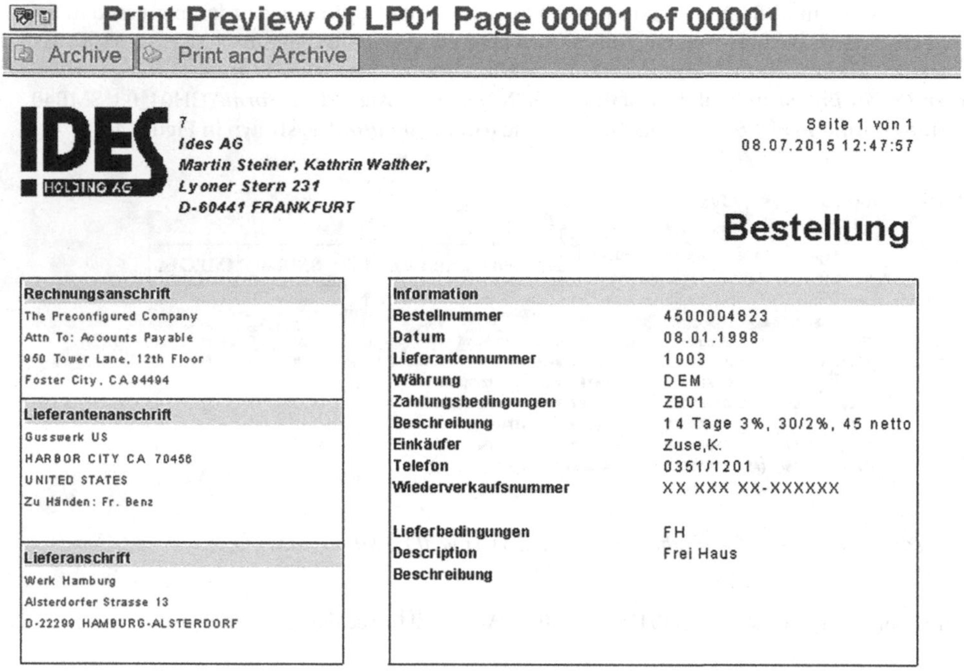

*Figure 4-61.* *Output with Form YCH04_03_SMB40_MMPO_A: PO No. 4500004823*

This purchase order outputs in one page. As you can see in Figure 4-62, the total of the purchase order expressed in text is output.

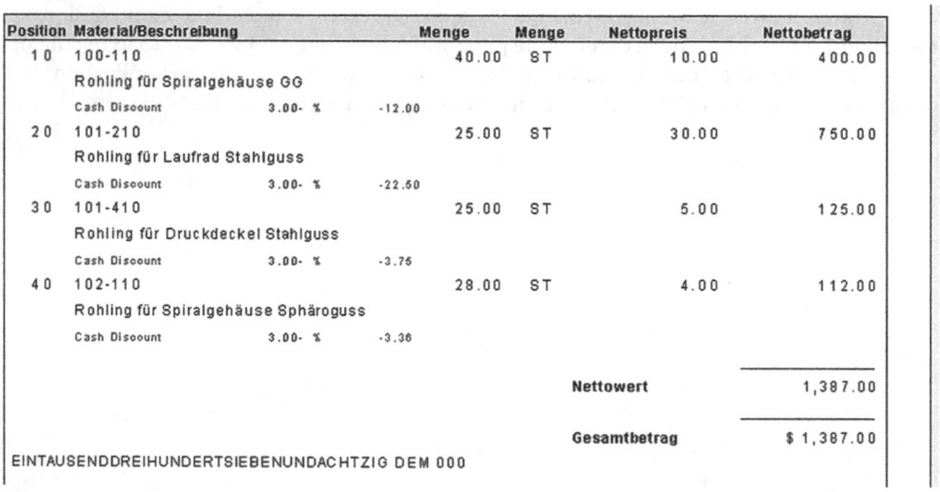

| Position | Material/Beschreibung | | | Menge | Menge | Nettopreis | Nettobetrag |
|---|---|---|---|---|---|---|---|
| 10 | 100-110 | | | 40.00 | ST | 10.00 | 400.00 |
| | Rohling für Spiralgehäuse GG | | | | | | |
| | Cash Discount | 3.00- % | -12.00 | | | | |
| 20 | 101-210 | | | 25.00 | ST | 30.00 | 750.00 |
| | Rohling für Laufrad Stahlguss | | | | | | |
| | Cash Discount | 3.00- % | -22.50 | | | | |
| 30 | 101-410 | | | 25.00 | ST | 5.00 | 125.00 |
| | Rohling für Druckdeckel Stahlguss | | | | | | |
| | Cash Discount | 3.00- % | -3.75 | | | | |
| 40 | 102-110 | | | 28.00 | ST | 4.00 | 112.00 |
| | Rohling für Spiralgehäuse Sphäroguss | | | | | | |
| | Cash Discount | 3.00- % | -3.36 | | | | |
| | | | | | | Nettowert | 1,387.00 |
| | | | | | | Gesamtbetrag | $ 1,387.00 |

EINTAUSENDDREIHUNDERTSIEBENUNDACHTZIG DEM 000

*Figure 4-62.* *Output with Form YCH04_03_SMB40_MMPO_A: PO No. 4500004823*

In a similar manner, we produced the print preview of the purchase order number 4500009520. The output of purchase order number 4500009520 runs for ten pages as shown in Figures 4-63, 4-64, 4-65, and 4-66.

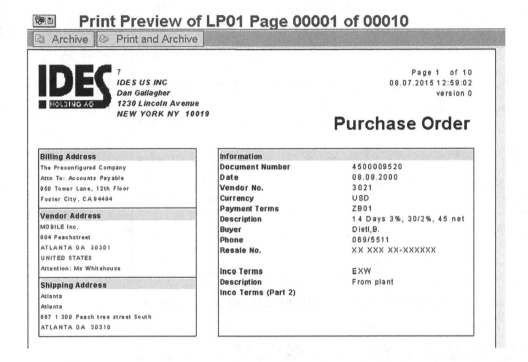

**Figure 4-63.** *Output with Form YCH04_03_SMB40_MMPO_A: PO No. 4500009520—I*

| Item | Material/Description | | Quantity | U M | Net Price | Net Amount |
|------|---------------------|--|----------|-----|-----------|------------|
| 1 0 | ISA-0002 | | 1 0 0 . 0 0 | PC | 265.00 | 26,500.00 |
| | AKAN DE LUXE | | | | | |
| | Cash Discount | 3.00- % | -795.00 | | | |
| 2 0 | ISA-0003 | | 1 0 0 . 0 0 | PC | 160.00 | 16,000.00 |
| | VANITY | | | | | |
| | Cash Discount | 3.00- % | -480.00 | | | |
| 3 0 | ISA-0009 | | 1 0 0 . 0 0 | PC | 240.00 | 24,000.00 |
| | PRIDE | | | | | |
| | Cash Discount | 3.00- % | -720.00 | | | |
| 4 0 | ISA-0010 | | 1 0 0 . 0 0 | PC | 240.00 | 24,000.00 |
| | SONIC | | | | | |
| | Cash Discount | 3.00- % | -720.00 | | | |
| 5 0 | ISA-0011 | | 1 0 0 . 0 0 | PC | 250.00 | 25,000.00 |
| | TWIN LETTI | | | | | |
| | Cash Discount | 3.00- % | -750.00 | | | |
| 6 0 | ISA-0012 | | 1 0 0 . 0 0 | PC | 260.00 | 26,000.00 |
| | V.W. | | | | | |
| | Cash Discount | 3.00- % | -780.00 | | | |
| 7 0 | ISA-0018 | | 1 0 0 . 0 0 | PC | 150.00 | 15,000.00 |
| | SLING | | | | | |
| | Cash Discount | 3.00- % | -450.00 | | | |
| 8 0 | ISA-0019 | | 1 0 0 . 0 0 | EA | 480.00 | 48,000.00 |
| | TEMPO | | | | | |
| | Cash Discount | 3.00- % | -1,440.00 | | | |

*Figure 4-64.* *Output with Form YCH04_03_SMB40_MMPO_A: PO No. 4500009520—II*

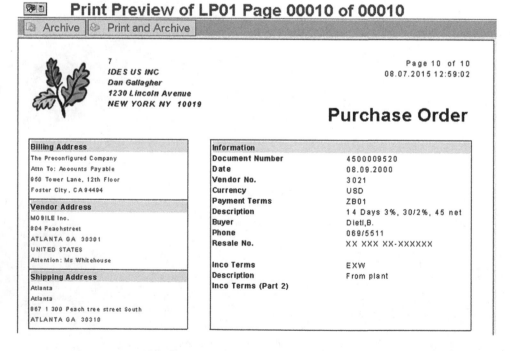

*Figure 4-65.* *Output with Form YCH04_03_SMB40_MMPO_A: PO No. 4500009520—III*

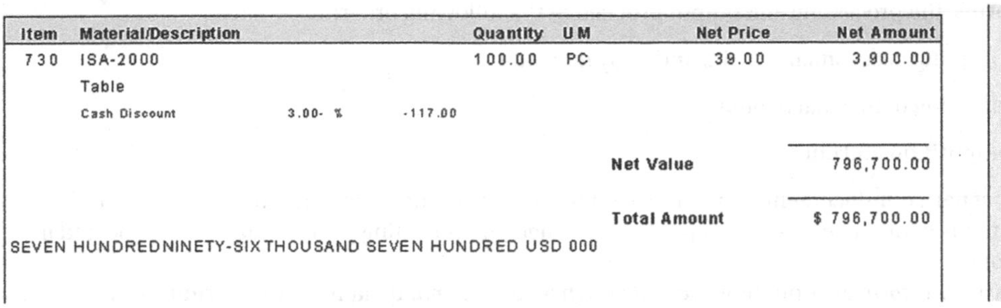

| Item | Material/Description | | Quantity | U M | Net Price | Net Amount |
|------|--------------------|--|----------|-----|-----------|------------|
| 7 3 0 | ISA-2000 | | 1 0 0 .0 0 | PC | 3 9 .0 0 | 3 ,9 0 0 .0 0 |
| | Table | | | | | |
| | Cash Discount | 3 .0 0 - % | - 1 1 7 .0 0 | | | |
| | | | | | Net Value | 7 9 6 ,7 0 0 .0 0 |
| | | | | | Total Amount | $ 7 9 6 ,7 0 0 .0 0 |

SEVEN HUNDRED NINETY-SIX THOUSAND SEVEN HUNDRED USD 000

***Figure 4-66.*** *Output with Form YCH04_03_SMB40_MMPO_A: PO No. 4500009520—IV*

This purchase order outputs in ten pages. As you can see in Figure 4-66, the total of the purchase order expressed in text is output.

## Hands-on Exercise Recapitulation

We generated the output twice in this hands-on exercise. We generated the output, first, with SAP delivered *form* YSM_SMB40_MMPO_A and next with a modified and customized version of the original *form*: YCH04_03_SMB40_MMPO_A. The focus in this hands-on exercise was on the modification of the driver program so that it incorporates the functionality of using Smartforms *form*, the output settings in transaction code NACE,

The *form* YCH04_03_SMB40_MMPO_A and the *style* it uses along with modified versions of driver programs YCH04_ SAPFM06P and YCH04_ FM06PE02 are available in the E-resource file for this book (www.apress.com/9781484212345).

## Smartforms System Fields: SFSY-PAGE and SFSY-FORMPAGES

In the SAP script forms environment, we used the system symbol &PAGE& and the general SAP script field &SAPSCRIPT-FORMPAGES&. The system symbol &PAGE& contained the current page number of the current document being output. The general SAP script field &SAPSCRIPT-FORMPAGDS& contained the total number of pages in current document being output.

The equivalent of SAP script system symbol &PAGE& in Smartforms is SFSY-PAGE. The equivalent of general SAP script field &SAPSCRIPT-FORMPAGES& in Smartforms is SFSY-FORMPAGES.

In the SAP script *forms* environment, using the system symbol &PAGE& and the field &SAPSCRIPT-FORMPAGES&, you can determine whether you are at the stage of outputting the last page or the second to last page of a document.

In the Smartforms environment, using the system fields SFSY-PAGE and SFSY-FORMPAGES&, you cannot determine in the *program lines* whether you are at the stage of outputting the last page or the second to last page of a document.

When the value of the system field SFSY-FORMPAGES is interrogated in the *Program Lines* node, through a static breakpoint, the ABAP runtime system will show the value of SFSY-FORMPAGES same as the value of current page (i.e., SFSY-PAGE). This statement applies to the secondary, main, and copy *windows*. In the final *window*, the value of SFSY-FORMPAGES is equal to the total number of pages in the document being output. And the value of SFSY-FORMPAGES outputs correctly, in whichever *window* type you locate it for output.

In Smartforms, the processing and output proceed in the following order:

1. Processing of secondary, main, and copy *windows*.

2. Processing of the final *window*.

3. Composition and output.

For the most part, our document output is driven by the data in the main window. This is because most business documents contain items—data repeating in a page and repeating page to page—to be located in the main *window*.

In the Smartforms *form* environment, we can assign a *page format* dynamically or at runtime. And, within the main *window*, using the fields SFSY-PAGE and SFSY-FORMPAGES, we are unable to determine whether we are on the last or second to last page of a document. So, from the main *window*, if we want to assign at runtime a *page format* dependent on the number of pages in a document (i.e., value of the system field SFSY-FORMPAGES), we are unable to do so.

# Three *Page Formats* and Runtime Assignment of *Page Format* with *Command* Node

In the E-resource file for this book (www.apress.com/9781484212345), one additional *form* YCH04_03_ SMB40_MMPO_A _EXT is available. It is an extension of the *form* YCH04_03_SMB40_MMPO_A. The *form* YCH04_03_SMB40_MMPO_A _EXT demonstrates the following:

- Use of three *page formats* in a *form*

- Runtime assignment of *page format* using the *command* node

The *form* YCH04_03_SMB40_MMPO_A _EXT has three *page formats*: FIRST, NEXT, and LAST. The output of the *window* NOTE is to appear on the last page of a purchase order. When a purchase order consists of a single page, the output of the *window* NOTE must appear on the first physical page (*page format* FIRST). When a purchase order consists of two pages, the output of the *window* NOTE must appear on the second physical page (*page format* LAST). When a purchase order consists of more than two pages, the output of the *window* NOTE need not appear on the intermediate pages (*page format* NEXT). Since the output of the *window* NOTE is not to appear on the intermediate pages (*page format* NEXT), the vertical space occupied by the *window* NOTE can be assigned to the main *window* in the *page format* NEXT.

In our present scenario, if a purchase order outputs only to one page (*page format*: FIRST), it does not involve runtime assignment of *page format*.

If a purchase order outputs in two pages, the first page of the purchase order will output in *page format* FIRST. By default, the second page of the purchase order will output with *page format* NEXT through static assignment in the *Next Page*. But, we want the second page of the purchase order to output with *page format* LAST. So before the commencement of processing the second page of the purchase order, we must dynamically assign the *page format* LAST for output of the purchase order's second page.

If a purchase order outputs in more than two pages, the first page of the purchase order will output in *page format* FIRST. By default, the subsequent page(s) of the purchase order will output with *page format* NEXT through static assignment in the *Next Page*. But, we want the last page of the purchase order to output with *page format* LAST. So before the commencement of processing the last page of the purchase order, we must dynamically assign the *page format* LAST for output of the purchase order's last page.

In effect, we must know during processing that we are about to commence the output of last page of a purchase order, and dynamically assign the *page format* LAST for output of the last page of a purchase order.

Since we cannot determine the total number of pages in a purchase order through the system field SFSY-FORMPAGES in the main *window*, we have resorted to using the number of items being output on different *page formats* to determine when we are about to commence the output of the last page of a purchase order.

We are outputting eight items in the *page formats* FIRST and LAST. We are outputting ten items in the *page format* NEXT. We are maintaining two counters, ICOUNT and LICOUNT. The counter ICOUNT is a running counter and contains the number of the current item of a purchase order being output. The counter ICOUNT will start from 1 for every purchase order. The counter LICOUNT contains the total number of items in a purchase order excluding the number of items on the last page of the purchase order.

In our processing, when the counter ICOUNT is equal to the counter LICOUNT, we are about to commence the processing of the last page of a purchase order.

We are using two more variables, FPAGES and TLINES. You can go through the code in the *Initialization* tab of the *Global Definitions* node of the *form*. The code starts with the comment line: ***** `Calculate Form Pages Etc.` *****

If font types and sizes change or the main *window* sizes change, then the number of items being output in different *page formats* have to be reexamined and reworked.

We created in the main *window*, under the *loop* element EKPO_LOOP, a *command* node GO_TO_LAST_PAGE with the context menu option: Create ➤ Flow Logic ➤ Command. In the *Conditions* tab of the *command* node, we entered the condition ICOUNT = LICOUNT. In the *General Attributes* tab of the *command* node GO_TO_LAST_PAGE, we enabled the check box *Go to New Page* and assigned the *page format* LAST_PAGE. In effect, if a purchase order is outputting to more than two pages, before output of the last physical page of the purchase order commences, the *page format* LAST_PAGE will be assigned to output the last page of the purchase order. This was a case of utilizing space more optimally.

You can upload the *form* YCH04_03_SMB40_MMPO_A _EXT from the E-resource file for this book (`www.apress.com/9781484212345`), perform the required settings in transaction code NACE, and generate the print preview. You can observe the output of the print preview.

## *Forms*: /BPR3PF/MMPO_L, /BPR3PF/MMPO_A, and Driver Program /BPR3PF/FM06P

SAP also provides the following for output of purchase orders:

- Smartforms *forms*: /BPR3PF/MMPO_L (letter-size stationery) and /BPR3PF/MMPO_A (A4 size stationery)

- Driver program: /BPR3PF/FM06P

- Transaction code for purchase order output settings: M/34

As for the purchase orders, SAP provides Smartforms *forms* and driver programs for other business documents.

The *forms* and the driver program mentioned previously do not come as part of the normal SAP installation. They are available as an add-on from `http://service.sap.com/`. To install the add-on, an authorization is required.

You might not be able to install the add-on into an IDES server. We have not described the above-mentioned *forms* and driver program for this reason.

# Hands-on Exercise: IV–Generate Material Bar Code Labels

In this hands-on exercise, we will output material bar code labels using a Smartforms *form* similar to the vendor address labels we output in hands-on exercise I in this chapter. Along with the material bar code, we will output also the material number/code and the material description. We will create a new custom bar code. The bar codes like fonts are maintained in transaction code SE73. In the Smartforms *form* environment, bar code output is implemented by assigning a *character format* of a *style* to the variable to be output as a bar code. The *character formats* of a *style* to be used to output variables as bar codes are to be assigned the bar codes (just like fonts) maintained in transaction code SE73. We will start off by specifying the output layout of material bar code labels.

## Output Specification, Major Tasks, etc.

The output of the material bar code labels will look like that in Figure 4-67.

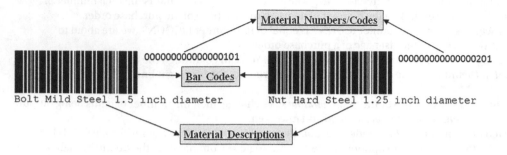

**Figure 4-67.** *Rough layout of material bar code label output*

The bar codes of materials must appear along with their respective numbers/codes and descriptions as shown in Figure 4-67.

The material number or code is being output as bar code as well as simple material number, and it is being output twice across the page.

Our data originates in the database table MAKT. We will retrieve data of the logged-in language only from the database table MAKT. We will use the letter-size stationery in landscape mode: 279X215MM. We will output 12 materials' data in one page, two across (Figure 4-67) and six down. To repeat data twice across a page, we will load in the driver program, an internal table having a structure with two sets of fields: MATNR1, MAKTX1, MATNR2, and MAKTX2. This is similar to the manner we loaded an internal table to output address labels of vendors in hands-on exercise I in this chapter. We have created an ABAP dictionary structure YCH04_MATR_STRU consisting of the four fields MATNR1, MAKTX1, MATNR2, and MAKTX2. The ABAP dictionary structure YCH04_MATR_STRU will be referred to to declare data in the driver program and the *Form Interface*.

The present hands-on exercise will involve the following major tasks:

1.  Creation of a custom bar code—transaction code SE73.

2.  Assignment of the created custom bar code to a device type (print device)—transaction code SE73.

3.  Creation of a *style* with a bar code *character format*—transaction code SMARTFORMS.

4.  Creation of a Smartforms *form* to output material bar code labels—transaction code SMARTFORMS.

5.  Creation of a driver program—transaction code SE38.

6.  Execution of the driver program to test or print preview (output) the material bar code labels.

The driver program will retrieve the data in the requisite internal table and invoke the function module of the Smartforms *form*.

A description of each of these tasks follows.

## Creation of Custom Bar Code YCH_04BC, Assignment to a Print Device

To create a custom bar code, we navigated to the opening screen of transaction code SE73. We selected the Radio button *System Bar Codes* and clicked the Change button. A screen like the one shown in Figure 4-68 appeared.

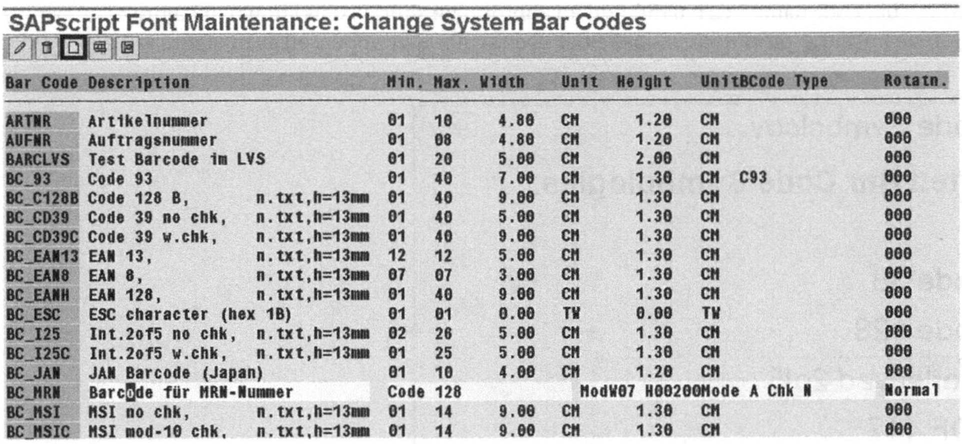

## SAPscript Font Maintenance: Change System Bar Codes

| Bar Code | Description | | Min. | Max. | Width | Unit | Height | Unit | BCode Type | Rotatn. |
|----------|-------------|---|------|------|-------|------|--------|------|-----------|---------|
| ARTNR | Artikelnummer | | 01 | 10 | 4.80 | CM | 1.20 | CM | | 000 |
| AUFNR | Auftragsnummer | | 01 | 08 | 4.80 | CM | 1.20 | CM | | 000 |
| BARCLVS | Test Barcode im LVS | | 01 | 20 | 5.00 | CM | 2.00 | CM | | 000 |
| BC_93 | Code 93 | | 01 | 40 | 7.00 | CM | 1.30 | CM | C93 | 000 |
| BC_C128B | Code 128 B, | n.txt,h=13mm | 01 | 40 | 9.00 | CM | 1.30 | CM | | 000 |
| BC_CD39 | Code 39 no chk, | n.txt,h=13mm | 01 | 40 | 5.00 | CM | 1.30 | CM | | 000 |
| BC_CD39C | Code 39 w.chk, | n.txt,h=13mm | 01 | 40 | 9.00 | CM | 1.30 | CM | | 000 |
| BC_EAN13 | EAN 13, | n.txt,h=13mm | 12 | 12 | 5.00 | CM | 1.30 | CM | | 000 |
| BC_EAN8 | EAN 8, | n.txt,h=13mm | 07 | 07 | 3.00 | CM | 1.30 | CM | | 000 |
| BC_EANH | EAN 128, | n.txt,h=13mm | 01 | 40 | 9.00 | CM | 1.30 | CM | | 000 |
| BC_ESC | ESC character (hex 1B) | | 01 | 01 | 0.00 | TW | 0.00 | TW | | 000 |
| BC_I25 | Int.2of5 no chk, | n.txt,h=13mm | 02 | 26 | 5.00 | CM | 1.30 | CM | | 000 |
| BC_I25C | Int.2of5 w.chk, | n.txt,h=13mm | 01 | 25 | 5.00 | CM | 1.30 | CM | | 000 |
| BC_JAN | JAN Barcode (Japan) | | 01 | 10 | 4.00 | CM | 1.20 | CM | | 000 |
| BC_MRN | Barcode für MRN-Nummer | | Code 128 | | | | ModW07 H00200 | | Mode A Chk N | Normal |
| BC_MSI | MSI no chk, | n.txt,h=13mm | 01 | 14 | 9.00 | CM | 1.30 | CM | | 000 |
| BC_MSIC | MSI mod-10 chk, | n.txt,h=13mm | 01 | 14 | 9.00 | CM | 1.30 | CM | | 000 |

*Figure 4-68.* *Change System Bar Codes*

To create a new custom bar code, we clicked the Create button on the application toolbar. The system prompted with options to create bar codes with new or old technology as shown in Figure 4-69.

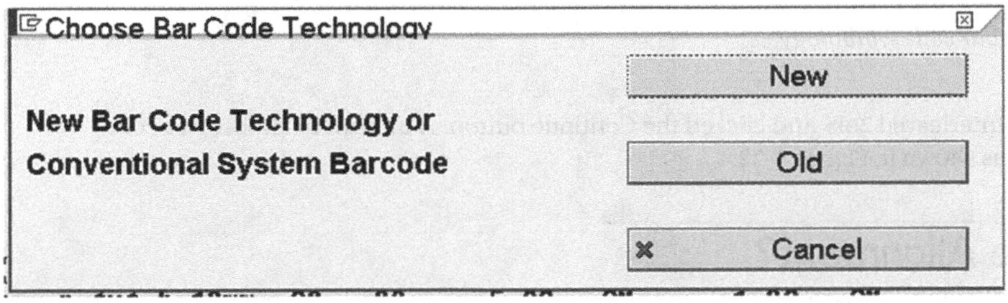

*Figure 4-69.* *Choose Bar Code Technology*

We selected the option to create bar code with new technology. The system prompted for bar code name and text as shown in Figure 4-70.

*Figure 4-70.* *Create New System Bar Code*

We entered the bar code name YCH_04BC and an appropriate short text as shown in Figure 4-70. We clicked the Continue button. A prompt to choose a bar code symbology appeared as in Figure 4-71.

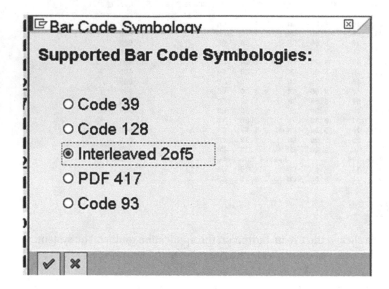

*Figure 4-71.* *Choose bar code symbology*

We selected the Interleaved 2of5 and clicked the Continue button. A prompt to choose bar code alignment appeared as shown in Figure 4-72.

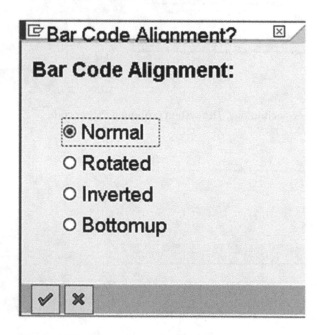

*Figure 4-72.* *Choose bar code alignment*

We selected the normal alignment and clicked the Continue button. A prompt appeared to enter the bar code parameters appeared as shown in Figure 4-73.

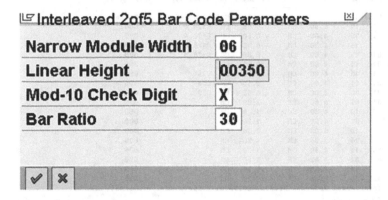

**Figure 4-73.** *Bar code parameters*

We accepted the proposed default values for all the fields except *Linear Height*. We changed the default *Linear Height* value from 250 to 350 since we wanted a bar code slightly higher. We clicked the Continue button. Prompts for Save Bar Code definition and Workbench request appeared as shown in Figure 4-74.

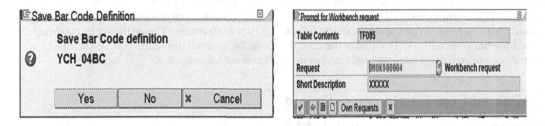

**Figure 4-74.** *Save Bar Code definition and Workbench request*

The created bar code YCH_04BC appeared in the list as shown in Figure 4-75.

**SAPscript Font Maintenance: Change System Bar Codes**

| Bar Code | Description | Min. | Max. | Width | Unit | Height | UnitBCode Type | Rotatn. |
|----------|-------------|------|------|-------|------|--------|----------------|---------|
| C128A | Code 128 Autoswitch, h=0.5 in | Code 128 | | | | ModV06 H00150 | Mode A Chk N | Normal |
| C128A_00 | Code 128A,        n.txt,h= 5mm | 01 | 15 | 4.00 | CM | 0.50 | CM C128_A | 000 |
| C128A_01 | Code 128A, r=090, n.txt,h= 5mm | 01 | 15 | 4.00 | CM | 0.50 | CM C128_A | 090 |
| C128B_00 | Code 128B,        n.txt,h= 5mm | 01 | 15 | 4.00 | CM | 0.50 | CM C128_B | 000 |
| C128B_01 | Code 128B, r=090, n.txt,h= 5mm | 01 | 15 | 4.00 | CM | 0.50 | CM C128_B | 090 |
| CD39C_00 | Code39 w.chk,     n.txt,h= 5mm | 01 | 15 | 4.00 | CM | 0.50 | CM C39 | 000 |
| CD39C_01 | Code39 w.chk,r=090,n.txt,h=5mm | 01 | 15 | 4.00 | CM | 0.50 | CM C39 | 090 |
| CD39__00 | Code39 n.chk,     n.txt,h= 5mm | 01 | 15 | 4.00 | CM | 0.50 | CM C39 | 000 |
| CD39__01 | Code39 n.chk,r=090,n.txt,h=5mm | 01 | 15 | 4.00 | CM | 0.50 | CM C39 | 090 |
| EAN8 | Barcode EAN8 für Schulung | 07 | 07 | 5.00 | CM | 2.00 | CM | 000 |
| KUNAUNR | Kundenauftragsnummer | 10 | 10 | 4.80 | CM | 1.20 | CM | 000 |
| KUNAUPS | Kundenauftragsposition | 06 | 06 | 4.80 | CM | 1.20 | CM | 000 |
| MBBARC | Test Barcode Bestandsführung | 10 | 10 | 5.00 | CM | 2.00 | CM | 000 |
| MBBARC1 | Test Barcode 1 Bestandsführung | 10 | 14 | 5.00 | CM | 1.20 | CM | 000 |
| RSNUM | Reservierungsnummer | 10 | 10 | 4.80 | CM | 1.20 | CM | 000 |
| RSPOS | Reservierungsposition | 04 | 04 | 4.80 | CM | 1.20 | CM | 000 |
| RUECKNR | Rueckmeldenummer | 08 | 14 | 4.80 | CM | 1.20 | CM | 000 |
| TYPNR | Typennummer | 10 | 10 | 8.00 | CM | 1.20 | CM | 000 |
| YCH_04BC | Own New Bar Code | Interleaved 2of5 | | | | ModV06 H00350 | Chk Y Ratio 30 | Normal |

Bar Code: YCH_04BC

*Figure 4-75.* *Bar code YCH_04BC created*

We need to assign the custom bar code YCH_04BC to a device type (print device). To determine device types available on the application server, refer to the section "Assigning the Font to a Device Type" in Chapter 1. To assign a bar code to a device type, we selected the Radio button *Printer Bar Codes* and clicked the Change button on the opening screen of transaction code SE73. We located the print device HPLJIIID and clicked the Create button on the application toolbar. The *Font Maintenance Create* dialog box appeared. We entered the bar code name YCH_04BC in the field *Bar Code*. We entered the values SBP12 and SBS12 in the fields: *Bar code prefix* and *Bar code suffix,* respectively. Figure 4-76 illustrates.

**SAPscript Font Maintenance: Create**

| | |
|---|---|
| Device type | HPLJIIID |
| Bar code | YCH04_BC |
| Bar code prefix | SBP12 |
| Bar code suffix | SBS12 |
| Baseline Alignment | ☐ |

*Figure 4-76.* *Font Maintenance: Create*

We created *Bar code prefix* SBP12 and *Bar code suffix* SBS12 using the application toolbar button: *Maint. Print Control.* For a description of the process of the creation of print controls, refer to section titled 'True Type Font Installation" in Chapter 1.

## Creation of *Style* YCH04_04

We navigated to transaction code SMARTFORMS. We clicked the Radio button *Style*, entered the name of the *style* as YCH04_04, and clicked the Create button. We created a *paragraph format* SP with the default values. We assigned the *paragraph format* SP as the standard paragraph in the *header data* of the *style*.

We next created a *character format* BC. In the *Standard Settings* tab of *character format* BC, in the *Bar Code* area, we selected from the drop-down list, the custom bar code YCH_04BC as shown in Figure 4-77.

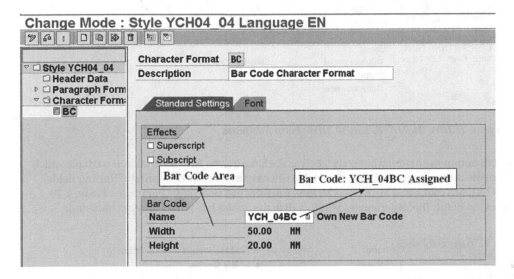

***Figure 4-77.*** *Style: YCH04_04Character Format: BC*

We saved and activated *style* YCH04_04.

This concludes the creation of *style* YCH04_04. We will use the *character format* BC in the *form* YCH04_04_MATERIAL_BCODES to output material number/code as bar code.

## Creation of *Form* YCH04_04_MATERIAL_BCODES

We navigated to transaction code SMARTFORMS. We clicked the Radio button *Form*, entered the name of the *form* as YCH04_04_MATERIAL_BCODES, and clicked the Create button.

In the *Output Options* tab of the node *Form Attributes*, we assigned the page LETTER and the *style* YCH04_04. Figure 4-78 illustrates.

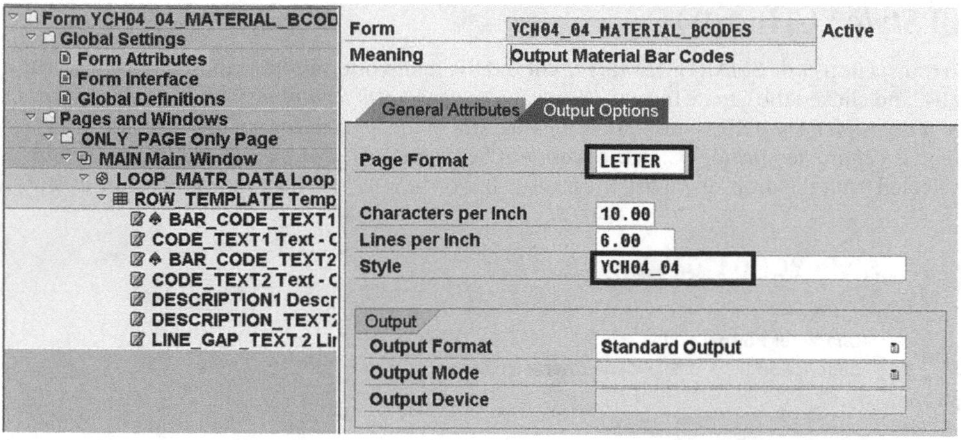

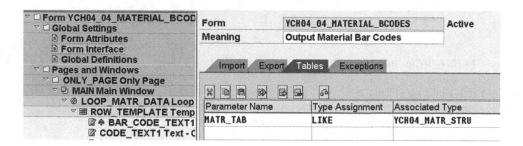

**Figure 4-78.** *Form: YCH04_04_MATERIAL_BCODESForm Attributes*

We intend to output the material bar code labels in the Smartforms *form* from an internal table which will be loaded in the driver program. The internal table will have a structure consisting of the four fields: MATNR1, MAKTX1, MATNR2, and MAKTX2. The *form* will have just one *Tables* parameter. Figure 4-79 shows the definition of the *Tables* parameter MATR_TAB in the *Tables* tab of the *Form Interface* node.

**Figure 4-79.** *Form: YCH04_04_MATERIAL_BCODESTables parameter: MATR_TAB*

The *Tables* parameter is referring to the ABAP dictionary structure YCH04_MATR_STRU. A structure of the same name as the *Tables* parameter name, that is, a header line, gets created by default.

We renamed the default created *page format* as ONLY_PAGE and set the page alignment as landscape. Figure 4-80 illustrates.

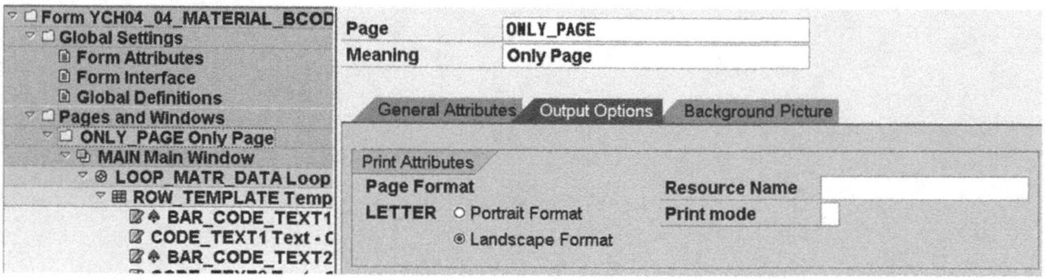

**Figure 4-80.** *Form: YCH04_04_MATERIAL_BCODESPage Format: ONLY_PAGE*

336

As all of the information to be outputtedmaterial number as bar code, material number, and material description  is repetitive, we will use only the main *window*. The dimensions of the main *window* are as follows:

- Left margin: 5MM

- Upper margin: 5MM

- Window width: 269MM

- Window height: 205MM

We created the *form* element *loop* named LOOP_MAIN_DATA under the main *window*. The *form* element *loop* operates just like the LOOP AT.....ENDLOOP construct in an ABAP program; it serially fetches one row at a time from an internal table into a structure. Figure 4-81 shows the element *loop* named LOOP_ MAIN_DATA.

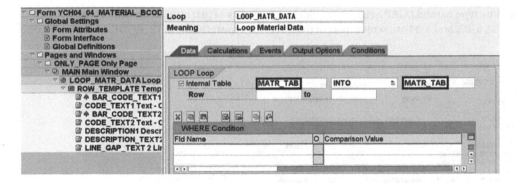

*Figure 4-81.* *Form: YCH04_04_MATERIAL_BCODESLoop: LOOP_MAIN_DATA*

Under the element *loop* named LOOP_MAIN_DATA, we created the *form* element *template* named ROW_TEMPLATE. The element *template* named ROW_TEMPLATE consists of just one row. A *template* row can consist of multiple lines.

A *template* like a *table* has the ability to define line types. We have defined three line types for the *template* ROW_TEMPLATE. The first line type named CODE_BAR_CODE's height is four lines and consists of seven cells as listed in Table 4-11.

*Table 4-11.* *Line Type CODE_BAR_CODE of Element Template ROW_TEMPLATE*

| Cell | Dimensions | Data/Field |
|------|-----------|------------|
| Cell 1 | 10MM | Gap |
| Cell 2 | 56MM | Bar code MATNR1 |
| Cell 3 | 63MM | MATNR1 |
| Cell 4 | 13MM | Gap |
| Cell 5 | 56MM | Bar code MATNR2 |
| Cell 6 | 63MM | MATNR2 |
| Cell 7 | 08MM | Gap |

The height of the bar code is determining the height of the line type CODE_BAR_CODE as four lines. We fixed this height after trial-and-error attempts.

The second line type named DESCRIPTION is two lines in height and consists of four *cells* as listed in Table 4-12:

***Table 4-12.** Line Type DESCRIPTION of Element Template ROW_TEMPLATE*

| Cell | Dimensions | Data/Field |
|------|-----------|-----------|
| *Cell 1* | 10MM | Gap |
| *Cell 2* | 127MM | MAKTX1 |
| *Cell 3* | 5MM | Gap |
| *Cell 4* | 127MM | MAKTX2 |

The third line type named LGAP height is two lines and consists of just one *cell* of width 269MM

Figures 4-82, 4-83, and 4-84 are screenshots of the three line types: CODE_BAR_CODE, DESCRIPTION, and LGAP.

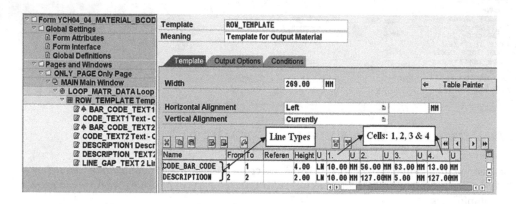

***Figure 4-82.** Template: ROW_TEMPLATEline types: CODE_BAR_CODE & DESCRIPTION1*

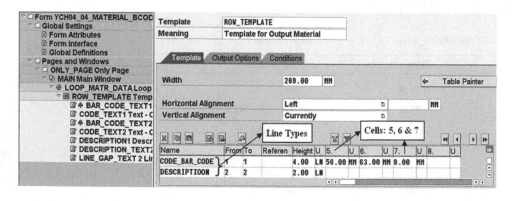

***Figure 4-83.** Template: ROW_TEMPLATEline types: CODE_BAR_CODE & DESCRIPTION2)*

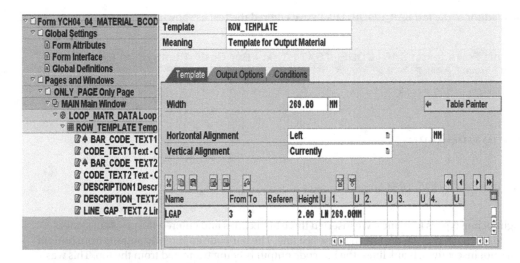

*Figure 4-84.* *Template: ROW_TEMPLATEline type: LGAP*

We have to create the element *texts* in the *template* ROW_TEMPLATE. Each of the element *texts* in the *template* has to be assigned or identified with a line type and *cell* of the *template*. The line types are identified by numbers 1, 2, etc. In our present context, the line type CODE_BAR_CODE is identified as 1, the line type DESCRIPTION is identified as 2, and the line type LGAP is identified as 3. In a similar manner, the *cells* in the line types are identified as 1, 2, etc.

A *text* in a *template* is assigned a line type and a *cell* in the *Output structure* area of the *Output Options* tab of the *text*.

We created the *text* BAR_CODE_TEXT1 for the first material number in the row to output as bar code. In the *Output structure* area of the *Output Options* tab of the *text* BAR_CODE_TEXT1, we assigned 1 to the field *Line* (Line type CODE_BAR_CODE) and 2 to the field *Column* (*cell* number 2). Figure 4-85 illustrates.

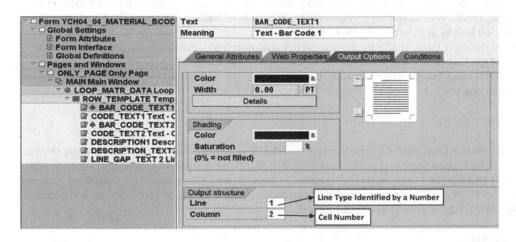

*Figure 4-85.* *Text: BAR_CODE_TEXT1line type and cell assignment*

In the text editor of the *text* BAR_CODE_TEXT1, we entered the text as shown in Figure 4-86.

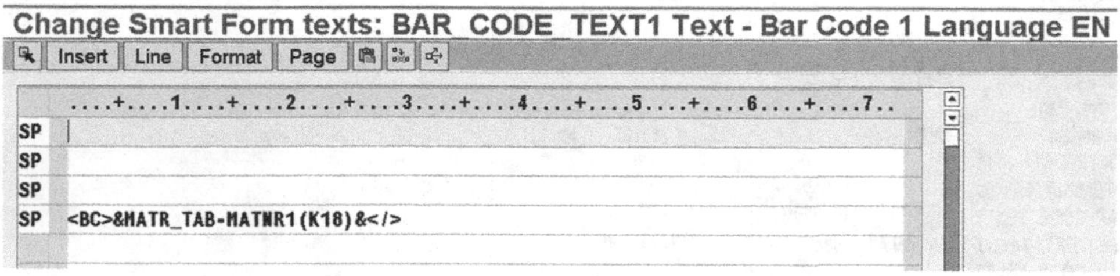

**Change Smart Form texts: BAR_CODE_TEXT1 Text - Bar Code 1 Language EN**

| 🔍 | Insert | Line | Format | Page | 🖺 | ⠿ | ⊹ |

```
....+....1....+....2....+....3....+....4....+....5....+....6....+....7..
SP  |
SP
SP
SP  <BC>&MATR_TAB-MATNR1 (K18) &</>
```

*Figure 4-86.*  *Text: BAR_CODE_TEXT1*

The height of line type is four lines. We inserted three blank lines and entered the program symbol &MATR_TAB-MATNR1(K18)& on the fourth or the last line. The bar code apparently outputs from bottom to top. If we do not insert three blank lines, the bar code output is being truncated from the top. This was determined by trial and error. We have assigned the *character format* BC to the program symbol as shown in Figure 4-86. To ensure that a blank material code does not output as bar code, we have entered in the *Conditions* tab of *texts* BAR_CODE_TEXT1 and BAR_CODE_TEXT2 the following conditions: MATR_TAB-MATNR1 NE INITIAL and MATR_TAB-MATNR2 NE INITIAL.

We created the *text* CODE_TEXT1 for the first material number in the row to output. In the *Output structure* area of the *Output Options* tab of the *text* CODE_TEXT1, we assigned 1 to the field *Line* (line type CODE_BAR_CODE) and 3 to the field *Column* (*cell* number 3). In the text editor of the *text* CODE_TEXT1, we entered the following text:

&MATR_TAB-MATNR1(K18)&

We created the *text* BAR_CODE_TEXT2 for the second material number in the row to output as bar code. In the *Output structure* area of the *Output Options* tab of the *text* BAR_CODE_TEXT2, we assigned 1 to the field *Line* (line type CODE_BAR_CODE) and 5 to the field *Column* (*cell* number 5) In the text editor of the *text* BAR_CODE_TEXT2, we entered the text <BC>&MATR_TAB-MATNR2(K18)&</> on the fourth line; the first three lines left blanks as shown in Figure 4-86.

We created the *text* CODE_TEXT2 for the second material number in the row to output. In the *Output structure* area of the *Output Options* tab of the *text* CODE_TEXT2, we assigned 1 to the field *Line* (line type CODE_BAR_CODE) and 7 to the field *Column* (*cell* number 7). In the text editor of the *text* CODE_TEXT2, we entered the following text:

&MATR_TAB-MATNR2(K18)&

We created the *text* DESCRIPTION1 for the first material description in the row to output. In the *Output structure* area of the *Output Options* tab of the *text* DESCRIPTION1, we assigned 2 to the field *Line* (line type DESCRIPTION) and 2 to the field *Column* (*cell* number 2) As per our naming pattern, we should have named this *text* DESCRIPTION_TEXT1. By mischance, we have named the *text* DESCRIPTION1. In the text editor of the *text* DESCRIPTION1, we entered the following text:

&MATR_TAB-MAKTX1&

We created the *text* DESCRIPTION_TEXT2 for the second material description in the row to output. In the *Output structure* area of the *Output Options* tab of the *text* DESCRIPTION_TEXT2, we assigned 2 to the field *Line* (line type DESCRIPTION) and 4 to the field *Column* (*cell* number 4). In the text editor of the *text* DESCRIPTION_TEXT2, we entered the following text:

&MATR_TAB-MAKTX2&

We created the *text* LINE_GAP to generate two lines gap. In the *Output structure* area of the *Output Options* tab of the *text* LINE_GAP, we assigned 3 to the field *Line* (line type LGAP) and 1 to the field *Column* (*cell* number 1). We did not enter anything in the text editor of the *text* LINE_GAP.

We saved, performed a consistency check, and activated the *form*.

## Creation of Driver Program YCH04_04_DPRG_YCH04_04_MBCODES

We created and activated an ABAP program YCH04_04_DPRG_YCH04_04_MBCODES. This will be the driver program for the *form* YCH04_04_MATERIAL_BCODES. The source lines of the driver program are as follows:

```
REPORT   YCH04_04_DPRG_YCH04_04_MBCODES.

*****************************************************
* Driver Program for Form: YCH04_04_MATERIAL_BCODES **
* Material Bar Code Label Print                    **
*****************************************************
TABLES MAKT.

DATA: MATR_TAB      TYPE STANDARD TABLE OF YCH04_MATR_STRU
                             WITH HEADER LINE,
      REM           TYPE I,
      FORM_NAME     TYPE TDSFNAME   "Form Name
                             VALUE 'YCH04_04_MATERIAL_BCODES',
      FM_NAME       TYPE RS38L_FNAM. "Function Module Name

***********************************************************
START-OF-SELECTION.

SELECT * FROM MAKT INTO MAKT UP TO 1000 ROWS
   WHERE SPRAS = SY-LANGU ORDER BY MATNR.

 REM = SY-DBCNT MOD 2.

 IF REM <> 0.
  MATR_TAB-MATNR1 = MAKT-MATNR.
  MATR_TAB-MAKTX1 = MAKT-MAKTX.
 ELSE.
  MATR_TAB-MATNR2 = MAKT-MATNR.
  MATR_TAB-MAKTX2 = MAKT-MAKTX.
  APPEND MATR_TAB TO MATR_TAB.
  CLEAR MATR_TAB.
 ENDIF.
```

```
ENDSELECT.
******************************************************
IF MATR_TAB IS NOT INITIAL.
 APPEND MATR_TAB TO MATR_TAB.
ENDIF.

IF LINES( MATR_TAB ) = 0.
 MESSAGE S001(YCH02_MCLASS) DISPLAY LIKE 'E'.
                           "No Data Retrieved
 EXIT.
ENDIF.

CALL FUNCTION 'SSF_FUNCTION_MODULE_NAME'
  EXPORTING
    FORMNAME                 = FORM_NAME
  IMPORTING
    FM_NAME                  = FM_NAME
  EXCEPTIONS
    NO_FORM                  = 1
    NO_FUNCTION_MODULE       = 2
    OTHERS                   = 3.
IF SY-SUBRC <> 0.
 MESSAGE ID SY-MSGID TYPE SY-MSGTY NUMBER SY-MSGNO
        WITH SY-MSGV1 SY-MSGV2 SY-MSGV3 SY-MSGV4.
ENDIF.

 CALL FUNCTION FM_NAME
*  EXPORTING
  TABLES
    MATR_TAB       = MATR_TAB
  EXCEPTIONS
    FORMATTING_ERROR         = 1
    INTERNAL_ERROR           = 2
    SEND_ERROR               = 3
    USER_CANCELED            = 4
    OTHERS                   = 5.
 IF SY-SUBRC <> 0.
  MESSAGE ID SY-MSGID TYPE SY-MSGTY NUMBER SY-MSGNO
        WITH SY-MSGV1 SY-MSGV2 SY-MSGV3 SY-MSGV4.
 ENDIF.
```

# Execution of Driver Program—Output

We executed the program YCH04_04_DPRG_YCH04_04_MBCODES. We fetched a thousand rows for output. The output will look like that in Figures 4-87, 4-88, and 4-89.

**Figure 4-87.** *Material bar code labels output—page 1/84, first eight materials*

**Figure 4-88.** *Material bar code labels output—page 1/84, last four materials*

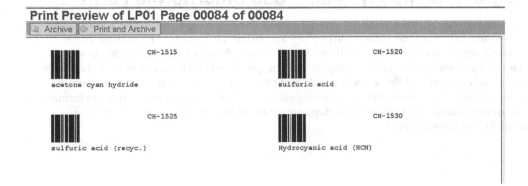

**Figure 4-89.** *Material bar code labels output—page 84/84*

343

## Hands-on Exercise Recapitulation

In this hands-on exercise, we demonstrated the output of material number/code as bar code. We started off by creating a custom bar code in SAP new bar code technology. We assigned the custom bar code to a device type. The tasks of creating the custom bar code and assigning it to a device type were carried out in transaction code SE73.

We defined a scenario to output material bar code labels. In the scenario to output the material bar code labels, we planned to output the material number as bar code, along with material number and material description. We planned to use the letter stationery in landscape mode: 279 X 215MM, to output the material bar code labels. We planned to output 2 labels across and 6 labels down in a page, a total of 12 labels in a page.

In the Smartforms environment, we created a *style*. Within the *style*, we created a *character format*. To the *character format*, we assigned the custom bar code created earlier. We activated the *style*.

We next created in the Smartforms environment a *form*. We assigned to the *form*, the *style* created earlier. We assigned to the *form*, the letter stationery. We entered in the *Tables* tab of the *Form Interface*, a single internal table parameter to receive the material data to be output. We renamed the default *page format* and enabled the page alignment as landscape.

As all of our information to be output was repetitive, we operated only the main *window* in the *form*. In the main *window*, we created the element *loop*. Within the element *loop*, we created the element *template* with one row. The element *template* consisted of three line types. We created element *texts* and assigned them the line types and *cells*. We entered in the element *text*, the program symbols to output material number as bar code material number and material description. We assigned to the program symbols to output material number as bar code, the *character format*.

We saved and activated the *form*.

We created a driver program. In the driver program, we loaded the internal table with four fields: MATNR1, MAKTX1, MATNR2, and MAKTX2. In the driver program, we invoked the function module of the *form*. We activated the driver program.

We executed the driver program and produced the output of material bar code labels.

We could have demonstrated the output of bar codes using the new bar code technology in SAP script environment. The demonstration of output of bar codes using the new bar code technology in SAP script environment requires uploading *SAP Service Marketplace*, a facility not available to the IDES user. You can peruse bar code technology specifics on the Internet.

# Hands-on Exercise V—Output Customer-wise Sales Summary of a Company code—Use Smartforms *Form*

As in Chapter 2, as a round-off to the hands-on exercises in this chapter, we will create a Smartforms *form* and its corresponding driver program which will produce a report much like a report produced by the features of classical reporting or ALV functionalities. We will create a *form* as layout of a customer-wise sales summary and its corresponding driver program. A report produced by a Smartforms *form* should use the extra formatting features like different fonts and different font styling in different parts of the output, enclosing outputs in box-like frames, imparting shading effect, etc. A requirement to use the extra formatting features of Smartforms *forms* will warrant the deployment of Smartforms *forms* over that of classical reporting or the ALV functionalities.

## Output Specification and Layout

Reproducing from Chapter 2, assume that a customer-wise sales summary is required with the following specifications:

- The column headings and the body of the report should be enclosed in box-like frames.

- The column headings and the body of the report should appear in shaded backgrounds.

- The column headings of the report should appear in bold font.

Figure 4-90 shows a rough layout of the report similar to the one in Chapter 2.

The number of Xs indicates the number of column positions for the field. The column headings and the body of the report will appear in a gray shaded background (not shown in this rough layout). The field names are marked. Most of the marked fields originate from tables. In the next section "Data Inputs," the originating tables of the fields will be identified. Some of the marked fields do not originate from tables: SFSY-PAGE is a Smartforms system field; SRL_NO and GTOTAL are variables defined in the Smartforms *form Global Data* tab of the *Global Definitions* node.

The output will be generated with data from the IDES server. The IDES server contains data of a number of company codes; each company code operates in a specific currency. So it becomes necessary to process and generate the customer-wise sales summary of one specified company code at a time. The driver program can provide for the input of a company code for which the customer-wise sales summary is to be generated through a PARAMETERS statement, and so on.

We will proceed to the identification of inputs and the processing of input involved in producing an output of Figure 4-90.

## Data Inputs

To produce the output of Figure 4-90, we will be required to access the following tables and their fields, as shown in Table 4-13.

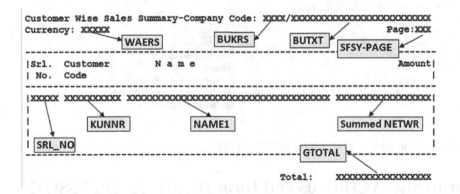

***Figure 4-90.*** *Customer-wise sales summary—rough layout*

**Table 4-13.** *Tables and Their Fields Required to Output Customer-wise Sales Summary*

| Srl. No. | Table | Field | Field Description |
|----------|-------|-------|-------------------|
| 01 | T001—Company code data | BUTXT | Company Code Name |
| 02 | | WAERS | Currency Key of Company Code |
| 03 | KNA1 Customer primary | KUNNR | Customer Code/Number |
| 04 | | NAME1 | Customer Name |
| 05 | VBRK-Billing document, header | BUKRS | Company Code |
| 06 | | NETWR | Total Net Amount |
| 07 | | KURRF | Exchange rate |

The database view YCH02_VBRK_KNA1 consisting of the tables VBRK and KNA1 created in Chapter 2 will be used again.

The currency of each billing document can be different. We have to convert the amount NETWR of individual billing documents into the currency of the company code by multiplying the amount field NETWR with the exchange rate field KURRF With the converted amounts; we have to summarize the data customer-wise. We are using the COLLECT statement to generate customer-wise summarized sales data.

## Create ABAP Dictionary Structure YCH04_SALES_SUMM_STRU

We created an ABAP dictionary structure YCH04_SALES_SUMM_STRU with the following fields: KUNNR, NAME1, KURRF, NETWR, and WAERK. The structure will be used to define or declare data in the ABAP driver program as well as in the Smartforms *form* environment. Figure 4-91 shows a screenshot of the structure.

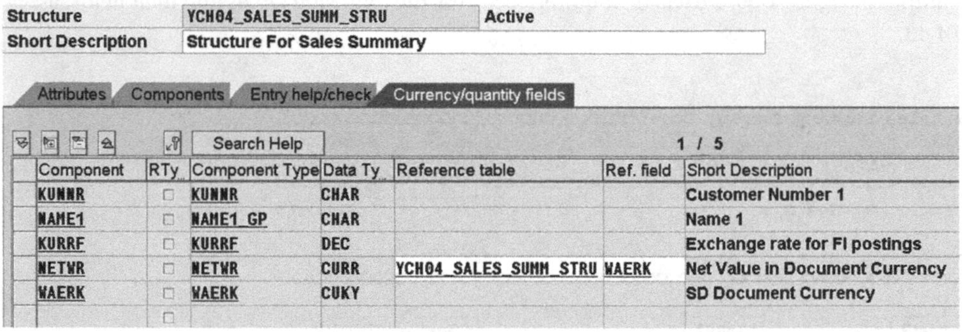

| Structure | YCH04_SALES_SUMM_STRU | | Active | |
|-----------|-----------------------|--|--------|--|
| Short Description | Structure For Sales Summary | | | |

Attributes  Components  Entry help/check  Currency/quantity fields

Search Help                                                    1 / 5

| Component | RTy | Component Type | Data Ty | Reference table | Ref. field | Short Description |
|-----------|-----|----------------|---------|-----------------|------------|-------------------|
| KUNNR | ☐ | KUNNR | CHAR | | | Customer Number 1 |
| NAME1 | ☐ | NAME1_GP | CHAR | | | Name 1 |
| KURRF | ☐ | KURRF | DEC | | | Exchange rate for FI postings |
| NETWR | ☐ | NETWR | CURR | YCH04_SALES_SUMM_STRU | WAERK | Net Value in Document Currency |
| WAERK | ☐ | WAERK | CUKY | | | SD Document Currency |
| | ☐ | | | | | |

**Figure 4-91.** *ABAP dictionary structure: YCH04_SALES_SUMM_STRU*

## Create Smartforms *Style* YCH04_05 and *Form* YCH04_05_SALESSUM

In transaction code SMARTFORMS, we created the *style* YCH04_05. We created a *paragraph format* SP with default values. We assigned the *paragraph format* SP as the standard paragraph of the *style* YCH04_05.

We next created a *character format* BL in the *style* YCH04_05. We accepted the default values of the font family as Courier and font size as 12 points. We assigned the *Font Style* as Bold. The *character format* BL will be applied to the column heading of the report to make column heads appear in bold lettering.

We performed a consistency check and activated the *style* YCH04_05.

In transaction code SMARTFORMS, we created the *form* YCH04_05_SALESSUM.

We assigned the DINA4 stationery to the *form*. We assigned the *style* YCH04_05 to the *form*.

We entered in *Import* tab of the *Form Interface* node, an import parameter T001 as shown in Figure 4-92.

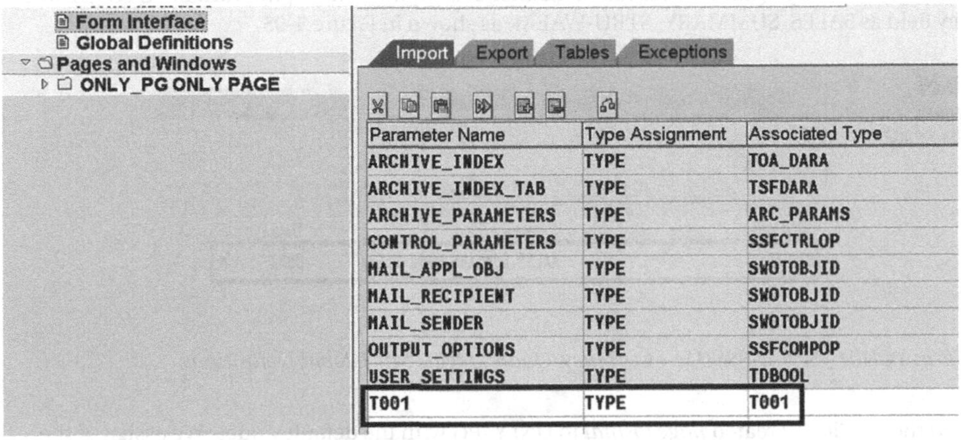

**Figure 4-92.** *Form YCH04_05_SALESSUM—Import tab, Form Interface*

We entered in the *Tables* tab of the *Form Interface* node, an internal table parameter SALES_SUMMARY_TAB as shown in Figure 4-93.

**Figure 4-93.** *Form YCH04_05_SALESSUM—Tables tab, Form Interface*

We entered in the *Global Data* tab of the *Global Definitions* node, the variables SRL_NO, GTOTAL, and SALES_SUMMARY_STRU as shown in Figure 4-94.

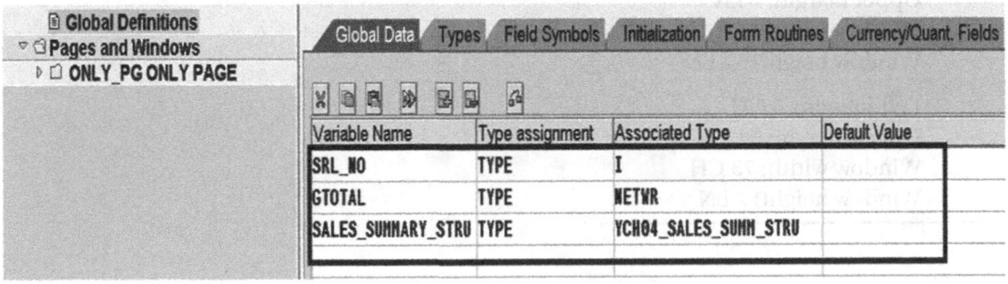

**Figure 4-94.** *Form YCH04_05_SALESSUM—Global Data tab, Global Definitions*

347

We will increment and output the variable SRL_NO as a serial number in the report, as the ABAP system field SY-TABIX will not work in the Smartforms environment. We will build the grand total in the variable GTOTAL and output it at the end of the loop processing. We will fetch a row of data from the internal table parameter SALES_SUMMARY_TAB into the structure SALES_SUMMARY_STRU. Strictly, this is unnecessary. We could have used the header line SALES_SUMMARY_STRU. We are avoiding the use of a header line.

We entered in the *Currency/Quant. Fields* tab of the *Global Definitions* node, the variable GTOTAL and the currency key field as SALES_SUMMARY_STRU-WAERK as shown in Figure 4-95.

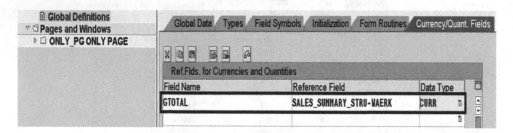

***Figure 4-95.*** *Form YCH04_05_SALESSUM—Currency/Quant. Fields tab, Global Definitions*

We renamed the implicitly created *page format* to ONLY_PG with the default values. We assigned the next page for *page format* ONLY_PG as ONLY_PG. We enabled the Radio button *Landscape Format* to output the report in landscape mode: 297 X 210MM.

For the only *page format* ONLY_PG, we created the *windows* as per the entries in Table 4-14. The horizontal dimensions of the *windows* have been specified in characters (CH) and the vertical dimensions of the *windows* have been specified in lines (LN).

***Table 4-14.*** *Page Format ONLY_PG—Windows*

| Window | Window Dimensions |
|---|---|
| 1. RHEADING | Left margin: 5 CH<br>Upper margin: 1 LN<br>Window width: 73 CH<br>Window height: 3 LN |
| 2. CHEADING | Left margin: 5 CH<br>Upper margin: 4 LN<br>Window width: 73 CH<br>Window height: 3 LN |
| 3. MAIN | Left margin: 5 CH<br>Upper margin: 7 LN<br>Window width: 73 CH<br>Window height: 57 LN |
| 4. GTOTAL | Left margin: 5 CH<br>Upper margin: 64 LN<br>Window width: 73 CH<br>Window height: 2 LN |

Further creations in the *windows* will be as follows.

## *Window* RHEADING

We created the element *text* in the *window* RHEADING and named it as RHEADING_TEXT. The following was entered in the *text* RHEADING_TEXT:

```
* Customer Wise Sales Summary-Company Code: &T001-BUKRS&/&T001-BUTXT&
*                           Currency: &T001-WAERS&         ,,,,,,,,,,,
= Page:&SFSY-PAGE(3)&
```

## *Window* CHEADING

As per our output specifications, the column headings must be enclosed in a box-like frame with a shaded background. This is achieved by settings in *Output Options* tab of the *window* CHEADINGS as shown in Figure 4-96.

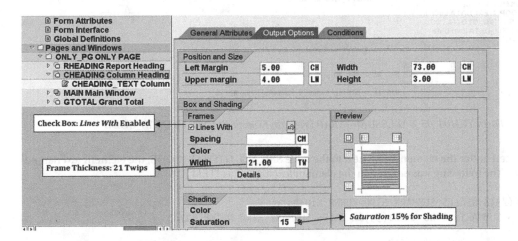

***Figure 4-96.*** *Form YCH04_05_SALESSUM—window CHEADING: tab Output Options*

We created the element *text* in the *window* CHEADING and named it as CHEADING_TEXT. The following was entered in the *text* CHEADING_TEXT:

```
*
* <BL> Srl.  Customer      N a m e</>
= <BL>                                    Amount</>
* <BL> No.   Code</>
```

## Window MAIN

The data in the main *window* has to output repeatedly; hence, we created the element *loop* named LOOP_ITEM_DATA. Figure 4-97 illustrates.

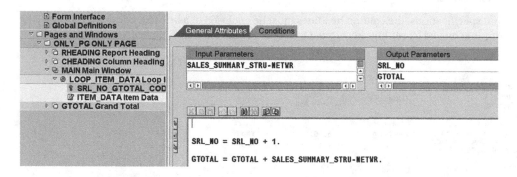

**Figure 4-97.** *Form YCH04_05_SALESSUM—loop: LOOP_ITEM_DATA*

To increment the serial number field SRL_NO and build the grand total field GTOTAL, we created under the element *loop* LOOP_ITEM_DATA, a node of *ABAP Program Lines*. We named this node of *ABAP Program Lines* SRL_NO_GTOTAL_CODE as shown in Figure 4-98.

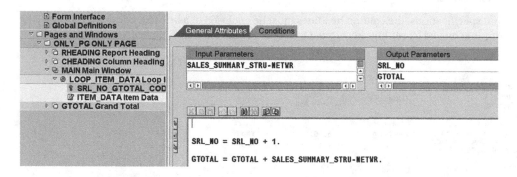

**Figure 4-98.** *Form YCH04_05_SALESSUM—ABAP Program Lines: SRL_NO_GTOTAL_CODE*

We created under the element *loop*, next to the node SRL_NO_GTOTAL_CODE, the element *text* named ITEM_DATA. The following was entered in the element *text* named as ITEM_DATA:

```
*    &SRL_NO(Z5)& &SALES_SUMMARY_STRU-KUNNR(K10)&
     & SALES_SUMMARY _STRU-NAME1(35)&& SALES_SUMMARY_STRU-NETWR(R17)&
```

## Window GTOTAL

We created the element *text* in the *window* GTOTAL and named it GTOTAL_TEXT. The following was entered in the *text* GTOTAL_TEXT:

```
*    ,,,,,,,,,,,,,,,,,,,,,    Total: &GTOTAL(17)&
```

We want the grand total to output once all the data is output in the main *window*. Hence, in the *Conditions* tab of the element *text* named GTOTAL_TEXT, we enabled the check box *Only After End of Main Window*.

After creation of the all the requisite *form* elements as described, we saved and activated the *form*.

## Driver Program YCH04_05_DPRG_YCH04_05_SALESUM for Smartforms *Form* YCH04_05_SALESUM

We created an ABAP program YCH04_05_DPRG_YCH04_05_SALESUM. This will be the driver program for the *form* YCH04_05_SALESUM. The source lines of the driver program are as follows:

```
REPORT   YCH04_05_DPRG_YCH04_05_SALESUM.

*************************************************
* Driver Program for Form: YCH04_05_SALESUM    **
* Customer Wise Sales Summary of a Company Code **
*************************************************

TABLES: T001.

DATA: CUST_SUMM_TAB  TYPE STANDARD TABLE OF
                          YCH04_SALES_SUMM_STRU,
      CUST_SUMM_STRU TYPE YCH04_SALES_SUMM_STRU,
      FORM_NAME      TYPE TDSFNAME VALUE
                          'YCH04_05_SALESUM', "Form Name
      FM_NAME        TYPE RS38L_FNAM. "Function Module Name
************************************************************
PARAMETERS COMP_CD TYPE VBRK-BUKRS DEFAULT 3000 VALUE CHECK.

START-OF-SELECTION.

SELECT SINGLE * FROM T001 WHERE BUKRS = COMP_CD.

SELECT KUNNR NAME1 KURRF NETWR WAERK FROM YCH02_VBRK_KNA1 INTO
      CUST_SUMM_STRU WHERE BUKRS = COMP_CD.

 CUST_SUMM_STRU-NETWR =
                CUST_SUMM_STRU-NETWR * CUST_SUMM_STRU-KURRF.
 CUST_SUMM_STRU-KURRF = 0.

 COLLECT CUST_SUMM_STRU INTO CUST_SUMM_TAB.
ENDSELECT.

IF LINES( CUST_SUMM_TAB ) = 0.
 MESSAGE S001(YCH02_MCLASS) DISPLAY LIKE 'E'.
                            "No Data Retrieved
 EXIT.
ENDIF.
```

351

```
SORT CUST_SUMM_TAB BY KUNNR.

CALL FUNCTION 'SSF_FUNCTION_MODULE_NAME'
  EXPORTING
    FORMNAME                = FORM_NAME
 IMPORTING
    FM_NAME                 = FM_NAME
  EXCEPTIONS
    NO_FORM                 = 1
    NO_FUNCTION_MODULE      = 2
    OTHERS                  = 3.
IF SY-SUBRC <> 0.
 MESSAGE ID SY-MSGID TYPE SY-MSGTY NUMBER SY-MSGNO
         WITH SY-MSGV1 SY-MSGV2 SY-MSGV3 SY-MSGV4.
ENDIF.

 CALL FUNCTION FM_NAME
  EXPORTING
*     CONTROL_PARAMETERS     = CONTROLS
*     EKKO                   = EKKO
    T001                    = T001
  TABLES
    SALES_SUMMARY_TAB       = CUST_SUMM_TAB
  EXCEPTIONS
    FORMATTING_ERROR        = 1
    INTERNAL_ERROR          = 2
    SEND_ERROR              = 3
    USER_CANCELED           = 4
    OTHERS                  = 5.
IF SY-SUBRC <> 0.
 MESSAGE ID SY-MSGID TYPE SY-MSGTY NUMBER SY-MSGNO
         WITH SY-MSGV1 SY-MSGV2 SY-MSGV3 SY-MSGV4.
ENDIF.
```

We saved, performed a syntax check, and activated the program.

# Output

We executed the program YCH04_05_DPRG_YCH04_05_SALESUM. We executed with the company code 3000. The company code 3000 has substantial billing document data. The output will look like that in figures 4-99, 4-100 and 4-101.

## Print Preview of LP01 Page 00001 of 00002

[ Archive ] [ Print and Archive ]

```
Customer Wise Sales Summary-Company Code: 3000/IDES US INC
                              Currency: USD                    Page: 1
```

| Srl. No. | Customer Code | N a m e | Amount |
|---|---|---|---|
| 1 | 0000000255 | Emma Bull | 2,207.00 |
| 2 | 0000000257 | John Evans | 2,299.00 |
| 3 | 0000000258 | Roger Zahn | 1,912.00 |
| 4 | 0000000260 | Chelsa Quinn Yates | 2,124.00 |
| 5 | 0000000262 | Robert Jensen | 3,720.00 |
| 6 | 0000000266 | Charles Scott | 2,995.00 |
| 7 | 0000000272 | Joe Masson | 748.00 |
| 8 | 0000000281 | Tracy Collins | 1,567.50 |
| 9 | 0000000470 | Alex Lynch | 11,860.80 |
| 10 | 0000000471 | Steve Martin | 8,415.50 |
| 11 | 0000000473 | Albert Brooks | 10,911.80 |
| 12 | 0000000474 | Edward Burns | 12,427.70 |
| 13 | 0000000481 | Peter King | 10,542.10 |
| 14 | 0000000482 | Douglas Barker | 1,614.26 |
| 15 | 0000000504 | Janett Adams | 2,957.16 |
| 16 | 0000000505 | David Lynch | 366.00 |
| 17 | 0000001508 | Deutsche Computer AG | 3,012.50 |
| 18 | 0000003000 | Thomas Bush Inc. | 7,602.00 |
| 19 | 0000003001 | Industrial Supplies Inc. | 4,320.00 |
| 20 | 0000003028 | Live Insurance Inc. | 12,038.25 |
| 21 | 0000003034 | Insurance Company | 299.00 |
| 22 | 0000003060 | Candid International Technology | 28,089.25 |
| 23 | 0000003221 | Andyna and Dynana Laboratories, Inc | 6,153.60 |
| 24 | 0000003250 | Department of Defense | 50,000.00 |
| 25 | 0000003251 | Palo Alto Airways Inc. | 202,496.00 |

*Figure 4-99.* *Customer-wise sales summary: Company Code 30000—1/2*

**Print Preview of LP01 Page 00002 of 00002**

| Archive | Print and Archive |

```
Customer Wise Sales Summary-Company Code: 3000/IDES US INC
                        Currency: USD                        Page:2
```

| Srl. No. | Customer Code | N a m e | Amount |
|---|---|---|---|
| 58 | 0000300719 | Hall Manufacturing | 12,313,262.00 |
| 59 | 0000301090 | Townsend Company | 2,350.00 |
| 60 | 0000401075 | LORI WINTER | 862.00 |
| 61 | 0000401076 | MARIE WITENBURG | 862.00 |
| 62 | 0000401078 | MARIE ZDROK | 862.00 |
| 63 | 0000401079 | LORI ZINNY | 862.00 |
| 64 | 0000401081 | JANET ZUSSIN | 862.00 |
| 65 | 0000401082 | JANE CASTILLO | 862.00 |
| 66 | 0000401083 | JANE SANCHEZ | 862.00 |
| 67 | 0000401258 | ALAN FAITH | 862.00 |
| 68 | 0000401259 | JIM FARAIZL | 862.00 |
| 69 | 0000401260 | ALAN FARRAR | 862.00 |
| 70 | 0000401262 | JAMES FERENCY | 862.00 |
| 71 | 0000401263 | BILL FERNANCE | 3,165.10 |
| 72 | 0000401264 | BILL FERRARA | 862.00 |
| 73 | 0000401266 | ALAN FINER | 862.00 |
| 74 | 0000401267 | JAMES GRUPER | 862.00 |
| 75 | 0000401268 | JOHN GRÖNROS | 862.00 |
| 76 | 0000401269 | ALAN GUETTEL | 862.00 |
| 77 | 0000401270 | BEN GUIER | 862.00 |
| 78 | 0000401272 | ALAN GWARA | 862.00 |
| 79 | A300015 | IDES AG | 2,000.00 |
| 80 | CMS0000001 | Crocodile Enterprise | 4,495.00 |
| 81 | IDESCUST | IDES Customer | 21,000.00 |

***Figure 4-100.*** *Customer-wise sales summary: Company Code 30000—2/2*

```
                              Total:    54,469,355.10
```

***Figure 4-101.*** *Customer-wise sales summary: Company Code 30000—2/2 total*

## Hands-on Exercise Recapitulation

In this hands-on exercise, we created a *form*, a driver program, and required workbench objects to produce not a business document but a report—customer-wise sales summary of a specific company code. The source of data for the report was the tables VBRK (billing document header), KNA1 (Customer Primary), and T001 (company code). The *form* consisted of two secondary *windows* to output the report and column headings. The body of the report was located in the main *window*. A third secondary *window* was used to output the grand total. The report column heading was produced in bold lettering. The report column heading and body was enclosed in a box-like frame with background shading.

While processing data for the report, we have ignored to filter out or skip billing document data not relating to actual sales like pro forma invoice, etc. (VBTYP = 'U', etc.). In the training and teaching paradigm we are in, this can be overlooked. If you are very particular, you can incorporate the condition to skip the data not relating to actual sales in the WHERE condition of the SELECT statement as follows:

```
SELECT KUNNR NAME1 KURRF NETWR FROM YCH02_VBRK_KNA1 INTO
    CUST_SUMM_STRU WHERE BUKRS = COMP_CD
    AND VBTYP NE 'U' AND.....
```

# Smartforms Tidbits

Following are some miscellaneous tidbits of Smartforms *forms*.

## Smartforms Opening Screen Menu Options

A brief on the menu options on the opening screen of Smartforms follows:

- Copy, rename, and delete—*forms*, *styles,* and *text modules*:

- To copy *forms*, select the menu option Smart Forms ➤ Copy. The copied *form* will be in inactive mode.

- To delete *forms*, select the menu option Smart Forms ➤ Delete.

- To rename *forms*, select the menu option Smart Forms ➤ Rename. The renamed *form* will appear in active mode, though no function module is generated. When you generate the function module for the renamed *form*, the function module name will be different than the function module name prior to renaming.

- On parallel basis, menu options are available to copy, delete, and rename *styles* and *text modules*. The menu options to copy, delete, and rename *styles* will appear on selection of the Radio button *Styles*. The menu options to copy, delete, and rename *text modules* will appear on selection of the Radio button *Text Modules*.

- Reassign package.

- To reassign a package to a *form*, *style,* or *text module*, select the menu option Goto ➤ Object Directory Entry.

- Settings:

- To make default settings in the Smartforms environment, select the menu option Utilities(M) ➤ Settings.

- Download forms, styles, or text modules:

- To download *forms*, *styles,* or *text modules* to presentation server files, select the menu option Utilities(M) ➤ Download Form/ Download Style/ Download Text Module on the Smartforms opening screen. You have to select the appropriate Radio button to download *forms*, *styles,* or *text modules*. The downloaded *forms*, *styles,* or *text modules* can be uploaded into the same or other SAP systems, providing portability to the Smartforms components.

- You can also download *forms*, *styles,* or *text modules* when you have opened these elements in change or display mode.

- Upload forms, styles, or text modules:

- The uploading of the downloaded files into SAP systems is enabled with the menu option Utilities(M) ➤ Upload Form/ Upload Style/Upload Text Module on the Smartforms opening screen. The uploaded objects will be in inactive mode. We have used the menu options to download our *forms*, *styles*, and *text modules* to make them part of our E-resource file for this book (www.apress.com/9781484212345). You can try out the menu options to upload our *forms*, *styles*, and *text modules* into your SAP systems.

- You can also upload *forms*, *styles*, or *text modules* when you have opened these elements in change mode.

- Download subtree:

- Within a *form* opened in change or display mode, you can download a node of the Smartforms *form* by double-clicking the node for node selection and making the menu selection Utilities(M) ➤ Download Subtree.

- Upload subtree:

- Within a *form* opened in change mode, you can upload a node of the Smartforms *form* by making the menu selection Utilities(M) ➤ Upload. This will load the node into the clipboard. You have to perform a paste operation for the clipboard contents to be copied to the *form* tree.

- Migration—SAP script *forms* and *styles* to Smartforms

- You can migrate SAP script *styles* to Smartforms *styles* by selecting the menu option Utilities(M) ➤ Convert SAPscript Style.

- You can migrate SAP script *forms* to Smartforms *forms* by selecting the menu option Utilities(M) ➤ Migration ➤ Import SAPscript Form. The SAP script control commands in the text area of the migrating SAP script *form* are treated as comments in the destination Smartforms *form*.

- Final and copy *windows*.

- In all our demonstration and hands-on exercises, we used only two *window* types: secondary and main. The Smartforms supports two more *window* types: (1) final *window* and (2) copy *window*. These *window* types are used in special contexts. A brief description of these *windows* types follows.

# Final *Window*

The final *window* output is processed after the conclusion of the processing of secondary main and copy *windows*.

In a scenario, assume that you are totaling the amounts of individual items of a document within the element *loop* or *table* of the Smartforms *form* environment to derive the total amount of a document. Further, in this scenario, suppose you want the total amount of the document to appear on the document's first page. Normally, all the items are not processed when you are on the first page of the document. If you locate the output of total amount of the document in a secondary or main *window*, the total amount will output incorrectly as all the items in the document might not have been processed. But, if you locate the output of total amount of the document in a final *window*, the total amount will output correctly.

The value of the Smartforms system field SFSY-FORMPAGES, when interrogated through a static breakpoint in the *Program Lines* node located in the final *window*, will display the total number of pages in the document.

The value of the Smartforms system field SFSY-FORMPAGES, when interrogated through a static breakpoint in the *Program Lines* node located in a *window* other than the final *window*, will display the current page of the document.

## Copy Window

The copy *window* can be deployed in the context of generating multiple copies of documents.

Suppose you are generating multiple, say, two, copies of a document, say, purchase order—PO. The first of the two copies is designated as the internal copy. The second of the two copies is designated as the vendor copy (meant for the business partner).

You want some data, text to appear on the internal copy and not appear on the vendor copy. And you want some data, text to appear on the vendor copy and not appear on the internal copy.

The Smartforms provides the facility of copy *windows* to manage the scenario described. When you designate a *window* as a copy *window*, in the *General Attributes* tab, the *Output to* area under the *Window type* appears. With the Radio buttons provided in the *Output to* area, you specify and control the output of copy *windows* in the multiple copies of a document.

You can also use the Smartforms system fields SFSY-COPYCOUNT and SFSY-COPYCOUNT0 to control the output of copy *windows*.

The Smartforms system field SFSY-COPYCOUNT contains 1 for the original copy and 2, 3… for subsequent copies.

The Smartforms system field SFSY-COPYCOUNT0 contains 0 for the original copy and 1, 2… for subsequent copies.

# Conclusion

This chapter consisted for most part of implementations of specific business scenarios using the Smartforms concepts and features introduced and described in Chapter 3. I called the implementation of the business scenarios hands-on exercises. We performed five hands-on exercises in this chapter.

In the first hands-on exercise, we created a *form*, a driver program, and other required workbench objects to produce vendors' address labels of a specific company code.

In the second hands-on exercise, we created a *form*, a driver program, and other required workbench objects to output standard purchase orders. The specialty or peculiarity of the *form* was that it can generate multiple language outputs with a single language version of the *form*. This was implemented through all text in the text area of the *form* originating from the ABAP dictionary data element text.

In the third hands-on exercise, we modified and customized a copy of the SAP delivered *form* /SMB40/ MMPO_A to output purchase orders. The modifications and customizations were carried out as per laid-out specifications. The hands-on exercise involved the copying of SAP delivered driver programs FM06PE02 and SAPFM06P into Y namespace and modifying them. The hands-on exercise involved the output settings in transaction code NACE. The output was tested in transaction code ME22N.

The fourth hands-on exercise output material bar code labels. The hands-on exercise involved the creation of custom bar codes in transaction code SE73. The custom bar codes created were deployed through *character format* in a *style*.

The fifth hands-on exercise involved a *form* to output a customer-wise sales summary of a specific company code. The hands-on exercise demonstrated that a list normally produced with reporting features like ABAP WRITE statement and ALV functionalities can also be produced using a Smartforms *form* and a driver program.

We concluded the chapter with Smartforms miscellaneous tidbits.

■ ■ ■

# CHAPTER 5

# Migration Using Batch Input Session and Call Transaction Methods

There are situations in which a large volume of data is required to be imported into the SAP system from non-SAP systems on a one-time basis as well as on a periodic or routine basis.

When SAP is implemented in an enterprise for the very first time, the enterprise could already be using some software to run its business. We will call this software existing in an enterprise before the SAP implementation as the legacy system. The legacy system will be maintaining data such as customer data, vendor data, material data, accounts data, and so on. The customer, vendor, material, accounts, etc., data is the so-called master data. Each category of master data—customer, vendor, etc.—consists of thousands or tens of thousands of rows. The master data already existing in the legacy system can be transferred into the SAP system as part of SAP implementation. Otherwise, the master data will have to be created manually from scratch in the SAP system—a laborious and error-prone exercise. Subsequently, post-SAP implementation, new customers, vendors, and materials will be created manually in SAP system. The master data is transferred from the legacy system into the SAP system only once during the SAP implementation phase—a case of one-time exercise of transferring data from a non-SAP system into the SAP system.

An enterprise might be using SAP for some of its business processes and might be using some other software for some other of its business processes. For example, in India, some banks use the software *Finacle* for their front-end operations and SAP for their back-end operations. Some of the data generated by the front-end software *Finacle* can be used by the back-end software SAP. The back-end software SAP might not use the data generated by the front-end software *Finacle* in the exact form in which it is generated. The data generated by the front-end software *Finacle* probably would have to be converted and summarized before transferring it to the back-end software SAP. The necessary programs/software can be written (a one-time exercise) to convert and summarize the front-end data which is to be transferred to the back-end SAP. The data transfer will have to be on a periodic basis—daily or weekly, etc. Thus, through the means of data transfer from the front-end software *Finacle* to the back-end software SAP, manual entry of transferred data in the SAP software is avoided. This is an instance of data transfer from a non-SAP system into the SAP system on a periodic or routine basis.

These were scenarios of data transfer from a non-SAP system into the SAP system as a one-time exercise as well as a periodic or routine exercise.

We will henceforth also call the data transfer from a non-SAP system into the SAP system as data migration.

© Sushil Markandeya 2017
S. Markandeya, *Pro SAP Scripts, Smartforms, and Data Migration*,
https://doi.org/10.1007/978-1-4842-3183-8_5

# Data Migration–Issues and Considerations

When data is transferred from a non-SAP system (source) into the SAP system (destination), there could be issues. Some common issues are listed here.

- The form of the data in the source can be different from the form in which it is expected to be stored in the destination. To cite a random example: suppose the customer name is stored in the source as 3x40. That is, each line of customer name has 40 characters and there are a maximum of three lines of customer name. In the destination, the customer name is stored as 4x35. That is, each line of customer name has 35 characters and there are a maximum of four lines of customer name. In such a case as described in the foregoing lines, string manipulation needs to be performed to the source data to convert it into a form expected in the destination. This is an issue of conversion of source data to the form expected in the destination. There might be more fields requiring such conversions. In the exercises we perform in this chapter and the next, we will not be addressing this issue. We are assuming that the source data has already been converted to the form expected in the destination.

- Certain data types in the destination are not supported in the source. For example, the ABAP type P—packed decimal —might not be supported in the source. Generally, the variations in the types supported at the source and destination are overcome by converting all of the source data into character (Unicode) type. The character (Unicode) type is universally supported. In all of our exercises, all of the source data will always be character oriented.

  Mostly, master data like customers, vendors, materials, etc., do not contain mandatory numeric fields in the SAP system. But if you are migrating transaction data like billing documents and purchasing documents, the data will consist of mandatory numeric fields like quantities and currency amounts. In our exercises, we will specify the numeric source fields as character oriented. The character-oriented numeric data can consist of numerals (0-9), a sign (+/-), and a decimal (.). During the assignment of source fields to the destination fields, the character-oriented numeric source data will automatically get converted to destination type.

- When you are migrating data, mandatory foreign key fields are involved. For example, if you are migrating customers, you need to provide valid values for *company code, account group, reconciliation account, sales organization, distribution channel,* and *division*. All of these fields are foreign key fields in the customer database tables. Hence, values should have been created for these fields in the respective primary database tables. Values are created for these fields in the primary database tables through the process of functional module configuration.

  The rows in the primary database tables for fields, *company code, account group,* and *reconciliation account,* are created through the configuration of the finance (FI) functional module.

  The rows in the primary database tables for fields, *sales organization, distribution channel,* and *division* are created through the configuration of the sales and distribution (SD) functional module.

  Thus, before migrating data of customers, you must ensure that the functional modules FI and SD are configured.

Before migration of any data, you must ensure that the appropriate functional modules are fully configured.

- When any new data is created manually in the SAP system, like, for example, customer data using the transaction code XD01, rigorous checks and validations are performed. When data is migrated from legacy systems into SAP systems, the migratory data must undergo the same checks and validations as when data is manually created in the SAP system. The SAP data migration tools and facilities provide for such checks and validations; you do not have to write ABAP code to perform such checks and validations.

# Data Migration–A Brief on Tools and Facilities Available

SAP provides the following methods for data migration from non-SAP systems into the SAP system:

- Direct input.

SAP provides a separate program for migration of each of business objects like customers, vendors, materials, accounting documents, purchasing documents, and so on. The *direct input* programs use function modules to perform the requisite validation of input legacy data. To view the *direct input* programs available, you can navigate to the transaction code SXDA and use the following menu option: Goto ➤ DX Program Library.

We will be migrating data using the *direct input* method under the Legacy System Migration Workbench (LSMW) in Chapter 6.

- Batch input or batch data communication (BDC)

With the *batch input* method, you initially perform recording of a transaction. Recording a transaction generally involves the manual creation of a sample business object like a customer, vendor, material, purchasing document, etc., with the appropriate transaction code. For instance, if you want a recording of customer creation, you will use the transaction code XD01 to create one sample customer. Some transaction codes, especially those involving controls of the control framework—CFW—are not accessible for recording.

Once the recording of the creation of a business object is over, you can generate an ABAP program from that recording. The generated ABAP program contains statements that simulate the screens of the created business object data. The generated ABAP program can then be appropriately modified to carry out data migration of the business object. In effect you are creating your own ABAP program for migration of data of a specific business object. Most of the code of the ABAP program is generated from the recording of the transaction.

When the modified version of the generated ABAP program is run with the converted data from the legacy system, data is not inserted into the SAP functional module tables. Instead, the converted data from the legacy system is inserted into queue or session database tables. You can then run a background session using transaction code SM35 to transfer the data from the queue or session database tables into the SAP functional module database tables. The running of the session produces a detailed log of data transfer from the queue or session database tables into the SAP functional module database tables.

A detailed description of the data flow is contained in the hands-on exercise of data migration using the *batch input* method in this chapter.

- Call transaction

The modified version of the generated ABAP program from the recording of a business object has the option to use the *batch input* method or the *call transaction* method. The same program can be run using either of the methods: *batch input* or *call transaction*. With the *call transaction* method, data is inserted directly from the converted data of the legacy system into the SAP functional module database tables. By default, no log is produced during the run of the program using the *call transaction* method.

This chapter contains a detailed description of the data flow in the hands-on exercise of data migration using the *call transaction* method.

- *Call dialog* (obsolete, not covered)

In addition to the methods, SAP provides two data migration workbenches.

- Data Transfer Workbench—transaction code: SXDA

- Legacy System Migration Workbench transaction code: LSMW

The two workbenches provide a single point or a screen from where you can perform all the required operations to migrate data.

The Data Transfer Workbench has been superseded by the LSMW workbench. The LSMW workbench provides the following four methods for data migration:

- Standard batch/direct input

- Batch input recording

- Business object method (BAPI)

- IDoc (intermediate document)

The LSMW provides an easy-to-use user interface to perform the requisite steps for data migration. When you perform data migration with LSMW, it could be possible that no program development will be required. When no program development is required, a non-programmer can perform the setup for data migration with LSMW. I will cover all the four methods of LSMW in Chapters 6 and 7.

In this chapter, using hands-on exercises, I will demonstrate data migration using the *batch input* method and the *call transaction* method.

# Recording a Transaction, BDCDATA Table, and the Include Program BDCRECX1

Before we venture to perform the hands-on exercises, we must understand the processing of recording a transaction, the data definitions, and functionalities incorporated in the ABAP include program: BDCRECX1.

When a recording is performed of a transaction code, the recording captures all the data entered on the screens and the operations performed on the screens. When an ABAP program is generated from the recording, the generated ABAP program invokes the include program BDCRECX1. The ABAP program generated from the recording is a screen simulation of the data entered and operations performed on the screen.

Mostly a recording is performed for one specimen entity. The program generated from recording will then support the creation of one entity. The generated program from the recording needs to be modified to read data of multiple entities from text file(s) residing on the application or presentation server and pass on the data from text file(s) to the creation of entities in the SAP database tables.

Descriptions of transaction recording and the include program BDCRECX1 follow.

# Recording a Transaction, BDCDATA Table

When we generate an ABAP program from the recording of any transaction code, the generated program invokes the include program BDCRECX1. The program BDCRECX1 is using the ABAP dictionary structure BDCDATA to declare an internal table of the same name as the ABAP dictionary structure. The ABAP dictionary structure BDCDATA consists of the following fields:

PROGRAM
DYNPRO
DYNBEGIN
FNAM
FVAL

I will refer to the internal table declared by referring to the ABAP dictionary structure BDCDATA as BDCDATA table. The BDCDATA table at runtime contains rows of the screen simulation of entered data and operations performed.

The BDCDATA table is filled up with rows for each entity (a customer, a vendor, a document number, etc.). The BDCDATA table is filled up in the following manner: for any row in the BDCDATA table, either the first three fields are filled up or the last two (fourth and fifth) fields are filled up. That is, when the first three fields contain values, the last two fields must be blank; when the last two fields contain values, the first three fields must be blank.

In the SAP environment, for most of the master and transaction data, there are multiple screens. When a new screen commences, the field PROGRAM is filled with the name of the dynpro program, the field DYNPRO is filled with the screen number and the field DYNBEGIN is filled with the value 'X' indicating the commencement of a new screen. The last two fields, FNAM and FVAL, should be blank. For every screen navigated to, a row with values in the first three fields will be created in the BDCDATA table.

Within a screen, for data entered in a field/every operation, the field FNAM is filled with the field name/ operation name and the field FVAL is filled with the value entered in the field/function code. The first three fields—PROGRAM, DYNPRO, and DYNBEGIN—should be blank. For every screen field into which data is entered or an operation like the positioning of a cursor is performed, a row with values entered in the last two fields will be created in the BDCDATA table.

To illustrate how the BDCDATA table is filled as a simulation of screen operations, we have performed a recording of the transaction code FI01. The transaction code FI01 creates bank master data in the single database table BNKA. With the transaction code FI01 in recording mode, we will fill the following fields of the database table BNKA:

- BANKS        Bank country (key)

- BANKL        Bank key

- BANKA        Bank name

- PROVZ        Region (Province or state code)

- STRAS        Street

- ORT01        City

- BRNCH        Bank Branch

The transaction code FI01 contains two screens and serves our present purpose of the demonstration of recording with minimum number of multiple screens.

To record a transaction, we use the transaction code SHDB. The opening screen of transaction code SHDB should look like the one in Figure 5-1.

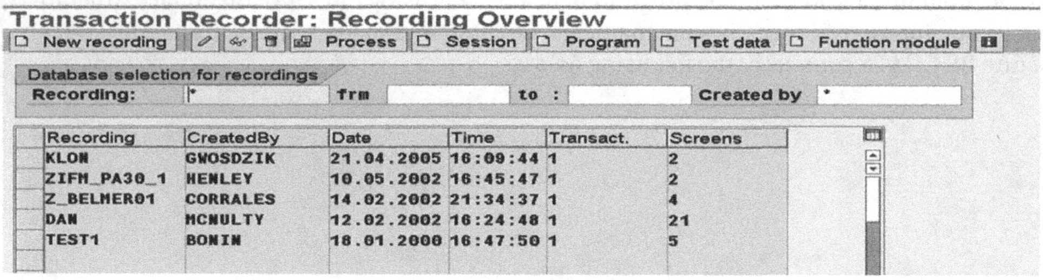

**Figure 5-1.** *Transaction recorder—opening screen*

To create a new recording, we clicked the *New recording* button. Clicking the *New recording* button popped up the dialog box shown in Figure 5-2.

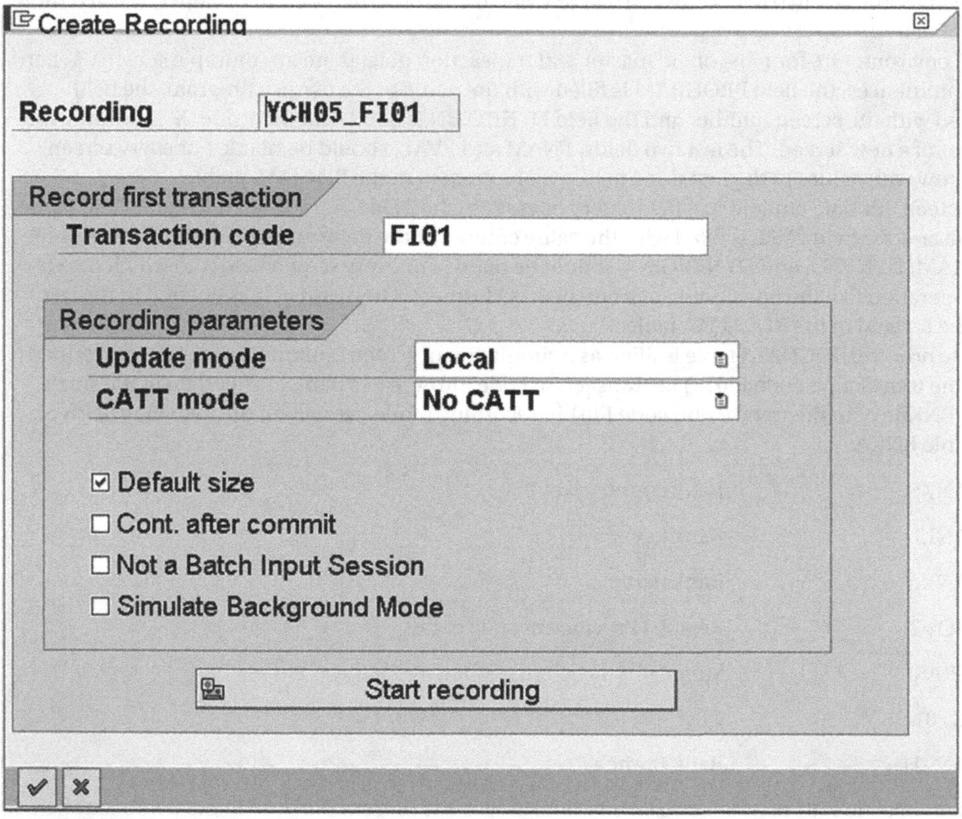

**Figure 5-2.** *Transaction recorder—create recording*

We entered the *Recording* name as YCH05_FI01, the *Transaction code* as FI01, and the *Update mode* as local and accepted the rest as default values. The *Update mode* and other items on this dialog box will be elaborated upon when we perform the hands-on exercise: data migration using the *batch input* method. To perform recording, we clicked on the Continue button. The *Create Bank: Initial Screen* appeared. Figure 5-3 shows the *Create Bank: Initial Screen* with entered data.

## Create Bank : Initial Screen

| Bank Country | IN |
| Bank Key | 987987987 |

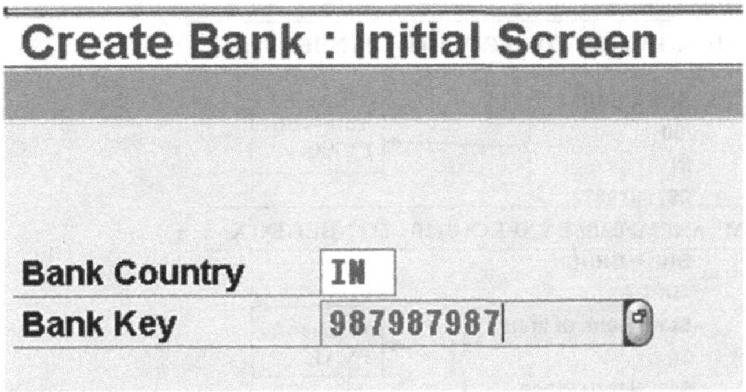

*Figure 5-3. Create Bank: Initial Screen with data*

By pressing the <enter > key, we navigated to the next (final) screen. The final screen—Figure 5-4 shows *Create Bank: Detail Screen* with entered data.

## Create Bank : Detail Screen

| Bank Country | IN | India |
| Bank Key | 987987987 | |

**Address**

| Bank name | State Bank of India |
| Region | 30 |
| Street | 555, Nehru Place |
| City | Delhi |
| Bank Branch | Nehru Place Branch |

**Control data**

| SWIFT code | |
| Bank group | |
| ☐ Postbank Acct | |
| Bank number | |

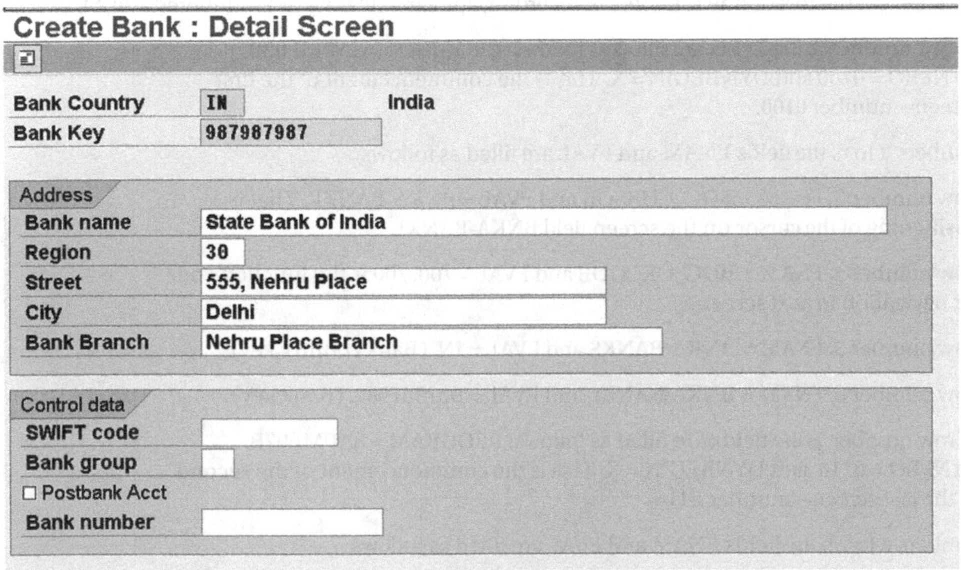

*Figure 5-4. Create Bank: Detail Screen with data*

We clicked the save button. The control returned to the *Transaction Recorder* screen as shown in Figure 5-5.

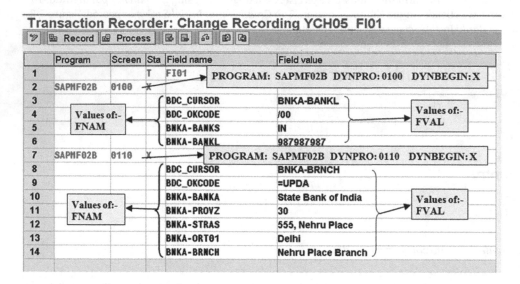

**Figure 5-5.** *Transaction Recorder: Change Recording YCH05_FI01*

On the extreme left, the row or line numbers of recording appear. The rows are numbered 1 to 14.

1. In row number 2, the fields are filled as follows: PROGRAM = SAPMF02B, DYNPRO = 0100 and DYNBEGIN = X. This is the commencement of the first screen—number 0100.

In row numbers 3 to 6, the fields FNAM and FVAL are filled as follows:

2. Row number 3, FNAM = BDC_CURSOR and FVAL = BNKA-BANKL. That is, positioning of the cursor on the screen field BNKA-BANKL.

3. Row number 4, FNAM = BDC_OKCODE and FVAL = /00. /00 is the function code for navigation to next screen.

4. Row number 5, FNAM = BNKA-BANKS and FVAL = IN. (Bank country key)

5. Row number 6, FNAM = BNKA-BANKL and FVAL = 987987987. (Bank key)

   In row number 7, the fields are filled as follows: PROGRAM = SAPMF02B, DYNPRO = 0110, and DYNBEGIN = X. This is the commencement of the second or the last screen—number 0110.

In row numbers 8 to 14, the fields FNAM and FVAL are filled as follows:

6. Row number 8, FNAM = BDC_CURSOR and FVAL = BNKA-BRNCH. That is, positioning of the cursor on the screen field BNKA-BRNCH.

7. Row number 9, FNAM = BDC_OKCODE and FVAL = UPDA. UPDA is the function code for saving data.

8.  Row number 10, FNAM = BNKA-BANKA and FVAL = State Bank of India (bank name).

9.  Row number 11, FNAM = BNKA-PROVZ and FVAL = 30 (region or province/state code).

10. Row number 12, FNAM = BNKA-STRAS and FVAL = 555, Nehru Place (street).

11. Row number 13, FNAM = BNKA-ORT01 and FVAL = Delhi (city).

12. Row number 14, FNAM = BNKA-BRNCH and FVAL = Nehru Place Branch (bank branch).

Table 5-1 shows what the contents of the BDC_DATA table will be upon the recording operation of transaction code FI01 described in the preceding lines.

*Table 5-1.* *BDCDATA Table Contents on Recoding of Transaction Code: FI01*

| Row No. | PROGRAM | DYNPRO | DYNBEGIN | FNAM | FVAL |
|---|---|---|---|---|---|
| 2 | SAPMF02B | 0100 | X | | |
| 3 | | | | BDC_CURSOR | BNKA-BANKL |
| 4 | | | | BDC_OKCODE | /00 |
| 5 | | | | BNKA-BANKS | IN |
| 6 | | | | BNKA-BANKL | 987987987 |
| 7 | SAPMF02B | 0110 | X | | |
| 8 | | | | BDC_CURSOR | BNKA-BRNCH |
| 9 | | | | BDC_OKCODE | =UPDA |
| 10 | | | | BNKA-BANKA | State Bank of India |
| 11 | | | | BNKA-PROVZ | 30 |
| 12 | | | | BNKA-STRAS | 555, Nehru Place |
| 13 | | | | BNKA-ORT01 | Delhi |
| 14 | | | | BNKA-BRNCH | Nehru Place Branch |

We can save the recording and generate an ABAP program from the recording. We are not saving the recording and or generating an ABAP program for now. We will save the recordings and generate ABAP programs from the recording when we perform the hands-on exercises. Recordings are client dependent.

The recording lines can be modified. You can insert and delete lines of recording; buttons are available on the application tool bar to enable insertion and deletion of recording lines.

You can delete complete recordings.

You can export the recording lines to a presentation server text file. Conversely, you can import the contents of a presentation server text file into a recording. Buttons are available on the application toolbar to enable the export and import operations.

You can generate a function module instead of an executable ABAP program from the recording. You will generate a function module from the recording if you expect to call a modified version of the generated function module from a number of ABAP programs.

In a single recording, you can include multiple transactions or transaction codes. When you include multiple transactions in a single recording and generate an ABAP program, you can run the ABAP program using the *batch input* method only. The *call transaction* method does not support multiple transactions. We are not demonstrating multiple transactions in a recording.

# Include Program BDCRECX1

This section provides an overview of the include program BDCRECX1. When you generate an ABAP program from the saved recording of a transaction, the generated ABAP program invokes the include program BDCRECX1.

In the data declaration area of the program BDCRECX1, the BDCDATA table has been declared as follows:

```
*---------------------------------------------------------*
*   data definition
*---------------------------------------------------------*
*       Batchinputdata of single transaction
DATA:   BDCDATA LIKE BDCDATA    OCCURS 0 WITH HEADER LINE.
```

The program BDCRECX1 contains, at the very beginning, selection screen statements to input various runtime options. As we mentioned earlier, the same ABAP program generated from recording a transaction, with suitable modifications, can be run using either the *batch input* method or the *call transaction* method. A Radio button selection determines which of the methods is to be used during the runtime. Two Radio buttons are provided using selection screen statements for enabling runtime method selection. The selection screen statements for the Radio buttons in the program BDCRECX1 are as follows:

```
SELECTION-SCREEN BEGIN OF LINE.
  PARAMETERS SESSION RADIOBUTTON GROUP CTU.  "create session
  SELECTION-SCREEN COMMENT 3(20) TEXT-S07 FOR FIELD SESSION.
  selection-screen position 45.
  PARAMETERS CTU RADIOBUTTON GROUP  CTU.     "call transaction
  SELECTION-SCREEN COMMENT 48(20) TEXT-S08 FOR FIELD CTU.
SELECTION-SCREEN END OF LINE.
```

Other selection screen statements in the program BDCRECX1 will be discussed during performance of the hands-on exercises.

There are two subroutines, BDC_DYNPRO and BDC_FIELD, in the program BDCRECX1. These two subroutines will be continually invoked or called from the generated program from recording a transaction.

The first subroutine, BDC_DYNPRO, fills the first three fields—PROGRAM, DYNPRO, and DYNBEGIN—of the BDCDATA table structure with the supplied parameter values. It appends a row to the BDCDATA table with the assigned values. The subroutine BDC_DYNPRO lines are as follows:

```
*------------------------------------------*
*        Start new screen                  *
*------------------------------------------*
FORM BDC_DYNPRO USING PROGRAM DYNPRO.
  CLEAR BDCDATA.
  BDCDATA-PROGRAM  = PROGRAM.
  BDCDATA-DYNPRO   = DYNPRO.
  BDCDATA-DYNBEGIN = 'X'.
  APPEND BDCDATA.
ENDFORM.
```

The second subroutine, BDC_FIELD, fills the last two fields—FNAM and FVAL—of the BDCDATA table structure with the supplied parameter values. It appends a row to the BDCDATA table with the assigned values. The subroutine BDC_FIELD lines are as follows:

```
*------------------------------*
*         Insert field         *
*------------------------------*
FORM BDC_FIELD USING FNAM FVAL.
  IF FVAL <> NODATA.
    CLEAR BDCDATA.
    BDCDATA-FNAM = FNAM.
    BDCDATA-FVAL = FVAL.
    APPEND BDCDATA.
  ENDIF.
ENDFORM.
```

If you run the program using the *batch input* method, before you create data for a new session, you need to open this new session once (analogous to the opening of a new file). The program BDCRECX1 provides a subroutine OPEN_GROUP to perform this task of opening a new session. The function module BDC_OPEN_GROUP is called to open a new session. Program lines of subroutine OPEN_GROUP in the program BDCRECX1 are as follows:

```
*-------------------------------------------------*
*   create batchinput session                     *
*   (not for call transaction using...)           *
*-------------------------------------------------*
FORM OPEN_GROUP.
  IF SESSION = 'X'.
    SKIP.
    WRITE: /(20) 'Create group'(I01), GROUP.
    SKIP.
*   open batchinput group
    CALL FUNCTION 'BDC_OPEN_GROUP'
         EXPORTING  CLIENT   = SY-MANDT
                    GROUP    = GROUP
                    USER     = USER
                    KEEP     = KEEP
                    HOLDDATE = HOLDDATE.
    WRITE: /(30) 'BDC_OPEN_GROUP'(I02),
            (12) 'returncode:'(I05),
                 SY-SUBRC.
  ENDIF.
ENDFORM.
```

When you run the program using the *batch input* method, an opened session must be closed in the end (analogous to the closing of a file). The function module BDC_CLOSE_GROUP is called to close an opened session. Program lines of the subroutine CLOSE_GROUP in the program BDCRECX1 are as follows:

```
*----------------------------------------------*
*   end batchinput session                      *
*   (call transaction using...: error session)  *
*----------------------------------------------*
FORM CLOSE_GROUP.
  IF SESSION = 'X'.
*   close batchinput group
    CALL FUNCTION 'BDC_CLOSE_GROUP'.
```

369

```
      WRITE: /(30) 'BDC_CLOSE_GROUP'(I04),
             (12) 'returncode:'(I05),
                   SY-SUBRC.
    ELSE.
      IF E_GROUP_OPENED = 'X'.
        CALL FUNCTION 'BDC_CLOSE_GROUP'.
        WRITE: /.
        WRITE: /(30) 'Fehlermappe wurde erzeugt'(I06).
        E_GROUP_OPENED = ' '.
      ENDIF.
    ENDIF.
ENDFORM.
```

Once the table BDCDATA is filled with the screen simulation of one entity—a customer or a vendor or a material or a document, etc.—the data has to be transferred from the BDCDATA table to either the queue/session database tables or the functional module database tables depending on which method you are using while running the program: the *batch input* or the *call transaction*.

If the *batch input* method is being used when running the program, the function module BDC_INSERT is called to transfer the data from the BDCDATA table to the queue/session database tables. If the *call transaction* method is being used when running the program, the ABAP statement CALL TRANSACTION..... is used to transfer the data from the BDCDATA table to the functional module database tables.

The tasks of determining what method is being used to run the program, the calling of the function module BDC_INSERT, or using the ABAP statement CALL TRANSACTION...... are performed in the subroutine BDC_TRANSACTION of the program BDCRECX1. Partial lines of the subroutine BDC_TRANSACTION are as follows:

```
*----------------------------------------------------------*
*          Start new transaction according to parameters *
*----------------------------------------------------------*
FORM BDC_TRANSACTION USING TCODE.
  DATA: L_MSTRING(480).
  DATA: L_SUBRC LIKE SY-SUBRC.
* batch input session
  IF SESSION = 'X'.
    CALL FUNCTION 'BDC_INSERT'
         EXPORTING TCODE     = TCODE
         TABLES    DYNPROTAB = BDCDATA.
    IF SMALLLOG <> 'X'.
      WRITE: / 'BDC_INSERT'(I03),
               TCODE,
               'returncode:'(I05),
               SY-SUBRC,
               'RECORD:',
               SY-INDEX.
    ENDIF.
* call transaction using
  ELSE.
    REFRESH MESSTAB.
    CALL TRANSACTION TCODE USING BDCDATA
                     MODE   CTUMODE
                     UPDATE CUPDATE
                     MESSAGES INTO MESSTAB.
```

```
    L_SUBRC = SY-SUBRC.
.....
.....
      CALL FUNCTION 'BDC_INSERT'
           EXPORTING TCODE    = TCODE
           TABLES    DYNPROTAB = BDCDATA.
    ENDIF.
  ENDIF.
  REFRESH BDCDATA.
ENDFORM.
```

This was an overview of the include program BDCRECX1 invoked by the generated program from the transaction recording. An overview of the include program BDCRECX1 touched upon the following:

- Selection screen statements

- Data declaration

- Subroutine BDC_DYNPRO

- Subroutine BDC_FIELD

- Subroutine OPEN_GROUP

- Subroutine CLOSE_GROUP

- Subroutine BDC_TRANSACTION

SAP provides the means for any transaction to be recorded; an ABAP program generated which can be modified to suit specific requirements. So, a custom program for the migration of any data can be created with little effort, as the core of the program is generated by the system from the recording of the transaction.

Transaction recording does not support OOPS screen controls in the SAP enjoy transactions.

# Determine Program Name, Screen Numbers, Screen Field Names

In the SAP environment, on any screen, you can determine the technical information such as the dynpro program name, screen number, field name, etc. You can determine the technical information of a specific screen field by first positioning the cursor on the screen field and pressing the function key F1. Pressing the function key F1 will pop up the help text dialog box of the field. The help text for most part is the text created in the data element assigned to the screen field. On the help text dialog box of a field (titled the *Performance Assistant*), buttons appear at the top. Clicking the fourth button from the left will fetch the dialog box detailing the technical information of the screen field.

As an example, we navigated to the opening screen of transaction code XD01—create customer. On the opening screen of transaction code XD01, we positioned the cursor on the first field *Account group* and pressed the function key F1 which popped up the *Performance Assistant* screen as shown in Figure 5-6:

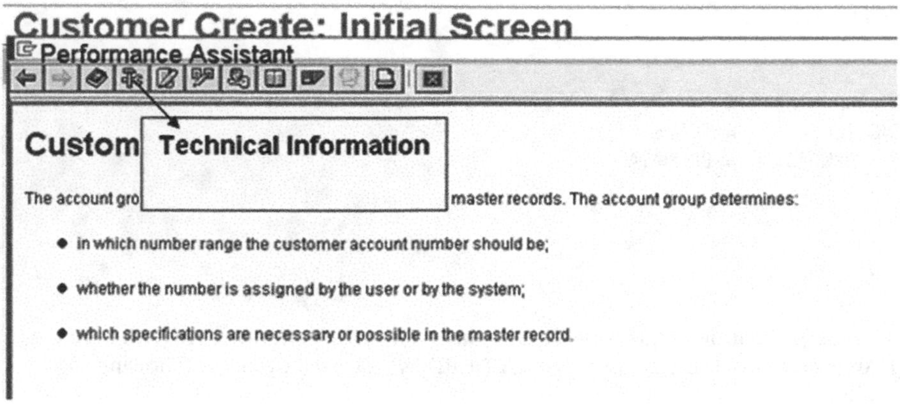

*Figure 5-6. Transaction code XD01 opening screen: function key F1 on the first field*

Clicking the fourth button from the left on the *Performance Assistant* screen fetched the *Technical Information* screen as shown in Figure 5-7:

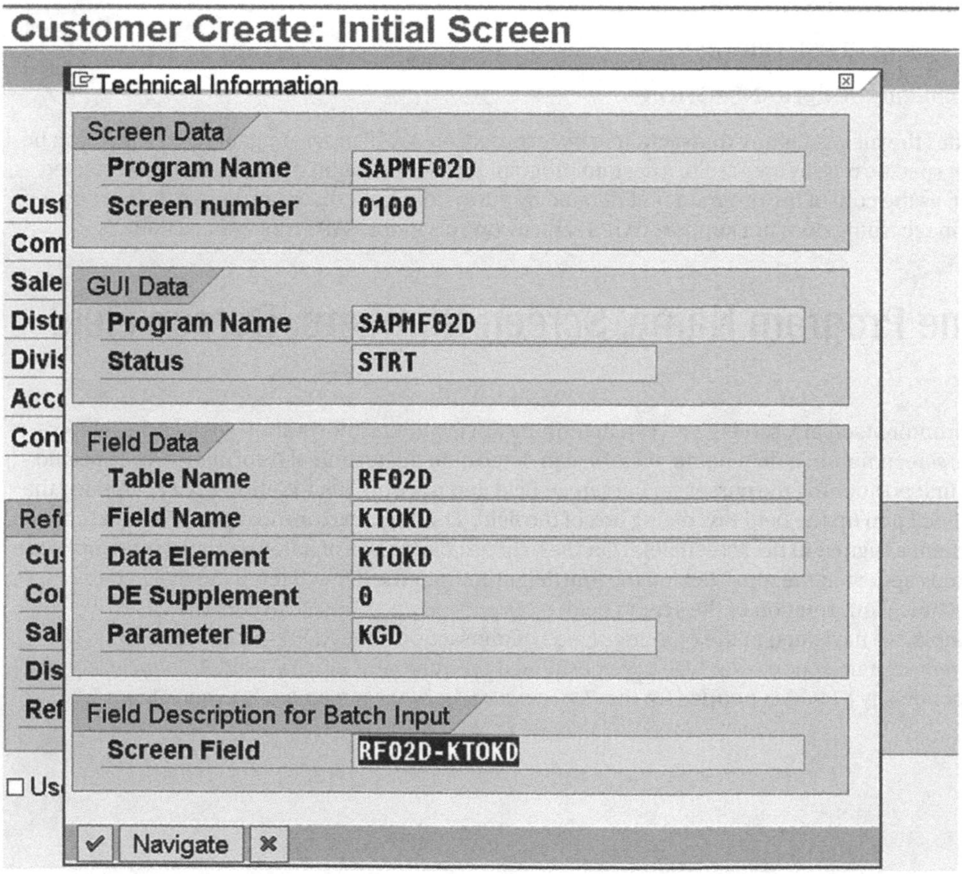

*Figure 5-7. Transaction code XD01: technical information of field account group*

From Figure 5-7, you can deduce that the dynpro program name is SAPMF02D, the screen number is 0100, GUI status is STRT, the screen field name is RF02D-KTOKD, etc. The fields on the screen number 0100 originate from more than one database table; hence have been grouped into the structure RF02D. The structure RF02D is not a database table. On subsequent screens of transaction code XD01, all the fields on one screen originate from one database table. Hence the field structure names are the same as database table names from where the fields originate. You can check this out for any of the fields: *Name, Street,* etc., on the next screen by clicking the function key F1 on any of these fields and next clicking the *Technical Information* button on the *Performance Assistant* screen. For instance, the screen field name for *Street* will be KNA1-STRAS.

In this manner, you can gather technical information of fields, one field at a time. You are able to co-relate field labels on the screen with the field names or technical names. The field names or technical names are available in the recording as well as in the generated program from the recording. When you are determining technical information as described in the preceding lines, do not save data, recording, and generate program from recording.

In our hands-on exercises, we will modify and use the modified generated program. The generated program will contain screen simulation statements. We will not manually write screen simulation statements. If we were manually writing screen simulation statements, then the technical information of fields would need to be determined by pressing function key F1, and so on.

Up to now, we have described the tools and facilities available in the SAP environment for data migration. The hands-on exercises follow.

# Hands-on Exercise I: Migrate Vendor Data Using *Batch Input* Method

We will start off the hands-on exercise by describing its specification and scope.

## Specification and Scope

The hands-on exercise will transfer data from text files into the vendor master functional module database tables using the *batch input* method. It is assumed that input data in the form of text files is in the required form, and conversions, etc., have been effected. The input data in the form of text files will reside on the presentation server. In the next hands-on exercise, we will locate the input data in the form of text files on the application server.

We do not have a large volume of vendor input data. For our purposes, we need to have only a small amount of representative vendor input data which can be used to demonstrate the efficacy of SAP tools and facilities available for data migration. We will use a text editor to create representative vendor input data on the presentation server. In a real-life scenario, data will never be created using a text editor. The data will be extracted from the legacy database systems into text files.

Data migration presupposes you/one or more of the team have some background knowledge of database tables and screens associated with specific data migration being undertaken—in our present case, the vendors. The focus in the hands-on exercise will be on the deployment of data migration tools and facilities. We will restrict ourselves to inserting data into all of the mandatory fields and only a few nonmandatory fields.

The following transaction codes are used to create vendors:

- Vendor—Central perspectives     XK01     Material Management and Accounts Payable

- Vendor—Purchasing     MK01     Material Management perspective

- Vendor—Accounting     FK01     Accounts Payable perspective

We will employ the transaction code XK01, Vendor—Central, for hands-on exercise I.

The following convention is used for transactions codes involving data maintenance:

- Transaction codes ending with 01 for creation of data

- Transaction codes ending with 02 for changes to existing data

- Transaction codes ending with 03 to display existing data

The recording will involve data entry on screen numbers: 100, 110, 130, 210, 215, 220, and 310. The recording will involve navigating the screen numbers: 100, 110, 120, 130, 210, 215, 220, 310, and 320.

The input data: text files will reside on the presentation server. The input will consist of two text files: (1) main data and (2) bank data. The two text files will be related through the vendor number—which of the bank(s) belongs to which vendor.

Table 5-2 lists the selected fields for which values will be entered, along with the table names and screen numbers. The order of the fields is the order in which they are encountered on the screens when you enter data while recording the transaction code XK01.

*Table 5-2.* *Fields Which Will Assume Values and the Corresponding Tables.*

| Srl. No. | Field Name | Field Description | Table Name | Screen Number | Remarks |
|---|---|---|---|---|---|
| 1 | LIFNR | Vendor (Number) | LFA1 | 0100 | Mandatory |
| 2 | BUKRS | Company Code | LFB1 | 0100 | Mandatory |
| 3 | EKORG | Purchasing Organization | LFM1 | 0100 | Mandatory |
| 4 | KTOKK | Account Group | LFA1 | 0100 | Mandatory |
| 5 | ANRED | Title | LFA1 | 0110 | |
| 6 | NAME1 | Name | LFA1 | 0110 | Mandatory |
| 7 | SORTL | Search term | LFA1 | 0110 | Mandatory |
| 8 | STRAS | Street | LFA1 | 0110 | Mandatory |
| 9 | ORT01 | City | LFA1 | 0110 | |
| 10 | PSTLZ | Postal Code | LFA1 | 0110 | |
| 11 | LAND1 | Country (Key) | LFA1 | 0110 | Mandatory |
| 12 | SPRAS | Language Key | LFA1 | 0110 | Mandatory |
| 13 | BANKS | Ctry (Bank Country Key) | LFBK | 0130 | |
| 14 | BANKL | Bank Key | LFBK | 0130 | Mandatory if Bank Country Key entered |
| 15 | BANKN | Bank Account | LFBK | 0130 | Mandatory if Bank Country Key entered |
| 16 | AKONT | Recon. Account | LFB1 | 0210 | Mandatory |
| 17 | FDGRV | Cash mgmnt. group | LFB1 | 0210 | Mandatory |
| 18 | ZTERM | Payt. Terms | LFB1 | 0215 | |
| 19 | MAHNA | Dunn. Procedure | LFB5 | 0220 | |
| 20 | WAERS | Order currency | LFM1 | 0310 | Mandatory |

## Multiple Rows on a Screen—Case of Table Control

Enterprises transact with their business partners using electronic fund transfer technologies. To use electronic fund transfer technologies, enterprises will require information of the bank of their business partners. A business partner can transact electronically using more than one bank—multiple banks. There has to be a provision to create multiple banks' data for a business partner. The transaction code XK01 provides for the creation of multiple banks' data for a vendor on screen number 0130. As you know your dynpro programming, the creation of multiple rows on a screen is achieved with the table control.

For business documents (purchasing, billing, etc.), there can be multiple line items for a document, again a case of multiple rows on a screen. Multiple line items of business documents are maintained using the table control.

The table control screens involve specific coding in the data migration program. This will be demonstrated when we modify the program generated from the recording of transaction code XK01.

## Value Assignment to Fields

We are specifying how the 20 fields listed in Table 5-2 will assume values.

As our main objective is to demonstrate the use the tools and facilities of data migration, we will locate the bare minimum data in the text files. We will assume that all the vendors being migrated have the same constant values for each of the following 11 fields shown in Table 5-3.

***Table 5-3.*** *Fields with Constant Values*

| Srl. No. | Field Name | Field Description | Value |
|----------|-----------|-------------------|-------|
| 1 | BUKRS | Company Code | 0001 |
| 2 | EKORG | Purchasing Organization | 0001 |
| 3 | KTOKK | Account Group | 0001 |
| 4 | ANRED | Title | Company |
| 5 | LAND1 | Country Key | IN |
| 6 | SPRAS | Language Key | EN |
| 7 | AKONT | Reconciliation Account | 160000 |
| 8 | FDGRV | Cash Management Group | A1 |
| 9 | ZTERM | Payment Terms | 0001 |
| 10 | MAHNA | Dunning Procedure | 0001 |
| 11 | WAERS | Order Currency | INR |

Before you adopt these values for your hands-on exercise, check the validity of these field values on your system. If you are operating on an IDES server and logged into client 800, the foregoing values should be all right.

We are resorting to assigning constant values to the fields listed in the Table 5-3 to minimize and simplify the data in the text files.

The values for the five fields shown in Table 5-4 will originate from the text file—main data.

**Table 5-4.** *Fields with Values Originating from Text File—Main Data*

| Srl. No. | Field Name | Field Description |
|---|---|---|
| 1 | LIFNR | Vendor (Code or Number) |
| 2 | NAME1 | Vendor Name |
| 3 | STRAS | Street |
| 4 | ORT01 | City |
| 5 | PSTLZ | Postal Code |

The values for the three fields shown in Table 5-5 will originate from the text file—bank data.

**Table 5-5.** *Fields with Values Originating from Text File—Bank Data*

| Srl. No. | Field Name | Field Description |
|---|---|---|
| | LIFNR | Vendor (to relate with the Main Data) |
| 1 | BANKS | Bank Country Key |
| 2 | BANKL | Bank Key |
| 3 | BANKN | Bank Account |

Note, the field LIFNR in the bank data is only for connecting the bank data with the main data—which banks belong to which vendor?

We are still left with one field SORTL, for which we have not specified what value it will assume. We will pick the first word of the field NAME1 (vendor name) and assign it to the field SORTL—SPLIT statement, etc.

The contents of the field SORTL (search term) are to provide the end user with an additional means to search for vendors in large volume of data. Assigning it, the first word from the field NAME1 in practical terms, is not a good proposition. We are assigning the field SORTL, the first word from the field NAME1, in the present learning paradigm only to demonstrate a case of the value of a field being derived from the value of another field.

This was a detailed specification of how the selected 20 fields will assume values during the data migration.

# Data Flow When Running Program Using *Batch Input* Method

When a modified version of the generated ABAP program from recording of XK01 is executed using the *batch input* method, the diagram in Figure 5-8 traces the data flow from the text files on the presentation server into the queue or session database tables.

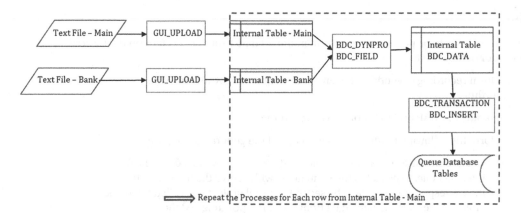

***Figure 5-8.*** *Data flow diagram: execution of program using batch input method*

To start with, data will be fetched from the two text files (main and bank) residing on the presentation server into two internal tables: internal table-main and internal table-bank. The function module GUI_ UPLOAD is used to transfer data from text files into the internal tables.

The internal table—main will contain one row for one vendor. A loop (LOOP AT.....) is set up for the internal table-main. Within this main loop, as new screens are navigated, the subroutine BDC_DYNPRO is invoked with the following parameters: PROGRAM and DYNPRO. Within a screen the subroutine BDC_ FIELD is invoked with the following parameters: FNAM and FVAL. Data will be passed from the structure of the internal table-main or through literals to the parameter FVAL. When the subroutines BDC_DYNPRO and BDC_FIELD are invoked, the BDCDATA table is being filled up.

Within this main loop, a nested loop with internal table-bank is set up to fetch data of banks belonging to the vendor fetched in the main loop. (WHERE.....) The subroutine BDC_FIELD is invoked with the parameters FNAM and FVAL to pass data from the structure of internal table-bank to the parameter FVAL. When the subroutines BDC_DYNPRO and BDC_FIELD are invoked, the BDCDATA table is being filled up

Once the BDC_DATA table has been filled for a vendor, the data from BDCDATA table is transferred to the queue or session database tables by invoking the subroutine BDC_TRANSACTION. The subroutine BDC_TRANSACTION calls the function module BDC_INSERT to transfer data from the BDCDATA table to the queue or session database tables.

The process is repeated as the next vendor is fetched in the main loop from the internal table-main. The process repeats until the main loop is exhausted.

Subsequently, when the created session is executed, data is extracted from the queue database tables and inserted into the functional module database tables. Checks and validations are carried out before the data is inserted into the functional module database tables.

When a batch input session is run, the mode of database update is synchronous only. During the processing, no transaction is started until the previous transaction has been written to the database tables.

This was a trace of the data as it traverses from the text files on the presentation server to their destination, the queue database tables, when you execute the program using the *batch input* method.

## Task List

Following is a list of tasks to be performed for the migration of data from the text files on the presentation server into vendor database tables.

(1) Perform recording of vendor creation—transaction code XK01. Save the recording.

(2) Generate an ABAP program from saved recording.

(3) Perform the following modifications to a copy of the generated program:

    (a) Declare two internal tables to receive data from the two text files. The first internal table, to be called the main table, will receive the main data from the corresponding text file. The second internal table, to be called the bank table, will receive the bank data from the corresponding text file.

    (b) Provide selection screen statements with appropriate selection list (F4 facility) to input the two text files' names along with folder location on the presentation server.

    (c) Provide statements to transfer data from the text files into the internal tables (main table and bank table)—use the function module GUI_UPLOAD.

    (d) Set up nested loops (LOOP AT.....) to fetch data from the main and bank tables. From the structure fields of the main table, the bank table, and literal assignments, data is to be passed to the subroutine BDC_FIELD.

    (e) Perform program check and activate the modified program.

(4) Prepare text data files.

(5) Run the program with the *batch input* option (default) for creation of a batch.

(6) Run the batch input session in foreground mode with transaction code SM35

(7) Check and verify migration of vendor data from the text files using transaction code XK02 or XK03

(8) Repeat steps 4, 5, 6, and 7, running the batch input session in background mode instead of foreground mode

What follows is a detailed description of the listed tasks.

## Perform Recording of Vendor Creation Using Transaction Code XK01 and Save It

We will create a recording of transaction code XK01, thereby manually creating a new vendor. We will enter values for the fields listed in Table 5-2.

To record transaction XK01, we navigated to transaction code SHDB. We clicked the *New recording* button. The *Create Recording* dialog box popped up. We entered the *Recording* (recording name) as YCH05_XK01_A and the *Transaction code* as XK01.

We selected the option *Local* for the field *Update mode* and the option *No CATT* for the field *CATT mode*.

Check box options in the *Recording parameters* area correspond to some of the fields in ABAP dictionary structure CTU_PARAMS. When you use the ABAP statement CALL TRANSACTION, you can supply the parameters related to the check box options in the *Recording parameters* area using the key phrase OPTIONS FROM followed by an internal table declared referring to the ABAP dictionary structure CTU_PARAMS.

When you call the function module BDC_INSERT, you can supply the export parameter CTUPARAMS related to the check boxes in the *Recording parameters* area. This export parameter is again an internal table declared referring to the ABAP dictionary structure CTU_PARAMS.

For further elaboration of check box options in the *Recording parameters* area, you can refer to the documentation of the ABAP statement CALL TRANSACTION or the function module BDC_INSERT.

For now, for the check boxes in the *Recording parameters* area, the proposed defaults will serve our purpose. By default, the check box *Default size* is enabled.

Figure 5-9 shows the *Create Recording* dialog box with the entered values.

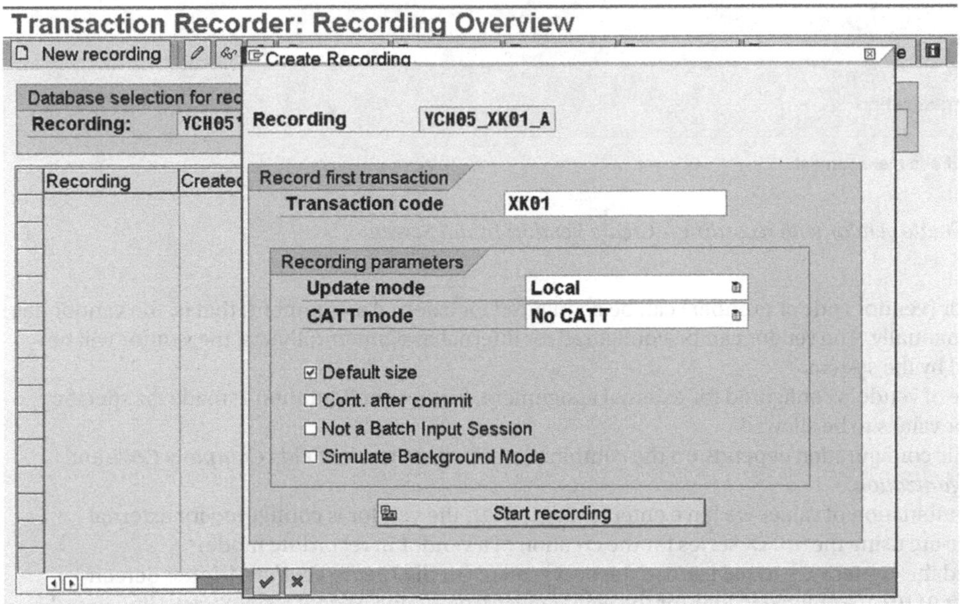

***Figure 5-9.*** *Create Recording: transaction code XK01*

We clicked the Continue button. The control navigated to *Create Vendor: Initial Screen*. During the creation of a vendor with recording, do not perform any extraneous steps. Do not perform any corrections/ revisions during the data creation. Do not navigate to previous screens. The extraneous steps will generate unnecessary extra ABAP statements during program generation. You use function key F4 to make selection from lists though. Enter data during recording smoothly.

Preferably, use the tab key to navigate to the next field and the <enter> key to navigate to the next screen.

Figure 5-10 shows the *Create Vendor: Initial Screen* (screen number 0100) with entered values for the four fields *Vendor, Company Code, Purchasing Organization,* and *Account group.*

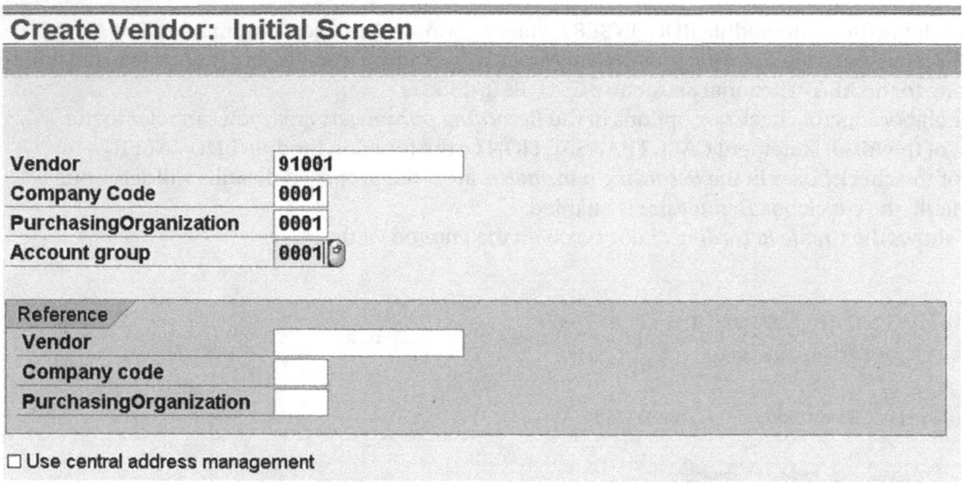

**Create Vendor: Initial Screen**

| Vendor | 91001 |
|---|---|
| Company Code | 0001 |
| PurchasingOrganization | 0001 |
| Account group | 0001 |

| Reference | |
|---|---|
| Vendor | |
| Company code | |
| PurchasingOrganization | |

☐ Use central address management

***Figure 5-10.*** *Create vendor with recording—Create Vendor: Initial Screen*

The vendor (vendor code or number) can be configured for external assignment; that is, the vendor has to be entered manually. The vendor can be configured for internal assignment; that is, the vendor will be auto-generated by the system.

In the case of vendors configured for external assignment, further configuration is made for specific range of vendor values to be allowed.

The specific configuration depends on the combination of values for the fields *Company Code* and *Purchasing Organization.*

For the combination of values we have entered, 0001, 0001, the vendor is configured for external assignment. We are using the 910XX series for the creation of a vendor in recording mode.

We pressed the <enter> key to navigate to the next screen. On the *Create Vendor: Address* Screen (screen number 0110), we entered values for the eight fields: *Title, Name, Search term, Street, City, Postal Code, Country* (key), and *Language Key.* Figure 5-11 shows the screen with entered values.

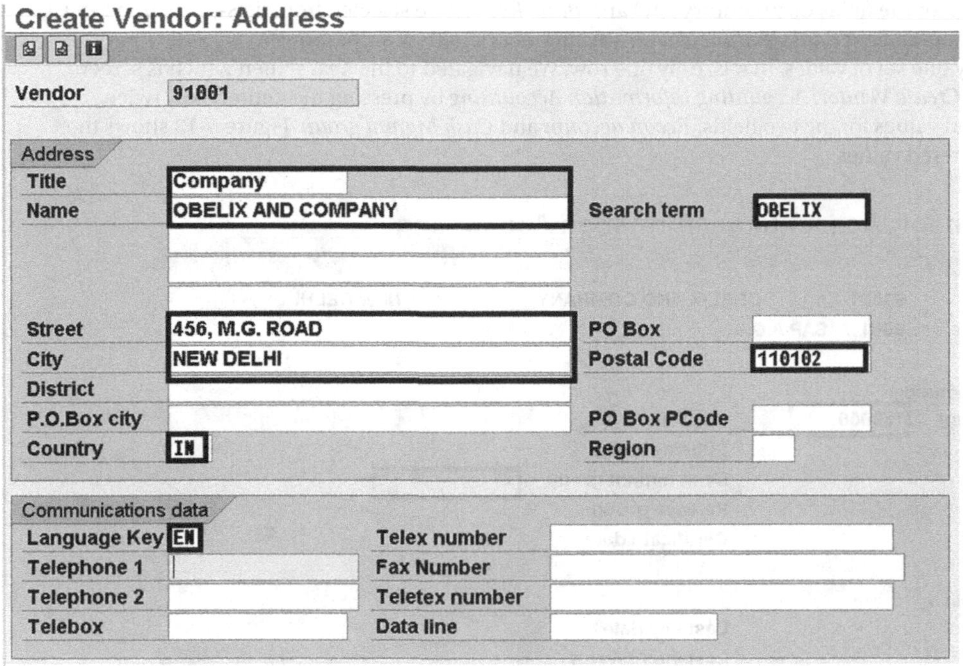

## Create Vendor: Address

| Vendor | 91001 |
|---|---|

**Address**

| Title | Company | | |
|---|---|---|---|
| Name | OBELIX AND COMPANY | Search term | OBELIX |

| Street | 456, M.G. ROAD | PO Box | |
|---|---|---|---|
| City | NEW DELHI | Postal Code | 110102 |
| District | | | |
| P.O.Box city | | PO Box PCode | |
| Country | IN | Region | |

**Communications data**

| Language Key | EN | Telex number | |
|---|---|---|---|
| Telephone 1 | | Fax Number | |
| Telephone 2 | | Teletex number | |
| Telebox | | Data line | |

*Figure 5-11. Create vendor with recording—Create Vendor: Address*

We navigated to the next screen, that is, screen number 0120, by pressing the <enter> key. We are not entering any values on screen number 0120, so we pressed the <enter> key again to navigate to screen number 0130, *Create Vendor: Payment transactions*. On screen number 0130, you can enter multiple bank particulars through the table control.

We entered one set of values for the three fields: *Ctry, Bank Key,* and *Bank Account.* Figure 5-12 shows the screen with entered values.

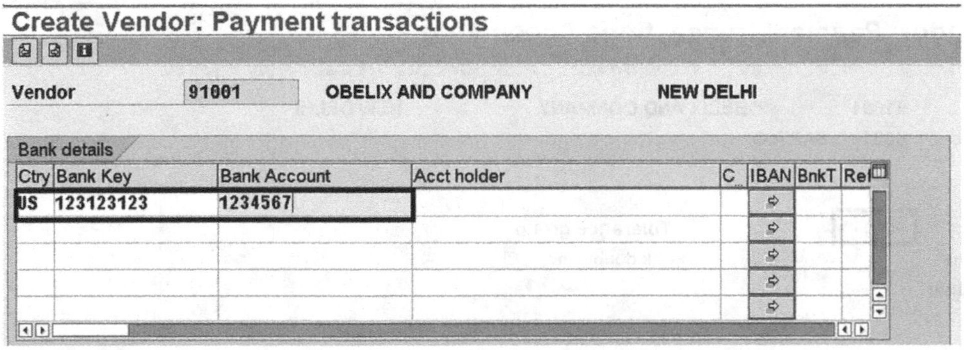

## Create Vendor: Payment transactions

| Vendor | 91001 | OBELIX AND COMPANY | NEW DELHI |
|---|---|---|---|

**Bank details**

| Ctry | Bank Key | Bank Account | Acct holder | C | IBAN | BnkT | Ref |
|---|---|---|---|---|---|---|---|
| US | 123123123 | 1234567 | | | ⇨ | | |
| | | | | | ⇨ | | |
| | | | | | ⇨ | | |
| | | | | | ⇨ | | |
| | | | | | ⇨ | | |

*Figure 5-12. Create vendor with recording—Create Vendor: Payment transactions*

The values for the fields *Ctry* (country key) and *Bank Key* can be selected from lists—function key F4, etc. The value for the field *Bank Account* can be any number (length of six or more).

Enter only one set of values, that is, only one row. We navigated to the next screen which is screen number 0210, *Create Vendor: Accounting information Accounting* by pressing the <enter> key twice.

We entered values for the two fields: *Recon.account* and *Cash Mgmnt group*. Figure 5-13 shows the screen with entered values.

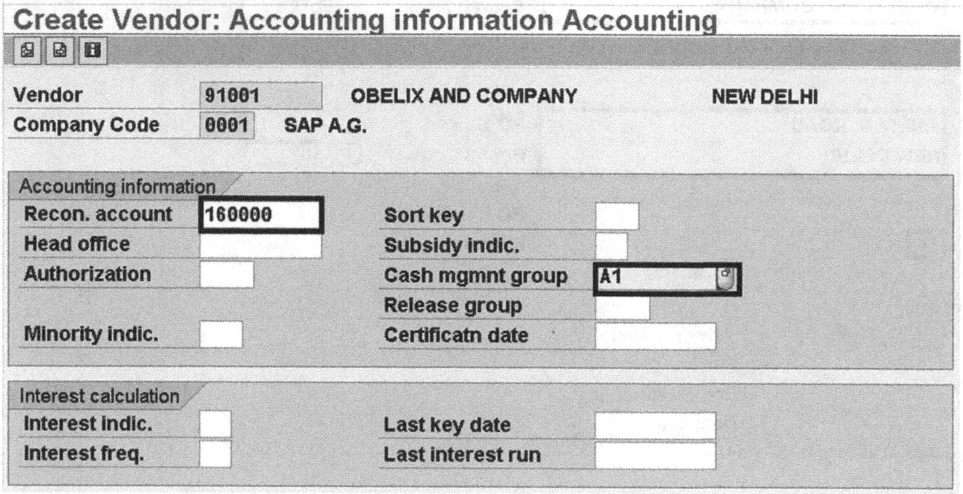

*Figure 5-13.* *Create vendor with recording—Create Vendor: Accounting information Accounting*

We navigated to the next screen, which is screen number 0215, *Create Vendor: Payment transactions Accounting,* by pressing the <enter> key.

We entered a value for the field: *Payt Terms*. Figure 5-14 shows the screen with the entered value.

We navigated to the next screen, which is screen number 0220, *Create Vendor: Correspondence Accounting,* by pressing the <enter> key.

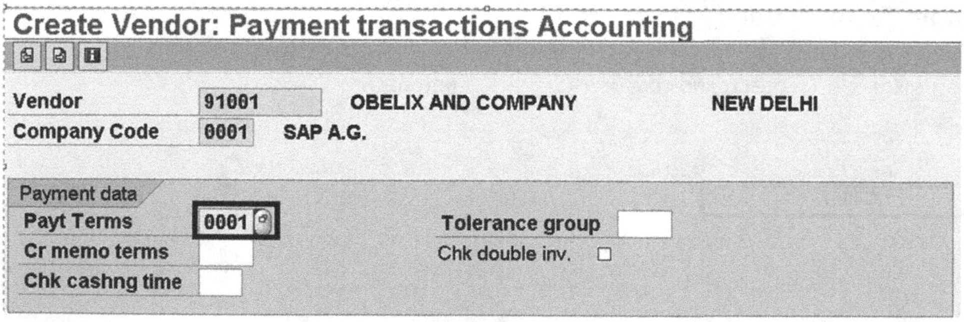

*Figure 5-14.* *Create vendor with recording—Create Vendor: Payment transactions Accounting*

We entered value for the field: *Dunn.Procedure.* Figure 5-15 shows the screen with the entered value.

## Create Vendor: Correspondence Accounting

| Vendor | 91001 | OBELIX AND COMPANY | NEW DELHI |
| Company Code | 0001 | SAP A.G. | |

Dunning data

| Dunn.Procedure | 0001 | Dunning block | |
| Dunn.recipient | | Legal dunn.proc. | |
| Last dunned | | Dunning level | |
| Dunning clerk | | Grouping key | |
| Dunn. Areas | | | |

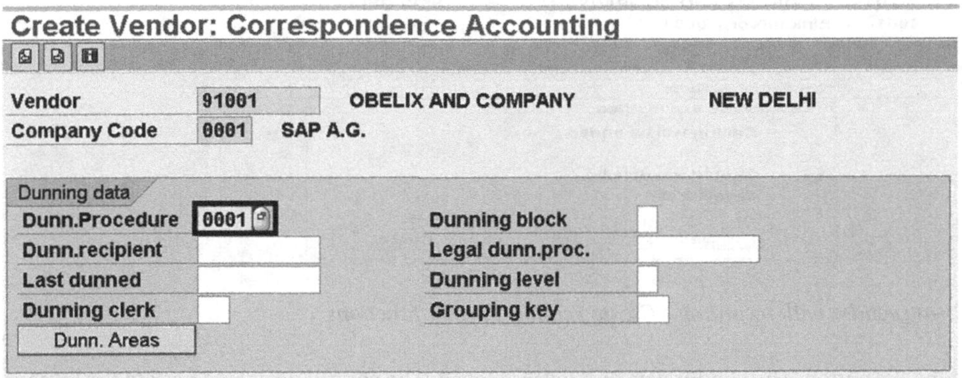

*Figure 5-15. Create vendor with recording—Create Vendor: Correspondence Accounting*

We navigated to the next screen, which is screen number 0310, *Create Vendor: Purchasing data,* by pressing the <enter> key.

We entered value for the field: *Order currency.* Figure 5-16 shows the screen with the entered value.

## Create Vendor: Purchasing data

Alternative data   Sub-ranges

| Vendor | 91001 | OBELIX AND COMPANY | NEW DELHI |
| Purchasing Org. | 0001 | Einkaufsorg. 0001 | |

Conditions

| Order currency | INR |
| Terms of paymnt | |
| Incoterms | |

*Figure 5-16. Create vendor with recording – Create Vendor: Purchasing data*

We navigated to the next screen, which is screen number 0320, *Create Vendor: Partner functions,* by pressing the <enter> key.

This is the last screen. We do not have to enter any data on this screen. We pressed the <enter> key which popped up the dialog box to save the data as shown in Figure 5-17:

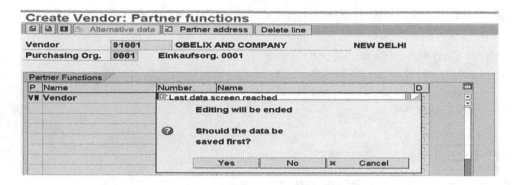

**Figure 5-17.** *Create vendor with recording—Create Vendor: Partner functions*

We clicked the *Yes* button. The vendor data entered was saved. The control navigated back to the screen of *Transaction Recorder*. We clicked the save button to save the recording. The *Transaction Recorder* screen after saving will look as shown in Figure 5-18.

| | Program | Screen | Sta | Field name | Field value |
|---|---|---|---|---|---|
| 1 | | | T | XK01 | |
| 2 | SAPMF02K | 0100 | X | | |
| 3 | | | | BDC_CURSOR | RF02K-KTOKK |
| 4 | | | | BDC_OKCODE | /00 |
| 5 | | | | RF02K-LIFNR | 91001 |
| 6 | | | | RF02K-BUKRS | 0001 |
| 7 | | | | RF02K-EKORG | 0001 |
| 8 | | | | RF02K-KTOKK | 0001 |
| 9 | SAPMF02K | 0110 | X | | |
| 10 | | | | BDC_CURSOR | LFA1-TELF1 |
| 11 | | | | BDC_OKCODE | /00 |
| 12 | | | | LFA1-ANRED | Company |
| 13 | | | | LFA1-NAME1 | OBELIX AND COMPANY |
| 14 | | | | LFA1-SORTL | OBELIX |
| 15 | | | | LFA1-STRAS | 456, M.G. ROAD |
| 16 | | | | LFA1-ORT01 | NEW DELHI |

Line  1 - 16 Fr. 60

⊘ Recording was saved

**Figure 5-18.** *Transaction recorder: vendor created with recording and recording saved*

Now that we created and saved a recording of transaction code XK01, the next step is to generate an ABAP program from the saved recording.

## Generate an ABAP Program from Saved Recording

After saving the recording, we navigated back to the previous screen, *Transaction Recorder: Recording Overview,* by pressing the function key F3. We want to generate an ABAP program from the recording YCH05_XK01_A of vendor creation. So, we selected the recording YCH05_XK01_A through the row selector and then, clicked the *Program* button on the application toolbar. Clicking the *Program* button popped up the dialog box titled *Generate Program for Recording.* We entered the *Program Name* as YCH05_XK01_PROGRAM_GENERATED. We clicked the Radio button *Transfer from recording* in the *Field contents* area. We did not enter anything in the *Test data* area; we do not want test data to be generated. Figure 5-19 shows the *Generate Program for Recording* dialog box with the entered values.

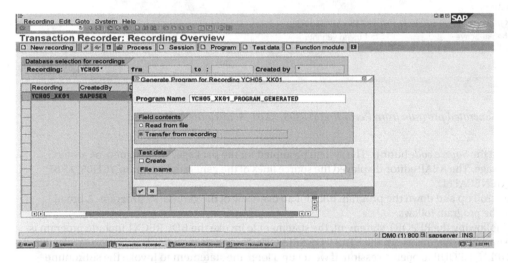

***Figure 5-19.*** *Generate program for recording YCH05_XK01_A*

We clicked the Continue button and the program attributes screen popped up. We entered a suitable program title and selected the program type as executable (default) (illustrated in Figure 5-20).

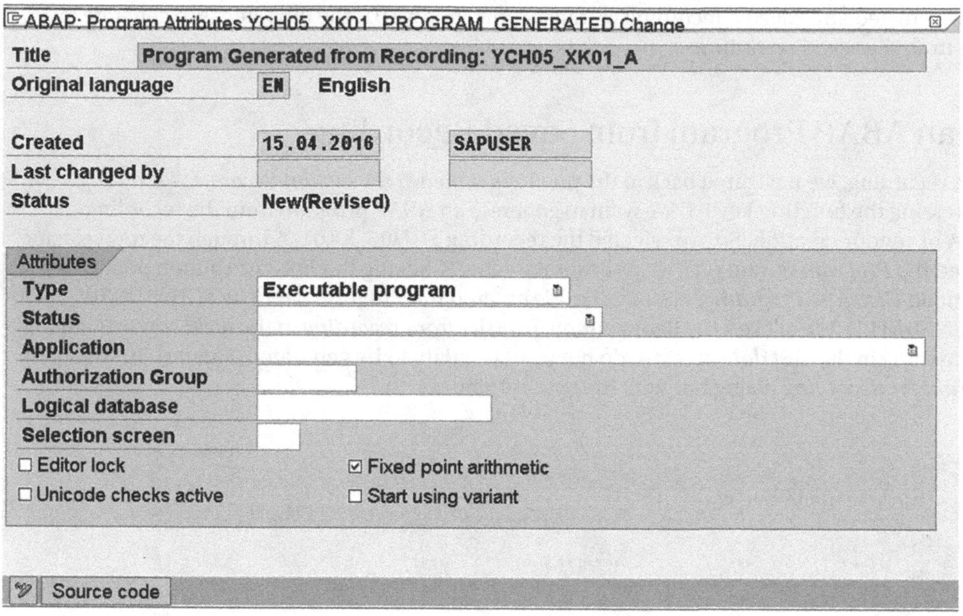

*Figure 5-20. Generated program from Recording YCH05_XK01_A: attributes screen*

We clicked the *Source code* button. The system prompted for the package. We assigned, as always, the $TMP package. The ABAP editor displayed the source lines of the generated program YCH05_XK01_ PROGRAM_GENERATED.

You can scroll up and down the program lines for an overview of the generated program. A broad discussion of the program follows.

Initially, following the REPORT statement, the statement to invoke the BDCRECX1 include program is located. The next two statements are the START-OF-SELECTION statement and a statement to invoke the subroutine OPEN_GROUP to open a session. If we set up a loop, the statement to invoke the subroutine OPEN_GROUP must be outside the loop. A session is opened just once, not repeatedly.

The statements following the statement to invoke the subroutine OPEN_GROUP are the ones simulating the data entry and screen operations. Whenever a new screen commences, the subroutine BDC_DYNPRO is invoked. Within a screen, whenever data is entered or operations performed, the subroutine BDC_FIELD is invoked. Whatever values we entered for fields from the keyboard are passed as literals to the FVAL parameter of the subroutine BDC_FIELD – '91001' for RF02K-LIFNR, '0001' for RF02K-BUKRS, and so on.

Figure 5-21 shows the initial segment of the generated program YCH05_XK01_PROGRAM_ GENERATED.

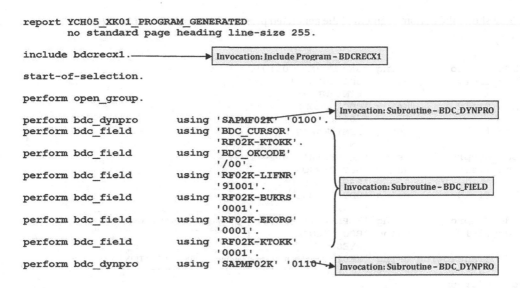

**Figure 5-21.** *Program YCH05_XK01_ PROGRAM_GENERATED: Initial Segment*

Figure 5-22 shows the segment of the generated program YCH05_XK01_ PROGRAM_GENERATED when data was entered for the fields in the table control, that is, screen number 130.

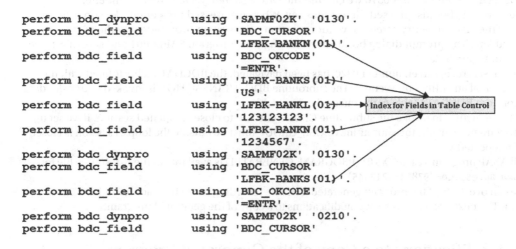

**Figure 5-22.** *Program YCH05_XK01_ PROGRAM_GENERATED: segment related to table control*

When data is entered for fields in a table control, the index of the field is indicated like BANKS(01), etc. The index is the visible row number of the data in the table control. Since, in the present context, we entered one set of field values or one bank for the vendor, the variables BANKS, BANKL, and BANKN carry the index 01. If we had entered two or more banks for the vendor, there would have been two or more sets of generated statements.

Figure 5-23 shows the bottom segment of the generated program YCH05_XK01_PROGRAM_ GENERATED.

```
perform bdc_dynpro        using  'SAPMF02K'  '0310'.
perform bdc_field         using  'BDC_CURSOR'
                                 'LFM1-WAERS'.
perform bdc_field         using  'BDC_OKCODE'
                                 '/00'.
perform bdc_field         using  'LFM1-WAERS'
                                 'INR'.
perform bdc_dynpro        using  'SAPMF02K'  '0320'.
perform bdc_field         using  'BDC_CURSOR'
                                 'RF02K-LIFNR'.
perform bdc_field         using  'BDC_OKCODE'
                                 '=ENTR'.
perform bdc_dynpro        using  'SAPLSPO1'  '0300'.      Dialog Box Prompt to Save Data etc.
perform bdc_field         using  'BDC_OKCODE'
                                 '=YES'.
perform bdc_transaction using  'XK01'.          Invocation: Subroutine – BDC_TRANSACTION

perform close_group.
```

*Figure 5-23.* *Program YCH05_XK01_ PROGRAM_GENERATED: bottom segment*

Figure 5-23 lists the lines related to data entered and operations performed on screen numbers 0310 and 0320. On screen number 0310 we entered the *Order Currency*. On screen number 0320 we did not enter any data but just pressed the <enter> key. When we pressed the <enter> key on screen number 0320 (the last data entry screen of vendor creation), the system prompted whether data is to be saved, aborted, etc. The prompt dialog box displays through the program SAPLSPO1 and screen number 0300 marked in Figure 5-23.

When the last screen, screen number 0320, has been navigated, the BDCDATA table is filled with the screen simulation of an entity—one vendor. The subroutine BDC_TRANSACTION is invoked to transfer data of one vendor from BDCDATA table to the queue database tables.

The last statement is to invoke the subroutine CLOSE_GROUP to close an opened session. If we set up a loop, the statement to invoke the subroutine CLOSE_GROUP must be outside the loop. A session is closed just once, not repeatedly.

The full ABAP program YCH05_XK01_PROGRAM_GENERATED is available in the E-resource file for this book (www.apress.com/9781484212345).

This was an overview of the program generated from the recording of the transaction code XK01— create vendor. The next step is to carry out modifications to a copy of the generated program.

## Perform Modifications to a Copy of the Generated Program

On the opening screen of the ABAP editor, we made a copy of the generated program YCH05_XK01_ PROGRAM_GENERATED into YCH05_XK01_PROGRAM_BATCH_INPUT. After copying, we activated the program text elements. We have resorted to carrying out modifications to a copy of the generated program instead of the generated program as a procedure.

Detailed descriptions of modifications to the program YCH05_XK01_PROGRAM_BATCH_INPUT follow.

## Declare Two Internal Tables to Receive Data from Text Files

We located the data declaration statements at the very beginning, following the REPORT statement. The program lines to declare two internal tables which will receive data from the text files residing on the presentation server with the requisite structures are as follows:

```
DATA: BEGIN OF MAIN_STRU,
        LIFNR     TYPE LIFNR,
        NAME1     TYPE NAME1_GP,
        STRAS     TYPE STRAS_GP,
        ORTO1     TYPE ORTO1_GP,
        PSTLZ     TYPE PSTLZ,
      END OF MAIN_STRU,

      BEGIN OF BANK_STRU,
        LIFNR     TYPE LIFNR,
        BANKS     TYPE BANKS,
        BANKL     TYPE BANKL,
        BANKN     TYPE BANKN,
      END OF BANK_STRU,

      MAIN_TAB  LIKE STANDARD TABLE OF MAIN_STRU,
  BANK_TAB  LIKE STANDARD TABLE OF BANK_STRU,

    MAIN_FL   TYPE IBIPPARMS-PATH, "F4-select file from
                                   "presentation server
    BANK_FL   TYPE IBIPPARMS-PATH.
```

When a user presses function key F4 on the text file PARAMETERS statement and makes a file selection, the function module F4_FILENAME returns the selected file name as ABAP dictionary type IBIPPARMS-PATH. Hence the declarations MAIN_FL and BANK_FL.

## SELECTION-SCREEN Statements (with F4 Facility) to Input Text File Names

We located the SELECTION-SCREEN statements following the data declaration statements. The program lines to input text file names with facility to make file selections using function key F4 are as follows:

```
PARAMETERS: MFILE TYPE STRING,
            BFILE TYPE STRING.

************************************************
AT SELECTION-SCREEN ON VALUE-REQUEST FOR MFILE.

CALL FUNCTION 'F4_FILENAME'
  IMPORTING
    FILE_NAME            = MAIN_FL.
```

```
MFILE = MAIN_FL.

***********************************************
AT SELECTION-SCREEN ON VALUE-REQUEST FOR BFILE.

CALL FUNCTION 'F4_FILENAME'
 IMPORTING
   FILE_NAME            = BANK_FL.

BFILE = BANK_FL.
```

The event AT SELECTION-SCREEN ON VALUE-REQUEST was triggered for both MFILE and BFILE. In the event AT SELECTION-SCREEN ON VALUE-REQUEST, we invoked the function module F4_FILENAME to enable the end user to make a file selection from the presentation server with function key F4.

The assignments MFILE = MAIN_FL and BFILE = BANK_FL are because the function module F4_FILENAME accepts the export parameter FILE_NAME as ABAP dictionary type IBIPPARMS-PATH and the function module GUI_UPLOAD accepts the import parameter FILENAME as the elementary type STRING.

We created selection texts for PARAMETERS variables MFILE and BFILE as follows:

- Text File: Main

- Text File: Bank

## Transfer Data from Text Files into Internal Tables

We located the statements to transfer data from text files to internal tables following the START-OF-SELECTION statement. The program lines to transfer data from text files to internal tables and no data alert are as follows:

```
*****************************************************************
CALL FUNCTION 'GUI_UPLOAD'
  EXPORTING
    FILENAME                   = MFILE
  TABLES
    DATA_TAB                   = MAIN_TAB.

CALL FUNCTION 'GUI_UPLOAD'
  EXPORTING
    FILENAME                   = BFILE
  TABLES
    DATA_TAB                   = BANK_TAB.

IF LINES( MAIN_TAB ) = 0.
 MESSAGE S001(YCH02_MCLASS) DISPLAY LIKE 'E'. "No Data Retrieved
 EXIT.
ENDIF.
```

## Set Up Loops to Fetch Data from the Internal Tables, Pass Data, etc.

We will set up two loops—the main loop and the bank loop. The bank loop will be nested under the main loop. The bank loop will operate with a condition—WHERE LIFNR = MAIN_STRU-LIFNR. That is, fetch only rows from the BANK_TAB belonging to the vendor fetched in the main loop.

The main loop statement is to be located following the statement PERFORM OPEN_GROUP. The main loop ending statement must precede the last program statement PERFORM CLOSE_GROUP.

The main loop structure should look as follows:

```
perform open_group.
LOOP AT MAIN_TAB INTO MAIN_STRU. "main loop
......
.....
ENDLOOP.
perform close_group.
```

In the copy of the generated program we are modifying, the subroutine BDC_FIELD is invoked by passing both the parameters FNAM (field name) and FVAL (field value) as literals.

The values for the following fields are originating from the internal table-main:

```
LIFNR
NAME1
STRAS
ORT01
PSTLZ
```

Also, we are deriving the value of field SORTL by assigning it the first word from the field NAME1. The derivation of value for SORTL from the value of NAME1 involved declaration of data items like the following:

```
DATA: .....
.....
      SORTL   TYPE STRING,
      GSTRING TYPE STRING.
```

We need to modify the statements which pass values for these fields through the FVAL parameters from literals to variables when invoking the subroutine BDC_FIELD. The modified lines which pass the field values as variables (MAIN_STRU-NAME1, SORTL, MAIN_STRU-STRAS, etc.) are listed.

```
perform bdc_field        using 'LFA1-NAME1'
                               MAIN_STRU-NAME1. "'OBELIX AND COMPANY'.

SPLIT MAIN_STRU-NAME1 AT ' ' INTO SORTL GSTRING.

perform bdc_field        using 'LFA1-SORTL'
                               SORTL. "'OBELIX'.
perform bdc_field        using 'LFA1-STRAS'
                               MAIN_STRU-STRAS. "'456, M.G. ROAD'.
perform bdc_field        using 'LFA1-ORT01'
                               MAIN_STRU-ORT01. "'NEW DELHI'.
perform bdc_field        using 'LFA1-PSTLZ'
                               MAIN_STRU-PSTLZ. "'110102'.
```

The original literal values in the statements have been retained as side comments to make changes apparent.

We need to set up the inner nested loop for passing the bank data of a vendor. A vendor can have nil or n number of banks. The index of the bank data variables BANKS, BANKL, and BANKN has to be a variable instead of a literal. In the lines of the generated program, when invoking the subroutine BDC_FIELD, the parameter FNAM is passed as a literal like 'LFBK-BANKS(01)'. We will construct this string—concatenate, etc.—at runtime and assign it to a string variable. We will then pass this string variable as the FNAM parameter when invoking the subroutine BDC_FIELD for the bank variables.

We need to declare a variable which can be operated as an index for the bank variables. We have declared the variable INDX to be operated as index. We declared it as type N so it can used in a concatenate statement directly. We have specified its length as two—can support a maximum of 99 banks for a vendor.

```
DATA: .....
      .....
      INDX(2)   TYPE N. "bank data index
```

We located the nested loop statement: LOOP AT BANK_TAB INTO BANK_STRU WHERE LIFNR = MAIN_STRU-LIFNR just before the statement PERFORM BDC_FIELD USING 'LFBK-BANKS(01)'.....The initial positioning of cursor on the first field, first row should not be part of looping process.

The ENDLOOP statement was located after the statements relating to last reference to the screen number 0130 as you can see in the forthcoming program lines.

Before the nested loop commences, we initialized the index variable INDX, INDX = 0. Immediately after the commencement of the nested loop we are incrementing the index variable INDX: INDX = INDX + 1.

1. We are concatenating 'LFBK-BANKS(' INDX ')' INTO GSTRING. We are passing the variable GSTRING as the FNAM parameter when invoking the subroutine BDC_FIELD.

2. We are passing the BANK_STRU-BANKS as the FVAL parameter when invoking the subroutine BDC_FIELD.

Steps (1) and (2) were performed for the variable BANKS. Steps (1) and (2) were repeated for variables BANKL and BANKN.

The modified program lines relating to the nested loop are as follows:

```
INDX = 0.

LOOP AT BANK_TAB INTO BANK_STRU WHERE
                LIFNR = MAIN_STRU-LIFNR. "inner bank loop
INDX = INDX + 1.

CONCATENATE 'LFBK-BANKS(' INDX ')' INTO GSTRING.
perform bdc_field      using GSTRING "'LFBK-BANKS(01)'
                             BANK_STRU-BANKS. "'US'.

CONCATENATE 'LFBK-BANKL(' INDX ')' INTO GSTRING.
perform bdc_field      using GSTRING "'LFBK-BANKL(01)'
                             BANK_STRU-BANKL. "'123123123'.

CONCATENATE 'LFBK-BANKN(' INDX ')' INTO GSTRING.
perform bdc_field      using GSTRING "'LFBK-BANKN(01)'
                             BANK_STRU-BANKN. "'1234567'.
```

```
perform bdc_dynpro      using 'SAPMF02K' '0130'.
perform bdc_field       using 'BDC_CURSOR'
                              'LFBK-BANKS(01)'.
perform bdc_field       using 'BDC_OKCODE'
                              '=ENTR'.
ENDLOOP.
```

The original literal values in the statements have been retained as side comments to make changes apparent.

This was the incorporation of nested loop modifications to pass the parameters FNAM and FVAL as variables in the nested loop. This was all that was needed to enable the creation of bank data for a vendor. This also concludes modifications to the program YCH05_XK01_PROGRAM_BATCH_INPUT.

The complete source lines of program YCH05_XK01_PROGRAM_BATCH_INPUT are available in the E-resource file for this book (www.apress.com/9781484212345).

## Syntax Check and Program Activation

We performed a syntax check and activated the program YCH05_XK01_PROGRAM_BATCH_INPUT. The program YCH05_XK01_PROGRAM_BATCH_INPUT is ready for execution.

## Prepare Text Data Files

As I mentioned earlier, we will migrate only representative vendor data to demonstrate the working of data migration tools and facilities available in the SAP environment. We are locating the migrating source data, the text files, on the presentation server. We are operating in the Microsoft windows operating system. We created a separate folder TEMP on drive D (D:\TEMP) of our presentation server. You can also locate the text files in a separate folder on the presentation server. There will be two text files, the first text file containing the main data of fields listed in Table 5-4 and the second text file containing the bank data of fields listed in Table 5-5. The data in the two text files are linked by the vendor number or code.

We have adopted free-flowing text layout for our text files; that is, there will be no field separators, no field names, etc. Each line in the text file will represent one row.

For the first text file containing the main data, the layout will be as shown in Table 5-6.

***Table 5-6.*** *Layout of Text File—Main Data*

| Srl. No. | Character Positions | Field Description | Field Name |
|----------|---------------------|-------------------|------------|
| 1 | First 10 characters | Vendor Number or Code | LIFNR |
| 2 | Next 35 characters | Vendor Name | NAME1 |
| 3 | Next 35 characters | Street | STRAS |
| 4 | Next 35 characters | City | ORT01 |
| 5 | Last 10 characters | Postal Code | PSTLZ |

For the second text file containing the bank data, the layout will be as shown in Table 5-7.

***Table 5-7.*** *Layout of Text File—Bank Data*

| Srl. No. | Character Positions | Field Description | Field Name |
|---|---|---|---|
| 1 | First 10 characters | Vendor Number or Code | LIFNR |
| 2 | Next 3 characters | Country Key | BANKS |
| 3 | Next 15 characters | Bank Key | BANKL |
| 4 | Last 18 characters | Bank Account | BANKN |

If the data in a field has fewer characters than the allotted characters, the extra characters must appear as trailing blanks. Like, for example, the field city is allotted 35 characters. Suppose, for a vendor, city data is only 10 characters. Then the city data in this context must be entered with 25 trailing blanks—blanks on the right.

We have taken care to declare the internal table structures in the program to correspond exactly with these layouts. The data from these two text files will be loaded into two internal tables using the function module GUI_UPLOAD.

We are using the 902XX series for the migration of vendors.

Using notepad editor, we created main data for three vendors: 0000090201, 0000090202, and 0000090203, shown in Figure 5-24.

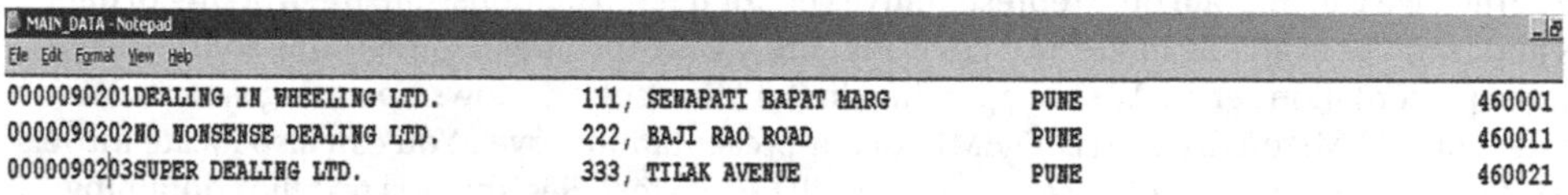


```
0000090201DEALING IN WHEELING LTD.      111, SENAPATI BAPAT MARG      PUNE      460001
0000090202NO NONSENSE DEALING LTD.      222, BAJI RAO ROAD            PUNE      460011
0000090203SUPER DEALING LTD.            333, TILAK AVENUE             PUNE      460021
```

***Figure 5-24.*** *Vendors Main Data—text file*

Entering the leading zeroes for vendor number in the text files is not necessary; the ALPHA routine inserts leading zeroes automatically. We are following, all through this book, the convention of specifying the leading zeroes in our text files.

In a like manner, we created bank data for two vendors: 0000090202 and 0000090203. We created one bank for the vendor 0000090202 and two banks for vendor 0000090203. Vendor 0000090201 has no bank data. In effect, we are testing three cases: a vendor with no bank data, a vendor with one bank, and a vendor with more than one bank but not more than the number of visible rows in the table control area. The case of testing the number of banks for a vendor greater than the number of visible rows in the table control area is being deferred for now. Figure 5-25 shows the bank data in the text file.

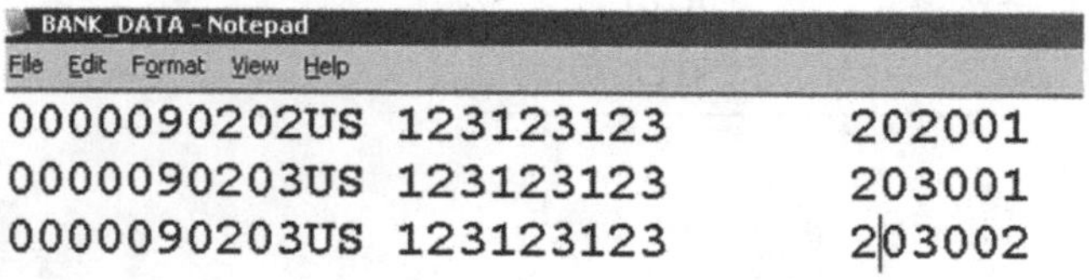


```
0000090202US 123123123      202001
0000090203US 123123123      203001
0000090203US 123123123      203002
```

***Figure 5-25.*** *Vendors Bank Data—text file*

Recall that the combination of the values of country key (US) and bank key (123123123) must exist in the bank master. Before using a combination, you should check for its existence in the bank master. If you are using IDES server and logged into client 800, we recommend you use the same combination of country key and bank key we have used here. The bank key value 123123123 is easy to remember.

We have used the same value of country key and bank key in our bank data. This is to make matters simple in our present context of emphasizing demonstrativeness. The bank data for vendors resides in the database table LFBK. The primary key of this database table is client, country key (BANKS), bank key (BANKL), and bank account (BANKN). In our bank data we used the same values for the two fields BANKS and BANKL and varied only the value of the last field BANKN.

In real-life scenarios, text data is not prepared in the manner we have done so in the present hands-on exercise.

This completes the preparation of input text files residing on the presentation server.

## Run the Program with the *Batch Input* Option (Default) for Creation of a Batch Input Session

Now that we have modified a copy of the generated program from recording as per laid-down specifications and created the input text files on the presentation server, we are ready to run and test the program YCH05_XK01_PROGRAM_BATCH_INPUT.

One of the pitfalls which could occur is that the data in the text files is skewed or misaligned—the trailing blanks are fewer or more than required in field(s). Another of the pitfalls could be that the structure of internal tables receiving data from text files is not properly declared. To detect the occurrences of such fallacies, if any, we can set a dynamic break point just after the internal tables receiving data from the text files are loaded, and view the data of internal tables in the debugger.

We navigated to the opening screen of transaction code SE38 and entered the program name as YCH05_XK01_PROGRAM_BATCH_INPUT. We clicked the *Change* button. We set a dynamic breakpoint on the statement PERFORM OPEN_GROUP, just after the internal tables are loaded from text files. After setting the breakpoint, we clicked the execute button. A selection screen as shown in Figure 5-26 appeared.

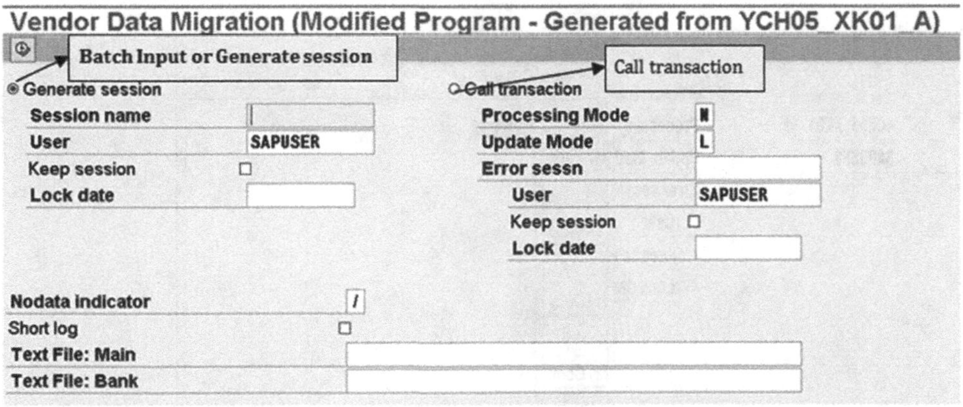

*Figure 5-26.* *Program YCH05_XK01_PROGRAM_BATCH_INPUT—selection screen*

The same program can be run using either *the batch input/Generate session* method or the *call transaction* method. If you enable left-side Radio buttons at the top, the *batch input/Generate session* method will be used. If you enable right-side Radio buttons at the top, the *call transaction* method will be used. This is indicated in Figure 5-26. Our present hands-on exercise pertains to migrating vendor data using the *batch input/Generate session* method and so we will execute this present program using only the *batch input/Generate session* method.

For now, we will elaborate on the items under *Generate session* on the selection screen. The items under *call transaction* on the selection screen will be elaborated upon when we perform the next hands-on exercise. In the next hands-on exercise, vendor data migration will be performed the using the *call transaction* method.

In the *Session name*, we have to enter the name of the session and maximum length of 12 characters; it need not start with letter Y or Z. There can be multiple sessions of the same name, since a session's uniqueness is through its name, date, and time of its creation. We entered the session name as YCH05_XK01.

We have to enter the user name. The user name entered here will have authorization to run the created session. The system proposes the logged user as a default.

If a batch session runs successfully without any errors, the batch session by default gets deleted automatically. If a batch session runs encountering errors, the batch session is retained. If a batch session runs successfully without any errors, and you want the batch session to be retained, you can enable the check box *Keep session*. If you want the batch session to be run beyond a specific date, you can enter the date in the *Lock date*. The session will remain locked until the date entered in the *Lock date*. We are not retaining the session; hence we did not enable the check bo: *Keep session*. We do not want to lock the session either, so we are leaving the *Lock date* blank.

The system uses by default the no data indicator '/' for fields with no data.

When you run a session, by default, an elaborate log is created. If you desire a short log, you can enable the check box *Short log*.

The inputs prompts described until now, as well as the input prompts under *Call transaction*, are through the selection screen statements in the include program BDCRECX1. Our own selection screen statements are for input of text file names located on the presentation server.

To select *Text File: Main*, we pressed the function key F4. A dialog box to select a file from the presentation server popped up. We navigated to presentation folder D:\TEMP as shown in Figure 5-27.

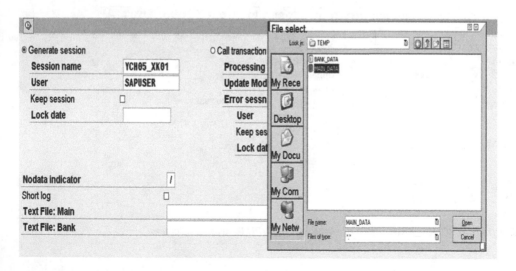

**Figure 5-27.** *Dialog box to select a file from presentation Server*

We selected the file MAIN_DATA. In a similar manner, we selected the file BANK_DATA. Figure 5-28 shows the screen with all the input values.

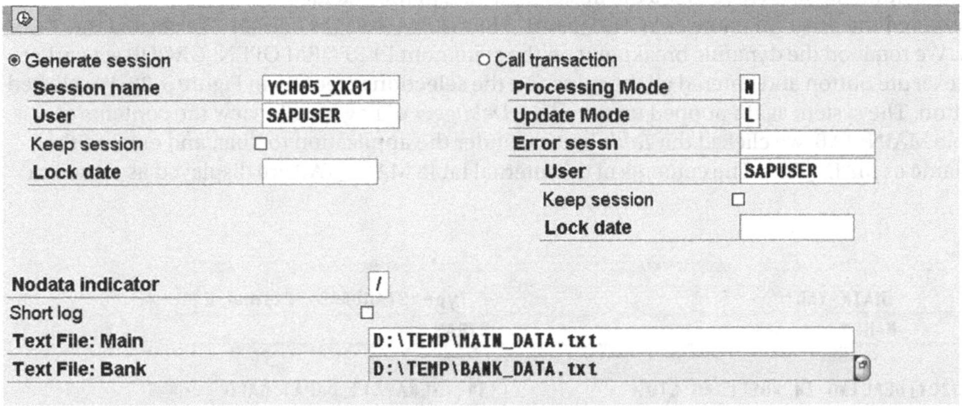

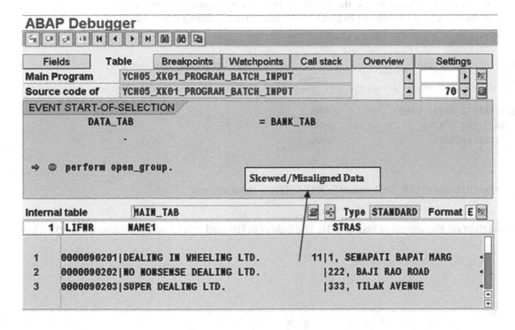

**Figure 5-28.** *Program YCH05_XK01_PROGRAM_BATCH_INPUT—inputs*

We clicked the execute button. The system popped up the *ABAP Debugger* dialog box just before the execution of the statement PERFORM OPEN_GROUP. We will view the contents of the internal table MAIN_TAB. So we clicked the *Table* button, under the application toolbar, and entered the *internal table* name as MAIN_TAB. The contents of the internal table MAIN_TAB were displayed as shown in Figure 5-29.

**Figure 5-29.** *Contents of Internal Table MAIN_TAB—data misaligned*

We had deliberately entered two fewer trailing blanks in the vendor name for the first vendor 0000090201 to demonstrate the occurrence of misaligned data as marked in Figure 5-29.

It is no use executing the program further. So we exited the program by entering /NSE38 (transaction code SE38) in the command box. We rectified the misaligned data in the text file.

We again entered the program name as YCH05_XK01_PROGRAM_BATCH_INPUT. We clicked the *Change* button. We retained the dynamic breakpoint on the statement PERFORM OPEN_GROUP set earlier. We clicked the execute button and entered all the values on the selection screen as in Figure 5-28. We clicked the execute button. The system again popped up the *ABAP Debugger* dialog box. To view the contents of the internal table MAIN_TAB, we clicked the *Table* button, under the application toolbar, and entered the *internal table* name as MAIN_TAB. The contents of the internal table MAIN_TAB are displayed as shown in Figure 5-30.

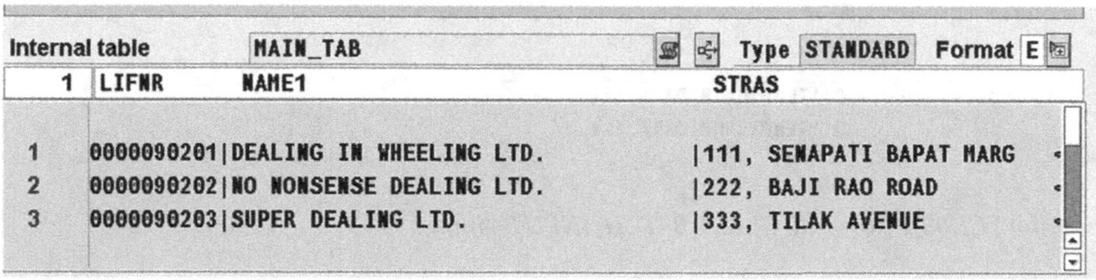

| Internal table | MAIN_TAB | | | Type STANDARD | Format E |
|---|---|---|---|---|---|
| 1 | LIFNR | NAME1 | | STRAS | |
| 1 | 0000090201 | DEALING IN WHEELING LTD. | | \|111, SENAPATI BAPAT MARG | |
| 2 | 0000090202 | NO NONSENSE DEALING LTD. | | \|222, BAJI RAO ROAD | |
| 3 | 0000090203 | SUPER DEALING LTD. | | \|333, TILAK AVENUE | |

*Figure 5-30.* *Internal table MAIN_TAB, fields: LIFNR NAME1 STRAS—data aligned*

The data for three fields LIFNR, NAME1, and STRAS is aligned and okay. To view the data of the two other fields ORT01 and PSTLZ, you can use the scroll buttons on the application tool bar. ◄ ◄ ► ► We scrolled right and the screen was as shown in Figure 5-31, displaying fields STRAS and ORT01.

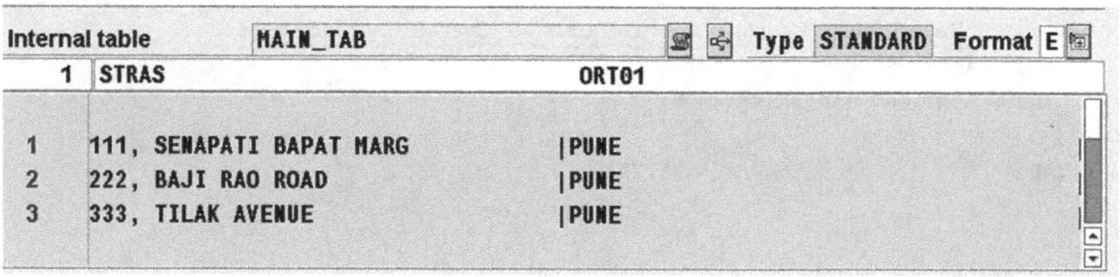

| Internal table | MAIN_TAB | | Type STANDARD | Format E |
|---|---|---|---|---|
| 1 | STRAS | ORT01 | | |
| 1 | 111, SENAPATI BAPAT MARG | \|PUNE | | |
| 2 | 222, BAJI RAO ROAD | \|PUNE | | |
| 3 | 333, TILAK AVENUE | \|PUNE | | |

*Figure 5-31.* *Internal table MAIN_TAB, fields: STRAS ORT01—data aligned*

We scrolled right on the screen of Figure 5-31. The fields ORT01 and PSTLZ were displayed as shown in Figure 5-32.

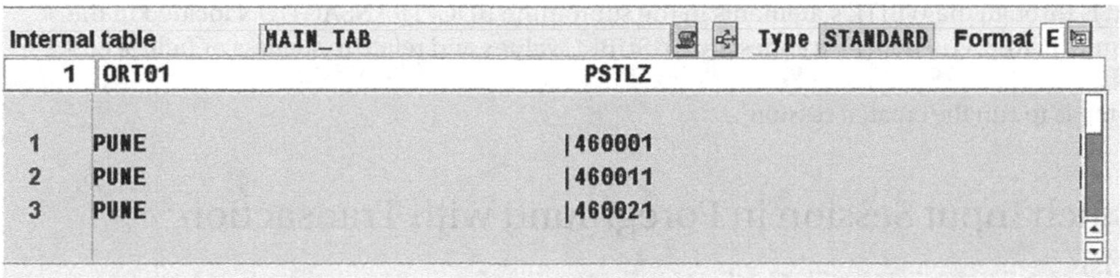

| Internal table | MAIN_TAB | | | Type STANDARD Format E |
|---|---|---|---|---|
| 1 | ORT01 | | PSTLZ | |
| 1 | PUNE | | \|460001 | |
| 2 | PUNE | | \|460011 | |
| 3 | PUNE | | \|460021 | |

*Figure 5-32. Internal table MAIN_TAB, Fields: ORT01 PSTLZ—data aligned*

The data in the internal table MAIN_TAB is okay.

To view the data of the internal table BANK_TAB, we entered in the *internal table* BANK_TAB. Figure 5-33 shows the contents of the internal table BANK_TAB:

| Internal table | BANK_TAB | | | Type STANDARD Format E |
|---|---|---|---|---|
| 1 | LIFNR | BANKS BANKL | BANKN | |
| 1 | 0000090202\|US | \|123123123 | \|202001 | |
| 2 | 0000090203\|US | \|123123123 | \|203001 | |
| 3 | 0000090203\|US | \|123123123 | \|203002 | |

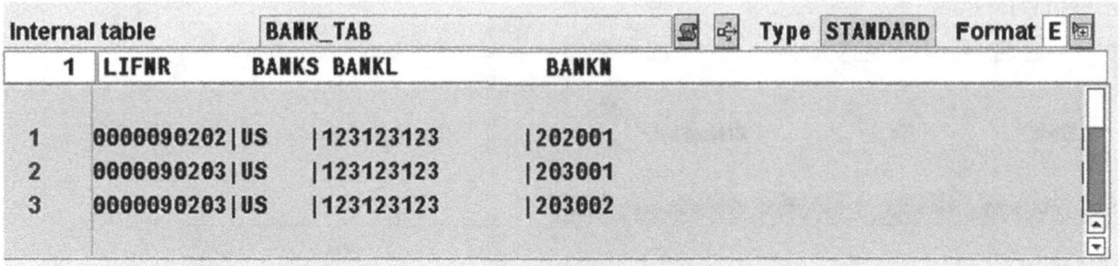

*Figure 5-33. Internal table BANK_TAB, Fields: BANKS BANKL BANKN—data aligned*

The data in the internal table BANK_TAB is okay. So we clicked the *Run* button on the *ABAP Debugger* dialog box. You can alternatively press function key F8.

It is a good practice to run the program in debugging mode, when you are executing a newly created data migration program for the very first time. Any mistakes committed in input data preparation and data declarations to receive input data can be detected and rectified.

The data is inserted into the queue database tables. The validation of data does not occur when data is inserted into the queue database tables and a session is created. The validation of data occurs only when the session is run and data is transferred from the queue database tables into the functional module database tables.

An output as shown in Figure 5-34 appeared.

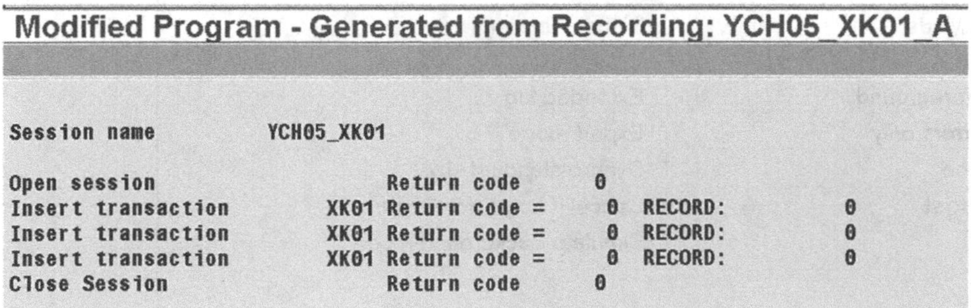

### Modified Program - Generated from Recording: YCH05_XK01_A

```
Session name          YCH05_XK01

Open session                   Return code      0
Insert transaction      XK01 Return code =      0   RECORD:          0
Insert transaction      XK01 Return code =      0   RECORD:          0
Insert transaction      XK01 Return code =      0   RECORD:          0
Close Session                  Return code      0
```

*Figure 5-34. Output—Execution of program YCH05_XK01_PROGRAM_BATCH_INPUT*

The output is through the WRITE statements in the subroutine BDC_TRANSACTION located in the include program BDCRECX1. The return codes are SY-SUBRC values and relate to success or failure of session creation.

The next step is to run the created session.

## Run the Batch Input Session in Foreground with Transaction Code SM35

To run the batch input session created in the previous step, we navigated to the *Batch Input Session Overview* screen using transaction code SM35. This is shown in Figure 5-35.

We filtered out session names starting with YCH05 by entering YCH05* in the field *Sess*. In our present context, there is only one session starting with YCH05. There is additional facility to view sessions by session status through the eight tabs: *New, Incorrect, Processed,* etc.

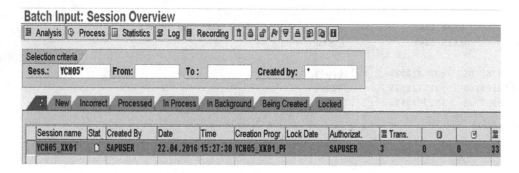

*Figure 5-35.* *Batch input session overview—session names starting with YCH05*

Session attributes like *Status, Created By, Date, Time,* etc., appear as different columns of the session. Our session has the *Status* as new (create icon).

You can also delete sessions.

To run a session, we selected the session through the row selector as shown in Figure 5-35; then we clicked the *Process* button on the application bar. Clicking the *Process* button popped up the *Process Session* dialog box as shown in Figure 5-36.

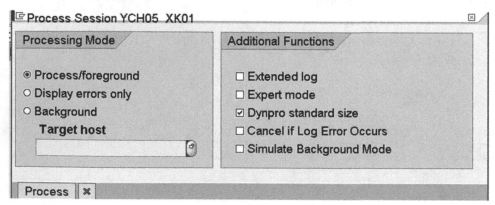

*Figure 5-36.* *Process Session YCH05_XK01*

The *Process Session* dialog box consists of the *Processing Mode* area on the left and the *Additional Functions* area on the right.

Under the *Processing Mode* area, three alternative options are available through Radio buttons.

- *Process/foreground.* When you run a session with this option, screens will appear as when you create a vendor manually. When we created a vendor manually, data was entered from the keyboard. When you run a session with *Process/foreground* option, the data passed as FVAL parameter to the subroutine BDC_FIELD will appear on the screen fields. You can edit this data. You will run a session with *Process/foreground* option mostly to test your program with small amount of data. We will run the session now initially with *Process/foreground* option. Subsequently, with another set of data, we will run the session with *Background* option.

- *Display errors only.* With this option, only error screens, if any, will be displayed. You can edit the data on the error screens.

- *Background.* With this option, the session will run in background. No screens will be displayed.

The *Target host* is to be entered if you want your session to be executed in background on specific application server. If we do not enter any value, the runtime system will select the next free system.

Under the *Additional Functions* area, the following options are available through check boxes:

- *Extended log.* This check box is to control the inclusion of message types I and S in the log, when you run a session using either of the first two Radio button options in the *Processing Mode* area: *Process/foreground* or *Display errors only*. If you enable this check box, all message types I are not written to the log and only the last of the message type S, if happens to be the last message, is written to the log.

- *Expert mode.* This is applicable only when you run a session using either of the first two Radio buttons options in the *Processing Mode* area: *Process/foreground* or *Display errors only*. If you enable this check box, you suppress the repeated appearance of the error message: 'Batch input data not available for this screen'.

- *Dynpro standard size.* Enabling the check box resets the screen to the standard size during batch input processing.

- Cancel *if Log Error Occurs.* Enabling the check box will halt the processing of the batch input session if an error occurs in a transaction.

- *Simulate Background Mode.* Some transactions behave differently in the background and in foreground. If you are running the session in the foreground and want the background behavior, you will enable this check box.

By default, the check box *Dynpro standard size* is enabled.

We executed the session in this step using the *Process/foreground* option. We clicked the *Process* button of the *Process Session* dialog box. The *Create Vendor: Initial Screen* (screen number 100) appeared with the data as shown in Figure 5-37.

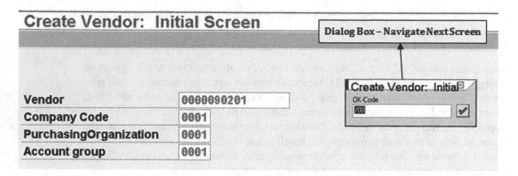

*Figure 5-37. Vendor 0000090201—Create Vendor: Initial Screen*

The data pertains to the first row of MAIN_TAB, vendor = 0000090201.

There is a dialog box marked as *Navigate—Next Screen* in Figure 5-37; this dialog box will appear on every screen to navigate to the next screen or next entity if any. The screens will appear in the same manner as when we created the vendor manually under the recording mode of transaction code XK01. The difference is that under the recording mode, we entered the data from the keyboard, whereas in the present situation, whatever FVAL values we passed to the subroutine BDC_FIELD are appearing on the screen fields.

Since the vendor creation screens are familiar, we are not incorporating screenshots of other screens except for screen number 130—*Payment transactions*. The bank data of vendors is entered on this screen. We want to demonstrate and display the *Payment transactions* for (a) a vendor with no banks, (b) a vendor with one bank, and (c) a vendor with more than one bank. Figure 5-38 shows the *Payment transactions* for vendor 0000090201.

---

**Create Vendor: Payment transactions**

| | | | | Create Vendor: Paym⊡ | | | | | |
|---|---|---|---|---|---|---|---|---|---|
| Vendor | 90201 | **DEALING IN WHEELING LTD.** | | OK-Code ◄ENTR | ✔ | | | | |

| Bank details | | | | | | | | |
|---|---|---|---|---|---|---|---|---|
| Ctry | Bank Key | Bank Account | Acct holder | | C | IBAN | BnkT | Rel |
| | | | | | | ⇨ | | |

*Figure 5-38. Vendor 0000090201—Create Vendor: Payment transactions*

We navigated to the last screen: *Partner functions*. When we clicked the button to navigate next, the dialog box *Last data screen reached* popped up, prompting us to save the data: yes/no, etc. We clicked the yes button. The data of vendor 0000090201 was saved.

Next, the *Create Vendor: Initial Screen* appeared for vendor 0090202 as shown in Figure 5-39.

Create Vendor: Initial Screen
Create Vendor: Initial
OK-Code
/00
Vendor
0000090202
Company Code
0001
PurchasingOrganization
0001
Account group
0001

*Figure 5-39.* *Vendor 0000090202—Create Vendor: Initial Screen*

We navigated to the *Payment transactions* screen, the bank data of vendor 0000090202. Vendor 0000090202 has one bank as shown in Figure 5-40.

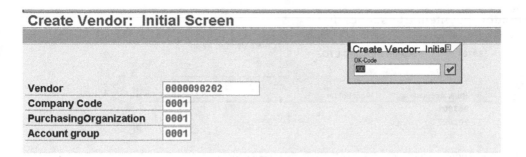

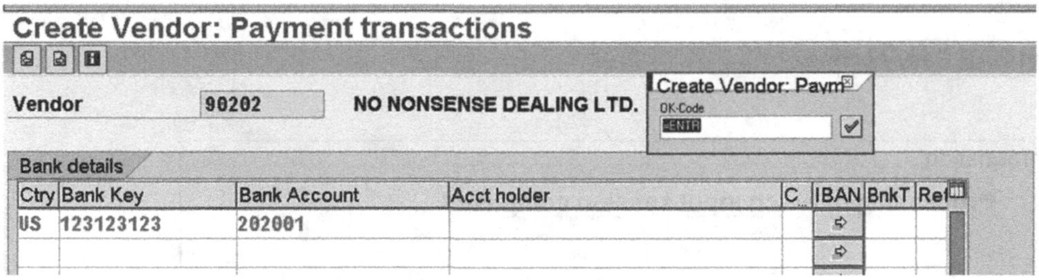

Create Vendor: Payment transactions
Vendor
90202
NO NONSENSE DEALING LTD.
Create Vendor: Paym
OK-Code
=ENTR
Bank details
Ctry
Bank Key
Bank Account
Acct holder
C
IBAN
BnkT
Ref
US
123123123
202001

*Figure 5-40.* *Vendor 0000090202—Create Vendor: Payment transactions*

We navigated to the last screen: *Partner functions.* We clicked the button to navigate next; the dialog box *Last data screen reached* popped up, prompting us to save the data: yes/no, etc. We clicked the yes button. The data of vendor 0000090202 was saved.

Next, the *Create Vendor: Initial Screen* appeared for vendor 0090203 as shown in Figure 5-41.

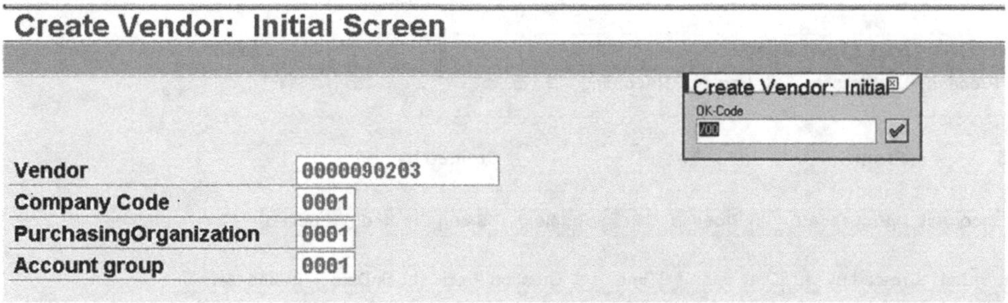

Create Vendor: Initial Screen
Create Vendor: Initial
OK-Code
/00
Vendor
0000090203
Company Code
0001
PurchasingOrganization
0001
Account group
0001

*Figure 5-41.* *Vendor 0000090203—Create Vendor: Initial Screen*

We navigated to the *Payment transactions* screen, the bank data of vendor 0000090203. Vendor 0000090203 has two banks as shown in Figure 5-42.

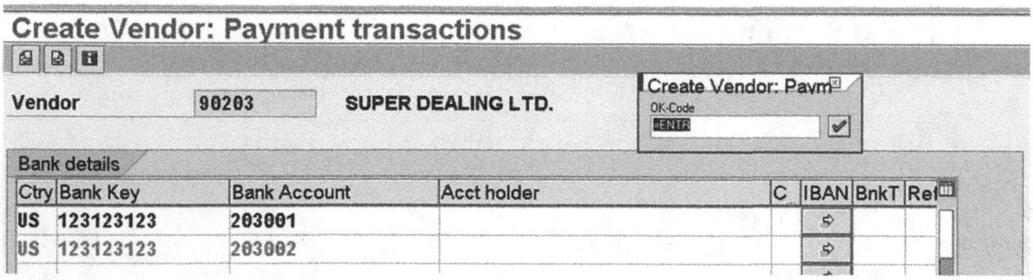

**Create Vendor: Payment transactions**

| Vendor | 90203 | SUPER DEALING LTD. |
|--------|-------|--------------------|

Create Vendor: Paym
OK-Code
+ENTR

**Bank details**

| Ctry | Bank Key | Bank Account | Acct holder | C | IBAN | BnkT | Ref |
|------|----------|--------------|-------------|---|------|------|-----|
| US | 123123123 | 203001 | | | ⇨ | | |
| US | 123123123 | 203002 | | | ⇨ | | |

*Figure 5-42.* *Vendor 0000090203—Create Vendor: Payment transactions*

We navigated to the last screen: *Partner functions*. We clicked the button to navigate next; the dialog box *Last data screen reached* popped up, prompting us to save the data: yes/no, etc. We clicked the yes button. The data of vendor 0000090202 was saved.

Next, the dialog box as shown in Figure 5-43 appeared.

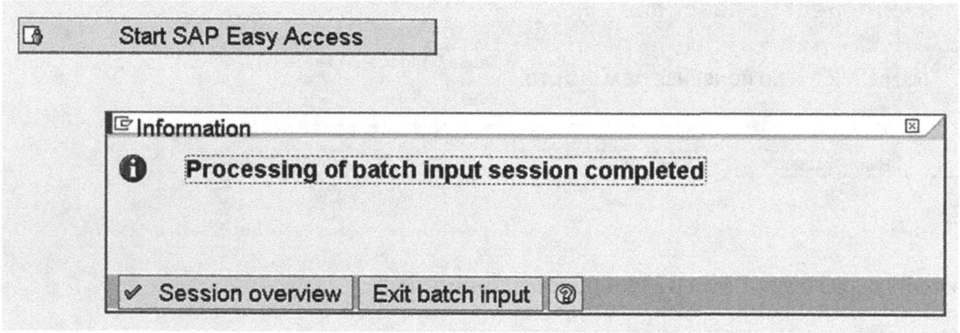

Start SAP Easy Access

**Information**

ℹ **Processing of batch input session completed**

✔ Session overview | Exit batch input | ⑦

*Figure 5-43.* *Processing of batch input session completed*

We clicked the *Session overview* button to get us back to the *Batch Input: Session Overview* screen as shown in Figure 5-44.

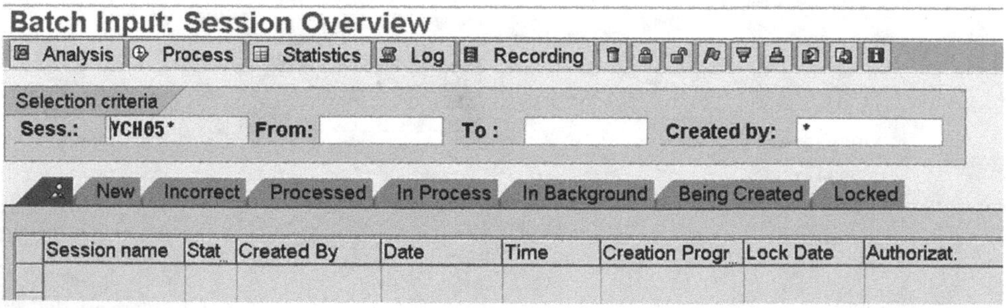

**Batch Input: Session Overview**

Analysis | Process | Statistics | Log | Recording

**Selection criteria**

| Sess.: | YCH05* | From: | | To : | | Created by: | * |
|--------|--------|-------|--|------|--|-------------|---|

| New | Incorrect | Processed | In Process | In Background | Being Created | Locked |
|-----|-----------|-----------|------------|---------------|---------------|--------|

| Session name | Stat | Created By | Date | Time | Creation Progr | Lock Date | Authorizat. |
|--------------|------|------------|------|------|----------------|-----------|-------------|

*Figure 5-44.* *Batch Input: Session Overview*

Since the session run was successful, without errors, the session was deleted by default as is apparent from Figure 5-44.

## Check and Verify Migration of Vendor Data—Transaction Code XK02 or XK03, etc.

A simple way to cross-verify that vendor data was migrated is to execute one of the transaction codes: XK02 or XK03—*Change Vendor* or *Display Vendor*. We executed, in the present instance, the transaction code XK02 - *Change Vendor*. On the opening screen of transaction code XK02; we pressed the function key F4 on the field *Vendor*. The filter dialog box which popped up was using the tab *Vendor by Company Code* as default. We entered the pattern 9020* in the field *Vendor*, the fifth field from the top. We clicked the Continue button. All the vendors starting with 9020 appeared in the list as shown in Figure 5-45.

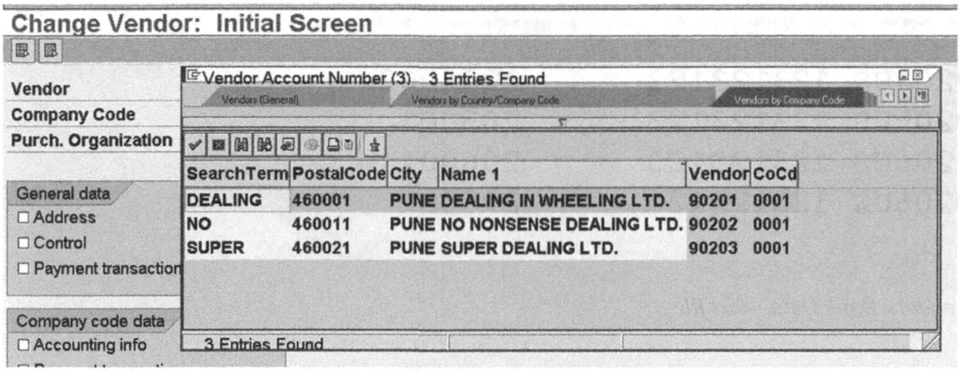

*Figure 5-45. Vendor List—Vendor Numbers with Pattern: 9020\**

Vendors 0000090201, 0000090202, and 0000090203 are appearing in the list of Figure 5-45. We selected each of the vendors in turn and navigated through all the screens for each of the vendors as to perform an individual field-wise cross-check of values.

This concludes the performance of steps 1 to 7 of the hands-on exercise.

## Prepare Text Files; Run Program with the *Batch Input* Option to Create a Session; Run Session in Background and Verify Migration of Data

We will prepare a new set of text data in the files on the presentation server main and bank. With the new set of data, we will run the program YCH05_XK01_PROGRAM_BATCH_INPUT using the *batch input* option to create a session. We will run the session in the background instead of the foreground as in the previous step. In real-life scenarios, for a substantial amount of data, sessions are always run in background. Sessions are run in the foreground for program testing purposes or for a small amount of erroneous data which can be corrected manually on the screens.

Using notepad editor, we created again a new set of main data for three vendors: 0000090204, 0000090205, and 0000090206, as shown in Figure 5-46.

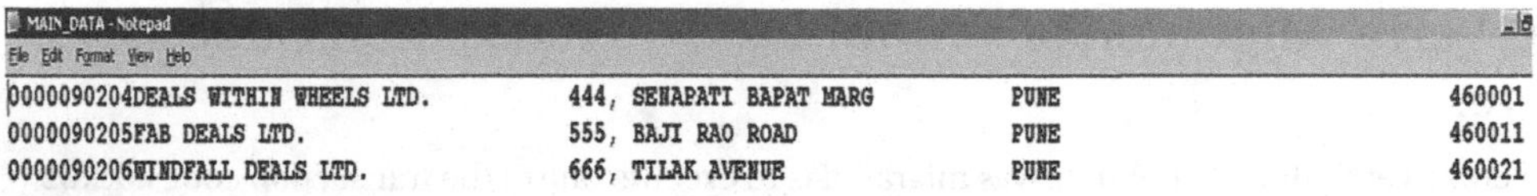
MAIN_DATA - Notepad
File Edit Format View Help
0000090204DEALS WITHIN WHEELS LTD. 444, SENAPATI BAPAT MARG PUNE 460001
0000090205FAB DEALS LTD. 555, BAJI RAO ROAD PUNE 460011
0000090206WINDFALL DEALS LTD. 666, TILAK AVENUE PUNE 460021

***Figure 5-46.*** *Vendors' Main Data—text file*

We created a new set of bank data for all three vendors: 0000090204, 0000090205, and 0000090206. Figure 5-47 shows the bank data in the text file.

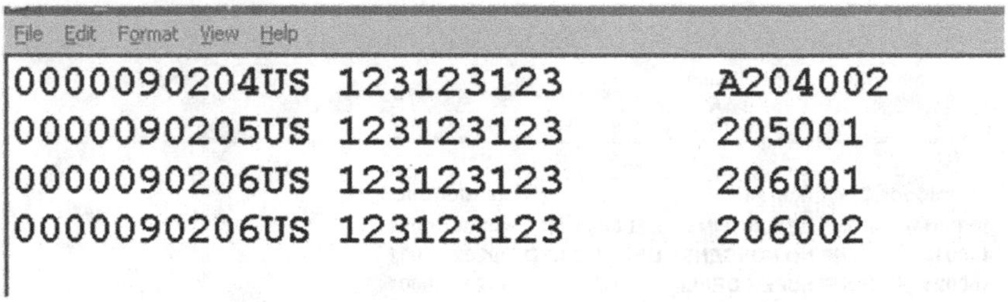
File Edit Format View Help
0000090204US 123123123 A204002
0000090205US 123123123 205001
0000090206US 123123123 206001
0000090206US 123123123 206002

***Figure 5-47.*** *Vendors' Bank Data—text file*

Vendor 0000090204 has an invalid bank account—A204002. The bank account cannot contain non-numeric data. This is deliberately created to demonstrate how erroneous data is handled.

After the text files were prepared, we executed the program YCH05_XK01_PROGRAM_BATCH_INPUT. Figure 5-48 shows the selection screen with values filled.

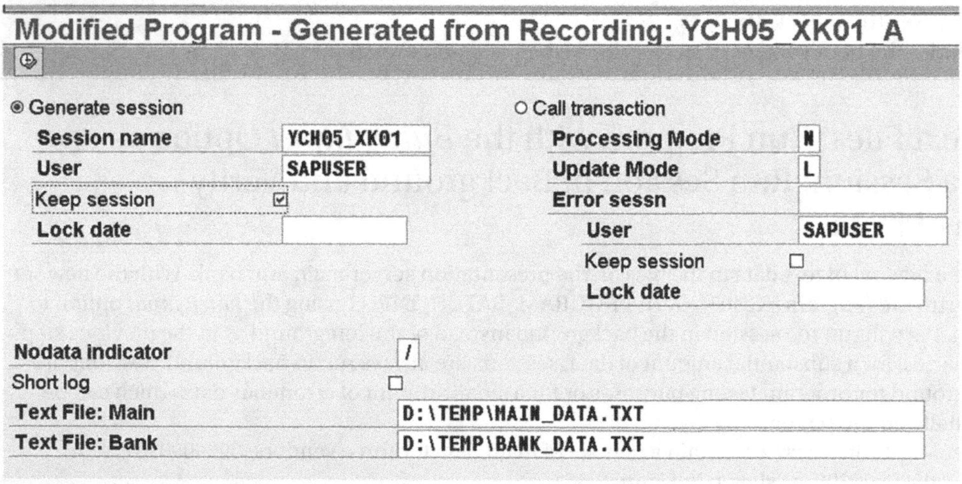
Modified Program - Generated from Recording: YCH05_XK01_A
Generate session
Session name YCH05_XK01
User SAPUSER
Keep session
Lock date
Call transaction
Processing Mode N
Update Mode L
Error sessn
User SAPUSER
Keep session
Lock date
Nodata indicator /
Short log
Text File: Main D:\TEMP\MAIN_DATA.TXT
Text File: Bank D:\TEMP\BANK_DATA.TXT

***Figure 5-48.*** *Program YCH05_XK01_PROGRAM_BATCH_INPUT—inputs*

We enabled the check box *Keep session*. Except for this, the inputs are the same as in the previous step. We clicked the execute button.

An output as shown in Figure 5-49 appeared.

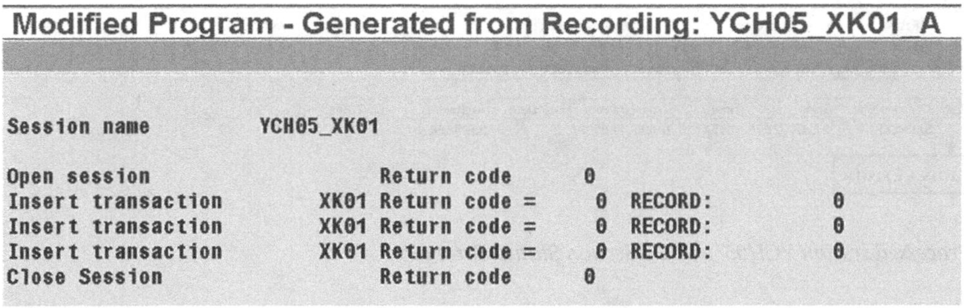

---

**Modified Program - Generated from Recording: YCH05_XK01_A**

```
Session name          YCH05_XK01

Open session                  Return code      0
Insert transaction    XK01 Return code =       0  RECORD:          0
Insert transaction    XK01 Return code =       0  RECORD:          0
Insert transaction    XK01 Return code =       0  RECORD:          0
Close Session                 Return code      0
```

---

*Figure 5-49. Output—execution of program YCH05_XK01_PROGRAM_BATCH_INPUT*

To run the batch input session created in the previous step, we navigated to the *Batch Input Session Overview* screen using transaction code SM35.

We filtered out session names starting with YCH05—in our present context, there is only one session starting with YCH05. To run the session, we selected the session through the row selector and then clicked the *Process* button on the application bar. Clicking the *Process* button popped up the *Process Session* dialog box as shown in Figure 5-50.

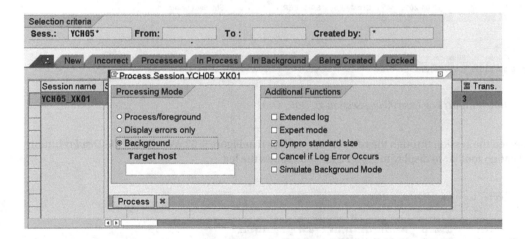

*Figure 5-50. Batch input session overview—process session YCH05_XK01*

On the *Process Session* dialog box, we clicked the *Background* option. We clicked the *Process* button of the *Process Session* dialog box.

It took some time for the session to run. You can refresh the *Batch Input: Session Overview* screen by pressing the <enter> key with the pattern YCH05* in the field: *Sess.*

Our session ended up with the status Errors as shown in Figure 5-51.

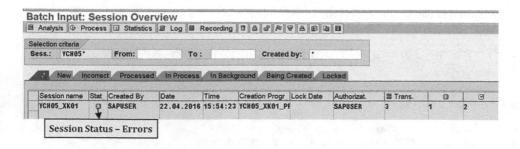

**Figure 5-51.** *Processed session YCH05_XK01—Session Status: Errors*

Sessions ending with errors are retained even though you might not have enabled the check box *Keep session* on the selection screen of Figure 5-48.

To determine the error(s) in the run session, we selected the error session through the row selector and clicked the *Log* button on the application toolbar. Clicking the *Log* button fetched the *Batch input: Log Overview* screen as shown in Figure 5-52.

### Batch Input: Log Overview

| | | | | | | | |
|---|---|---|---|---|---|---|---|
| Date | Time | Sess. name | Session status | User | Queue ID | | Appl. server |
| 22.04.2016 | 15:56:07 | YCH05_XK01 | Errors | SAPUSER | 16042215542328842455 | | sapserver |

**Log information**

Session QueueID 16042215542328842455   Sess.name: YCH05_XK01

Created on   22.04.2016   Created by SAPUSER   Standard selection

**Figure 5-52.** *Batch Input: Log Overview—Session YCH05_XK01*

We selected the session through the row selector as shown in Figure 5-52. We clicked the *Display* button on the application toolbar to display the log. Figure 5-53 shows the log.

### Batch Input Log for Session YCH05_XK01

**Log attributes**

Name  YCH05_XK01   Queue ID  16042215542328842455   User  SAPUSER

Created On  22.04.2016   TemSe ID  BDCLG232884245529146   ☐ Details

| Time | Message | Transacti | Ind | Modul | Scre | Ind | Type |
|---|---|---|---|---|---|---|---|
| 15:56:07 | Session YCH05_XK01 is being processed by user SAPUSER in mode N on server | 0 | | | 0 | | S |
| 15:56:08 | A numeric entry is expected in field Bank Acct. No. | XK01 | 1 | SAPHF02K | 0130 | 4 | E |
| 15:56:08 | Transaction error | XK01 | 1 | | 0 | | S |
| 15:56:08 | Vendor 0000090205 has been created for company code 0001 purchasing organ | XK01 | 2 | SAPHF02K | 0320 | 11 | S |
| 15:56:09 | Transaction was processed successfully | XK01 | 2 | | 0 | | S |
| 15:56:09 | Vendor 0000090206 has been created for company code 0001 purchasing organ | XK01 | 3 | SAPHF02K | 0320 | 12 | S |
| 15:56:09 | Transaction was processed successfully | XK01 | 3 | | 0 | | S |
| 15:56:09 | Processing statistics | | 0 | | 0 | | S |
| 15:56:09 | 3 transactions read | | 0 | | 0 | | S |
| 15:56:09 | 2 transactions processed | | 0 | | 0 | | S |
| 15:56:09 | 1 transactions with errors | | 0 | | 0 | | S |
| 15:56:09 | 0 transactions deleted | | 0 | | 0 | | S |

13 Messages read

**Figure 5-53.** *Batch Input: Log for Session YCH05_XK01*

The bank account (*Bank Acct. No.*) for the first vendor 0000090204 in the text file contained non-numeric data which is disallowed in the field BANKN. Vendor 0000090204 was not created because of the error in bank data. The next two vendors, 0000090205 and 0000090206, were created. The text in the log describes this elaborately and at the end summarizes the transactions read, transactions created, transactions with errors, etc.

To cross-verify whether the vendor data was migrated, we again executed transaction code XK02—*Change Vendor*. On the opening screen of transaction code XK02, we pressed the function key F4 on the field *Vendor*. The filter dialog box which popped up was using the tab *Vendor by Company Code* as default. We entered the pattern 9020* in the field *Vendor*, the fifth field from the top. We clicked the Continue button. All the vendors starting with the digits 9020 appeared in the list. A total of five vendors appeared in the list, three vendors created in the previous step and two vendors, 0000090205 and 0000090206, created in the current step. The list should appear as shown in Figure 5-54.

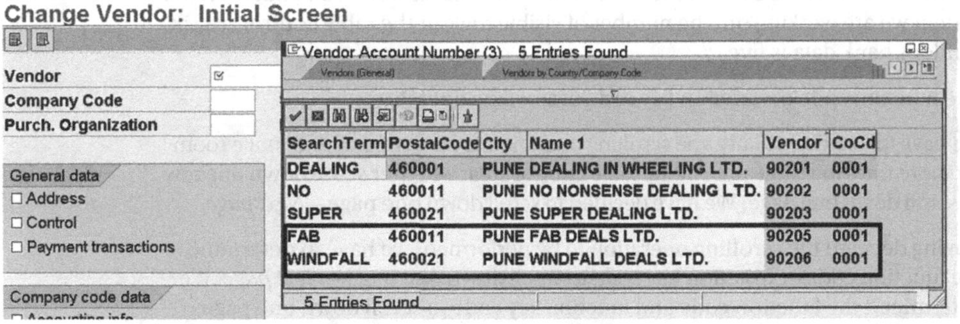

*Figure 5-54. Vendor list—Vendor numbers with pattern: 9020\**

We selected each of the vendors, 0000090205 and 0000090206, in turn and navigated through all the screens for each of these vendors to perform an individual field-wise cross-check of values.

Sessions are, for the most part, run in the background.

This concludes the process of creating a new set of data in text files, creating a session by running the program YCH05_XK01_PROGRAM_BATCH_INPUT, running the created session in background, examining the log of the run session, and finally cross-verifying the migrated data with transaction code XK02.

# Issue of Number of Rows Greater Than Visible Number of Rows in Table Control Area

The program YCH05_XK01_PROGRAM_BATCH_INPUT will perform successfully the migration of vendor data as long as the number of banks for a vendor is not greater than the number of visible rows in the table control area of the bank data. Recall from the dynpro programming concepts that the index of a variable in the table control area indicates the visible row number. When you attempt to insert a row with an index greater than the number of visible rows, an error will occur.

If you were creating bank data manually, in the recording mode or otherwise, you filled up the visible area with data and wanted to create more rows; you would scroll down either one row or a complete page to make room for new row(s) in the visible area of the table control. You will have to simulate the scrolling operation in the program: BDC_OKCODE being assigned the function code or function key code of scrolling operation.

For a scrolling operation to be simulated, you need to know the following:

1. The number of visible rows in the table control area:

   The number of visible rows in the table control area will depend, among other things, upon the dynpro or screen size.

   When recording the transaction XK01, on the *Create Recording* dialog box, in the *Recording parameters* area, we ensured that the check box *Default size* is enabled.

   When running the session, on the *Process Session* dialog box, in the *Additional Functions* area, we ensured that the check box *Dynpro standard size* is enabled.

   The objective was to make sure that we operated in the same screen size when recording and running a session—the standard size. You can visually determine the number of visible rows in the table control area of vendor's bank data. On the system we are working on, the number of visible rows in the table control area of vendor's bank data is five.

2. The function code or function key code of scrolling operation:

   We have to decide, initially, the scrolling operation to be performed to make room for more rows in visible area of the table control area: whether scroll down one row or scroll down one page. We have decided to scroll down one page—*Next page*.

   Having decided the scrolling operation to be performed, we have to determine the function code or function key code to scroll down one page—*Next page*. We determined the function code and function key code to scroll down one page through the screen technical information of the screen number 0130, dynpro program SAPMF02K.

   To determine the function code and function key code to scroll down one page, we performed a dummy recording for transaction XK01. The recording was a dummy in the sense that we did not save the data, did not save this recording or generated a program, etc. During the dummy recording of transaction XK01, while on the screen number 0130, that is the screen with table control of bank data, we positioned the cursor on any of the fields in the table control area, clicked function key F1, and then clicked the *Technical Information* button on the *Performance Assistant* dialog box. In the *GUI Data* area of the *Technical Information* dialog box, the *Status* was specified as 130V. We double-clicked the *Status* specified as 130V. In the *Status* 130V, we expanded the node *Function Keys*. From the expansion of the node *Function Keys*, we could determine the following:

   - Function key assignment for *Next page*: shift+F11

   - Function code for *Next page*: P+

Alternatively, you can determine the function code for *Next page* by creating banks more than the number of visible rows in the table control area during the dummy recording of transaction XK01. The recording will simulate the scrolling operation as you create banks more than the number of visible rows in the table control area. The function code for scrolling will appear in the recording. But you cannot determine the function key assignment from the recording.

Between the two methods of determining the function codes for scrolling, we recommend the first one: through the function key assignment in the *GUI status*.

We advise that you do not straight away adopt the values of visible rows in the table control area and the function code for scrolling mentioned here. You should visually examine on your system, the screen number

0130 to determine the visible rows in the table control area. You should perform the steps described in the preceding paragraphs to determine the function code and the function key assignment from the *GUI status* of screen number 0130. The function code and function key assignment depend on the operating system on which you are running the presentation server. We are running our presentation server under the windows operating system.

Now that we know the number of visible rows in the table control area of the vendor's bank data as well as function code and the function key assignment for *Next page*, we can proceed to incorporate ABAP code in the nested inner loop of our data migration program. This incorporation of ABAP code in the nested inner loop of our data migration program will enable the creation of banks for a vendor exceeding the number of visible rows in the table control area.

We copied the data migration program YCH05_XK01_PROGRAM_BATCH_INPUT to YCH05_XK01_PROGRAM_BI_TB_SC. We incorporated extra ABAP code in the nested inner loop of the copied program YCH05_XK01_PROGRAM_BI_TB_SC.

We incorporated the following ABAP code in the nested inner loop of the program YCH05_XK01_PROGRAM_BI_TB_SC:

```
CONCATENATE 'LFBK-BANKN(' INDX ')' INTO GSTRING.
perform bdc_field      using GSTRING "'LFBK-BANKN(01)'
                             BANK_STRU-BANKN. "'1234567'.

***** start of incorporated code *****
*************************************
IF INDX = ROWS_IN_TB. " no of rows visible in table control
  INDX = 0.            " reached, trigger next page scroll

  CONCATENATE 'LFBK-BANKN(' ROWS_IN_TB ')' INTO GSTRING.
  perform bdc_field      using 'BDC_CURSOR'
                               GSTRING. "'LFBK-BANKN(05)'.

  perform bdc_field      using 'BDC_OKCODE'
                               '/23'. " '=P+'. " P+ function
                               " code for next page

ENDIF.

***** end of incorporated code *****
*************************************
perform bdc_dynpro      using 'SAPMF02K' '0130'.

perform bdc_field      using 'BDC_CURSOR'
                             'LFBK-BANKS(01)'.
perform bdc_field      using 'BDC_OKCODE'
                             '=ENTR'.
ENDLOOP.

perform bdc_dynpro      using 'SAPMF02K' '0210'.
```

We commenced the extra incorporated code with the following comment line:

```
***** start of incorporated code *****
```

We concluded the extra incorporated code with the following comment line:

```
***** end of incorporated code *****
```

We included the program extra lines above and below the incorporated code as to clearly indicate the location of the incorporated code. The location of the incorporated code is significant for the scrolling to operate. We located the incorporated code between the following two ABAP statements:

```
perform bdc_field       using GSTRING "'LFBK-BANKN(01)'
                              BANK_STRU-BANKN. "'1234567'.

perform bdc_dynpro      using 'SAPMF02K' '0130'.
```

We arrived at the location of the incorporated code by trial and error.

We declared the data object ROWS_IN_TB as a constant with value 5—the number of rows in visible area of the table control on our system. You can alternatively make it a runtime input parameter variable. We are checking the value of INDX—current row number in the visible area. If the value of INDX is equal to ROWS_IN_TB, scroll *Next page* is being performed and current row number in the visible area INDX is being initialized. We are using the key combination shift+F11 to scroll *Next page*. The code for the key combination shift+F11 in the windows operating system is 23 ('/23'). We could have used the function code P+ ('=P+') to scroll *Next page*.

The program YCH05_XK01_PROGRAM_BI_TB_SC is available in the E-resource file for this book (www.apress.com/9781484212345).

We tested the program YCH05_XK01_PROGRAM_BI_TB_SC with data of vendors as follows:

- Vendor with 12 banks 2 scroll *Next page*

- Vendor with 7 banks 1 scroll *Next page*

- Vendor with 2 banks no scroll

- Vendor with 1 bank no scroll

- Vendor with no bank 723 no scroll

This test data is available as text files in the E-resource file for this book (www.apress.com/9781484212345). You can use this test data, but before you use it, ensure that the vendor codes in text file do not exist on your system.

We have covered the issue of the number of banks for vendors exceeding the number of visible rows in the table control area under a separate subheading. The technical aspects to this were considerable and so warranted a description under a separate subheading.

This concludes tackling the issue of the number of rows being greater than the visible number of rows in the table control area.

This also concludes the hands-on exercise of data migration using the *batch input* method.

# Recapitulation—Hands-on Exercise I: Migrate Vendor Data Using *Batch Input* Method

We specified the scope of the hands-on exercise as migrating vendor data using the *batch input* method.

The source data would reside on the presentation server. We decided to prepare representative vendor data—3/4 vendors. The main focus of the hands-on exercise is the deployment of SAP data migration tools.

We identified the fields that will be assigned values—all mandatory fields and a few non-mandatory fields.

We identified the fields that will be assigned constants; that is, all the vendors will share the same values for a field.

We identified the fields that will assume different values for each vendor. These fields will be assigned values from text files.

We identified a field that will derive its value from another field.

We determined that there will be two text files, one text file designated as containing main data and the second designated as containing bank data. The two text files were to be located on the presentation server.

A data flow diagram traced the flow of data when the data migration program would be run using the *batch input* method.

We prepared a task list listing the tasks to be carried out for the migration of data from the text files on presentation to the queue tables.

The first of the tasks involved the creation of a recording. Using transaction code SHDB, we created a recording of transaction code XK01—create vendor centrally. We saved the recording and generated an ABAP program from the recording of transaction code XK01.

The following modifications were carried out to the program generated from the recording:

- We declared two internal tables, main table and bank table, to be loaded with data from text files—main and bank. We declared the corresponding structures for the two internal tables. We declared other required variables.

- We coded selection screen statements to input text file names, with facility for the end user to make file selections from the presentation server.

- We used the function module GUI_UPLOAD to transfer data from the text files to the respective internal tables.

- We set up loops to fetch data from the internal tables into the structures. We set up the outer loop to fetch data from the main table and the nested loop to fetch data from the bank table.

- The appropriate data was passed from the table structure fields to the subroutine BDC_FIELD through the FVAL parameters. The bank variable names with their indexes were built as strings. The strings were passed to the subroutine BDC_FIELD through the FNAM parameters.

- One field SORTL was derived from the field NAME1. The requisite code was written to derive the field SORTL.

We performed a check on the modified program and activated it.

We prepared representative data of three vendors in the text files.

Initially, we executed the program in debugging mode. In the debugger, we checked the contents of the internal table to ascertain the correctness of the input data format, internal table structures declarations, etc.

After we ascertained the correctness of the input data format, internal table structures declarations, etc., we executed the program using the *batch input* option.

We createda session. Navigating to transaction code SM35, we ran the session in the foreground. All the screens appeared with the data which was passed on to the fields as FVAL parameter to the subroutine BDC_FIELD. Each of the vendors was saved.

We cross-verified the migration of data of three vendors using the transaction code XK02—change vendors.

We prepared new data of three vendors in the text files.

We executed the program using again the *batch input* option. The program used the newly created data.

We created a session. Navigating to transaction code SM35, we ran the created session in the background. The session was retained because there was erroneous input data for the first vendor. This was a deliberate action to create error status for a run session. We viewed and checked the log.

We cross-verified the migration of data of three vendors using transaction code XK02—change vendors.

We tackled the issue of the number of rows being greater than the visible number of rows in the table control area of bank data of a vendor.

# Hands-on Exercise II: Migrate Vendor Data Using *Call Transaction* Method

Hands-on exercise II will migrate the vendor data using the *call transaction* method. We can use the program from the previous hands-on exercise: YCH05_XK01_PROGRAM_BI_TB_SC. As I stated earlier, the program generated from a recording of a transaction supports two methods of data migration: the *batch input* and the *call transaction* methods.

We will be migrating vendor data using the *call transaction* method the same way we performed data migration using the *batch input* method. Only the 20 fields listed in Table 5-2 will assume values. The 11 fields listed in Table 5-3 will assume constant values—the same values for the field for all vendors. The data of the five fields listed in Table 5-4 will originate from the text file—main data. The data of the three fields listed in Table 5-5 will originate from the text file—bank data. The field SORTL was assigned the first word of the field NAME1 (vendor name).

We are planning to incorporate two extra features in this hands-on exercise, so will use a new program. We are making a copy of the earlier program YCH05_XK01_PROGRAM_BI_TB_SC (source) into YCH05_XK01_PROGRAM_CALL_TRAN (destination). After the copying process, we activated the text elements in the destination program.

## Extra Features in the Program

We are planning to incorporate the following two extra features in the program YCH05_XK01_PROGRAM_CALL_TRAN:

- Locate the text files on the application server. This will require that we use the ABAP statements OPEN DATASET, READ DATASET, and CLOSE DATASET to retrieve data from text files. In the previous hands-on exercise, with the text files located on the presentation server, we used the function module GUI_UPLOAD to retrieve and transfer data from the text files.

- Create a log as a text file on the application server. We plan to locate the ABAP statements for creation of the log file on the application server in a copy of the include program BDCRECX1. Since we cannot modify the include program BDCRECX1, we are making a copy of it into YCH05_BDCRECX1. We will incorporate ABAP statements for creation of the log file on the application server in the include program YCH05_BDCRECX1. In the main program YCH05_XK01_PROGRAM_CALL_TRAN, the statement INCLUDE BDCRECX1 will be replaced by the following statement: INCLUDE YCH05_BDCRECX1.

We will incorporate the two program features in two stages. In the first stage, we will incorporate the feature of locating the text files on the application server and test this incorporated feature. In the second stage, we will further incorporate the feature of creating a log file on the application server and test this incorporated feature.

# Migrate Data of Text Files on Application Server Using *Call Transaction* Method

A detailed description of the implementation of location of text files on the application server, migrating data from the text files using the *call transaction* method, follows.

## Locate Text Files on Application Server

To start with, we are detailing the process we are adopting to locate text files on the application server.

If you are working on an IDES server installed on a desktop or a laptop, as I am, all three components of the three-tier architecture—the database server, the application server, and the presentation server—reside on the same physical system/machine. So you have access to the text files residing on the application server at the operating system level. But we will pretend that we do not have access to the text files residing on the application server at the operating system level. We will access the text files residing on the application server from within the SAP system as a logged-in user. We will continue to create and maintain the text files on the presentation server. We will copy the text files created and maintained on the presentation server on to the application server from within the SAP system. To copy and view the text files on the application server, we will use the transaction code USS_FAS. The transaction code USS_FAS enables you to view the folders and files on the application server, copy files from presentation server to the application server, view contents of files on the application server, etc.

We created a new set of main and bank data on the presentation server.

Using notepad editor, we created the new set of main data for three vendors: 0000090207, 0000090208, and 0000090209. Figure 5-55 provides an illustration.

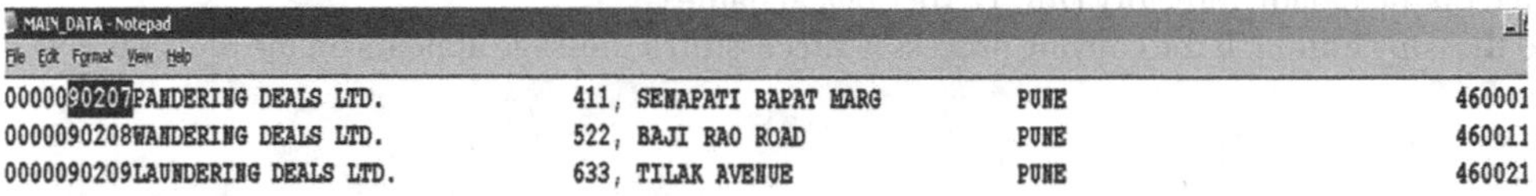

| MAIN_DATA - Notepad |
| File Edit Format View Help |
| 0000090207PANDERING DEALS LTD.    411, SENAPATI BAPAT MARG    PUNE    460001 |
| 0000090208WANDERING DEALS LTD.    522, BAJI RAO ROAD    PUNE    460011 |
| 0000090209LAUNDERING DEALS LTD.    633, TILAK AVENUE    PUNE    460021 |

***Figure 5-55.*** *Vendors' Main Data—text file*

We created a new set of bank data for all three vendors: 0000090207, 0000090208, and 0000090209. Figure 5-56 shows the bank data in the text file.

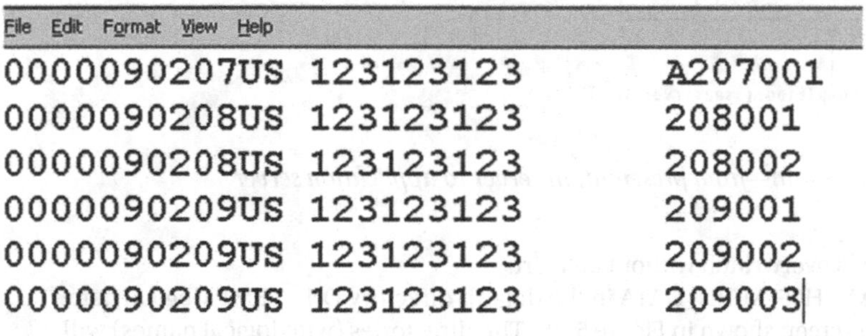

File Edit Format View Help
```
0000090207US 123123123      A207001
0000090208US 123123123      208001
0000090208US 123123123      208002
0000090209US 123123123      209001
0000090209US 123123123      209002
0000090209US 123123123      209003
```

***Figure 5-56.*** *Vendors' bank data—text file*

Vendor 0000090207 has an invalid bank account—A207001. As in the earlier hands-on exercise, this is deliberately created to demonstrate how erroneous data is handled.

To copy files from the presentation server to the application server from within the SAP system, we navigated to the opening screen of transaction code USS_FAS. We selected text file—main from the presentation server using the *Select* button and entered the file name on application server as YCH05_MAIN_DATA. Figure 5-57 illustrates.

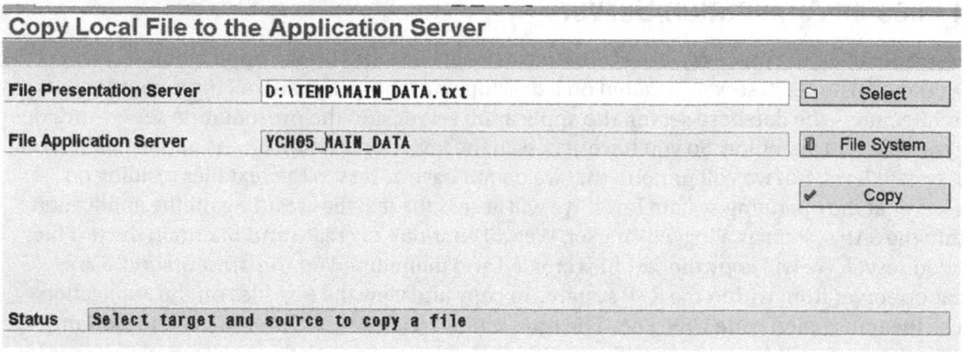

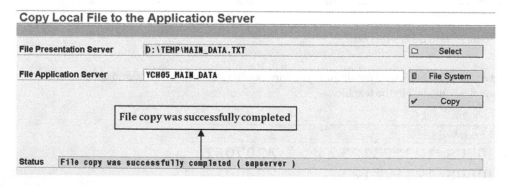

**Figure 5-57.** *Copy main data—from presentation server to application server*

We have deliberately provided a prefix YCH05_ to the file name to make it distinct on the application server. We have deliberately not provided any directory or folder for the file on the application server. The file will be copied on the default directory DIR_TEMP (logical name).

We clicked the *copy* button. If the copying process is successful, a message appears on the *Status* bar as shown in Figure 5-58.

---

**Copy Local File to the Application Server**

| File Presentation Server | D:\TEMP\MAIN_DATA.TXT | Select |
| File Application Server | YCH05_MAIN_DATA | File System |
| | | Copy |

File copy was successfully completed

Status  File copy was successfully completed ( sapserver )

---

**Figure 5-58.** *Successful copy of main data—from presentation server to application server*

If the destination file exists, it is overwritten without an alert.

If you want to look up the file YCH05_MAIN_DATA in the default directory DIR_TEMP (logical name) click the *File System* button on the screen shown in Figure 5-58. The directories (with logical names) will appear as in Figure 5-59.

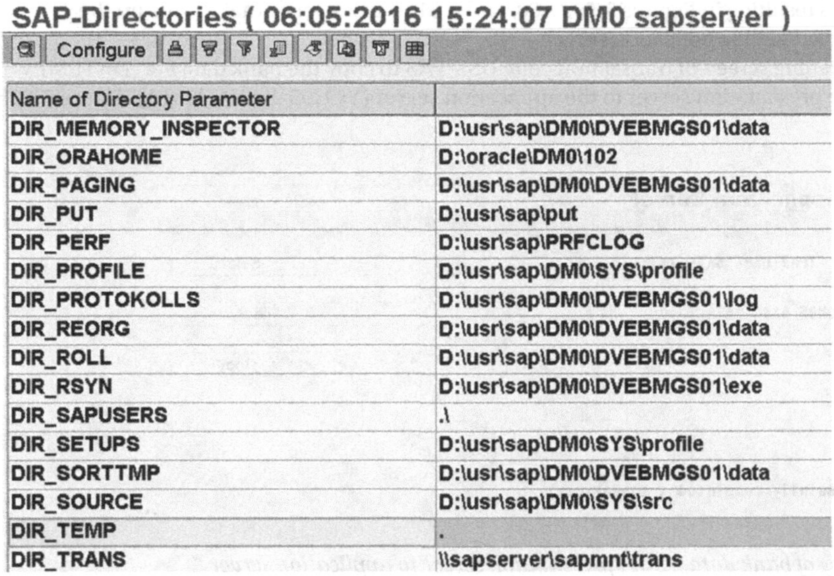

## SAP-Directories ( 06:05:2016 15:24:07 DM0 sapserver )

| Name of Directory Parameter | |
|---|---|
| DIR_MEMORY_INSPECTOR | D:\usr\sap\DM0\DVEBMGS01\data |
| DIR_ORAHOME | D:\oracle\DM0\102 |
| DIR_PAGING | D:\usr\sap\DM0\DVEBMGS01\data |
| DIR_PUT | D:\usr\sap\put |
| DIR_PERF | D:\usr\sap\PRFCLOG |
| DIR_PROFILE | D:\usr\sap\DM0\SYS\profile |
| DIR_PROTOKOLLS | D:\usr\sap\DM0\DVEBMGS01\log |
| DIR_REORG | D:\usr\sap\DM0\DVEBMGS01\data |
| DIR_ROLL | D:\usr\sap\DM0\DVEBMGS01\data |
| DIR_RSYN | D:\usr\sap\DM0\DVEBMGS01\exe |
| DIR_SAPUSERS | .\ |
| DIR_SETUPS | D:\usr\sap\DM0\SYS\profile |
| DIR_SORTTMP | D:\usr\sap\DM0\DVEBMGS01\data |
| DIR_SOURCE | D:\usr\sap\DM0\SYS\src |
| DIR_TEMP | . |
| DIR_TRANS | \\sapserver\sapmnt\trans |

***Figure 5-59.*** *Directories with logical names on application server*

Double-click the directory DIR_TEMP. The files appear as an ALV list. Our copied file name starts with the alphabet Y. To make the copied file appear at the beginning of the list, we selected the file name column, clicked the ▼ (sort descending) button. The files list appeared with the file YCH05_MAIN_DATA at the top of the list as in Figure 5-60.

**Button – Sort Descending**

**Column - File Name**

### Directory : .

| Useable | Viewe | Changed | Length | Owner | Lastchange | Lastchange | |
|---|---|---|---|---|---|---|---|
| X | | | 369 | SAPServi | 06.05.2016 | 11:57:31 | YCH05_MAIN_DATA |
| X | | | 992 | SAPServi | 05.03.2016 | 09:56:45 | YBLAH1_YBLAH1_YBLAH1.lsmw.read |
| X | | | 1504 | SAPServi | 11.02.2016 | 10:47:01 | YBLAH_YBLAH_YBLAH.lsmw.read |
| X | | | 5568 | SAPServi | 17.03.2016 | 11:00:46 | yblah |
| X | | | 3260 | SAPServi | 15.02.2016 | 11:17:41 | Y_060000 |
| X | | | 4 | SAPServi | 06.05.2016 | 10:36:46 | wd.pid |

***Figure 5-60.*** *Partial list of files in the directory DIR_TEMP*

We double-clicked the line of the file YCH05_MAIN_DATA; Figure 5-61 displays the contents of the file.

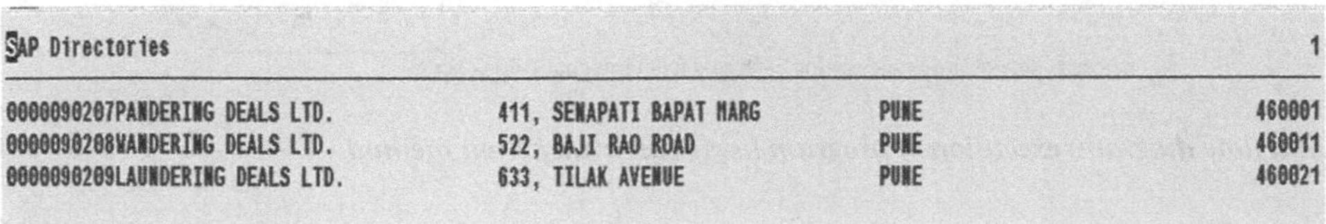

| SAP Directories | | | 1 |
|---|---|---|---|
| 0000090207PANDERING DEALS LTD. | 411, SENAPATI BAPAT MARG | PUNE | 460001 |
| 0000090208WANDERING DEALS LTD. | 522, BAJI RAO ROAD | PUNE | 460011 |
| 0000090209LAUNDERING DEALS LTD. | 633, TILAK AVENUE | PUNE | 460021 |

***Figure 5-61.*** *Contents of file YCH05_MAIN_DATA*

We performed the steps resulting in Figures 5-59, 5-60, and 5-61 to cross-verify that the file on the presentation server was copied to the application server.

We navigated to the opening screen of transaction code USS_FAS to copy the bank data file (D:\TEMP\ BANK_DATA.TXT) from the presentation server to the application server (YCH05_BANK_DATA). Figure 5-62 illustrates.

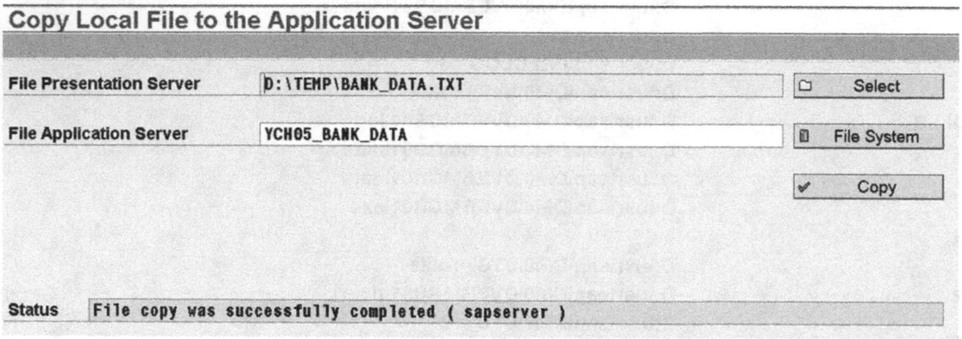

| **Copy Local File to the Application Server** | | |
|---|---|---|
| **File Presentation Server** | D:\TEMP\BANK_DATA.TXT | ▢    Select |
| **File Application Server** | YCH05_BANK_DATA | ▣    File System |
| | | ✔    Copy |
| **Status** | File copy was successfully completed ( sapserver ) | |

*Figure 5-62.* *Successful copy of bank data—from presentation server to application server*

You can cross-verify the copying of the bank data file from the presentation server to the application server by repeating the steps we performed to cross-verify the copying of the main data file from the presentation server to the application server.

This completes the process of copying the files from the presentation server to the application server.

## Data Flow in *Call Transaction* Method

This is a description of the data flow when you execute a modified version of the generated ABAP program from a recording of XK01 using the *call transaction* method. The diagram in Figure 5-63 traces the data flow from the text files on the application server into the functional module database tables.

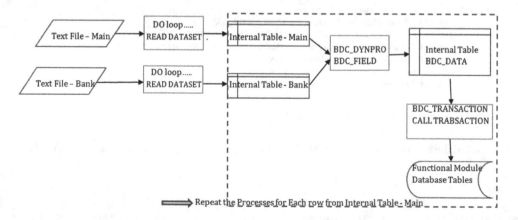

*Figure 5-63.* *Data flow diagram: execution of program using call transaction method*

To start with, data will be fetched from the two text files (main and bank) residing on the application server into two internal tables: internal table-main and internal table-bank. One DO loop is set up to continually read one line of data at a time (READ DATASET.....), from the main text file into the structure of internal table-main; append the data from the structure to the internal table-main. A second DO loop is set up to continually read one line of data at a time (READ DATASET.....), from the bank text file into the structure of internal table-bank; append the data from the structure to the internal table-bank.

The internal table-main will contain one row for one vendor. A loop (LOOP AT.....) is set up for the internal table-main. Within this main loop, as new screens are navigated, the subroutine BDC_DYNPRO is invoked with the parameters PROGRAM and DYNPRO. Within a screen the subroutine BDC_FIELD is invoked with the parameters FNAM and FVAL. Data will be passed from the structure of the internal table-main or through literals to the parameter FVAL. When the subroutines BDC_DYNPRO and BDC_FIELD are invoked, the BDCDATA table is being filled up.

Within this main loop, a nested loop with internal table-bank is set up to fetch data of banks belonging to the vendor fetched in the main loop. (WHERE.....) The subroutine BDC_FIELD is invoked with the parameters FNAM and FVAL to pass data from the structure of internal table-bank to the parameter FVAL. When the subroutines BDC_DYNPRO and BDC_FIELD are invoked, the BDCDATA table is being filled up

Once the BDC_DATA table has been filled for a vendor, the data from BDCDATA table is transferred to the functional module database tables by invoking the subroutine BDC_TRANSACTION. The subroutine BDC_TRANSACTION contains the ABAP statement CALL TRANSACTION to transfer data from the BDCDATA table to the functional module database tables.

The process is repeated as the next vendor is fetched in the main loop from the internal table-main. The process repeats until the main loop is exhausted.

When you execute the program using the *call transaction* method, the mode of database update can be either synchronous or asynchronous. The mode of database update is supplied at runtime through a selection screen parameter variable. The system executes a database commit immediately before and after the CALL TRANSACTION USING....statement.

This was a trace of the data as it traverses from the text files on the application server to their final destination, the functional module database tables, when you execute the program using the *call transaction* method.

## Modifications to Program to Support Input Text Files on Application Server, etc.

We copied the include program BDCRECX1 into YCH05_BDCRECX1. We activated the program YCH05_BDCRECX1. We will be carrying out modifications to the program YCH05_BDCRECX1 to create a log file on the application server as part of the second stage of the hands-on exercise.

The program YCH05_XK01_PROGRAM_CALL_TRAN being a copy of the program YCH05_XK01_PROGRAM_BI_TB_SC supports text files only on the presentation server. Suitable modifications are to be carried out so that it supports text files only on the application server

The following lines describe the modifications to be carried out the program YCH05_XK01_PROGRAM_CALL_TRAN to support text files on the application server.

The function module F4_FILENAME works only for the end user making a file selection from the presentation server. In our present context, text files being located on the application server, all the program lines related to the context of text files being located on the presentation server have to be deleted or commented.

In the data declaration area, the following statements are not required, so are commented:

```
DATA:.....
* MAIN_FL   TYPE IBIPPARMS-PATH, "to select file from
                                 "presentation server
* BANK_FL   TYPE IBIPPARMS-PATH,
```

The INCLUDE statement is modified as follows:

```
include ycho5_bdcrecx1.
```

The DEFAULT clause has been incorporated into the PARAMETERS statements to input text file names.

```
PARAMETERS: MFILE TYPE STRING DEFAULT 'YCHO5_MAIN_DATA',
            BFILE TYPE STRING DEFAULT 'YCHO5_BANK_DATA'.
```

The event AT SELECTION-SCREEN ON VALUE-REQUEST was triggered to enable the end user to make a file selection from the presentation server. In the present context, the triggering of this event is irrelevant, as files are located on the application server. The statements relating to the triggering of the event AT SELECTION-SCREEN ON VALUE-REQUEST are commented, as follows:

```
*********************************************
*AT SELECTION-SCREEN ON VALUE-REQUEST FOR MFILE.
*
*CALL FUNCTION 'F4_FILENAME'
* IMPORTING
*   FILE_NAME           = MAIN_FL.
*
*MFILE = MAIN_FL.
*
**********************************************
*AT SELECTION-SCREEN ON VALUE-REQUEST FOR BFILE.
*
*CALL FUNCTION 'F4_FILENAME'
* IMPORTING
*   FILE_NAME           = BANK_FL.
*
*BFILE = BANK_FL.
*
```

The statement to transfer data from the text file on the presentation server to the internal table MAIN_TAB

```
CALL FUNCTION 'GUI_UPLOAD'
  EXPORTING
    FILENAME                = MFILE
    FILETYPE                = 'ASC'
  TABLES
    DATA_TAB                = MAIN_TAB
        .
```

is replaced with the following statements:

```
PERFORM OPEN_DATASET USING MFILE.

DO.
 READ DATASET MFILE INTO MAIN_STRU.
 IF SY-SUBRC NE 0.
  EXIT.
 ENDIF.
 APPEND MAIN_STRU TO MAIN_TAB.
ENDDO.

PERFORM CLOSE_DATASET USING MFILE.
```

The statement to transfer data from the text file on the presentation server to the internal table BANK_TAB

```
CALL FUNCTION 'GUI_UPLOAD'
  EXPORTING
    FILENAME                = BFILE
    FILETYPE                = 'ASC'
  TABLES
    DATA_TAB                = BANK_TAB
        .
```

is replaced with the following statements:

```
PERFORM OPEN_DATASET USING BFILE.

DO.
 READ DATASET BFILE INTO BANK_STRU.
 IF SY-SUBRC NE 0.
  EXIT.
 ENDIF.
 APPEND BANK_STRU TO BANK_TAB.
ENDDO.

PERFORM CLOSE_DATASET USING BFILE.
```

The program YCH05_XK01_PROGRAM_CALL_TRAN with modifications carried out supports text files on the application server only. The complete source lines of program YCH05_XK01_PROGRAM_CALL_TRAN are available in the E-resource file for this book (www.apress.com/9781484212345).

We saved and activated the program YCH05_XK01_PROGRAM_CALL_TRAN.

## Execute Program—Verify Data Migrated

We will execute the program YCH05_XK01_PROGRAM_CALL_TRAN using the *call transaction* method.

When the program YCH05_XK01_PROGRAM_CALL_TRAN is executed, the selection screen as shown in Figure 5-64 appears.

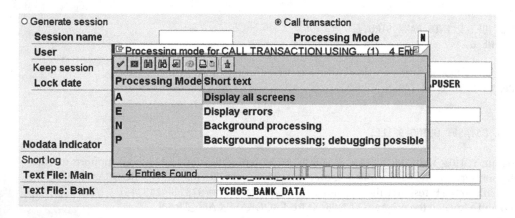

**Figure 5-64.** *Program YCH05_XK01_PROGRAM_CALL_TRAN—selection screen*

When the program is executed using the *call transaction* method, four options of *Processing Mode* are available.

- A—*Display all screens*, equivalent to *Process/foreground* option when running a session

- E—Display errors equivalent to *Display errors only* option when running a session

- N—*Background processing* equivalent to *background* option when running a session

- P—*Background processing debugging possible*

Figure 5-65 shows the *Processing mode* list of options.

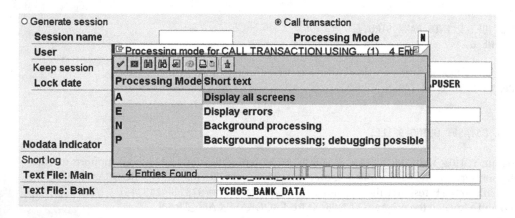

**Figure 5-65.** *Selection screen—processing modes*

For now, we selected the option *Background processing*.

Figure 5-66 shows the *Update mode* list of options:

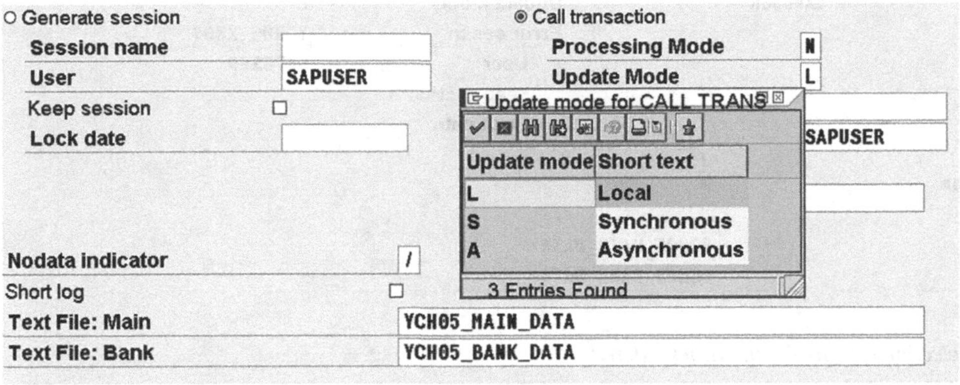

○ Generate session                                    ⦿ Call transaction
  **Session name**                                      **Processing Mode**          N
  **User**              SAPUSER                          **Update Mode**             L
  **Keep session**        ☐                    ⌐Update mode for CALL TRANS⌐
  **Lock date**                                  ✓ ⊠ 🔍 🔍 🔳  ⊡ 🗎 ⌐     ⌗        SAPUSER
                                                 **Update mode** **Short text**
                                                 L            Local
                                                 S            Synchronous
  **Nodata indicator**                    /       A            Asynchronous
  Short log                               ☐       3 Entries Found
  **Text File: Main**          YCH05_MAIN_DATA
  **Text File: Bank**          YCH05_BANK_DATA

*Figure 5-66.*  *Selection screen—update modes*

Table 5-8 gives a brief description of the three options available for the field *Update Mode*

*Table 5-8.*  *Update Modes*

| Update Mode | Description |
| --- | --- |
| L – *Local* | The database update does not occur in a separate process, but occurs in the process of calling program itself. |
| S – *Synchronous* | With this mode of update, the called transaction receives completion message including errors if any from update module. |
| A – *Asynchronous* | The transaction passes the updates to the SAP update service. It results in a faster execution of the program. This mode of update is not advisable with a large amount of data, as the calling program receives no completion message from update module. The calling program is not able to determine the success or failure of database update. |

You can refer to SAP documentation for a more elaborate description of *update modes*.

We entered YCH05_XK01 in the *Error sessn*. A session is automatically created for error data. A user has to be entered who has the authorization to run the session of error data. By default the logged-in user is proposed. We accepted the default logged-in user. The *Keep session* and *Lock date* have the same meaning when you execute the program using *batch input* or *Generate session* method.

Figure 5-67 shows the selection with the entered values.

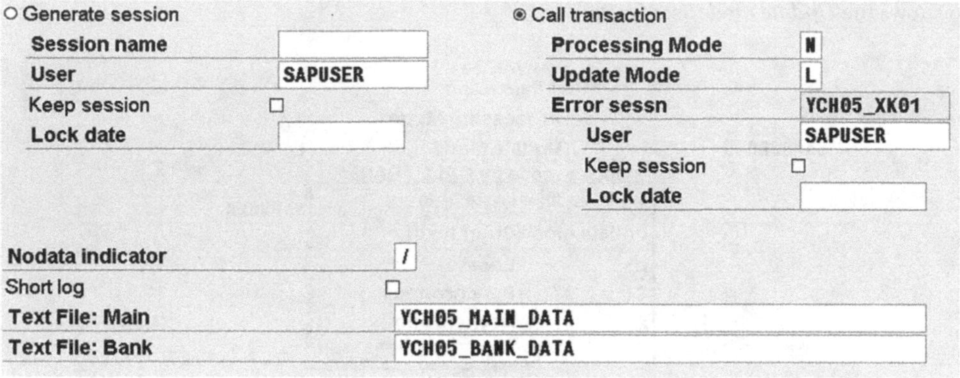

| ○ Generate session | | ◉ Call transaction | |
|---|---|---|---|
| **Session name** | | **Processing Mode** | **N** |
| **User** | **SAPUSER** | **Update Mode** | **L** |
| **Keep session** | ☐ | **Error sessn** | **YCH05_XK01** |
| **Lock date** | | **User** | **SAPUSER** |
| | | **Keep session** ☐ | |
| | | **Lock date** | |

| | |
|---|---|
| **Nodata indicator** | *I* |
| Short log | ☐ |
| **Text File: Main** | **YCH05_MAIN_DATA** |
| **Text File: Bank** | **YCH05_BANK_DATA** |

*Figure 5-67.* *Selection screen—input values entered*

When we clicked the execute button, the output as shown in Figure 5-68 was generated:

```
CALL_TRANSACTION XK01 Return code = 1,001  RECORD:        0
E A numeric entry is expected in field Bank Acct. No.

CALL_TRANSACTION XK01 Return code =    0  RECORD:        0
S Vendor 0000090208 has been created for company code 0001 purchasing organization 0001

CALL_TRANSACTION XK01 Return code =    0  RECORD:        0
S Vendor 0000090209 has been created for company code 0001 purchasing organization 0001


Error session created
```

*Figure 5-68.* *Program YCH05_XK01_PROGRAM_CALL_TRAN—output*

This output is the outcome of the WRITE statements located in the include program YCH05_BDCRECX1 following the ABAP statements CALL TRANSACTION...... (Subroutine BDC_TRANSACTION) and CALL FUNCTION BDC_CLOSE_GROUP (Subroutine CLOSE_GROUP).

The ABAP statement CALL TRANSACTION.....returns resultant information of system messages such as message id, message numbers, and so on into an internal table of ABAP dictionary structure BDCMSGCOLL. The internal table of ABAP dictionary structure BDCMSGCOLL is declared as MESSTAB in the include program YCH05_BDCRECX1. The information relating to messages such as message id, message numbers, and so on is extracted from the internal table MESSTAB. The message texts are retrieved using the message id and message numbers from the database tables; variable information is inserted into placeholders of the message texts and the resultant string output with the WRITE statements.

The first vendor (vendor number 0000090207) generated an error condition as the field BANKN contained non-numeric data. This is reported in the first two lines of the output of Figure 5-68.

The second and third vendors (vendor numbers: 0000090208, 0000090209) were created successfully. This is also reported in the output of Figure 5-68.

Since an error condition was generated by the first vendor, a session is created with the error data and this is reported on the last line of the output of Figure 5-68.

To cross-verify whether the vendor data was migrated, we again executed transaction code XK02—*Change Vendor*. On the opening screen of transaction code XK02, we pressed the function key F4. The filter dialog box which popped up was using the tab *Vendor by Company Code* as default. We entered the pattern

9020* in the field *Vendor*, the fifth field from the top. We clicked the Continue button. All the vendors starting with the digits 9020 appeared in the list. A total of seven vendors appeared in the list: five vendors created in the previous hands-on exercise and two vendors, 0000090208 and 0000090209, created in the current hands-on exercise. The list should appear as shown in Figure 5-69.

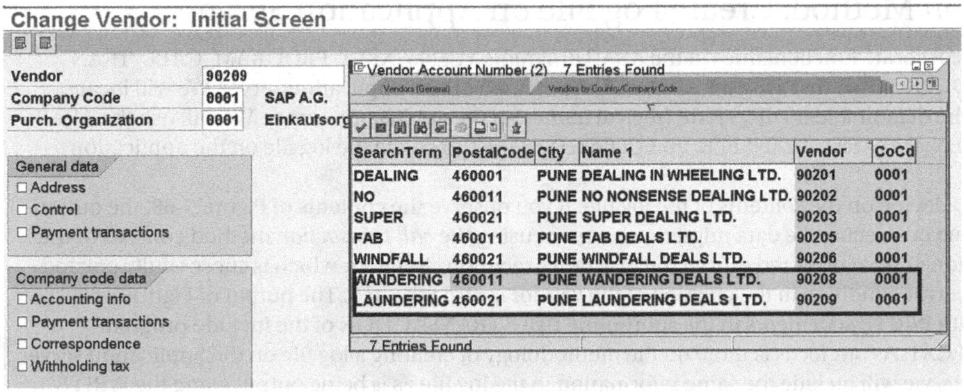

*Figure 5-69. Vendor list—vendor numbers with pattern: 9020\**

We selected each of the vendors 0000090208 and 0000090209 in turn and navigated through all the screens for each of these vendors to perform an individual field-wise cross-check of values.

The error condition in one of the vendors created a session with the error data. We navigated to the transaction code SM35 and entered YCH05* in the field *Sess*. Session names starting with YCH05 are listed. The first entry in the list, selected with the row selector, is the session with error data. Figure 5-70 illustrates.

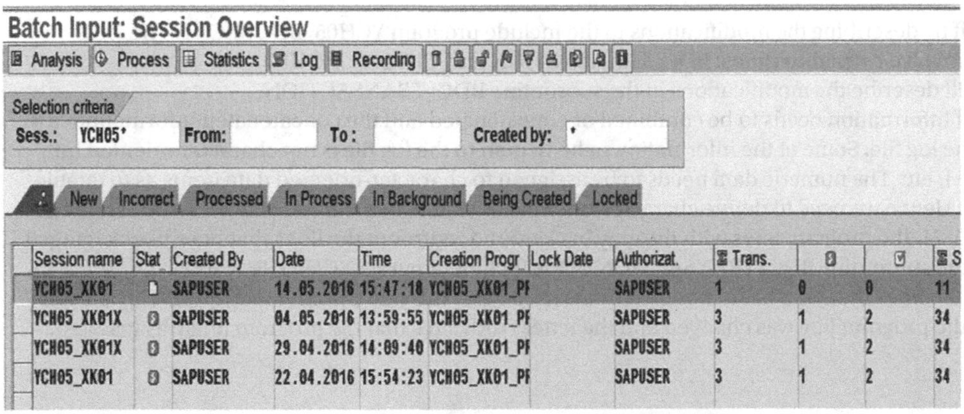

*Figure 5-70. Execute program YCH05_XK01_PROGRAM_CALL_TRAN—error session*

Note that this is a new session and as such will not have a log. When you execute the program using the *call transaction* method, no log is created. In the next or second stage of this hands-on exercise, we will create a log as a text file on the application server.

You can run the session with error data in the foreground and rectify the error(s) manually.

This concludes the first stage of the hands-on exercise: migrate vendor data of text files on application server using the *call transaction* method.

## Migrate Data of Text Files on Application Server Using *Call Transaction* Method, Create Log File on Application Server

We will now incorporate functionalities in the ABAP programs YCH05_XK01_PROGRAM_CALL_TRAN and YCH05_BDCRECX1 so that a log file as a text file is created on the application server. We will locate the log file on the default folder DIR_TEMP (logical name) on the application server. We will use the ABAP statements OPEN_DATASET, TRANSFER, and CLOSE DATASET to create the log file on the application server.

We have to decide on the contents of the log file. If you observe the contents of Figure 5-68, the output generated when you execute the data migration program using the *call transaction* method consists of the basic information of what occurred during the program execution. A vendor which is successfully created is reported. An error condition in the creation of the vendor is also reported. The output of Figure 5-68 is generated with WRITE statements in the subroutine BDC_TRANSACTION of the include program YCH05_BDCRECX1. As our focus is more on the methodology of creating a log file on the application server than its contents, we will include the same information in the log file as is being output using the WRITE statements in the subroutine BDC_TRANSACTION of the include program YCH05_BDCRECX1. Next to the WRITE statements related to the *call transaction* method, we will incorporate TRANSFER statements. The TRANSFER statements will write to the log file, the same information being output with the WRITE statements. At the very beginning of the log file, we will incorporate the following information, SY-UNAME—user name, SY-DATUM—system date, SY-UZEIT—system time, along with the related text.

The next step is to describe the modifications to be carried out in the programs YCH05_XK01_PROGRAM_CALL_TRAN and YCH05_BDCRECX1 to enable creation of log file on the application server.

## Modifications to the Include Program YCH05_BDCRECX1

We will start off by describing the modifications to the include program YCH05_BDCRECX1. The modifications involve two subroutines: BDC_TRANSACTION and CLOSE_GROUP.

Firstly, I will describe the modifications in the subroutine BDC_TRANSACTION.

Individual Information needs to be combined or concatenated and the concatenated information is to be written to the log file. Some of the information to be written to the log file is not character oriented but numeric—type I, etc. The numeric data needs to be assigned to character-oriented data items as to enable concatenation. Hence we need to define character-oriented data to which numeric data is to be assigned.

In Figure 5-71, the program lines with the gray background represent the lines that have been changed or inserted in the subroutine BDC_TRANSACTION of the include program YCH05_BDCRECX1.

The program lines that have been modified or inserted carry the side comment log file C/I. The letter C indicates that the program line was changed and the letter I indicates that the program line was inserted.

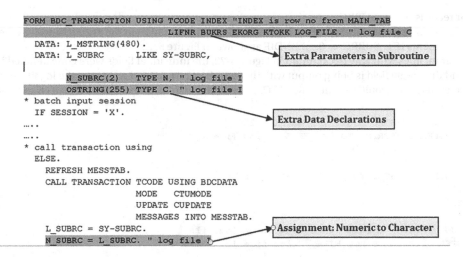

```
FORM BDC_TRANSACTION USING TCODE INDEX "INDEX is row no from MAIN_TAB
                     LIFNR BUKRS EKORG KTOKK LOG_FILE. " log file C
  DATA: L_MSTRING(480).
  DATA: L_SUBRC      LIKE SY-SUBRC,

        N_SUBRC(2)   TYPE N, " log file I
        OSTRING(255) TYPE C. " log file I
* batch input session
  IF SESSION = 'X'.
…..
…..
* call transaction using
  ELSE.
     REFRESH MESSTAB.
     CALL TRANSACTION TCODE USING BDCDATA
                      MODE   CTUMODE
                      UPDATE CUPDATE
                      MESSAGES INTO MESSTAB.
     L_SUBRC = SY-SUBRC.
     N_SUBRC = L_SUBRC. " log file I
```

**Extra Parameters in Subroutine**

**Extra Data Declarations**

**Assignment: Numeric to Character**

*Figure 5-71.* *Modifications to subroutine: BDC_TRANSACTION—I*

The original version of the subroutine BDC_TRANSACTION was receiving only one parameter TCODE. Six additional parameters are being received in the modified version. Extra data declarations are made in the modified version. An assignment is made to convert numeric data to character-oriented data in the modified version. Figure 5-71 marks the modifications.

Because of the constraints of vertical space, all the modifications could not be represented in a single figure. Hence Figures 5-72 and 5-73 are a continuation of modifications to the subroutine BDC_TRANSACTION.

```
IF SMALLLOG <> 'X'.
   CONCATENATE 'CALL_TRANSACTION' (I03) TCODE 'returncode:'(I05)
            N_SUBRC 'RECORD:' INDEX "changed from SY-INDEX
            INTO OSTRING SEPARATED BY ' '. " log file I


   WRITE: / OSTRING. " log file C
   TRANSFER OSTRING TO LOG_FILE. " log file I


LOOP AT MESSTAB.
   …..
   ENDIF.
   CONDENSE L_MSTRING.
   IF L_SUBRC <> 0. " log file I
      CONCATENATE 'Vendor:'(L03) LIFNR ' Company Code:'(L04) BUKRS
      ' Pur. Org.:'(L05) EKORG ' Account Group:'(L06) KTOKK
      INTO OSTRING. " log file I


      WRITE: / OSTRING. " log file I
      TRANSFER OSTRING TO LOG_FILE. " log file I
   ENDIF. " log file I
```

*Figure 5-72.* *Modifications to subroutine: BDC_TRANSACTION—II*

427

For error records (i.e., L_SUBRC <> 0), the information company code, vendor, purchasing organization, etc., were not appearing in the output. We are incorporating this information in the output as well as the log file with the statements IF L_SUBRC <> 0......ENDIF as shown in Figure 5-72.

In the program lines with gray background in Figure 5-72, the individual fields were concatenated into a single field, and this single field is being output with the WRITE statement and written to the log file with the TRANSFER statement. You could use the WRITE TO.....statement instead of the CONCATENATE statement.

```
      WRITE: / MESSTAB-MSGTYP, L_MSTRING(250).
      TRANSFER L_MSTRING TO LOG_FILE. " log file I
    ELSE.
      WRITE: / MESSTAB.
      TRANSFER MESSTAB TO LOG_FILE. " log file I
    ENDIF.
  ENDLOOP.
  SKIP.
  OSTRING = '|'. " create blank like row / log file I
  TRANSFER OSTRING TO LOG_FILE. " log file I
ENDIF.
```

*Figure 5-73.* *Modifications to subroutine: BDC_TRANSACTION—III*

In Figure 5-73, the TRANSFER statements have been inserted to write to the log file.
This concludes the modifications to the subroutine BDC_TRANSACTION.
The modifications to the subroutine CLOSE_GROUP involve the following:

- Providing the log file as a single parameter to the subroutine. The original version of the subroutine did not have any parameter.

- If an error condition arises during the data migration, a session with error data is created. The creation of a session with error data is reported with the WRITE statement and appears as the last line of the output. The reporting of the creation of a session with error data should also be written to the log file with the TRANSFER statement. Figure 5-74 shows the modifications to the subroutine CLOSE_GROUP.

```
FORM CLOSE_GROUP USING LOG_FILE. " log file C

IF E_GROUP_OPENED = 'X'.
  CALL FUNCTION 'BDC_CLOSE_GROUP'.
  WRITE: /.
  WRITE: /(30) 'Fehlermappe wurde erzeugt'(I06).

  TRANSFER 'Fehlermappe wurde erzeugt'(I06) TO LOG_FILE. " log file I

.....
```

*Figure 5-74.* *Modifications to subroutine: CLOSE_GROUP*

# Modifications to the Main Program YCH05_XK01_PROGRAM_CALL_TRAN

We are carrying out modifications to the program YCH05_XK01_PROGRAM_CALL_TRAN directly. You can, if you so desire, make a copy of the program YCH05_XK01_PROGRAM_CALL_TRAN and carry out modifications to the copy of the program YCH05_XK01_PROGRAM_CALL_TRAN. You can have two programs: (1) YCH05_XK01_PROGRAM_CALL_TRAN, not containing the feature of log file creation and (2) a modified copy of program YCH05_XK01_PROGRAM_CALL_TRAN, containing the extra feature of log file creation.

The following modifications were carried out to the program YCH05_XK01_PROGRAM_CALL_TRAN to incorporate the feature of log file creation.

Literal values were being assigned to the fields RF02K-BUKRS (company code), RF02K-EKORG (purch. organization), and RF02K-KTOKK (account group)—subroutine BDC_FIELD. The values of these three fields now have to be incorporated into the log file as well—subroutine BDC_TRANSACTION. So, instead of specifying the same literal parameters when invoking the two subroutines BDC_FIELD and BDC_TRANSACTION, we have declared them as constants and used these constants as parameters when invoking the two subroutines.

The program lines to declare constants are as follows:

```
* constants defined to create log file ***********
* being passed as parameters in two subroutines  *
* (1) BDC_FIELD (2) BDC_TRANSACTION              *
*************************************************
CONSTANTS: BUKRS    TYPE BUKRS VALUE '0001',
           EKORG    TYPE EKORG VALUE '0001',
           KTOKK    TYPE KTOKK VALUE '0001'.
```

The three constants BUKRS, EKORG, and KTOKK have been assigned the same value '0001'. You could argue that we can manage with the declaration of just one constant instead of three. The objective is that, when invoking subroutines, the parameters being passed must be apparent in terms of being assigned to which fields.

To be able to report correctly, the processed vendor/row number in the output as well as the log file, the variable ROW_NO was defined as follows:

```
INDX(2)   TYPE N, "bank data index
ROW_NO(6) TYPE N. " log file I
```

An additional entry with the PARAMETERS statement to input the log file name is as follows:

```
PARAMETERS.....
           LFILE TYPE STRING DEFAULT 'YCH05_LOG'. " log file I
```

To open the log file on the application server, write the information related to user, date, and time to the log file. The following program lines will be positioned preceding the statement: PERFORM OPEN_GROUP:

```
****** inserted for log file start ******
OPEN DATASET LFILE
               FOR OUTPUT
               IN TEXT MODE
               ENCODING DEFAULT WITH SMART LINEFEED.
********************************************************
CONCATENATE 'User: '(S02) SY-UNAME ' Date:'(L01)
            SY-DATUM+6(2) '/' SY-DATUM+4(2) '/'
            SY-DATUM+0(4) ' Time:'(L02) SY-UZEIT+0(2)
            ':' SY-UZEIT+2(2) ':' SY-UZEIT+4(2) INTO GSTRING.

TRANSFER GSTRING TO LFILE.

GSTRING = '|'.
TRANSFER GSTRING TO LFILE.
***** inserted for log file end
```

To maintain the row number being processed, the statement to increment the variable ROW_NO will follow the statement LOOP AT MAIN_TAB INTO MAIN_STRU as follows:

```
ROW_NO = ROW_NO + 1. "log file I
```

The subroutine BDC_FIELD for the fields BUKRS, EKORG, and KTOKK will be invoked with FVAL parameter as the respective declared constant instead of a literal.

```
perform bdc_field        using 'RFO2K-BUKRS'
                               BUKRS. "'0001' / log file C.
+perform bdc_field        using 'RFO2K-EKORG'
                               EKORG. "'0001' / log file C.
perform bdc_field        using 'RFO2K-KTOKK'
                               KTOKK. "'0001' / log file C.
```

The subroutine BDC_TRANSACTION will be invoked with six additional parameters.

```
perform bdc_transaction using 'XKO1'
                               ROW_NO " parameters to create
                                      " log file/log file C
                               MAIN_STRU-LIFNR
                               BUKRS
                               EKORG
                               KTOKK
                               LFILE.
```

The subroutine CLOSE_GROUP will be invoked with a parameter, the log file name.

```
perform close_group using lfile. " log file C
```

To close the log file on the application server, the last line of the program is as follows:

```
CLOSE DATASET LFILE. " log file I
```

This concludes the modifications to the program YCH05_XK01_PROGRAM_CALL_TRAN to incorporate the feature of log file creation on the application server.

We activated the program YCH05_XK01_PROGRAM_CALL_TRAN.

The programs YCH05_BDCRECX1 and YCH05_XK01_PROGRAM_CALL_TRAN are available in the E-resource file for this book (www.apress.com/9781484212345).

## Prepare Text Files; Copy Text Files to Application Server, etc.

We created new set of main and bank data on the presentation server.

Using notepad editor, we created the new set of main data for three vendors: 0000090201, 0000090232, and 0000090233. Figure 5-75 illustrates.

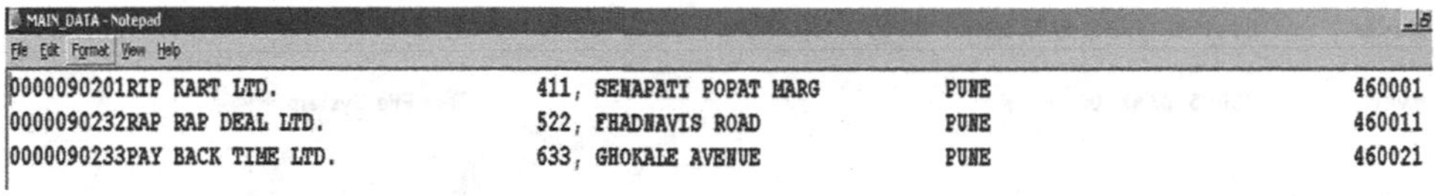

```
MAIN_DATA - Notepad                                                          _|5
File  Edit  Format  View  Help
0000090201RIP KART LTD.            411, SENAPATI POPAT MARG    PUNE           460001
0000090232RAP RAP DEAL LTD.        522, PHADNAVIS ROAD         PUNE           460011
0000090233PAY BACK TIME LTD.       633, GHOKALE AVENUE         PUNE           460021
```

**Figure 5-75.** *Vendors' main data—text file*

Vendor 0000090201 already exists. We deliberately created this already existing vendor in the input to demonstrate the handling of erroneous data.

We created a new set of bank data for all three vendors: 0000090201, 0000090232, and 0000090233. Figure 5-76 shows the bank data in the text file.

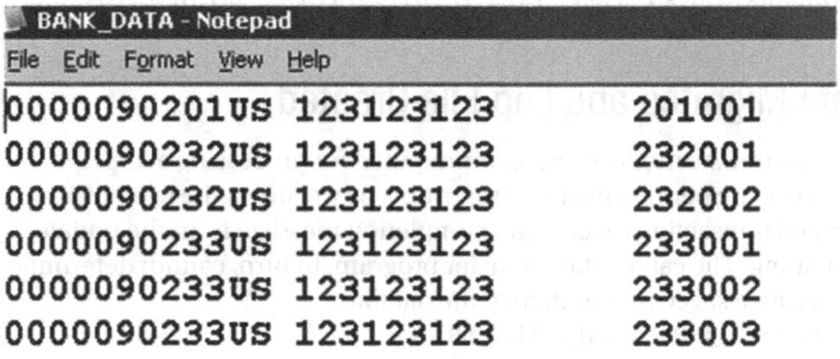

```
BANK_DATA - Notepad
File  Edit  Format  View  Help
0000090201US 123123123          201001
0000090232US 123123123          232001
0000090232US 123123123          232002
0000090233US 123123123          233001
0000090233US 123123123          233002
0000090233US 123123123          233003
```

**Figure 5-76.** *Vendors' bank data—text file*

To copy files from the presentation server to the application server from within the SAP system, we navigated to the opening screen of transaction code USS_FAS. We selected text file-main from the presentation server using the *Select* button and entered the file name on application server as YCH05_MAIN_DATA. We clicked the *Copy* button. The file was successfully copied from the presentation server on to the application server. Figure 5-77 illustrates.

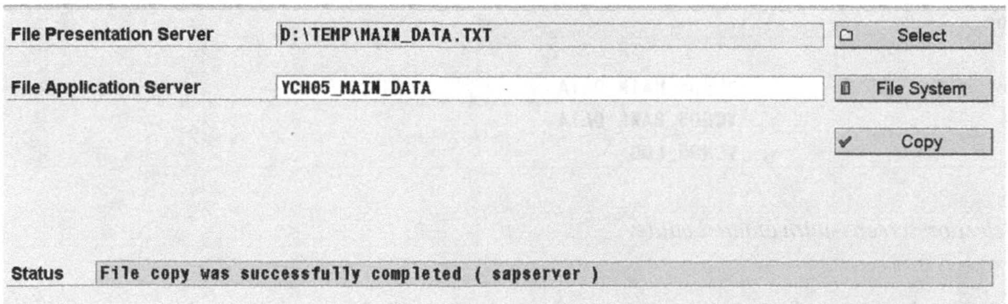

**Figure 5-77.** *Successful copy of main data—from presentation server to application server*

In a similar manner, we selected text file-bank from the presentation server using the *Select* button and entered the file name on application server as YCH05_BANK_DATA. We clicked the *Copy* button. The file was successfully copied from the presentation server on to the application server. Figure 5-78 illustrates.

431

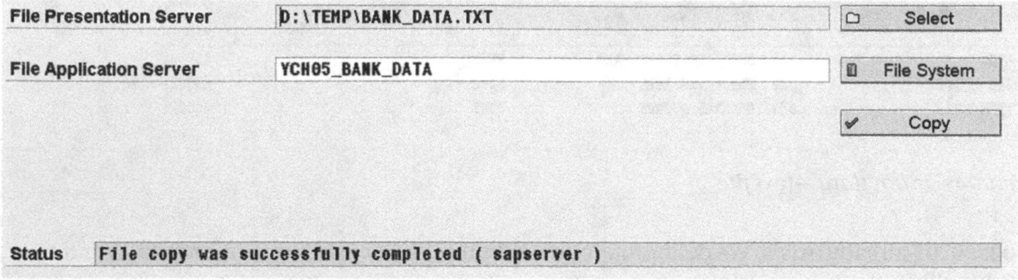

| File Presentation Server | D:\TEMP\BANK_DATA.TXT | | Select |
|---|---|---|---|
| File Application Server | YCH05_BANK_DATA | | File System |
| | | | Copy |

Status   File copy was successfully completed ( sapserver )

*Figure 5-78.* *Successful copy of bank data—from presentation server to application server*

We cross-verified by checking the contents of files YCH05_MAIN_DATA and YCH05_BANK_DATA.

## Execute Program—Verify Data Migrated and Log File Created

We would like to mention that asynchronous update mode is not recommended for processing a larger amount of data. This is especially so when you are performing error reporting, as we are, in the current hands-on exercise. This is because the called transaction receives no completion message from the update module in the asynchronous mode of updating. The calling data transfer program, in turn, cannot determine whether or not a called transaction ended with a successful update of the database.

We next executed the program YCH05_XK01_PROGRAM_CALL_TRAN.

Figure 5-79 shows the selection screen with the filled in values.

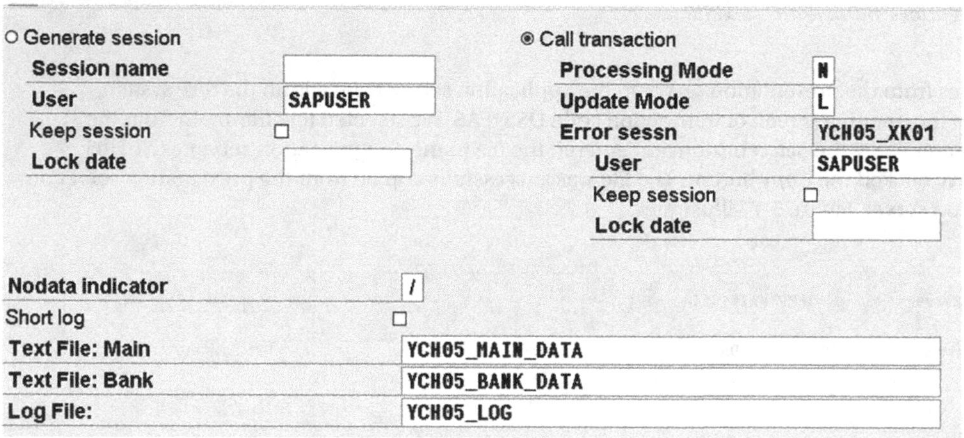

| O Generate session | | ◉ Call transaction | |
|---|---|---|---|
| **Session name** | | **Processing Mode** | **N** |
| **User** | **SAPUSER** | **Update Mode** | **L** |
| Keep session | ☐ | **Error sessn** | **YCH05_XK01** |
| **Lock date** | | User | **SAPUSER** |
| | | Keep session | ☐ |
| | | Lock date | |

| | |
|---|---|
| **Nodata indicator** | *I* |
| Short log | ☐ |
| **Text File: Main** | YCH05_MAIN_DATA |
| **Text File: Bank** | YCH05_BANK_DATA |
| **Log File:** | YCH05_LOG |

*Figure 5-79.* *Selection screen—with entered values*

When we clicked the execute button, the output as shown in Figure 5-80 was generated:

```
CALL_TRANSACTION XK01 Return code = 01 RECORD: 000001
Vendor:0000090201 Company Code:0001 Pur. Org.:0001 Account Group:0001
E Vendor 90201 already exists for company code 0001 and purchasing organizatn 0001

CALL_TRANSACTION XK01 Return code = 00 RECORD: 000002
S Vendor 0000090232 has been created for company code 0001 purchasing organization 0001

CALL_TRANSACTION XK01 Return code = 00 RECORD: 000003
S Vendor 0000090233 has been created for company code 0001 purchasing organization 0001


Error session created
```

***Figure 5-80.*** *Program YCH05_XK01_PROGRAM_CALL_TRAN—output*

The first vendor (vendor number 0000090201) generated an error condition: *Vendor 90201 already exists.....* This is reported in the first three lines of the output of Figure 5-80.

The second and third vendors (vendor numbers: 0000090232, 0000090233) were created successfully. This is also reported in the output of Figure 5-80.

Since an error condition was generated by the first vendor, a session is created with the error data and this is reported on the last line of the output of Figure 5-80.

To cross-verify whether the vendor data was migrated, we again executed transaction code XK02—*Change Vendor*. On the opening screen of transaction code XK02, we pressed the function key F4 on the field *Vendor*. The filter dialog box which popped up was using the tab *Vendors by Country/Company Code* as default. We entered the pattern 9023* in the field *Vendor*, the fifth field from the top. We clicked the Continue button. All the vendors starting with the digits 9023 appeared in the list. A total of two vendors appeared in the list. The list should appear as shown in Figure 5-81.

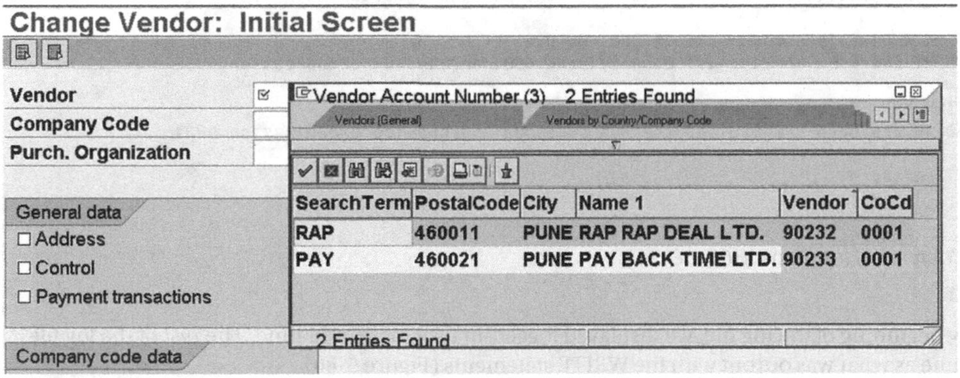

***Figure 5-81.*** *Vendor list—vendor numbers with pattern: 9023\**

We selected each of the vendors 0000090232 and 0000090233 in turn and navigated through all the screens for each of these vendors to perform an individual field-wise cross-check of values.

The crux of this part of the hands-on exercise was the creation of the log file on the application server. So let us check out the successful creation of the log file on the application server.

To view the log file created on the application server, we navigated to the opening screen of transaction code USS_FAS. We clicked the *File System* button and double-clicked the folder DIR_TEMP (logical name). The files in the folder DIR_TEMP are displayed. We clicked the file name column and further clicked the

(sort descending) button. The file names starting with YCH05 appeared at the beginning of the list shown in Figure 5-82.

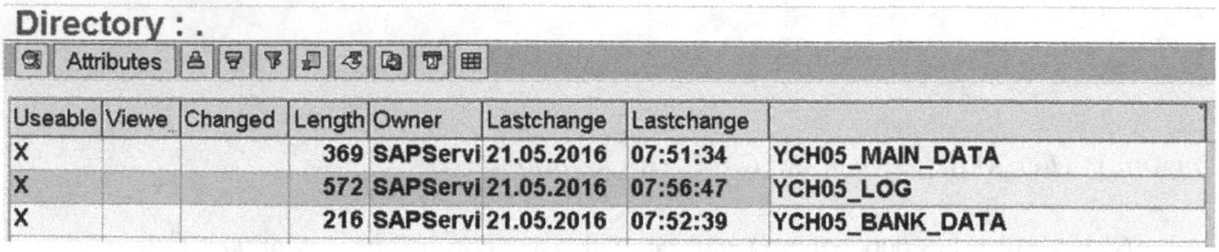

## Directory : .

| Useable | Viewe | Changed | Length | Owner | Lastchange | Lastchange | |
|---------|-------|---------|--------|-------|------------|------------|---|
| X | | | 369 | SAPServi | 21.05.2016 | 07:51:34 | YCH05_MAIN_DATA |
| X | | | 572 | SAPServi | 21.05.2016 | 07:56:47 | YCH05_LOG |
| X | | | 216 | SAPServi | 21.05.2016 | 07:52:39 | YCH05_BANK_DATA |

*Figure 5-82.* *Log file YCH05_LOG created on application server*

We double-clicked the row of log file YCH05_LOG. The contents of log file YCH05_LOG was displayed as shown in Figure 5-83.

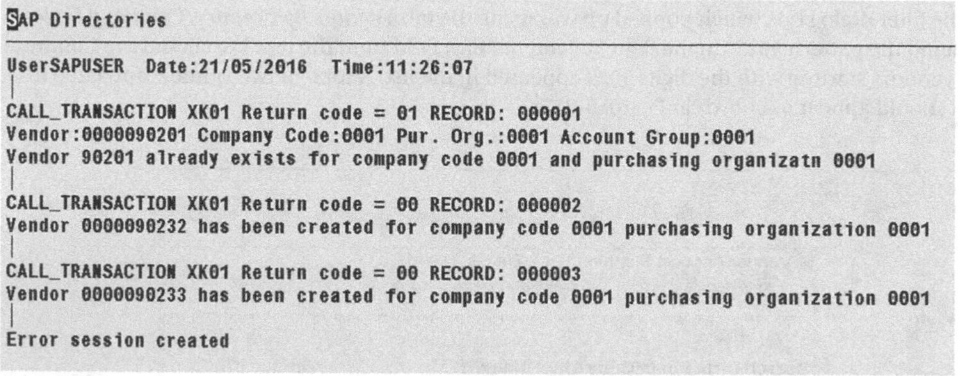

```
SAP Directories

UserSAPUSER   Date:21/05/2016   Time:11:26:07
|
CALL_TRANSACTION XK01 Return code = 01 RECORD: 000001
Vendor:0000090201 Company Code:0001 Pur. Org.:0001 Account Group:0001
Vendor 90201 already exists for company code 0001 and purchasing organizatn 0001
|
CALL_TRANSACTION XK01 Return code = 00 RECORD: 000002
Vendor 0000090232 has been created for company code 0001 purchasing organization 0001
|
CALL_TRANSACTION XK01 Return code = 00 RECORD: 000003
Vendor 0000090233 has been created for company code 0001 purchasing organization 0001
|
Error session created
```

*Figure 5-83.* *Contents of log file YCH05_LOG*

At the very beginning of the log file, we displayed logged-in user, date, and time. The rest of the log file contents are same as what was output with the WRITE statements (Figure 5-80).

The error condition in one of the vendors created a session with the error data. We navigated to transaction code SM35 and entered YCH05* in the field *Sess*. Session names starting with YCH05 are listed. The first entry in the list; selected with the row selector is the session with error data. Figure 5-84 illustrates.

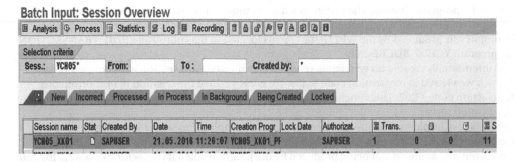

*Figure 5-84. Execution of program YCH05_XK01_PROGRAM_CALL_TRAN—error session*

This concludes the second stage of the hands-on exercise: migrate vendor data using *call transaction* method. The second stage of the hands-on exercise involved the creation of a log file on application server.

This also concludes the hands-on exercise: migrate vendor data using *call transaction* method.

## Recapitulation—Hands-on Exercise II: Migrate Vendor Data Using *Call Transaction* Method

This hands-on exercise also performed migration of vendor data using the *call transaction* method instead of the *batch input* method. The program we executed for migration of vendor data using *batch input* method could have been executed for migration of vendor data using *call transaction* method without any changes. But we changed our specifications of the present hands-on exercise. We specified that

1.  the text data files reside on the application server

2.  a log file as a text file be created on the application server

All other specifications remained the same as in hands-on exercise I.

We implemented hands-on exercise II in two stages; the first stage implemented item (1). The second stage was an extension to implement item (2).

The source data was created on the presentation server using a text editor and copied on the application server with the transaction code USS_FAS.

A data flow diagram traced the flow of data when the data migration program would be run using the *call transaction* method.

The implementation of (1) locating input text files on the application server and (2) creating a log file on the application server involved the modification of the main as well as the include program BDCRECX1. We copied the program (main) YCH05_XK01_PROGRAM_BI_TB_SC of the previous hands-on exercise into YCH05_XK01_PROGRAM_CALL_TRAN. This became the main program for the current hands-on exercise. We copied the include program BDCRECX1 into YCH05_BDCRECX1 and activated it. In the main program, we changed the statement INCLUDE BDCRECX1 to INCLUDE YCH05_BDCRECX1.

The implementation of locating the input text files on the application server involved modifications to the main program only. We modified the selection screen statements in the main program to input text file names located on the application server. We modified the main program to fetch data from text files on the application server into the internal tables—OPEN DATASET, READ DATASET, CLOSE DATASET, etc. We activated the main program.

We executed the program choosing the *call transaction* method. The execution of the program produced an output that reported which vendors were created and which vendors were generating errors. The program output was produced by the WRITE statements located in the subroutine BDC_TRANSACTION of the include program YCH05_BDCRECX1.

As we had intentionally created an erroneous vendor in the input data, a session with erroneous data was created which we viewed in transaction code SM35. We cross-verified the creation of non-erroneous vendors in transaction code XK02. This concluded the first stage of implementation—locating the input text files on the application server.

The second stage of implementation—create a log file on the application server—involved modifications to both the main program and the include program. We decided that the log file will have almost the same contents as the output being produced by the program when it is executed choosing the *call transaction* method.

We incorporated TRANSFER statements following WRITE statements associated with the *call transaction* method to write to the log file. The TRANSFER statements were incorporated in the subroutines BDC_TRANSACTION and CLOSE_GROUP. Additional parameters were required to be received by these subroutines.

Appropriate data declarations were created in the main program. The log file on the application server is to be opened in output mode. Hence the main program contained the statements OPEN DATASET..... and CLOSE DATASET..... statements. The subroutine invocation statements CALL BDC_TRANSACTION and CALL CLOSE_GROUP in the main program had to be modified to pass additional parameters.

After carrying out the modifications to the main and include programs for the creation of log files, we activated the programs.

New source data was created on the presentation server using a text editor and copied to the application server with transaction code USS_FAS.

We executed the program choosing the *call transaction* method. The execution of the program produced output which reported the vendors created successfully as well as the vendors generating errors.

As we had intentionally created an erroneous vendor in the input data, a session with erroneous data was created which we viewed in transaction code SM35. We cross-verified the creation of non-erroneous vendors in transaction code XK02. Finally, we displayed the log file using transaction code USS_FAS. This concluded the second stage of hands-on exercise implementation—the creation of a log file on the application server.

# Batch Input vis-à-vis Call Transaction Methods

The *batch input* and the *call transaction* methods are referred to as classical methods for data migration. If a BAPI method—*create from data* or *IDoc* type—is available for an entity, it should be the preferred mode for the data migration of the entity.

Table 5-9 presents a comparison of the *batch input* and the *call transaction* methods. The comparison is not comprehensive and lists only items related to our coverage in hands-on exercises I and II.

***Table 5-9.*** *Batch Input vs. Call Transaction*

| batch input | call transaction |
| --- | --- |
| There are two stages of processing: the first stage, when input data is written to the session database tables; the second stage when data is extracted from the session database tables, validated, and written to the SAP functional module database tables—running a session, etc. Because of the two stages, the processing time when compared to the *call transaction* method will be more. | The input data is validated and written to the SAP functional module database tables. Because of the single processing stage, the processing time when compared to the *batch input* method will be less. |
| There is a built-in error trapping and recovery mechanism in the running of a session—SM35 to view the error log, run the erroneous transactions again. | The error handling mechanism is not built-in and has to be incorporated into the data migration program by the developer. |
| If the data being migrated is large—tens of thousands of entities—and the expected erroneous data is high—3% or higher—then, between the two classical data migration methods, the *batch input* is to be preferred. | If the expected erroneous data is on the low side—less than 3%—then, between the two classical data migration methods, the *call transaction* is to be preferred. |
| Multiple transactions can be recorded in one session. | Only one transaction can be called with the ABAP statement: CALL TRANSACTION.... |
| The update mode is synchronous only. | The update mode can be specified at runtime. |

# Conclusion

We commenced the chapter with a description of the requirement for importing data from non-SAP systems into the SAP systems—scenarios for data import. We termed the non-SAP system a "legacy system," the data of the legacy system as "legacy data," and the import of legacy data into the SAP systems as "data migration."

Some commonly occurring issues and considerations associated with data migration were listed. A universal issue is the support of different data types on different systems and certain data types supported on one system and not supported on another. The character type or text-oriented type is supported universally. We decided that all of the input data in our data migration exercises will be character type or text oriented.

I introduced the different data migration methods and workbenches available in the SAP system.

I detailed the concept of recording a transaction and the generation of an ABAP program from a recorded transaction. As an illustration, we recorded transaction code FI01—create bank master. The generated ABAP program from recording simulated the process of data entered and operations performed on the screen. The generated ABAP program invoked the SAP-supplied include program BDCRECX1. The include program BDCRECX1 was overviewed, especially its subroutines BDC_OPEN_GROUP, BDC_CLOSE_GROUP, BDC_TRANSACTION, BDC_DYNPRO, BDC_FIELD, etc. I described the manner in which the internal table BDCDATA is filled up.

The generated program from the recording of a specific transaction can be modified suitably to accept data from text files residing either on the presentation server or the application server and migrate it to the SAP system. So, a custom program can be created for migration of any data. The core of the custom program is generated from the recording of the transaction.

If you wish to write screen simulation ABAP statements, you will require technical information such as the dynpro program name, screen number, field name, and so on. SAP provides the means to determine the technical information on any screen. To determine a field name on a screen, position the cursor on the screen field and press the function key F1. The *Performance Assistant* dialog box pops up. When you click the *Technical Information* button of the *Performance Assistant* dialog box, all the technical information related to screen including the field name is displayed.

After an exposure to the data migration tools, we proceeded to the first hands-on exercise: migrate vendor data using the *batch input* method. The execution of the program using the *batch input* method generates a session.

Initially, I described the specification and scope of the hands-on exercise. A vendor can consist of multiple banks. I also described the maintenance of multiple rows on a screen and the related programming to tackle multiple rows on a screen. The source data would reside on the presentation server. The source data would consist of two text files. A list of fields that would assume values was prepared. Because our primary focus was on the demonstration of deployment of data migration tools, I decided to assign values to the all mandatory fields and very few non-mandatory fields. For the fields to be assigned values, we determined which fields would be assigned constant values, which fields would be assigned values from text files, which fields would be derived from values of other fields, etc.

A data flow diagram traced the flow of data when executing a program using the *batch input* method.

I listed the tasks to be carried out to perform the hands-on exercise. I described and implemented each of the task listed. The data migration program was executed twice with two sets of data. The first time data migration program was executed, we processed the session in the foreground. The second time data migration program was executed, we processed the session in the background.

While performing the first hands-on exercise, I introduced a few transaction codes:

- SHDB—transaction recorder

- SM35—batch input sessions

- XK02—change vendor

We concluded the first hands-on exercise by tackling the issue when the number of banks for vendors exceeds the number of visible rows in the table control area.

Our second hands-on exercise was to migrate vendor data using the *call transaction* method. The program we created for the first hands-on exercise could very well have been used for migration of vendor data using the *call transaction* method. But I decided to change the specifications of the second hands-on exercise. I specified that (1) the input text files would reside on the application server instead of the presentation server and (2) we would create a log file on the application server since no log is created with the *call transaction* method by default. Except for these two features, the specifications of the second hands-on exercise were identical to the specifications of the first hands-on exercise.

We made a copy of the program we had created for the first hands-on exercise and made modifications in the copy to incorporate the features of our specifications. We incorporated the features in two stages.

In the first stage, we incorporated the feature of input text files residing on the application server into the program. We created a new set of data on the presentation server and copied this created data to the application server using transaction code USS_FAS. We executed the program using the *call transaction* method. We cross-verified the migration of vendor data.

In the second stage of the hands-on exercise, we had to incorporate the feature of creating a log file on the application server. We had to decide on the contents of the log file. When we execute the program using the *call transaction* method, an output is produced which provides details of each vendor created successfully/unsuccessfully. This output is produced by the WRITE statements in the subroutines BDC_TRANSCTION and BDC_CLOSE of the include program BDCRECX1. We decided that we could include the same information as was output with WRITE statements in our log file. This required the modification of the program BDCRECX1. We made a copy of the program BDCRECX1 and carried out the requisite modifications. We again created a new set of data on the presentation server and copied this created data to the application server using transaction code USS_FAS. We executed the program using the *call transaction* method. We cross-verified the migration of vendor data as well as the creation and contents of log file.

The program of the first hands-on exercise accepts input data from the presentation server and can be executed using either the *batch input* or the *call transaction* method. If the program is executed using the *call transaction* method, no log is produced.

The program of the second hands-on exercise accepts input data from the application serverand can be executed using either the *batch input* or the *call transaction* method. If the program is executed using the *call transaction* method, a log file is produced on the application server.

In Chapter 6, we will continue with the data migration hands-on exercises deploying LSMW.

■ ■ ■

# Data Migration Using Legacy System Migration Workbench LSMW-I

In Chapter 5, we performed migration of external data into the SAP system using custom-created ABAP programs, the core of these custom=created programs being generated by the system from the recording of transactions. We, as developers, had complete access and control over the custom-created programs.

In this chapter and the next, for migration of external data into SAP system, we are shifting to the legacy system migration workbench – LSMW. In the LSMW environment, a ready-to-use SAP supplied programs can be deployed for migration of external data into the SAP system for a host of common business objects like customers, vendors, materials, purchasing documents, billing documents, and so on.

In the LSMW environment, in addition to the ready-to-use SAP supplied programs, the feature of recording of transactions (with constraints) is also available. Recording can be utilized in the LSMW environment for migration of external data into the SAP system. But in the LSMW environment, you, as a developer, do not have access to modifications to the program generated from the recording.

If your data migration requirements map to any of the SAP supplied programs inside the LSMW environment, you can perform the migration of external data into the SAP system using the LSMW. If you require recording of a transaction without the necessity of the developer's access to the generated program, you can use the transaction recording feature of LSMW to perform the migration of external data into the SAP system. If your data migration requirements do not map to the SAP supplied programs inside the LSMW environment, or if you require access and control over the generated program from recording, you have to perforce resort to the data migration methods described in Chapter 5.

Depending on your requirements, you can choose the program to transfer external data into SAP systems. Three categories or types of programs are available: (1) *Standard Batch/Direct Input*, (2) *Business Object (BAPI)*, and (3) *IDoc (Intermediate Document)*.

Apart from these three types of programs, you can create and deploy custom data transfer using transaction recording with no control, as a developer, over the generated program from the recording.

The three types of programs along with the recording option are termed *Object Types*.

In the LSMW environment, you create a series of configuration steps. Once the configuration steps are created, you can execute the configured steps as you execute an ABAP program.

The first of the configuration step consists of the selection of one of the three program types—(1) *Standard Batch/Direct Input*, (2) *Business Object (BAPI)*, or (3) *IDoc (Intermediate Document)*—or, alternative to the three program types, a recorded transaction. If data is being migrated using one of the three program types, then, the first configuration step also involves the selection of a business object to be migrated like customers, vendors, materials, purchasing documents, billing documents, and so on.

© Sushil Markandeya 2017
S. Markandeya, *Pro SAP Scripts, Smartforms, and Data Migration*,
https://doi.org/10.1007/978-1-4842-3183-8_6

Once a program type and business object or recorded transaction has been specified, within the LSMW environment, you can specify further configuration steps like the following:

- The specification of input structures.

- The layout of input structures—fields in the input structures.

- The mapping of input structures to destination structures.

- Specification of how the destination fields will assume values: assignment to input fields, assignment to a constant value, deriving the destination fields from other fields, and so on. This configuration step allows ABAP code.

- Specification of input text files.

- Assignment of input text files to input structures.

The configuration steps will be mostly created once, like a program. The configuration steps are followed by execution steps:

- Read input text files data.

- Optionally, display the read data.

- Convert data. The convert data step involves the destination fields assuming values as per the configuring step—specification of how the destination fields will assume values.

- Optionally, display the converted data.

- Create session or create *IDocs*.

- Run direct input program or session or transfer *IDocs*.

If for a business object, the external data is to be migrated into the SAP system on a periodic basis, then the execution steps are to be performed repeatedly.

The configuration steps together with the execution steps will be called the process steps.

In the LSMW, for a business object, from a single screen, a series of configuration steps are performed mostly once. Then, from the same screen, a series of execution steps are performed every time external data is required to be migrated into the SAP system for the business object. If requirements or scenario does not need ABAP programming, the data migration configuration steps can be created by non-technical personnel.

# LSMW—*Project* Structure and an Overview of the Opening Screen

You can navigate to the LSMW environment by using the transaction code LSMW. The opening screen of LSMW will appear as shown in Figure 6-1.

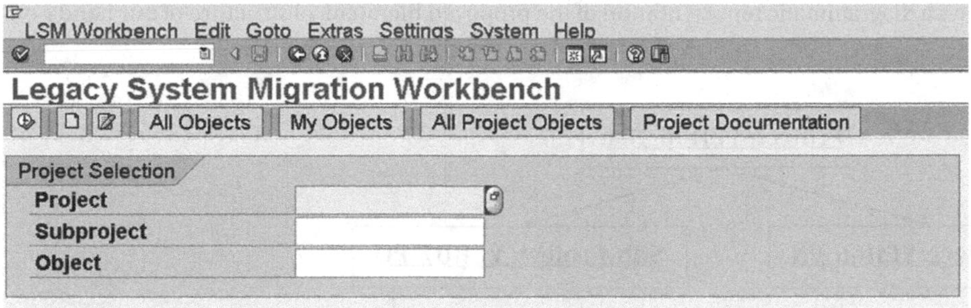

**Figure 6-1.** *LSMW—opening screen*

The opening screen of LSMW has the *Project Selection* area as shown in Figure 6-1. The *Project Selection* area prompts for *Project, Subproject,* and *Object*. The structure and nature are elaborated under the following subheading: *Project* structure.

## *Project* Structure

The *Project, Subproject,* and *Object* provide you with a hierarchical structure in which you can organize your objects created in the LSMW environment as per your requirements.

The *Project* is the first level of the hierarchical structure. A *Project* can contain under it, any number of *Subprojects*.

The *Subproject* is at the second level of the hierarchical structure. A *Subproject* can contain under it, any number of *Objects*.

The *Object* is at the last level of the hierarchical structure. An *Object* will map to a business object of which you want to migrate data, such as customer, vendor, material, purchasing document, billing document, and so on.

Apart from the Subprojects under a Project and Objects under Subprojects, a Project can contain optionally under it Recordings, Fixed Values, Translations, and User-Defined Routines. The Recordings, Fixed Values, Translations, and User-Defined Routines can be used across all Objects in a Project

You can create a new *Project*, a new *Subproject*, and a new *Object*. You can create a new *Subproject* and a new *Object* under an existing *Project*. You can create a new *Object* under an existing *Project* and *Subproject*. You can retrieve an existing *Project, Subproject,* and *Object*.

As an illustration, we are presenting the proposed hierarchical structure of our hands-on exercises to be performed in this chapter and Chapter 7. In the proposed hierarchical structure of our hands-on exercises, we will create a *Project* named YCH06_DM. Under the *Project* YCH06_DM, we will locate two *Subprojects*:

1. YCH06_VN—to migrate data of vendors

2. YCH07_PO—to migrate data of purchase orders

Under the *Subproject* YCH06_VN, we will locate two *Objects*:

1.1. YCH06_DI—to migrate data of vendors using the *Standard Batch/Direct Input*

1.2. YCH06_RC—to migrate data of vendors using the *Batch Input Recording*

Under the *Subproject* YCH07_PO, we will locate two *Objects*:

2.1. YCH07_IDOC—to migrate data of purchase orders using the *IDoc (Intermediate Document)*

2.2. YCH07_BAPI—to migrate data of purchase orders using the *Business Object (BAPI)*

Figure 6-2 shows a diagrammatic representation of the proposed hierarchical structure of our hands-on exercises.

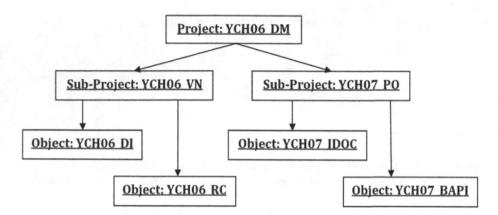

***Figure 6-2.*** *LSMW environment—hierarchical structure of Projects, Subprojects, and Objects*

We next present an overview of some of the application toolbar buttons and menu options available on the opening screen of the LSMW environment.

## LSMW Opening Screen Overview—Some Application Toolbar Buttons and Menu Options

In the LSMW environment, the names of *Projects, Subprojects,* and *Objects* can start with an alphabet letter (need not start with Y or Z) and the rest of the characters can be alphanumeric with embedded underscores and hyphens, a maximum of 15 characters.

When you click the application toolbar button *All Objects* on the LSMW opening screen (Figure 6-1), *Projects, Subprojects,* and *Objects* of all the users appear as a pop-up list and you can select from this list.

When you click the application toolbar button *My Objects* on the LSMW opening screen (Figure 6-1), *Projects, Subprojects,* and *Objects* of the logged-in user appear as a pop-up list and you can select an item from the list.

When you click the application toolbar button *All Project Objects* on the LSMW opening screen (Figure 6-1), *Projects, Subprojects,* and *Objects* of the specified values/pattern/all (of all users) appear in a tree form with modes, subnodes, etc.

We clicked the application toolbar button *All Project Objects* without any values in the three fields *Projects, Subprojects,* and *Objects* (all *Projects* of all users). A screen like the one in Figure 6-3 appeared.

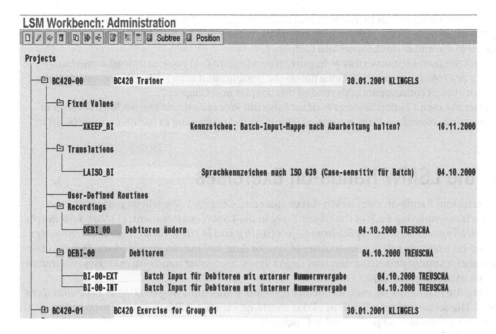

**Figure 6-3.** *LSMW Environment—All Project Objects screen*

All the *Projects* of all the users appear in tree form in Figure 6-3. The node of the *Project* BC420-00 has been fully expanded in Figure 6-3. You can perform the operations of create, delete, copy, and rename on any of the *Projects* and the objects under a *Project*.

In an IDES server, the BC420.....series of *Projects* meant for training are preloaded.

This was just to provide you with a preview of the *All Project Objects* screen.

You can maintain project documentation by clicking the button *Project Documentation* on the application toolbar.

Figure 6-4 shows the suboptions under the menu options *Goto, Extras,* and *Settings.*

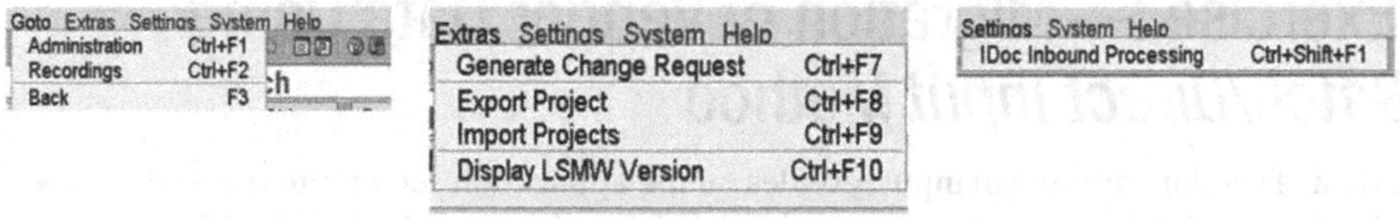

**Figure 6-4.** *LSMW Environment—menu options: Goto, Extras, and Settings*

When you select the menu option Goto ➤ Administration (Figure 6-4), all the *Projects, Subprojects,* and *Objects* of all users appear in a tree form with modes, subnodes, etc. You can perform the operations of create, delete, copy, and rename on any of the *Projects* and the objects under a *Project*. This menu option is similar to the application toolbar button *All Project Objects* except that you cannot retrieve specific value/pattern *Projects*.

When you select the menu option Goto ➤ Recordings (Figure 6-4) you can perform recordings of transactions. We will perform a recording of a transaction in hands-on exercise II in this chapter.

When you select the menu option Extras ➤ Generate Change Request (Figure 6-4) you can create a change request for the entire project for transportation to another system.

When you select the menu option Extras ➤ Export Project (Figure 6-4) you can download a *Project* or its specific constituents as a file on the presentation server. We will demonstrate the export of a *Project* or its specific constituents at the end of this chapter and Chapter 7.

When you select the menu option Extras ➤ Import Project (Figure 6-4) you can upload a previously downloaded *Project* or *Project* constituents from a file on the presentation server. We will demonstrate the import of a *Project* or *Project* constituents at the end of this chapter and Chapter 7.

When you select the menu option Settings ➤ IDoc Inbound Processing, you can perform settings of *IDoc* inbound processing. We will perform settings of *IDoc* inbound processing in hands-on exercise III in Chapter 7.

## A Brief on the LSMW Hands-on Exercises

We will be performing four hands-on exercises in this chapter and Chapter 7. We will be performing the four hands-on exercises employing each of the *Object Types* in the LSMW environment: (1) *Standard Batch/Direct Input*, (2) *Batch Input Recording*, (3) *Business Object (BAPI)*, and (4) *IDoc (Intermediate Document)*.

The four hands-on exercises will involve transfer of vendor data and purchase order data. Two hands-on exercises will transfer vendor data using different *Object Types*. Two other hands-on exercises will transfer purchase order data using different *Object Types*.

We will perform the first hands-on exercise involving vendor data employing the *Object Type*: *Standard Batch/Direct Input*. The scope and specifications of this hands-on exercise will be for the most part identical to those of the hands-on exercises we performed in Chapter 5.

We will perform the second hands-on exercise involving vendor data employing the *Object* Type: Batch *Input Recording*. The scope and specifications of this hands-on exercise will also be for the most part identical to those of the hands-on exercises we performed in Chapter 5.

The first and the second hands-on exercises will serve the purpose of comparing data migration deploying LSMW vis-à-vis data migration deploying a custom program created from a generated program of transaction recording.

We will perform the third hands-on exercise involving purchase order data employing the *Object Type*: IDoc (Intermediate Document). Finally, we will perform the fourth hands-on exercise involving purchase order data employing the *Object* Type: Business Object (BAPI).

In the performance of the four hands-on exercises, we will have employed most of the features of LSMW.

## Hands-on Exercise I—Migration of Vendor Data Using *Standard Batch/Direct Input* Method

We will transfer the data of vendors residing in input text files on the application server into the SAP functional module database tables deploying the *Standard Batch/Direct Input* method of LSMW. We will perform the data transfer with representative data of a three or four vendors. We will perform the data transfer for a few fields—all of the mandatory fields and very few non-mandatory fields. Of the fields designated for data transfer, most of the fields will be assigned the same constant value for all the vendors being transferred. We will locate in the input text files only the minimal data that varies from vendor to vendor. We will locate the input text data in two files. The first of the input files designated the main data will contain values for the following fields:

- LIFNR     Vendor/Vendor Number
- NAME1     Name
- STRAS     Street
- ORT01     City
- PSTLZ     Postal Code

The second of the input files designated the bank data, with a provision for multiple banks for a vendor, will contain values for the following fields:

- LIFNR     Vendor/Vendor Number
- BANKS     Country Key
- BANKL     Bank Key
- BANKN     Bank Account

The vendor number in the bank file is to connect the two files—which banks belong to which vendor.

The *Standard Batch/Direct Input* method of LSMW for vendors creates a batch input session as in hands-on exercise I in Chapter 5. The data is stored in the queue database tables when a batch input session is created. The created batch input session has to be executed subsequently, when data is extracted from queue database tables and transferred to the functional module database tables.

The *Standard Batch/Direct Input* method of LSMW for some business object-like materials does not create a batch input session but directly transfers data to the application database tables as in hands-on exercise II in Chapter 5.

All the foregoing descriptions must sound familiar. In fact, they are a brief recapitulation of specification and scope from Chapter 5. After all, we are performing the same task—transferring data of vendors from text files to the SAP systems. Only our methodology of transfer has changed from custom programs to LSMW.

A detailed description of specification, scope, and LSMW process steps follows.

## Specification and Scope

The hands-on exercise will transfer data from text files into the vendor master functional module database tables using the *Standard Batch/Direct input* method of LSMW. It is assumed that input data in the form of text files is in the required form and conversions have been effected. The input data in the form of text files will reside on and be accessed from the application server. The input will consist of two text files: (1) main data and (2) bank data. The two text files will be related through the vendor number—which of the bank(s) belongs to which vendor. We will maintain the text data with notepad editor on the presentation server and copy the text files from the presentation server to the application server using the transaction code USS_FAS, the same way we did it in chapter 5.

Other specifications of this hands-on exercise are identical to those of hands-on exercise I in Chapter 5.

We will assume that all the vendors being migrated have the same constant values for each of the following 11 fields (see Table 6-1, reproduced from Table 5-3 in Chapter 5):

*Table 6-1.* *Fields with Constant Values*

| Srl. No. | Field Name | Field Description | Value |
|----------|------------|-------------------|-------|
| 1 | BUKRS | Company Code | 0001 |
| 2 | EKORG | Purchasing Organization | 0001 |
| 3 | KTOKK | Account Group | 0001 |
| 4 | ANRED | Title | Company |
| 5 | LAND1 | Country Key | IN |
| 6 | SPRAS | Language Key | EN |
| 7 | AKONT | Reconciliation Account | 160000 |
| 8 | FDGRV | Cash Management Group | A1 |
| 9 | ZTERM | Payment Terms | 0001 |
| 10 | MAHNA | Dunning Procedure | 0001 |
| 11 | WAERS | Order Currency | INR |

■ **Caution**    Before you adopt these values, check the validity of these values on your system. If you are operating on an IDES server and logged into client 800, the above values should be all right.

The values for the following five fields will originate from the text file main data (see Table 6-2, reproduced from Table 5-4 in Chapter 5):

***Table 6-2.*** *Fields with Values Originating from Text File Main Data*

| Srl. No. | Field Name | Field Description |
|---|---|---|
| 1 | LIFNR | Vendor (Code or Number) |
| 2 | NAME1 | Vendor Name |
| 3 | STRAS | Street |
| 4 | ORT01 | City |
| 5 | PSTLZ | Postal Code |

The values for the following three fields will originate from the text file bank data (see Table 6-3, reproduced from Table 5-5 in Chapter 5):

***Table 6-3.*** *Fields with Values Originating from Text File Bank Data*

| Srl. No. | Field Name | Field Description |
|---|---|---|
|   | LIFNR | Vendor (To relate with the Main Data) |
| 1 | BANKS | Bank Country Key |
| 2 | BANKL | Bank Key |
| 3 | BANKN | Bank Account |

Recall, the field LIFNR in the bank data is for connecting the bank data with the main data, which banks belong to which vendor?

We will pick the first word of the field NAME1 (vendor name) and assign it to the field SORTL—SPLIT statement, etc.

There will be a total of 20 fields which will assume values—11 fields from Table 6-1, 5 fields from Table 6-2, 3 fields from Table 6-3, and 1 field, SORTL, being derived from another field, NAME1. (Refer to Table 5-2 in Chapter 5.)

Having described the specifications and scope of the hands-on exercise, we will proceed to the creation of a *Project*, a *Subproject,* and an *Object*. Following the creation of a *Project*, a *Subproject,* and an *Object* we will create and execute LSMW process steps.

## Create Project, Subproject, and Object

To create a *Project*, a *Subproject,* and an *Object*, we navigated to the opening screen of transaction code LSMW, entered *Project* name as YCH06_DM, entered *Subproject* name as YCH06_VN, and entered *Object* name as YCH06_DI as shown in Figure 6-5.

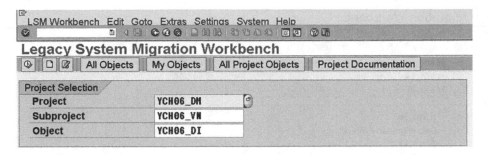

**Figure 6-5.** *LSMW—Create Project, Subproject, and Object*

We clicked the Create button on the application toolbar. The system successively popped up dialog boxes for descriptions of *Project, Subproject,* and *Object* as shown in Figures 6-6, 6-7, and 6-8.

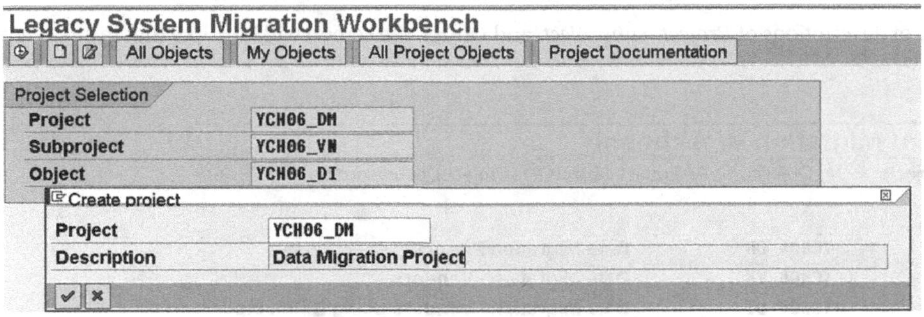

**Figure 6-6.** *LSMW—description for Project*

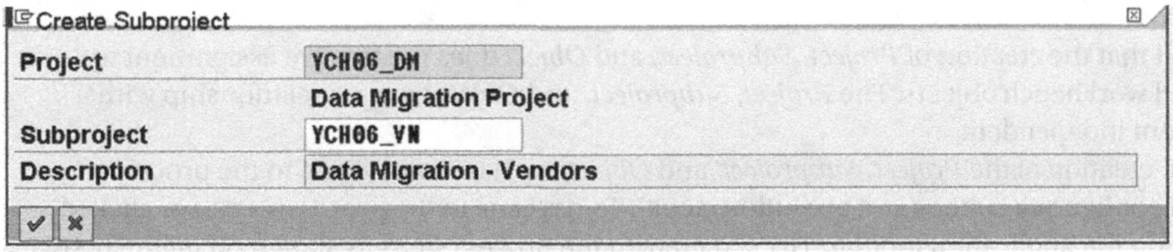

**Figure 6-7.** *LSMW—description for Subproject*

Legacy System Migration Workbench
All Objects
My Objects
All Project Objects
Project Documentation
Project Selection
Project YCH06_DM
Subproject YCH06_VN
Object YCH06_DI
Create Object
Project YCH06_DM
Data Migration Project
Subproject YCH06_VN
Data Migration - Vendors
Object YCH06_DI
Name Data Migration - Vendors Using Direct Input Method

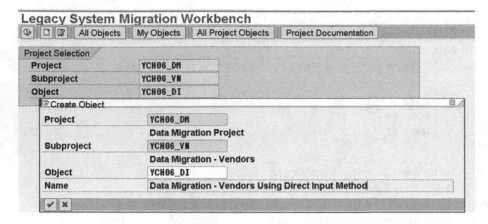

***Figure 6-8.*** *LSMW—description for Object*

After the entry of descriptions of *Project, Subproject,* and *Object,* the screen will look like that in Figure 6-9.

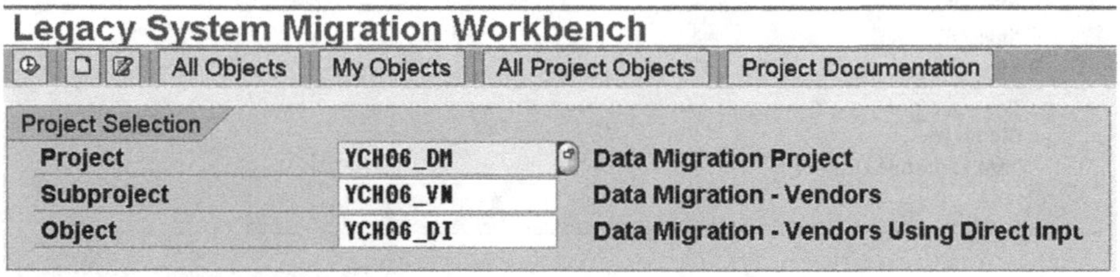

Legacy System Migration Workbench
All Objects
My Objects
All Project Objects
Project Documentation
Project Selection
Project YCH06_DM Data Migration Project
Subproject YCH06_VN Data Migration - Vendors
Object YCH06_DI Data Migration - Vendors Using Direct Inpu

***Figure 6-9.*** *LSMW—Project, Subproject, and Object created*

It is to be noted that the creation of *Project, Subproject,* and *Object* does not involve assignment to a package, unlike all workbench objects. The *Project, Subproject,* and *Object* have no relationship with a client—they are client independent.

After the initial creation of the *Project, Subproject,* and *Object,* we have to navigate to the process steps (consisting of configuration steps and execution steps). To navigate to the process steps, we clicked the Execute button on the application toolbar. The screen with the process steps as shown on Figure 6-10 appeared.

| Process Step | Last Action (Date, Time, User) |
|---|---|
| ● 1 Maintain Object Attributes | |
| ○ 2 Maintain Source Structures | |
| ○ 3 Maintain Source Fields | |
| ○ 4 Maintain Structure Relations | |
| ○ 5 Maintain Field Mapping and Conversion Rules | |
| ○ 6 Maintain Fixed Values, Translations, User-Defined Routines | |
| ○ 7 Specify Files | |
| ○ 8 Assign Files | |
| ○ 9 Read Data | |
| ○ 10 Display Read Data | |
| ○ 11 Convert Data | |
| ○ 12 Display Converted Data | |
| ○ 13 Create Batch Input Session | |
| ○ 14 Run Batch Input Session | |
| ○ 15 Start Direct Input Program | |
| ○ 16 Start IDoc Generation | |
| ○ 17 Start IDoc Processing | |
| ○ 18 Create IDoc Overview | |
| ○ 19 Start IDoc Follow-Up | |
| ○ 20 Frame Program for Periodic Data Transfer | |

**Figure 6-10.** *LSMW—process steps before executing process step 1*

The 20 numbered process steps appearing in Figure 6-10 apply to all *Object Types*: (1) *Standard Batch/Direct Input*, (2) *Batch Input Recording*, (3) *Business Object (BAPI)*, and (4) *IDoc (Intermediate Document)*. When you choose a specific *Object Type* in process step 1, the number of process steps will be reduced as applicable to the specific selected *Object Type*.

We will execute the process steps one after another. We will start off by executing process step 1 by selecting the Radio button and clicking the Execute button.

## Process Step 1—Maintain Object Attributes

When you navigate to any of the process step screens, the screen, by default, is in display mode. You use the Display/Change toggle button on the application toolbar to enable changes on the screen.

On the process step 1 screen, in the *Attributes area,* we entered and specified the following:

- Suitable description already entered during creation of the *Object.*

- The *Owner* as the logged-in user, which is the default. We can assign any other valid user name.

- The data transfer Radio button: *Once Only.*

  The Radio button nomenclature: *Once Only* is a trifle misleading, it does not mean that if you enable this Radio button, you can execute the LSMW process steps only once. You can, with this Radio button enabled, execute the process steps any number of times. Normally, you would repeat the process steps every time you want to mass transfer new data of an entity or a business object. When you want to mass transfer new data of an entity or a business object repeatedly, you would execute all the process steps the first time around. From second time onward, you would only execute the process step starting from process step 9—*Read Data.*

  If you enable the *Periodic* Radio button option, the LSMW system generates an extra process step appearing as the last process step.

The last process step—*Frame Program* (*/SAPDMC/SAP_LSMW_INTERFACE*)—is usually executed within the LSMW to specify runtime parameters for the *frame program* to be saved as a variant(s). The *frame program* can then be scheduled to run periodically in the background (from outside the LSMW environment) with a specific saved variant. The *frame program* expects input data on the application server only. The *frame program* executes the process steps one by one, commencing from the process step 9—*Read Data*. We are not demonstrating the enablement of the *Periodic* Radio button the creation and saving of variant(s), and a scheduled background execution of the *frame program*.

- The file names you are going to specify are not *System Specific*—check box disabled. With the *System Specific* option check box enabled, separate file names for separate SAP systems can be specified in process step 7—*Specify Files*

Figure 6-11 shows the *Attributes* area of the screen, with our entries and specifications.

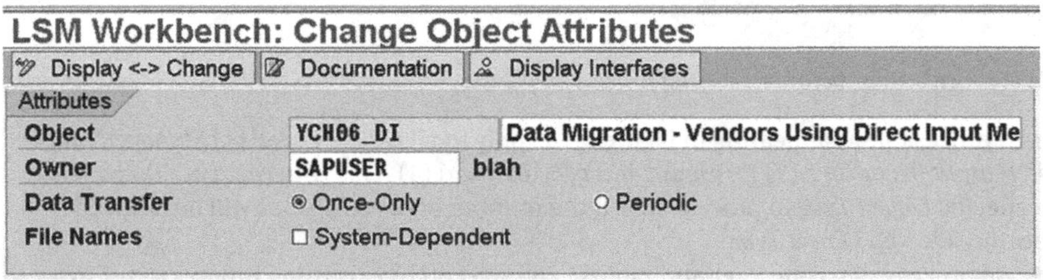

## LSM Workbench: Change Object Attributes

| ⅋ Display <-> Change | 🖋 Documentation | ⅋ Display Interfaces |
| --- | --- | --- |

| Attributes | | |
| --- | --- | --- |
| Object | YCH06_DI | Data Migration - Vendors Using Direct Input Me |
| Owner | SAPUSER | blah |
| Data Transfer | ◉ Once-Only | ○ Periodic |
| File Names | ☐ System-Dependent | |

***Figure 6-11.*** *Process step 1: Attributes area*

In the *Object Type and Import Method* area of the process step 1 screen, you select *Object Type* (Radio button) and *Object* (from a function key F4 list). We selected the *Object Type* as *Standard Batch/Direct Input* and popped up the *Object* list. Figure 6-12 illustrates.

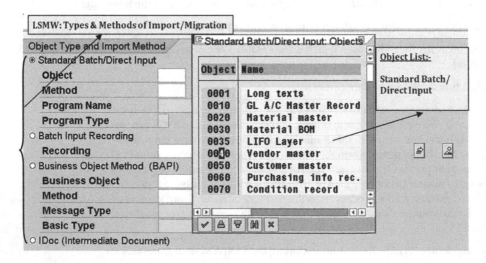

***Figure 6-12.*** *Process step 1—Object Type and Import Method area: Standard Batch/Direct Input Object list*

We selected from the *Object* list the following entry: 0040—vendor master. We selected the method as 001 standard. Figure 6-13 shows the screen with these assignments.

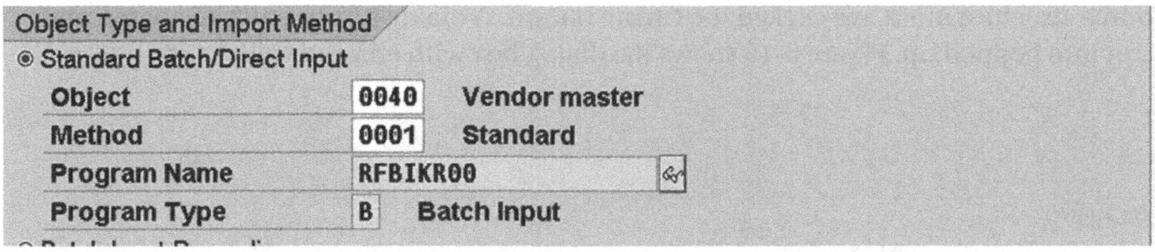

Object Type and Import Method
◉ Standard Batch/Direct Input

| | | |
|---|---|---|
| Object | 0040 | Vendor master |
| Method | 0001 | Standard |
| Program Name | RFBIKR00 | 🖉 |
| Program Type | B | Batch Input |

*Figure 6-13.* *Process step 1: Object Type and Import Method area*

When we saved and exited the screen of process step 1, the process steps screen looked like that in Figure 6-14.

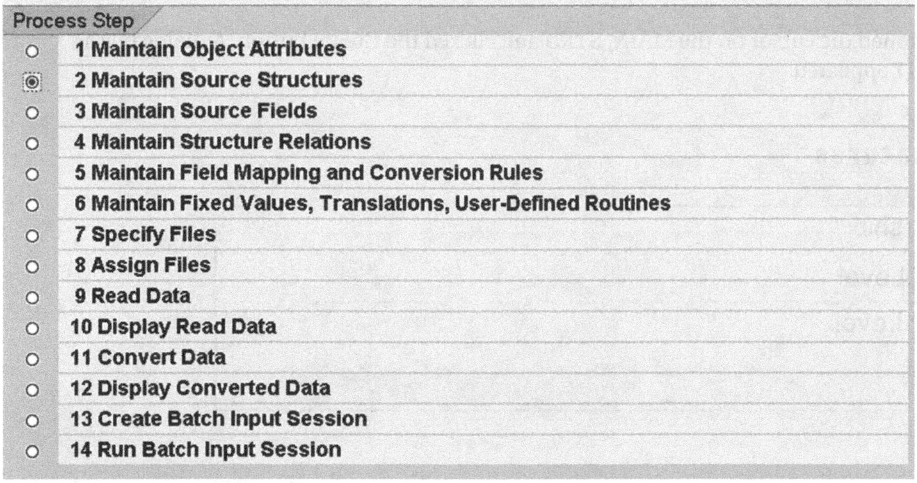

Process Step

| | |
|---|---|
| ○ | 1 Maintain Object Attributes |
| ◉ | 2 Maintain Source Structures |
| ○ | 3 Maintain Source Fields |
| ○ | 4 Maintain Structure Relations |
| ○ | 5 Maintain Field Mapping and Conversion Rules |
| ○ | 6 Maintain Fixed Values, Translations, User-Defined Routines |
| ○ | 7 Specify Files |
| ○ | 8 Assign Files |
| ○ | 9 Read Data |
| ○ | 10 Display Read Data |
| ○ | 11 Convert Data |
| ○ | 12 Display Converted Data |
| ○ | 13 Create Batch Input Session |
| ○ | 14 Run Batch Input Session |

*Figure 6-14.* *LSMW—Process steps after executing process step 1*

You can observe that the number of process steps stand reduced from 20 earlier to 14 after the execution of process step 1.

## Process Step 2—Maintain Source Structures

We navigated to the screen of process step 2. On the screen of process step 2, you specify the input or source structures. On the screen of process step 2, we first switched to change mode. Figure 6-15 shows the screen of process step 2.

LSM Workbench: Change Source Structures

🖉 □ 🖉 🗑 🖉 🖳 🔒 🗟 🗒 🗐 Subtree 🗐 Position

YCH06_DM - YCH06_VN - YCH06_DI Data Migration - Vendors Using Direct Input Method

Source Structures

*Figure 6-15.* *Process step 2—Maintain Source Structure*

In our proposed input, we are locating data in two text files—main and bank—which will map to two source structures. The bank structure is subservient to the main structure, since one vendor can have more than one bank.

To create the source structure main, we clicked the Create button. A dialog box to enter the name and description of the structure popped up. Figure 6-16 shows the dialog box with entered values.

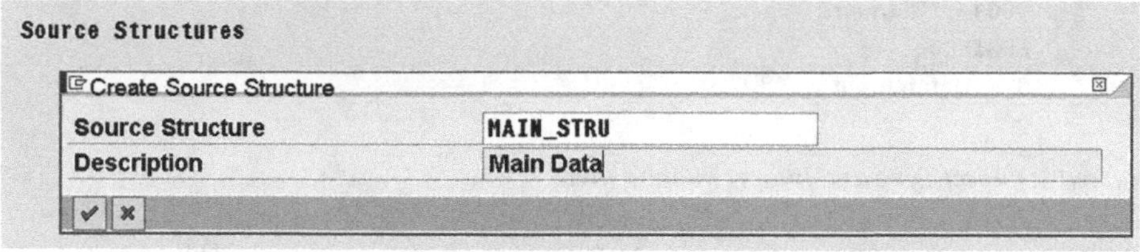

**Figure 6-16.** *Process step 2—Create Source Structure: MAIN_STRU*

Next, we positioned the cursor on the MAIN_STRU and clicked the Create button. A dialog box as shown in Figure 6-17 appeared.

**Figure 6-17.** *Process step 2—Create Source Structure: under MAIN_STRU*

As the structure bank is to be under the MAIN_STRU structure, we selected the Radio button *Lower Level*. Figure 6-18 shows the dialog box with entered values of name and description of the bank structure.

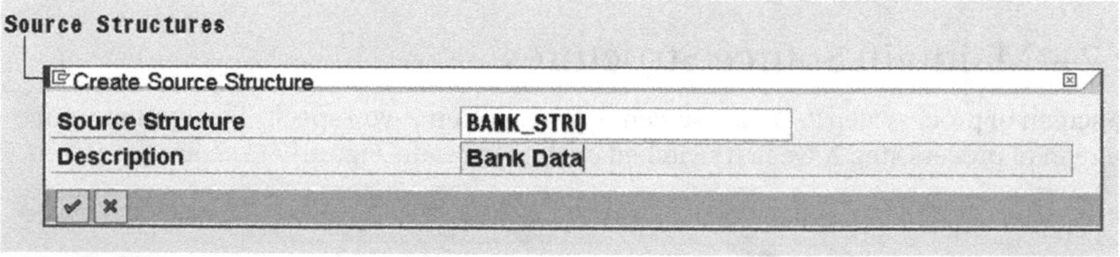

**Figure 6-18.** *Process step 2—Create Source Structure: BANK_STRU under MAIN_STRU*

Figure 6-19 shows the final source structures.

Source Structures
MAIN_STRU
Main Data
BANK_STRU
Bank Data

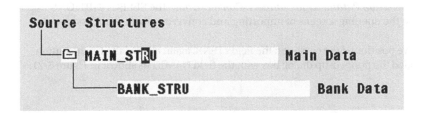

***Figure 6-19.*** *Process step 2—Create Source Structure: BANK_STRU under MAIN_STRU created*

We saved and returned to the screen with the process steps.

## Process Step 3—Maintain Source Fields

We executed process step 3. Process step 3 enables you to insert fields into the source structures. We switched the screen to change mode. We will, in the first stage, insert fields into source structure MAIN_STRU. To insert fields into source structure MAIN_STRU, we positioned the cursor on the MAIN_STRU and clicked the Create button. A screen prompting for field name, field description, field length, and field type appeared. We entered the field name as LIFNR, a suitable field description, field length as 10, and field type as C. Figure 6-20 shows the screen with entered values.

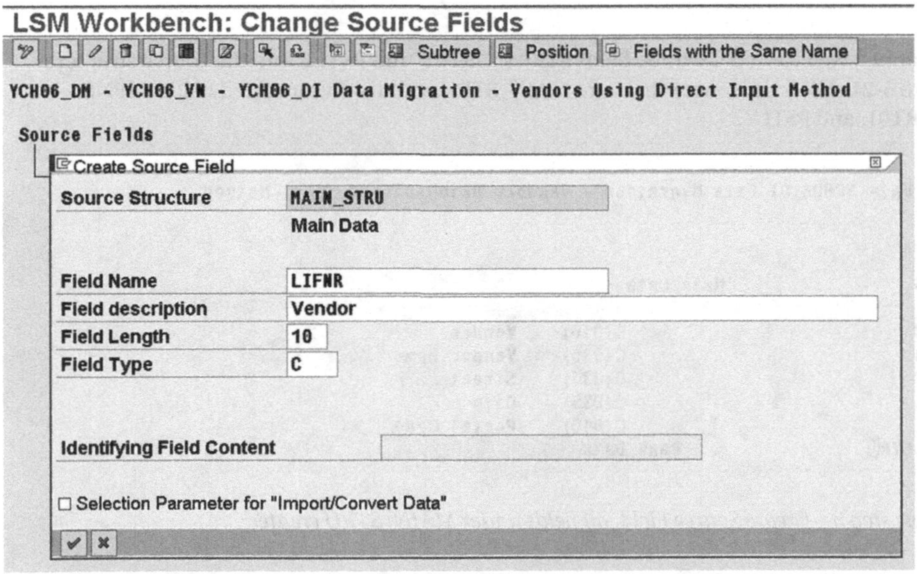

LSM Workbench: Change Source Fields
Subtree
Position
Fields with the Same Name
YCH06_DM - YCH06_VN - YCH06_DI Data Migration - Vendors Using Direct Input Method
Source Fields
Create Source Field
Source Structure
MAIN_STRU
Main Data
Field Name
LIFNR
Field description
Vendor
Field Length
10
Field Type
C
Identifying Field Content
Selection Parameter for "Import/Convert Data"

***Figure 6-20.*** *Process step 3—Create Source Field: LIFNR under MAIN_STRU*

We could have used a different field name, but LIFNR was convenient and it is preferable to use SAP database field names. We clicked the Continue button on the dialog box.

*Identifying Field Content* is applicable when you locate data of more than one structure in an input file. You enter the name of the structure in this field.

If you enable the check box *Selection Parameter for "Import/Convert Data,"* the SELECT-OPTIONS prompt of the field will appear on the opening screens of importing and converting data—process steps 9 and 11.

To continue creating fields, we positioned the cursor on the field LIFNR, again clicked the Create button on the application toolbar, and filled the popped-up dialog box with the field NAME1 as shown in Figure 6-21:

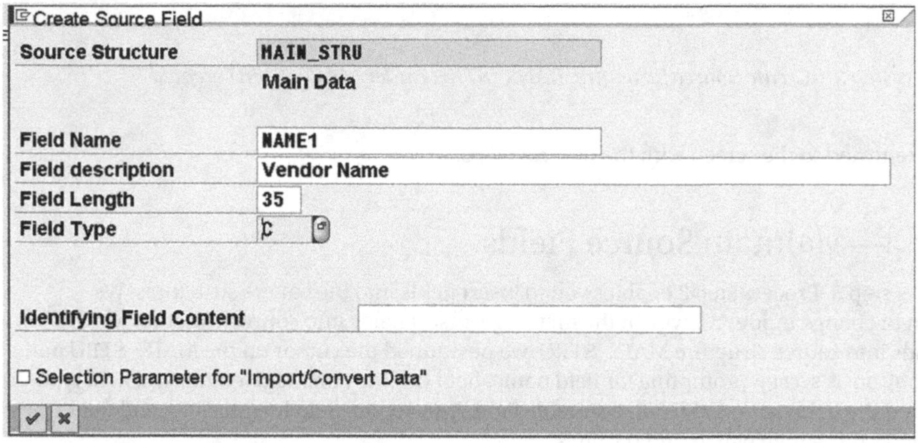

*Figure 6-21.* *Process step 3—Create Source Field: NAME1 under MAIN_STRU*

In a similar manner, we inserted the three fields STRAS, ORT01, and PSTLZ into the source structure MAIN_STRU. Figure 6-21 shows the source structure MAIN_STRU with the five inserted fields: LIFNR, NAME1, STRAS, ORT01, and PSTLZ.

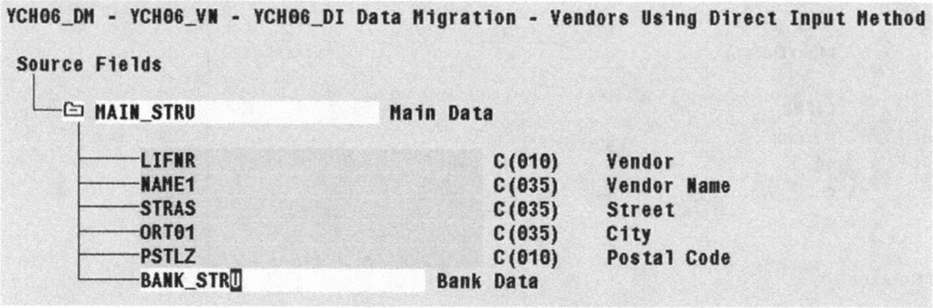

*Figure 6-22.* *Process step 3—Create Source Field: all fields under MAIN_STRU created*

The order of the fields in the source structure must be identical to the order in which data is located in the text files. The lengths of fields specified in the source structure must match the length of data in text files. We are using text files with one line for one vendor, with no field separators, and so on.

For each line in the main text file, the first 10 characters are designated for LIFNR, the next 35 characters are designated for NAME1, the next 35 are designated for STRAS, the next 35 are designated for ORT01, and the rest of the characters in the line (maximum of 10) are designated for PSTLZ.

For each line in the bank text file, the first 10 characters are designated for LIFNR, the next 3 characters are designated for BANKS, the next 15 are designated for BANKL, and the rest of the characters in the line (maximum of 18) are designated for BANKN.

The layout and the mode of text files are same as those we used in the hands-on exercises in Chapter 5.

We inserted the fields LIFNR, BANKS, BANKL, and BANKN into the source structure BANK_STRU. Figure 6-23 shows all the fields in the source structures MAIN_STRU and BANK_STRU.

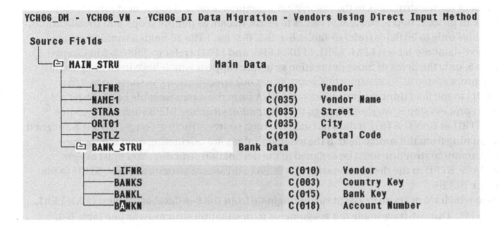

*Figure 6-23. Process step 3—Create Source Field: all fields under MAIN_STRU and BANK_STRU*

We saved and returned to the process steps screen.

## Process Step 4—Maintain Structure Relations

We executed process step 4 and switched the screen to change mode. In process step 4, you relate the destination structures to the source structures. In Figure 6-24, the destination structures appear on the left and source structure assigned to the destination structures appear on the extreme right.

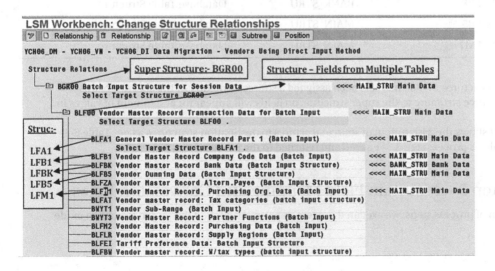

*Figure 6-24. Process step 4—Maintain Structure Relations*

457

First, we will focus on the organization of destination structures. At the very top of the destination structures tree is the super structure BGR00 marked in Figure 6-24. The structure BLF00 is located under the super structure BGR00, also marked in Figure 6-24. The structure BLF00 has fields originating from multiple database tables corresponding to the opening screen of transaction code XK01. Next to the structure BLF00 are located the database table structures BLFA1, BLFB1, BLFBK, BLFB5, BLFM1, and so on. These database table structures are also marked in Figure 6-24. The database table structures LFA1, LFB1, etc., are renamed with the prefix B in the destination structures' organization.

The assignment of source structures to the destination structures is related to the next process step (i.e., process step 5). In process step 5, you assign values to fields. Recall, as per the scope and specifications, we are assigning values only to 20 fields (refer to Tables 6-1, 6-2, 6-3, etc.) The 20 fields assuming values originate from the five database tables: LFA1, LFB1, LFBK, LFB5, and LFM1 (refer to Table 5-2 in Chapter 5)

In process step 5, only the fields of those destination structures appear which have been assigned a source structure in process step 4. To illustrate this point, as per our specifications, we have to assign a constant value (0001) to the field dunning procedure—MAHNA from the database table LFB5. To be able to implement this in process step 5, we should assign the destination structure BLFB5 any of the source structures: MAIN_STRU or BANK_STRU. It does not matter which source structure you assign if the assigned values are not originating from the source field. If the assigned values are originating from the source field, the appropriate source structure must be assigned to the destination structure. You must assign source structure MAIN_STRU to the destination structure BLFA1 and source structure BANK_STRU to the destination structure BLFBK.

The 20 fields to which we propose to assign values originate from the five database tables: LFA1, LFB1, LFBK, LFB5, and LFM1. Thus we have made the assignments to destination structures as per Table 6-4.

*Table 6-4. Source Structure Assignment to Destination Structures*

| Srl. No. | Destination Structure | Source Structure | Remarks |
|----------|----------------------|------------------|---------|
| 1 | BGR00 | MAIN_STRU | Super Structure |
| 2 | BLF00 | MAIN_STRU | Structure with Fields from Multiple Database Tables |
| 3 | BLFA1 | MAIN_STRU | Database Table Structure |
| 4 | BLFB1 | MAIN_STRU | Database Table Structure |
| 5 | BLFBK | BANK_STRU | Database Table Structure |
| 6 | BLFB5 | MAIN_STRU | Database Table Structure |
| 7 | BLFM1 | MAIN_STRU | Database Table Structure |

The super structures BGR00 has also been assigned a source structure. In the absence of this assignment of source structure to the super structure, no fields will appear for assignment of values in process step 5.

Figure 6-24 shows the assignment of source structures to destination structures as per Table 6-4. This completes process step 4. We saved and returned to the process steps screen.

# Process Step 5—Maintain Field Mapping and Conversion Rules

From the screen of process steps, we executed process step 5 and switched the screen to change mode.

In process step 5, you assign values to the destination fields. The destination fields can be assigned constants and fields of source structure, derived from other fields, and so on. Interfaces are available to make assignments. Whatever assignments made through interfaces will result in the generation of ABAP assignment statements by the LSMW system. Process step 5 is just one of the two areas in the LSMW environment where you can locate ABAP statements. Figure 6-25 shows the screen of process step 5 with tree nodes expanded.

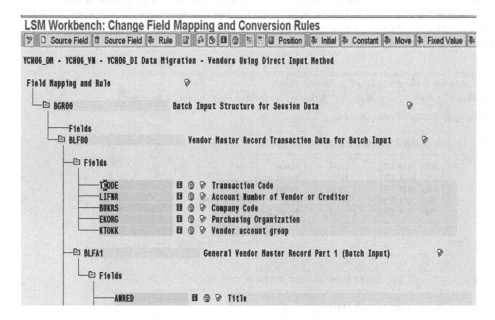

*Figure 6-25. Process step 5—Maintain Field Mapping and Conversion Rules*

At the head of the tree is the node of the super structure BGR00. Under the superstructure BGR00, the constituent structures BLF00, BLFA1, and so on appear with their fields. The first structure, BLF00, corresponds to the opening screen of transaction code XK01, except that it has one extra field. The extra field is the very first field, TCODE—transaction code. You have to assign the value XK01 to this field.

Let us go about assigning values to destination fields starting with BLF00-TCODE. In Figure 6-26, you can observe the application toolbar buttons available to perform assignments to destination fields. Two of application toolbar buttons we will employ most frequently, *Source Field* and *Constant,* are marked in Figure 6-26.

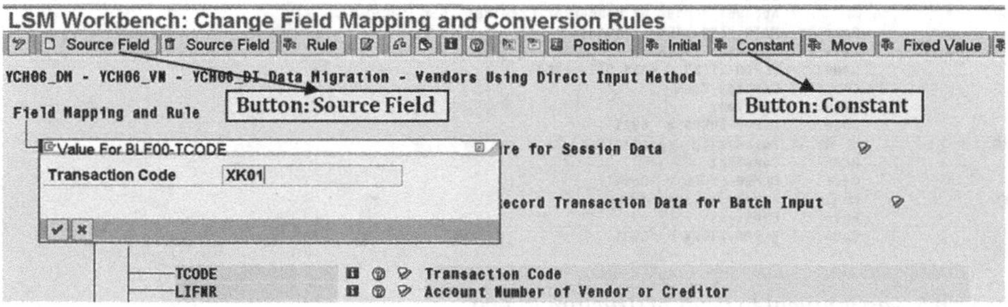

*Figure 6-26. Process step 5—value for BLF00-TCODE*

To assign the literal or constant 'XK01' to the destination field BLF00-TCODE, we first positioned the cursor on the destination field BLF00-TCODE and then clicked the application toolbar button *Constant*. A dialog box popped up prompting for the constant value. We entered the constant value XK01 as shown in Figure 6-26.

We clicked the Continue button on the popped-up dialog box.

Next, we will make an assignment to the destination field BLF00-LIFNR. The value of the destination field BLF00-LIFNR originates from source field MAIN_STRU-LIFNR. We positioned the cursor on the destination field BLF00-LIFNR and then clicked the application toolbar button *Source Field*. A selection list popped up listing all the fields of the source structure MAIN_STRU. We selected the field LIFNR from the selection list as shown in Figure 6-27.

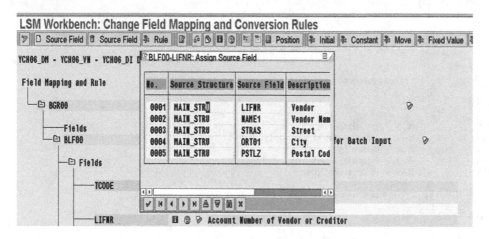

*Figure 6-27.* *Process step 5—BLF00-LIFNR: Assign Source Field*

The rest of the destination fields in the structure BLF00—BUKRS, EKORG, and KTOKK—have to be assigned constant values as per Table 6-1. We used the same procedure we used for the destination field BLF00-TCODE to assign values to the destination fields BLF00-BUKRS, BLF00-EKORG, and BLF00-KTOKK.

The screen after assignment to all the destination fields of structure BLF00 will look like that in Figure 6-28.

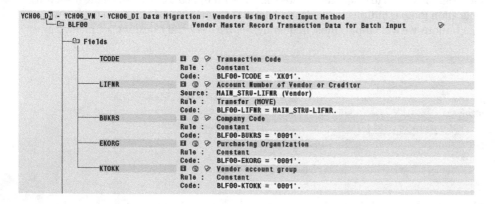

*Figure 6-28.* *Process step 5—assignment to fields of structure BLF00*

As you can observe in Figure 6-28, ABAP assignment statements have been generated from the assignments we made through the application toolbar buttons *Source Field* and *Constant*:

```
BLF00-TCODE = 'XK01'.
BLF00-LIFNR = MAIN_STRU-LIFNR.
.....
```

If you double-click any of these assignments on the *Field Mapping and Conversion Rules* screen, you will navigate to the ABAP line editor screen (not the ABAP text editor). You could have manually entered the ABAP assignment statements in the ABAP line editor by clicking the application toolbar button *Rule* and selecting *ABAP Code* from the list of options.

In the manner in which we assigned values to the destination fields of structure BLF00, we assigned values to the designated destination fields of the structure BLFA1. The screen after assignment to all the designated destination fields of structure BLFA1 will look like that in Figures 6-29 and 6-30.

```
YCH06_DM - YCH06_VM - YCH06_DI Data Migration - Vendors Using Direct Input Method
          ┌──ANRED            ⊞ ⊛ ∅ Title
          │                   Rule :  Constant
          │                   Code:   BLFA1-ANRED = 'Company'.
          ┌──NAME1            ⊞ ⊛ ∅ Name 1
          │                   Source: MAIN_STRU-NAME1 (Vendor Name)
          │                   Rule :  Transfer (MOVE)
          │                   Code:   BLFA1-NAME1 = MAIN_STRU-NAME1.
          ┌──NAME2            ⊞ ⊛ ∅ Name 2
          ┌──NAME3            ⊞ ⊛ ∅ Name 3
          ┌──NAME4            ⊞ ⊛ ∅ Name 4
          ┌──SORTL            ⊞ ⊛ ∅ Sort field
          ┌──STRAS            ⊞ ⊛ ∅ House number and street
          │                   Source: MAIN_STRU-STRAS (Street)
          │                   Rule :  Transfer (MOVE)
          │                   Code:   BLFA1-STRAS = MAIN_STRU-STRAS.
          ┌──PFACH            ⊞ ⊛ ∅ PO Box
          ┌──ORT01            ⊞ ⊛ ∅ City
          │                   Source: MAIN_STRU-ORT01 (City)
          │                   Rule :  Transfer (MOVE)
          │                   Code:   BLFA1-ORT01 = MAIN_STRU-ORT01.
          ┌──PSTLZ            ⊞ ⊛ ∅ Postal Code
          │                   Source: MAIN_STRU-PSTLZ (Postal Code)
          │                   Rule :  Transfer (MOVE)
```

***Figure 6-29.*** *Process step 5—assignment to fields of structure BLFA1*

```
YCH06_DM - YCH06_VM - YCH06_DI Data Migration - Vendors Using Direct Input Method
          ┌──PSTL2            ⊞ ⊛ ∅ P.O. Box Postal Code
          ┌──LAND1            ⊞ ⊛ ∅ Country Key
          │                   Rule :  Constant
          │                   Code:   BLFA1-LAND1 = 'IN'.
          ┌──REGIO            ⊞ ⊛ ∅ Region (State, Province, County)
          ┌──SPRAS            ⊞ ⊛ ∅ Language Acc. to ISO 639 (Batch Input Field)
          │                   Rule :  Constant
          │                   Code:   BLFA1-SPRAS = 'EN'.
          ┌──TELX1            ⊞ ⊛ ∅ Telex number
          ┌──TELF1            ⊞ ⊛ ∅ First telephone number
```

***Figure 6-30.*** *Process step 5—assignment to fields of structure BLFA1—continued*

We have not assigned value to the designated destination field SORTL in the structure BLFA1. The value of destination field BLFA1-SORTL is to be derived as the first word from the destination field BLFA1-NAME1. We will implement the derivation of the field in process step 6. After performing process step 6, we will return to process step 5 and make an assignment to destination field BLFA1-SORTL.

We assigned values to the designated destination fields of the structure BLFB1. The screen after assignment to all the designated destination fields of structure BLFB1 will look like that in Figure 6-31.

```
YCH06_DM - YCH06_VN - YCH06_DI Data Migration - Vendors Using Direct Input Method
            ──────AKONT                  ⬛ ⊚ ▽ Reconciliation Account in General Ledger
                                         Rule :   Constant
                                         Code:    BLFB1-AKONT = '0000016000'.
            ──────ZUAWA                  ⬛ ⊚ ▽ Key for sorting according to assignment numbers
            ──────LNRZE                  ⬛ ⊚ ▽ Head office account number
            ──────BLNKZ                  ⬛ ⊚ ▽ Subsidy indicator for determining the reduction rates
            ──────XDEZV                  ⬛ ⊚ ▽ Indicator: Local processing?
            ──────FDGRV                  ⬛ ⊚ ▽ Planning group
                                         Rule :   Constant
                                         Code:    BLFB1-FDGRV = 'A1'.
            ──────BEGRU                  ⬛ ⊚ ▽ Authorization Group
```

***Figure 6-31.*** *Process step 5—assignment to fields of structure BLFB1*

We deliberately assigned an invalid value 0000016000 instead of the valid value 0000160000 to the destination field BLFB1-AKONT to highlight the effect of the assignment of invalid values to destination fields (refer to Table 6-1).

Whenever a destination field is a foreign key field, function key F4 facility is expected when a constant is to be assigned to the destination field. The function key F4 facility is not always available when a constant is to be assigned to a destination field that is also a foreign key field.

We assigned values to the designated destination fields of the structure BLFBK. The screen after assignment to all the designated destination fields of structure BLFBK will look like that in Figure 6-32.

```
YCH06_DM - YCH06_VN - YCH06_DI Data Migration - Vendors Using Direct Input Method
        ──⬛ BLFB1                          Vendor Master Record Company Code Data (Batch Input)        ▽
        ──⬛ BLFBK                          Vendor Master Record Bank Data (Batch Input Structure)      ▽

            └─⬛ Fields

            ──────XDELE                  ⬛ ⊚ ▽ Indicator: Delete entry using batch input ?
            ──────BANKS                  ⬛ ⊚ ▽ Bank country key
                                         Source:  BANK_STRU-BANKS (Country Key)
                                         Rule :   Transfer (MOVE)
                                         Code:    BLFBK-BANKS = BANK_STRU-BANKS.
            ──────BANKL                  ⬛ ⊚ ▽ Bank Keys
                                         Source:  BANK_STRU-BANKL (Bank Key)
                                         Rule :   Transfer (MOVE)
                                         Code:    BLFBK-BANKL = BANK_STRU-BANKL.
            ──────BANKN                  ⬛ ⊚ ▽ Bank account number
                                         Source:  BANK_STRU-BANKN (Account Number)
                                         Rule :   Transfer (MOVE)
                                         Code:    BLFBK-BANKN = BANK_STRU-BANKN.
```

***Figure 6-32.*** *Process step 5—assignment to fields of structure BLFBK*

We assigned values to the designated destination fields of the structures BLFB5 and BLFM1. The screen after assignment to all the designated destination fields of structures BLFB5 and BLFM1will look like that in Figure 6-33.

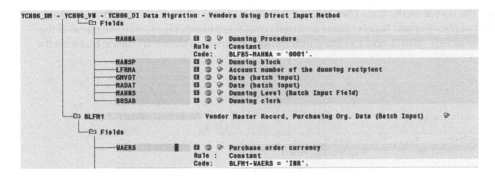

**Figure 6-33.** *Process step 5—assignment to fields of structure BLFB5 and BLFM1*

We performed a validity check ctrl+F2 or sixth button from the left on the application toolbar. We saved the changes and returned to the process steps screen.

Process step 5 is not yet complete. The destination field BFA1-SORTL is still to be assigned a value. The destination field BFA1-SORTL will be assigned a value by invoking a *User-Defined Routine* to be created in process step 6. After performing process step 6, we will return to process step 5 and assign value to the destination field BFA1-SORTL, thereby completing process step 5.

# Process Step 6—Maintain Fixed Values, Translations, and User-Defined Routines

Process step 6 is optional. If you do not have *Fixed Values*, *Translations,* and *User-Defined Routines* to be created for the *Project*, you can skip process step 6.

The Fixed Values, Translations, and User-Defined Routines, together termed "Reusable Rules," are located under a Project.

Whatever *Reusable Rules* you create are available for use across all the *Objects* in the *Project*.

The *Fixed Values* are akin to definitions of constants in an ABAP program. The defined *Fixed Values* can be accessed in all the *Objects* of a *Project*.

The *Translations* transform input strings to output strings on 1:1 translation basis and/or interval translation basis. The defined *Translations* can be invoked from all the *Objects* of a *Project*.

The subroutines defined under *User-Defined Routines* can be invoked from all the *Objects* of a *Project*.

We are creating a *User-Defined Routine* which will derive the value of the destination field BLFA1-SORTL. The *User-Defined Routine* to be created will receive one input parameter as the field BLFA1-NAME1. It will extract the first word from the input parameter BLFA1-NAME1 and return the extracted first word of BLFA1-NAME1 in the output parameter BLFA1-SORTL.

Though this proposed *User-Defined Routine* appears a little trivial, it serves the purpose of demonstration. So let us proceed to the creation of the proposed *User-Defined Routine*.

From the screen of process steps, we executed process step 6 and switched the screen to change mode. A screen like the one shown in Figure 6-34 appeared.

**Figure 6-34.** *Process step 6—Maintain Fixed Values, Translations, and User-Defined Routines*

We positioned the cursor on the node *User-Defined Routine* and clicked the Create button. A dialog box prompting for input of *User-Defined Routine* name and description appeared. We entered the name of the *User-Defined Routine* as GET_SORTL and a suitable description. Figure 6-35 shows the dialog box with the entered values.

Reusable Rules

└ 🖻 YCH06_DM        Data Migration Project                                    12.06.2016 SAPUSE

🖻 Create User-Defined Routine                                                          ⊠

| Project | YCH06_DM | Data Migration Project |
|---|---|---|
| Name | GET_SORTL | |
| Name | Derive SORTL | |

✔ ✖

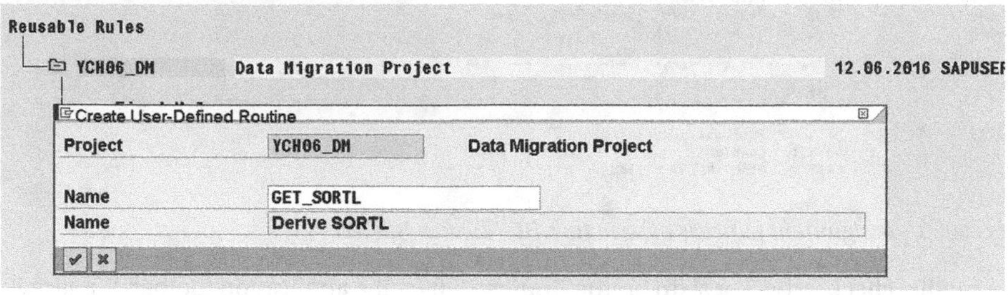

*Figure 6-35.*  *Process step 6—Create User-Defined Routines*

When we clicked the Continue button, another dialog box appeared prompting for the number of input and output parameters. Figure 6-36 shows the dialog box with the entered values of the number of input and output parameters.

Reusable Rules

└ 🖻 YCH06_DM        Data Migration Project                                    12.06.2016 SAPUSER

🖻 Create User-Defined Routine        ⊠

| Number of Entry Parameters | 1 |
|---|---|
| Number Output Parameters | 1 |

✔ ✖

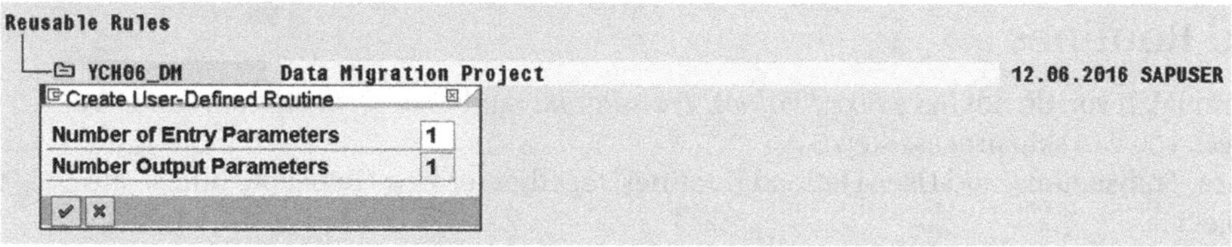

*Figure 6-36.*  *Process step 6—provide number of parameters to User-Defined Routine*

When we clicked the Continue button, the tree with the *User-Defined Routine* node looked like the screen in Figure 6-37.

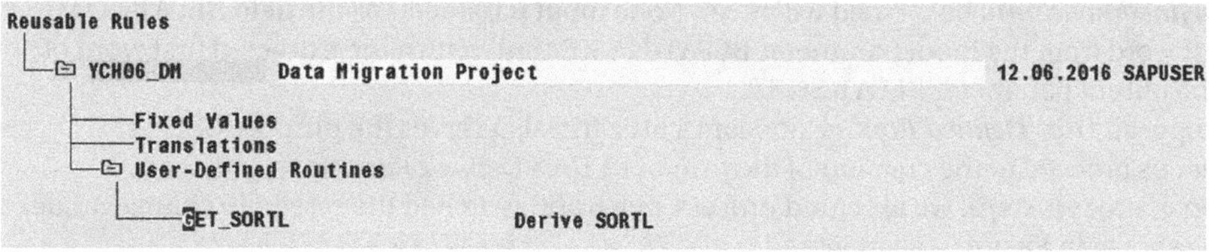

Reusable Rules

└ 🖻 YCH06_DM        Data Migration Project                                    12.06.2016 SAPUSER

├── Fixed Values
├── Translations
└── 🖻 User-Defined Routines

        └── GET_SORTL                Derive SORTL

*Figure 6-37.*  *Process step 6—User-Defined Routine GET_SORTL definition*

We double-clicked the GET_SORTL node and the ABAP line editor with subroutine template code appeared.

```
form ur_GET_SORTL
     using p_in
   changing p_out.
* ...
endform.
```

The LSMW system has appended the prefix ur_ to the node name GET_SORTL for the name of the subroutine. When invoking the subroutine, we must use the name: ur_GET_SORTL. You can change the formal parameter names p_in and p_out if you so desire. We added the following lines to the template code:

```
DATA BUF TYPE STRING.
SPLIT p_in AT ' ' INTO p_out BUF.
```

Figure 6-38 shows the subroutine with added lines to the original template lines.

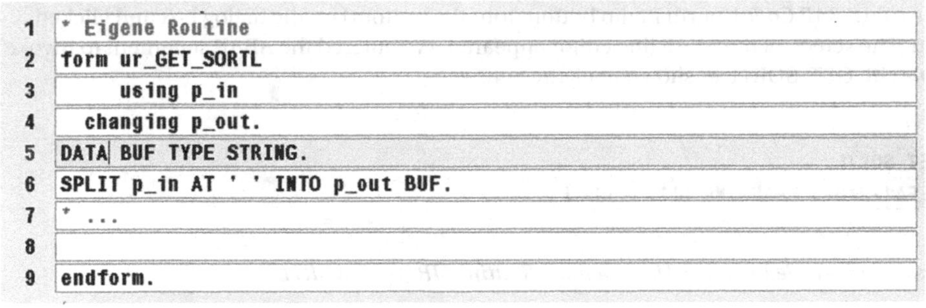

| | |
|---|---|
| 1 | * Eigene Routine |
| 2 | form ur_GET_SORTL |
| 3 | using p_in |
| 4 | changing p_out. |
| 5 | DATA BUF TYPE STRING. |
| 6 | SPLIT p_in AT ' ' INTO p_out BUF. |
| 7 | * ... |
| 8 | |
| 9 | endform. |

*Figure 6-38.* *Process step 6—User-Defined Routine UR_GET_SORTL code*

We saved the ABAP source lines and performed a syntax check.

This completes the creation of the *User-Defined Routine* UR_GET_SORTL to derive the destination field BLFA1-SORTL.

We navigated back to the process steps screen.

# Process Step 5—Revisited

From the screen of process steps, we executed process step 5 and switched the screen to change mode.

In this revisit of process step 5, we want to assign value to the destination field BLFA1-SORTL by invoking *User-Defined Routine* UR_GET_SORTL. To invoke *User-Defined Routine* UR_GET_SORTL, we positioned the cursor on the destination field BLFA1-SORTL and clicked the application toolbar button *Rule*. A dialog box to select a rule appeared as shown in Figure 6-39.

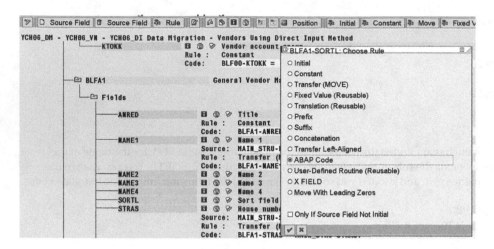

**Figure 6-39.** *Process step 5—create code to invoke User-Defined Routine UR_GET_SORTL*

We selected the rule *ABAP Code* (fourth Radio button from the bottom) on the dialog box and clicked the Continue button. The screen of the ABAP line editor appeared. We entered the ABAP statement to invoke *User-Defined Routine* UR_GET_SORTL as shown in Figure 6-40.

```
1  PERFORM UR_GET_SORTL
2       USING BLFA1-NAME1 CHANGING BLFA1-SORTL.
```

**Figure 6-40.** *Process step 5—code to invoke User-Defined Routine UR_GET_SORTL*

We saved and performed the syntax check of ABAP source lines. We exited the ABAP line editor and navigated back to the screen of process step 5. On the screen of process step 5, we performed the validity check and saved the changes to the screen of process step 5.

We could have located the following two ABAP statements:

```
DATA BUF TYPE STRING.
SPLIT BLFA1-NAME1 AT ' ' INTO BLFA1-SORTL BUF.
```

In place of the subroutine we invoked statement PERFORM UR_GET_SORTL.....saving ourselves the effort of defining a *User-Defined Routine*. The objective was to demonstrate the definition of *User-Defined Routine*.

In the dialog box of Figure 6-39, we could have selected the third rule from the bottom *User-Defined Routine (Reusable)* and generated the ABAP code to invoke *User-Defined Routine* UR_GET_SORTL.

We could have double-clicked the destination field BLFA1-SORTL and navigated to the ABAP line editor screen instead of clicking the application toolbar button *Rule*, etc.

These were alternative modes to generate or create ABAP program lines for the invocation of *User-Defined Routine* UR_GET_SORTL.

Now that we assigned value to the field BLFA1-SORTL, process step 5 is concluded. We navigated back to the process steps screen.

## Process Step 7—*Specify Files*

From the screen of process steps, we executed the process step 7 and switched the screen to change mode.

In process step 7, we specify the input text files. You can specify input text files on the presentation server (PC—Frontend) and the application server. As per our specifications, we are locating the two input text files on the application server.

The initial screen to specify input text files appears as shown in Figure 6-41.

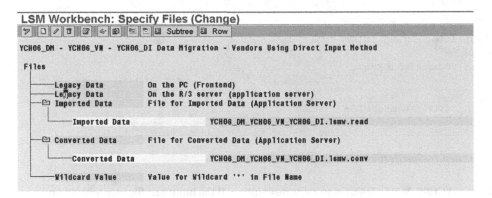

**Figure 6-41.** *Process step 7—specify files*

To specify input text files, we positioned the cursor on the node *Legacy Data on the R/3 Server* and clicked the Create button. A dialog box as shown in Figure 6-42 appeared.

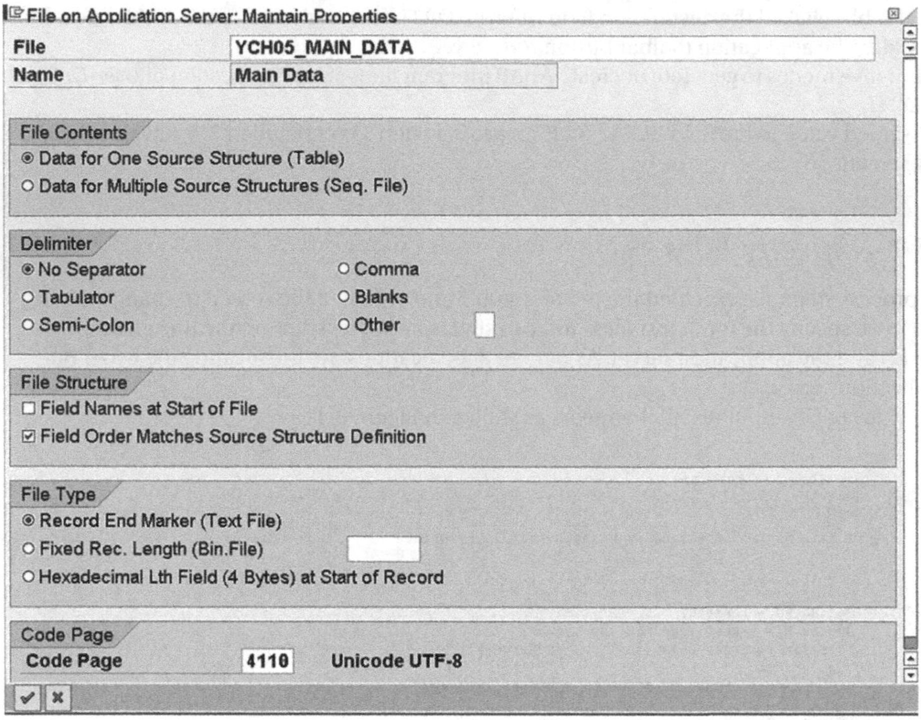

**Figure 6-42.** *Process step 7—Specify file YCH05_MAIN_DATA*

We entered *File* as YCH05_MAIN_DATA, a suitable description. If the input text files are located on the presentation server, function key F4 facility is available to make a file selection from a dialog box listing folders and files on the presentation server. If the input text files are located on the application server, function key F4 facility is unavailable; you have to manually enter the file name and so must take care to do so correctly.

The options for the remaining entries on the dialog box of Figure 6-42 are self-explanatory. For the remaining, the defaults will serve our purpose. We clicked the Continue button on the dialog box of Figure 6-42.

In a similar manner, we specified the second of our input text files, YCH05_BANK_DATA. After the specification of the two input text files, the screen will look like that in Figure 6-43.

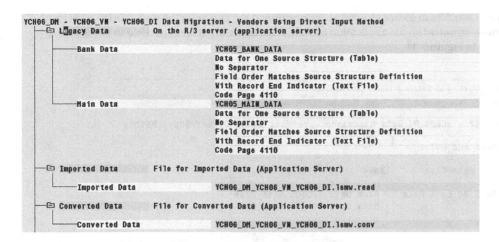

**Figure 6-43.** *Process step 7—Files YCH05_MAIN_DATA, YCH05_BANK_DATA specified*

We saved the changes on the screen of process step 7.

In Figure 6-43, you can observe the node *Imported Data*. Under the node *Imported Data* is a file whose name is a concatenation of the names of *Project, Subproject,* and *Object* with embedded underscores and ending with the following postfix: .lsmw.read. The number of characters in the file name must not exceed 45 characters. If the number of characters exceeds 45 characters, you must rename the file to ensure that the number of characters in the file name <= 45 characters. The LSMW system retrieves and stores the data of all the input text files together in this file.

In Figure 6-43, you can also observe the node *Converted Data*. Under the node *Converted Data* is a file whose name is again a concatenation of the names of *Project, Subproject,* and *Object* with embedded underscores and ending with the following postfix: .lsmw.conv. The number of characters in the file name must not exceed 45 characters. If the number of characters in the file name exceeds 45 characters, rename the file to ensure that the number of characters in the file name <= 45 characters. The LSMW system stores all the data to be migrated—that is, all the data assigned values as per specifications of process step 5 in this file.

In Figure 6-41, at the very bottom, is a node with the label *Wildcard Value.* You can enter wildcard file values, patterns in this field. By default, by specifying explicit file names in this process step, you are fixing the file names (input files, .lsmw.read file, and .lsmw.conv) and they cannot be specified or changed at runtime. If you enter values in the field *Wildcard Value,* input prompts will appear, as follows:

- In process step 9 (*Read Data*) for input files and .lsmw.read file

- In process step 11 (*Convert Data*) for .lsmw.read and .lsmw.conv files

This feature enables multiple users to use the same LSMW *Object.* Each user of the LSMW *Object* can operate his or her own input files, .lsmw.read file and .lsmw.conv file, and not overwrite on others, .lsmw. read file and .lsmw.conv file.

This concludes process step 7. We navigated back to the process steps screen.

## Process Step 8—*Assign Files*

From the screen of process steps, we executed process step 8 and switched the screen to change mode.

In process step 8, we co-relate or assign the input text files specified in process step 7 to the source structure defined in process step 2.

To assign input text files to source structures, we positioned the cursor on the node MAIN_STRU and clicked the button *Assignment* on the application toolbar. A list of the input files specified in process step 7 appeared as shown in Figure 6-44.

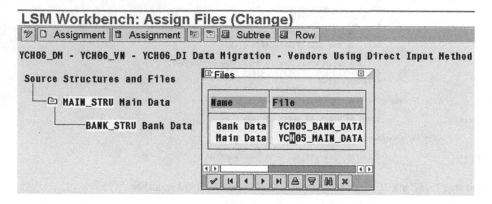

**Figure 6-44.** *Process step 8—Assign files to source structures*

We selected the input file YCH05_MAIN_DATA from the list.

In a similar manner, we assigned the input file YCH05_BANK_DATA to the source structure BANK_STRU. Figure 6-45 shows the screen after the assignment of two input files to the two source structures.

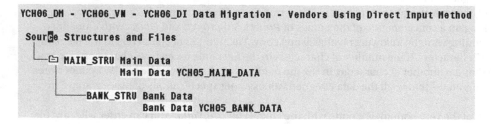

**Figure 6-45.** *Process step 8—files assigned to source structures*

We saved the changes on the screen of process step 8.

This concludes process step 8. We navigated back to the process steps screen.

# Data Creation on Presentation Server, Copy to Application Server

I am going to digress a bit from the process steps of LSMW to describe the creation of input text files on the presentation server, copying the created input text files to the application server. This procedure has already been described in hands-on exercise II in Chapter 5.

Figure 6-46 shows the main data of three vendors: 0000090236, 0000090237, and 0000090238.

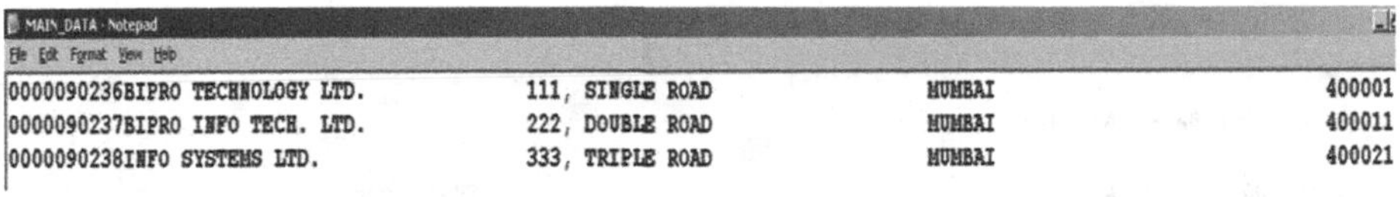

Figure 6-46. Vendors' main data—text file

Figure 6-47 shows the bank data of three vendors: 0000090236, 0000090237, and 0000090238. Vendor 0000090236 has one bank account, vendor 0000090237 has two bank accounts, and vendor 0000090238 has three bank accounts, respectively.

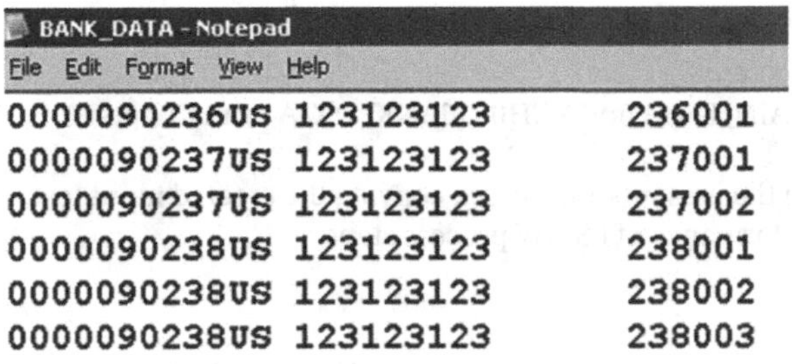

Figure 6-47. Vendors' bank data—text file

Figure 6-48 shows the successful copying of the main file on the presentation server to YCH05_MAIN_DATA on the application server using transaction code USS_FAS.

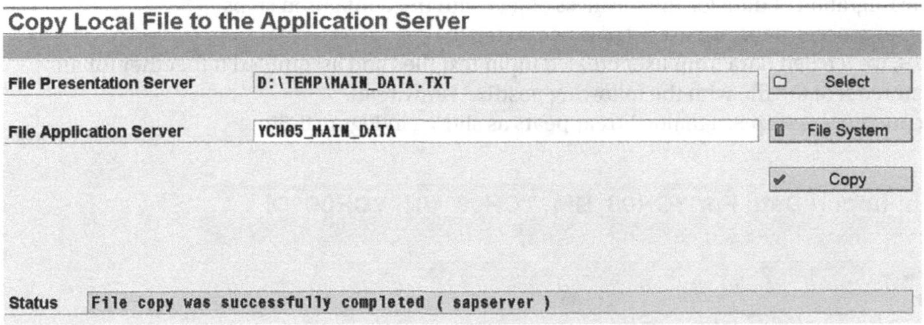

Figure 6-48. Successful copy of main data—from presentation server to application server

Figure 6-49 shows the successful copying of the bank file on the presentation server to YCH05_BANK_DATA on the application server.

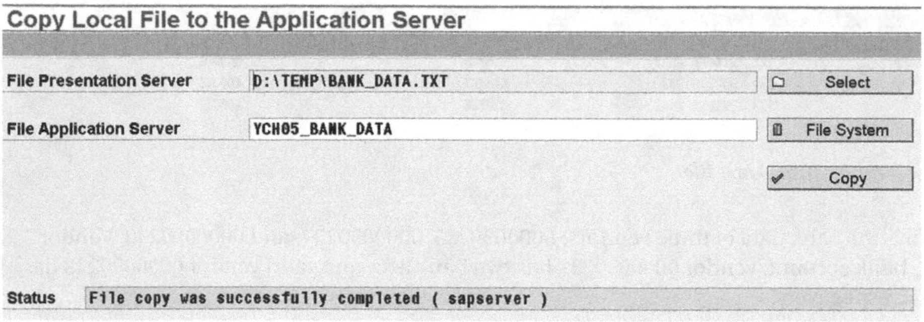

**Copy Local File to the Application Server**

| | | |
|---|---|---|
| File Presentation Server | D:\TEMP\BANK_DATA.TXT | 🗀 Select |
| File Application Server | YCH05_BANK_DATA | 🗐 File System |
| | | ✔ Copy |

| Status | File copy was successfully completed ( sapserver ) |
|---|---|

*Figure 6-49.* *Successful copy of bank data—from presentation server to application server*

We retained the input text file names YCH05_MAIN_DATA and YCH05_BANK_DATA from Chapter 5. You can use some other file names if you so desire.

This concludes the creation of input text files on the presentation server, copying the created input text files to the application server. We will resume the performance of LSMW process steps.

# Process Step 9—*Read Data*

Process steps 1–8 constituted what we termed "the configuration steps" in the initial sections of this chapter. If you are migrating data on a periodic or regular basis, process steps 1–8 need not be performed repeatedly unless something has changed in the configuration, like, for example, the input text file name(s). Even if some things changed, like the input text file name(s), the process steps pertaining to the changes need to be performed again.

Process steps 9 onward, termed "execution steps" in the initial sections of this chapter, need to be repeated for periodic migration of data for the business object with the configured steps.

From the screen of process steps, we executed process step 9.

In process step 9, we fetched data from user created input text files and assembled it together for an entity–vendor, and stored it in the file with the following postfix: .lsmw.read.

When you execute process step 9, a dialog box appears as shown in Figure 6-50.

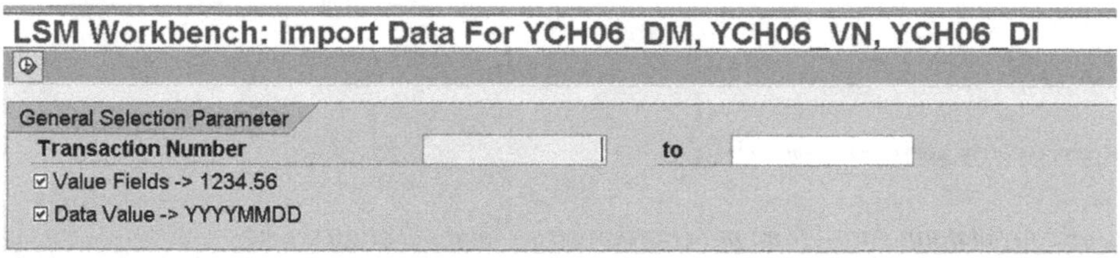

**LSM Workbench: Import Data For YCH06_DM, YCH06_VN, YCH06_DI**

🔘

General Selection Parameter
| Transaction Number | | to | |
|---|---|---|---|

☑ Value Fields -> 1234.56
☑ Data Value -> YYYYMMDD

*Figure 6-50.* *Process step 9-Import Data input screen*

You can filter data to be read based on a range of transactions or row numbers. The check boxes *Value Fields* and *Data Value* indicate how numeric decimal type data and date type data are stored.

We clicked the Execute button. The execution produced an output of statistics of input text data read and written or imported as shown in Figure 6-51.

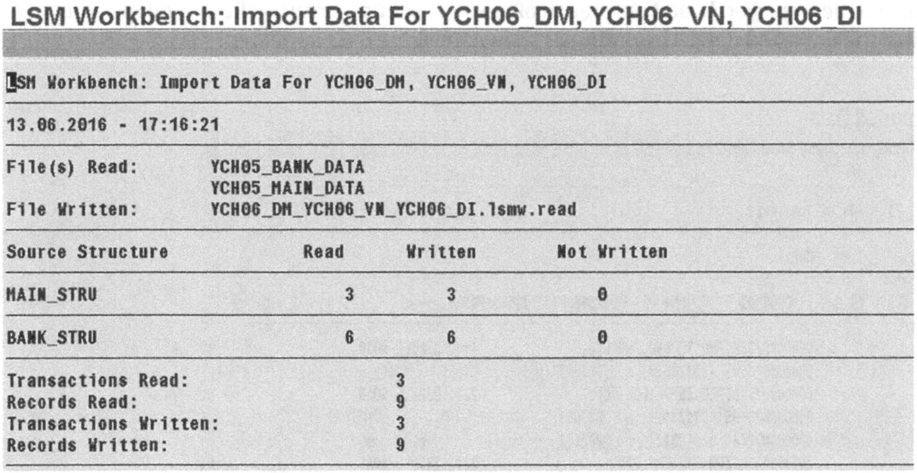

## LSM Workbench: Import Data For YCH06_DM, YCH06_VN, YCH06_DI

LSM Workbench: Import Data For YCH06_DM, YCH06_VN, YCH06_DI

13.06.2016 - 17:16:21

| File(s) Read: | YCH05_BANK_DATA |
| | YCH05_MAIN_DATA |
| File Written: | YCH06_DM_YCH06_VN_YCH06_DI.lsmw.read |

| Source Structure | Read | Written | Not Written |
| --- | --- | --- | --- |
| MAIN_STRU | 3 | 3 | 0 |
| BANK_STRU | 6 | 6 | 0 |

| Transactions Read: | 3 |
| --- | --- |
| Records Read: | 9 |
| Transactions Written: | 3 |
| Records Written: | 9 |

*Figure 6-51.* *Process step 9–Import Data output screen*

The number of rows or transactions read into MAIN_STRU is three for the three vendors.

The number of rows read into BANK_STRU is six-one row for the first vendor, two rows for the second vendor, and three rows for the third vendor.

The number of rows read into each of the source structures MAIN_STRU and BANK_STRU is indicated in the output report of Figure 6-51.

The number of rows written to the file with the postfix .lsmw.read must be identical to the number of rows read. If a mismatch occurs between the number of rows read and the number of rows written, it warrants an investigation of the data in the input text files.

This concludes process step 9. We navigated back to the process steps screen.

## Process Step 10–*Display Read Data*

This process step is optional. The process step displays the data imported into the file with the postfix: .lsmw. read from the input text files. The process step provides a visual means of verifying that data was imported correctly. Data in the imported file is assembled entity or vendor-wise.

When you execute process step 10, a dialog box appears as shown in Figure 6-52.

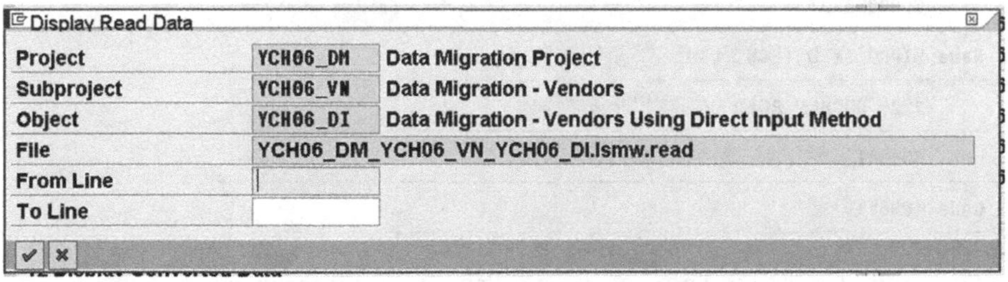

| Display Read Data | | |
| --- | --- | --- |
| Project | YCH06_DM | Data Migration Project |
| Subproject | YCH06_VN | Data Migration - Vendors |
| Object | YCH06_DI | Data Migration - Vendors Using Direct Input Method |
| File | YCH06_DM_YCH06_VN_YCH06_DI.lsmw.read | |
| From Line | | |
| To Line | | |

*Figure 6-52.* *Process step 10–Display Read Data: filter dialog box*

You can filter data to be displayed based on a range of line or row numbers. We clicked the Execute button to display all of the imported data. The output as shown in Figure 6-53 appeared.

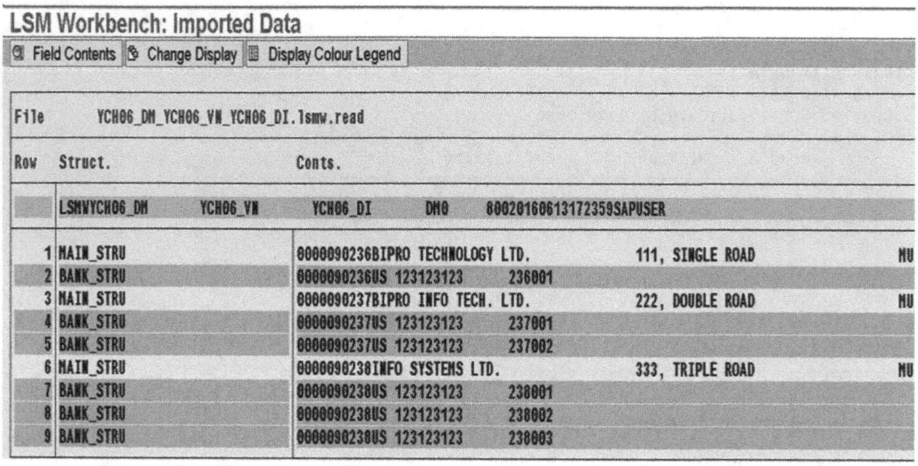

## LSM Workbench: Imported Data

| Field Contents | Change Display | Display Colour Legend |
|---|---|---|

File      YCH06_DM_YCH06_VN_YCH06_DI.1smw.read

| Row | Struct. | | Conts. | | | |
|---|---|---|---|---|---|---|
| | LSMWYCH06_DM | YCH06_VN | YCH06_DI | DM0 | 80020160613172359SAPUSER | |
| 1 | MAIN_STRU | | 0000090236BIPRO TECHNOLOGY LTD. | | 111, SINGLE ROAD | MU |
| 2 | BANK_STRU | | 0000090236US 123123123 | 236001 | | |
| 3 | MAIN_STRU | | 0000090237BIPRO INFO TECH. LTD. | | 222, DOUBLE ROAD | MU |
| 4 | BANK_STRU | | 0000090237US 123123123 | 237001 | | |
| 5 | BANK_STRU | | 0000090237US 123123123 | 237002 | | |
| 6 | MAIN_STRU | | 0000090238INFO SYSTEMS LTD. | | 333, TRIPLE ROAD | MU |
| 7 | BANK_STRU | | 0000090238US 123123123 | 238001 | | |
| 8 | BANK_STRU | | 0000090238US 123123123 | 238002 | | |
| 9 | BANK_STRU | | 0000090238US 123123123 | 238003 | | |

*Figure 6-53.* Process step 10–display Imported Data

As you can observe in Figure 6-53, all of a vendor's data appears together, the main data followed by the bank data under it. If you want to view a particular line, you click that particular line.

We clicked the main data line and subsequently the first bank data line of the second vendor: 0000090237.

Figure 6-54 detaild the main data and Figure 6-55 details the first bank data for vendor 0000090237.

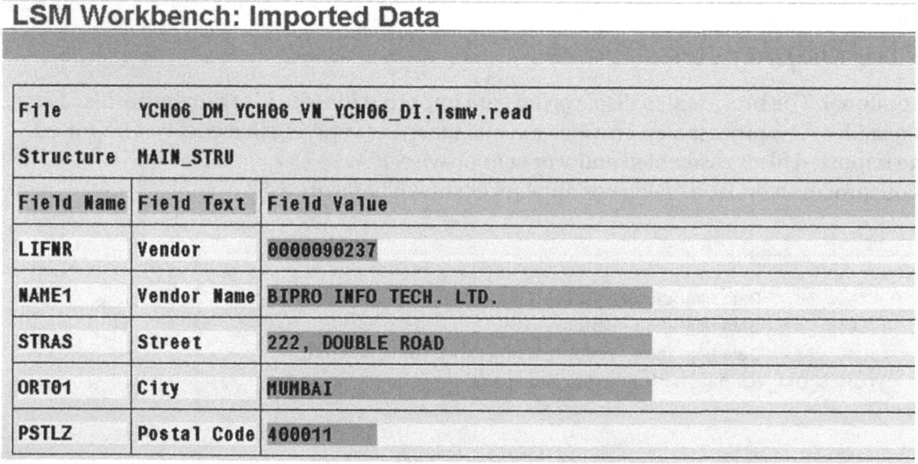

## LSM Workbench: Imported Data

| | | |
|---|---|---|
| File | YCH06_DM_YCH06_VN_YCH06_DI.1smw.read | |
| Structure | MAIN_STRU | |
| Field Name | Field Text | Field Value |
| LIFNR | Vendor | 0000090237 |
| NAME1 | Vendor Name | BIPRO INFO TECH. LTD. |
| STRAS | Street | 222, DOUBLE ROAD |
| ORT01 | City | MUMBAI |
| PSTLZ | Postal Code | 400011 |

*Figure 6-54.* Process step 10–display Imported Data: main mata of vendor 0000090237

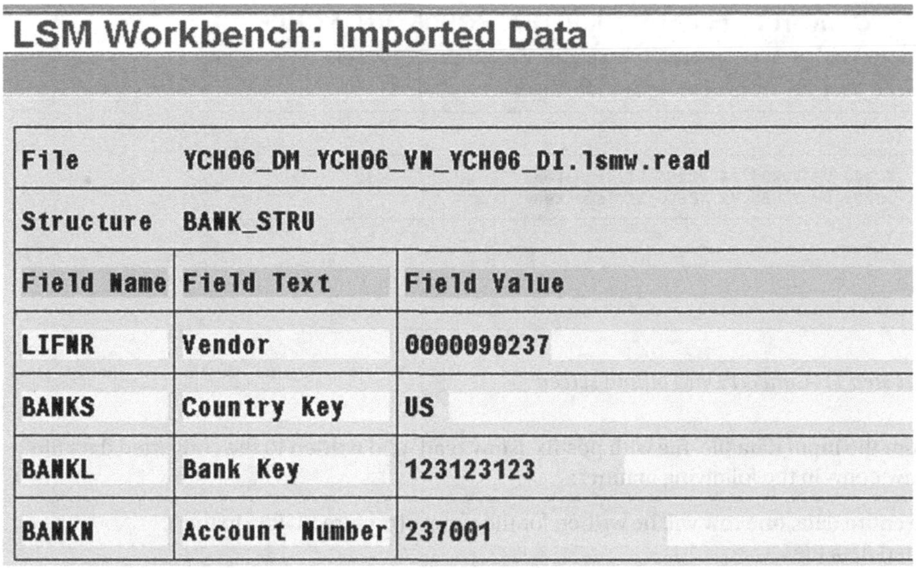

## LSM Workbench: Imported Data

| File | YCH06_DM_YCH06_VN_YCH06_DI.lsmw.read | |
|------|------|------|
| Structure | BANK_STRU | |
| Field Name | Field Text | Field Value |
| LIFNR | Vendor | 0000090237 |
| BANKS | Country Key | US |
| BANKL | Bank Key | 123123123 |
| BANKN | Account Number | 237001 |

*Figure 6-55.* *Process step 10–display Imported Data: First bank data of vendor 0000090237*

It is a good practice to view random, sample data when the volume of data is large.
This concludes the optional process step 10. We navigated back to the process steps screen.

## Process Step 11–*Convert Data*

From the screen of process steps, we executed process step 11.

In process step 11, we assigned data to the destination fields as per the specifications in process step 5 and wrote to the file with the postfix: .lsmw.conv.

When you execute process step 11, a dialog appears as shown in Figure 6-56.

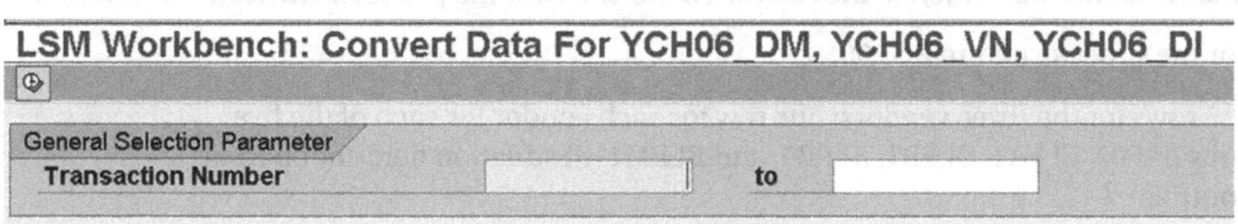

## LSM Workbench: Convert Data For YCH06_DM, YCH06_VN, YCH06_DI

General Selection Parameter
Transaction Number [          ]   to   [          ]

*Figure 6-56.* *Process step 11–Convert Data input screen*

You can filter data to be converted based on a range of line or row numbers. We clicked the Execute button to convert all of the input data. The execution produced an output of statistics of converted data written as shown in Figure 6-57.

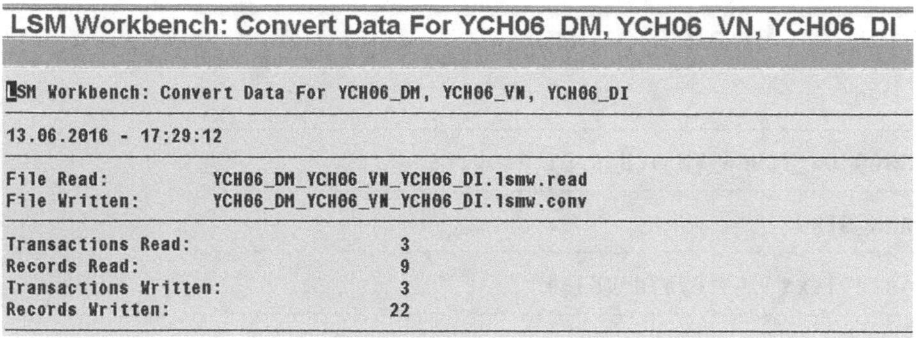

## LSM Workbench: Convert Data For YCH06_DM, YCH06_VN, YCH06_DI

```
LSM Workbench: Convert Data For YCH06_DM, YCH06_VN, YCH06_DI

13.06.2016 - 17:29:12

File Read:          YCH06_DM_YCH06_VN_YCH06_DI.lsmw.read
File Written:       YCH06_DM_YCH06_VN_YCH06_DI.lsmw.conv

Transactions Read:          3
Records Read:               9
Transactions Written:       3
Records Written:            22
```

***Figure 6-57.*** *Process step 11–Convert Data output screen*

Data is read from the input data file–file with postfix .lsmw.read–and written to the converted data file–file with postfix .lsmw.conv–in the following manner:

- For the entire data, one row will be written for the super structure BGR00 to the converted data file

- For each transaction or vendor:

  ✓ In case of destination fields not part of table control, a row will be written to the converted data file for each of the destination structures with designated fields (i.e., structures whose field(s) have been assigned value(s)). In our hands-on exercise, the destination structures with designated fields are BLF00, BLFA1, BLFB1, BLFB5, and BLFM1. Hence five rows will be written to the converted data file for each transaction or vendor.

  ✓ In case of destination fields being part of table control, a row will be written to the converted data file for each row in the input data file. In this hands-on exercise, the destination structure being part of table control is BLFBK.

In the present case, the data in the input file, the file with the postfix .lsmw.read, consists of three vendors and six banks. Data will be written to the converted file–file with the postfix .lsmw.conv–as follows:

- 1 row for the super structure BGR00.

- 3 x 5 = 15 rows for the three vendors: one row for each vendor for each of the five structures BLF00, BLFA1, BLFB1, BLFB5, and BLFM1–destination fields not part of table control.

- 6 rows corresponding to the 6 rows of banks–destination fields part of table control.

The total number of rows written to the converted file–file with the postfix .lsmw.conv–will be: 1 + 15 + 6 = 22 rows.

The rows written to the converted file appear as on the line *Records Written* in Figure 6-57. The audit or cross-check must be performed to ensure that all of the data from the input file is converted and written to the converted file.

This concludes process step 11. We navigated back to the process steps screen.

## Process Step 12–Display Converted Data

This process step is also optional. The process step displays the data assigned to the destination fields and written to the file with the following postfix: .lsmw.conv. The process step provides a visual means of verifying that data was converted correctly.

When you execute process step 12, a dialog appears as shown in Figure 6-58.

| Display Converted Data | | |
|---|---|---|
| Project | YCH06_DM | Data Migration Project |
| Subproject | YCH06_VN | Data Migration - Vendors |
| Object | YCH06_DI | Data Migration - Vendors Using Direct Input Method |
| File | YCH06_DM_YCH06_VN_YCH06_DI.lsmw.conv | |
| From Line | | |
| To Line | | |

**Figure 6-58.** *Process step 12—Display Converted Data: filter dialog box*

You can filter data to be displayed based on a range of line or row numbers. We clicked the Execute button to display all of the converted data. The output as shown in Figure 6-59 appeared.

LSM Workbench: Converted Data

🔲 Field Contents   📖 Change Display   🔳 Display Colour Legend

File   YCH06_DM_YCH06_VN_YCH06_DI.lsmw.conv

| Row | Struct. | Contents | | | | | | | |
|---|---|---|---|---|---|---|---|---|---|
| 1 | BGR00 | 0YCH06_DI | 800SAPUSER | / | | | | | |
| 2 | BLF00 | 1XK01 | 0000090236000100010001 | | | | | | |
| 3 | BLFA1 | 2BLFA1 | Company | BIPRO TECHNOLOGY LTD. | | | | / | |
| 4 | BLFB1 | 2BLFB1 | 0000016000/ | / | / /A1 | / | / / | / | |
| 5 | BLFBK | 2BLFBK | /US 123123123 | 236001 | | / / | / / | | |
| 6 | BLFB5 | 2BLFB5 | 0001// | / | / | / / | | | |
| 7 | BLFM1 | 2BLFM1 | INR / | / / | | / | | | |
| 8 | BLF00 | 1XK01 | 0000090237000100010001 | | | | | | |
| 9 | BLFA1 | 2BLFA1 | Company | BIPRO INFO TECH. LTD. | | | | / | |
| 10 | BLFB1 | 2BLFB1 | 0000016000/ | / | / /A1 | / | / / | / | |
| 11 | BLFBK | 2BLFBK | /US 123123123 | 237001 | | / / | / / | | |
| 12 | BLFBK | 2BLFBK | /US 123123123 | 237002 | | / / | / / | | |
| 13 | BLFB5 | 2BLFB5 | 0001// | / | / | / / | | | |
| 14 | BLFM1 | 2BLFM1 | INR / | / / | | / | | | |
| 15 | BLF00 | 1XK01 | 0000090238000100010001 | | | | | | |
| 16 | BLFA1 | 2BLFA1 | Company | INFO SYSTEMS LTD. | | | | / | |
| 17 | BLFB1 | 2BLFB1 | 0000016000/ | / | / /A1 | / | / / | / | |

**Figure 6-59.** *Process step 12—display Converted Data*

The destination fields of an entity–vendor appear together. Each line is an assemblage of fields of a structure: BLF00, BLFA1, and so on. You click a line for a detailed display of that line as shown in Figure 6-60.

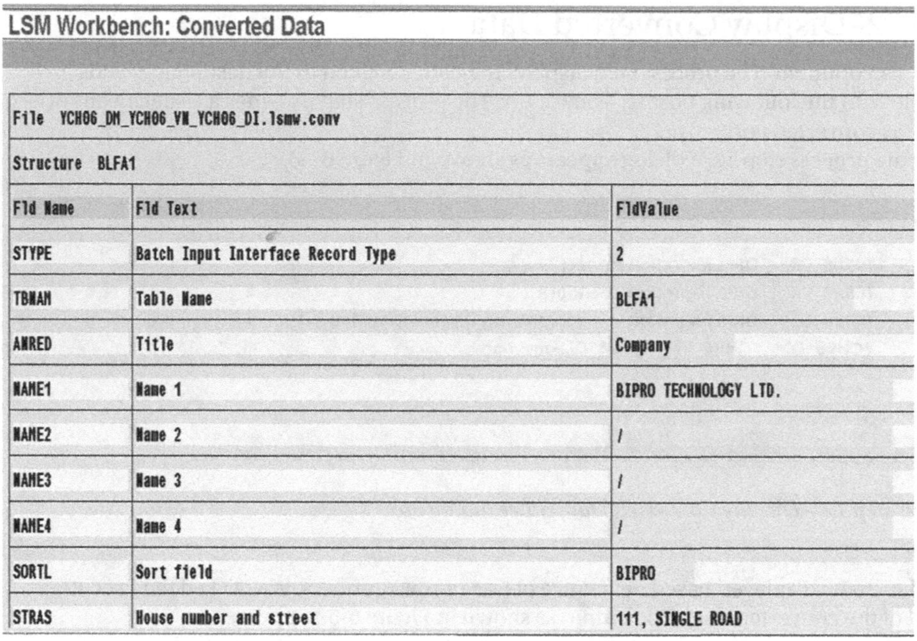

## LSM Workbench: Converted Data

File  YCH06_DM_YCH06_VN_YCH06_DI.lsmw.conv

Structure  BLFA1

| Fld Name | Fld Text | FldValue |
|----------|----------|----------|
| STYPE | Batch Input Interface Record Type | 2 |
| TBNAM | Table Name | BLFA1 |
| ANRED | Title | Company |
| NAME1 | Name 1 | BIPRO TECHNOLOGY LTD. |
| NAME2 | Name 2 | / |
| NAME3 | Name 3 | / |
| NAME4 | Name 4 | / |
| SORTL | Sort field | BIPRO |
| STRAS | House number and street | 111, SINGLE ROAD |

*Figure 6-60.* *Process step 12–display Converted Data: BLFA1, vendor 0000090236*

This concludes the optional process step 12. We navigated back to the process steps screen.

## Process Step 13–Create Batch Input Session

From the screen of process steps, we executed process step 13.

In process step 13, you create a batch input session from the converted data, that is, the data in the file with the following postfix: .lsmw.conv.

When you execute process step 13, a dialog box appears as shown in Figure 6-61.

## Batch Input Interface for Vendors

File path name        YCH06_DM_YCH06_VN_YCH06_DI.lsmw.conv

Selection of structures that are used
- ☐ Structures from Release < 4.0

Program control
- ☐ Check file only
- ☐ File has Non-Unicode Format

Info Messages
- ○ Dialog Box
- ◉ Log
- ○ No Information Message

*Figure 6-61.* *Process step 13–create batch input session*

On the dialog of Figure 6-61, if you enable the check box *Check file only*, the batch input file is checked and no session is created.

On the dialog of Figure 6-61, in the *Info Messages* area,

- If you enable the Radio button *Dialog Box*, each info message appears as a dialog box; you have to keep pressing <enter> key to continue.

- If you enable the Radio button *Log*, info messages will be gathered and output at the end of processing.

- If you enable the Radio button *No Information Message*, info messages will be suppressed.

We clicked the Execute button and an output of info messages as shown in Figure 6-62 appeared.

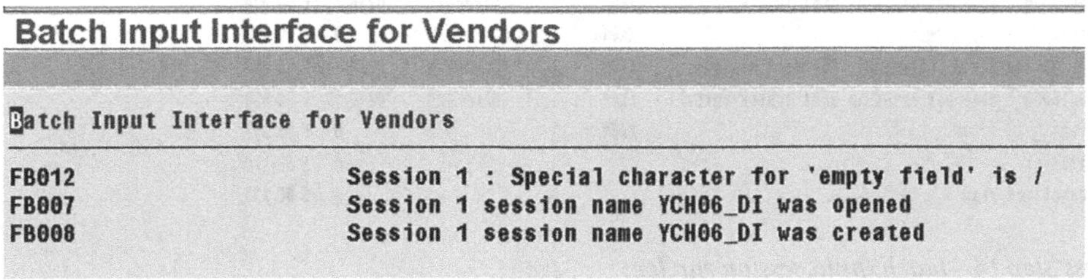

**Batch Input Interface for Vendors**

| Batch Input Interface for Vendors |
|---|
| FB012      Session 1 : Special character for 'empty field' is / |
| FB007      Session 1 session name YCH06_DI was opened |
| FB008      Session 1 session name YCH06_DI was created |

***Figure 6-62.*** *Process step 13–Batch Input session created*

As you can observe in Figure 6-62, a session of the same name as the *Object* name YCH06_DI was created.

This concludes process step 13. We navigated back to the process steps screen.

## Process Step 14—Run Batch Input Session

From the screen of process steps, we executed process step 14.

In process step 14, you run the batch input session created in process step 13.

When you execute process step 14, you navigate to the session overview screen as shown in Figure 6-63.

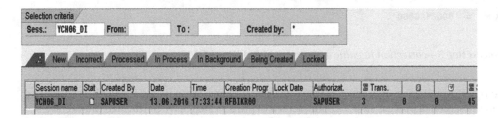

***Figure 6-63.*** *Process step 14—batch input session overview screen*

We selected the session and executed it in background. The execution of the session generated errors. We opened the log for the session as shown in Figure 6-64.

| Log attributes | | | | | |
|---|---|---|---|---|---|
| Name | YCH06_DI | Queue ID | 16061317334433840056 | User | SAPUSER |
| Created On | 13.06.2016 | TemSe ID | BDCLG443384005680086 | ☐ Details | |

| Time | Message | Transacti | Index | Modul | Scre | Ind | T | M | Me |
|---|---|---|---|---|---|---|---|---|---|
| 17:36:34 | Session YCH06_DI is being processed by user SAPUSER in mode N on | | 0 | | | 0 | S | 00 | 300 |
| 17:37:08 | Formatting error in the field LFB1-AKONT; see next message | XK01 | 1 | SAPMF02K | 0210 | 9 | E | 00 | 298 |
| 17:37:08 | Entry 0001 0000016000  does not exist in SKB1 (check entry) | XK01 | 1 | SAPMF02K | 0210 | 9 | E | 00 | 058 |
| 17:37:08 | Transaction error | XK01 | 1 | | | 0 | S | 00 | 357 |
| 17:37:09 | Formatting error in the field LFB1-AKONT; see next message | XK01 | 2 | SAPMF02K | 0210 | 11 | E | 00 | 298 |
| 17:37:09 | Entry 0001 0000016000  does not exist in SKB1 (check entry) | XK01 | 2 | SAPMF02K | 0210 | 11 | E | 00 | 058 |
| 17:37:09 | Transaction error | XK01 | 2 | | | 0 | S | 00 | 357 |
| 17:37:09 | Formatting error in the field LFB1-AKONT; see next message | XK01 | 3 | SAPMF02K | 0210 | 13 | E | 00 | 298 |
| 17:37:09 | Entry 0001 0000016000  does not exist in SKB1 (check entry) | XK01 | 3 | SAPMF02K | 0210 | 13 | E | 00 | 058 |
| 17:37:09 | Transaction error | XK01 | 3 | | | 0 | S | 00 | 357 |
| 17:37:09 | Processing statistics | | 0 | | | 0 | S | 00 | 370 |
| 17:37:09 |     3 transactions read | | 0 | | | 0 | S | 00 | 363 |

**Figure 6-64.** *Process Step 14—batch input session run log*

The error was generated because of invalid value in the destination field LFB1-AKONT. The error is highlighted in the log. This was a deliberate exercise on our part as to see the effect of erroneous data and its rectification.

We need to assign a correct or valid value to the destination field LFB1-AKONT in process step 5—*Maintain Field Mapping and Conversion Rules*—and after correction, perform the execution steps again.

We navigated back to the screen of process steps. From the screen of process steps, we executed process step 5 and switched the screen to change mode.

On the screen of process step 5, we double-clicked the destination field BLFB1-AKONT and rectified the ABAP program assignment statement as shown in Figure 6-65.

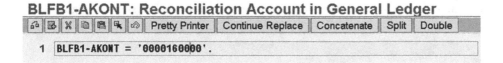

## BLFB1-AKONT: Reconciliation Account in General Ledger

| 🔍 | 🖹 | ✂ | 📋 | 📑 | 🔍 | ↶ | Pretty Printer | Continue Replace | Concatenate | Split | Double |

```
1  BLFB1-AKONT = '0000160000'.
```

**Figure 6-65.** *Process step 5—correction to value assignment of BLFB1-AKONT*

We saved and performed the syntax check on the ABAP source lines. We exited the ABAP line editor and navigated back to the screen of process step 5. On the screen of process step 5, we performed the validity check and saved the changes to the screen of process step 5.

We navigated back to the screen of process steps.

As there was no error in the input text files, we need not reexecute process step 9—*Read Data*. We reexecuted the following process steps:

- Process step 11—*Convert Data*

- Process step 13—*Create Batch Input Session*

- Process step 14—*Run Batch Input Session in background*

The created session executed successfully without errors. Vendors 0000090236, 0000090237, and 0000090238 were created successfully.

This concludes process step 14.

## Vendor Data Creation—Cross-Verification

We cross-checked the creation of the vendors by executing transaction code XK02. Figure 6-66 marks the created vendors.

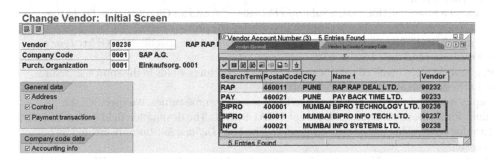

**Figure 6-66.** *Vendor list—vendor numbers with pattern: 9023\**

We selected each of the vendors in turn and navigated through all the screens to cross-check the migration of all the data correctly.

Figure 6-67 shows the *Payment transactions* (bank data) screen of vendor 0000090238.

**Change Vendor: Payment transactions**

| Vendor | 90238 | INFO SYSTEMS LTD. | | | MUMBAI | | | |
|---|---|---|---|---|---|---|---|---|

**Bank details**

| Ctry | Bank Key | Bank Account | Acct holder | C | IBAN | BnkT | Reference details | C | Name of bank |
|---|---|---|---|---|---|---|---|---|---|
| US | 123123123 | 238001 | | | | | | ☐ | Citibank |
| US | 123123123 | 238002 | | | | | | ☐ | Citibank |
| US | 123123123 | 238003 | | | | | | ☐ | Citibank |
| | | | | | | | | ☐ | |
| | | | | | | | | ☐ | |

**Figure 6-67.** *Vendor 0000090238—Payment transactions screen*

We successfully performed the migration of vendor data deploying the *Standard Batch/Direct Input* method of LSMW.

We have not tried out the condition where the number of banks for a vendor exceeds the visible rows in the bank data table control area. You can try out this condition by creating the appropriate data and performing the execution steps.

This concludes the cross-verification of vendor data created and hands-on exercise I.

# Hands-on Exercise I—Recapitulation

The hands-on exercise set out to transfer the data of vendors from text files residing on the application server into the SAP functional module database tables from the LSMW environment.

We started off by describing the scope and specifications of the hands-on exercise.

The input mode, destination fields to be assigned values, is the same as hands-on exercise II in Chapter 5. In fact, the whole of the scope and specifications of this hands-on exercise is identical to that of hands-on exercise II in Chapter 5 except for the creation of a log file on the application server. Only the paradigm has changed—instead of deploying a custom program, a ready-to-use program of LSMW environment is being deployed.

We initially created a *Project* YCH06_DM, a *Subproject* YCH06_VN, and an *Object* YCH06_DI. In the LSMW environment, you perform or execute a series of steps called the process steps.

Process step 1 mainly involved specifying the *Object Type* and *Object*. We specified the *Object Type* as *Standard Batch/Direct Input* and the *Object* as *0040—vendor master*.

The next three process steps involved specification of source structures, fields in the source structures, and relationships between source and destination structures.

In process step 5, we specified how the destination fields would assume values. We specified the assumption of values for all the destination fields except BLFA1-SORTL. The destination field BLFA1-SORTL is to be assigned a value by invoking a *User-Defined Routine*. The *User-Defined Routines* are created by performing process step 6.

In process step 6, you can create *Fixed Values, Translations,* and *User-Defined Routines*. We created a *User-Defined Routine* UR_GET_SORTL to derive the value of the field BLFA1-SORTL from the field BLFA1-NAME1.

We reverted to process step 5 to assign value to the destination field BLFA1-SORTL by invoking a *User-Defined Routine* UR_GET_SORTL.

In process step 7, we specified the input text files. We assigned the input text files to the source structures in process step 8.

We created representative input text data files of three vendors on the presentation server using the notepad editor. We copied the input text data files from on the presentation server to the application server in the transaction code USS_FAS.

We executed process step 9, where data is retrieved from the input text files and written to the file with the postfix .lsmw.read. In process step 10, we viewed the data from the file with the postfix .lsmw.read.

We executed process step 11, where the designated destination fields, which are assigned values as per specifications in process step 5, are written to the file with the postfix .lsmw.conv. In process step 12, we viewed the data from the file with the postfix .lsmw.conv.

Process steps 13 created a session.

In process step 14, we executed the created session in the background. The execution of the session generated errors (we had deliberately assigned an invalid value to the field BLFB1-AKONT). In process step 5, we had assigned a valid value to the field BLFB1-AKONT. We repeated process steps 11, 13, and 14. The session executed successfully. We verified the migration of vendor data from text files into SAP functional module database tables in transaction code XK02.

In the custom programs (from Chapter 5) vis-à-vis the LSMW system, no ABAP program lines were written

- For data declarations—internal tables, structures, etc.

- To retrieve data from input text files.

- To set up of nested loops.

- To take care of number of rows in the table control area exceeding the number of visible rows.

If, for a business object, a program exists in the LSMW system, then the LSMW should be the preferred mode of data migration.

# Hands-on Exercise II—Migration of Vendor Data Using *Batch Input Recording* Method

We will again transfer the data of vendors residing in input text files on the application server into the SAP functional module database tables deploying the *Batch Input Recording* method of LSMW. The specification and scope of hands-on exercise II is identical to that of hands-on exercise I in this chapter. We will perform the data transfer for 20 fields, 19 of them listed in Tables 6-1, 6-2, 6-3, and SORTL. Of the 20 fields designated for data transfer, 11 fields will be assigned the same constant value for all the vendors being transferred (see Table 6-1). In the two input text files, we will locate the fields listed in Tables 6-2 and 6-3, respectively. The field SORTL will be derived from the field NAME1.

The *Batch Input Recording* method of LSMW creates a batch input session. When this session is created, data is stored in the queue database tables. The created batch input session has to be executed subsequently, when data is extracted from queue database tables and transferred to the functional module database tables.

The first task is to create a new *Object* YCH06_RC under the existing *Project* and *Subproject*: YCH06_DM, YCH06_VN. The next task is to create a recording of transaction code XK01 in the LSMW followed by the LSMW process steps. A detailed description of the creation the new *Object* YCH06_RC and a recording of transaction code XK01 and LSMW process steps follows.

## Create *Object* YCH06_RC and Recording YCH06_XK01 of Transaction Code XK01

We navigated to the opening screen of transaction code LSMW. To create the new *Object* YCH06_RC under the existing *Project* and *Subproject*—YCH06_DM and YCH06_VN, we entered the names of the *Project*, *Subproject,* and *Object* in the respective fields, clicked the Create button, and entered a suitable description for the *Object*. The screen after the creation of the *Object* YCH06_RC will look like that in Figure 6-68.

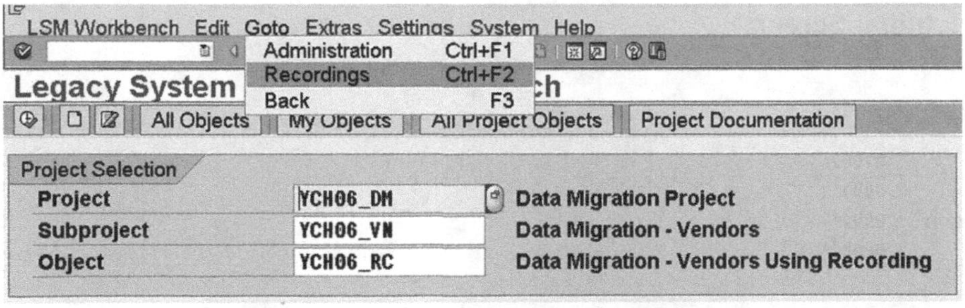

***Figure 6-68.*** *LSMW—Object created under Project, Subproject: menu option for recordings*

In the LSMW environment, a recording is always created under a *Project;* a recording cannot exist independent of a *Project*. A recording is available in all the *Objects* of a *Project*.

To create a recording, you select the menu option Goto ➤ Recordings as shown in Figure 6-68. When we made this menu selection, a dialog box popped up prompting for *Recording* (name), *Description,* and *Owner*. Figure 6-69 shows the screen with the entered values.

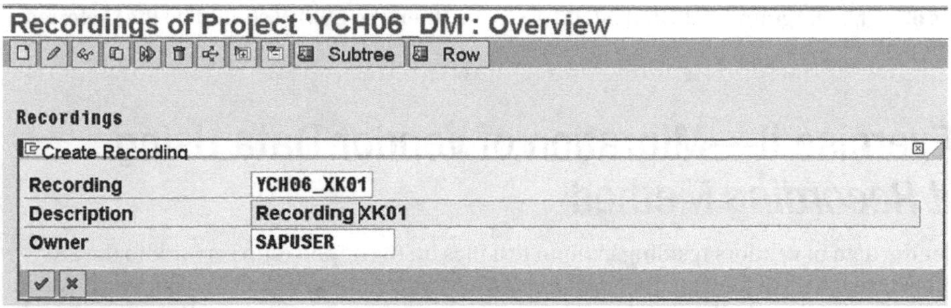

**Recordings of Project 'YCH06_DM': Overview**

Recordings

Create Recording

| | |
|---|---|
| Recording | YCH06_XK01 |
| Description | Recording XK01 |
| Owner | SAPUSER |

*Figure 6-69.* *LSMW—create recording*

We clicked the Continue button. Another dialog box popped up prompting for the transaction code. We entered the transaction code XK01 as shown in Figure 6-70.

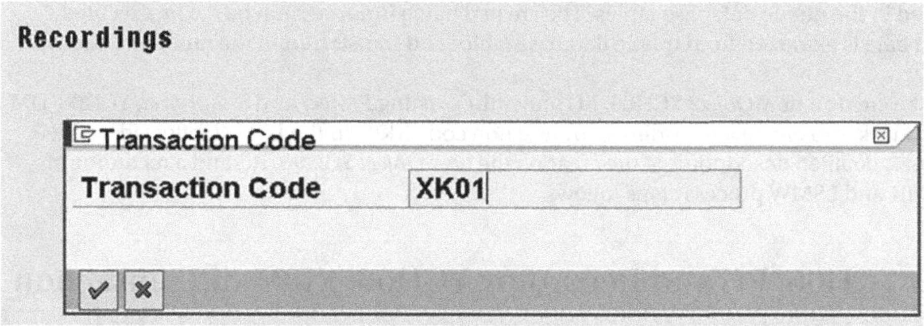

**Recordings**

Transaction Code

| Transaction Code | XK01 |
|---|---|

*Figure 6-70.* *LSMW—create recording for transaction code XK01*

We clicked the Continue button. The control transferred to the *Create Vendor: Initial Screen*. Figure 6-71 shows the screen with the entered values.

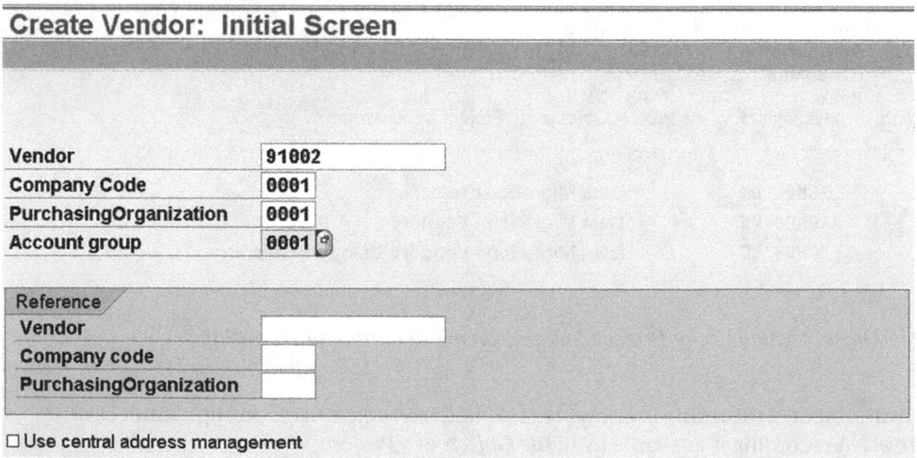

**Create Vendor: Initial Screen**

| | |
|---|---|
| Vendor | 91002 |
| Company Code | 0001 |
| PurchasingOrganization | 0001 |
| Account group | 0001 |

| Reference | |
|---|---|
| Vendor | |
| Company code | |
| PurchasingOrganization | |

☐ Use central address management

*Figure 6-71.* *LSMW—create a vendor under recording; Initial Screen*

Figure 6-72 shows the *Create Vendor: Address* screen with the entered values.

## Create Vendor: Address

| Vendor | 91002 |
|---|---|

**Address**

| | | | |
|---|---|---|---|
| Title | Company | | |
| Name | ASTERIX AND COMPANY | Search term | ASTERIX |
| Street | 999, S.P. ROAD | PO Box | |
| City | MUMBAI | Postal Code | 400078 |
| District | | | |
| P.O.Box city | | PO Box PCode | |
| Country | IN | Region | |

**Communications data**

| | | | |
|---|---|---|---|
| Language Key | EN | Telex number | |
| Telephone 1 | | Fax Number | |
| Telephone 2 | | Teletex number | |
| Telebox | | Data line | |

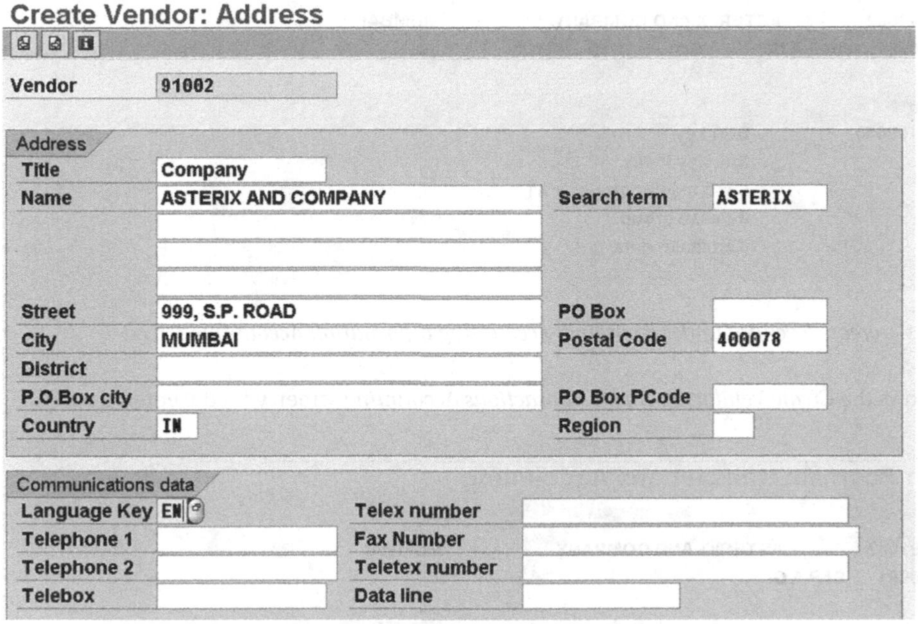

*Figure 6-72.* *LSMW—create a vendor under recording; Address screen*

Figure 6-73 shows the *Create Vendor: Payment transactions* screen with the entered values.

## Create Vendor: Payment transactions

| Vendor | 91002 | ASTERIIX AND COMPANY | MUMBAI |
|---|---|---|---|

**Bank details**

| Ctry | Bank Key | Bank Account | Acct holder | C | IBAN |
|---|---|---|---|---|---|
| US | 23123123 | 00201 | | | ⇨ |
| US | 123123123 | 00202 | | | ⇨ |
| US | 123123123 | 00203 | | | ⇨ |
| | | | | | ⇨ |
| | | | | | ⇨ |

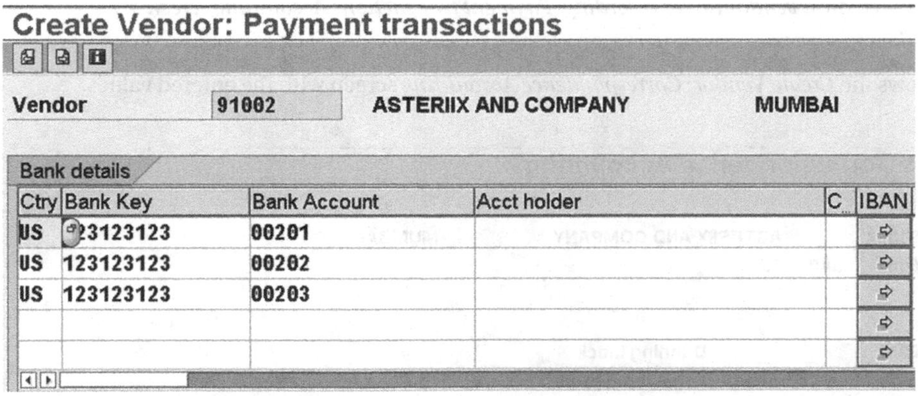

*Figure 6-73.* *LSMW—create a vendor under recording; Payment transactions screen*

We created three bank accounts for the vendor.

Figure 6-74 shows the *Create Vendor: Accounting information accounting* screen with the entered values.

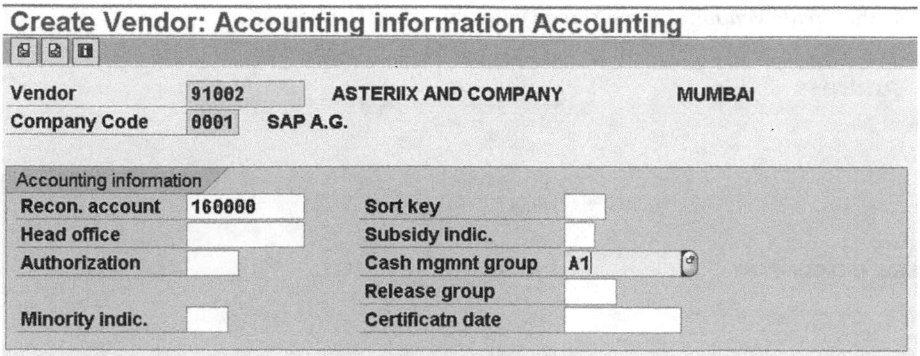

**Create Vendor: Accounting information Accounting**

| Vendor | 91002 | ASTERIIX AND COMPANY | MUMBAI |
|---|---|---|---|
| Company Code | 0001 | SAP A.G. | |

Accounting information

| Recon. account | 160000 | Sort key | |
|---|---|---|---|
| Head office | | Subsidy indic. | |
| Authorization | | Cash mgmnt group | A1 |
| | | Release group | |
| Minority indic. | | Certificatn date | |

*Figure 6-74. LSMW—create a vendor under recording; Accounting information Accounting screen*

Figure 6-75 shows the *Create Vendor: Payment transactions Accounting* screen with the entered values.

**Create Vendor: Payment transactions Accounting**

| Vendor | 91002 | ASTERIIX AND COMPANY | MUMBAI |
|---|---|---|---|
| Company Code | 0001 | SAP A.G. | |

Payment data

| Payt Terms | 0001 | Tolerance group | |
|---|---|---|---|
| Cr memo terms | | Chk double inv. | ☐ |
| Chk cashng time | | | |

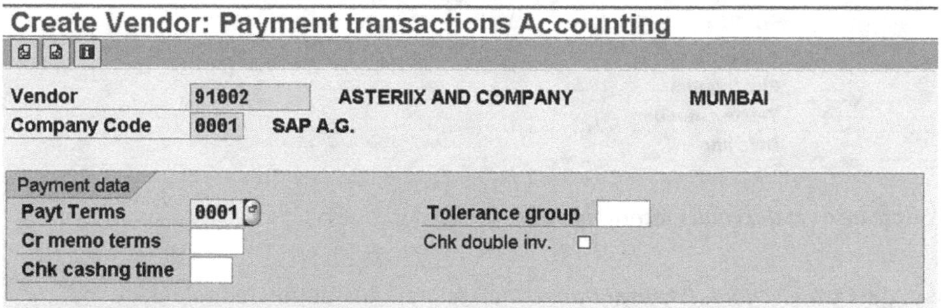

*Figure 6-75. LSMW—create a vendor under recording; Payment transactions Accounting screen*

Figure 6-76 shows the *Create Vendor: Correspondence Accounting* screen with the entered values.

**Create Vendor: Correspondence Accounting**

| Vendor | 91002 | ASTERIIX AND COMPANY | MUMBAI |
|---|---|---|---|
| Company Code | 0001 | SAP A.G. | |

Dunning data

| Dunn.Procedure | 0001 | Dunning block | |
|---|---|---|---|
| Dunn.recipient | | Legal dunn.proc. | |
| Last dunned | | Dunning level | |
| Dunning clerk | | Grouping key | |
| Dunn. Areas | | | |

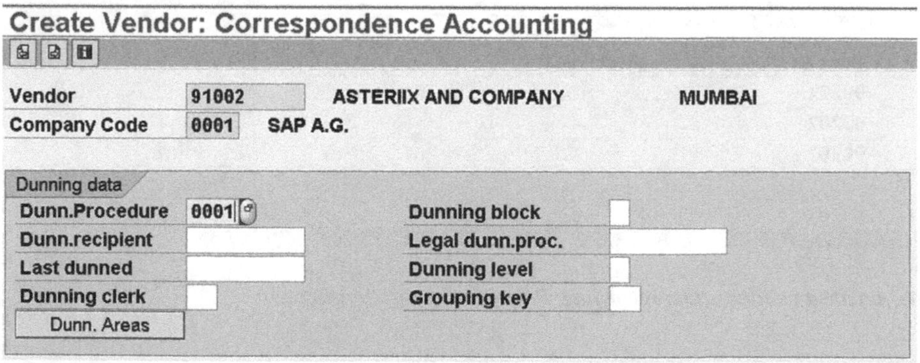

*Figure 6-76. LSMW—create a vendor under recording; Correspondence Accounting screen*

Figure 6-77 shows the *Create Vendor: Purchasing data* screen with the entered values.

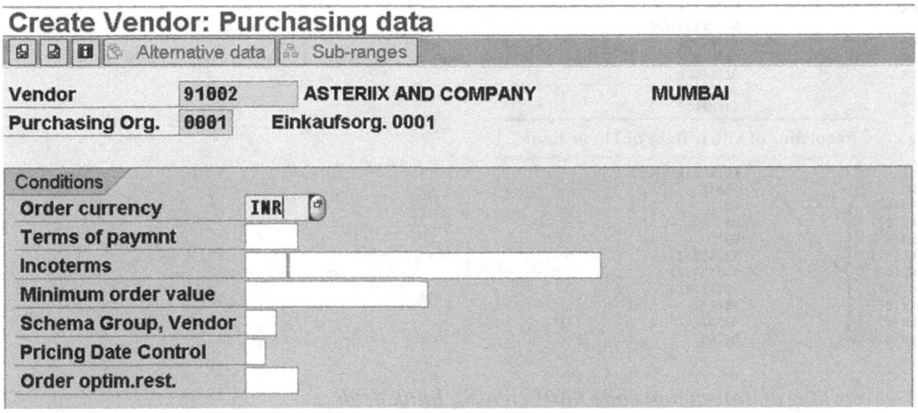

## Create Vendor: Purchasing data

| 🗗 | 🗗 | 🗗 | 🗞 Alternative data | 🗗 Sub-ranges |

| | | | |
|---|---|---|---|
| Vendor | 91002 | ASTERIIX AND COMPANY | MUMBAI |
| Purchasing Org. | 0001 | Einkaufsorg. 0001 | |

**Conditions**

| | |
|---|---|
| Order currency | INR |
| Terms of paymnt | |
| Incoterms | |
| Minimum order value | |
| Schema Group, Vendor | |
| Pricing Date Control | |
| Order optim.rest. | |

*Figure 6-77. LSMW—create a vendor under recording: Purchasing data screen*

Figure 6-78 shows the *Create Vendor: Partner functions* screen.

## Create Vendor: Partner functions

| 🗗 | 🗗 | 🗗 | 🗞 Alternative data | 🗗 Partner address | Delete line |

| | | | |
|---|---|---|---|
| Vendor | 91002 | ASTERIIX AND COMPANY | MUMBAI |
| Purchasing Org. | 0001 | Einkaufsorg. 0001 | |

**Partner Functions**

| P | Name | Number | Name | D |
|----|--------|--------|----------------------|---|
| VN | Vendor | 91002 | ASTERIIX AND COMPANY | ☐ |
| | | | | ☐ |

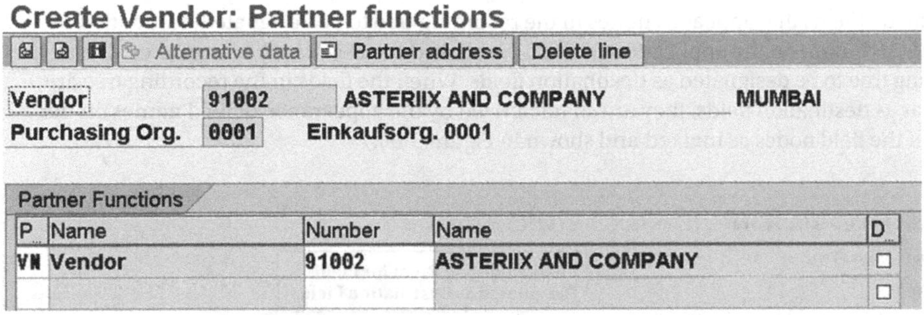

*Figure 6-78. LSMW—create a vendor under recording: Partner functions screen*

We saved the vendor data and navigated back to the *Create Recording* screen. The recording tree with the nodes will appear as shown in Figure 6-79.

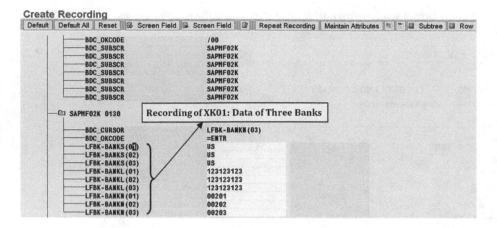

**Figure 6-79.** *LSMW—recording of transaction code XK01 created: bank fields*

We deliberately created three bank accounts for the vendor marked in Figure 6-79.

You can edit the recording—insert and delete lines, edit existing lines, etc., the same way you could edit a recording in transaction code SHDB. For illustrative purposes, we deleted the field LFA1-PSTLZ from the recording tree. The field LFA1-PSTLZ is no more a node in the recording tree and will not appear as a destination field.

If you require all the fields that appear as nodes in the recording tree to be designated destination fields, you click the *Default All* button on the application toolbar. We clicked the *Default All* button to enable all the fields in the recording tree to be designated as destination fields. When the fields in the recording tree are designated to appear as destination fields, they are characterized by the appearance of field names on the extreme right side of the field nodes as marked and shown in Figure 6-80.

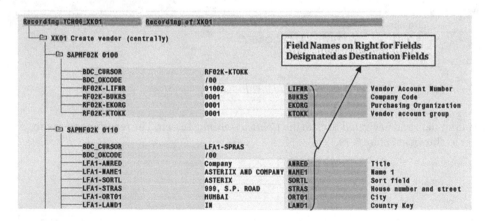

**Figure 6-80.** *LSMW—recording of transaction code XK01 after clicking default all button*

If you want to designate fields as destination fields on an individual or a single field basis, position the cursor on the field you desire to be designated a destination field and then click the *Default* button on the application toolbar.

If you want to annul the designation of fields as destination fields, you position the cursor on the field you desire to and click the *Reset* button on the application toolbar.

We earlier deleted the field LFA1-PSTLZ from the recording tree so that it does not appear as a destination field. An alternative way of making the field LFA1-PSTLZ not appear as a destination field is not to delete it but to annul the designation as destination field—position cursor on the field LFA1-PSTLZ and click the *Reset* button on the application toolbar.

We navigated back to the screen *Recordings of Project 'YCH06_DM': Overview* as shown in Figure 6-81.

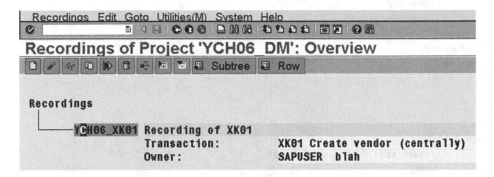

*Figure 6-81. LSMW—recording of Project 'YCH06_DM': Overview*

The following should be borne in mind in regard to LSMW recordings vis-à-vis the recordings created with transaction code SHDB:

- The LSMW recordings and the recordings created with transaction code SHDB exist in segregated environments and there is no way to migrate these recordings from one environment to another.

- The BDC_CURSOR and the BDC_OKCODE fields cannot be modified in the LSMW recording.

- There is no developer access to the program generated from LSMW recordings.

We navigated back to the LSMW opening screen and clicked the Execute button to get to the LSMW process steps screen.

We will commence executing the process steps. Since the process steps are similar and mostly identical to the process steps in hands-on exercise I, I will be less elaborate in describing them.

We started by executing process step 1 by selecting the Radio button and clicking the Execute button.

# Process Step 1—Maintain Object Attributes

We clicked the Display/Change toggle button on the application toolbar to enable changes on the screen.

On the process step 1 screen, in the *Attributes area,* we accepted the default values.

In the *Object Type and Import Method* area, we selected the second Radio button (*Object Type*) *Batch Input Recording.* We clicked the field *Recording* and selected the recording YCH06_XK01 created earlier—function key F4, etc. We clicked the Save button on the screen of process step 1.

Figure 6-82 shows the *Object Attributes* screen with the entries and selections.

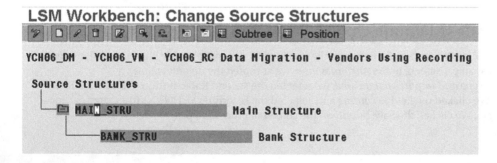

**Figure 6-82.** *Process step 1—Maintain Object Attributes*

We navigated back to the LSMW process steps screen.

## Process Step 2—Maintain Source Structures

We navigated to the screen of process step 2. On the screen of process step 2 we switched to change mode. We then created the input structure MAIN_STRU and under it, the input structure BANK_STRU as in hands-on exercise I.

Figure 6-83 shows the source structures.

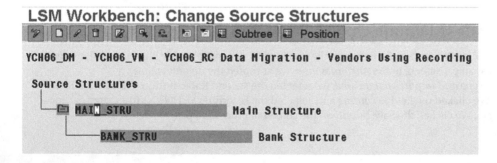

**Figure 6-83.** *Process step 2—create source structure: BANK_STRU under MAIN_STRU ceated*

We saved and returned to the screen with the process steps.

## Process Step 3—Maintain Source Fields

We executed process step 3 and switched the screen to change mode. We must insert fields into the source structures MAIN_STRU and BANK_STRU. The fields in these source structures are identical to the fields in the source structures of hands-on exercise I. There is a provision to copy fields from a source structure of another *Object* in another *Project*. We will utilize this facility instead of inserting fields in the source structures all over again. To copy fields from a source structure of another *Object* in another *Project* into MAIN_STRU, we positioned the cursor on MAIN_STRU and clicked the Copy button (fifth button from the left on the application toolbar). A dialog box appeared on clicking the Copy button as shown in Figure 6-84.

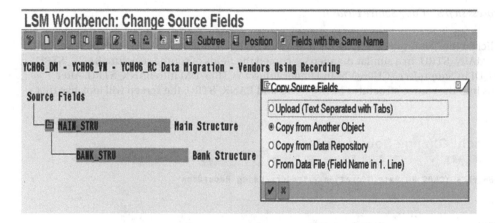

*Figure 6-84.* *Process step 3—Copy Source Fields I*

You can copy fields from

- A text file with field names separated by tabs

- Another *Object* in another *Project*—the option we are employing

- ABAP dictionary structure

- Data file with field names in the first line

On the dialog box of Figure 6-84, we clicked the second Radio button and then clicked the Continue button. Another dialog box popped up prompting for *Project, Subproject, Object,* and source structure name. Figure 6-85 shows the dialog box with entered values (YCH06_DM, YCH06_VN, YCH06_DU, and MAIN_STRU).

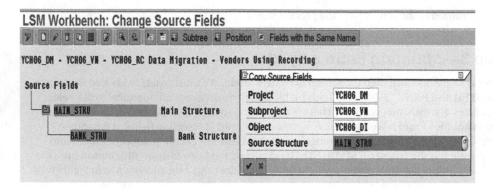

**Figure 6-85.** *Process step 3—Copy Source Fields II*

When we clicked the Continue button on the dialog box of Figure 6-85, the fields got copied into the source structure MAIN_STRU. In a similar manner, we copied the fields of source structure BANK_STRU in *Object* YCH06_DI in *Subproject* YCH06_VN and under *Project* YCH06_DM into BANK_STRU. After copying the fields into the source structures MAIN_STRU and BANK_STRU, the screen will look like that in Figure 6-86.

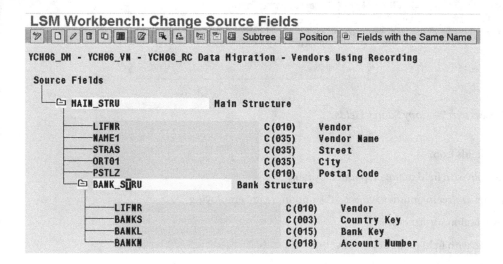

**Figure 6-86.** *Process step 3—create source field: all fields under MAIN_STRU and BANK_STRU*

This concludes process step 3. We saved and returned to the process steps screen.

## Process Step 4—Maintain Structure Relations

We executed process step 4 and switched the screen to change mode.

Recollect the organization of destination structures in hands-on exercise I. At the very top of the destination structures tree was the super structure BGR00. The structure BLF00 was located under the super structure BGR00 The structure BLF00 had fields originating from multiple database tables corresponding to the opening screen of transaction code XK01. Next to the structure BLF00 are located the database table structures BLFA1, BLFB1, BLFBK, BLFB5, BLFM1, and so on. In the present hands-on exercise II, the destination consists of only one structure, YCH06_XK01. Under this single destination structure YCH06_XK01, all the destination fields are located. Recall, we assigned values to 20 fields of non-table control area during recording and deleted one field PSTLZ from the recording subsequently. Figure 6-87 shows the single destination structure YCH06_XK01.

**Figure 6-87.** *Process step 4—Maintain Structure Relations*

As you can observe in Figure 6-87, the single destination structure YCH06_XK01 has been assigned the source structure MAIN_STRU.

Perhaps we should have located all of the input data, main and bank, in one input file instead of two input files. We will discuss this issue further when performing process step 5. For now, we accepted the default assignment of source structure MAIN_STRU to sole destination structure YCH06_XK01.

This completes process step 4. We saved and returned to the process steps screen.

## Process Step 5—Maintain Field Mapping and Conversion Rules

From the screen of LSMW process steps, we executed process step 5 and switched the screen to change mode. To recall, in process step 5, you assign values to the destination fields

Figure 6-88 shows the single destination structure with all the destination fields.

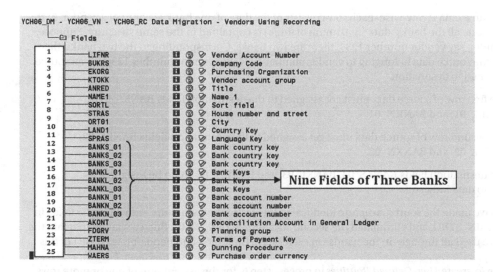

**Figure 6-88.** *Process step 5—Maintain Field Mapping and Conversion Rules*

Only fields for which data was entered during recording will appear in the destination structure. In Figure 6-88, the destination fields are marked with numbers 1–25. The nine fields of three banks are also marked in the Figure 6-88.

While recording, we had created data for three banks for the vendor. Corresponding to the data for three banks, the LSMW system incorporated nine fields in the sole destination structure YCH06_XK01 as follows:

```
BANKS_01
BANKS_02
BANKS_03
BANKL_01
BANKL_02
BANKL_03
BANKN_01
BANKN_02
BANKN_03
```

If we had created data for two banks for the vendor during recording, the LSMW system would have incorporated six fields in the destination structure.

And if we had not created any data for banks for the vendor during recording, the destination structure would not have consisted of any fields related to bank data.

As it is, with the creation of three banks for the vendor during recording, this configuration will support a maximum of three banks for a vendor. Beyond three banks, no fields can be assigned values. The configuration will support only a maximum of that many banks for a vendor as were created during recording.

Also, if you have created data of one or more bank(s) for the vendor during recoding, the LSMW system is generating an error condition during data migration if no bank data is submitted for a vendor.

The bank data of the vendors is being captured on the screen in a table control. From the discussions, it is apparent that if table control is featured in a data migration, it is not advisable to deploy the *Batch Input Recording* method of LSMW. We are featuring the table control in this hands-on exercise to highlight the issue.

The bank source data is row-wise–each row consists of the data of one bank account of a vendor. In the destination structure, all the banks' data (maximum of three) is contained in the same structure. Suppose, for a specific vendor, say vendor number 1234, there are two banks. Corresponding to the two banks, there will two rows in the source data belonging to vendor number 1234. For vendor number 1234, when source data is to be assigned to destination

- The first row of source data must get assigned to the destination fields BANKS_01, BANKL_01, and BANKN_01.

- The second row of source data must get assigned to the destination fields BANKS_02, BANKL_02, and BANKN_02.

- The destination fields BANKS_03, BANKL_03, and BANKN_03 are to be assigned '/'– the no data indicator.

We could have made the source structure identical to the destination structure with all the 25 fields in one structure, MAIN_STRU, and eliminated the second structure, BANK_STRU. But we wanted to retain the input text files we used all through–in the hands-on exercises of Chapter 5 and hands-on exercise I of this chapter.

We propose to create *User-Defined Routines* in process step 6, for the assignment of one or more rows (maximum of three) of bank data of a vendor in the source to the destination fields in a single row.

Except for the bank data fields, the assignments to other destination fields are a repetition of assignments in hands-on exercise I. Figure 6-89 shows the assignments to destination field nos. 1–4.

```
YCH06_DM - YCH06_VN - YCH06_RC Data Migration - Vendors Using Recording
   └─ Fields
        ├───LIFNR                 Vendor Account Number
        │                Source:  MAIN_STRU-LIFNR (Vendor)
        │                Rule  :  Transfer (MOVE)
        │                Code:    YCH06_XK01-LIFNR = MAIN_STRU-LIFNR.
        ├───BUKRS                 Company Code
        │                Rule  :  Constant
        │                Code:    YCH06_XK01-BUKRS = '0001'.
        ├───EKORG                 Purchasing Organization
        │                Rule  :  Constant
        │                Code:    YCH06_XK01-EKORG = '0001'.
        ├───KTOKK                 Vendor account group
        │                Rule  :  Constant
        │                Code:    YCH06_XK01-KTOKK = '0001'.
        ├───ANRED                 Title
```

*Figure 6-89.* *Process step 5—assignment to destination field Nos. 1-4*

Figure 6-90 shows the assignments to destination field nos. 5, 6, 8, 9, 10, and 11.

```
YCH06_DM - YCH06_VN - YCH06_RC Data Migration - Vendors Using Recording
        ├───ANRED                 Title
        │                Rule  :  Constant
        │                Code:    YCH06_XK01-ANRED = 'Company'.
        ├───NAME1                 Name 1
        │                Source:  MAIN_STRU-NAME1 (Vendor Name)
        │                Rule  :  Transfer (MOVE)
        │                Code:    YCH06_XK01-NAME1 = MAIN_STRU-NAME1.
        ├───SORTL                 Sort field
        ├───STRAS                 House number and street
        │                Source:  MAIN_STRU-STRAS (Street)
        │                Rule  :  Transfer (MOVE)
        │                Code:    YCH06_XK01-STRAS = MAIN_STRU-STRAS.
        ├───ORT01                 City
        │                Source:  MAIN_STRU-ORT01 (City)
        │                Rule  :  Transfer (MOVE)
        │                Code:    YCH06_XK01-ORT01 = MAIN_STRU-ORT01.
        ├───LAND1                 Country Key
        │                Rule  :  Constant
        │                Code:    YCH06_XK01-LAND1 = 'IN'.
        ├───SPRAS                 Language Key
        │                Rule  :  Constant
        │                Code:    YCH06_XK01-SPRAS = 'E'.
```

*Figure 6-90.* *Process step 5—assignment to destination field nos. 5, 6, 8, 9, 10, and 11*

The assignment to destination field no. 7 (SORTL) is by the invocation of the *User-Defined Routine* UR_GET_SORTL created during hands-on exercise I. Figure 6-91 shows the assignment to destination field no. 7 (SORTL).

```
* Target Field: YCH06_XK01-SORTL Sort field
PERFORM UR_GET_SORTL USING  YCH06_XK01-NAME1
                     CHANGING  YCH06_XK01-SORTL.
```

*Figure 6-91.* *Process step 5—assignment to destination field no. 7*

Figure 6-92 shows the assignments to destination field nos. 21-25.

```
---------            -----------------
----AKONT            ■ ⊟ ⊘ ⊗  Reconciliation Account in General Ledger
                     Rule :   Constant
                     Code:    YCH06_XK01-AKONT = '0000160000'.
----FDGRV            ⊟ ⊗ ⊘    Planning group
                     Rule :   Constant
                     Code:    YCH06_XK01-FDGRV = 'A1'.
----ZTERM            ⊟ ⊗ ⊘    Terms of Payment Key
                     Rule :   Constant
                     Code:    YCH06_XK01-ZTERM = '0001'.
----MAHNA            ⊟ ⊗ ⊘    Dunning Procedure
                     Rule :   Constant
                     Code:    YCH06_XK01-MAHNA = '0001'.
----WAERS            ⊟ ⊗ ⊘    Purchase order currency
                     Rule :   Constant
                     Code:    YCH06_XK01-WAERS = 'INR'.
```

*Figure 6-92. Process step 5—assignment to destination field nos. 21-25*

We performed a validity check (ctrl+F2 or sixth button from the left on the application toolbar). We saved the changes and returned to the process steps screen.

Process step 5 is still incomplete. The nine destination fields—BANKS_01, BANKS_02, BANKS_03, BANKL_01, BANKL_02, BANKL_03, BANKN_01, BANKN_02, and BANKN_03—are still to be assigned values. These destination fields will be assigned values by invoking *User-Defined Routines* to be created in process step 6. After performing process step 6, we will return to process step 5 and assign value to the nine destination fields, thereby completing process step 5.

## Process Step 6—Maintain Fixed Values, Translations, and User-Defined Routines

In process step 6, we are creating two *User-Defined Routines* for the assignment of one or more rows (maximum of three) of bank data of a vendor in the source to the destination fields in a single row.

The first *User-Defined Routine* UR_GET_BANK_FLD_VAL will receive three input parameters as

- The field YCH06_XK01-LIFNR

- SUFFIX containing suffix value: 01 or 02 or 03

- FNAME containing field name: BANKS or BANKL or BANKN

The first *User-Defined Routine* will return, in RET_VAL, the value to be assigned to the bank field.

The second *User-Defined Routine* UR_GET_BANKS will be invoked by the first *User-Defined Routine* and receive three input parameters as

- WBANK_TAB—the internal table containing bank data of a vendor

- SUFFIX containing suffix value: 01 or 02 or 03

- FIELD containing field name: BANKS or BANKL or BANKN

The second *User-Defined Routine* will return, in BANKS, the value to be assigned to the bank field.

From the screen of the LSMW process steps, we navigated to the screen of process step 6. We toggled the screen of process step 6 to change mode.

We created two *User-Defined Routine* nodes, GET_BANK_FLD_VAL and GET_BANKS, as shown in Figure 6-93.

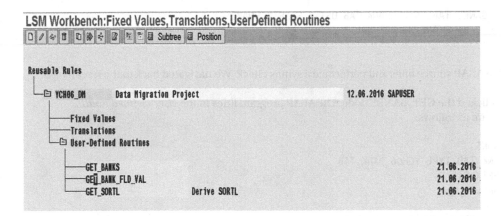

*Figure 6-93. Process step 6—User-Defined Routines GET_BANK_FLD_VAL and GET_BANKS*

We double-clicked the GET_BANK_FLD_VAL node. The ABAP program lines in the *User-Defined Routine* UR_GET_BANK_FLD_VAL are as follows:

```
form ur_GET_BANK_FLD_VAL
     using LIFNR SUFFIX FNAME
  changing RET_VAL.

STATICS: BANK_TAB    TYPE YCH06_BANK_TAB,
         WBANK_TAB   TYPE YCH06_BANK_TAB,
         ONCE(1)     TYPE C.
DATA BANK_STRU TYPE YCH06_BANK_STRU.

IF ONCE = ' '.
 ONCE = 'X'.
 OPEN DATASET 'YCH05_BANK_DATA' FOR INPUT IN TEXT MODE
   ENCODING DEFAULT.

 DO.
  READ DATASET 'YCH05_BANK_DATA' INTO BANK_STRU.
  IF SY-SUBRC NE 0.
   EXIT.
  ENDIF.
  APPEND BANK_STRU TO BANK_TAB.
 ENDDO.
ENDIF.
IF FNAME = 'BANKS' AND SUFFIX = '01'.
 REFRESH WBANK_TAB.
 LOOP AT BANK_TAB INTO BANK_STRU.
  IF BANK_STRU-LIFNR <> LIFNR.
   CONTINUE.
  ENDIF.
  APPEND BANK_STRU TO WBANK_TAB.
 ENDLOOP.
ENDIF.
```

```
PERFORM UR_GET_BANKS TABLES    WBANK_TAB USING SUFFIX FNAME
                          CHANGING RET_VAL.
endform.
```

We saved the ABAP source lines and performed a syntax check. We navigated back to the screen of process step 6.

We double-clicked the GET_BANKS node. The ABAP program lines in the *User-Defined Routine* UR_GET_BANKS are as follows:

```
form UR_GET_BANKS
   TABLES WBANK_TAB TYPE YCH06_BANK_TAB
     using SUFFIX FIELD
  changing BANKS.

  STATICS: BANK_STRU1 TYPE YCH06_BANK_STRU,
          SUBRC      TYPE SY-SUBRC.
  CLEAR BANK_STRU1.
  READ TABLE WBANK_TAB INTO BANK_STRU1 INDEX SUFFIX.
  SUBRC = SY-SUBRC.
 IF SUBRC NE 0.
  BANKS = '/'.
  ELSE.
  CASE FIELD.
  WHEN 'BANKS'.
   BANKS = BANK_STRU1-BANKS.
  WHEN 'BANKL'.
   BANKS = BANK_STRU1-BANKL.
  WHEN 'BANKN'.
   BANKS = BANK_STRU1-BANKN.
  ENDCASE.
  ENDIF.

endform.
```

We saved the ABAP source lines and performed a syntax check. We navigated back to the screen of process step 6.

This completes the creation of the *User-Defined Routines* UR_GET_BANK_FLD_VAL and UR_GET_BANKS. We navigated back to the process steps screen.

## Process Step 5—Revisited

From the screen of process steps, we executed the process step 5 and switched the screen to change mode.

In this revisit of process step 5, we want to assign value to the nine destination fields YCH06_XK01-BANKS_01, YCH06_XK01-BANKL_01, YCH06_XK01-BANKN_01.....by invocation of *User-Defined Routine* UR_GET_BANK_FLD_VAL. To invoke *User-Defined Routine* UR_GET_BANK_FLD_VAL, we double-clicked the BANKS_01 node and entered the following lines in the ABAP line editor:

```
DATA RETVAL1 TYPE STRING.
PERFORM ur_GET_BANK_FLD_VAL
       USING YCH06_XK01-LIFNR '01' 'BANKS'
     CHANGING RETVAL1.
YCH06_XK01-BANKS_01 = RETVAL1.
```

Note that the second parameter '01' is the suffix of the node BANKS_01; the third parameter 'BANKS' is the name of the field in the database table LFBK.

We saved, performed a syntax check, and navigated back to the screen of process step 5.

In a similar manner, we inserted ABAP code in the eight nodes of BANKS_01, BANKN_01, BANKS_02, BANKL_02, BANKN_02, BANKS_03, BANKL_03, and BANKN_03 with appropriate second and third parameter values when invoking the *User-Defined Routine* UR_GET_BANK_FLD_VAL.

Each time we inserted ABAP code under a node, we saved and performed a syntax check.

The assignment to destination fields of bank data involved a lot of extra work. We could have saved ourselves all the extra work by locating the source data in one structure instead of in two structures.

Now that we assigned values to the nine fields relating to bank data, process step 5 is concluded. We saved and performed a validity check. We navigated back to the process steps screen.

## Process Step 7—*Specify Files*

From the screen of process steps, we executed the process step 7 and switched the screen to change mode.

In process step 7, we specified the two input text files located on the application server.

The screen with the two input text files specified will appear as shown in Figure 6-94.

```
YCH06_DM - YCH06_VN - YCH06_RC Data Migration - Vendors Using Recording

Files

        ┌──────Legacy Data          On the PC (Frontend)
        ├─ 🗁 Legacy Data           On the█R/3 server (application server)

             ┌──────Bank Data            YCH05_BANK_DATA
             │                           Data for One Source Structure (Table)
             │                           No Separator
             │                           Field Order Matches Source Structure Definition
             │                           With Record End Indicator (Text File)
             │                           Code Page 4110
             └──────Main Data            YCH05_MAIN_DATA
                                         Data for One Source Structure (Table)
                                         No Separator
                                         Field Order Matches Source Structure Definition
                                         With Record End Indicator (Text File)
                                         Code Page 4110
```

*Figure 6-94.* *Process step 7—files YCH05_MAIN_DATA, YCH05_BANK_DATA specified*

We saved the changes on the screen of process step 7. This concludes process step 7. We navigated back to the process steps screen.

## Process Step 8—*Assign Files*

From the screen of process steps, we executed the process step 8 and switched the screen to change mode.

We assigned the two input text files specified in process step 7 to the respective source structures created in process step 2. This is shown in Figure 6-95.

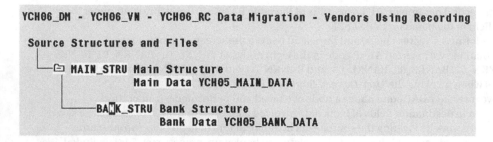

```
YCH06_DM - YCH06_VN - YCH06_RC Data Migration - Vendors Using Recording

Source Structures and Files

   └─ 🗁 MAIN_STRU Main Structure
                  Main Data YCH05_MAIN_DATA

      └─────BANK_STRU Bank Structure
                     Bank Data YCH05_BANK_DATA
```

*Figure 6-95.* *Process step 8—files assigned to source structures*

We saved the changes on the screen of process step 8. This concludes the process step 8. We navigated back to the process steps screen.

# Data Creation on Presentation Server, Copy to Application Server

We created the main and bank data on the presentation server using the notepad editor.

Figure 6-96 shows the main data of four vendors: 0000090241, 0000090242, 0000090243, and 0000090244:

```
MAIN_DATA - Notepad
File Edit Format View Help
0000090241GATA TECHNOLOGY LTD.      101, FIRST ROAD       MUMBAI       400001
0000090242GATA INFO TECH. LTD.      202, SECOND ROAD      MUMBAI       400011
0000090243KATA INFO SYSTEMS LTD.    303, TRIRD ROAD       MUMBAI       400021
0000090244PATA SYSTEMS LTD.         404, FOURTH ROAD      MUMBAI       400031
```

*Figure 6-96.* *Vendors' main data—text file*

Figure 6-97 shows the bank data of three vendors: 0000090242, 0000090243, and 0000090244. Vendor 0000090242, has one bank account, vendor 0000090243 has two bank accounts, and vendor 0000090244 has three bank accounts, respectively. No bank data was created for vendor 0000090241.

```
BANK_DATA - Notepad
File Edit Format View Help
0000090242US 123123123      242001
0000090243US 123123123      243001
0000090243US 123123123      243002
0000090244US 123123123      244001
0000090244US 123123123      244002
0000090244US 123123123      244003
```

*Figure 6-97.* *Vendors' bank data—text file*

The main file and bank file on the presentation server were copied to YCH05_MAIN_DATA and YCH05_BANK_DATA, respectively, on the application server using transaction code USS_FAS.

With the test data made available on the application server, we will execute process step 9 from the LSMW process steps screen.

500

## Process Step 9—*Read Data*

Recall, that in process step 9, data is fetched from input text files and assembled together for an entity-vendor and stored in the file with the following postfix: .lsmw.read.

On the screen of process step 9, we clicked the Execute button and then clicked the execute button on the dialog box that appeared. The execution produced an output of statistics of input text data read and imported or written as shown in Figure 6-98.

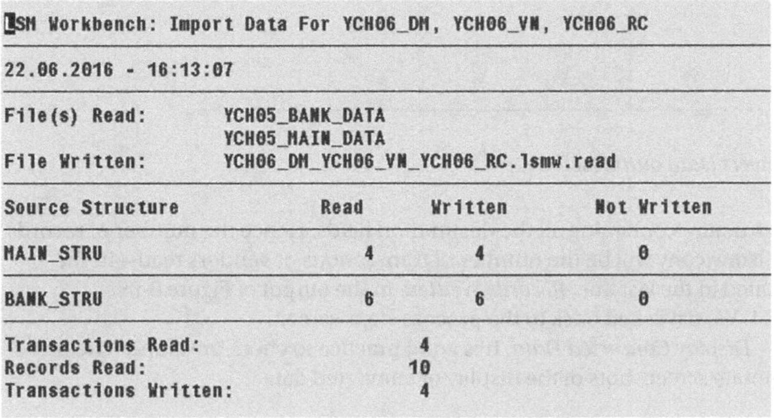

```
LSM Workbench: Import Data For YCH06_DM, YCH06_VN, YCH06_RC

22.06.2016 - 16:13:07

File(s) Read:      YCH05_BANK_DATA
                   YCH05_MAIN_DATA
File Written:      YCH06_DM_YCH06_VN_YCH06_RC.1smw.read

Source Structure         Read       Written      Not Written

MAIN_STRU                   4          4               0

BANK_STRU                   6          6               0

Transactions Read:          4
Records Read:              10
Transactions Written:       4
```

*Figure 6-98.* *Process step 9—Import Data output screen*

This concludes the process step 9. We navigated back to the process steps screen.

We executed process step 10. It is good practice to check or sample-check the imported data. We did not incorporate screenshots of the display of imported data.

## Process Step 11—*Convert Data*

From the screen of process steps, we executed process step 11.

In the of process step 11, data is assigned to the destination fields as per the specifications in process step 5 and written to the file with the postfix: .lsmw.conv.

On the screen of process step 11, we clicked the Execute button and then clicked the Execute button on the dialog box that appeared. The execution produced an output of statistics of converted data written as shown in Figure 6-99.

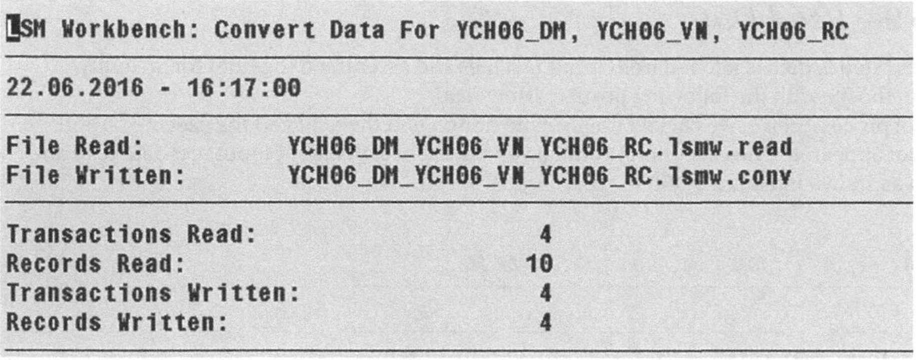

```
┃SM Workbench: Convert Data For YCH06_DM, YCH06_VN, YCH06_RC

22.06.2016 - 16:17:00

File Read:          YCH06_DM_YCH06_VN_YCH06_RC.lsmw.read
File Written:       YCH06_DM_YCH06_VN_YCH06_RC.lsmw.conv

Transactions Read:              4
Records Read:                  10
Transactions Written:           4
Records Written:                4
```

*Figure 6-99.* *Process step 11—Convert Data output screen*

There is a single destination structure containing all the destination fields. Hence the number of records written to the file with the postfix .lsmw.conv will be the number of transactions or vendors read—in the present context: four. This is indicated in the last line, *Records Written,* in the output of Figure 6-99.

This concludes process step 11. We navigated back to the process steps screen.

We executed process step 12—*Display Converted Data*. It is good practice to check or sample-check the converted data. We did not incorporate screenshots of the display of converted data.

## Process Step 13—Create Batch Input Session

From the screen of process steps, we executed process step 13.

In process step 13, we will create a batch input session from the converted data, that is, the data in the file with the postfix .lsmw.conv.

When you execute process step 13, a dialog appears as shown in Figure 6-100.

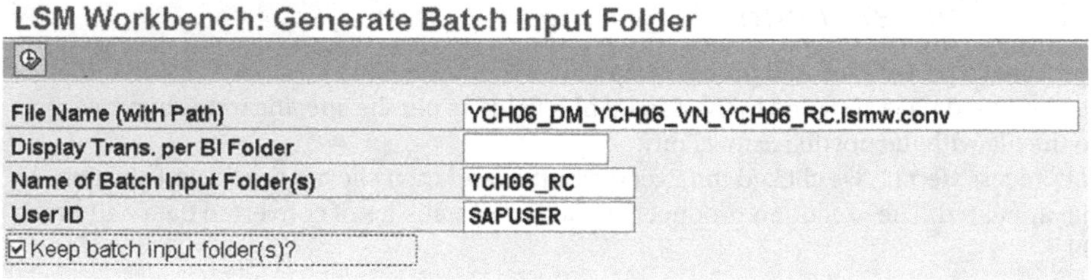

### LSM Workbench: Generate Batch Input Folder

| | |
|---|---|
| File Name (with Path) | YCH06_DM_YCH06_VN_YCH06_RC.lsmw.conv |
| Display Trans. per BI Folder | |
| Name of Batch Input Folder(s) | YCH06_RC |
| User ID | SAPUSER |
| ☑ Keep batch input folder(s)? | |

*Figure 6-100.* *Process step 13—create batch input session*

If the volume of data is very large, you can split the data into multiple batch input folders by specifying a number in the field *Display Trans. per BI Folder.*

We clicked the Execute button and an output of info message as shown in Figure 6-101 appeared.

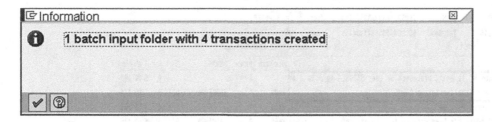

*Figure 6-101.* *Process step 13—batch input folder created*

This concludes process step 13. We navigated back to the process steps screen.

## Process Step 14—Run Batch Input Session

From the screen of process steps, we executed process step 14.

In process step 14, we will execute the batch input session created in process step 13.

When you execute process step 14, you navigate to the session overview screen. We selected the session YCH06_RC and clicked the *Process* button on the application toolbar.

*Process Session YCH06_RC* popped up. We selected the *Processing Mode* as *Background* and clicked the *Process* button on the dialog box as shown in Figure 6-102.

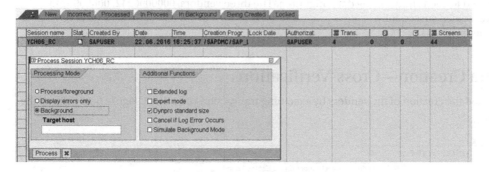

*Figure 6-102.* *Process step 14—batch input session overview screen*

The execution of the session generated errors. We opened the log for the session as shown in Figure 6-103.

| | | | |
|---|---|---|---|
| **Log attributes** | | | |
| Name | YCH06_RC | Queue ID | 16062216433633566411 | User | SAPUSER |
| Created On | 22.06.2016 | TemSe ID | BDCLG363356641134419 | ☐ Details | |

| Time | Message | Transacti | Index | Modul | Scre | Ind | T | M | Me |
|---|---|---|---|---|---|---|---|---|---|
| 16:45:14 | Session YCH06_RC is being processed by user SAPUSER in mode N or | | 0 | | | 0 | S | 00 | 300 |
| 16:45:34 | No batch input data for screen SAPMF02K 0210 | XK01 | 1 | SAPMF02K | 0210 | 5 | S | 00 | 344 |
| 16:45:34 | Transaction error | XK01 | 1 | | | 0 | S | 00 | 357 |
| 16:46:13 | Vendor 0000090242 has been created for company code 0001 purchas | XK01 | 2 | SAPMF02K | 0320 | 11 | S | F2 | 175 |
| 16:46:56 | Transaction was processed successfully | XK01 | 2 | | | 0 | S | 00 | 355 |
| 16:46:56 | Vendor 0000090243 has been created for company code 0001 purchas | XK01 | 3 | SAPMF02K | 0320 | 11 | S | F2 | 175 |
| 16:47:02 | Transaction was processed successfully | XK01 | 3 | | | 0 | S | 00 | 355 |
| 16:47:12 | Vendor 0000090244 has been created for company code 0001 purchas | XK01 | 4 | SAPMF02K | 0320 | 11 | S | F2 | 175 |
| 16:47:22 | Transaction was processed successfully | XK01 | 4 | | | 0 | S | 00 | 355 |
| 16:47:22 | Processing statistics | | 0 | | | 0 | S | 00 | 370 |
| 16:47:22 | 4 transactions read | | 0 | | | 0 | S | 00 | 363 |
| 16:47:22 | 3 transactions processed | | 0 | | | 0 | S | 00 | 364 |

*Figure 6-103.* *Process step 14—batch input session run log*

The error marked in Figure 6-103 was generated because of non-availability of bank data for vendor 0000090241 on screen number 210. In the LSMW environment, when employing the *Batch Input Recording* method, if you created data in the table control area during recording, at least one row of table control data needs to be provided to each entity during data migration. The three vendors, 0000090242, 0000090243, and 0000090244, were created successfully.

This concludes process step 14.

# Vendor Data Creation—Cross-Verification

We crossed-checked the creation of the vendors by executing transaction code XK02. Figure 6-104 shows the created vendors.

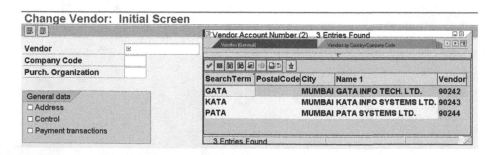

*Figure 6-104.* *Vendor list—vendor numbers with pattern: 9024\**

We selected each of the vendors in turn and navigated through all the screens to cross-check the migration of all the data correctly.

Figure 6-105 shows the *Payment transactions* (bank data) screen of vendor 0000090242 with one bank account.

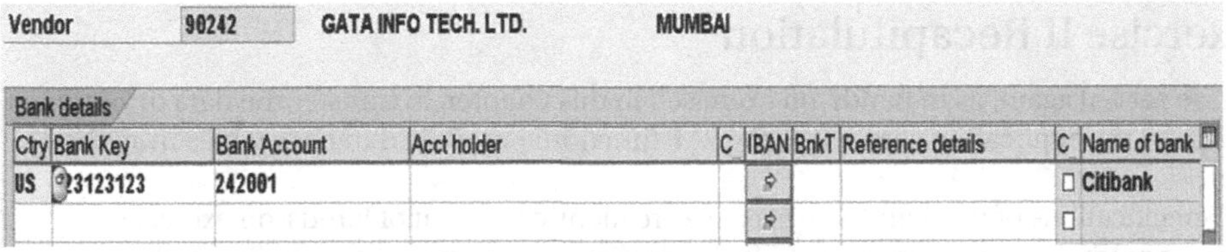

| Vendor | 90242 | GATA INFO TECH. LTD. | | MUMBAI | | | | | | |
|--------|-------|----------------------|--|--------|--|--|--|--|--|--|

| **Bank details** | | | | | | | | | |
|------|----------|--------------|------------|---|------|------|------------------|---|--------------|
| Ctry | Bank Key | Bank Account | Acct holder | C | IBAN | BnkT | Reference details | C | Name of bank |
| US | 123123123 | 242001 | | | ф | | | □ | Citibank |
| | | | | | ф | | | □ | |

*Figure 6-105. Vendor 0000090242—Payment transactions screen: one bank account*

Figure 6-106 shows the *Payment transactions* (bank data) screen of vendor 0000090243 with two bank accounts.

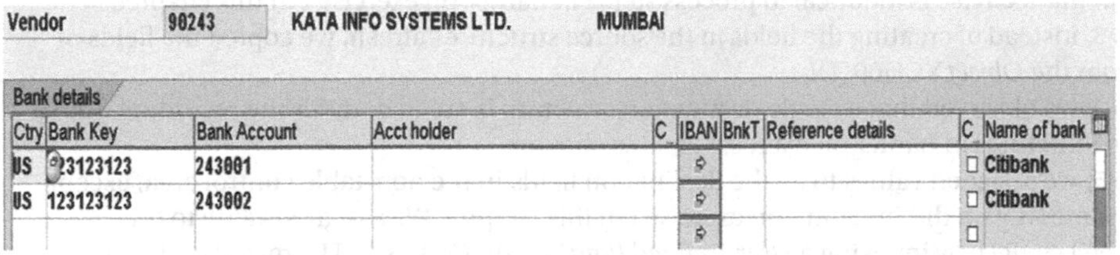

| Vendor | 90243 | KATA INFO SYSTEMS LTD. | | MUMBAI | | | | | | |
|--------|-------|------------------------|--|--------|--|--|--|--|--|--|

| **Bank details** | | | | | | | | | |
|------|----------|--------------|------------|---|------|------|------------------|---|--------------|
| Ctry | Bank Key | Bank Account | Acct holder | C | IBAN | BnkT | Reference details | C | Name of bank |
| US | 123123123 | 243001 | | | ф | | | □ | Citibank |
| US | 123123123 | 243002 | | | ф | | | □ | Citibank |
| | | | | | ф | | | □ | |

*Figure 6-106. Vendor 0000090243—Payment transactions screen: two bank accounts*

Figure 6-107 shows the *Payment transactions* (bank data) screen of vendor 0000090244 with three bank accounts.

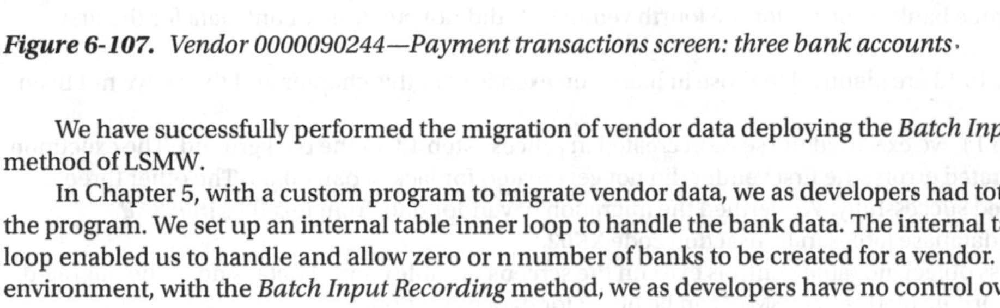

| Vendor | 90244 | PATA SYSTEMS LTD. | | MUMBAI | | | | | | |
|--------|-------|-------------------|--|--------|--|--|--|--|--|--|

| **Bank details** | | | | | | | | | |
|------|----------|--------------|------------|---|------|------|------------------|---|--------------|
| Ctry | Bank Key | Bank Account | Acct holder | C | IBAN | BnkT | Reference details | C | Name of bank |
| US | 123123123 | 244001 | | | ф | | | □ | Citibank |
| US | 123123123 | 244002 | | | ф | | | □ | Citibank |
| US | 123123123 | 244003 | | | ф | | | □ | Citibank |
| | | | | | ф | | | □ | |

*Figure 6-107. Vendor 0000090244—Payment transactions screen: three bank accounts·*

We have successfully performed the migration of vendor data deploying the *Batch Input Recording* method of LSMW.

In Chapter 5, with a custom program to migrate vendor data, we as developers had total control over the program. We set up an internal table inner loop to handle the bank data. The internal table inner loop enabled us to handle and allow zero or n number of banks to be created for a vendor. In the LSMW environment, with the *Batch Input Recording* method, we as developers have no control over the program generated from a recording. The single destination structure contains fields for as many banks only as were created during recoding and affords no scope for a repetitive looping process. If data migration involves table control, it is not advisable to deploy the *Batch Input Recording* method of LSMW.

This concludes the cross-verification of vendor data created and hands-on exercise II.

# Hands-on Exercise II Recapitulation

The hands-on exercise set out again, as in hands-on exercise I in this chapter, to transfer the data of vendors from text files residing on the application server into the SAP functional module database tables from the LSMW environment.

The scope and specifications of this hands-on exercise are identical to that of hands-on exercise I. Instead of deploying a ready-to-use program of LSMW environment, we created a recording of the transaction code XK01 and deployed the recording for migration of vendor data.

We created a new *Object* YCH06_RC under the existing *Project* YCH06_DM and *Subproject* YCH06_VN. A recording is created under a *Project* from the opening screen of LSMW. We created a recording YCH06_XK01 of transaction code XK01.

In process step 1, we selected the *Object Type* as *Batch Input Recording* and assigned the recording YCH06_XK01 to the field *Recording*.

Process step 2 in this exercise is identical to process step 2 in hands-on exercise I in this chapter.

In process step 3, instead of creating the fields in the source structures afresh, we copied the fields of source structures from the *Object* YCH06_DI.

In process step 4, we observed that a single destination structure is created under the recording unlike multiple destination structures in hands-on exercise I in this chapter.

In process step 5, we assigned values to all the destination fields in the non-table control area, except BLFA1-SORTL, the same way we did in hands-on exercise I in this chapter. We assigned value to the destination field BLFA1-SORTL by invoking a *User-Defined Routine* UR_GET_SORTL created earlier in hands-on exercise I of this chapter.

For destination fields in the table control area (i.e., the bank data), data from one or more rows in the source is to be assigned to multiple fields in a single destination structure. To implement the assignment from one or more rows in the source to multiple fields in a single destination structure, we created *User-Defined Routines* in process step 6.

In process step 6—*Fixed Values, Translations,* and *User-Defined Routines,* we created two *User-Defined Routines*: UR_GET_BANK_FLD_VAL and UR_GET_BANKS. The second routine UR_GET_BANKS is being invoked from the first routine, UR_GET_BANK_FLD_VAL. The two routines implement the assignment from one or more rows in the source to multiple fields in a single destination structure.

We reverted to process step 5 to assign values to the nine destination fields, YCH06_XK01-BANKS_01, YCH06_XK01-BANKL_01....., by invoking a *User-Defined Routine* UR_GET_BANK_FLD_VAL with appropriate parameters.

We created representative input text data files of four vendors on the presentation server using the notepad editor. We copied the input text data files from the presentation server to the application server in transaction code USS_FAS. We created one bank account for the second vendor, two bank accounts for the third vendor, and three bank accounts for the fourth vendor. We did not create any bank data for the first vendor.

Process steps 7 to 13 are identical to those in hands-on exercise I of this chapter and thus have not been elaborated upon.

In process step 14, we executed the session created in process step 13, in the background. The execution of the session generated errors; the first vendor did not get created for lack of bank data. The other three vendors were created successfully. We verified the migration of vendor data from text files into SAP functional module database tables in transaction code XK02.

If, for a business object, no table controls exist on the screens or table control data is not to be migrated, the *Batch Input Recording* method of LSMW can be opted for data migration.

# Process Steps Screen—Menu Options

This is a brief on the major menu options available on the LSMW process step screen.

The available menu options on the LSMW process step screen will look like those in Figure 6-108.

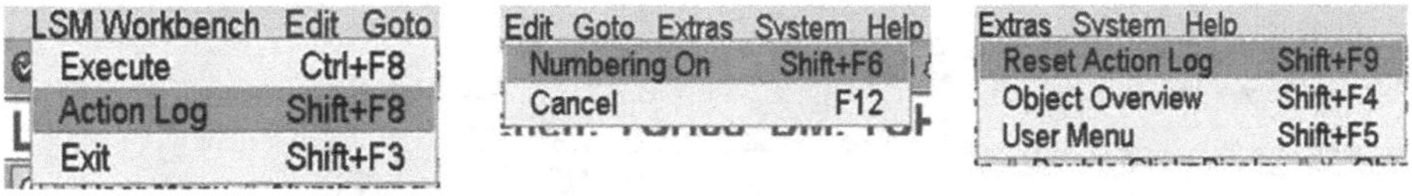

*Figure 6-108. Menu options—LSMW process steps screen*

- The LSMW system maintains a log of all changes made to process steps of an *Object* under a *Subproject* and *Project*. The log of the changes made to the process steps, the *Action Log,* contains user name, date, time, etc. To view the *Action Log*, you make the following menu selection: LSMW Workbench ➤ Action Log. Figure 6-109 shows a screenshot of the *Action Log.*While executing the process steps from the LSMW process steps screen, you have observed, all through, that numbers appear against the process steps. The numbers appearing against the process steps can be made to appear or disappear by choice by making the following menu selection: Edit ➤ Numbering On/Off.

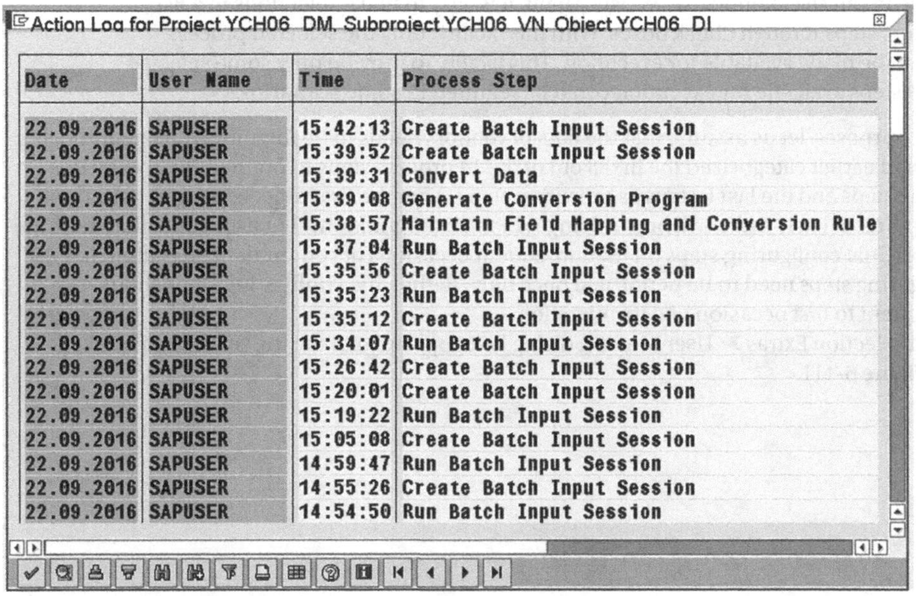

*Figure 6-109. LSMW Action Log*

- The *Action Log* maintained by the LSMW system for the changes made to the process steps can be initialized by making the following menu selection: Extras ➤ Reset Action Log.

- You can view complete details of destination structures, the fields of destination structures, source fields if any assigned to the fields of destination structures, etc., with the following menu selection: Extras ➤ Object Overview. The *Object Overview* can be displayed in either table or list mode. Figure 6-110 is a screenshot of the *Object Overview* in table mode.

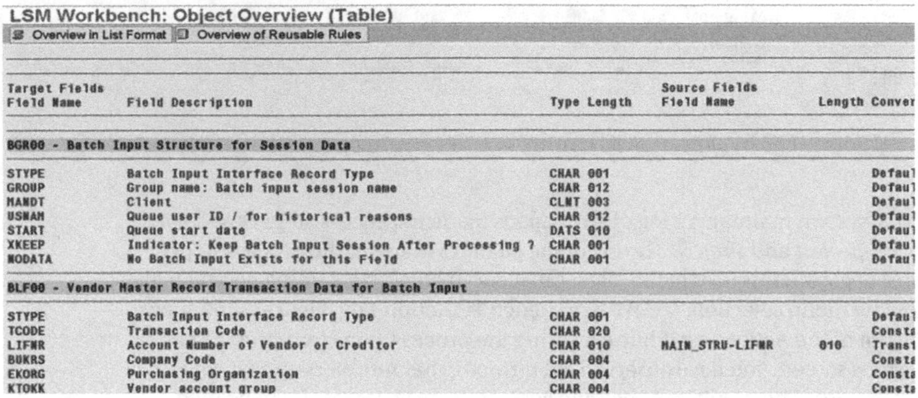

**LSM Workbench: Object Overview (Table)**

| Overview in List Format | Overview of Reusable Rules |

| Target Fields Field Name | Field Description | Type Length | Source Fields Field Name | Length Conver |
|---|---|---|---|---|
| **BGR00 - Batch Input Structure for Session Data** | | | | |
| STYPE | Batch Input Interface Record Type | CHAR 001 | | Defaul |
| GROUP | Group name: Batch input session name | CHAR 012 | | Defaul |
| MANDT | Client | CLNT 003 | | Defaul |
| USNAM | Queue user ID / for historical reasons | CHAR 012 | | Defaul |
| START | Queue start date | DATS 010 | | Defaul |
| XKEEP | Indicator: Keep Batch Input Session After Processing ? | CHAR 001 | | Defaul |
| NODATA | No Batch Input Exists for this Field | CHAR 001 | | Defaul |
| **BLF00 - Vendor Master Record Transaction Data for Batch Input** | | | | |
| STYPE | Batch Input Interface Record Type | CHAR 001 | | Defaul |
| TCODE | Transaction Code | CHAR 020 | | Consta |
| LIFNR | Account Number of Vendor or Creditor | CHAR 010 | MAIN_STRU-LIFNR | 010 Transl |
| BUKRS | Company Code | CHAR 004 | | Consta |
| EKORG | Purchasing Organization | CHAR 004 | | Consta |
| KTOKK | Vendor account group | CHAR 004 | | Consta |

*Figure 6-110.* *LSMW Object Overview*

- With the menu selection Extras ➤ User Menu, it is easy to make selections in a list of process steps through check boxes. With this facility, only the selected process steps can be made available for execution. This facility to provide only some selected process steps available for execution could be required in some scenarios.

For illustrative purposes, let us assume that the data of vendors needs to be migrated repeatedly on a periodic basis. We had earlier categorized the first 8 out of the 14 process steps in our hands-on exercises I and II as configuring steps and the last 6 steps as execution steps. After the first time, when you performed the configuring steps, most likely there will be no changes in the configurations. Let us assume that there are no changes to the original configuring steps on the subsequent occasions of vendor data migration. In this scenario, the configuring steps need to be performed once only. Rather, the configuring steps should not appear at all subsequent to first occasion of data migration.

With the menu selection Extras ➤ User Menu, a dialog box pops up to make the selection of process steps as shown in Figure 6-111.

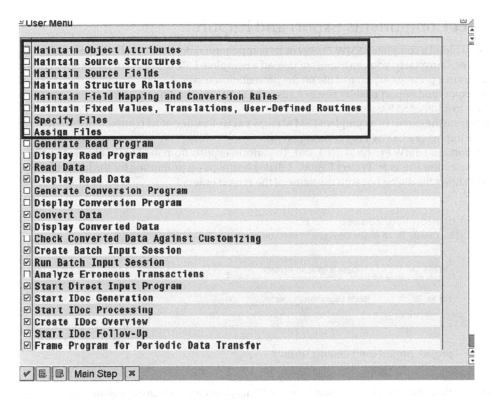

*Figure 6-111.* *User Menu—process step selections*

In Figure 6-111, the process steps *Generate Read Program, Display Read Program, Generate Conversion Program,* and *Display Conversion Program* were already in a disabled state. These process steps are meant to be executed to explicitly generate the programs.

As marked in Figure 6-111, we disabled the check boxes for the first eight process steps—the configuring steps. Disabling the check boxes for the configuring steps produced a process step screen as shown in Figure 6-112.

### LSM Workbench: YCH06_DM, YCH06_VN, YCH06_DI: Data Migration - Vendors

| ⊕ | User Menu | Numbering On | Double Click=Display | ⚖ Object Overview | ⊠ Action Log |

| Process Step | Last Action (Date, Time, User) |
| --- | --- |
| ○ 1 Read Data | 22.09.2016, 14:46:25 h, SAPUSER |
| ○ 2 Display Read Data | 22.09.2016, 14:18:38 h, SAPUSER |
| ○ 3 Convert Data | 22.09.2016, 15:39:31 h, SAPUSER |
| ○ 4 Display Converted Data | 22.09.2016, 14:19:36 h, SAPUSER |
| ○ 5 Create Batch Input Session | 22.09.2016, 15:42:13 h, SAPUSER |
| ◉ 6 Run Batch Input Session | 22.09.2016, 15:37:04 h, SAPUSER |

*Figure 6-112.* *Process step screen—without configuring steps*

The vendor data is categorized as master data. In practical terms, master data is mostly migrated on a one-time basis. It was just to illustrate the setup of process steps—making them appear or disappear on choice—that we assumed that data of vendors needed to be migrated on a periodic basis.

This concludes the process step screen—menu options.

## Project, Project Components Export and Import

You can export or download a complete LSMW *Project* or its component(s) down to a leaf node to a file on the presentation server. Conversely, you can import or upload a complete LSMW *Project* or its component(s) down to a leaf node from a previous export to a file on the presentation server.

The process of export and import enables you to transport LSMW projects and its parts or components from one SAP system to another SAP system.

We will demonstrate the export of a complete LSMW *Project* as well as one of its components. We will also demonstrate the import of a LSMW *Project's* component.

First, we will export our LSMW *Project* YCH06_DM. To perform exports from the LSMW opening screen, you make the menu selection Extras ➤ Project Export. A dialog box pops up prompting for the name of the *Project*. Figure 6-113 shows the dialog box with the name of the *Project* entered.

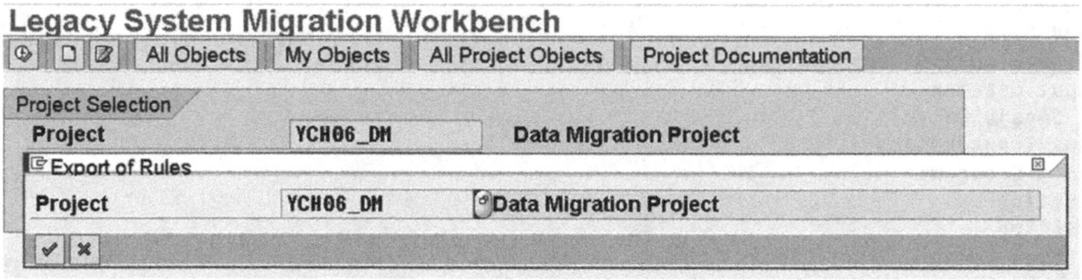

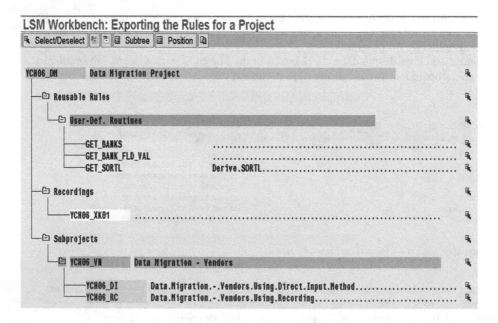

*Figure 6-113. LSMW—project, project component(s) export*

We clicked the Continue button. The complete *Project* with its components is presented in a tree form. We expanded all the nodes of the *Project* tree as shown in Figure 6-114.

*Figure 6-114. LSMW—project, project component(s) export: selection*

You can position the cursor on a node; use the *Select/Deselect* button (first button from the left) on the application bar to toggle between selection and deselection of the node. When a node is selected, the selection button 🔖 appears against the selected node on the extreme right as shown in Figure 6-118. If a node is selected, the subnodes under it, if any, are also selected by default.

When the screen of Figure 6-118 appears for the first time, the node corresponding to the *Project* and all the subnodes under it are selected by default. We want to export the complete *Project*; the default selection serves our present purpose, so we clicked the Export button on the application toolbar (the first button from the right). The dialog box to make folder selection and input the file name appeared as shown in Figure 6-115.

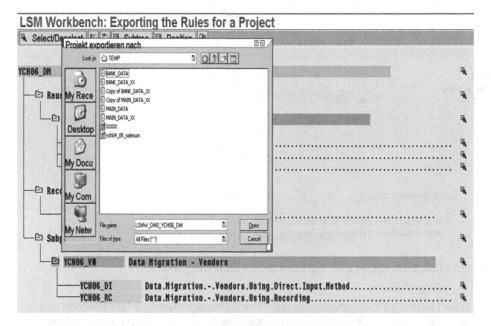

*Figure 6-115.* *LSMW—project export: select folder and input file name*

By default, the system proposes the name of the *Project* with the prefix LSMW_DM0_ (DM0 is our system id) as the file name. You can change the file name if you desire. We selected the folder, accepted the proposed file name, and clicked the *Open* button. The system issued an info message of successful export as shown in Figure 6-116.

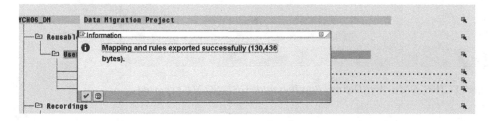

*Figure 6-116.* *LSMW—project exported*

Next, we want to demonstrate the export of a component of our LSMW *Project* YCH06_DM. To perform exports, from the LSMW opening screen, we made the menu selection Extras ➤ Project Export. The dialog box for the name of the *Project* appeared. We entered the name of the *Project* as YCH06_DM and clicked the Continue button.

The complete *Project* with its components is presented in a tree form with all the nodes selected by default. We will export only the node GET_SORTL corresponding to the *User-Defined Routines* UR_GET_SORTL. We positioned the cursor on the *Project* node YCh06_DM and deselected all the nodes. We next positioned the cursor on the node GET_SORTL and selected it. Figure 6-117 illustrates.

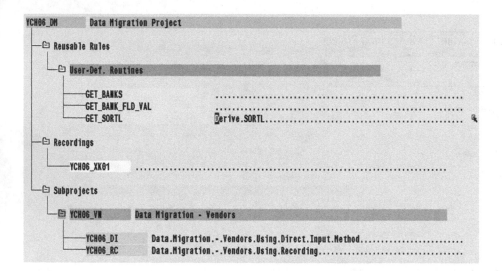

*Figure 6-117.* *Project YCH06_DM—export User-Defined Routines node GET_SORTL*

We clicked the Export button on the application toolbar. The dialog box to make folder selection and input the file name appeared. We selected the folder and changed the file name to LSMW_DM0_YCH06_DM_SORTL since we do not want to overwrite the earlier export file LSMW_DM0_YCH06_DM. We clicked the *Open* button. The system issued an info message of successful export as shown in Figure 6-118.

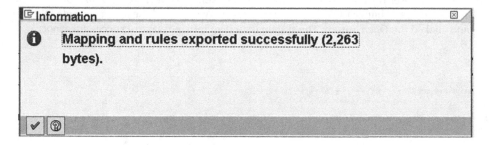

*Figure 6-118.* *Project YCH06_DM—User-Defined Routines node GET_SORTL exported*

We have successfully exported the complete *Project* YCH06_DM as well as a component GET_SORTL of it.

Finally, I want to demonstrate the import of a component into our LSMW *Project* YCH06_DM.

To start with, we will delete the *User-Defined Routines* node GET_SORTL in our LSMW *Project* YCH06_DM. We will then import the *User-Defined Routines* node GET_SORTL from export file LSMW_DM0_YCH06_DM_SORTL to restore the *Project* YCH06_DM to predeletion status.

To delete a node from a *Project*, we made the following menu selection from the LSMW opening screen: Goto ➤ Administration. The system navigated to the screen with *Projects* of all users. We scrolled down to our *Project* YCH06_DM. We expanded all the nodes of the *Project* YCH06_DM. We positioned the cursor on the *User-Defined Routines* node GET_SORTL and clicked the Delete button on the application toolbar. The system popped a warning alert as shown in Figure 6-119.

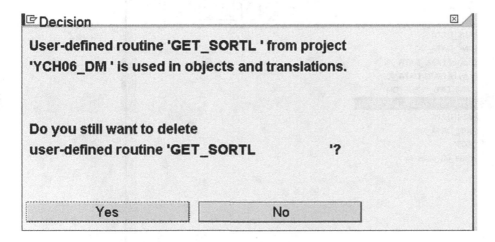

*Figure 6-119. User-Defined Routines node GET_SORTL—delete confirmation*

We clicked the Yes button. The *User-Defined Routines* node GET_SORTL was deleted. Figure 6-120 reflects the deletion.

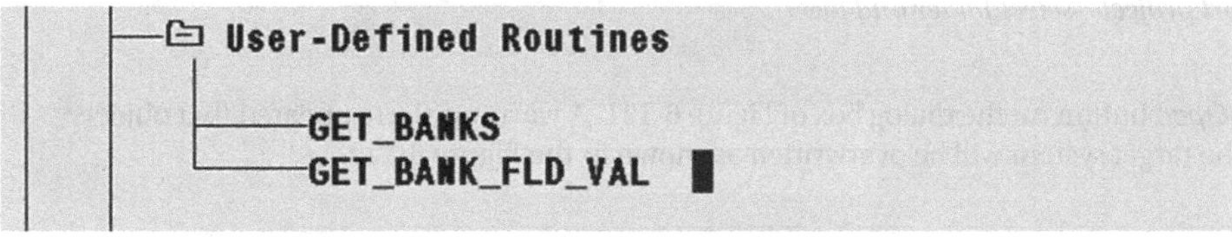

*Figure 6-120. User-Defined Routines Node GET_SORTL—deleted*

We will restore the *User-Defined Routines* node GET_SORTL by an import. We can import the *User-Defined Routines* node GET_SORTL from either of the following files:

- LSMW_DM0_YCH06_DM Full Project export

- LSMW_DM0_YCH06_DM_SORTL Project component GET_SORTL export

We will import from the file LSMW_DM0_YCH06_DM. To perform an import from the LSMW opening screen, we made the menu selection Extras ➤ Project Import. The dialog box to make folder and file selection appeared. We made the folder and file selection as shown in Figure 6-121.

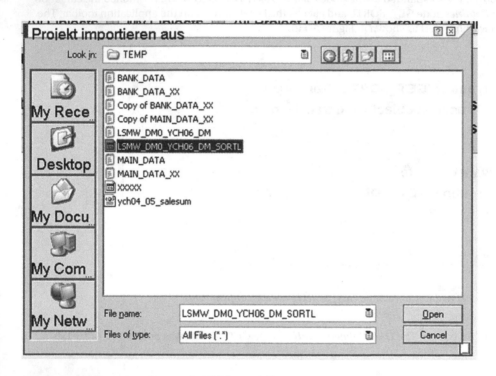

*Figure 6-121.* *Import project—select folder and file*

We clicked the *Open* button on the dialog box of Figure 6-121. A warning alert appeared that objects already existing in the target system will be overwritten as shown in the Figure 6-122.

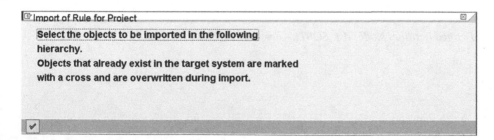

*Figure 6-122.* *Import project—warning alert*

514

We clicked the Continue button. The components or nodes from the export file were displayed in a tree form. We selected the node GET_SORTL as shown in the Figure 6-123.

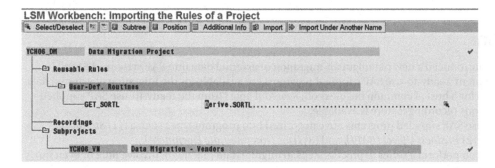

*Figure 6-123. Import project—select components or nodes*

There is a provision to import nodes with a different name: *Import Under Another Name*. We clicked the *Import* button on the application toolbar. The system issued an info message of successful import as shown in Figure 6-124.

*Figure 6-124. User-Defined Routines Node GET_SORTL imported—info message*

To cross-verify the import of the *User-Defined Routines* node GET_SORTL into the *Project*, we made the following menu selection from the LSMW opening screen: Goto ➤ Administration. The system navigated to the screen with *Projects* of all users. We scrolled down to our *Project* YCH06_DM. We expanded all the nodes of the *Project* YCH06_DM. The *User-Defined Routines* node GET_SORTL has been imported as shown in Figure 6-125.

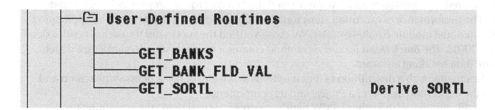

*Figure 6-125. User-Defined Routines node GET_SORTL imported into project*

We demonstrated an export of a full *Project*, an export of a component of a *Project,* and an import of a component of a *Project.*

This concludes the demonstration of export and import of a *Project.*

# Conclusion

In this chapter, we introduced a new paradigm for migration of external data into SAP system—LSMW. In the LSMW environment, ready-to-use SAP supplied programs are available for the migration of external data into the SAP system for a host of common business objects. And apart from the ready-to-use SAP supplied programs, transactions recording feature is available.

The ready-to-use SAP supplied programs are categorized into program types such as (1) *Standard Batch/Direct Input*, (2) *Business Object (BAPI)*, and (3) *IDoc (Intermediate Document)*.

In the LSMW, you perform a series of process steps to migrate data that might involve little or even no coding of ABAP program lines.

We presented an overview of the LSMW opening screen. We introduced the hierarchical structure of objects created in the LSMW environment—a *Project* with *Subprojects* under it, a *Subproject* with *Objects* under it. Apart from *Subprojects* a *Project* can contain *Recordings, Fixed Values, Translations,* and *User-Defined Routines*. We described the hierarchical structure of proposed hands-on exercises to be performed in this chapter and in Chapter 7.

After the introduction to LSMW, an overview of its opening screen, we set about performing hands-on exercise I. We proposed to transfer vendor data from text files on the application server to the SAP functional module database tables. I described the scope and specifications of hands-on exercise I. The scope and specifications of the hands-on exercise I is mostly similar to the scope and specifications of hands-on exercise II in Chapter 5. We created a *Project* YCH06_DM, a *Subproject* YCH06_VN under the *Project,* and an *Object* YCH06_DI under the *Subproject*. We performed the first eight process steps which we termed "configuring steps." The LSMW *Object Type* we chose for data transfer was *Standard Batch/Direct Input*. The *Object Type: Standard Batch/Direct Input* for vendors creates a session. We created representative data. We performed the last six process steps which we termed "execution steps." The performance of execution steps transferred the data from text files on the application server to the SAP functional module database tables. We crossverified the successful transfer of vendor data in transaction code XK02.

In hands-on exercise II, we again proposed to transfer vendor data from text files on the application server to the SAP functional module database tables. But the LSMW *Object Type* we chose for data transfer was *Batch Input Recording*. The *Object Type: Batch Input Recording* creates a session. The scope and specifications of hands-on exercise II are same as the scope and specifications of hands-on exercise I in this chapter. We created an *Object* YCH06_RC under the already created *Project* YCH06_DM and *Subproject* YCH06_VN. From the LSMW opening screen, we created a recording YCH01_XK01 of transaction code XK01. We performed the first eight process steps which we termed "configuring steps." On the screen of process step 1—*Maintain Object Attributes*—we clicked in the field *Recording* and selected the recording YCH06_XK01. We created representative data. We performed the last six process steps which we termed "execution steps." The performance of execution steps transferred the data from text files on the application server to the SAP functional module database tables. We cross-verified the successful transfer of vendor data in transaction code XK02. The *Batch Input Recording* method creates a single destination structure which makes table control data handling awkward.

I concluded the chapter with a description of menu options available on the process steps screen and demonstrations of the export and import of a *Project* and its components.

In Chapter 7, I will continue with further LSMW hands-on exercises deploying the remaining two LSMW *Object Types: Business Object (BAPI)* and *IDoc (Intermediate Document)*.

# CHAPTER 7

■ ■ ■

# Data Migration Using Legacy System Migration Workbench LSMW–II

In Chapter 6, we performed migration of external data into SAP system in the legacy system migration workshop LSMW environment. We performed two hands-on exercises employing LSMW *Object Types*: (1) *Standard Batch/Direct Input* and (2) *Batch Input Recording*.

In this chapter, we will perform two hands-on exercises employing the remaining two LSMW *Object Types*: (a) *IDoc (Intermediate Document)* and (b) *Business Object (BAPI)*. Thus, we would have employed all of the four *Object Types* provided in the LSMW environment.

We located the two hands-on exercises (corresponding to two *Objects*) of Chapter 6 in the *Project* YCH06_DM and the *Subproject* YCH06_VN. We will locate the two hands-on exercises (corresponding to two *Objects*) to be performed in this chapter in the *Project* YCH06_DM, which we created in Chapter 6. We will create a new *Subproject* YCH07_PO and locate the two hands-on exercises—*Objects*: YCH07_IDOC and YCH07_BAPI—to be performed in this chapter in this *Subproject*. (Refer to the Figure 6-2 in Chapter 6.)

Before we undertake the performance of the hands-on exercises of this chapter, we must cover someprerequisite topics. The prerequisite topics follow.

## Hands-on Exercises in This Chapter—Issues and Considerations

We will be performing two hands-on exercises in the present chapter involving transfer of purchase order data from operating system text files into the SAP functional module database tables. A purchase order is a business document and its data is categorized as transaction data. Until now, in all the hands-on exercises of Chapters 5 and 6, we were transferring vendor data. The vendor data is categorized as master data distinct from transaction data.

Most business documents (purchase orders, sales orders, billing documents, etc.) have multiple items in a business document. The data of multiple items in a business document will be invariably captured on the data entry screen using a table control. The data entry screens of most business documents contain multiple table controls.

© Sushil Markandeya 2017
S. Markandeya, *Pro SAP Scripts, Smartforms, and Data Migration*,
https://doi.org/10.1007/978-1-4842-3183-8_7

We are taking into account the following when migrating the data of purchase orders:

- When data of purchase orders is created, some fields are assigned default values depending on entry of values in some other fields. For example, when you enter a vendor number/code, the company code, currency key and language key are picked from the vendor database tables and assigned as default values to the corresponding fields of the purchase order. Also, the net prices for materials are assigned values from info records by default. The info records contain past net prices maintained material-wise, material group-wise, vendor-wise, etc.

- Further, when data of a purchase order is created, values of some field are calculated from fields of same/other database tables. For example, you need to enter for materials, only the delivery quantities; the ordered quantities for materials are calculated from the delivery quantities.

- Also, while migrating, the transaction data, the structure and form of the input data will depend on the data model of the transaction data in the SAP database tables. We will be describing the data model of purchase order database tables.

- The assignment of default values to some fields and the calculation for some other fields make the data migration of transaction data require technofunctional knowledge of the process of a higher degree than when migrating master data like vendors. We will highlight some of the technofunctional issues during the performance of the two hands-on exercises.

- The two hands-on exercises in this chapter employing the *Object Types—IDoc BAPI*—generate *IDocs*. To be able to generate the *IDocs*, you need to create *IDoc Inbound Settings*. The *IDoc* and related communication technology are substantial topics and cannot be dealt with in this book. Excellent books dealing with *IDoc* and related communication technology are available. We are describing only the *IDoc Inbound Settings* required to perform the hand-on exercises, with sketchy explanations. We are providing a brief on the *IDocs*.

This concludes the issues and considerations of hands-on exercises.

# Purchase Order Database Tables

A purchase order is generated when an order is placed for supply of goods or services with a vendor or supplier. In the SAP environment, a purchase order would contain the following minimal information:

- Document or purchase order number

- Document or purchase order date

- Vendor or supplier

- Purchasing organization

- Purchasing group

- Materials ordered with delivery dates, delivery quantities, net prices, plants where delivery to be made, etc.

In the hands-on exercises for data migration of purchase orders, our main focus will be on the deployment of LSMW, but I will be highlighting a few technofunctional issues. Because our main focus is on deployment of LSMW, I will be assigning values to representative, minimal, mostly mandatory fields, involving the following three database tables:

- EKKO purchasing document—header

- EKPO purchasing document—item

- EKET purchasing document—scheduling agreement schedule lines

The database tables are designated as purchasing document tables since they contain, apart from the purchase order data, data of other documents related to purchasing: requisition, request for quotation, etc. A description of the three database tables follows.

## Database Table EKKO

The database Table EKKO contains the document header information. We will be concerned with the fields in the database table EKKO (see Table 7-1).

**Table 7-1.** *Fields of Interest in Database Table EKKO*

| Srl. No. | Field Name | Field Description | Remarks |
|---|---|---|---|
| 1 | EBELN (PK) | Purchasing Document Number | Primary Key Field |
| 2 | BEDAT | Purchasing Document Date | |
| 3 | BSTYP | Purchasing Document Category | = F—for Purchase Order |
| 4 | BSART | Purchasing Document Type | = NB—Standard PO |
| 5 | LIFNR | Vendor Number/Code | |
| 6 | EKORG | Purchasing Organization | |
| 7 | EKGRP | Purchasing Group | |
| 8 | BUKRS | Company Code | Derived—Assigned from Vendor Database Table LFB1 |
| 9 | WAERS | Currency Key | Derived—Assigned from Vendor Database Table LFA1 |
| 10 | SPRAS | Language Key | Derived—Assigned from Vendor Database Table LFA1 |

We are not specifying the client code field MANDT. It is implicit.

For our hands-on exercises, we will create only data of standard purchase orders, which entails that the fields BSTYP = 'F' and BSART = 'NB' (field nos. 3 and 4).

In Table 7-1, fields are marked as derived—BUKRS, WAERS, and SPRAS. There are more fields being assigned derived values than appearing in Table 7-1. By default, these fields are assigned derived values. You might, in some cases, want to override the derived values with data from input text files.

## Database Table EKPO

The database table EKPO contains the material ordered information. We will be concerned with the following fields in the database table EKPO (see Table 7-2).

*Table 7-2.* *Fields of Interest in Database Table EKPO*

| Srl. No. | Field Name | Field Description | Remarks |
|---|---|---|---|
| 1 | EBELN (PK, FK) | Purchasing Document Number | Primary and Foreign Key Field |
| 2 | EBELP (PK) | Item Number of Purchasing Document | Primary Key Field |
| 3 | MATNR | Material Number/Code | |
| 4 | MENGE | Purchase Order Quantity | Calculated from Rows in Database Table EKET |
| 5 | MEINS | Purchase Order Unit of Measure | Derived—Assigned from Material Database Table MARA |
| 6 | NETPR | Net Price in Purchasing Document | Derived—Assigned from Info Records |
| 7 | MATKL | Material Group | |
| 8 | WERKS | Plant to which Material to be Delivered | |
| 9 | NETWR | Net Order Value in PO Currency | Calculated as (MENGE * NETPR) |

The tables EKKO and EKPO are linked through the field EBELN—purchasing document number, which materials belong to which purchasing document?

The field EBELP is a kind of serial number within a purchasing document and is used as a reference to a material ordered.

The considerations we described for derived fields in the database table EKKO hold good for the database table EKPO as well.

## Database Table EKET

The database table EKET contains the material delivery schedule information. A single material in a purchase order can have multiple delivery dates; hence, a separate database table for material delivery schedule. We will be concerned with the following fields in the database table EKET (see Table 7-3).

*Table 7-3.* *Fields of Interest in Database Table EKET*

| Srl. No. | Field Name | Field Description | Remarks |
|---|---|---|---|
| 1 | EBELN (PK, FK) | Purchasing Document Number | Primary and Foreign Key Field |
| 2 | EBELP (PK, FK) | Item Number of Purchasing Document | Primary and Foreign Key Field |
| 3 | ETENR (PK) | Delivery Schedule Line Counter or Number | Primary Key Field |
| 4 | MENGE | Scheduled Quantity | |
| 5 | EINDT | Item Delivery Date | |

The tables EKPO and EKET are linked through the fields EBELN and EBELP, which delivery schedule line numbers belongs to which purchasing item number of which purchasing document?

The field ETENR is a kind of count or serial number within a purchasing document and is used as a reference.

The field MENGE is occurring in both the database tables EKPO and EKET. The field MENGE in the database table EKET represents quantity to be delivered on a specified date of an item number; there can be multiple delivery dates with specified quantities for an item number in a purchase order. The field MENGE in the database table EKPO represents quantity ordered for an item number in a purchase order. The value in the field MENGE in the database table EKPO for an item number in a particular purchase order will be sum of the values in the field MENGE in the database table EKET for the item number in the purchase order.

Notice, in Table 7-3, that the field EBELN is foreign key in the database table EKET. The check table for the field EBELN in the database table EKET is EKKO.

Notice, in Table 7-3, that the field EBELP is foreign key in the database table EKET. The check table for the field EBELP in the database table EKET is EKPO.

Figure 7-1 is a screenshot of the foreign key relationship between the database tables EKET and EKPO.

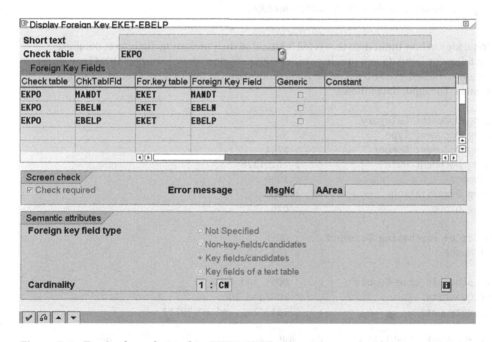

*Figure 7-1.* *Foreign key relationship: EKET-EKPO*

The database table EKET is linked to the database table EKPO through the field EBELP. The database table EKET is also linked to the database table EKKO through the field EBELN; you can view this relationship as an exercise.

## Database Tables of Purchasing Documents–ER Diagram and Data Storage

I would like to highlight the hierarchical order of the database tables EKKO, EKPO, and EKET. The database table EKPO is secondary to EKKO. The database table EKET is secondary to EKPO and EKKO. Figure 7-2 shows an ER diagram or data model of the database tables EKKO, EKPO, and EKET.

521

## ER Diagram / Data Model – Purchasing Documents

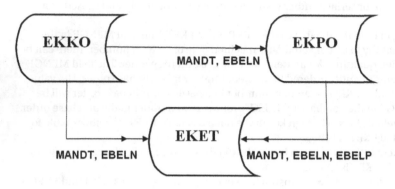

**Figure 7-2.** *ER diagram–database tables EKKO, EKPO, and EKET*

To give you some idea of how input data that is fed is stored in the purchasing document database tables, consider the following input data: a purchase order with a single material number 101-110, scheduled quantity 200 to be delivered on a date and scheduled quantity 300 to be delivered on another date–two delivery dates. The input data follows:

```
BSTYP - Purchasing Document Category        : F
BSART - Purchasing Document Type            : NB
EBELN - Purchasing Document Number          : 1234
BEDAT - Purchasing Document Date            : 20161226
LIFNR - Vendor Number                       : 1000
EKORG - Purchasing Organization             : 1000
EKGRP - Purchasing Group                    : 026

EBELP - Item Number of Purchasing Document  : 0010
MATNR - Material Number                     : 101-110
.....
ETENR - Delivery Schedule Line Number       : 0001 and 0002
MENGE - Schedule Quantity                   : 200 and 300
EINDT - Item Delivery Date                  : 20170202 and 20170217
```

Data storage in the database table EKKO will be as follows:

```
EBELN       : 1234
BEDAT       : 20161226
LIFNR       : 1000
EKORG       : 1000
EKGRP       : 026
BUKRS       : 1000   (derived from LFB1)
SPRAS       : D      (derived from LFA1)
WAERS       : EUR    (derived from LFA1)
.....
```

Data storage in the database table EKPO will be as follows:

```
EBELP    MATNR        MEINS                    MENGE
-----------------------------------------------------------------------------------
0010     101-110      PC (derived from MARA)   500 (derived - 200 + 300 from EKET)
```

Data storage in the database table EKET will be as follows:

```
EBELP    ETENR        MENGE         EINDT
---------------------------------------------------------------------------
0010     0001         200           20170202
0010     0002         300           20170217
```

This concludes the description of purchase order database tables.

# A Brief on *IDocs*

The *IDoc* is a substantial topic; adetailed description of its nitty-gritty would occupy more than a couple of chapters. We are briefly outlining its basics so that you get a fair idea of its features in the context of the hands-on exercises in this chapter.

## *IDoc*–A Data Container

The term "*IDoc*" is short for Intermediate Document. An *IDoc* is just a super structure (often called a data container) used to exchange data between two processes which can understand the syntax and semantics of the exchanged data. A super structure means a complex structure containing embedded structures and internal tables (called segments) within the super structure. The *IDoc* super structure can contain within it the complete data of one entity like a customer or a vendor or a purchase order. Different versions of *IDoc* can be maintained and backward compatibility is assured.

An *IDoc* created initially is called a basic *IDoc* type. A basic *IDoc* type can be enhanced or extended and is called an extended *IDoc* type. The basic *IDoc* type and the extended *IDoc* type together are called an *IDoc* type. If no extended *IDoc* type exists, the basic *IDoc* type and *IDoc* type are synonymous.

The *IDoc* is a loose term; it means different things in different contexts. In one context, it means the super structure or the object you create using transaction code WE30–basic and extended *IDoc* types. In another context, the term "*IDoc*" refers to a specific *IDoc* number. When an *IDoc* is generated, it is assigned a number just like a document number. Each *IDoc* bearing a number will contain information of one entity-customer, vendor, purchase order, etc. An *IDoc* number can be viewed as an instance of the *IDoc* type.

A *Message Type* can be assigned to one or more *IDoc* types and vice versa. A specific *Message Type* is associated with or attached to specific programs and function modules. The specific programs and function modules associated with a specific combination of an *IDoc* and a *Message Type* contain all the specific functionalities required to exchange data between processes.

In addition to the specific programs and function modules associated with a specific combination of an *IDoc* type and a *Message Type*, there are generic programs and function modules available to help in various stages of *IDoc* processing.

## *IDoc*–Deployment Scenarios

There are two very typical scenarios of *IDoc* deployment.

- **Master data distribution**: It involves control and maintenance of master data on a central system within an enterprise. The master data being maintained on a central system is distributed to other systems in the enterprise. A specific master data is to be distributed only to particular units within the enterprise dealing with that data. Further, the units of the enterprise receiving the data, might receive only be a subset or specific items of data–fields they are concerned with. The master data in an enterprise is distributed by deploying *IDocs*. A typical example of master data distribution is material master distribution.

- **Message control**: When business documents such as purchase orders, sales orders, billing documents, and so on (transactional data) are generated in an enterprise, they can be sent to the business partners–customers or vendors or banks deploying the *IDocs*.

A deployment of *IDocs* that does not fit into the master data distribution or message control scenarios can be called a custom scenario.

## *IDocs*–Storage in Database Tables

In the most common *IDoc* scenario, the *IDoc* is being deployed to transfer data from one system–source to other system(s)–recipient(s). Data is extracted from the SAP functional module database tables in the source system and *IDocs* are generated from the extracted data. Information of each entity of the extracted data–customer, vendor, purchase order, etc.–is stored in a separate *IDoc* which is assigned a number, just like a document number. The part of the *IDocs* containing the extracted data from SAP functional module database tables is called data records.

Communication or control information, called control records, is incorporated into the *IDocs* containing data records. The control information is generated from communication settings.

The success or failure at each stage of *IDoc* processing is carried along with the *IDocs* and is called *IDoc* status records.

To sum up, *IDocs* contain control records, data records, and status records. The *IDocs* are stored in the SAP database tables. The *IDoc* control records are stored in the database table EDIDC, the *IDoc* data records are stored in the database table EDID4, and the *IDoc* status records are stored in the database table EDIDS.

When *IDoc* data records are stored in the SAP database tables, mostly, there will be multiple data records bearing the same *IDoc* number for a single entity, because the database table structures must be flat structures.

## *IDocs*–*Outbound* and *Inbound* Processing

The *IDocs* with the control, data, and status information generated at the source system are called *outbound IDocs*. Figure 7-3 depicts roughly the generation and dispatch of *outbound IDocs*.

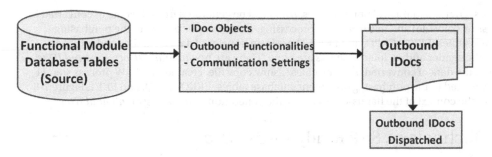

*Figure 7-3.* *Outbound IDocs–generation and dispatch*

The symbol used to represent the *outbound IDocs* in Figure 7-3 is to depict the generation of multiple *IDocs* and does not represent hard copy of *IDocs*. Recall, the *IDocs* are stored in the database tables: EDIDC, EDID4, and EDIDS. In Figures 7-4 and 7-5, the same symbol is used to represent multiple *IDocs*.

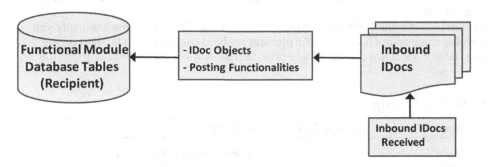

*Figure 7-4.* *Inbound IDocs at a recipient system–receipt and posting*

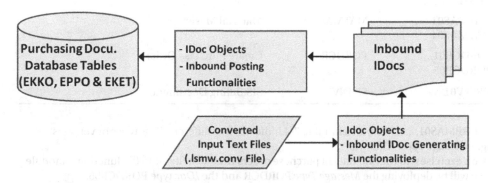

*Figure 7-5.* *Hands-on exercises context–inbound IDocs generation and posting*

The *outbound IDocs* are transmitted to the recipient system(s) and when they reach the recipient system(s) are called the *inbound IDocs*. From the *inbound IDocs* at each recipient system, data is transferred or posted to the SAP functional module database tables. At a recipient system, Figure 7-4 roughly depicts the receipt and posting of *inbound IDocs* to the SAP functional module database tables.

In the LSMW scenario of our hands-on exercises, *IDocs* will be generated from the data of converted input text files (.lsmw.conv file) and in subsequent processing, transferred or posted to the purchasing document database tables–EKKO, EKPO, and EKET. There is no transfer of data from the sender to the recipient. Rather, the sender and recipient systems are same. There are no *outbound IDocs*. *Inbound IDocs* are generated from the data of converted input text files (.lsmw.conv file, created in LSMW process step 11) and subsequently posted to the purchasing document database tables–EKKO, EKPO, and EKET. Figure 7-5 depicts roughly, in the context of the hands-on exercises, the generation and posting of *inbound IDocs*.

## *IDocs*–ALE Technology, SAP Ready-to-Use *IDocs*

Application Linking and Enabling (ALE) is a SAP proprietary technology used along with *IDocs* for data distribution between loosely coupled SAP and SAP or non-SAP systems.

ALE settings for data distribution deploying *IDocs* would normally involve the creation of *logical systems*, *RFC destinations*, *partner numbers*, *partner profiles*, and a *distribution model*. Since we are logged into an IDES server, we can use a preexisting *partner number* and only change the *partner profile* of the preexisting *partner number*. Also, since we are not distributing data as such, but transferring data from the operating system text files into the SAP database tables (Figure 7-5) through *IDocs*, we are saved from creating a *distribution model*.

You can create your own custom *IDoc* types with the related functionalities. But, more frequently, you will deploy SAP provided ready-to-use *IDoc* types. SAP provides ready-to-use *IDoc* types for most master and transaction data. Table 7-4 lists just a few of the SAP provided ready-to-use *IDoc* types along with the *Message Types*.

*Table 7-4.* *SAP Ready-to-Use IDoc Types and Message Types*

| Srl. No. | *IDoc* Types | Message Type | Description |
|---|---|---|---|
| 1 | CREMAS01..... CREMAS05 | CREMAS | Vendor Master Data Distribution |
| 2 | DEBMAS01..... DEBMAS05 | DEBMAS | Customer Master Data Distribution |
| 3 | MATMAS01..... MATMAS04 | MATMAS | Material Master |
| 4 | PORDCR01.... PORDCR05 | PORDCR | Create Purchase Order |
| 5 | SISINV01 | SISINV | SIS Billing Document |

The notation CREMAS01.....CREMAS05 in Table 7-4 indicates five different *IDoc* types or versions assigned to a single *Message Type*, CREMAS.

In the hands-on exercises, to transfer data of purchase orders from text files into the functional module database tables, we will be deploying the *Message Type* PORDCR and the *IDoc* type PORDCR05.

## *IDoc* Components–A Look at the *IDoc* Type PORDCR05

An *IDoc* type is a super structure having structures and internal tables embedded with it. The structures and internal table structures within the *IDoc* type are called *segments*. The components of a *segment* are *segment types*, *segment definitions*, and fields. Different versions of a *segment* can be maintained. The different versions of a *segment* are contained in a *segment* type. The *segments* are assigned to an *IDoc* type through the *segment* types. Figure 7-6 is a diagrammatic representation of components of *segments*: *segment types*, *segment definitions*, and fields.

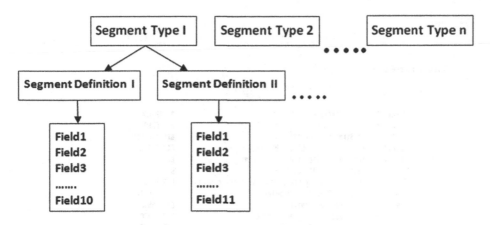

*Figure 7-6.* *Segment types, segment definitions, and fields*

As you can observe in Figure 7-6, the *segments* are somewhat like the ABAP dictionary (flat) structures. The attributes of fields like type, length, etc., in the *segments* are controlled through the data elements and domains. The process of creation of an *IDoc* type starts with the creation of domains and data elements, next the creation of *segment types* and *segment definitions*, and finally the creation of the *IDoc* type.

Fields within a *segment* can only be of ABAP dictionary types: CHAR, CLNT, CUKY, DATS, LANG, NUMC, and TIMS–all character-oriented types. The length of a *segment* is not to exceed 1,000 bytes.

The *IDoc* type being deployed in our hands-on exercises is PORCR05. Let us view the components: *segment types*, *segment definitions*, and fields of the *IDoc* type PORDCR05. To view the components of an *IDoc* type, we navigated to the opening screen of transaction code WE30 as shown in Figure 7-7.

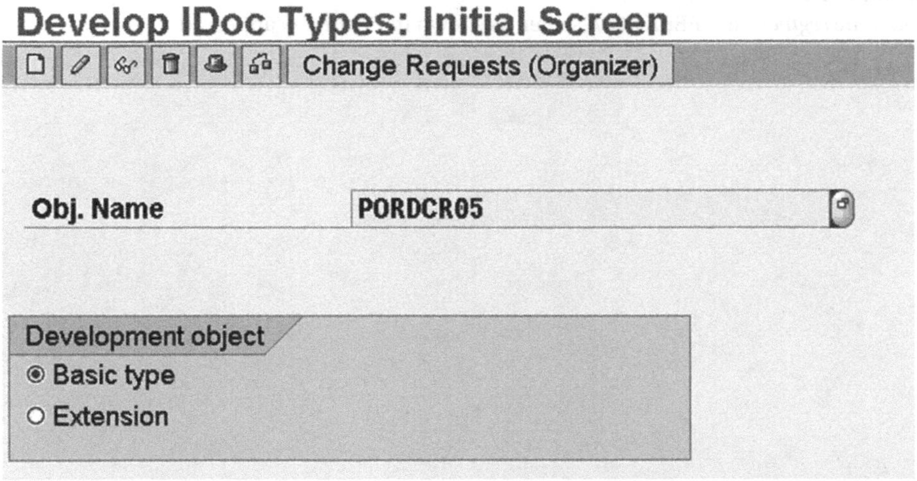

## Develop IDoc Types: Initial Screen

| □ | ✎ | ✂ | 🗑 | 🖨 | 🔅 | Change Requests (Organizer) |

Obj. Name             **PORDCR05**

Development object
◉ Basic type
○ Extension

*Figure 7-7.* *Develop IDoc Types: Initial Screen*

We entered the value PORDCR05 in the field *Obj. Name* and clicked the Display button on the application toolbar. A screen with the *segments* in the *IDoc* type PORDCR05 appeared as shown in Figure 7-8.

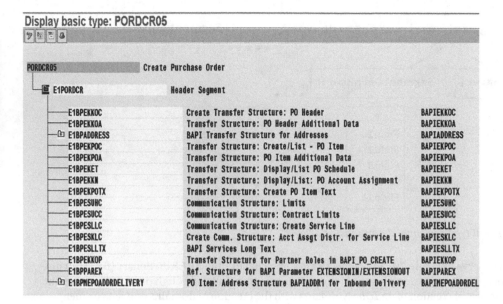

**Figure 7-8.** *Segments of IDoc type PORDCR05*

The first *segment* is E1PORDCR. Under the *segment* E1PORDCR, other *segments* E1BPEKKOC, E1BPEKKOA, etc. (total of 16 *segments*) are located.

In the context of our hands-on exercises, we are concerned with the three *segments* E1BPEKKOC (second *segment*), E1BPEKPOC (fifth), and E1BPEKET. (Seventh) These three *segments* map to the database tables EKKO, EKPO, and EKET.

We double-clicked the *segment* E1BPEKKOC. A screen as shown in Figure 7-9 appeared.

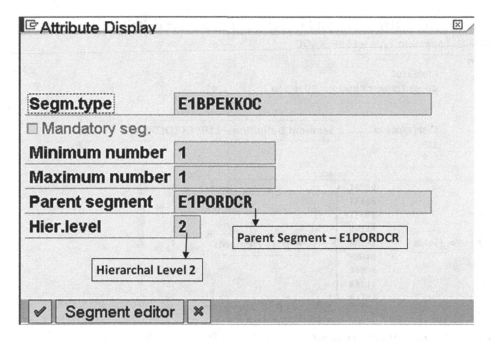

*Figure 7-9. Segment type E1BPEKKOC–attributes*

The *Parent segment* (parent *segment type*) and the *Hier.level* (hierarchical level) of the *segment type* E1BPEKKOC are marked in Figure 7-9. To view the fields of the *segment,* we double-clicked the *segment type* E1BPEKKOC on the screen of Figure 7-9. Figure 7-10 presents a screen showing the fields of the *segment definition.*

529

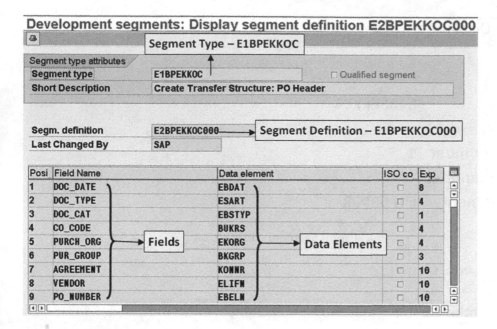

*Figure 7-10. Segment definition E1BPEKKOC000-fields*

The *segment* field names are different from the corresponding cryptic field names in the database table structure. For example, the field BEDAT of the database table structure EKKO bears the name DOC_DATE in the *segment*. In all forthcoming descriptions, I will specify, as far as possible, the field names of database table structures along their corresponding *segment* field names.

Returning to the screen of Figure 7-8, which displays the *segment types* in *IDoc* type PORDCR05, we double-clicked the *segment* E1BPEKPOC. A screen as shown in Figure 7-11 appeared.

Since, for a specific purchase order, multiple items can exist, the field *Maximum number* on the screen of the Figure 7-11 contains the value 999,999,999–making this object in the *IDoc* type an internal table.

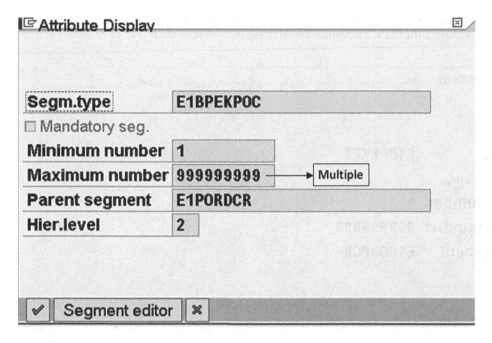

**Figure 7-11.** *Segment type E1BPEKPOC—Attributes*

The *Parent segment* (parent *segment type*) and the *Hier.level* (hierarchical level) of the *segment type* E1BPEKPOC are same as the *segment type* E1BPEKKOC. To view the fields of the *segment,* we double-clicked the *segment type* E1BPEKPOC on the screen of Figure 7-11. Figure 7-12 shows a screen displaying the fields of the *segment definition.*

## Development segments: Display segment definition E2BPEKPOC004

| Segment type attributes | | |
|---|---|---|
| Segment type | E1BPEKPOC | ☐ Qualified segment |
| Short Description | Transfer Structure: Create/List - PO Item | |

| | | |
|---|---|---|
| Segm. definition | E2BPEKPOC004 | ☐ Released |
| Last Changed By | SAP | |

| Posi | Field Name | Data element | ISO co | Exp |
|---|---|---|---|---|
| 1 | PO_NUMBER | EBELN | ☐ | 10 |
| 2 | PO_ITEM | EBELP | ☐ | 5 |
| 3 | ADDRESS | ADRNR | ☐ | 10 |
| 4 | MATERIAL | MATNR | ☐ | 18 |
| 5 | PUR_MAT | EMATNR | ☐ | 18 |
| 6 | INFO_REC | INFNR | ☐ | 10 |
| 7 | ITEM_CAT | PSTYP | ☐ | 1 |
| 8 | ACCTASSCAT | KNTTP | ☐ | 1 |
| 9 | AGREEMENT | KONNR | ☐ | 10 |

**Figure 7-12.** *Segment definition E1BPEKPOC004–fields*

We returned to the screen in Figure 7-8 displaying the *segment types* in the *IDoc* type PORDCR05. We double-clicked the *segment* E1BPEKET. A screen as shown in Figure 7-13 appeared.

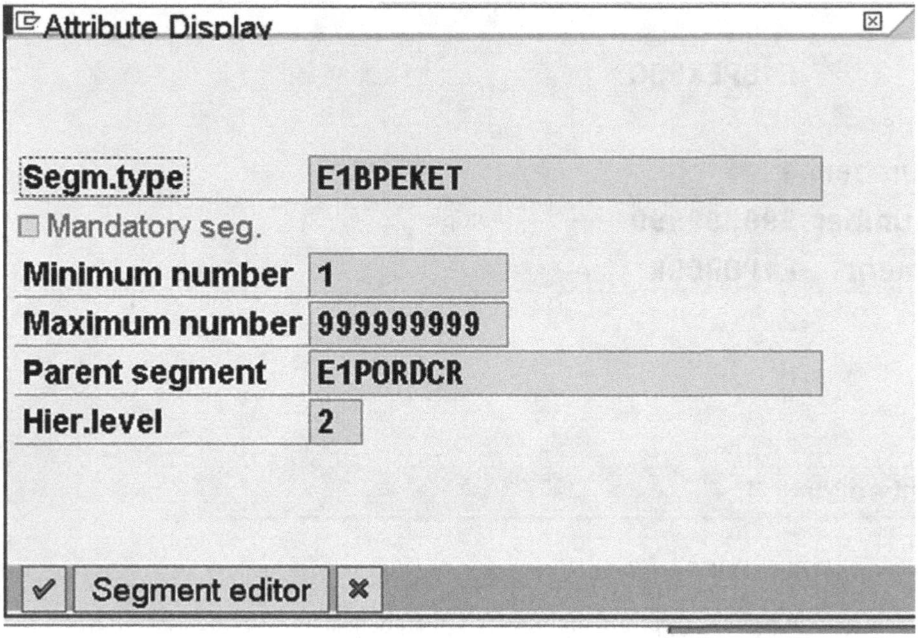

*Figure 7-13. Segment type E1BPEKET-attributes*

Since, for a specific purchase order, multiple items can exist with multiple delivery dates for an item, the field *Maximum number* on the screen of the Figure 7-13 contains the value 999,999,999–making this object in the *IDoc* type an internal table.

The *Parent segment* (parent *segment type*) and the *Hier.level* (hierarchical level) of the *segment type* E1BPEKET are same as those of the *segment type* E1BPEKKOC. To view the fields of the *segment*, we double-clicked the *segment type* E1BPEKET on the screen of Figure 7-13. Figure 7-14 displays a screen showing the fields of the *segment definition*.

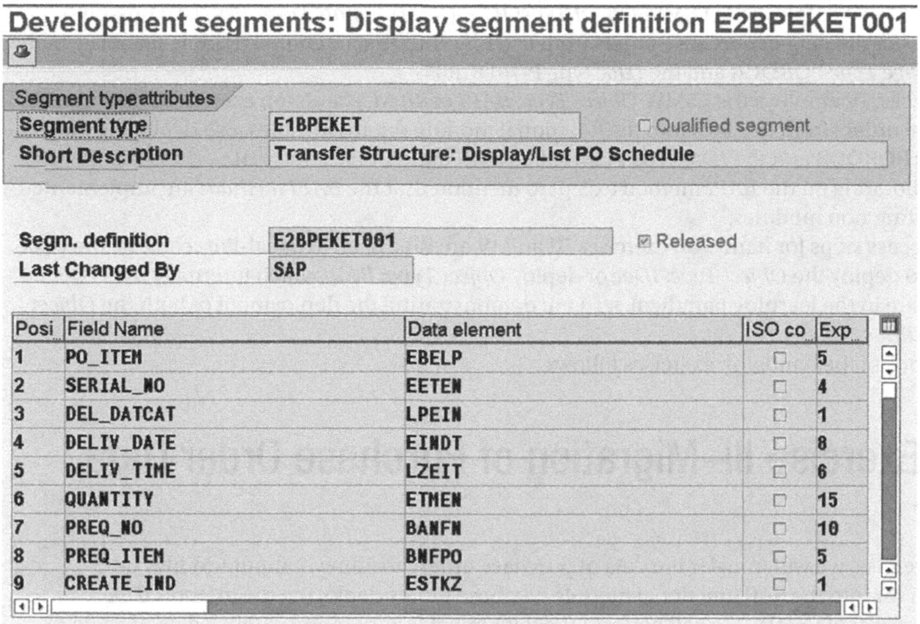

## Development segments: Display segment definition E2BPEKET001

**Segment type attributes**

| | | |
|---|---|---|
| **Segment type** | E1BPEKET | ☐ Qualified segment |
| **Short Description** | Transfer Structure: Display/List PO Schedule | |

| | | |
|---|---|---|
| **Segm. definition** | E2BPEKET001 | ☑ Released |
| **Last Changed By** | SAP | |

| Posi | Field Name | Data element | ISO co | Exp |
|---|---|---|---|---|
| 1 | PO_ITEM | EBELP | ☐ | 5 |
| 2 | SERIAL_NO | EETEN | ☐ | 4 |
| 3 | DEL_DATCAT | LPEIN | ☐ | 1 |
| 4 | DELIV_DATE | EINDT | ☐ | 8 |
| 5 | DELIV_TIME | LZEIT | ☐ | 6 |
| 6 | QUANTITY | ETMEN | ☐ | 15 |
| 7 | PREQ_NO | BANFN | ☐ | 10 |
| 8 | PREQ_ITEM | BNFPO | ☐ | 5 |
| 9 | CREATE_IND | ESTKZ | ☐ | 1 |

*Figure 7-14.  Segment definition E1BPEKET001–fields*

The *segment definition* E1BPEKET001 does not contain the field PO_NUMBER.

We have viewed the relevant components of the *IDoc* type PORDCR05.

The *IDoc* type PORDCR05 is assigned to *Message Type* PORDCR. The *Message Type* is maintained in transaction code WE81.

The *IDoc* type assignments to *Message Types* are maintained in transaction code WE82. Figure 7-15 shows the assignment of *IDoc* type PORDCR05 to *Message Type* PORDCR.

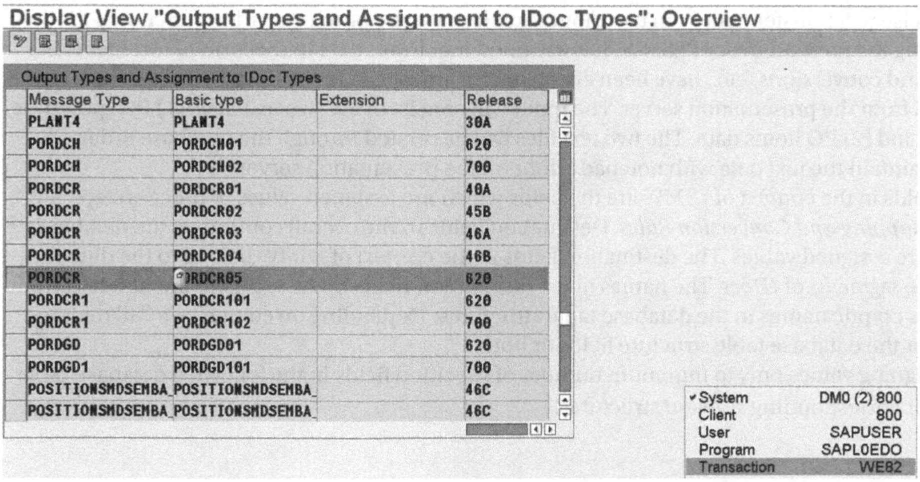

## Display View "Output Types and Assignment to IDoc Types": Overview

**Output Types and Assignment to IDoc Types**

| Message Type | Basic type | Extension | Release |
|---|---|---|---|
| PLANT4 | PLANT4 | | 30A |
| PORDCH | PORDCH01 | | 620 |
| PORDCH | PORDCH02 | | 700 |
| PORDCR | PORDCR01 | | 40A |
| PORDCR | PORDCR02 | | 45B |
| PORDCR | PORDCR03 | | 46A |
| PORDCR | PORDCR04 | | 46B |
| PORDCR | PORDCR05 | | 620 |
| PORDCR1 | PORDCR101 | | 620 |
| PORDCR1 | PORDCR102 | | 700 |
| PORDGD | PORDGD01 | | 620 |
| PORDGD1 | PORDGD101 | | 700 |
| POSITIONSMDSEMBA | POSITIONSMDSEMBA_ | | 46C |
| POSITIONSMDSEMBA | POSITIONSMDSEMBA_ | | 46C |

| | |
|---|---|
| System | DMO (2) 800 |
| Client | 800 |
| User | SAPUSER |
| Program | SAPLOEDO |
| Transaction | WE82 |

*Figure 7-15.  IDoc type PORDCR05 assigned to Message Type PORDCR*

533

Hands-on exercise III employs the LSMW *Object Type*: *IDoc (Intermediate Document)*. Hands-on exercise III will transfer the data of purchase orders from text files into the functional module database tables deploying the *Message Type* PORDCR and the *IDoc* type PORDCR05.

Hands-on exercise IV employs the LSMW *Object Type*: *BAPI method*. Hands-on exercise IV will transfer the data of purchase orders from text files into the functional module database tables also deploying the same *Message Type* PORDCR and the *IDoc* type PORDCR05 as in hands-on exercise III.

We are not elaborating on the *BAPI* method except to mention that the *BAPI methods* are implemented using RFC enabled function modules.

The LSMW process steps for hands-on exercises III and IV are identical. In a real-life scenario, the issue will arise whether to deploy the *Object Type*: *IDoc* or deploy *Object Type*: *BAPI* which internally uses *IDocs* only. For now, you are in the learning paradigm, so, I am demonstrating the deployment of both the *Object Types*: *IDoc* and *BAPI*.

The performance of the hands-on exercises follows.

# Hands-on Exercise III–Migration of Purchase Order Data Using *IDoc*

In this hands-on exercise, we will transfer the data of purchase orders residing in input text files on the presentation server into the SAP functional module database tables deploying the method *IDoc (Intermediate Document)* of LSMW. We will perform the data transfer with representative data of a two or three purchase orders. We will perform the data transfer providing values for a few representative fields, mostly mandatory fields.

The method *IDoc* of LSMW for purchase orders generates *IDocs*. When deploying the method *IDoc* to create purchase orders, we will use the *Message Type* PORDCR and the *IDoc Basic Type* PORDCR05. We will perform the *Settings* for *IDoc Inbound Processing* before proceeding to the LSMW process steps.

A description of specification and scope; *IDoc Inbound Settings*; creation of *Subproject, Object*; and LSMW process steps follows.

## Specification and Scope

The hands-on exercise will transfer data from two input text files into the purchase orders functional module database tables using the method *IDoc* of LSMW. It is assumed that input data in the form of text files is in the required form and conversions, etc., have been effected. The input data in the form of text files will reside on and be accessed from the presentation server. The input will consist of the two text files: (1) PO (purchase order) header data and (2) PO items data. The two text files will be related through the purchase order number. We will maintain the text data with notepad editor on the presentation server.

Destination fields in the context of LSMW are the fields which are assigned values in process step 5–*Maintain Field Mapping and Conversion Rules*. Destination fields in the overall context are the database table fields which are assigned values. The destination fields in the context of LSMW belong to the different structures called the *segments* of *IDocs*. The names of the destination fields in the *segments* are different from their corresponding cryptic names in the database table structures. Depending on context, we will refer to the *segment* fields or the database table structure fields or both.

We will be assigning values only to minimum number of specified fields in the following database table structures with their corresponding *segment* structures.

The fields belonging to the three structures listed in Table 7-5 will only be assigned values.

***Table 7-5.*** *Structures Whose Fields Will Assume Values*

| Srl. No. | Database Table Structure | Database Table Structure Description | *IDoc Segment* Structure |
|---|---|---|---|
| 1 | EKKO | Purchasing Document Header | E1BPEKKOC |
| 2 | EKPO | Purchasing Document Item | E1BPEKPOC |
| 3 | EKET | Purchasing Document Scheduling Agreement Schedule Lines | E1BPEKET |

***Table 7-6.*** *Fields Which Will Be Assigned Values*

| Srl. No. | Field Name (Database Table) | Field Name (*IDoc Segment*) | Field Description |
|---|---|---|---|
| 1 | EKKO-EBELN | E1BPEKKOC-PO_NUMBER | Purchasing Document Number |
| 2 | EKKO-BEDAT | E1BPEKKOC-DOC_DATE | Purchasing Document Date |
| 3 | EKKO-BSTYP | E1BPEKKOC-DOC_CAT | Purchasing Document Category |
| 4 | EKKO-BSART | E1BPEKKOC-DOC_TYPE | Purchasing Document Type |
| 5 | EKKO-LIFNR | E1BPEKKOC-VENDOR | Vendor Number/Code |
| 6 | EKKO-EKORG | E1BPEKKOC-PURCH_ORG | Purchasing Organization |
| 7 | EKKO-EKGRP | E1BPEKKOC-PUR_GRP | Purchasing Group |
| 8 | EKPO-EBELN | E1BPEKPOC-PO_NUMBER | Purchasing Document Number |
| 9 | EKPO-MATNR | E1BPEKPOC-PUR_MAT | Material Number/Code |
| 10 | EKPO-EBELP | E1BPEKPOC-PO_ITEM | Item Number of Purchasing Document |
| 11 | EKPO-NETPR | E1BPEKPOC-NET_PRICE | Net Price Purchasing Document |
| 12 | EKPO-MATKL | E1BPEKPOC-MAT_GRP | Material Group |
| 13 | EKPO-WERKS | E1BPEKPOC-PLANT | Plant to which Material to be Delivered |
| 14 | EKET-EBELN | E1BPEKET-PO_NUMBER | Purchasing Document Number |
| 15 | EKET-EBELP | E1BPEKET-PO_ITEM | Item Number of Purchasing Document |
| 16 | EKET-ETENR | E1BPEKET-SERIAL_NO | Delivery Schedule Line Counter or Number |
| 17 | EKET-MENGE | E1BPEKET-QUANTITY | Scheduled Quantity |
| 18 | EKET-EINDT | E1BPEKET-DELIV_DATE | Item Delivery Date |

The field EBELN is repeating in database table structures EKKO and EKPO for relationship. The fields EBELN and EBELP are repeating in database table structures EKPO and EKET for relationship.

We will now specify the manner in which the destination or *segment* fields will assume values.

The fields of *segment* E1BPEKKOC will assume the same constant values for all the purchase orders being migrated.

*Table 7-7. Fields with Constant Values*

| Srl. No. | Field Name (Database Table) | Field Name (*IDoc Segment*) | Field Description | Value |
|---|---|---|---|---|
| 1 | EKKO-BEDAT | E1BPEKKOC-DOC_DATE | Purchasing Document Date | SY-DATUM |
| 2 | EKKO-BSTYP | E1BPEKKOC-DOC_CAT | Purchasing Document Category | F |
| 3 | EKKO-BSART | E1BPEKKOC-DOC_TYPE | Purchasing Document Type | NB |

■ **Caution**    Before you adopt the values for field numbers 2 and 3, check the validity of these values on your system. If you are operating on an IDES server and logged into client 800, the foregoing values should be all right.

The values for the fields of *segment* E1BPEKKOC in Table 7-8 will originate from the text file–PO header data.

*Table 7-8. Fields with Values Originating from Text File–PO Header Data*

| Srl. No. | Field Name (Database Table) | Field Name (IDoc *Segment*) | Field Description |
|---|---|---|---|
| 1 | EKKO-EBELN | E1BPEKKOC-PO_NUMBER | Purchasing Document Number |
| 2 | EKKO-LIFNR | E1BPEKKOC-VENDOR | Vendor Number/Code |
| 3 | EKKO-EKORG | E1BPEKKOC-PURCH_ORG | Purchasing Organization |
| 4 | EKKO-EKGRP | E1BPEKKOC-PUR_GROUP | Purchasing Group |

The field EBELN is autogenerated on the system we are working upon. With autogeneration, whatever value provided for field PO_NUMBER from the input does not get assigned to the field EBELN in the database tables. The field PO_NUMBER has been incorporated into the PO header data for LSMW processing–connecting the PO items data with it, which items belong to which PO?

We are combining the fields to be assigned values for *segments* E1BPEKPOC and E1BPEKET into one input text file–PO items data. We are doing this deliberately, to demonstrate that while configuring the input data, we must bear in mind the data model of database tables: EKKO, EKPO, and EKET. Table 7-9 lists the fields.

***Table 7-9.*** *Fields with Values Originating from Text File–PO Items Data*

| Srl. No. | Field Name (Database Table) | Field Name (*IDoc Segment*) | Field Description |
|---|---|---|---|
| 1 | EKPO-EBELN | E1BPEKPOC-PO_NUMBER | Purchasing Document Number |
| 2 | EKPO-MATNR | E1BPEKPOC-PUR_MAT | Material Number/Code |
| 3 | EKPO-EBELP | E1BPEKPOC-PO_ITEM | Item Number of Purchasing Document |
| 4 | EKPO-NETPR | E1BPEKPOC-NET_PRICE | Net Price in Purchasing Document |
| 5 | EKPO-MATKL | E1BPEKPOC-MAT_GRP | Material Group |
| 6 | EKPO-WERKS | E1BPEKPOC-PLANT | Plant to which Material to be Delivered |
| 7 | EKET-ETENR | E1BPEKET-SERIAL_NO | Delivery Schedule Line Counter or Number |
| 8 | EKET-MENGE | E1BPEKET-QUANTITY | Scheduled Quantity |
| 9 | EKET-EINDT | E1BPEKET-DELIV_DATE | Item Delivery Date |

The field PO_NUMBER in the PO items data is for connecting the PO items data with the PO header data, which items belong to which PO?

Having described the specifications and scope of the hands-on exercise, we will first perform the *Settings for IDoc Inbound Processing*. Next, we will create *Subproject* YCH_07_PO under the existing *Project* YCH06_DM. We will then proceed to create the *Object* YCH07_PO_IDOC under the *Project* and *Sub-Project* YCH06_DM/YCH_07_PO. After creating the *Object* YCH07_PO_IDOC, create and execute LSMW process steps.

# Perform IDoc Inbound Settings

The *IDoc Inbound Settings* is attached to a *Project* in the LSMW. The different *Objects* under a *Project* can use the same *IDoc Inbound Settings*. Different *Projects* will have different *IDoc Inbound Settings*.

We navigated to the LSMW opening screen, entered the *Project* name as YCH06_DM. To perform the *IDoc Inbound Settings*, we made the following menu selection: Settings ➤ IDoc Inbound Settings. A screen as shown in Figure 7-16 appeared.

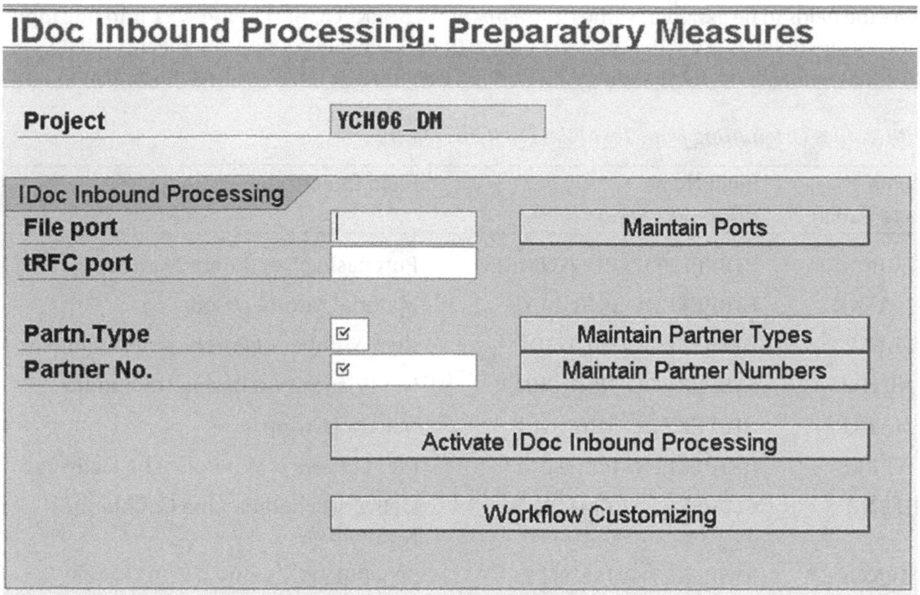

**Figure 7-16.** *LSMW–Settings for IDoc Inbound Processing*

We will have to enter the three mandatory fields: *File port, Partn.Type,* and *Partner No.*

The *File port* is required only if the EDI subsystem is operative. In our hands-on exercise execution, the EDI subsystem is inoperative. But, we have to provide the *File port* as it is a mandatory field on the screen of Figure 7-16. When the EDI subsystem is operative, *inbound IDocs* are generated as operating system files. The *inbound IDocs* generated as operating system files must reside in a folder. The value in the field *File port* on the screen of Figure 7-16 specifies the folder. To specify a *File port*, we clicked the button *Maintain Ports* on the screen of Figure 7-16. A screen as shown in Figure 7-17 appeared.

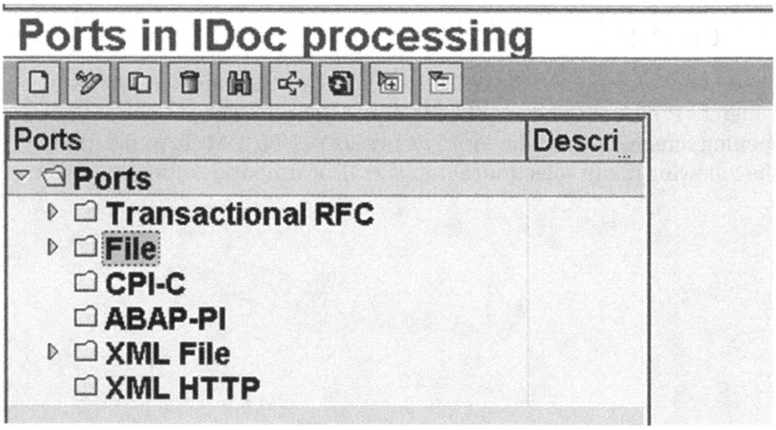

**Figure 7-17.** *Ports in IDoc Processing*

We positioned the cursor on the node *File* and clicked the Create button. A screen to create a new *File port* appeared. We made the appropriate selections and entries as shown in Figure 7-18.

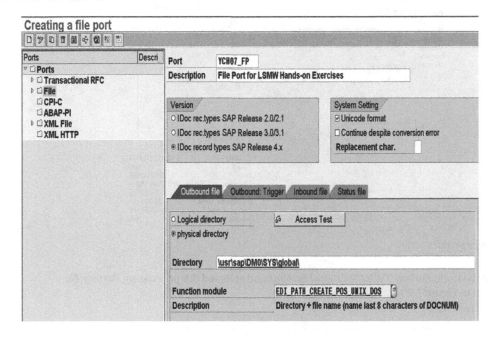

**Figure 7-18.** *Creating a file port*

We entered the *Port* name as YCH07_FP. We accepted the following defaults: Radio button *IDoc record types SAP Release 4.x* and check box *Unicode format*. We selected the Radio button *Physical Directory*. We assigned value to the field *Directory* by pressing function key F4 and making a selection from the list. We assigned a value to the field *Function module* by pressing function key F4 and making a selection from the list. The assigned function module generates the *IDoc* file names. The creation of a *File port* can be performed from transaction code WE21 as well.

We saved the screen and navigated back to the *IDoc Inbound Processing* screen. We clicked the button *Maintain Partner Numbers*. A screen as shown in Figure 7-19 appeared.

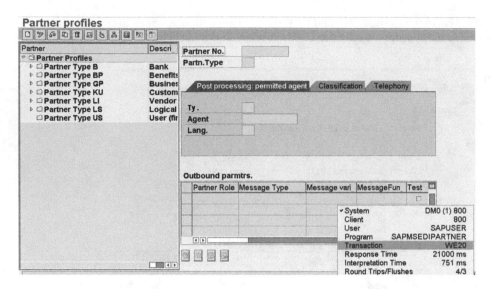

*Figure 7-19. Partner profiles*

We expanded the node *Partner Type LS–Logical Systems* and selected the preexisting *Partner No.* XI_00_800 as shown in Figure 7-20.

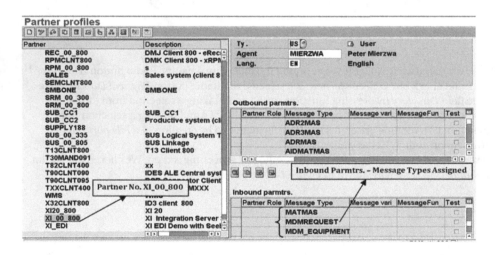

*Figure 7-20. Partner profile–Partner No. XI_00_800*

In the bottom left corner of Figure 7-20, the selected Partner No. XI_00_800 is marked. In the bottom right half of Figure 7-20, the *Outbound parmtrs.* and the *Inbound parmtrs.* appear. The *Outbound parmtrs.* and the *Inbound parmtrs,* essentially, consist of the *IDoc Message Types* assigned to the *Partner No.* XI_00_800 for generation of *outbound* and *inbound IDocs,* respectively.

Since, in our scenario, *inbound IDocs* are to be generated, we must ensure that the *IDoc Message Type* PORDCR is assigned to the *Inbound parmtrs.* of the *Partner No.* XI_00_800. On the IDES system, we are operating upon, we have to assign *IDoc Message Type* PORDCR to the *Inbound parmtrs.* of the *Partner No.*

540

XI_00_800. To assign an *IDoc Message Type* to the *Inbound parmtrs.* of a *Partner No.*, we clicked the Insert  button available under the *Inbound parmtrs.*, not visible in Figure 7-20. Figure 7-21 shows the screen for the assignment of an *IDoc Message Type* to *Partner No.* with the entered values and selections.

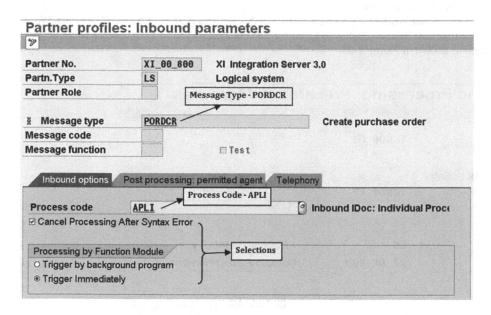

*Figure 7-21.* *Partner No. XI_00_800–Inbound parameters*

We saved the screen and navigated back to the *Partner Profiles* screen of *Partner No.* XI_00_800. We scrolled down to confirm the assignment of *IDoc Message Type* PORDCR to the *Inbound parmtrs.* of the *Partner No.* XI_00_800 as shown in Figure 7-22.

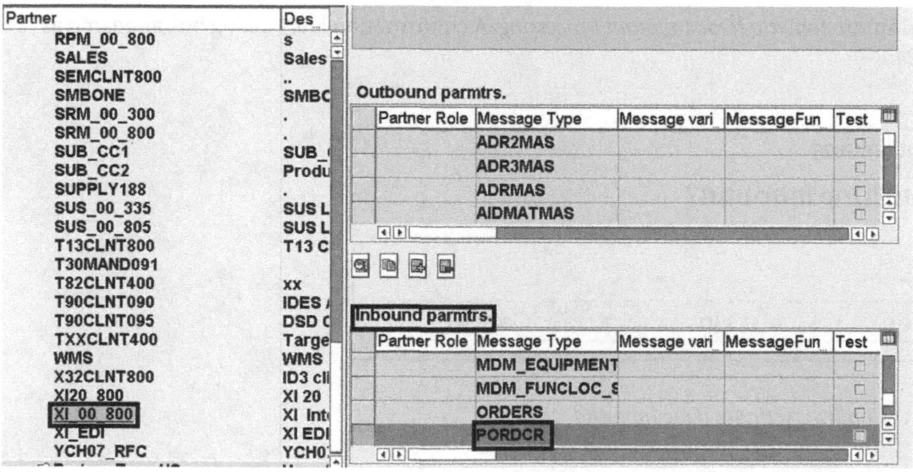

*Figure 7-22.* *Partner No. XI_00_800–inbound parameters: Message Type PORDCR*

The *Partner Profiles* can be maintained with transaction code WE20 as well.

If you are working in client 800 of the IDES server, you can use the *Partner No.* B3TCLNT800 instead of XI_00_800. A *Partner No.* is associated with a client. The names of *Partner No.* in the IDES server contain the client as the last three characters. If you are not working on the IDES server, you will have to create a *Partner No.* along with its underlying components.

From the screen of Partner Profiles, we navigated back to the Settings of *IDoc Inbound Processing*. We entered the values for the three fields: *File port* as YCH07_FP, *Partn.Type* as LS, and *Partner No.* as XI_00_800 and saved the screen as shown in Figure 7-23.

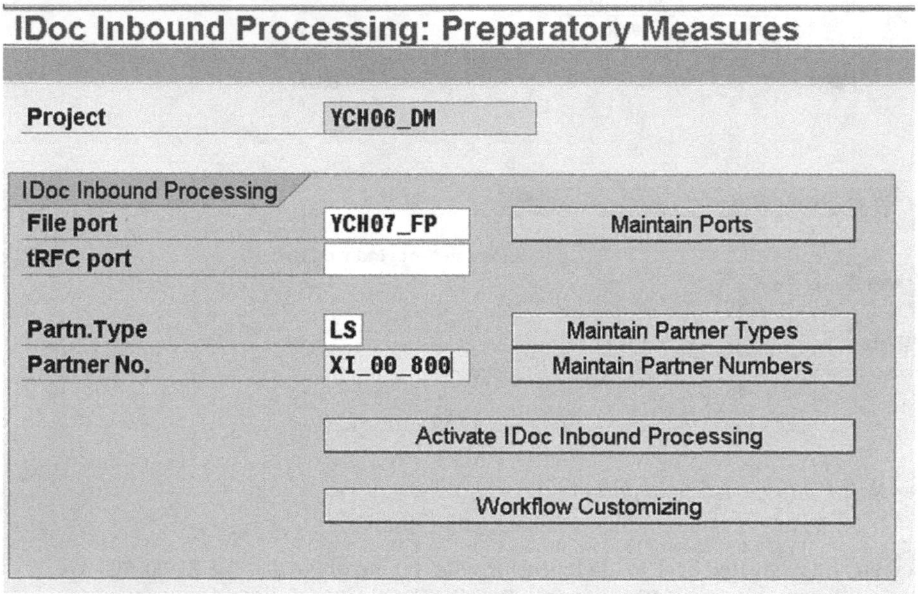

## IDoc Inbound Processing: Preparatory Measures

| Project | YCH06_DM |
| --- | --- |

**IDoc Inbound Processing**

| File port | YCH07_FP | Maintain Ports |
| --- | --- | --- |
| tRFC port | | |

| Partn.Type | LS | Maintain Partner Types |
| --- | --- | --- |
| Partner No. | XI_00_800 | Maintain Partner Numbers |

| Activate IDoc Inbound Processing |
| --- |

| Workflow Customizing |
| --- |

*Figure 7-23.  LSMW–Settings performed for IDoc Inbound Processing*

We clicked the button *Activate IDoc Inbound Processing*. A confirmation alert dialog box appeared as shown in Figure 7-24.

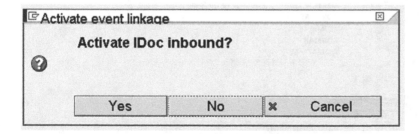

*Figure 7-24.  LSMW–Confirm Activate IDoc Inbound*

We clicked the Yes button on the dialog box.

This concludes the *Settings* for *IDoc Inbound Processing.* We navigated to the opening screen of LSMW.

## Create Subproject YCH07_PO

To create the *Subproject* YCH07_PO under the existing *Project* YCH06_DM, we entered YCH06_DM in the field *Project* on the opening screen of LSMW and clicked the button *All Project Objects* of the application toolbar. The hierarchical tree with nodes and subnodes of the *Project* YCH06_DM appeared as shown in Figure 7-25.

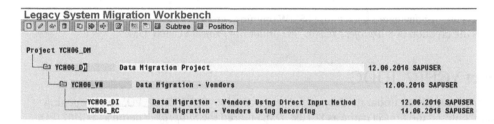

*Figure 7-25.  Project YCH06_DM – Hierarchical Tree*

We positioned the cursor on *Project* node YCH06_DM and clicked the Create button on the application toolbar. A dialog box for entry of *Subproject* name and description appeared. Figure 7-26 shows the dialog box with the entered values.

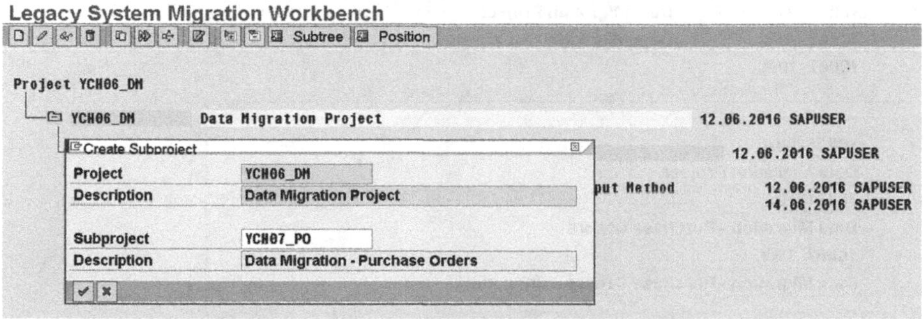

**Legacy System Migration Workbench**

```
Project YCH06_DM

      YCH06_DM          Data Migration Project                      12.06.2016 SAPUSER

         Create Subproject                                          12.06.2016 SAPUSER

         Project            YCH06_DM                    put Method   12.06.2016 SAPUSER
         Description        Data Migration Project                   14.06.2016 SAPUSER

         Subproject         YCH07_PO
         Description        Data Migration - Purchase Orders

         ✔ ✗
```

*Figure 7-26.  Create Subproject YCH07_PO under Project YCH06_DM*

We clicked the Continue button on the *Create Subproject* dialog box. The *Subproject* YCH07_PO was created as shown in Figure 7-27.

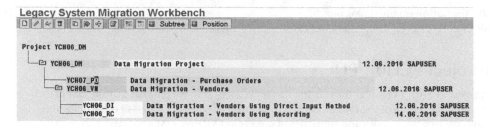

*Figure 7-27. Subproject YCH07_PO under Project YCH06_DM created*

We saved the screen and navigated back to the LSMW opening screen.

This concludes the creation of *Subproject* YCH07_PO under the *Project* YCH06_DM.

# Create Object YCH07_IDOC

To create the *Object* YCH07_IDOC under the *Project/Subproject* YCH06_DM/YCH07_PO, on the opening screen of LSMW, we entered the *Project* name as YCH06_DM, entered the *Subproject* name as YCH07_PO, and entered the *Object* name as YCH07_IDOC. We positioned the cursor on the *Object* field and clicked the Create button on the application toolbar. The dialog box to enter a description of the *Object* popped up. We entered a suitable description as shown in Figure 7-28.

**Legacy System Migration Workbench**

| | | | All Objects | My Objects | All Project Objects | Project Documentation |

Project Selection

| **Project** | YCH06_DM | Data Migration Project |
| **Subproject** | YCH07_PO | Data Migration - Purchase Orders |
| **Object** | YCH07_IDOC | |

Create Object

| **Project** | YCH06_DM |
| | **Data Migration Project** |
| **Subproject** | YCH07_PO |
| | **Data Migration - Purchase Orders** |
| **Object** | YCH07_IDOC |
| **Name** | **Data Migration - Purchase Orders usinng Idoc** |

*Figure 7-28. LSMW–create Object YCH07_IDOC*

We clicked the Continue button and the *Object* YCH07_IDOC was created in the *Project* YCH06_DM and the *Subproject* YCH07_PO. Next, we have to perform the process steps.

To perform the process steps, we clicked the Execute button on the application toolbar of LSMW opening screen.

Our descriptions of process steps 1 to 12 will be brief, since they were described elaborately in the hands-on exercises I and II in Chapter 6.

We started off by executing process step 1 by selecting the Radio button and clicking the Execute button.

# Process Step 1–Maintain Object Attributes

We clicked the Display/Change toggle button on the application toolbar to enable changes on the screen. On the process step 1 screen, in the *Attributes area,* we entered and specified the following:

- Suitable description already entered during creation of the Object appears.

- The *Owner* as the logged-in user, which is the default. We can assign any other valid user name.

- The data transfer Radio button: *Once Only.*

- The file names you are going to specify are not *System Specific*-check box disabled.

In the *Object Type and Import Method* area of the process step 1 screen, we clicked the *Object Type* Radio button as *IDoc.* We positioned the cursor in the field *Message Type,* and pressed the function key F4. Next, we pressed the keys ctrl + F to invoke the search dialog box. We entered the word "Purchase" in the search dialog box as shown in Figure 7-29.

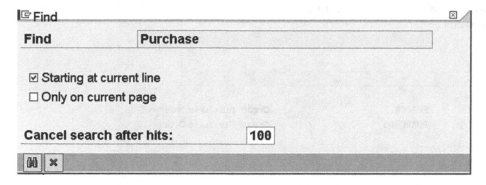

*Figure 7-29.*  *Select Message Type –search dialog box*

We clicked the Continue button on the search dialog box. A list of entries with the word "purchase" was returned as shown in Figure 7-30.

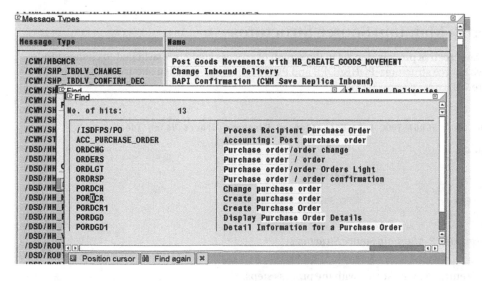

*Figure 7-30.*  *Select Message Type–list with word "purchase"*

We selected, from the *Select Message Type* list, the entry PORDCR–Create Purchase Order. Similarly, we assigned as PORDCR05 to the field *Basic Type*. Figure 7-31 shows the screen with all the entries and assignments.

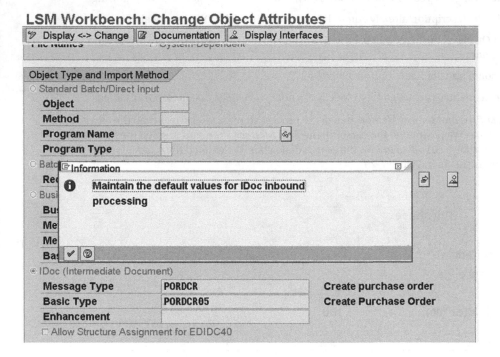

*Figure 7-31.* *Process step 1: all entries and assignments*

Then we saved and exited the screen of process step 1.

You can observe that the number of process steps is 16 after the execution of process step 1.

## Process Step 2–Maintain Source Structures

We navigated to the screen of process step 2. On the screen of process step 2, we switched to change mode. We created the two source structures–POHEADER and POITEMS–corresponding to our two input text files as shown in Figure 7-32.

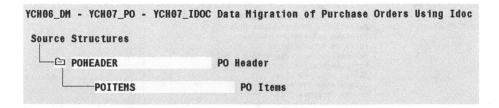

*Figure 7-32.* *Process step 2–Maintain Source Structures*

We saved and returned to the screen with the process steps.

## Process Step 3–Maintain Source Fields

We executed process step 3 and switched the screen to change mode. We inserted the fields in the two source structures POHEADER and POITEMS as shown in Figure 7-33.

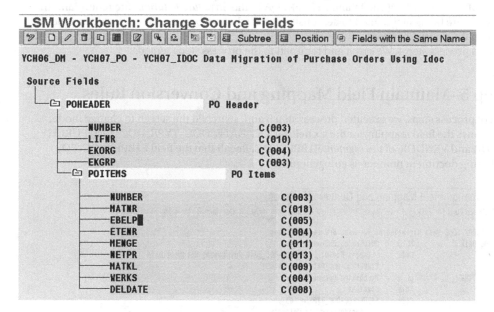

**Figure 7-33.** *Process step 3–create source field: all fields under two source structures created*

The order of the fields in the source structure must be identical to the order in which data is located in the text files. We are using text files with one line for one row of data, with comma (,) as a field separator.

We saved and returned to the process steps screen.

## Process Step 4–Maintain Structure Relations

We executed process step 4 and switched the screen to change mode.

Our destination structures are the *segments* (structures) including the super structure *segment* E1PORDCR (see Figure 7-34).

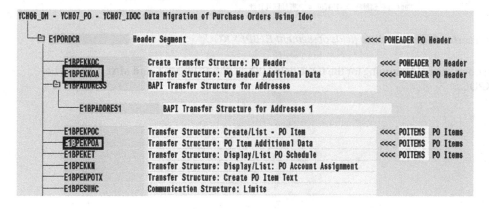

**Figure 7-34.** *Process step 4–Maintain Structure Relations*

The 18 fields to which we propose to assign values originate from the three *segments*: E1BPEKKOC, E1BPEKPOC, and E1BPEKET. The fields in the *segment* E1BPEKKOC map to the source structure POHEADER; the fields in the *segments* E1BPEKPOC and E1BPEKET map to the source structure POITEMS

Figure 7-34 shows the assignment of source structures to destination *segments* or structures.

The selection of *segments* E1BPEKKOA and E1BPEKPOA in the *Structure Relations* are redundant; the redundant selections are being maintained to demonstrate that whatever *segments* are selected in process step 4 will appear in the reviews of *IDocs*.

This completes process step 4. We saved and returned to the process steps screen.

## Process Step 5–Maintain Field Mapping and Conversion Rules

From the screen of process steps, we executed process step 5 and, switched the screen to change mode.

Figure 7-35 shows the field mapping for the six fields, DOC_DATE, DOC_TYPE, DOC_CAT, PURCH_ORG, PUR_GROUP, and VENDOR, of the *segment* E1BPEKKOC. Recall that the field E1BPEKKOC-PO_NUMBER–purchasing document number–is autogenerated.

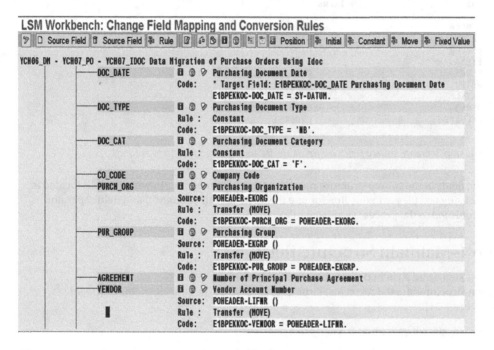

*Figure 7-35.* *Process step 5–assignment to fields of segment E1BPEKKOC*

Figure 7-36 shows the field mapping for the three fields PO_ITEM, PUR_MAT, and MAT_GRP of the *segment* E1BPEKPOC.

```
YCH06_DM - YCH07_PO - YCH07_IDOC Data Migration of Purchase Orders Using Idoc
     └─ Fields
          ├─PO_NUMBER          ⊟ ⊚ ⊳ Purchasing Document Number
          ├─PO_ITEM            ⊟ ⊚ ⊳ Item Number of Purchasing Document
                             Source:  POITEMS-EBELP ()
                             Rule :   Transfer (MOVE)
                             Code:    E1BPEKPOC-PO_ITEM = POITEMS-EBELP.
          ├─ADDRESS            ⊟ ⊚ ⊳ Address
          ├─MATERIAL           ⊟ ⊚ ⊳ Material Number
          ├─PUR_MAT            ⊟ ⊚ ⊳ Material Number
                             Source:  POITEMS-MATNR ()
                             Rule :   Transfer (MOVE)
                             Code:    E1BPEKPOC-PUR_MAT = POITEMS-MATNR.
          ├─INFO_REC           ⊟ ⊚ ⊳ Number of Purchasing Info Record
          ├─ITEM_CAT           ⊟ ⊚ ⊳ Item Category in Purchasing Document
          ├─ACCTASSCAT         ⊟ ⊚ ⊳ Account Assignment Category
          ├─AGREEMENT          ⊟ ⊚ ⊳ Number of Principal Purchase Agreement
          ├─AGNT_ITEM          ⊟ ⊚ ⊳ Item Number of Principal Purchase Agreement
          ├─STORE_LOC          ⊟ ⊚ ⊳ Storage Location
          ├─MAT_GRP            ⊟ ⊚ ⊳ Material Group
                             Source:  POITEMS-MATKL ()
                             Rule :   Transfer (MOVE)
                             Code:    E1BPEKPOC-MAT_GRP = POITEMS-MATKL.
```

***Figure 7-36.*** *Process step 5–assignment to fields of segment E1BPEKPOC–I*

Figure 7-37 shows the field mapping for the two fields PLANT and NET_PRICE of the *segment* E1BPEKPOC.

```
YCH06_DM - YCH07_PO - YCH07_IDOC Data Migration of Purchase Orders Using Idoc
          ├─KANBAN_IND         ⊟ ⊚ ⊳ Kanban Indicator
          ├─PLANT              ⊟ ⊚ ⊳ Plant
                             Source:  POITEMS-WERKS ()
                             Rule :   Transfer (MOVE)
                             Code:    E1BPEKPOC-PLANT = POITEMS-WERKS.
          ├─ALLOC_TBL          ⊟ ⊚ ⊳ Allocation Table Number
          ├─AT_ITEM            ⊟ ⊚ ⊳ Item number of allocation table
          ├─UNIT               ⊟ ⊚ ⊳ Purchase Order Unit of Measure
          ├─NET_PRICE          ⊟ ⊚ ⊳ Net price in purchasing document (in document currency)
                             Source:  POITEMS-NETPR ()
                             Rule :   Transfer (MOVE)
                             Code:    E1BPEKPOC-NET_PRICE = POITEMS-NETPR.
          └─PRICE_UNIT         ⊟ ⊚ ⊳ Price Unit
```

***Figure 7-37.*** *Process step 5–assignment to fields of segment E1BPEKPOC–II*

Figure 7-38 shows the field mapping for four fields PO_ITEM, SERIAL_NO, DELV_DATE, and QUANTITY of the *segment* E1BPEKET.

```
YCH06_DM - YCH07_PO - YCH07_IDOC Data Migration of Purchase Orders Using Idoc
     └─ E1BPEKET               Transfer Structure: Display/List PO Schedule        ⊳
          └─ Fields
              ├─PO_ITEM            ⊟ ⊚ ⊳ Item Number of Purchasing Document
                             Source:  POITEMS-EBELP ()
                             Rule :   Transfer (MOVE)
                             Code:    E1BPEKET-PO_ITEM = POITEMS-EBELP.
              ├─SERIAL_NO          ⊟ ⊚ ⊳ Delivery Schedule Line Counter
                             Source:  POITEMS-ETENR ()
                             Rule :   Transfer (MOVE)
                             Code:    E1BPEKET-SERIAL_NO = POITEMS-ETENR.
              ├─DEL_DATCAT         ⊟ ⊚ ⊳ Category of Delivery Date
              ├─DELIV_DATE         ⊟ ⊚ ⊳ Item Delivery Date
                             Source:  POITEMS-DELDATE ()
                             Rule :   Transfer (MOVE)
                             Code:    E1BPEKET-DELIV_DATE = POITEMS-DELDATE.
              ├─DELIV_TIME         ⊟ ⊚ ⊳ Delivery Date Time-Spot
              ├─QUANTITY           ⊟ ⊚ ⊳ Scheduled Quantity
                             Source:  POITEMS-MENGE ()
                             Rule :   Transfer (MOVE)
                             Code:    E1BPEKET-QUANTITY = POITEMS-MENGE.
```

***Figure 7-38.*** *Process step 5–assignment to fields of segment E1BPEKET*

We performed a validity check, ctrl+F2 or sixth button from the left on the application toolbar. We saved the changes and returned to the process steps screen.

## Process Step 7–*Specify Files*

From the screen of process steps, we executed process step 7 and switched the screen to change mode.

As the input text files are to be located on the presentation server, we positioned the cursor on the node *Legacy Data on the PC (Frontend)* and clicked the Create button on the application toolbar. The dialog box to input file entries appeared. We selected the file PO_HEADER.txt from the folder D:TEMP, entered a suitable description, and selected comma (,) as field separator in the *Delimiter* area. Figure 7-39 illustrates.

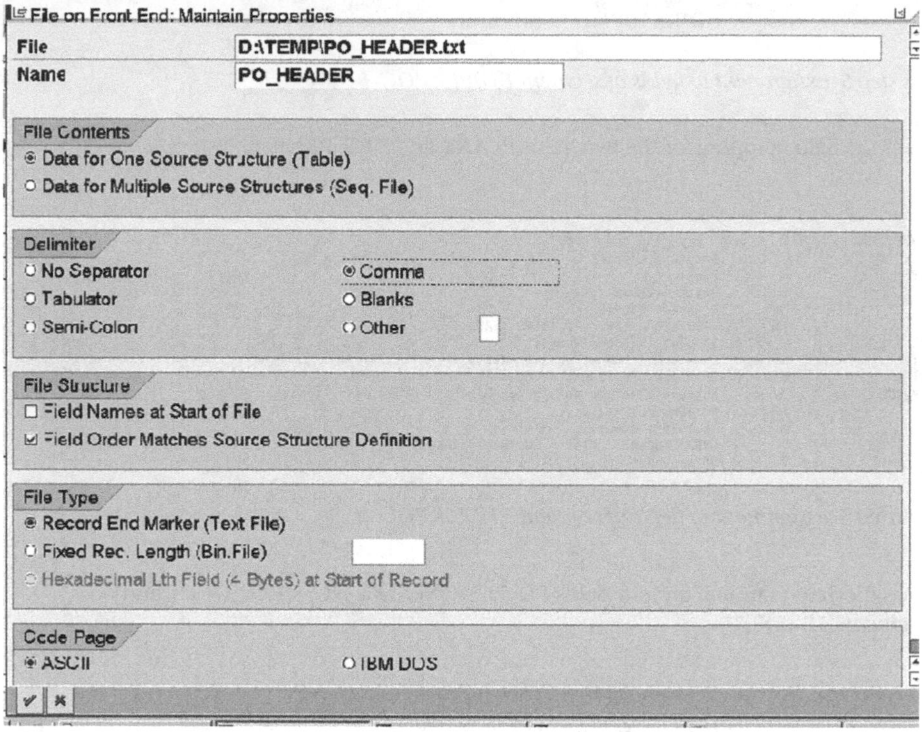

*Figure 7-39. Process step 7–specify file: PO_HEADER.txt*

We clicked the Continue button on the dialog box. The file PO_HEADER.txt got specified. In a similar manner we specified the second files: PO_ITEM.txt. Figure 7-40 shows the screen with both the two files specified.

```
YCH06_DM - YCH07_PO - YCH07_IDOC Data Migration of Purchase Orders Using Idoc

Files

    ├─ 🗀 Legacy Data          On the PC (Frontend)

        ├──PO_ITEM                     D:\TEMP\PO_ITEM.txt
        │                              Data for One Source Structure (Table)
        │                              Separator Comma
        │                              Field Order Matches Source Structure Definition
        │                              With Record End Indicator (Text File)
        │                              Code Page ASCII
        └──PO_HEADER                   D:\TEMP\PO_HEADER.txt
                                       Data for One Source Structure (Table)
                                       Separator Comma
                                       Field Order Matches Source Structure Definition
                                       With Record End Indicator (Text File)
                                       Code Page ASCII
```

*Figure 7-40.* *Process step 7-files PO_HEADER and PO_ITEM*

We saved the changes on the screen of process step 7.
This concludes process step 7. We navigated back to the process steps screen.

## Process Step 8–*Assign Files*

From the screen of process steps, we executed process step 8 and switched the screen to change mode.
We assigned the input text files to the respective source structures.
Figure 7-41 shows the screen after the assignment of two input files to the two source structures.

```
YCH06_DM - YCH07_PO - YCH07_IDOC Data Migration of Purchase Orders Using Idoc

Source Structures and Files

    └─ 🗀 POHEADER PO Header
                PO_HEADER D:\TEMP\PO_HEADER.txt

        └──POITEMS PO Items
                PO_ITEM D:\TEMP\PO_ITEM.txt
```

*Figure 7-41.* *Process step 8-files assigned to Source Structures*

We saved the changes on the screen of process step 8.
This concludes process step 8. We navigated back to the process steps screen.

## Data Creation on Presentation Server

We are digressing from the process steps of LSMW to describe the creation of input text files on the presentation server.

We created in the input file, two purchase orders. The first purchase order –101 contains two materials, and both the materials have a single delivery date. For PO 101, one row must be created in the database table EKKO and two rows each must be created in the database tables EKPO and EKET, respectively. The second purchase order–102 has one material, with two delivery dates. For PO 102, one row each must be created in the database tables EKKO and EKPO, respectively, and two rows must be created in the database table EKET.

We can use the same input data (i.e., PO 101 and PO 102) repeatedly as these do not get assigned to the destination EBELN. EBELN is autogenerated.

Figure 7-42 shows the PO header data of two purchase orders, 101 and 102.

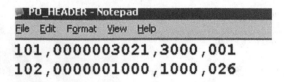

**Figure 7-42.** *PO header data–text file*

The PO header data consists of four fields: EBELN, LIFNR, EKORG, and EKGRP. We are using comma (,) as a field separator. We have entered the data of the field LIFNR with leading zeroes although it is not necessary. The values for the field EBELN (101 and 102) serve the purpose of linking the items and deliveries to the purchasing documents. The purchasing document numbers will be autogenerated in the database tables.

Confirm the validity of values for the fields LIFNR, EKORG, and EKGRP on your system. If you are logged into client 800 or its equivalent of IDES server, the adoption of values being provided here should be all right.

Figure 7-43 shows the PO items (and delivery) data of two purchase orders, 101 and 102.

The po items data consists of nine fields: EBELN, MATNR, EBELP, ETENR, MENGE, NETPR, MATKL, WERK, and EINDT. We deliberately provided zero value to the field NETPR in the first, third, and fourth rows (double comma). We are using comma (,) as a field separator.

```
PO_ITEM - Notepad
File  Edit  Format  View  Help
101,ISA-0023,0010,0001,10,,060,3200,20170202
101,ISA-1016,0020,0001,70,125,060,3200,20170202
102,101-110,0010,0001,200,,001,1000,20170202
102,101-110,0015,0002,300,,001,1000,20170217
```

**Figure 7-43.** *PO items data–text file*

Confirm the validity of values for the fields MATNR, MATKL, and WERK on your system. If you are logged into client 800 or its equivalent of IDES server, the adoption of values being provided here should be all right.

This concludes the creation of input text files on the presentation server. We will resume the performance of LSMW process steps.

## Process Step 9–*Read Data*

From the screen of process steps, we executed process step 9.

In process step 9, data is fetched from user created input text files and assembled together for an entity-purchase order and stored in the file with the postfix: .lsmw.read.

The execution of process step 9 produced an output of statistics of input text data read and written or imported as shown in Figure 7-44.

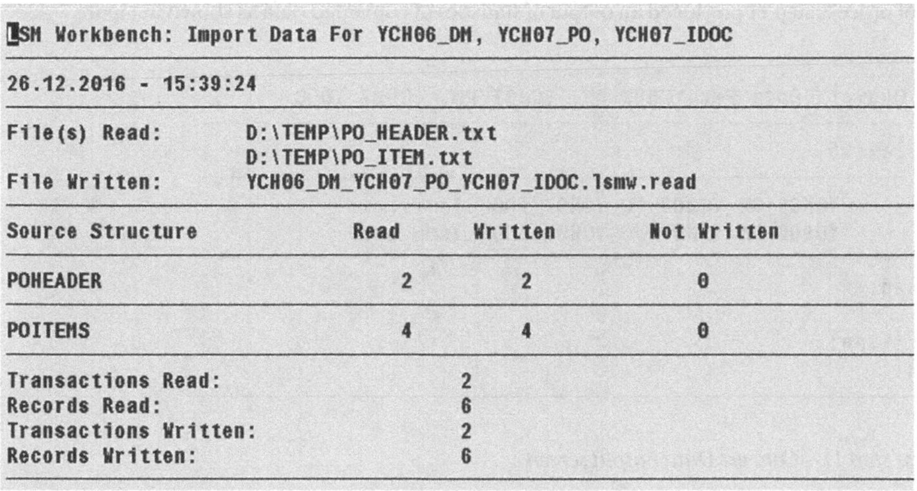

```
LSM Workbench: Import Data For YCH06_DM, YCH07_PO, YCH07_IDOC

26.12.2016 - 15:39:24

File(s) Read:        D:\TEMP\PO_HEADER.txt
                     D:\TEMP\PO_ITEM.txt
File Written:        YCH06_DM_YCH07_PO_YCH07_IDOC.lsmw.read
```

| Source Structure | Read | Written | Not Written |
|---|---|---|---|
| POHEADER | 2 | 2 | 0 |
| POITEMS | 4 | 4 | 0 |

```
Transactions Read:         2
Records Read:              6
Transactions Written:      2
Records Written:           6
```

*Figure 7-44.* *Process step 9—Import Data output screen*

The output report of Figure 7-44 indicates the number of rows read into each of the source structures POHEADER and POITEMS.

This concludes process step 9. We navigated back to the process steps screen.

## Process Step 10—*Display Read Data*

The execution of process step 10 produced an output of the input text data read and written or imported as shown in Figure 7-45.

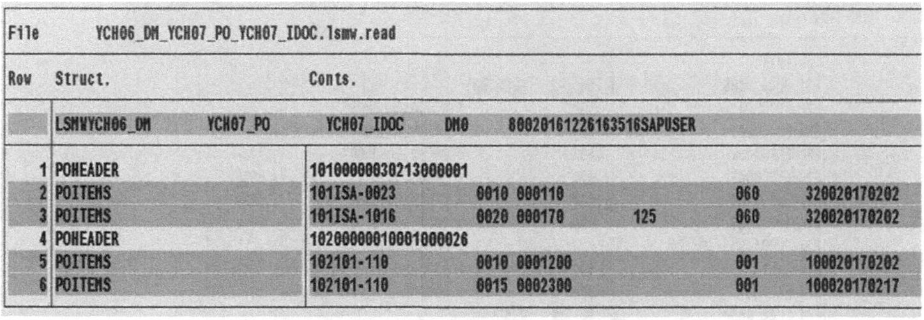

| File | YCH06_DM_YCH07_PO_YCH07_IDOC.lsmw.read | | | | | | |
|---|---|---|---|---|---|---|---|
| Row | Struct. | | Conts. | | | | |
| | LSMWYCH06_DM | YCH07_PO | YCH07_IDOC | DM0 | 80020161226163516SAPUSER | | |
| 1 | POHEADER | | 10100000030213000001 | | | | |
| 2 | POITEMS | | 101ISA-0023 | 0010 000110 | | 060 | 320020170202 |
| 3 | POITEMS | | 101ISA-1016 | 0020 000170 | 125 | 060 | 320020170202 |
| 4 | POHEADER | | 10200000010001000026 | | | | |
| 5 | POITEMS | | 102101-110 | 0010 0001200 | | 001 | 100020170202 |
| 6 | POITEMS | | 102101-110 | 0015 0002300 | | 001 | 100020170217 |

*Figure 7-45.* *Process step 10—display imported data*

You can click any of the lines to view the detail on a single screen.

This concludes the optional process step 10. We navigated back to the process steps screen.

## Process Step 11—*Convert Data*

From the screen of process steps, we executed process step 11.

Recall, in process step 11, data is assigned to the destination fields as per the specifications in process step 5 and written to the file with the following postfix: .lsmw.conv.

The execution of process step 11 produced an output of statistics of converted data as shown in Figure 7-46.

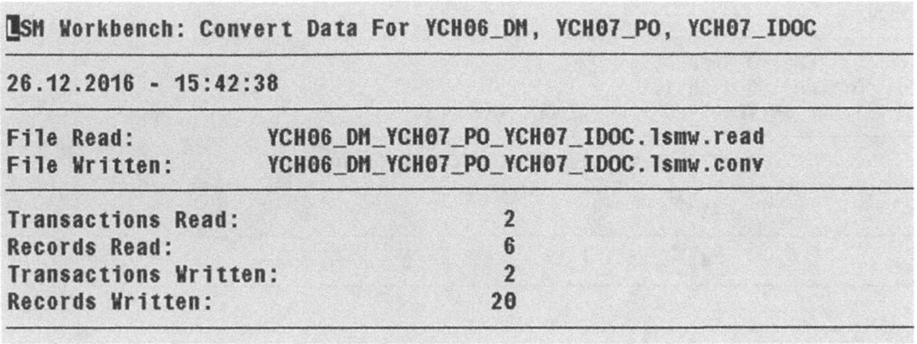

```
LSM Workbench: Convert Data For YCH06_DM, YCH07_PO, YCH07_IDOC

26.12.2016 - 15:42:38

File Read:              YCH06_DM_YCH07_PO_YCH07_IDOC.lsmw.read
File Written:           YCH06_DM_YCH07_PO_YCH07_IDOC.lsmw.conv

Transactions Read:              2
Records Read:                   6
Transactions Written:           2
Records Written:               20
```

*Figure 7-46.*  *Process step 11—Convert Data output screen*

Data is read from the input data file—file with postfix .lsmw.read—and written to the converted data file—file with postfix .lsmw.conv.

The rows written to the converted file appear as the line *Records Written* in Figure 7-46. The number of rows written to the converted file, 20, will become apparent when you execute the next process step—process step 12.

This concludes process step 11. We navigated back to the process steps screen.

## Process Step 12—Display Converted Data

The execution of process step 12 produced an output of the converted data as shown in Figure 7-47.

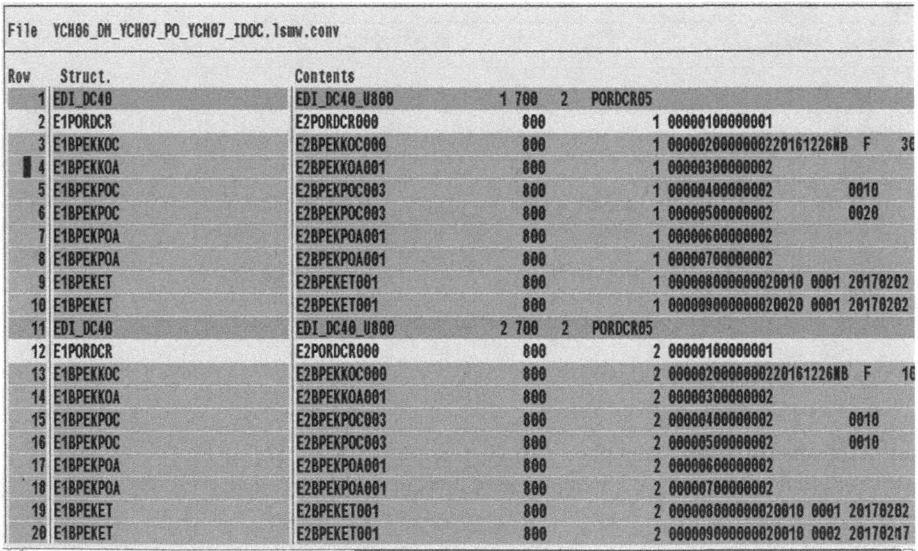

| File | YCH06_DM_YCH07_PO_YCH07_IDOC.lsmw.conv | | | | |
|---|---|---|---|---|---|
| Row | Struct. | Contents | | | |
| 1 | EDI_DC40 | EDI_DC40_U800 | 1 700 | 2 | PORDCR05 |
| 2 | E1PORDCR | E2PORDCR000 | 800 | 1 00000100000001 | |
| 3 | E1BPEKKOC | E2BPEKKOC000 | 800 | 1 000002000000220161226NB  F   36 | |
| 4 | E1BPEKKOA | E2BPEKKOA001 | 800 | 1 00000300000002 | |
| 5 | E1BPEKPOC | E2BPEKPOC003 | 800 | 1 00000400000002        0010 | |
| 6 | E1BPEKPOC | E2BPEKPOC003 | 800 | 1 00000500000002        0020 | |
| 7 | E1BPEKPOA | E2BPEKPOA001 | 800 | 1 00000600000002 | |
| 8 | E1BPEKPOA | E2BPEKPOA001 | 800 | 1 00000700000002 | |
| 9 | E1BPEKET | E2BPEKET001 | 800 | 1 00000800000002 0010  0001 20170202 | |
| 10 | E1BPEKET | E2BPEKET001 | 800 | 1 00000900000002 0020  0001 20170202 | |
| 11 | EDI_DC40 | EDI_DC40_U800 | 2 700 | 2 | PORDCR05 |
| 12 | E1PORDCR | E2PORDCR000 | 800 | 2 00000100000001 | |
| 13 | E1BPEKKOC | E2BPEKKOC000 | 800 | 2 000002000000220161226NB  F   16 | |
| 14 | E1BPEKKOA | E2BPEKKOA001 | 800 | 2 00000300000002 | |
| 15 | E1BPEKPOC | E2BPEKPOC003 | 800 | 2 00000400000002        0010 | |
| 16 | E1BPEKPOC | E2BPEKPOC003 | 800 | 2 00000500000002        0010 | |
| 17 | E1BPEKPOA | E2BPEKPOA001 | 800 | 2 00000600000002 | |
| 18 | E1BPEKPOA | E2BPEKPOA001 | 800 | 2 00000700000002 | |
| 19 | E1BPEKET | E2BPEKET001 | 800 | 2 00000800000002 0010  0001 20170202 | |
| 20 | E1BPEKET | E2BPEKET001 | 800 | 2 00000900000002 0010  0002 20170217 | |

*Figure 7-47.*  *Process step 12—Display Converted Data*

In process step 4—*Maintain Structure Relations*—we assigned source structure to five segments (destination structures): E1BPEKKOC, E1BPEKKOA, E1BPEKPOC, E1BPEKPOA, and E1BPEKET.

Since, in a purchase order, there will be one row for each of the segments E1BPEKKOC and E1BPEKKOA, it will work out to four rows for two purchase orders.

Since, for every item in a purchase order, there will be one row for each of the segments E1BPEKPOC, E1BPEKPOA, E1BPEKET, for four deliveries, this will work out to 12 rows.

Process step 11 is generating two additional rows for each entity or purchase order in segments EDI_DC40 and E1PORDCR. For two purchase orders, this will work out to four rows. The total number of rows in the converted data will be 4 + 12 + 4 = 20, as shown in Figure 7-47.

This concludes the optional process step 12. We navigated back to the process steps screen.

## Process Step 13—Start IDoc Generation

From the screen of process steps, we executed process step 13. Process step 13 generates *IDocs* from the converted data—file with secondary name .lsmw.conv. When we executed process step 13, a prompt appeared for input of converted data file and proposing a default converted data file as shown in Figure 7-48.

**LSM Workbench: Generate IDocs**

| File with Converted Data | YCH06_DM_YCH07_PO_YCH07_IDOC.lsmw.conv |

*Figure 7-48. Process step 13—generate IDocs*

We clicked the Execute button and an output of an info message as shown in Figure 7-49 appeared.

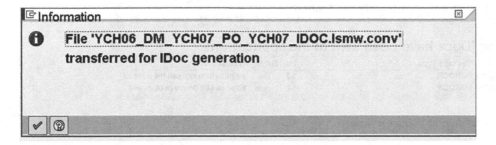

**Information**

❶ File 'YCH06_DM_YCH07_PO_YCH07_IDOC.lsmw.conv' transferred for IDoc generation

*Figure 7-49. Process step 13—IDocs generated*

Corresponding to our two purchase orders, two *IDocs* are generated.
This concludes process step 13. We navigated back to the process steps screen.

## Process Step 14—Start IDoc Processing

From the screen of process steps, we executed process step 14. Process step 14 transfers data from the *IDocs* to the *Application documents*—in our case the purchase order database tables EKKO, EKPO, and EKET.

When you execute process step 14, an elaborate selection screen for input appears. The values from the creation of the latest *IDocs* for the fields *Created on, Created at, Message Type,* and so on, are picked up and appear as default values on the selection screen as shown in Figure 7-50.

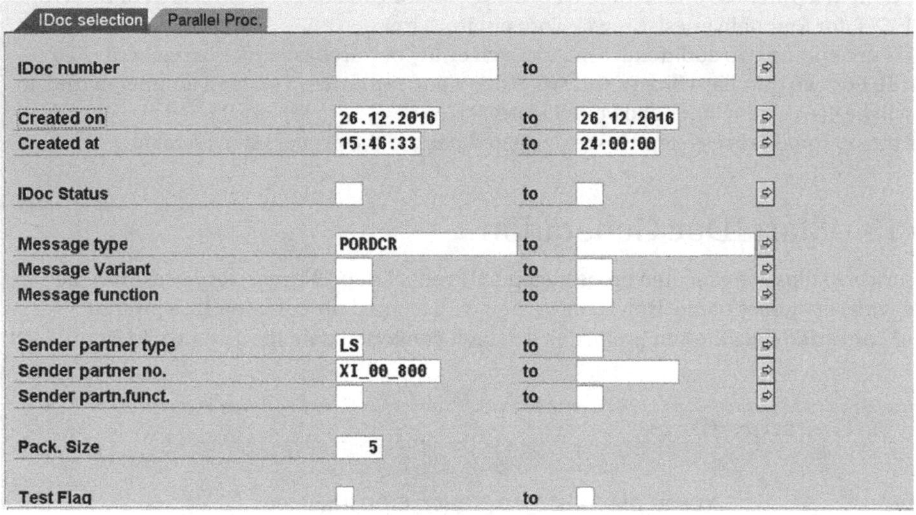

**Figure 7-50.** *Process step 14—IDocs processing*

We accepted the default values and clicked the Execute button.
When all the *IDocs* were processed, the system navigated to the screen shown in Figure 7-51.

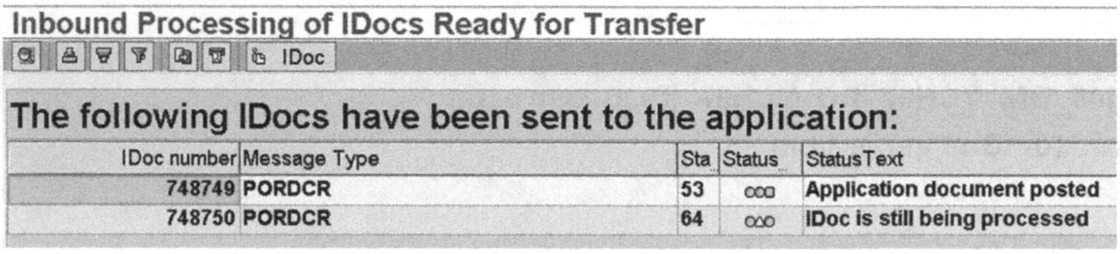

**Figure 7-51.** *Process dtep 14—IDocs processed*

The screen in Figure 7-51 lists the *IDocs* processed. *IDoc* 743749 has been successfully posted and purchase order created—status code 53, as shown in Figure 7-51. We can view the details of each *IDoc* (e.g., control info, data, and status info) by double-clicking an *IDoc*. Let us view the details of the erroneous and unposted *IDoc* 743750 corresponding to purchase order 102 with two (multiple) delivery dates for the single item in it. We double-clicked *IDoc* 743750 and the screen shown in Figure 7-52 appeared.

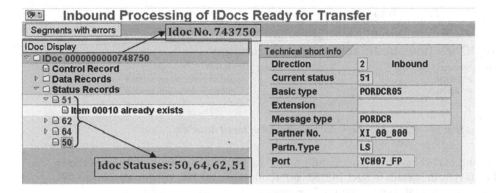

*Figure 7-52. Process step 14—IDoc 743750 details*

On the top lefthand corner of Figure 7-52, the nodes *Control record, Data Records,* and *Status records* appear. We expanded node *Status records* in Figure 7-52. The statuses which the *IDoc* 743750 attained—50, 64, 62, 51—are marked in the figure. *IDoc* 743750 did not get posted as *Item 00010 already exists.*

In the database table EKPO, for a specific purchase order, the field EBELP cannot be assigned duplicate values since the fields EBELN and EBELP constitute the primary key fields.

In the database table EKET, for a specific purchase order, the field EBELP can be assigned duplicate, triplicate, etc. values (multiple delivery dates of an item) since the fields EBELN, EBELP, and ETENR constitute the primary key fields.

Since we have two deliveries dates for the single item in PO 102 and we have combined the data of items and delivery into one input file, the field EBELP of the database table EKPO is being assigned duplicate value which is generating an error. The input data of PO 102 was rejected.

For now, for PO 102, we will provide data of two delivery dates with two item numbers, 0010 and 0015. This will create two rows in the database table EKPO and two rows in the database table EKET. This is contrary to our specifications: in a specific purchase order, for an item with multiple delivery dates, only one row is to be created in the database table EKPO and multiple rows are to be created in the database table EKET.

In hands-on exercise IV, we will rectify the situation by providing the item data and delivery dates data in two separate input files instead of combining them into one input file.

We changed the last line in PO items (and delivery) data from the existing
102,101-110,0010,0002,300,,001,1000,20170202 to 102,101-110,0015,0002,300,,001,1000,20170217.
With the change in input, we again performed the following process steps:

    9. *Read Data*

    11. *Convert Data*

    13. *Start IDoc Generation*

    14. *Start IDoc Processing*

When all the *IDocs* were processed, the system navigated to the screen shown in Figure 7-53.

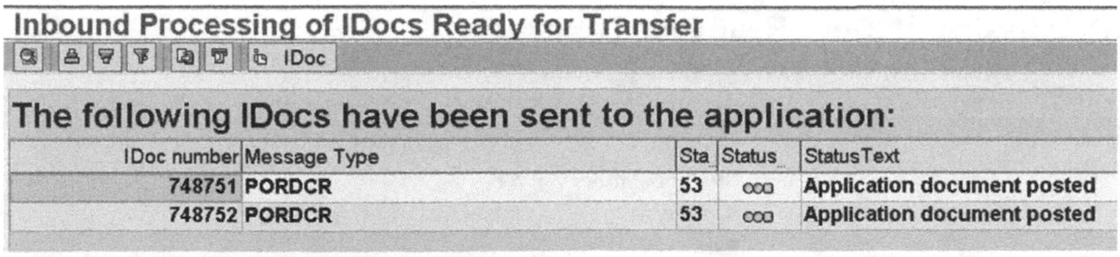

**Inbound Processing of IDocs Ready for Transfer**

| | | IDoc |

**The following IDocs have been sent to the application:**

| IDoc number | Message Type | Sta | Status | StatusText |
|---|---|---|---|---|
| 748751 | PORDCR | 53 | ∞ | Application document posted |
| 748752 | PORDCR | 53 | ∞ | Application document posted |

*Figure 7-53.* *Process step 14—IDocs processed after correction of input data, etc.*

*IDocs* 743751 and 743752 have been successfully posted snf PO created—status code 53, as shown in Figure 7-53. Let us view the details of *IDoc* 743752 corresponding to PO 102. We double-clicked *IDoc* number 743750 and the screen shown in Figure 7-54 appeared.

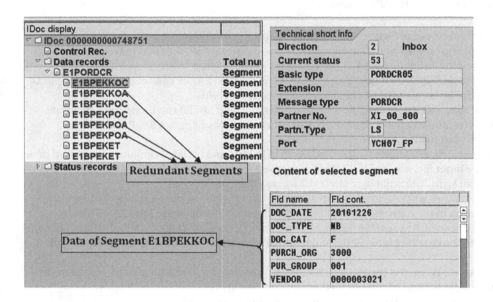

*Figure 7-54.* *Process step 14—IDoc 743752 details*

In Figure 7-54, we expanded the node *Data records* and the subnode E1PORDCR under it. The redundant *segments—segments* whose fields were not assigned any values—E1BPEKKOA and E1BPEKPOA are marked in Figure 7-54. We had incorporated the redundant *segments* to demonstrate that whatever *segments* you make assignments to in process step 4—*Maintain Structure Relations*—will appear in the *IDoc* reviews.

We selected the *segment* E1BPEKKOC. The field values of the selected *segments* appear in the bottom right corner of Figure 7-54.

The first time we had submitted the data of input PO 101 and PO 102, the input of PO 101 was accepted and the input of errorprone PO 102 was rejected, and so one purchase order was successfully created.

After correction to the input text file of PO 102, we submitted the input data of POs 101 and 102. The input data of POs 101 and 102 was accepted, thereby resulting in the successful creation of two purchase orders. In total, three purchase orders were created in the two submissions of input data.

This concludes process step 14. We navigated back to the process steps screen.

# Process Step 15—Create IDoc Overview

From the screen of process steps, we executed process step 15. In process step 15, we can view the *IDocs* created and processed. When you execute process step 15, the elaborate selection screen exactly like the one in process step 14 for input appears. The values from creation of latest *IDocs* for the fields *Created on*, *Created at*, *Message Type*, etc., are picked up and appear as default values on the selection screen. When you click the Execute button on the selection screen, the *IDocs* fulfilling field values on the selection screen are listed.

We entered 26.12.2016 in the field *Created on* and clicked Execute button. A list containing the four *IDocs* created in the current hands-on exercise appeared as shown in Figure 7-55.

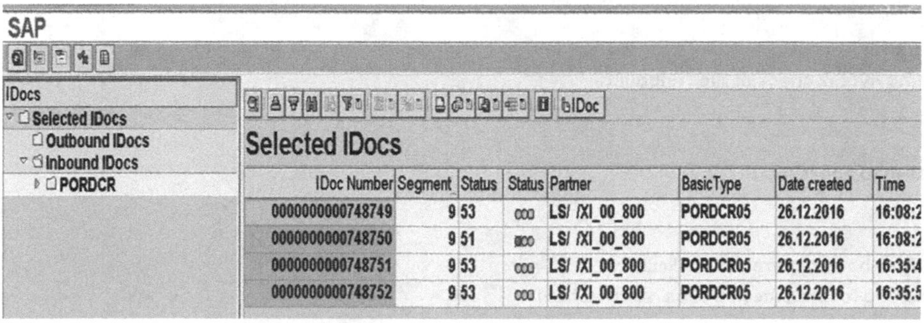

*Figure 7-55.* *Process step 15—selected IDocs list*

You can view details of each *IDoc* like control info, data, and status info by double-clicking an *IDoc* as in process step 14.

The *IDocs* list produced in this process step contains more columns than the *IDocs* list produced in process step 14.

# Process Step 16—Start IDoc Follow-Up

Process step 16 is to resubmit error *IDocs* again for processing. When the process step is executed, a screen as shown in Figure 7-56 appeared.

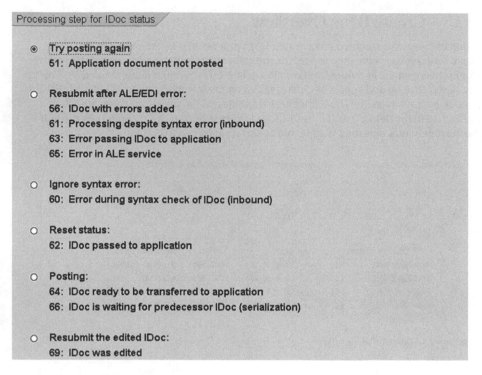

**Figure 7-56.** *Process step 16—Start IDoc Follow-Up*

The screen in Figure 7-56 offers of the ability to select a scenario of error *IDocs* to be resubmitted for processing.

There are whole lot of facilities to make corrections to error *IDocs*, submit corrected *IDocs* for processing, etc. The description of these facilities is beyond the scope of this book.

This concludes the process step 16, the last process step.

## Purchase Orders Created—Cross-Verification with Input Data

We will now verify the three purchase orders that were created as per the input data. To verify the creation of purchase orders, we navigated to the opening screen of transaction code ME22N—*Change Purchase Order*. On the opening screen of transaction code ME22N, we made the menu selection Purchase Orders ➤ Other Purchase Order as shown in Figure 7-57.

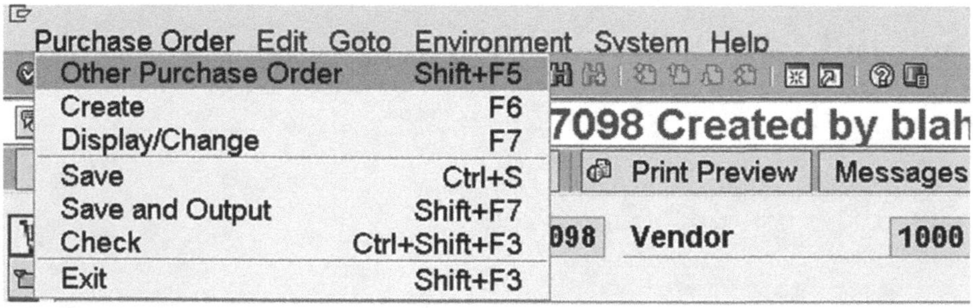

**Figure 7-57.** *Transaction code ME22N—menu selection*

The menu selection popped up a dialog box as shown in Figure 7-58.

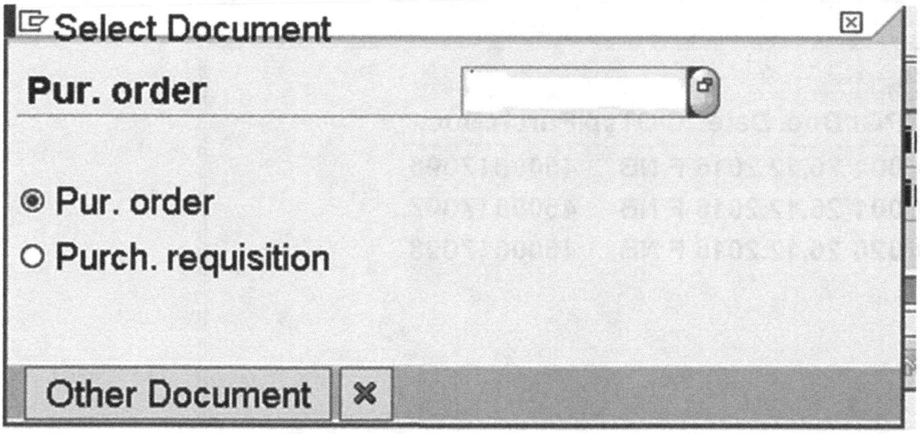

**Figure 7-58.** *Select Document—purchase order*

We pressed function key F4 for a selection list. The dialog box to filter purchasing documents appeared as shown in Figure 7-59.

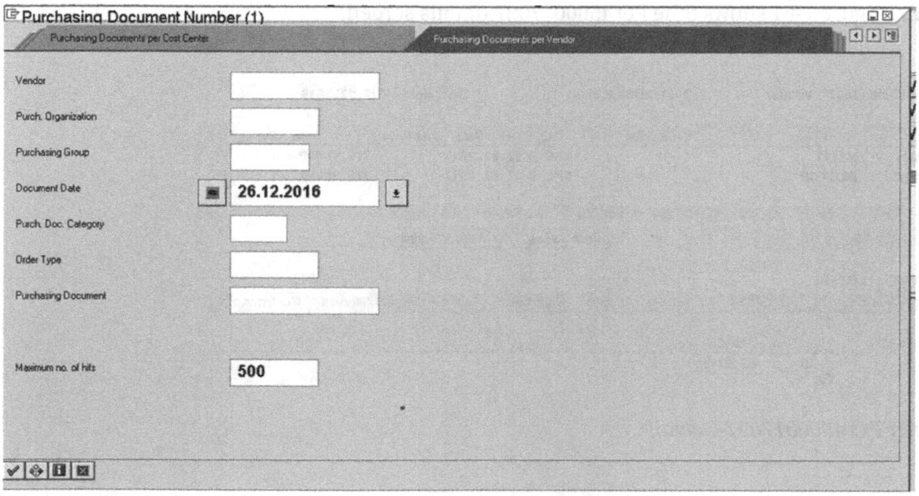

**Figure 7-59.** *Select Document—purchase order: filter dialog box*

We want to view a list containing only the purchase orders created through the current hands-on exercise. We are able to filter out the purchase orders created in the current hands-on exercise by entering in the field *Document Date* the value of 26.12.2016 as shown in Figure 7-59. We clicked the Continue button on the filter dialog box. A list containing the three purchase orders with *Document Date* as 26.12.2016 appeared as shown in Figure 7-60.

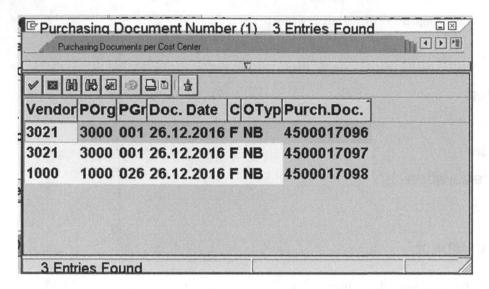

*Figure 7-60. Selected purchase orders—document date = 26.12.2016*

The POs 4500017096 and 4500017097 have identical data; each of them contains two materials, with a single delivery date for each of materials. Viewing any one of them for verification will suffice.

From the list, we selected PO 4500017097, which contains two materials, with a single delivery date for each of the materials. Figure 7-61 shows thhe PO 4500017097 details screen.

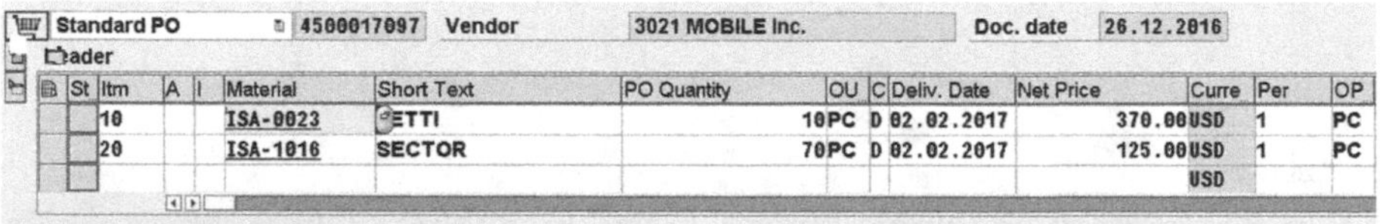

*Figure 7-61. Selected PO 4500017097—detail*

As you can observe in Figure 7-61, the header data has been created as per our input data.

> *Document Type and Category*: Standard PO

> *Vendor*: 3021

> *Doc. Date*: 26.12.2016

If you click the button ⊡ at the top left corner, you can view the two additional fields of the header data (tab—Org. Data) as shown in Figure 7-62.

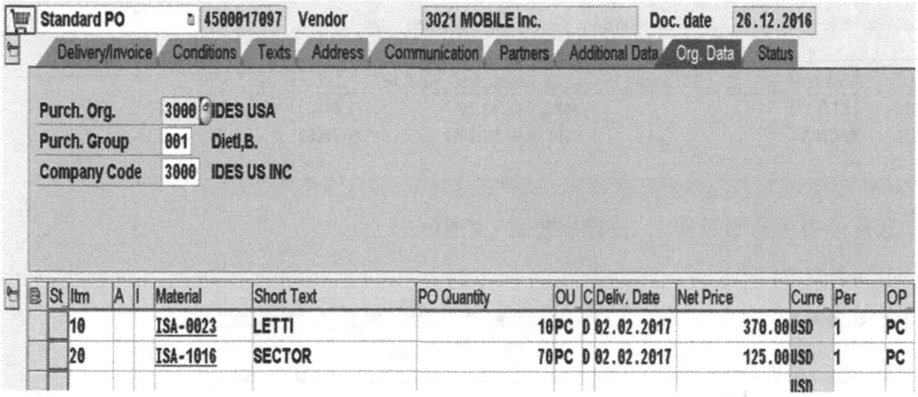

**Figure 7-62.** *Purchase Order 4500017097—tab: Org. Data*

As you can see in Figure 7-62, the additional header data has been created as per our input data.

*Purch. Org.*: 3000

*Purch. Group*: 001

The item data for the two materials except for net price has been created as per our input data.

*Itm*: 10 and 20

*Material*: ISA-0023 and ISA-1016

*PO Quantity*: 10 PC and 70 PC

*Net Price*: 370.00 and 125.00 [not as per input data]

If you scroll to the right, you can view the two additional fields *Matl. Group* and *Plnt.* of the item data as shown in Figure 7-63.

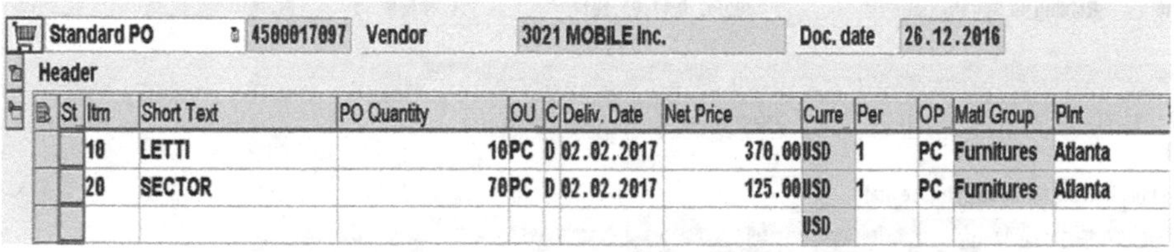

**Figure 7-63.** *Purchase Order 4500017097—item data: Matl. Group and Plnt*

The additional item data has been created as per our input data.

*Matl Group (Material Group)*: 060 and 060 (Furnitures)

*Plnt (Plant)*: 3200 and 3200 (Atlanta)

Figure 7-64 shows the delivery data for the two materials.

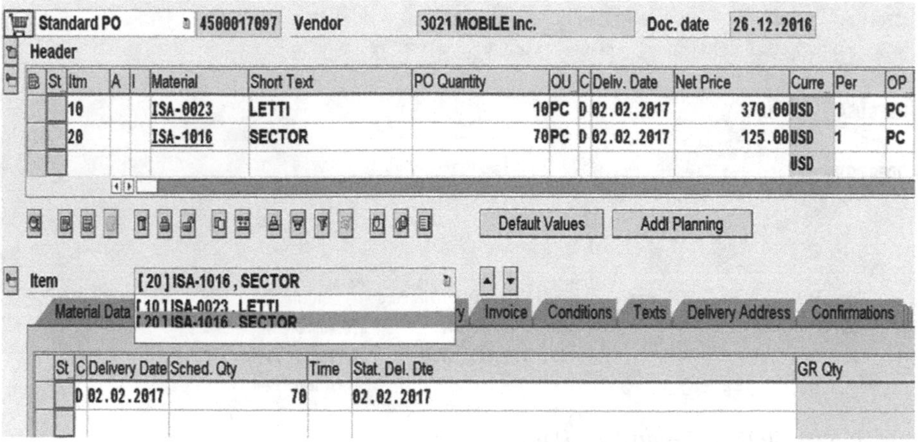

*Figure 7-64.* *Purchase Order 4500017097—item 20 delivery date*

The delivery data for the two materials has been created as per our input data.

> *Itm*: 10 and 20
>
> *Delivery Date*: 02.02.2017 and 02.02.2017
>
> *Sch. Qty*: 10 PC and 70 PC

Having verified the creation of PO 4500017097 as per the input data except net price, we next fetched the details of PO 4500017098, which contains only one material, with two delivery dates for the material. Figure 7-65 shows the PO 4500017098 details screen.

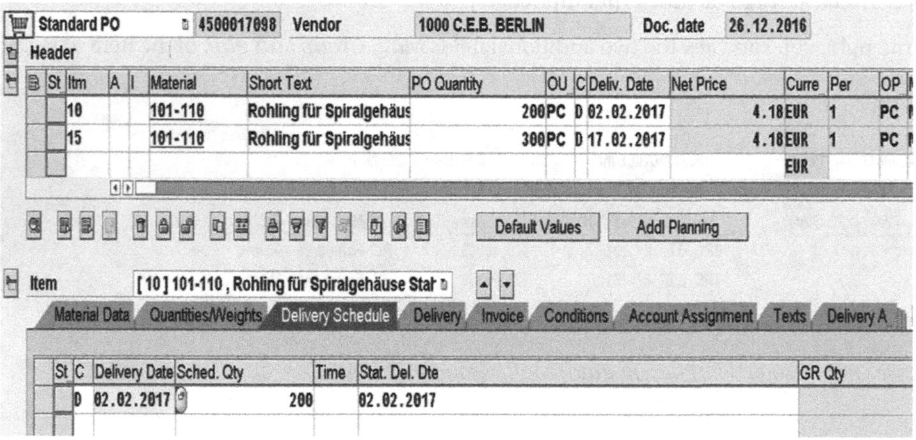

*Figure 7-65.* *Selected PO 4500017098—detail*

As you can see in Figure 7-65, the header data has been created as per our input data.

> *Document Type and Category*: Standard PO
>
> *Vendor*: 1000
>
> *Doc. Date*: 26.12.2016

If you click on the button ⬚ at the top left corner, you can view the two additional fields of the header data (tab—Org. Data) as follows:

*Purch. Org.*: 1000

*Purch. Group*: 026

The item data for the single material (101-110 split into two items) except for net price has been created as per our input data.

*Itm*: 10 and 15

*Material*: 101-110 and 101-110

*PO Quantity*: 200 PC and 300 PC

*Net Price*: 5.05 and 5.05 [not as per input data]

If you scroll to the right, you can view the two additional fields of the item data as follows:

*Matl Group (Material Group)*: 001 and 001 (Metal processing)

*Plnt (Plant)*: 1000 and 1000 (Werk Hamburg)

Figure 7-66 shows the delivery data for the single material.

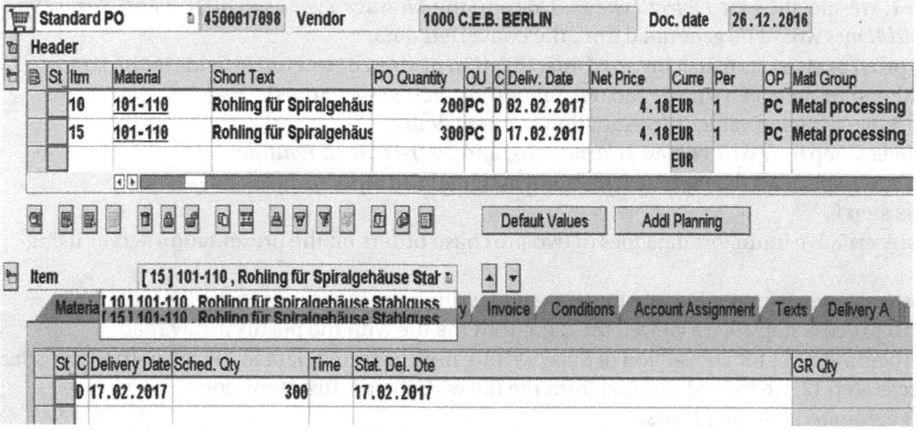

***Figure 7-66.*** *Purchase Order 4500017098—item 15 delivery date*

The delivery data for the single material has been created as per our input data.

*Itm*: 10 and 15

*Delivery Date*: 02.02.2017 and 17.02.2017

*Sch. Qty*: 200 PC and 300 PC

We have verified that the two purchase orders were created as per the input data and specifications except for the following:

- The net price destination field E1BPEKPOC-NET_PRICE is not getting assigned a value from the input data, but instead is being assigned a value from info records.

- Multiple delivery dates for a material is getting created only if you have as many items as number of delivery dates.

We will rectify these deficiencies in the next hands-on exercise.

This concludes the cross-verification of purchase orders created with input data.

# Hands-on Exercise III—Recapitulation

The hands-on exercise set out to transfer the data of purchase orders from two text files residing on the presentation server into the SAP functional module database tables from the LSMW environment deploying the *Object Type* as *IDoc*.

We started off by describing the scope and specifications of the hands-on exercise. We identified the database tables whose fields will assume values. We further identified which of the fields will assume constant values and which of the fields will be assigned values from input files, etc.

We performed the *Settings* for *IDoc Inbound Processing*.

We initially created the *Subproject* YCH07_PO under the existing *Project* YCH06_DM.

We then created the *Object* YCH07_IDOC under the *Project* YCH06_DM and *Subproject* YCH07_PO.

In process step 1, we specified the *Object Type* as *IDoc* and the *Message Type* as PORDCR and *Basic Type* PORDCR05. *Inbound IDocs* would be generated from the converted data,

The next three process steps, as usual, involved specification of source structures, fields in the source structures, and relationships between source and destination *segments* (structures).

In process step 5, we assigned values to destination *segment* fields.

We skipped process step 6—*Fixed Values, Translations,* and *User-Defined Routines*.

In process step 7, we specified the input text files and assigned the input text files to the source structures in process step 8.

We created representative input text data files of two purchase orders on the presentation server using the note pad editor.

We executed process step 9 for reading of input data and writing the input data to the file with the postfix .lsmw.read. In process step 10, we viewed the data from the file with the postfix .lsmw.read.

We executed process step 11 for conversion of data, writing the converted data to the file with the postfix .lsmw.conv. In process step 12, we viewed the data from the file with the postfix .lsmw.conv.

Process step 13 generated *inbound IDocs*.

In process step 14, the generated *inbound IDocs* were processed or posted to the application—transferred to the SAP functional module database tables. Process step 14 also provided for a review of just processed *IDocs*.

Process step 15 provided for a review of *IDocs*. Process step 16 provided for the resubmission of *IDocs* with errors for posting. We did not perform process step 16.

We performed a visual cross-verification that the purchase orders were created as per the input data (with certain exceptions) using transaction code ME22N.

This concludes hands-on exercise III.

# Hands-on Exercise IV—Migration of Purchase Order Data Using *Business Object Method*

In this hands-on exercise, we will transfer the data of purchase orders residing in input text files on the presentation server into the SAP functional module database tables deploying the *BAPI method* of LSMW. We will perform the data transfer with representative data of two or three purchase orders. We will perform the data transfer providing values for the 18 fields as in hands-on exercise III.

The *BAPI* method of LSMW for purchase orders creates *IDocs* as in hands-on exercise III of this chapter. The *BAPI* method to create purchase orders uses the same *Message Type/IDoc Basic Type* as in hands-on exercise IIIPORDCR/PORDCR05. So, the LSMW process steps in the current hands-on exercise are identical to those process steps of hands-on exercise III. The *Settings for IDoc Inbound Processing* performed in hands-on exercise III will serve us in the current hands-on exercise as well.

## Deficiencies of Hands-on Exercise III—Rectification

We will rectify the deficiencies of hands-on exercise III. In hands-on exercise III, the net price—destination field E1BPELPOC-NET_PRICE—was not getting assigned the value we were supplying from the input text file PO items data. By default, the destination field E1BPELPOC-NET_PRICE is assigned a value from info records. If you want the default value assignment from the info records to the destination field E1BPELPOC-NET_PRICE to be overruled, you have to set the destination field E1BPEKPOC-PO_PRICE to X.

Again, in hands-on exercise III, we were unable to create properly multiple delivery dates for an item. For instance, a purchase order has an item A with quantity 500 pieces. Item A is to be delivered in two lots. The first lot quantity 300 pieces is to be delivered on a specified date and the second lot quantity 200 pieces is to be delivered on another specified date. For the scenario described, the database table EKPO must contain one row for the item A, with the total quantity of 500 pieces. The database table EKET must contain two rows for the item A, with the corresponding quantities of 300 pieces and 200 pieces to be delivered on different dates.

In hands-on exercise III, the problem was the manner in which we were providing the input data of items and item deliveries. The destination field E1BPEKPOC-PO_ITEM cannot receive duplicate values for a purchase order. The destination field E1BPEKET-PO_ITEM can receive duplicate values for a purchase order—multiple delivery dates. We had combined the data of fields of the *segments* E1BPEKPOC and E1BPEKET into single input file, thus creating the possibility of providing duplicate values for the destination field E1BPEKPOC-PO_ITEM.

In the present hands-on exercise, we will provide the data for fields of the *segments* E1BPEKPOC and E1BPEKET from two separate input files. The values for the destination fields E1BPEKPOC-PO_ITEM and E1BPEKET-PO_ITEM will be received from two different input structure fields instead of a single input structure field as in hands-on exercise III.

So, in the current hands-on exercise, we will locate the input data in three text files instead of the two input text files in hands-on exercise III. The first input file will be designated the PO header data. The second input file will be designated the PO items data. The third input file will be designated the PO delivery data.

A detailed description of specification, scope, and LSMW process steps follows.

## Specification and Scope

The hands-on exercise will transfer data from three text files into the purchase orders' functional module database tables using the *BAPI* method of LSMW. It is assumed that input data in the form of text files is in the required form and conversions have been effected. The input data in the form of text files will reside on and be accessed from the presentation server. The input will consist of the three text files: (1) PO header data, (2) PO items data, and (3) PO delivery data. The three text files will be related through the purchase order number. We will maintain the text data with notepad editor on the presentation server.

Other specifications of the current hands-on exercise are identical to those of hands-on exercise III in this chapter.

The following fields (see Table 7-10) will assume the same constant values for all the purchase orders being migrated.

*Table 7-10.* *Fields with Constant Values*

| Srl. No. | Field Name (Database Table) | Field Name (*IDoc Segment*) | Field Description | Value |
|---|---|---|---|---|
| 1 | EKKO-BEDAT | E1BPEKKOC-DOC_DATE | Purchasing Document Date | SY-DATUM |
| 2 | EKKO-BSTYP | E1BPEKKOC-DOC_CAT | Purchasing Document Category | F |
| 3 | EKKO-BSART | E1BPEKKOC-DOC_TYPE | Purchasing Document Type | NB |
| 4 | | E1BPEKPOC-PO_PRICE | Indicator – Adopt Price | X |

■ **Caution**    Before you adopt the values for field numbers 2 and 3, check the validity of these values on your system. If you are operating on an IDES server and logged into client 800, the foregoing values should be all right.

The values for the fields in Tablle 7-11 will originate from the text file PO header data.

*Table 7-11.* *Fields with Values Originating from Text File—PO Header Data*

| Srl. No. | Field Name (Database Table) | Field Name (*IDoc Segment*) | Field Description |
|---|---|---|---|
| 1 | EKKO-EBELN | E1BPEKKOC-PO_NUMBER | Purchasing Document Number |
| 2 | EKKO-LIFNR | E1BPEKKOC-VENDOR | Vendor Number/Code |
| 3 | EKKO-EKORG | E1BPEKKOC-PURCH_ORG | Purchasing Organization |
| 4 | EKKO-EKGRP | E1BPEKKOC-PUR_GROUP | Purchasing Group |

The values for the fields in Table 7-12 will originate from the text file PO items data.

***Table 7-12.*** *Fields with Values Originating from Text File—PO Items Data*

| Srl. No. | Field Name (Database Table) | Field Name (*IDoc Segment*) | Field Description |
|---|---|---|---|
| 1 | EKPO-EBELN | E1BPEKPOC-PO_NUMBER | Purchasing Document Number |
| 2 | EKPO-MATNR | E1BPEKPOC-PUR_MAT | Material Number/Code |
| 3 | EKPO-EBELP | E1BPEKPOC-PO_ITEM | Item Number of Purchasing Document |
| 4 | EKPO-NETPR | E1BPEKPOC-NET_PRICE | Net Price in Purchasing Document |
| 5 | EKPO-MATKL | E1BPEKPOC-MAT_GRP | Material Group |
| 6 | EKPO-WERKS | E1BPEKPOC-PLANT | Plant to which Material to be Delivered |

Recall, the field EBELN in the PO items data is for connecting the PO items data with the PO header data, which items belong to which PO?

The values for the fields in Table 7-13 will originate from the text file PO delivery data.

***Table 7-13.*** *Fields with Values Originating from Text File—PO Delivery Data*

| Srl. No. | Field Name (Database Table) | Field Name (*IDoc Segment*) | Field Description |
|---|---|---|---|
| 1 | EKET-EBELN | E1BPEKET-PO_NUMBER | Purchasing Document Number |
| 2 | EKET-EBELP | E1BPEKET-PO_ITEM | Item Number of Purchasing Document |
| 3 | EKET-ETENR | E1BPEKET-SERIAL_NO | Delivery Schedule Line Counter or Number |
| 4 | EKET-MENGE | E1BPEKET-QUANTITY | Scheduled Quantity |
| 5 | EKET-EINDT | E1BPEKET-DELIV_DATE | Item Delivery Date |

The fields EBELN and EBELP in the PO delivery data are for connecting the PO delivery data with the PO items data, which of the scheduled line numbers belongs to which PO and item number?

There will be a total of 19 fields which will assume values—four fields from Table 7-10, four fields from Table 7-11, six fields from Table 7-12, and five fields from Table 7-13.

Having described the specifications and scope of the hands-on exercise, we will proceed to the creation of the *Object* YCH07_PO_BAPI under the *Project* and *Subproject* YCH06_DM/YCH_07_PO. After the creation of the *Object* YCH07_PO_BAPI, we will look at the LSMW process steps.

## Create Object YCH07_BAPI

To create the *Object* YCH07_BAPI under the *Project/Subproject* YCH06_DM/YCH07_PO, we navigated to the opening screen of transaction code LSMW, entered the *Project* name as YCH06_DM, entered the *Subproject* name as YCH07_PO, and entered the *Object* name as YCH07_BAPI. We positioned the cursor on the *Object* field and clicked the Create button on the application toolbar. The dialog box to enter a description of the *Object* popped up. We entered a suitable description as shown in Figure 7-67.

| Create Object | | ⊠ |
|---|---|---|
| Project | YCH06_DM | |
| | Data Migration Project | |
| Subproject | YCH07_PO | |
| | Data Migration - Purchase Orders | |
| Object | YCH07_BAPI | |
| Name | Data Migration of Purchase Orders Using BAPI | |

| ✓ | ✗ |

*Figure 7-67.* *LSMW—Create Object YCH07_BAPI*

We clicked the Continue button and the *Object* YCH07_BAPI was created in the *Project* YCH06_DM and the *Subproject* YCH07_PO. Next, we have to perform the process steps.

To perform the process steps, we clicked the Execute button on the application toolbar on the LSMW opening screen.

We started off by executing process step 1 by selecting the Radio button and clicking the Execute button.

## Process Step 1—Maintain Object Attributes

We clicked the Display/Change toggle button on the application toolbar to enable changes on the screen.

On process step 1 screen, in the *Attributes area,* we entered and specified the following:

- Suitable description, which was already entered during creation of the Object.

- The *Owner* as the logged-in user, which is the default. We can assign any other valid user name.

- The data transfer Radio button: *Once Only.*

- The file names you are going to specify are not *System Specific*—check box disabled.

In the *Object Type and Import Method* area of the process step 1 screen, we clicked the *Object Type* Radio button as *Business Object Method (BAPI)*. We positioned the cursor in the field *Business Object* and pressed function key F4. Next, we pressed the keys ctrl + F to invoke the search dialog box. We entered the word "Purchase" in the search dialog box as shown in the Figure 7-68.

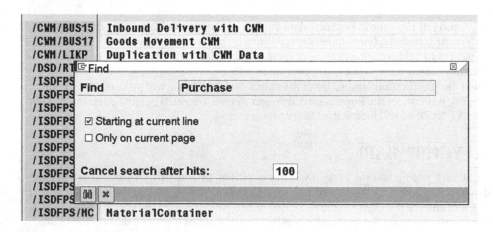

*Figure 7-68.* *Select business object—search dialog box*

We clicked the Continue button on the search dialog box. A list of entries with the word "Purchase" was returned as shown in Figure 7-69.

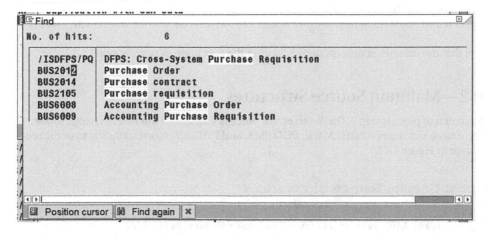

*Figure 7-69.* *Select business object—list with word "purchase"*

From the *Business Object* list, we selected the entry BUS2012 —Purchase Order. We selected the method as CREATEFROMDATA. Figure 7-70 shows the screen with all the entries and assignments.

| Object | YCH07_BAPI | Data Migration of Purchase Orders Using BAPI |
| --- | --- | --- |
| Owner | SAPUSER | blah |
| Data Transfer | ⊙ Once-Only | ○ Periodic |
| File Names | ☐ System-Dependent | |

**Object Type and Import Method**

○ Standard Batch/Direct Input

| Object | |
| --- | --- |
| Method | |
| Program Name | |
| Program Type | |

○ Batch Input Recording

| Recording | |
| --- | --- |

⊙ Business Object Method (BAPI)

| Business Object | BUS2012 | Purchase Order |
| --- | --- | --- |
| Method | CREATEFROMDATA | Create Purchase Order |
| Message Type | PORDCR | Create purchase order |
| Basic Type | PORDCR05 | Create Purchase Order |

○ IDoc (Intermediate Document)

*Figure 7-70.* *Process step 1: all entries and assignments*

From Figure 7-70, you can observe the *IDoc Message Type* assigned as PORDCR and the *IDoc Basic Type* assigned as PORDCR05. These values of the *IDoc Message Type* and the *IDoc Basic Type* are same as in hands-on exercise III. The *BAPI* method for creation or transfer of purchase orders uses the same *IDoc Message Type* and the *IDoc Basic Type* as the *IDoc* method.

We saved the screen and exited the screen of process step 1 to navigate back to the screen with process steps.

You can observe that the number of process steps is 16 after the execution of process step 1.

## Process Step 2—Maintain Source Structures

We navigated to the screen of process step 2. On the screen of process step 2, we switched to change mode. We created the three source structures—POHEADER, POITEMS, and PODELV—corresponding to our three input text files as shown in Figure 7-71.

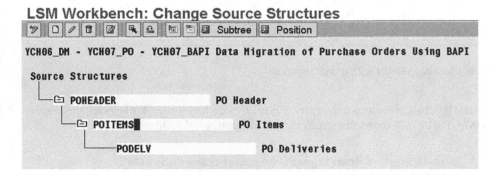

*Figure 7-71.* *Process step 2—Maintain Source Structure*

We saved and returned to the screen with process steps.

## Process Step 3—Maintain Source Fields

We executed process step 3. We switched the screen to change mode. We inserted the fields in the three source structures—POHEADER, POITEMS, and PODELV—as shown in Figure 7-72.

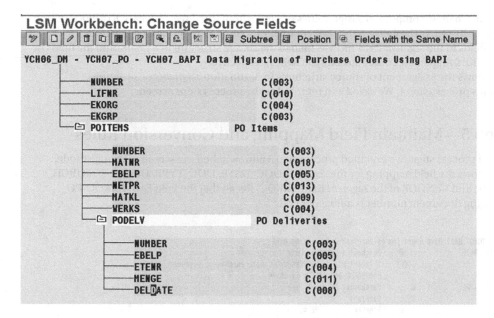

**Figure 7-72.** *Process step 3—create source field: all fields under three source structures created*

The order of the fields in the source structure must be identical to the order in which data is located in the text files. We are using text files with one line for one row of data, with comma (,) as a field separator.

We saved and returned to the process steps screen.

## Process Step 4—Maintain Structure Relations

We executed process step 4 and switched the screen to change mode.

Our destination structures are the *segments* (structures) including the super structure *segment* E1PORDCR (see Figure 7-73).

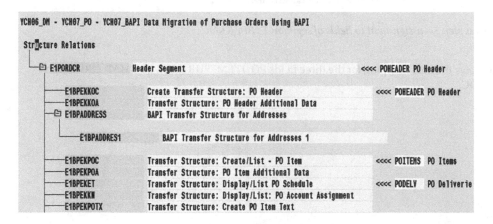

**Figure 7-73.** *Process step 4—Maintain Structure Relations*

The 19 fields to which we propose to assign values originate from the three *segments*: E1BPEKKOC, E1BPEKPOC, and E1BPEKET. The fields in the *segment* E1BPEKKOC map to the source structure POHEADER, the fields in the *segment* E1BPEKPOC map to the source structure POITEMS, and the fields in the *segment* E1BPEKET map to the source structure PODELV, respectively.

Figure 7-73 shows the assignment of source structures to destination *segments* or structures.

This completes process step 4. We saved and returned to the process steps screen.

## Process Step 5—Maintain Field Mapping and Conversion Rules

From the screen of process steps, we executed process step 5 and switched the screen to change mode.

Figure 7-74 shows the field mapping for the six fields DOC_DATE, DOC_TYPE, DOC_CAT, PURCH_ORG, PUR_GROUP, and VENDOR of the *segment* E1BPEKKOC. Recall that the field E1BPEKKOC-PO_NUMBER purchasing document number is autogenerated.

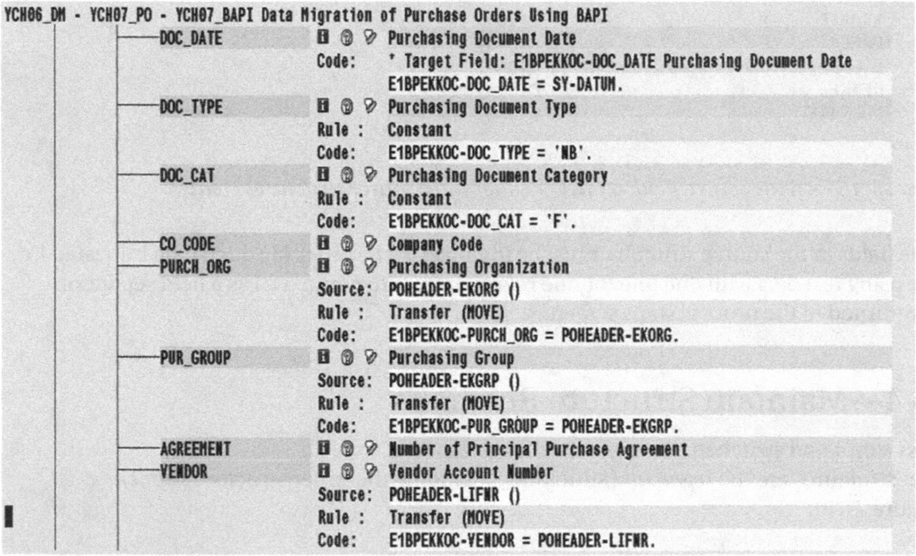

```
YCH06_DM - YCH07_PO - YCH07_BAPI Data Migration of Purchase Orders Using BAPI
          ──DOC_DATE          ⊞ ⊕ ▽ Purchasing Document Date
                              Code:   ' Target Field: E1BPEKKOC-DOC_DATE Purchasing Document Date
                                      E1BPEKKOC-DOC_DATE = SY-DATUM.
          ──DOC_TYPE          ⊞ ⊕ ▽ Purchasing Document Type
                              Rule :  Constant
                              Code:   E1BPEKKOC-DOC_TYPE = 'NB'.
          ──DOC_CAT           ⊞ ⊕ ▽ Purchasing Document Category
                              Rule :  Constant
                              Code:   E1BPEKKOC-DOC_CAT = 'F'.
          ──CO_CODE           ⊞ ⊕ ▽ Company Code
          ──PURCH_ORG         ⊞ ⊕ ▽ Purchasing Organization
                              Source: POHEADER-EKORG ()
                              Rule :  Transfer (MOVE)
                              Code:   E1BPEKKOC-PURCH_ORG = POHEADER-EKORG.
          ──PUR_GROUP         ⊞ ⊕ ▽ Purchasing Group
                              Source: POHEADER-EKGRP ()
                              Rule :  Transfer (MOVE)
                              Code:   E1BPEKKOC-PUR_GROUP = POHEADER-EKGRP.
          ──AGREEMENT         ⊞ ⊕ ▽ Number of Principal Purchase Agreement
          ──VENDOR            ⊞ ⊕ ▽ Vendor Account Number
                              Source: POHEADER-LIFNR ()
                              Rule :  Transfer (MOVE)
                              Code:   E1BPEKKOC-VENDOR = POHEADER-LIFNR.
```

*Figure 7-74. Process step 5—assignment to fields of segment E1BPEKKOC*

Figure 7-75 shows the field mapping for the three fields PO_ITEM, PUR_MAT, and MAT_GRP of the *segment* E1BPEKPOC.

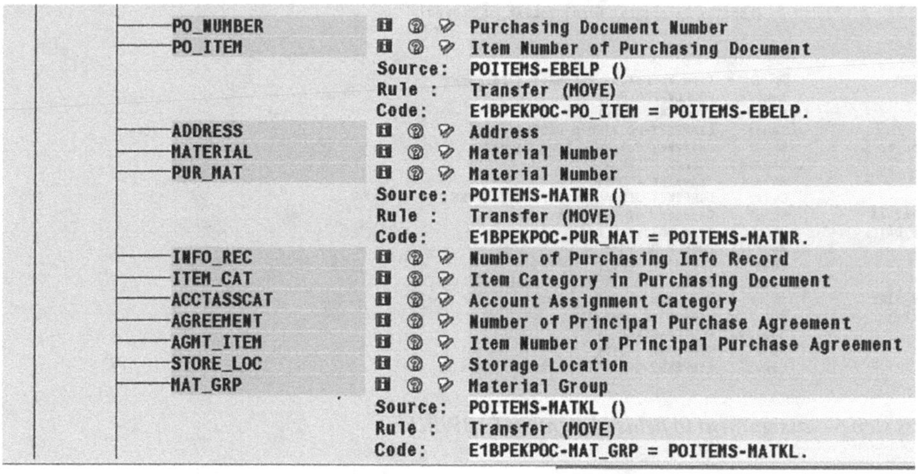

```
       PO_NUMBER        ⊞ ⊗ ▽ Purchasing Document Number
       PO_ITEM          ⊞ ⊗ ▽ Item Number of Purchasing Document
                        Source:  POITEMS-EBELP ()
                        Rule :   Transfer (MOVE)
                        Code:    E1BPEKPOC-PO_ITEM = POITEMS-EBELP.
       ADDRESS          ⊞ ⊗ ▽ Address
       MATERIAL         ⊞ ⊗ ▽ Material Number
       PUR_MAT          ⊞ ⊗ ▽ Material Number
                        Source:  POITEMS-MATNR ()
                        Rule :   Transfer (MOVE)
                        Code:    E1BPEKPOC-PUR_MAT = POITEMS-MATNR.
       INFO_REC         ⊞ ⊗ ▽ Number of Purchasing Info Record
       ITEM_CAT         ⊞ ⊗ ▽ Item Category in Purchasing Document
       ACCTASSCAT       ⊞ ⊗ ▽ Account Assignment Category
       AGREEMENT        ⊞ ⊗ ▽ Number of Principal Purchase Agreement
       AGMT_ITEM        ⊞ ⊗ ▽ Item Number of Principal Purchase Agreement
       STORE_LOC        ⊞ ⊗ ▽ Storage Location
       MAT_GRP          ⊞ ⊗ ▽ Material Group
                        Source:  POITEMS-MATKL ()
                        Rule :   Transfer (MOVE)
                        Code:    E1BPEKPOC-MAT_GRP = POITEMS-MATKL.
```

***Figure 7-75.*** *Process step 5—assignment to fields of segment E1BPEKPOC - I*

Figure 7-76 shows the field mapping for the two fields PLANT and NET_PRICE of the *segment* E1BPEKPOC.

```
       KANBAN_IND       ⊞ ⊗ ▽ Kanban Indicator
       PLANT            ⊞ ⊗ ▽ Plant
                        Source:  POITEMS-WERKS ()
                        Rule :   Transfer (MOVE)
                        Code:    E1BPEKPOC-PLANT = POITEMS-WERKS.
       ALLOC_TBL        ⊞ ⊗ ▽ Allocation Table Number
       AT_ITEM          ⊞ ⊗ ▽ Item number of allocation table
       UNIT             ⊞ ⊗ ▽ Purchase Order Unit of Measure
       NET_PRICE        ⊞ ⊗ ▽ Net price in purchasing document (in document currency)
                        Source:  POITEMS-NETPR ()
                        Rule :   Transfer (MOVE)
                        Code:    E1BPEKPOC-NET_PRICE = POITEMS-NETPR.
```

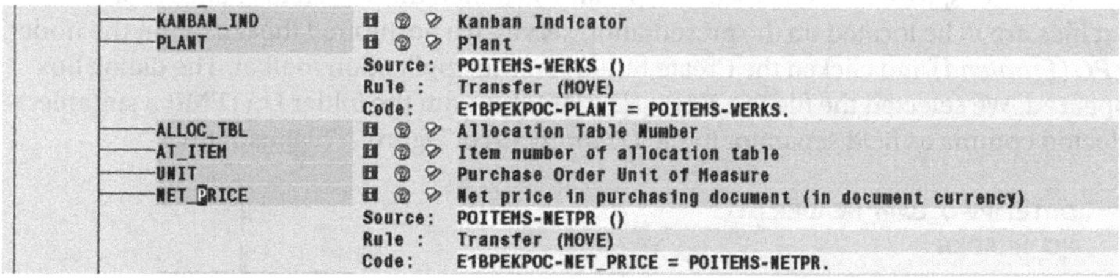

***Figure 7-76.*** *Process step 5—assignment to fields of segment E1BPEKPOC—II*

Figure 7-77 shows the field mapping for the field PO_PRICE of the *segment* E1BPEKPOC.

```
       MFR_NO_EXT       ⊞ ⊗ ▽ External manufacturer code name or number
       PO_PRICE         ⊞ ⊗ ▽ Indicator: adopt price - do not use info record
                        Code:    * Target Field: E1BPEKPOC-PO_PRICE Indicator: adopt price - do n
                                 E1BPEKPOC-PO_PRICE = 'X'.
       SHIPPING         ⊞ ⊗ ▽ Shipping Instructions
```

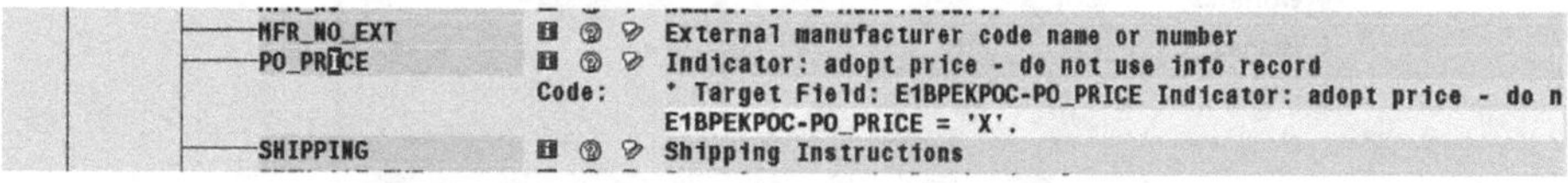

***Figure 7-77.*** *Process step 5—assignment to fields of segment E1BPEKPOC—III*

Figure 7-78 shows the field mapping for four fields PO_ITEM, SERIAL_NO, DELV_DATE, and QUANTITY of the *segment* E1BPEKET.

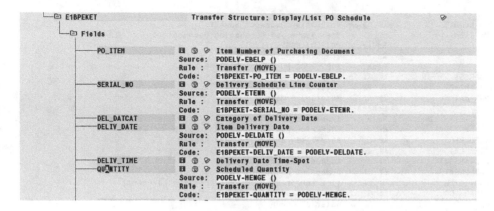

**Figure 7-78.** *Process step 5—assignment to fields of segment E1BPEKET*

We performed a validity check (ctrl + F2 or sixth button from the left on the application toolbar). We saved the changes and returned to the process steps screen.

## Process Step 7—*Specify Files*

From the screen of process steps, we executed process step 7 and switched the screen to change mode.

As the input text files are to be located on the presentation server, we positioned the cursor on the node *Legacy Data on the PC (Frontend)* and clicked the Create button on the application toolbar. The dialog box input file entries appeared. We selected the file PO_BAPI_HEADER.txt from the folder D:\TEMP, a suitable description, and selected comma as field separator in the *Delimiter* area. Figure 7-79 illustrates.

| File | D:\TEMP\PO_BAPI_HEADER.txt |
| --- | --- |
| Name | PO_HEADER |

**File Contents**
- ⦿ Data for One Source Structure (Table)
- ○ Data for Multiple Source Structures (Seq. File)

**Delimiter**
- ○ No Separator
- ○ Tabulator
- ○ Semi-Colon
- ⦿ Comma
- ○ Blanks
- ○ Other

**File Structure**
- ☐ Field Names at Start of File
- ☑ Field Order Matches Source Structure Definition

**File Type**
- ⦿ Record End Marker (Text File)
- ○ Fixed Rec. Length (Bin.File)
- ○ Hexadecimal Lth Field (4 Bytes) at Start of Record

**Code Page**
- ⦿ ASCII
- ○ IBM DOS

**Figure 7-79.** *Process step 7—specify file: PO_BAPI_HEADER.txt*

We clicked the Continue button on the dialog box. The file PO_BAPI_HEADER.txt got specified. In a similar manner we specified the two other files: PO_BAPI_ITEM.txt and PO_BAPI_DELV.txt. Figure 7-80

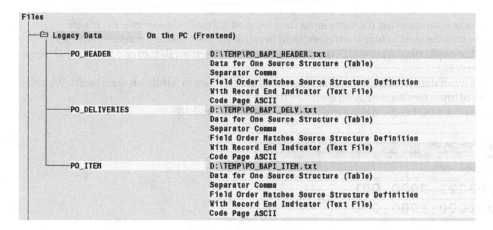

**Figure 7-80.** *Process step 7—files PO_BAPI_HEADER, PO_BAPI_ITEM, PO_BAPI_DELV*

shows the screen with all the three files specified.

We saved the changes on the screen of process step 7.

This concludes the process step 7. We navigated back to the process steps screen.

## Process Step 8—*Assign Files*

From the screen of process steps, we executed process step 8 and switched the screen to change mode.

We assigned the input text files to the respective source structures.

Figure 7-81 shows the screen after the assignment of three input files to the three source structures.

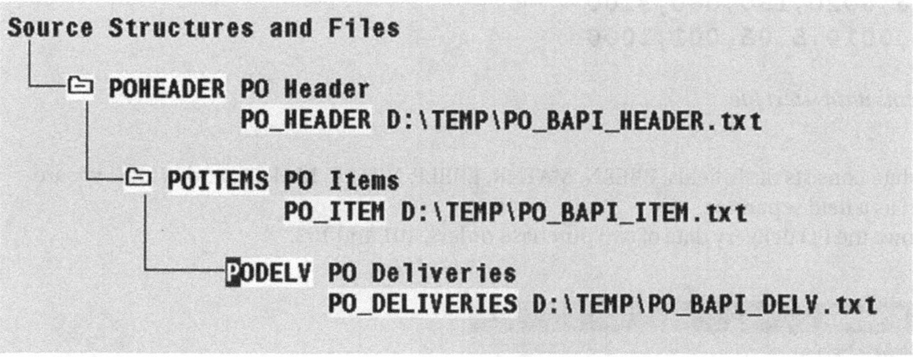

```
Source Structures and Files
    └─ 🗁 POHEADER PO Header
                PO_HEADER D:\TEMP\PO_BAPI_HEADER.txt

        └─ 🗁 POITEMS PO Items
                    PO_ITEM D:\TEMP\PO_BAPI_ITEM.txt

            └─ 🗁 PODELV PO Deliveries
                        PO_DELIVERIES D:\TEMP\PO_BAPI_DELV.txt
```

**Figure 7-81.** *Process step 8—files assigned to source structures*

We saved the changes on the screen of process step 8.

This concludes process step 8. We navigated back to the process steps screen.

## Data Creation on Presentation Server

I will digress from the process steps of LSMW to describe the creation of input text files on the presentation server.

In terms of contents, we are using the same input data we used in hands-on exercise III. We are able to use the same data we used in hands-on exercise III because the purchasing document number is autogenerated. We have split the data of the PO items file of hands-on exercise III into two files: (1) PO items file and (2) PO delivery file.

So, we have the input data located in three files instead of the two files in hands-on exercise III. We are using a different set of input files for hands-on exercises III and IV.

Figure 7-82 shows the PO header data of two purchase orders, 101 and 102.

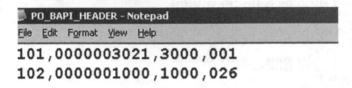

```
PO_BAPI_HEADER - Notepad
File  Edit  Format  View  Help
101,0000003021,3000,001
102,0000001000,1000,026
```

*Figure 7-82.* PO header data—text file

The PO header data consists of four fields: EBELN, LIFNR, EKORG, and EKGRP. We are using comma (,) as a field separator. We have entered the data of the field LIFNR with leading zeroes, although it is not necessary. The values for the field EBELN (101 and 102) serve the purpose of linking the items and deliveries to the purchasing documents. The purchasing document numbers will be autogenerated in the database tables. The PO header data is the same as we used in hands-on exercise III.

Figure 7-83 shows the PO items data of two purchase orders, 101 and 102.

```
PO_BAPI_ITEM - Notepad
File  Edit  Format  View  Help
101,ISA-0023,0010,380,060,3200
101,ISA-1016,0020,130,060,3200
102,101-110,0010,5.05,001,1000
```

*Figure 7-83.* PO items data—text file

The PO items data consists of six fields: EBELN, MATNR, EBELP, NETPR, MAKTL, and WERK. We are using the comma (,) as a field separator.

Figure 7-84 shows the PO delivery data of two purchase orders, 101 and 102.

```
PO_BAPI_DELV - Notepad
File  Edit  Format  View  Help
101,0010,0001,10,20170210
101,0020,0001,70,20170205
102,0010,0001,200,20170205
102,0010,0002,300,20170220
```

*Figure 7-84.* PO delivery data—text file

578

The PO delivery data consists of five fields: EBELN, EBELP, ETENR, MENGE, and EINDT. We are using the comma (,) as a field separator. PO 102 consists of a single item, item number 0010. This single item is delivered on two dates.

The data in the PO items and PO delivery files is the same as the data in the PO items file of hands-on exercise III.

This concludes the creation of input text files on the presentation server. We will resume performance of LSMW process steps.

## Process Step 9—*Read Data*

From the screen of process steps, we executed process step 9.

In process step 9, data is fetched from the user-created input text files and assembled together for an entity–purchase order and stored in the file with the following postfix: .lsmw.read.

The execution of process step 9 produced an output of statistics of input text data read and written or imported as shown in Figure 7-85.

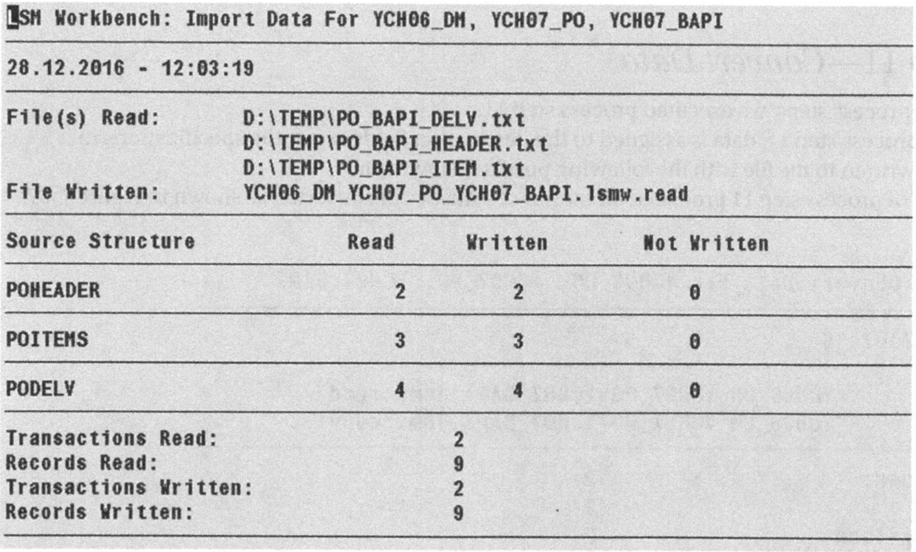

```
LSM Workbench: Import Data For YCH06_DM, YCH07_PO, YCH07_BAPI

28.12.2016 - 12:03:19

File(s) Read:      D:\TEMP\PO_BAPI_DELV.txt
                   D:\TEMP\PO_BAPI_HEADER.txt
                   D:\TEMP\PO_BAPI_ITEM.txt
File Written:      YCH06_DM_YCH07_PO_YCH07_BAPI.lsmw.read
```

| Source Structure | Read | Written | Not Written |
|---|---|---|---|
| POHEADER | 2 | 2 | 0 |
| POITEMS | 3 | 3 | 0 |
| PODELV | 4 | 4 | 0 |

```
Transactions Read:       2
Records Read:            9
Transactions Written:    2
Records Written:         9
```

*Figure 7-85. Process step 9—import data Output Screen*

The number of rows read into each of the source structures POHEADER, POITEMS, and PODELV is indicated in the output report of Figure 7-85.

This concludes process step 9. We navigated back to the process steps screen.

## Process Step 10—*Display Read Data*

The execution of process step 10 produced an output of the input text data read and written or imported as shown in Figure 7-86.

```
File      YCH06_DM_YCH07_PO_YCH07_BAPI.1smw.read

Row    Struct.                      Conts.

       LSMWYCH06_DM       YCH07_PO       YCH07_BAPI     DM0      80020161228120242SAPUSER

   1   POHEADER                      10100000030213000001
   2   POITEMS                       101ISA-0023           0010 380         060       3200
   3   PODELV                        1010010 000110            20170210
   4   POITEMS                       101ISA-1016           0020 130         060       3200
   5   PODELV                        1010020 000170            20170205
   6   POHEADER                      10200000010001000026
   7   POITEMS                       102101-110            0010 5.05        001       1000
   8   PODELV                        1020010 0001200           20170205
   9   PODELV                        1020010 0002300           20170220
```

*Figure 7-86.  Process step 10—display imported data*

You can click any of the lines to view the detail on a single screen.

This concludes the optional process step 10. We navigated back to the process steps screen.

# Process Step 11—*Convert Data*

From the screen of process steps, we executed process step 11.

Recall that in process step 11, data is assigned to the destination fields as per the specifications in process step 5 and written to the file with the following postfix: .lsmw.conv.

The execution of process step 11 produced an output of statistics of converted as shown in Figure 7-87.

```
LSM Workbench: Convert Data For YCH06_DM, YCH07_PO, YCH07_BAPI

28.12.2016 - 12:07:16

File Read:           YCH06_DM_YCH07_PO_YCH07_BAPI.1smw.read
File Written:        YCH06_DM_YCH07_PO_YCH07_BAPI.1smw.conv

Transactions Read:        2
Records Read:             9
Transactions Written:     2
Records Written:         13
```

*Figure 7-87.  Process step 11—Convert Data output screen*

Data is read from the input data file—file with postfix .lsmw.read—and written to the converted data file—file with postfix .lsmw.conv.

The rows written to the converted file appear as the *Records Written* line in Figure 7-87. The number of rows written to the converted file—13—will become apparent when you execute process step 12.

This concludes process step 11. We navigated back to the process steps screen.

## Process Step 12—Display Converted Data

The execution of process step 12 produced an output of the converted data as shown in Figure 7-88.

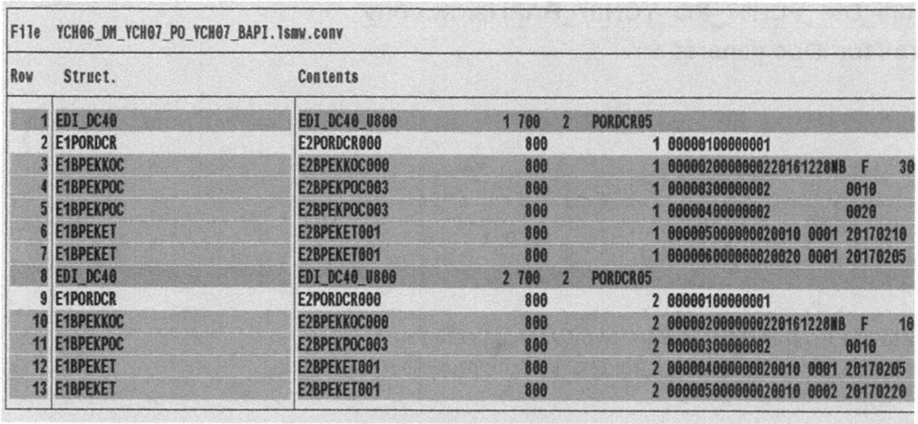

| File | YCH06_DM_YCH07_PO_YCH07_BAPI.lsmw.conv | | | | | |
|---|---|---|---|---|---|---|
| **Row** | **Struct.** | **Contents** | | | | |
| 1 | EDI_DC40 | EDI_DC40_U800 | 1 700 | 2 | PORDCR05 | |
| 2 | E1PORDCR | E2PORDCR000 | 800 | | 1 00000100000001 | |
| 3 | E1BPEKKOC | E2BPEKKOC000 | 800 | | 1 0000020000000220161228NB | F    30 |
| 4 | E1BPEKPOC | E2BPEKPOC003 | 800 | | 1 00000300000002      0010 | |
| 5 | E1BPEKPOC | E2BPEKPOC003 | 800 | | 1 00000400000002      0020 | |
| 6 | E1BPEKET | E2BPEKET001 | 800 | | 1 00000500000020010 0001 20170210 | |
| 7 | E1BPEKET | E2BPEKET001 | 800 | | 1 00000600000020020 0001 20170205 | |
| 8 | EDI_DC40 | EDI_DC40_U800 | 2 700 | 2 | PORDCR05 | |
| 9 | E1PORDCR | E2PORDCR000 | 800 | | 2 00000100000001 | |
| 10 | E1BPEKKOC | E2BPEKKOC000 | 800 | | 2 0000020000000220161228NB | F    10 |
| 11 | E1BPEKPOC | E2BPEKPOC003 | 800 | | 2 00000300000002      0010 | |
| 12 | E1BPEKET | E2BPEKET001 | 800 | | 2 00000400000020010 0001 20170205 | |
| 13 | E1BPEKET | E2BPEKET001 | 800 | | 2 00000500000020010 0002 20170220 | |

***Figure 7-88.*** *Process step 12—Display Converted Data*

We are assigning values to the fields of three *segments* (destination structures) E1BPEKKOC, E1BPEKPOC, and E1BPEKET. These *segments* map to our source structures POHEADER, POITEMS, and PODELV, Hence, the nine rows from imported data will appear as nine rows in the converted data. Process step 11 is generating two additional rows for each entity or purchase order in segments EDI_DC40 and E1PORDCR. For two purchase orders, this will result in four rows. The total number of rows in the converted data will be 9 + 4 = 13 as shown in Figure 7-88.

This concludes the optional process step 12. We navigated back to the process steps screen.

## Process Step 13—Start IDoc Generation

From the screen of process steps, we executed process step 13. Process step 13 generates *IDocs* from the converted data—file with secondary name .lsmw.conv. When we executed process step 13, a prompt appeared for input of converted data file and proposing a default converted data file as shown in Figure 7-89.

**LSM Workbench: Generate IDocs**

| **File with Converted Data** | YCH06_DM_YCH07_PO_YCH07_BAPI.lsmw.conv |
|---|---|

***Figure 7-89.*** *Process step 13—Generate IDocs*

We clicked the Execute button and an output of an info message as shown in Figure 7-90 appeared.

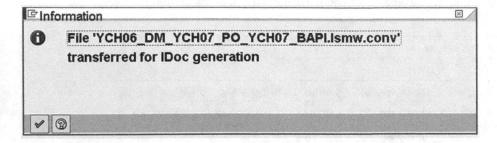

> ⌐ Information                                                          ⊠
>
> ⓘ    **File 'YCH06_DM_YCH07_PO_YCH07_BAPI.lsmw.conv'**
>      **transferred for IDoc generation**
>
> ✔ ⑦

*Figure 7-90.* *Process step 13—IDocs generated*

Corresponding to our two purchase orders, two *IDocs* are generated.
This concludes process step 13. We navigated back to the process steps screen.

## Process Step 14—Start IDoc Processing

From the screen of process steps, we executed process step 14. Process step 14 transfers data from the *IDocs* to the *Application documents*—in our case the purchase order database tables: EKKO, EKPO, and EKET.

When you execute process step 14, an elaborate selection screen for input appears. The values from creation of latest *IDocs* for the fields *Created on, Created at, Message Type,* etc. are picked up and appear as default values on the selection screen as shown in Figure 7-91.

| IDoc selection | Parallel Proc. | | | |
|---|---|---|---|---|
| IDoc number | | to | | ⮾ |
| Created on | 28.12.2016 | to | 28.12.2016 | ⮾ |
| Created at | 12:11:08 | to | 24:00:00 | ⮾ |
| IDoc Status | | to | | ⮾ |
| Message type | PORDCR | to | | ⮾ |
| Message Variant | | to | | ⮾ |
| Message function | | to | | ⮾ |
| Sender partner type | LS | to | | ⮾ |
| Sender partner no. | XI_00_800 | to | | ⮾ |
| Sender partn.funct. | | to | | ⮾ |
| Pack. Size | 5 | | Idoc Nos. 750745 & 46 Being Processed | |
| Test Flag | | to | | |

(0000002 of 0000002) IDoc 0000000000750746 currently being processed ▷

*Figure 7-91.* *Process step 14—IDocs processing*

The status bar in Figure 7-91 is displaying the message of two *IDocs,* 750745 and 750746, being processed.

When all the *IDocs* were processed, the system navigated to the screen shown in Figure 7-92.

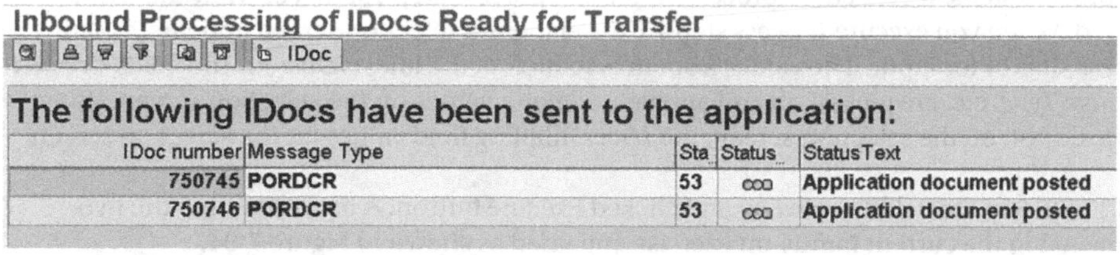

### Inbound Processing of IDocs Ready for Transfer

| ◰ | ▤ | ▽ | ▼ | ◱ | ▤ | ▷ | IDoc |

## The following IDocs have been sent to the application:

| IDoc number | Message Type | Sta | Status | StatusText |
|---|---|---|---|---|
| 750745 | PORDCR | 53 | ∞ | Application document posted |
| 750746 | PORDCR | 53 | ∞ | Application document posted |

***Figure 7-92.*** *Process step 14—IDocs posted to application documents*

The screen in Figure 7-92 lists the *IDocs* processed. Both our *IDocs* have been successfully posted—status code 53, as shown in Figure 7-92. We can view details of each *IDoc* (e.g., control info, data, status info) by double-clicking an *IDoc*. We double-clicked *IDoc* number 750745 and the screen shown in Figure 7-93 appeared.

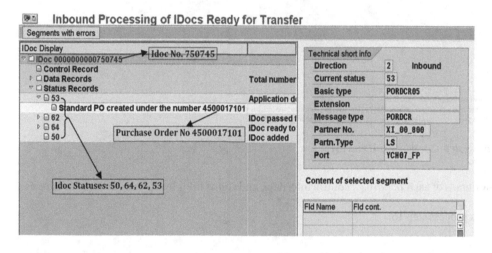

***Figure 7-93.*** *Process step 14—IDoc number 750745 details*

On the top left-hand corner of Figure 7-93, the nodes *Control Record, Data Records,* and *Status Records* appear. We expanded node *Status Records* in Figure 7-93. The statuses which the *IDoc* 750745 attained, 50, 64, 62, and 53, are marked in the figure. *IDoc* 750745 was posted as standard PO number 4500017101, which is also marked in the figure. If you click the node *Data Records*, the *segments* E1BPEKKOC, E1BPEKPOC, and E1BPEKET will appear as subnodes. If you click a *segment* subnode, each field name and its contents will appear under the head *Content of selected segment* at the bottom right corner of Figure 7-93.

This concludes process step 14. We navigated back to the process steps screen.

## Process Step 15—Create IDoc Overview

From the screen of process steps, we executed process step 15. In process step 15, we can view the *IDocs* created and processed. When you execute process step 15, the elaborate selection screen appears, exactly like the one in process step 14 for input. The values from the creation of the latest *IDocs* for the fields *Created on*, *Created at*, *Message Type*, etc. are picked up and appear as default values on the selection screen. When you click the Execute button on the selection screen, the *IDocs* fulfilling field values on the selection screen are listed.

We entered 28.12.2016 in the field *Created on* and clicked Execute button. A list containing the two *IDocs* created and posted in the current hands-on exercise appeared as shown in Figure 7-94.

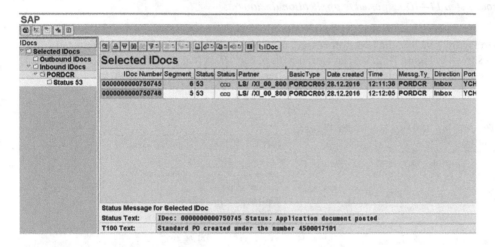

**Figure 7-94.** *Process step 15—selected IDocs list*

You can view details of each *IDoc* (e.g., control info, data, and status info) by double-clicking an *IDoc* as in process step 14.

This concludes process step 15.

## Process Step 16—Start IDoc Follow-Up

Process step 16 is to resubmit error *IDocs* again for processing. Since we did not encounter any *IDocs* with error status, we are not required to perform this process step. When the process step is executed, a screen as shown in Figure 7-95 appears.

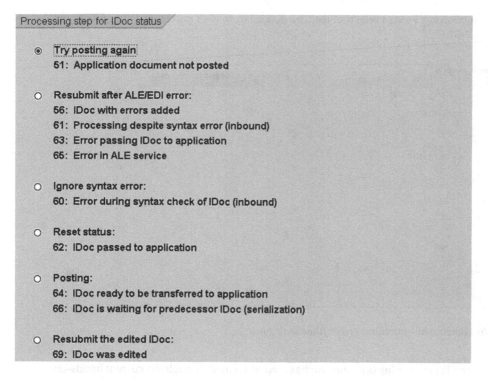

**Figure 7-95.** *Process step 16—Start IDoc Follow-Up*

The screen in Figure 7-95 offers of the ability to select a scenario of error *IDocs* to be resubmitted for processing.

This concludes process step 16, the last process step.

## Purchase Orders Created—Cross-Verification with Input Data

We will now verify that the purchase orders were created as per the input data. To verify the creation of purchase orders, we navigated to the opening screen of transaction code ME22N—*Change Purchase Order*. On the opening screen of transaction code ME22N, we made the following menu selection: Purchase Orders ➤ Other Purchase Order. The menu selection popped up a dialog box as shown in Figure 7-96.

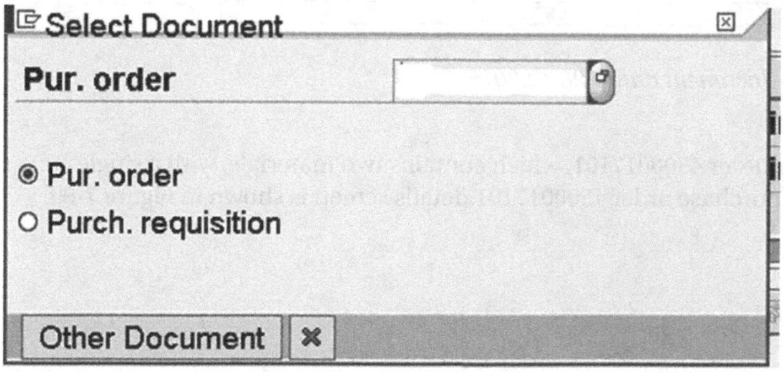

**Figure 7-96.** *Select Document—purchase order*

We pressed function key F4 for a selection list. The dialog box to filter purchasing documents appeared as shown in Figure 7-97.

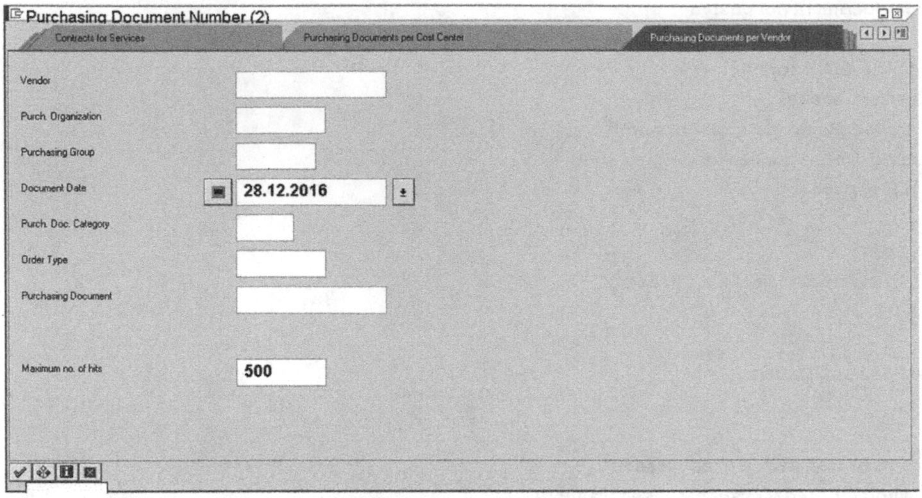

**Figure 7-97.** *Select document—purchase order: filter dialog box*

We want to view a list containing only the purchase orders created through the current hands-on exercise. We are able to filter out the purchase orders created in the current hands-on exercise by entering in field *Document Date* the value of 28.12.2016 as shown in Figure 7-97. We clicked the Continue button on the filter dialog box. A list containing the two purchase orders with *Document Date* as 28.12.2016 appeared as shown in Figure 7-98.

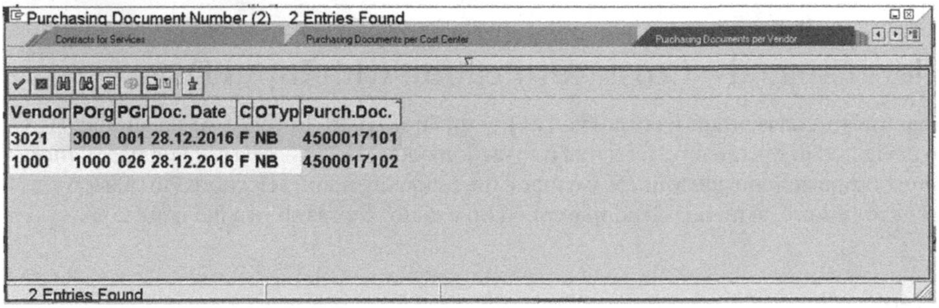

**Figure 7-98.** *Selected purchase orders—document date = 28.12.2016*

From the list, we selected purchase order 4500017101, which contains two materials, with a single delivery date for each of materials. The purchase order 4500017101 details screen is shown in Figure 7-99.

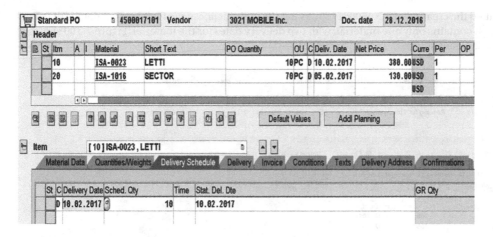

**Figure 7-99.** *Selected purchase order 4500017101—detail*

As you can observe in Figure 7-99, the header data has been created as per our input data.

*Document Type and Category*: Standard PO

*Vendor*: 3021

*Doc. Date*: 28.12.2016

If you click the button ![button] at the top left corner, you can view the two additional fields of the header data (tab—Org. Data) as follows:

*Purch. Org.*: 3000

*Purch. Group*: 001

The item data for the two materials has been created as per our input data.

*Itm*: 10 and 20

*Material*: ISA-0023 and ISA-1016

*PO Quantity*: 10 PC and 70 PC

*Net Price*: 380.00 and 130.00

If you scroll to the right, you can view the two additional fields of the item data as follows:

*Matl Group (Material Group)*: 060 and 060 (Furnitures)

*Plnt (Plant)*: 3200 and 3200 (Atlanta)

The delivery data for the two materials has been created as per our input data.

*Itm*: 10 and 20

*Delivery Date*: 10.02.2017 and 05.02.2017

*Sch. Qty*: 10 PC and 70 PC

Having verified the creation of PO 4500017101 as per the input data, we next fetched the details of PO 4500017102, which contains only one material, with two delivery dates for the material. Figure 7-100 shows the PO 4500017102 details screen.

**Figure 7-100.** *Selected purchase order 4500017102—detail*

As you can observe in Figure 7-100, the header data has been created as per our input data.

> *Document Type and Category*: Standard PO

> *Vendor*: 1000

> *Doc. Date*: 28.12.2016

If you click the button ![icon] at the top left corner, you can view the two additional fields of the header data (tab—Org. Data) as follows:

> *Purch. Org.*: 1000

> *Purch. Group*: 026

The item data for the single material has been created as per our input data.

> *Itm*: 10

> *Material*: 101-110

> *PO Quantity*: 500 PC

> *Net Price*: 5.05

If you scroll to the right, you can view the two additional fields of the item data as follows:

> *Matl Group (Material Group)*: 001 (Metal processing)

> *Plnt (Plant)*: 1000 (Werk Hamburg)

The delivery data for the single material has been created as per our input data.

> *Itm*: 10

> *Delivery Date*: 05.02.2017 and 20.02.2017

> *Sch. Qty*: 200 PC and 300 PC

We have verified that the two purchase orders were created as per the input data and as per our specifications. We have rectified the two deficiencies of hands-on exercise III:

- The net price destination field E1BPEKPOC-NET_PRICE was not getting assigned a value from the input data; instead, it was being assigned a value from info records. We enabled the assignment to the field E1BPEKPOC-NET_PRICE to a value from input data by setting the field E1BPEKPOC-PO_PRICE to X.

- Multiple delivery dates for an item are being created properly. We enabled the creation of multiple delivery dates for an item by providing the item data and item delivery data from two separate inputs files.

This concludes the cross-verification of purchase orders created with input data.

# Hands-on Exercise IV—Recapitulation

The hands-on exercise set out to transfer the data of purchase orders from three text files residing on the presentation server into the SAP functional module database tables from the LSMW environment deploying the *Object Type* as *the BAPI method.*

We started off by describing the scope and specifications of the hands-on exercise. Which of the fields will assume constant values? Which of the fields will be assigned values from input files, etc.?

We initially created the *Object* YCH07_BAPI under the existing *Project* YCH06_DM and *Subproject* YCH07_PO.

In process step 1, we specified the *Object Type* as *the BAPI method* and the *Business Object* as BUS2012 and the *Method* as CREATEFROMDATA. The LSMW system assigned the *IDoc Message Type* PORDCR and *IDoc Basic Type* PORDCR05. The *IDoc Message Type* PORDCR and *IDoc Basic Type* PORDCR05 are same as in that the hands-on exercise III. *Inbound IDocs* would be generated from the converted data. The *IDoc Inbound Settings* performed for *File port, Partner Type,* and *Partner No.* in hands-on exercise III were used again in the current hands-on exercise.

The next three process steps, as usual, involved specification of source structures, fields in the source structures, and relationships between source and destination *segments* (structures).

In process step 5, we assigned of values to destination *segment* fields.

We skipped process step 6, *Fixed Values, Translations,* and *User-Defined Routines.*

In process step 7, we specified the input text files and assigned the input text files to the source structures in process step 8.

We created representative input text data files of two purchase orders on the presentation server using the notepad editor.

We executed process step 9 for reading of input data and writing the input data to the file with the postfix .lsmw.read. In process step 10, we viewed the data from the file with the postfix .lsmw.read.

We executed process step 11 for conversion of data, writing the converted data to the file with the postfix .lsmw.conv. In process step 12, we viewed the data from the file with the postfix .lsmw.conv.

Process step 13 generated *inbound IDocs.*

In process step 14, the generated *inbound IDocs* were processed or posted to the application— transferred to the SAP functional module database tables. Process step 14 also provided for a review of just processed *IDocs.*

Process step 15 provided for a review of *IDocs.* Process step 16 provided for resubmission of *IDocs* with errors for posting. We did not perform process step 16; we did not generate *IDocs* with errors.

We performed a visual cross-verification that the purchase orders were created as per the input data using transaction code ME22N.

This concludes hands-on exercise IV.

# Project Components Export

At the end of Chapter 6, we demonstrated the export and import of LSMW *Project* components to and from files on the presentation server, respectively.

We exported the complete *Project* YCH06_DM, as it existed at the end of Chapter 6, to a file on the presentation server. *Project* YCH06_DM, at the end of Chapter 6, consisted of the following:

- *User-Defined Routines*—GET_BANKS, GET_BANK_FLD_VAL and GET_SORTL

- *Recording*—YCH06_XK01

- *Subproject*—YCH06_VN with *Objects* YCH06_DI and YCH06_RC

The *Project* CH06_DM was exported to the file LSMW_DM0_YCH06_DM on the presentation server.

In this chapter, we added the *Subproject* YCH07_PO to the *Project* YCH06_DM. We further incorporated the *Objects* YCH07_IDOC and YCH07_BAPI to the the *Subproject* YCH07_PO.

We will now export whatever LSMW *Project* components we created in the current chapter to a separate file on the presentation server.

To export LSMW *Project* components, we entered the *Project* name as YCH06_DM on the opening screen of LSMW and made the following menu selection Extras ➤ Export Project. A dialog box appeared with the Project name as shown in Figure 7-101.

*Figure 7-101. LSMW—project component(s) export*

We clicked the Continue button. The complete *Project* with its components is presented in a tree form. We expanded all the nodes of the *Project* tree. We deselected all the nodes except YCH07_PO as shown in Figure 7-102.

```
YCH06_DM          Data Migration Project
  └─ Reusable Rules
      └─ User-Def. Routines
              GET_BANKS              ...............................................
              GET_BANK_FLD_VAL       ...............................................
              GET_SORTL              Derive.SORTL.....................................
  └─ Recordings
          YCH06_XK01            ...............................................
  └─ Subprojects
      └─ YCH06_VN        Data Migration - Vendors
              YCH06_DI          Data.Migration.-.Vendors.Using.Direct.Input.Method....................
              YCH06_RC          Data.Migration.-.Vendors.Using.Recording.............................
      └─ YCH07_PO        Data Migration - Purchase Orders
```

*Figure 7-102. LSMW—project, project components export: selection*

We clicked the Export button on the application toolbar—the first button from the right. The dialog box to make folder selection and input the file name appeared as shown in Figure 7-103.

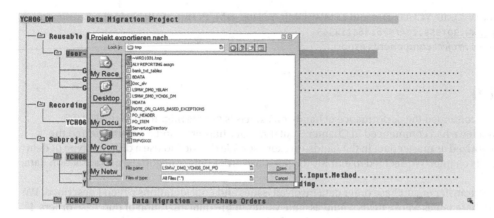

**Figure 7-103.** *LSMW—project export: select folder and input file name*

By default, the system proposes the name of the *Project* with the prefix LSMW_DM0_ (DM0 is our system id) as the file name. We selected the folder D:\TMP, changed the proposed file name to LSMW_DM0_ YCH06_DM_PO, and clicked the *Open* button. The system issued an info message of successful export as shown in Figure 7-104.

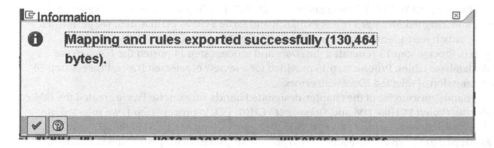

**Figure 7-104.** *LSMW—project components exported*

We have successfully exported the *Subproject* component YCH07_PO of the *Project* YCH06_DM.

The file LSMW_DM0_YCH06_DM contains the exported *Project* components created in Chapter 6.
The file LSMW_DM0_YCH06_DM_PO contains the exported *Project* components created in this chapter.

We located the *Project* components export files in the folder D:\TMP. Figure 7-105 shows the two files.

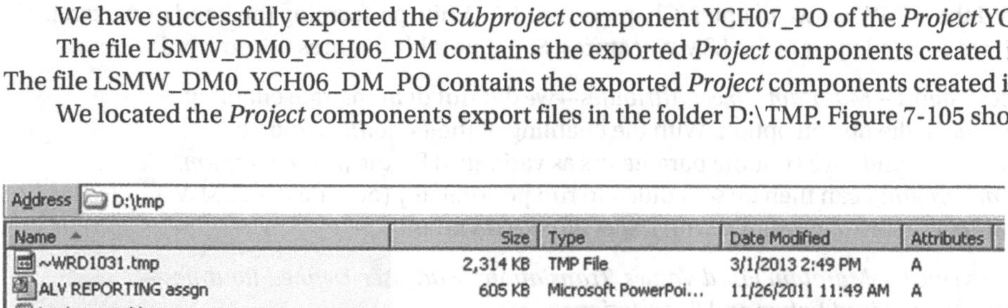

| Address | D:\tmp | | | |
|---|---|---|---|---|
| Name ▲ | Size | Type | Date Modified | Attributes |
| ~WRD1031.tmp | 2,314 KB | TMP File | 3/1/2013 2:49 PM | A |
| ALV REPORTING assgn | 605 KB | Microsoft PowerPoi... | 11/26/2011 11:49 AM | A |
| bank_txt_tables | 1 KB | Text Document | 2/8/2016 6:46 PM | A |
| BDATA | 1 KB | Text Document | 3/5/2016 1:47 PM | A |
| Doc_alv | 1,142 KB | Microsoft Word Doc... | 7/12/2013 4:15 PM | A |
| LSMW_DM0_YBLAH | 20 KB | Text Document | 2/7/2016 1:11 PM | A |
| LSMW_DM0_YCH06_DM | 128 KB | Text Document | 6/22/2016 5:03 PM | A |
| LSMW_DM0_YCH06_DM_PO | 128 KB | File | 2/3/2017 12:53 PM | A |
| MDATA | 1 KB | Text Document | 3/5/2016 1:47 PM | A |

**Figure 7-105.** *Project components export files*

The files LSMW_DM0_YCH06_DM and LSMW_DM0_YCH06_DM_PO are available in the E-resource file for this book (www.apress.com/9781484212345).

This concludes *Project* components export.

# Conclusion

In this chapter, we continued the performance of hands-on exercises of data migration in the LSMW environment, which we had commenced in Chapter 6. All through Chapters 5 and 6, we transferred the vendor data categorized as master data in the hands-on exercises. We decided to use a different type of data for migration in this chapter. We decided to employ the purchase order data, categorized as transaction data, for migration.

The proposed transfer of purchase order data involved issues and considerations which I described. We identified the database tables whose fields would assume values in the data migration of purchase orders. I described the data model or the ER diagram of the identified purchase order database tables.

It was proposed to transfer the purchase order data deploying each of the LSMW *Object Types—IDoc* and *BAPI*—as separate hands-on exercise. The deployment of both the LSMW *Object Types, IDoc* and *BAPI,* generates *IDocs*. Hence, we provided a brief description of *IDocs* in the context of the hands-on exercises.

To be able to generate the *IDocs*, we needed to perform the *IDoc Inbound Settings* from the LSMW environment.

We created the *Subproject* YCH07_PO under the *Project* YCH06_DM.

For the first hands-on exercise of this chapter designated as hands-on exercise III, we created the *Object* YCH07_IDOC under the *Project* YCH06_DM and *Subproject* YCH07_PO. In process step 1, we selected the *Object Type* as *IDoc* and assigned *Message Type* as PORDCR and *Basic Type* as PORDCR05. We performed process steps 2 to 12, which were identical to the process steps 2 to 12 we performed in the hands-on exercises in Chapter 6. Process step 13 generated the *IDocs* and process step 14 posted the *IDocs* to the functional module database tables. Process step 15 provided for a review of selected *IDocs*. Process step 16 provided for a resubmission of selected *IDocs* with errors.

For the second hands-on exercise of the chapter, designated hands-on exercise IV, we created the *Object* YCH07_BAPI under the *Project* YCH06_DM and *Subproject* YCH07_PO. In process step 1, we selected the *Object Type* as *BAPI, and* assigned *Business Object* as BUS2012 and *Method* as CREATEFROMDATA. We performed process steps 2 to 14, which were identical to process steps 2 to 14 we performed in hands-on exercise III,

We concluded the chapter with the export of components in the *Project* YCH06_DM created in this chapter.

We have covered the LSMW in two chaptersChapters 6 and 7. While performing the hands-on exercises in Chapters 6 and 7, we covered most of the LSMW features. Some notable features not covered were:

- In process step 1—*Maintain Object Attributes*—we did not demonstrate enabling the *Periodic* Radio button option. With the enabling of the *Periodic* Radio button, you can specify and save runtime parameters as variant(s) for the *frame program*. The *frame program* can then be scheduled to run periodically (outside the LSMW environment) in the background with a specific saved variant.

- In process step 6—*Maintain Fixed Values, Translations, and User-Defined Routines*— we did not cover *Fixed Values* and *Translations*.

- In process step 7—*Specify Files*—we did not cover the feature *Wildcard Values*, which enables the runtime specification of input files .lsmw.read file and .lsmw.conv file.

# Index

© Sushil Markandeya 2017
S. Markandeya, *Pro SAP Scripts, Smartforms, and Data Migration*,
https://doi.org/10.1007/978-1-4842-3183-8

## ■ W, X, Y, Z

# Get the eBook for only $5!

Why limit yourself?

With most of our titles available in both PDF and ePUB format, you can access your content wherever and however you wish—on your PC, phone, tablet, or reader.

Since you've purchased this print book, we are happy to offer you the eBook for just $5.

To learn more, go to http://www.apress.com/companion or contact support@apress.com.

# Apress®

Printed in the United States
By Bookmasters